D0181739

500

THINGS TO EAT
BEFORE IT'S
TOO LATE

New England

Mid Atlantic

South

Midwest

Southwest

West

JANE & MICHAEL STERN

500

THINGS TO EAT BEFORE IT'S TOO LATE

and the
Very Best Places
to Eat Them

Houghton Mifflin Harcourt
Boston New York 2009

New England

Mid Atlantic

South

Midwest

Southwest

West

www.hmhbooks.com

Library of Congress Cataloging-in-Publication Data

Stern, Jane.
500 things to eat before it's too late and the very best places to
eat them / Jane and Michael Stern.
p. cm.
Includes index.
ISBN-13: 978-0-547-05907-5
ISBN-10: 0-547-05907-8
1. Restaurants—United States—Guidebooks. I. Stern, Michael, date.
II. Title. III. Title: Five hundred things to eat before it's too
late and the very best places to eat them.
TX907.2.S836 2009
647.9573—dc22   2008053317

Book design by Anne Chalmers
Typefaces: Archer, Meta, Minion

Printed in the United States of America
DOC 10 9 8 7 6 5 4 3 2

Page 88, photo courtesy of Stephen Rushmore Jr.;
pages 111, 112, and 218 (bottom), photos courtesy of Bruce Bilmes;
pages 196, 265, 285, and 286, photos courtesy of Cliff Strutz;
all other photos © Michael Stern.

ACKNOWLEDGMENTS

There is no way to fully acknowledge the countless cooks and customers who have provided us with information, advice, encouragement, and vividly spiced opinions over the course of the millions of miles we have traveled in search of great things to eat. It is their passions that make food-hunting so much fun. Were it not for the tenacity of independent restaurateurs and the zeal of eaters who celebrate dishes that define American cooking at its best, we could be a nation of nothing but monotonous unhappy meals.

We are especially grateful to the community of food-focused partisans who share the joys of edible adventuring at our website, Roadfood.com. We offer heartfelt thanks to all who participate in the forums, who post trip reports and Roadfooddigest.com blog entries, and who take time to contribute their own reviews. Roadfood.com would not exist if not for the inspiration of our partner, Stephen Rushmore Jr., who continues to expand horizons on the Internet and beyond. Our own vision is consistently enhanced by the contributions of team members Marc Bruno, Bruce Bilmes and Sue Boyles, Kristin Little, Chris Ayers and Amy Briesch, Cliff Strutz, Billyboy, Al "the Mayor" Bowen, Tony Bad, Mike S., Larry the Ribrater, Sundancer, enthusiastic participants on our annual eating tours, and too many other regulars to name. What a blessing it is to be part of this ebullient crowd. Special thanks are owed to Stephen Rushmore Jr., Bruce Bilmes, and Cliff Strutz for photos that add extra flavor to this book.

For the past fifteen years we have enjoyed the best gig in the food-writing world: contributing a monthly column to *Gourmet* magazine, for which we have discovered so many of the must-eats described in this book. Abetting, aiding, and always supporting our quest for memorable meals and the right words to describe them are Ruth Reichl,

James Rodewald, John "Doc" Willoughby, and Larry Karol. Each week we talk about our findings with Lynne Rossetto Kasper of American Public Radio's *The Splendid Table*. Lynne, Sally Swift, and Jen Russell make these weekly reports one of the happiest parts of what we do.

As always, we are inexpressibly grateful to our literary agent, Doe Coover, who enables us to spend the vast majority of our time eating and writing rather than worrying about publishing. Our editor, Rux Martin, is an author's dream, always inspiring us to go farther, eat more, and write better. Thanks to Rux, as well as to Sara Shaffer, Clare O'Keeffe, Liz Duvall, Jacinta Monniere, and designer Anne Chalmers, the sometimes tortuous road from vaporous notion to finished book has been a magic carpet ride.

CONTENTS

New England

Mid Atlantic

South

Midwest

Southwest

West

INTRODUCTION

Finding a great dish—whether it's one you've never heard about or one of legendary status—is an experience never to be forgotten. It can happen on a cross-country road trip or during an impromptu Sunday drive: you sit down at a Nashville cafe counter and are rocked by the cool fusion of sweet and tart in the creamiest lemon icebox pie on earth; you gasp in awe at petals of griddle-crisped cheese that encircle a Sacramento Squeezeburger like chewy cheddar rings of Saturn. You find what surely is the juiciest fried chicken in Kansas City or the crumbliest crumb cake in New Jersey. To savor a treasured edible alongside people who love it as theirs in its natural setting—a town cafe, a lobsterman's wharf, a humble hot dog stand—is a slice of life good eaters know as bliss.

Since the first edition of *Roadfood*, in 1978, our goal has been to seek out America's unique restaurants and unforgettable dishes. After downing some 100,000 meals in our quest for the nation's best, the time has come to name and rank the pièces de résistance. That is what this book is: a life list of superlative dishes everyone ought to try. Some of the honorees are all-American. We want to tell you where to find the country's best ice cream, pancakes, pizza, hamburgers, ribs, and French fries. Other must-eats are little known outside their home but unforgettable once you've tasted them: the delirious duet of South Tucson *pico de gallo,* in which nectarous fresh fruit is sprinkled with lime and fiery red pepper; a Sheboygan brat broiled over charcoal and gilded with melted Dairy State butter; Rhode Island's east-of-the-bay flint-corn jonnycakes as thin as flannel, with edges fine as lace.

500 Things to Eat Before It's Too Late tells you where to find the best dishes that are unique to this country. Its focus is more on the food itself than on the places that serve it. Of course, we provide names, addresses, phone numbers, and website links, as well as mail-order information. Recommended sources go beyond ordinary eateries to include grocery stores, roadside stands, farmers' markets, butcher shops, and state fairs. We even recommend a handful of high-dollar dining rooms that happen to be home of such not-to-be-missed delights as red velvet cake (page 197) and lobster pizza (page 54).

To make this book as useful as possible, we also include sidebars: recipes to cook at home, places to shop for great food while on the road (or at your computer), plus a handful of favorite roadside stores, museums, and indefinable attractions you might want to visit between meals. Have you been to the Northern Hemisphere's largest crucifix? Do you know where to be fitted for lizard-skin boots by the Michelangelo of bordertown leather crafters? Do you want to visit the exact place on the beach where surfing began in Southern California or the scariest maximum-security prison in the East, complete with its Rube Goldberg electric chair? Do you need to purchase sturdy Amish work clothes, a healing crystal pipe of amethyst, or a voodoo candle that promises death unto your enemies? How about an underwater watsu massage or a hike through the Sitka spruce rainforest at ocean's edge in Oregon? All are side trips close to the destination dishes honored in this book.

It is our conviction that everything listed is worth a major detour, and in many cases a whole trip. Some unique regional specialties are absent. Recommendable New York bagels, Dubois County (Indiana) turtle soup, and Hopi mutton stew all eluded us, and we are still looking for a steady purveyor of Maryland's white potato pie. The once-great St. Louis fried brain sandwich seems to be history. Nor can we in good conscience direct readers to chitlins, a culinary euphemism for the last part of a pig's alimentary canal. Hog rectums are okay when deep-fried (what is not?), but steamed in vinegar, pale, and flaccid, as you find them in parts of southern Virginia? No thanks!

With many dishes, though, it was a huge challenge to winnow our choices down to the very best. As classicists, we tend to seek the paradigm. For instance, huevos rancheros. You'll find a textbook version of the eggs-and-salsa classic at Albuquerque's Frontier Restaurant. But what about the uniquely creamy huevos at the H&H Car Wash in El Paso and the totally iconoclastic baked ones at Hell's Kitchen in Minneapolis? No way can we list America's best huevos rancheros without including all three. Always, decision-making came down to one ultimate criterion: Is this a dish to remember, with joy, forever?

We do acknowledge that despite the hubris required to tell anyone what he or she ought to eat, we do not know everything! Even if we are still chowing down at age 100, we are quite certain we will be finding local favorites that we never knew existed. We welcome suggestions of regional specialties and unique dishes that ought to be included in subsequent editions of this book. E-mail us directly at roadfood123@ comcast.net; visit us at the website Roadfood.com, or write to us c/o Houghton Mifflin Harcourt, 222 Berkeley St., Boston, MA 02116.

Often, several places make excellent versions of essentially the same dish. In that case, we rank them in order, listing our favorites first. This is a way to help travelers prioritize visits. We know the ranking will engender controversy; the foods here are ones about which devotees feel tremendous passion. That's great. We love a good discussion about Chicago red hots versus New Jersey rippers or where the barbecue is finest and the custard freshest. In fact, we hope this book sparks enough debate to encourage people to hit the road to confirm that their favorites really are the best or to discover worthy challengers for the crown.

Know this: Even if your favorite ice cream in New England is #2 on the list in this book, its red ribbon means we love it only slightly less than #1. Indeed, being last on any one of these lists is in no way a poor showing. For example, in the rankings of the five best opportunities to eat Texas hot sausage links (page 342), #5 on the list is sensational, four-star, world class. Every single place itemized in this book, whether first in its ranking or #16, is one we consider a compelling culinary destination, a Holy Grail of deliciousness. So please, dig in!

500

THINGS TO EAT
BEFORE IT'S
TOO LATE

New England

Mid Atlantic

South

Midwest

Southwest

West

NEW ENGLAND

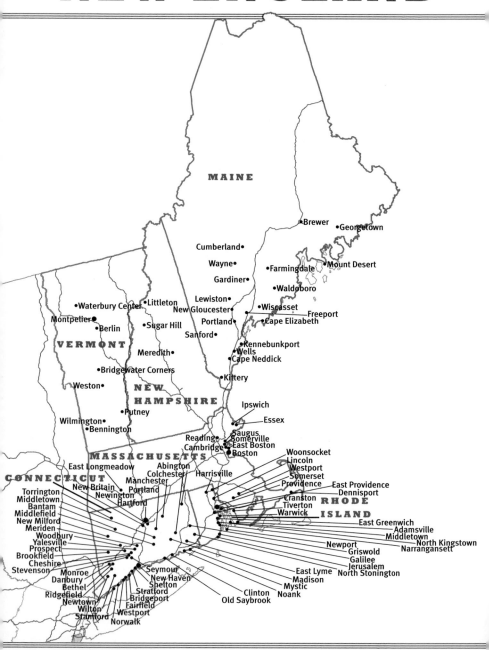

MAINE

Brewer • Georgetown •

Cumberland •

Wayne •   • Farmingdale   Mount Desert •

Gardiner •   • Waldoboro

                  Lewiston •   • Wiscasset
• Waterbury Center • Littleton   New Gloucester •   Freeport •
• Littleton   Portland •   • Cape Elizabeth
Montpelier •   • Sugar Hill Sanford •
   • Berlin
VERMONT   Meredith •   • Kennebunkport
                                            • Wells
        • Bridgewater Corners   • Cape Neddick

• Weston •   NEW   • Kittery
                     HAMPSHIRE
Wilmington •   • Putney   Ipswich •
     • Bennington   • Essex
                                    Saugus
MASSACHUSETTS   Reading • Somerville
                 Cambridge • East Boston
   East Longmeadow Abington   • Boston   Woonsocket •
                    Colchester •   Lincoln •
CONNECTICUT   Manchester Harrisville •   Westport •
Torrington   New Britain Portland •   Somerset •
Middletown   Newington   Providence • East Providence •
Bantam   Hartford •   Cranston • Dennisport •
Middlefield   Tiverton • RHODE
New Milford   Warwick •   ISLAND
Meriden •
Woodbury   East Greenwich •
Yalesville   Adamsville •
Prospect   Middletown •
Brookfield   Newport • North Kingstown •
Cheshire •   Griswold • Narragansett •
Stevenson • Monroe   Galilee •
     Danbury   Seymour   Jerusalem •
Bethel   New Haven   East Lyme • North Stonington •
Ridgefield   Shelton   Madison •
   Newtown Stratford   Mystic •
     Wilton Bridgeport   Noank •
Stamford Fairfield   Clinton •
       Norwalk Westport   Old Saybrook •

CONNECTICUT

Chicken Pie: Woodbury, 8
Chocolate Truffle: Brookfield, 48
Clam Chowder: East Lyme and Noank, 9
Crumb-Top Apple Pie: Shelton, 15
Deep-Fried Dog: Cheshire, Fairfield, and Torrington, 15
Dirt Bomb: Bantam, 18
Donut Bread Pudding: Woodbury, 22
Doughnut: Hartford, Westport, Woodbury, and Yalesville, 19
French Fries: Fairfield and Norwalk, 247
Fried Clams: Madison and Mystic, 23
Fried Dough and Doughboy: Newington, 27
Hamburger: Colchester, Manchester, New Haven, and New Milford, 328
Hot Dog: Danbury, Middlefield, Monroe, New Britain, Newington, Stevenson, and Stratford, 28
Hot Dog Wagon: Danbury, Portland, Ridgefield, and Seymour, 28
Ice Cream: Abington, Bethel, Bridgeport, Griswold, Manchester, Monroe, Prospect, and Ridgefield, 30
Lobster Roll: Clinton and Old Saybrook, 38
Lobstermania: North Stonington, 42
Pain de Campagne: Wilton, 47
Pierogi, Placki, and Golabki: Danbury, Hartford, and New Britain, 49
Pizza: Bethel, New Haven, Newtown, and Stamford, 50
Shore Dinner: Noank, 59
Steamed Cheeseburger: Hartford, Meriden, and Middletown, 63
Summer Sausage Sandwich: Danbury, 65

MAINE

Boiled Dinner: Gardiner, Portland, and Waldoboro, 6
Clam Chowder: Kennebunkport and Wells, 9
Flo Dog: Cape Neddick, 23
French Fries: Portland, 247
Fried Clams: Georgetown and Kennebunkport, 23
Ice Cream: New Gloucester, Sanford, and Wayne, 30
Indian Pudding: Wells, 35
Lobster Roll: Brewer, Kennebunkport, Kittery, Wells, and Wiscasset, 38
Lobstermania: Wells, 42
Maple Dessert: Waldoboro, 43
Real Italian: Portland, 58
Shore Dinner: Cape Elizabeth, Georgetown, Kennebunkport, Kittery, and Mount Desert, 59
Whoopie Pie: Cumberland, Farmingdale, Freeport, Gardiner, Kittery, and Lewiston, 66
Whoopie Pie Cake: Portland, 69

MASSACHUSETTS

Boiled Dinner: Boston, 6
Chacarero: Boston, 7
Chicken Pie: Reading, 8
Coffee Jell-O: Boston, 12
Doughnut: East Longmeadow, Saugus, and Somerset, 19
Fried Clams: Essex and Ipswich, 23
Hamburger: Somerville, 328
Ice Cream: Cambridge and Dennisport, 30
Indian Pudding: Boston and Essex, 35
Lobstermania: Boston, 42
Pizza: Boston and East Boston, 50
Shore Dinner: Essex, 59
Stuffie: Westport, 65

NEW HAMPSHIRE

Ice Cream: Littleton, 30
Maple Dessert: Sugar Hill, 43
Pancakes: Sugar Hill, 402
Turkey Dinner: Meredith, 66

RHODE ISLAND

Blackstone Valley Chicken Dinner: Harrisville and Woonsocket, 5
Clam Chowder: Galilee and Tiverton, 9
Coffee Milk: Lincoln, 12
Doughnut: North Kingstown, 19
Fried Dough and Doughboy: Warwick, 27
Gingerbread Pancakes: East Greenwich, 37
Ice Cream: Tiverton, 30
Jonnycakes: Adamsville, East Greenwich, and Newport, 36
Lobster Roll: Jerusalem, 38
Murderburger: Providence, 13
New York System: Cranston, East Providence, and Providence, 45
Shore Dinner: Narragansett, 59
Snail Salad: Cranston, Galilee, Narragansett, and Warwick, 62

BLACKSTONE VALLEY CHICKEN DINNER
Rhode Island

Here is a feast virtually unknown outside the Blackstone River Valley in Rhode Island — one of the nation's premier big feeds, notable not only because the chicken is so succulent and vividly seasoned, but because it is always served family-style in eating halls that bubble over with good cheer.

The tradition goes back to the 1930s, when Italian immigrants in Woonsocket used to gather to play bocce at the home of the Pavoni family. Mama Pavoni made roasted chicken and pasta, and when her step-daughter decided to open a restaurant in the basement of the family home, the **Bocce Club**, that was the meal she served. It became hugely popular among locals because it reflected their culinary heritage and also because the family-style service offered such a sense of community. Today's Bocce Club is huge and has a full menu, but roast chicken, its meat saturated with butter and olive oil and seasoned with rosemary, accompanied by an antipasto and olive oil–roasted potatoes as well as French fries and tomato-sauced pasta, is the meal that nearly everybody comes to eat.

Bocce Club chickens were originally sourced from a place called **Wright's Farm**, which began as a backyard barbecue and chicken ranch and has now become the biggest of the area's chicken dinner halls, with seats for 1,023 eaters at a time. Despite its cavernous accommodations, Wright's Farm is so popular that it's not uncommon to wait an hour before you dig into a quickly served meal of hot rolls, cool salad, macaroni shells with red sauce, thick-cut French fries, and big bowls full of roast chicken followed by a slice of ice cream roll. It's not intimate or

WRIGHT'S FARM GIFT SHOP

As a general rule of Roadfood, great eateries do not boast big gift shops. Call us purists, but we tend to prefer places that focus all their attention on serving delicious food; a really big inventory of souvenirs does not set our appetite aglow. But there is a point at which the profusion of knick-knacks grows so large that it takes on a life of its own, and as the authors of The Encyclopedia of Bad Taste, we cannot help but pay attention. Such a place is the 4,000-square-foot gift shop at Wright's Farm in Harrisville, Rhode Island. Of course the shop offers Wright's good salad dressing and its signature pasta sauce, but here you also can purchase Bearington Bear collectibles, Faerie Glen fairies, a wall tile that says "Because I'm the Mom, That's Why," sea monkeys and their aquaria, and an item called Poo-pourri, an air freshener made especially for bathrooms, available in a gift pack with a roll of toilet paper.

cozy, and whatever homey comfort the Blackstone Valley chicken dinner once suggested is long gone — the gift shop is a virtual museum of kitsch. But if you are looking for an all-you-can-eat blow-out feast in a pastoral setting of rolling meadows at a reasonable price (about $10), this is the place.

ESSENTIAL BLACKSTONE VALLEY CHICKEN DINNER

Bocce Club: 226 St. Louis Ave., Woonsocket, RI
401-767-2000
Wright's Farm Restaurant: 84 Inman Rd., Harrisville, RI
401-769-2856
www.wrightsfarm.com

BOILED DINNER
Northern New England

When it comes to eating plain and square, New Englanders have everybody else beat. This is the home of the plainest, squarest meat-and-potatoes meal in America, the New England

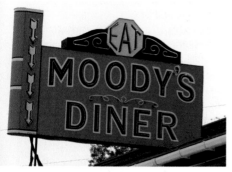

Moody's Diner, in Waldoboro, ME, serves hot boiled dinners every Thursday night.

boiled dinner. Picture it: brick-red slabs of corned beef brisket striated with juicy veins of fat accompanied on the plate by a faded rainbow of vegetables: beets in a crimson puddle that bleeds into the salty dampness of the beef; a cabbage wedge, steamy and pale green; a white hunk of boiled potato; a couple of lengths of cooked carrot and slices of turnip. No sauce, no gravy, nothing bright or gay; what emanates from this platter is a cloud of earthy, briny perfume. If you can set aside any prejudice and think of food as essential sustenance, there is nothing on earth more satisfying.

Compared to it, other contenders for the most basic plate of food in America — steak and French fries or ham and biscuits or turkey and dressing — are epicurean fare. If you doubt that, consider its name. You could not get more generic, prosaic, and neutral unless you called it Dinner, boiled.

There was a time when many New England restaurants and inns offered boiled dinner once a week, usually on Thursday. Now that many of them have an elevated culinary consciousness, such humble fare is a rarity. Not at **Doyle's Cafe**, an 1882-vintage neighborhood saloon in Boston's Jamaica Plain, which boasts such other local arcana as Grape-Nuts custard and old-fashioned (on a biscuit) strawberry shortcake. Like Doyle's, **Moody's Diner** of Waldoboro, Maine, puts boiled dinner on the menu every Thursday night. And if there is any left over in the kitchen, expect red flannel hash (named because beets tint it the color of a farmer's long johns) for breakfast the next morning.

Brisket, beets, potatoes, and more: New England's plain meal is a rarity.

At the **A-1 Diner** in Gardiner, Maine, where an ambitious modern menu offers the likes of wild mushroom ragout and Asian noodle bowls, not to mention both a wine list and an artisan beer list, you can still come on Thursday for a completely uncreative — and excellent — boiled dinner.

The **Wayside Restaurant and Bakery** of Montpelier, Vermont, is a modest family lunchroom where locals come to chat over breakfast and tourists stop for a piece of maple cream pie (page 43). Simple it may be, but it takes its role as a conservator of Yankee cooking seriously. We know of no other restaurant anywhere that serves the bygone country staple salt pork and milk gravy, on the menu here in cold-weather months, and there are precious few other places that still offer the old farmer favorite tripe (Moody's does!). Traditional boiled dinner is a Thursday night thing at the Wayside, but it is available only seasonally. (Who wants boiled dinner in August?)

We did not expect to eat boiled dinner at **Becky's Diner** in Portland,

Maine, but knowing Becky Rand's talents with meat and potatoes, we ordered the daily special one evening in autumn: pot roast. What arrived was not technically boiled dinner. The beef was not corned; there were no beets, turnips, or cabbage on the plate. Nevertheless, the tableau of big, extremely tender meat chunks, plain white boiled potatoes, unadorned carrots, and steam-softened leaves of sweet onion had all the austere beauty and profound, primal satisfaction of the Yankee classic.

5 BEST BOILED DINNERS

1. **Wayside Restaurant and Bakery:** 1873 U.S. Route 302, Montpelier, VT 802-223-6611
2. **Moody's Diner:** 1885 Atlantic Highway (Route 1), Waldoboro, ME 207-832-7785 www.moodysdiner.com
3. **Becky's Diner:** 390 Commercial St., Portland, ME 207-773-7070 www.beckysdiner.com
4. **A-1 Diner:** 3 Bridge St., Gardiner, ME 207-582-4804
5. **Doyle's Cafe:** 3484 Washington St., Jamaica Plain, MA 617-524-2345 www.doyles-cafe.com

CHACARERO
Boston, Massachusetts

Chacarero is the name of a restaurant and its specialty, a Chilean grilled-meat flatbread sandwich that Juan Hurtado started selling from a pushcart about ten years ago. It has since become the talk of Boston, and while the restaurant has expanded to a couple of locations, the sandwich remains supreme quick-eats lunch. The puffy bread is similar to Portuguese but with a nature that is more sourdough-buttery than bright and sweet. Onto the bread go pieces of marinated and grilled chicken and/or beef similar to what you'd get on a fajita, a slice of melty mild cheese, red peppers, steamed al dente green beans, mashed avocados, and spicy or extra-spicy green sauce. None of the ingredients are rarities, but Hurtado makes bread-baking and vegetable shopping an everyday event, so each ingredient is its best self, and while it sounds like a dizzying mix, all the notes come together to make a symphonic sandwich that Boston expatriates have learned to pine for.

Chacarero: 101 Arch St.,
  Boston, MA
  617-542-0392
  Second location: 26 Province St.,
  Boston, MA
  617-367-1167
  www.chacarero.com

CHICKEN PIE
Southern New England

As late as the mid-twentieth century, when much of Connecticut was still farmland, the wives of chicken farmers continued a tradition of making chicken pies and selling them from their back porches for people to take home, heat, and eat. The chicken farms are gone, but **Dottie's Diner**, located on rural Route 6 in Wood-

Farmland heritage: the all-chicken pies at Dottie's in Woodbury, CT

bury — known to collectors as "antiques row" for the old homes that are now whatnot shops — still offers farmworthy pies. No meal is more purely comfy. There is *no* filler packed inside these pies' savory crusts. Just a mass of gentle chicken meat — a few slices, some shreds, some chopped as fine as hash, a mix of white and dark, all of it moist and steamy. Crack through the crust, inhale the oven-roasted perfume, then pour on some of the gravy that comes on the side along with fine mashed potatoes, carrots, and peas. When Dottie Sperry took over the diner from the Phillips family in 2006, she knew she could not change anything about this legendary pie, but she did supplement it on the menu with more familiar chicken *pot* pies, with everything, including vegetables, packed inside the crust. Both are available frozen to take home and bake.

There is no place to eat at **Harrow's Chicken Pies**, in Reading, Massachusetts, but the takeout place will heat up your pie if you call ahead so it is ready to take home and enjoy immediately. Available with only chicken and gravy or with potatoes and carrots included, Harrow's pies come in four sizes: individual, apartment size (for two or three), family size (four), and jumbo (six). They are made using the same recipe that's been used here since the 1930s, based on chickens that are roasted every day and pulled into pieces so moist that they tend to fall apart when you fork into them.

TRUE CHICKEN PIES

Dottie's Diner: 740 S. Main St.,
Woodbury, CT
203-263-2516
Harrow's Chicken Pies:
126 Main St., Reading, MA
781-944-0410
www.chickenpie.com

CLAM CHOWDER
Yankee Shores

The way partisans debate the issue, you'd think there were only two kinds of clam chowder in the Northeast: red and white. In fact there are four: Manhattan chowder, which is red and contains tomatoes and other vegetables; New England chowder, which is white because it is made with milk or cream; South Coast chowder, which is clear, containing no dairy products or any vegetables other than potato and perhaps onions, and is almost always made with salt pork; and finally a chowder so little appreciated that it doesn't really have a name. That last one is pink, containing both cream and tomatoes. Once a common item on menus in the Ocean State's big shore dinner halls, where it was served alongside clam cakes, pink chowder has become a rarity.

HOLY LAND, USA

Holy Land, USA, has been closed to the public for more than twenty years, but a giant cross marking this miniature re-creation of the Land of the Lord still looms over Waterbury. And while they have fallen into disrepair, most of the two hundred one-tenth-sized buildings still stand. As you gaze over the mini Holy City and see modern Waterbury in the background, the feeling is surreal indeed, with the rumble of traffic along I-84 providing a bizarre audio backdrop to the ancient Middle East. All around the villages of Bethlehem and Jerusalem are glass-fronted sheds that contain "actual photographs of Jesus," a replica of the Dead Sea Scrolls, and jars alleged to contain ashes of Jesus' contemporaries. At one point the miniature version of the inn that turned away Joseph and Mary had a NO VACANCY sign on its door.

Holy Land, USA: Slocum St.,
Waterbury, CT
No phone
Visit at your own risk.

A pat of butter melts luxuriously into creamy New England chowder.

We won't spend much time with Manhattan chowder, which really is vegetable soup with clams in it. Not that it can't be good — it is chunky to the point of being forkworthy at New York's **Grand Central Oyster Bar.** Clams add a briny glow but are upstaged by everything else. In fact, the Oyster Bar's version of New England chowder, thick and creamy and radiant with clam flavor, puts the red stuff in the shade.

Many restaurants along southern New England shores serve both clear and white chowder, but only in Rhode Island will you find the pink. It can be especially elusive for the culinary explorer because so often it is listed on menus as red. **Champlin's Seafood Deck** in Narragansett originally was famous for its clear chowder but now also offers red and white. The red indeed is pink, containing cream and tomatoes, plus just enough clams and their juice to give it an ocean accent. **George's of Galilee** confuses the issue even more by noting on its menu that Rhode Island chowder is "not to be confused with

New England style or Manhattan style" (in other words, it's clear) but then adding that it is "served plain, with tomato or cream."

The best clear chowder we know is served at **Abbott's Lobster in the Rough,** a breezy picnic of a restaurant at the Noank, Connecticut, harbor, where the broth that is the chowder's soul radiates bracing saltwater flavor underpinned by the richness of pork. It would be delicious if it were only broth; the tender nuggets of potato and sweet bits of clam are a bonus. (If you need something creamy here, the lobster bisque is dramatically so.) In Rhode Island along Sakonnet Bay, **Evelyn's** is another superior source of South Coast chowder, here called "Rhode Island" style. This open-air drive-in is worth a visit also for its chorizo sausage–charged "stuffies" (stuffed quahogs; page 65) and that local oddity, a chow mein sandwich, which is a hamburger bun floating in a sea of chow mein.

The two adjectives most appropriate to traditional New England chowder are creamy and buttery. Some are emphatically more one than the other. At the **Maine Diner** in Wells, clam chowder is relatively thin because it is extremely buttery. The seafood chowder is buttery, too — one of the most scrumptious foods there is. It is packed with ocean sweetness in the form not just of clams but of shrimp and spoon-sized pieces of flaky white fish. It would be possible to eat the ultra-crowded brew with a fork, but then of course you would want to slurp up the golden broth from the bottom of the bowl. At **Mabel's Lobster Claw** in Kennebunkport, the clam chowder is nearly thick enough to support a spoon.

The very best New England clam chowder? Both buttery and rich, thick but in no way pasty, energized with the power of smoky bacon, the paradigm is served at the **Pearl Oyster Bar**, a hip little seafood restaurant located in . . . Manhattan.

Bisque, which is not chowder because it contains no potatoes, demands a footnote. Made with no vegetables at all, it is ultra-creamy and just might make you faint with pleasure at **Flanders Fish Market** in East Lyme, Connecticut, where the lobster bisque is spoon-sized hunks of moist pink meat immersed in butter-gilded cream with a jot of pepper and spice.

PAN ROAST

Oysters on the half shell are swell at the Grand Central Oyster Bar, but so are the pan roasts — rich, creamy stews made from your choice of shellfish instantaneously prepared in gleaming vessels that look like something from Diamond Jim Brady's kitchen. With oven-fresh baking powder biscuits to go along and the clatter of Grand Central Station just outside, a counter seat at the oyster bar with air perfumed by a piping hot pan roast is an only in New York experience.

Grand Central Oyster Bar: Grand Central Terminal, New York, NY
212-490-6650
www.oysterbarny.com

TOP 9 CHOWDERS

1. **Pearl Oyster Bar:** 18 Cornelia St., New York, NY
   212-691-8211
   www.pearloysterbar.com
2. **Maine Diner:** 2265 Post Rd., Wells, ME
   207-646-4441
   www.mainediner.com
3. **Abbott's Lobster in the Rough:** 117 Pearl St., Noank, CT
   860-536-7719
   www.abbotts-lobster.com
4. **Mabel's Lobster Claw:** 124 Ocean Ave., Kennebunkport, ME
   207-967-2562
5. **Champlin's Seafood Deck:** 256 Great Island Rd., Narragansett, RI
   401-783-3152
   www.champlins.com
6. **George's of Galilee:** 250 Sand Hill Cove Rd., Galilee, RI
   401-783-2306
   www.georgesofgalilee.com
7. **Flanders Fish Market:** 22 Chesterfield Rd., East Lyme, CT
   860-739-8866
   www.flandersfish.com

Travelers take refuge in New York City's temple to the oyster in Grand Central Station.

8. Grand Central Oyster Bar: Grand Central Terminal, New York, NY
212-490-6650
www.oysterbarny.com

9. Evelyn's: 2335 Main Rd., Tiverton, RI
401-624-3100
www.evelynsdrivein.com

COFFEE JELL-O
Boston, Massachusetts

James Hallett, proprietor of the august **Durgin-Park** restaurant from 1945 to 1993, abhorred waste. One morning he saw a waitress pouring out leftover coffee from the night before. "What are you doing with my coffee?" he asked her. She explained that no one wanted to drink yesterday's reheated brew, a point he couldn't argue with. Still, he thought, *There ought to be* something *we can do with it other than pour it away.* And so he came up with the idea of making it into coffee-flavored Jell-O.

Coffee Jell-O is beautiful, so darkly amber it can appear black, served in rectangular blocks that are each a

Cubes of coffee Jell-O crowned by fresh whipped cream at Boston's Durgin-Park

bit bigger than a domino and firm enough to jiggle in a buff sort of way. What makes it especially unusual — and true to Yankee taste — is how minimally sweet it is, hardly sugared at all. It is presented under a mantle of freshly whipped cream that, like the Jell-O itself, contains only a hint of sweetness. If you like saccharine desserts, this strangely dour concoction is not for you. If, however, you are a serious coffee lover and take yours with little or no sugar and enough cream to balance the java's acidity, it can be a revelation. We especially like it on a hot summer day — it's like iced coffee you can eat with a spoon.

Durgin-Park: 340 Faneuil Hall Marketplace, Boston, MA
617-227-2038
www.durgin-park.com

COFFEE MILK
Rhode Island

What's up with Rhode Island and coffee? The Ocean State is crazy for its flavor, which is not at all to suggest that you'll find an elevated coffee consciousness like that of Seattle (page 374). No, there are not too many terrific little coffee shops and virtuoso baristas other than a few hot spots in Providence, but everywhere you go on either side of Narragansett Bay, you will find coffee ice cream and coffee milk. In 1993 the state legislature declared coffee milk to be the official state drink. Diners sell it by the glass and convenience stores sell it in half-pint cardboard cartons. Home cooks make their own by infusing milk with coffee syrup. The leading brand of syrup is **Autocrat**, which sells six-packs of 16-ounce bottles of syrup as well as coffee milk T-shirts, all by mail.

Historians speculate that the popularity of coffee milk has something to do with the population's Italian heritage and an old-country tradition of gentling strong coffee with a lot of milk and sweetener. Another story is that a thrifty 1930s diner operator, not wanting to waste once-used grounds, mixed them with sugar and

---

MURDERBURGER AT MIDNIGHT

Haven Brothers of Providence, Rhode Island, has been around since the 1880s, when the original diner on wheels was pulled by horses. In true hash-house spirit, it is open all night, but *only* all night. It arrives at the corner of Fulton and Dorrance Streets at the foot of City Hall at dusk and drives away just before dawn. No ordinary food truck, it is a real sit-down diner with a cramped dining area where customers sit on stools at a narrow counter and enjoy such disreputable delights as a murderburger (twin patties with everything, including bacon, cheese, chili, lettuce, tomatoes, and pickles). Although there is a battery-powered mixer for milk shakes, the beverage of choice is, of course, coffee milk.

Haven Brothers: Fulton and Dorrance Sts., Providence, RI
   401-861-7777

---

milk to create coffee syrup, which could be used to flavor whole milk. Rhode Island coffee milk, like most of the coffee ice cream you find around the state, tends not to be strong at all; it is milk with a slightly sweet, mildly caffeinated flavor.

Add a scoop of ice cream to coffee milk and you have what Rhode Islanders know as a coffee cab, short for "coffee cabinet." Whir it and you've got what the rest of the nation might call a coffee milk shake and Bay State natives know as a frappe. On the subject of esoteric local mixological nomenclature, we should note that the term *milk shake* hereabouts means simply milk and flavoring without any ice cream.

Autocrat: 10 Blackstone Valley Place, Lincoln, RI
   401-333-3300
   www.autocrat.com
   Syrup available by mail-order

CRACKERS AND MILK
Weston, Vermont

Crackers and milk: there's a forthright sight! As served at the **Bryant House**, adjoining the well-known Vermont Country Store, the crackers are primitive: round, hard, white, and unflavored, the kind you'd expect to find in an old wooden cracker barrel. Known as common crackers, they originally were developed in Montpelier in 1828 and were considered essential for constructing a farmhouse chowder in the days when chowders were layered casseroles of crackers, potatoes, and salt pork. They were also used for cracker pudding or

Snacking Vermont-style: common crackers, cheddar, and milk at Weston's Bryant House

mock apple pie, or they were simply split, buttered, and toasted. They were the inspiration for their downsized brethren, oyster crackers, which

were developed when restaurateur John Isaacs of Green Bay, Wisconsin, wanted something more wieldy for customers to spoon up with their chili (page 245).

Common crackers pretty much disappeared until the Vermont Country Store started making them several decades ago. They are a true taste of Yankee folk life, and they are on the menu at the Bryant House, along with such other very local inamoratas as chicken pie (page 8), jonnycakes (page 36), and Indian pudding (page 35). "Crackers and Milk" is listed as something to have *with* your meal, but given that it comes with nice hunks of Vermont cheddar, it's a substantial dish. The customary way to enjoy it is to break some of the crack-

THE WILSON HOUSE

Bill Wilson, the cofounder of Alcoholics Anonymous, was born in East Dorset, Vermont, home of the family of Ethan Allen, who was a Revolutionary War hero before he became a furniture brand. Wilson's birthplace, built in 1852 and originally called the Mt. Aeolus Inn, was a halfway station for travelers along Route 7 between New York and Montreal, run by his grandmother and called the Wilson House when he came into the world in 1895. In the 1930s, when Prohibition ended, new owners made a bar out of his birth room. Later in life, Wilson used to joke that he was born in a barroom.

The Wilson House remained a public hostelry into the 1970s and

now operates as a nonprofit foundation with fourteen guest rooms. It includes a free museum of early AA memorabilia and hosts meetings of AA and other recovery programs. After Wilson died, in 1971, he was buried in the East Dorset Community Cemetery. His grave and that of his wife, Lois, have become compelling attractions for twelve-step tourists, who strew the simple plots with the medallions that recovering alcoholics earn for extended periods of sobriety as well as with flowers and bags of chopped walnuts, which Lois liked to snack on.
Wilson House: 378 Village St., Dorset, VT
802-362-5524
www.wilsonhouse.org

ers into cold whole milk and swirl them around a bit until they begin to soften (but not too much), then spoon up the farmy pabulum, punctuating its simple bliss with an occasional chaw on the cheese.

Bryant House: Main St. (Route 100), Weston, VT
802-824-6287
Crackers are available via mail-order: www.vermontcountrystore.com.

CRUMB-TOP APPLE PIE
Shelton, Connecticut

No human with a functional olfactory system can walk into **Beardsley's Cider Mill** and not yearn for pie. The spicy, hot smell of apples turning caramel-rich under a cloak of buttery gold pastry crumbles is agonizingly appetizing. On the short list of the nation's best apple pies, Beardsley's crumb earns highest marks for opu-

lence. The top is nearly cobbler-thick and so rich it seems moist despite its crunchiness. The apples underneath are neither mushy nor al dente but a joy to roll around on the tongue and to squeeze gently with the teeth, releasing the full, fruity essence of the Northern Spies. The apple pieces are suspended in a slurry of syrup of which there is just enough to mix with crumbs and make every forkful sheer bliss. Alas, there is no place to eat on the premises, nor does Beardsley's sell single slices, so we strongly suggest you bring a fork.

Beardsley's Cider Mill: 278 Leavenworth Rd., Shelton, CT
203-926-1098
www.beardsleyscidermill.com
Store hours are strictly seasonal, from mid-September through December 24.

DEEP-FRIED DOG
Connecticut

Historians believe that deep-fried hot dogs didn't make it to Connecticut until just after World War II, when a man remembered now only as "the southerner" set up shop along the Post Road in Fairfield. Boiled-in-oil franks have become a Connecticut signature dish, and the direct descendant of the southerner's enterprise, **Rawley's**, in Fairfield has become a cheap-eats superstar, its "Special" imitated throughout the state. A special is a hot dog deep-fried to succulent delectability, then turned on the grill until its skin becomes crisp. It is then bunned with mustard, raw onions, sauerkraut, and a

Apple crumb pie perfection from Beardsley's Cider Mill in Shelton, CT

Rawley's in Fairfield takes Connecticut's deep-fried dog to new heights.

big fistful of cooked bacon shreds. The sweetness, chewiness, and fatty luxury that the bacon adds to the wicked package is so good that some customers get theirs "heavy," with a double order of bacon. We find that configuration unbalanced, but clearly for those who love it, bacon is a foodstuff, like champagne and caviar, of which it is nearly impossible to have too much.

To many Connecticut connoisseurs, **Blackie's** of Cheshire is the be-all and end-all of deep-fried hot dogs. The staff at Blackie's refuses to call them deep-fried, preferring the term "boiled in oil." Whatever. The big, pink, Hummel's-brand plumpies emerge having blossomed with flavor quite literally, as their surface bursts from the heat. They are served plain in the bun, and customers top their

NOT FRIED BUT TOO GOOD TO IGNORE

Super Duper Weenie does not deep-fry hot dogs, and yet for reasons maybe too elusive to explain, it belongs here. Split and cooked on a griddle where the insides suck in maximum grill savor, SDW franks are, in our book, spiritually deep-fried. While they lack the wanton greasiness of a full oil bath (and in fact taste rather wholesome by comparison), their connection to the pantheon is irrefutable. Indeed, Super Duper Weenie actually offers a "New Englander," topped with kraut, bacon, mustard, relish, and onion, which is an ode to the Rawley's Special (page 15), which proprietor and chef Gary Zemola grew up eating. SDW is a goofy little place with torrents of kibitzing across the counter, but Gary, a graduate of the Culinary Institute of America, is serious not only about hot dogs (firm sausages he obtains from a local purveyor) but about condiments, too. Sauerkraut, chili, and onion sauce are all made from scratch, and relish is made from cucumbers that Gary pickles himself. You can build a dog any way you like, but SDW makes life easy by offering basic configurations. In addition to the New Englander, you can have a New Yorker, with sauerkraut, onion sauce, mustard, and hot relish, or a Chicagoan, buried beneath lettuce, tomato, mustard, hot relish, and a pickle spear and sprinkled with celery salt.

Super Duper Weenie: 306 Black Rock Turnpike, Fairfield, CT 203-334-DOGS www.superduperweenie.com

own with mustard and relish. Made from the same secret recipe that put the open-air drive-in on the map in 1928, Blackie's relish is luxuriously dense, dark green, and spicy enough to make your lips glow all afternoon. Customers are so devoted to this formula for frankfurter perfection that the kitchen does not bother to offer sauerkraut or chili. And other than a hamburger, there is nothing else on the menu. Nor will you hear "What will it be?" or other such extraneous palaver from the waitress at the counter. Customers enter, sit down, and call out a number, generally between one and six, indicating how many hot dogs are required.

Deep-fried dog connoisseurs frequently ask for their hot dogs well done so they're good and crusty at the edges of the fissures. At **Shiek's**

PATRICK BAKER & SONS

It had not occurred to us that church furnishings and clerical wardrobes need to be bought somewhere. We assumed that vestments, crucifixes, and holy statues somehow floated in through stained glass windows out of divine ether. Then one day on our way to Super Duper Weenie, we happened upon Patrick Baker & Sons, a one-stop-shopping opportunity for everything religious except faith itself. Here you can purchase Bibles that are big and leather-bound or vest-pocket-sized, palm ashes for Ash Wednesday, even red wine stain remover for sacramental accidents. Baker also operates a thriving church renovation business that can do everything from polishing old pews and restoring faded murals to supplying brand-new marble work, gold leaf, and mosaics.

Most of the upstairs ecclesiastical showroom is occupied by clerical garments, including gold-brocade chasubles and mitres that look grand enough to be a cardinal's Sunday best.

Unlike police uniforms, all attire is available to the public, many of whom buy clothing to bequeath to their church. The entire first floor of Patrick Baker & Sons is a retail store aimed more at the public than at the clergy. Here is a wealth of holy-themed cards, statuettes, and religious pictures for the wall, an inventory of wholesome videos (*The Bells of St. Mary's, The Sound of Music*), and holy medals of saints who offer support in dealing with any of life's problems. We were fascinated by a front-lawn Madonna that comes with strict strictures about proper installation: *WARNING! Grotto must be filled with 30 to 40 pounds of concrete or 30 to 40 pounds of gravel. ABSOLUTELY no sand or cat litter is to be used!*

Patrick Baker & Sons:
72 Chambers St., Fairfield, CT
203-366-5058
Second location: 1650 West St., Southington, CT
860-628-5566
www.churchgoods.com

of Torrington they are a Saturday special known as splitters — plump weenies that can be had with or without excellent chili but definitely must be tried with some of Shiek's peppery relish and most definitely topped with Shiek's sauerkraut, which is larded with bits of roast pork.

TOP DEEP-FRIED DOGS

1. **Blackie's:** 2200 Waterbury Rd., Cheshire, CT
   203-699-1819
2. **Rawley's:** 1886 Post Rd., Fairfield, CT
   203-259-9023
3. **Shiek's:** 235 E. Elm St., Torrington, CT
   860-489-5576

DIRT BOMB
Bantam, Connecticut

The **Bantam Bread Company,** a cramped little place down a flight of stairs in an old house in rural northwestern Connecticut, brought artisan bread to the Berkshire foothills over a decade ago, and while its loaves are wonderful, as are its flatbreads, tarts, and cookies, it's the dirt bomb we love most. It is a muffin that is vaguely spherical in shape, its exterior blanketed with a thick coat of cinnamon sugar that might be considered a confectionery version of dirt. In the world of muffins it is *the* bomb, as in *the best,* so much better than a nor-

---

DIRT BOMB

1 stick butter, softened
1 cup sugar
2 large eggs
3 cups all-purpose flour
1 tablespoon baking powder
¼ teaspoon baking soda
1 teaspoon salt
½ teaspoon ground nutmeg
1 cup milk

TOPPING
1 stick butter, melted
1 cup sugar mixed with 1 tablespoon ground cinnamon

Grease a 12-cup muffin tin and preheat the oven to 350 degrees.

Cream together the butter and sugar in a large bowl with an electric mixer.

Beat in the eggs, one at a time.

Combine the dry ingredients. Add one third of the dry ingredients and one third of the milk to the butter-sugar mixture. Beat at low speed until just barely mixed. Repeat twice, until all the ingredients are mixed together and the batter is smooth.

Fill the greased muffin tin and bake for about 20 minutes, until the muffins are golden brown. Cool on a rack. When cool enough to handle, dip each bomb in the melted butter and roll it in the cinnamon sugar.

Dirt bombs are best when served still slightly warm, but they will keep for several hours.

MAKES 12 MUFFINS

No ordinary muffin: the famous dirt bomb of Bantam Bread Company in CT

mal muffin, and in some ways so unlike one, that it almost seems wrong to label it as such. Its mouthfeel is more like that of a doughnut: slightly crisp exterior skin enveloping nutmeg-tinged tenderness that is as velvety as a whipped-cream pound cake. Its sumptuous character is owed to the fact that before it gets rolled in cinnamon sugar, the dirt bomb is fully immersed in melted butter. The butter seeps in and creates a halo of inexpressible opulence that separates the creamy interior from the golden, cinnamon-crisp skin.

(Local ordinance prohibits the Bantam Bread Company from offering coffee, which is a tragedy. No pastry goes better with a bottomless cup. To be truthful, a dirt bomb is too rich to have without coffee. So BYO.)

Bantam Bread Company:
853 Bantam Rd., Bantam, CT
860-567-2737
Second location: 333 Whiting St., Plainville, CT

860-747-1686
www.bantambread.com

DOUGHNUT
Inland New England

Almost any recently made doughnut from a national chain offers the undeniable satisfaction of sweet, deep-fried fat, but mass-produced ones cannot compare to the edible ecstasy of a fresh doughnut made by a master. New England is blessed with more than its fair share of the world's greatest sinkers, foremost among them the cinnamon doughnuts made each morning at **Dottie's Diner** in Woodbury, Connecticut. Fashioned from baking powder batter and cooked until the outside is dark brown, encasing creamy cake with enough body to pleasure teeth as well as taste buds, they are heavily coated with cinnamon sugar while still hot, so the first thing your teeth meet is the sandy-sweet veil that clings to their crisp skin. Dottie's chocolate doughnuts, made from the

Whisper-light cream puffs at Butler's in Somerset, MA, filled with real whipped cream

same heavy-cream batter, are robed in a silken fudge glaze that is far from upscale chocolate and yet infinitely satisfying in its blue-collar way.

At **Neil's Donut and Bake Shop**, just off the Merritt Parkway near Wallingford, Connecticut, Neil Bukowski makes lightweight glazed doughnuts and more substantial cake doughnuts as well as luxurious jam-filled crullers and big round yeast-dough Bismarks that are sliced in half and loaded with jelly. The glazed doughnuts are excellent, and the old-fashioned ones are addictive: dense and satisfying, with insides that are luxuriously unctuous from the time they spend in their hot oil bath. Early in the morning, when they're still warm, they virtually melt in your mouth.

In fact, every worthy doughnut is like a rose in bloom: its magic has something to do with the knowledge that its allure is evanescent. Freshness is decisive. Some of the greatest ones you will ever eat are the devil's food doughnuts served every morning at a little shop called **Coffee An'** in Westport, Connecticut. They are

The Bismark at Neil's in Wallingford, CT, a sugary orb of yeasted dough and jelly

truly devilish — delightfully oily with a roundhouse chocolate punch. But take home a bag and eat one the next morning: it's like waking up in bed next to a stranger whose night-before appeal is perplexing.

Allie's, in North Kingstown, Rhode Island, has two separate entrances and two adjoining order counters, just to handle the mobs who flood in for their morning pastry fix. Made in a giant open kitchen in back where the bakers heft mighty bags of flour and sheathe crullers with a gossamer glaze, Allie's doughnuts come in an eye-boggling variety, from plain cake to coconut-glazed solid chocolates to a rainbow of jimmie-topped extravaganzas. We love the hefty sugar sticks, with their crunchy exteriors and tender insides that are sweet but not cloying.

If you're looking for the biggest variety of the most colorful doughnuts, there is only one place to go: **Tastease**, a tiny Hartford bakeshop that makes modestly sized mini doughnuts with Kodachrome rainbows of frosting, sprinkles, nuts, coconut, and nuts in beautiful geometric patterns. Of the approximately three dozen varieties available on any one day, we recommend lemon-filled, orange cream, and caramel chocolate.

The doughnuts at **Butler's Colonial Donut House** in Somerset, Massachusetts, near Fall River, are so extraordinary that they barely qualify as doughnuts. In fact, they are holeless — giant, featherweight cream puffs, sliced in half and filled with whipped, sweetened cream that is either plain or mocha-flavored. They are made from raised yeast dough and are so frail that you want to hold them very gently, lest you dent the surface with a loutish thumb. The cool filling is pure and white (or, in the case of mocha, tan), and the counterpoise of silky whipped cream with ethereal cake, crowned by a spill of powdered sugar, is aristocratic. The doughnut-like pastry we recommend even more than these airy spheres is a Long John, a tubular puff that is sliced and filled not only with the dreamy cream filling but also with a ribbon of sweet raspberry jelly. Alex Kogler, who ran Butler's when we first came upon it many years ago, referred to the Long John as "the ultimate" — an assessment with which we would concur.

The cider doughnut of **Cold Hollow Cider Mill** in Waterbury Center, Vermont, is less than 3 inches across, unraised and unfrosted, with a crunch to its surface and insides as dark as gingerbread. Made with apple cider pressed on the premises and a good measure of cinnamon and clove, it is a spicy morsel, just sweet enough to harmonize with apple cider. That harmony is this doughnut's raison d'etre, for the principal business of this very popular roadside attraction is making cider. You can get it cold, hot and mulled, or mixed with cranberry juice, by the cup or the jug. It is flabbergasting to walk from the parking lot into the cider press room, where the smell of apples is as intense as fermenting mash in a bourbon distillery. Here you can help yourself to a sample from a big silver drum, watch apples being pressed, or view a video that shows exactly how an apple on a tree becomes cider in a glass. Walk from the cider press room

into the store and a second olfactory wallop awaits. Here the tantalizing smell of hot doughnuts rules the air, overwhelming even the aroma of the Vermont cheeses, maple candies, and baked breads for sale. At the back counter, uniform batches of doughnuts are always lined up for sale by the dozen or singly, with cider or coffee on the side. Behind the counter is the single small machine that turns out these happy doughnuts, and if you arrive when it's in use, the sight is spellbinding. Perfect circles of dough are mechanically plopped onto a kind of treadmill that takes them through the hot oil, flips them once, and sends them out into the air crusty and hot. When we asked the strapping teenage boy serving coffee if he personally liked doughnuts, he admitted, "I eat so many all day, they get kinda gross to me by dinnertime. But in the morning, when they're hot at eight o'clock, I always have a dozen."

The apple cider doughnuts made by **Donut Dip** in East Longmeadow, Massachusetts, are full-sized and magnificently crunchy-skinned. They smell like fresh-pressed cider and deliver a bushel's worth of apple flavor in every cinnamon-haloed bite. The stalwart Yankee varieties include tangy sour cream, plain home-cut (old-fashioned cake), devil's food, and, in autumn, pumpkin. Raised glazed doughnuts also are available, and the egg-batter French cruller, while it looks like the Dunkin' Donuts standard, is gossamer, melt-in-the-mouth swanky.

Neon signs in the window of **Kane's Donuts** advertise FRESH DONUTS and HOT COFFEE, but devotees know that as worthy and multifarious as the doughnuts are, it is the coffee roll that earns this decades-old bake-house in Saugus, Massachusetts, its place on the honor roll. A vast, hole-less, crumble-bottomed cinnamon roll topped with tender frosting and a shroud of sugar, it costs four times what a single doughnut costs but will easily feed four people. Although huge — maybe a foot across — it is fragile rather than doughy, so it's easy

The cinnamon doughnuts at Dottie's are reborn in heavenly bread pudding.

to pull wieldy sections away from the big pastry mother ship. It truly is the perfect coffee companion, too fragile to be dunkable but just what you want in your left hand if you are picking up the cup with your right.

DONUT BREAD PUDDING

You can head up to a certain heady Litchfield County, Connecti-cut, inn and enjoy donut bread pudding as the $10 exclamation point for a $50 meal. Or you can go to Dottie's Diner and have the same dessert for $3.50. Dottie's makes it for the inn, using its renowned cinnamon doughnuts. Rather than turning custardy the way ordinary bread tends to do, these substantial sinkers main-tain their doughnut avoirdupois, poising the pudding on the verge of cake. It comes as a quivery cream-and-tan cube swirled with luscious veins of cinnamon sugar and topped with crème anglaise and berries. Dottie's pies are very good and the éclairs divine, but if you are looking for an extra-spe-cial sweet to top off your supper of chicken pie (page 8), donut bread pudding is a once-in-a-lifetime extravagance.

9 SUPREME DOUGHNUTS

1. **Dottie's Diner:** 740 S. Main St., Woodbury, CT
   203-263-2516
2. **Butler's Colonial Donut House:** 1448 Grand Army Highway, Somerset, MA
   508-672-0865
3. **Neil's Donut & Bake Shop:** 83 N. Turnpike Rd., Yalesville, CT
   203-269-4255
4. **Donut Dip:** 648 N. Main St., East Longmeadow, MA
   413-736-2224
5. **Coffee An':** 343 Main St., Westport, CT
   203-227-3808
6. **Allie's Donuts:** 3661 Quaker Lane (Route 2), North Kingstown, RI
   401-295-8060

7. **Kane's Donuts:** 120 Lincoln Ave., Saugus, MA
781-233-8499
8. **Tastease Donuts:** 70 New Park Ave., Hartford, CT
860-233-2235
9. **Cold Hollow Cider Mill:** 300 Waterbury–Stowe Rd. (Route 100), Waterbury Center, VT
802-244-8771
www.coldhollow.com

FLO DOG
Cape Neddick, Maine

Hot dogs are the only thing on the menu at **Flo's**, so when you enter the low-slung, six-seat diner and peer through the pass-through window into the kitchen, the staff will ask just one question: "How many?" They are diminutive franks, so it's not unusual for regulars to call for four, six, even eight. We've seen normal-sized men consume a dozen at lunch, allotting no more than two hearty bites per dog.

As much as devotees adore them, Flo's are not gourmet hot dogs, that's

In Cape Neddick, ME, Flo's piles dogs high with hot relish and mayo.

for certain. They are blubbery little pinkies with squared-off ends that, frankly, all by themselves would not be very interesting. However, nobody gets Flo's dogs plain. They require an application of hot sauce. Nothing like the beefy chili on a chili dog, it is a meatless, dark, sweet/hot relish of stewed onions, glistening with spice and customarily finished with a sprinkling of celery salt. A "special" at Flo's is a hot dog with this sauce and a thin line of mayonnaise, a magical combination of heat and sweet that transforms the modest dog into a blue-ribbon champ. If instead of mayo you get mustard with the hot sauce, the kick of the sauce seems supercharged and every bite is a tastebuds exclamation mark. Each little package is nestled in a split-top Yankee bun, pulled fresh out of the steam box, with a fine, silky texture and an ineffable tenderness that are vital components of the singular culinary experience of dining at Flo's.

Flo's: 1359 Route 1, Cape Neddick, ME
No phone
Multiple locations: See www.floshotdogs.com for specifics. Note that Flo's is open only for lunch and is closed on Wednesdays.

FRIED CLAMS
Yankee Shore

"I'm a semiretired plumber, but I've dug clams all my life," said a cook at one of the great clam shacks of Essex, Massachusetts. "The ones you want to deep-fry are just about *soooo* long."

He held his thumb and middle finger a scant 2 inches apart. "Any bigger than that and a clam is good only for frying in a pan, or for people in Connecticut. If a clam is too small, like those that come from Canada, it won't have much taste. Eating little clams is no better than eating peanuts."

Strong convictions about clams are common among cooks, customers, and staff at restaurants all along the Atlantic shore north of Boston. This is America's fried clam belt, where a person who is serious about fried clams wants to know their size, exactly which beds they come from, what they're fried in, and how often the kitchen sifts its meal. The best clams for deep-frying — steamers large enough to pack a salty savor and yet not so big they wind up as fodder for crude-tongued Connecticuters — are hand-raked at low tide from beds in the Essex River, where smooth sand and pure water combine to yield the sweetest, most tender clams in the East. And it is along the winding marsh-lined roads that run among the fishing and resort villages east of Route 1 that you find a handful of casual restaurants that serve the most delicious ones on earth. After you have eaten them in Essex and Ipswich, you are spoiled for life. As long as your taste buds retain the memory of these bulging, crisp-fried beauties, any other fried clam will always seem a little flat.

Please don't misunderstand: There are excellent fried clams to be savored all along the Yankee shore. At **Lenny and Joe's** in Madison, Connecticut, the soft shells are crunchy and sweet and come with the added attraction of some of the most exquisitely crisp onion rings this side of Saturn. At **Sea Swirl** in Mystic, Connecticut, you want to call the fried clams debonair: They feel so fine and lithe when you heft them from their cardboard container. Sea Swirl also offers irresistibly downscale clam-shack atmosphere, with picnic tables sandwiched between Route 1 and an auto supply store and its best seats providing a view of the restaurant's storage area and such scenic wonders as giant drums of Eat-It-All Twinkle Cote ice cream topping. The **Clam Shack** of Kennebunkport, Maine, best known for its lobster roll (page 41), can dish out some of the plushest clams that will ever melt in your mouth. At **Five Islands Lobster Company** in Georgetown, Maine, the clams are right-sized and addictive, their briny marine essence encased in a microthin crust. Despite such worthies, though, it is Massachusetts's North Shore that is clam-eater paradise, where bivalves and hot lard are fused in Frialators to produce perfection on a paper plate, with tartar sauce on the side.

The great North Shore fried clam is a crusty, pale gold nugget big enough

The Clam Box in Ipswich, MA, proudly serving the sweetest clams since 1938

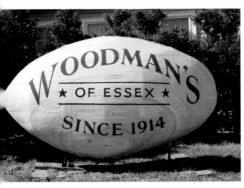

A Massachusetts landmark, the birthplace of the fried clam

It has a lot of bounce in your fingers, as if it is about to fall apart and as if the tenuous veil of crisp cooked cornmeal that envelops it wants to simply disintegrate. It is a piece of food on the verge of transformation. That's the magic. When you savor it, the crust fairly melts in your mouth. It has crunch, but like the crust of a blue-ribbon pie, the brittleness turns lush on the tongue. It is both rich and bracing, one of those wondrous foods that seems to provoke appetite long after hunger has been appeased. Most fried clam platters appear frighteningly enormous when you pick them up at the order window of the restaurant, and even pints are customarily served with so many clams that a surplus spills out of the box onto the plate or tray below, but it is amazing how easy it is to plow through order after order here in clam country.

The first stop on any clam-eating tour should be **Woodman's of Essex**, because it was here that the

to be one greedy mouthful. It is a heavy piece of food, the way steamer clams are, and although it first appears to be a twisted, free-form blob, close scrutiny reveals two distinct areas, the long, chewy neck and the tender belly. Frequently a fried clam resembles a bulbous cartoon ring (the neck) set with a giant stone (the belly). The belly yields the distinctive marine smack of a freshly opened mollusk. On the very finest fried clam platters, the bellies vary subtly in size, making each and every piece a unique eating experience. Some are, in fact, scarcely bigger than a Virginia peanut, making a package with more crust than clam, in which the chewy neck provides the prime sensation and the silky morsel of oceanic meat plays second fiddle. On others, the belly is so large that it reminds you of a steamer or a clam on the half shell, with a nectarous clamitude that has the quality of being cooked and yet maintains its fresh, briny wallop.

A good fried clam feels incredibly fragile when you lift it from the plate or from its cardboard pint container.

The keys to the frail crust of the Clam Box's fried clams are corn flour and ultra-clean oil.

fried clam was invented. The tale is that late in June 1916, Lawrence "Chubby" Woodman, who sold clams in the shell and freshly cooked potato chips from a small stand on the Essex Causeway, was approached by a friend named Mr. Tarr, who wanted something different. Tarr suggested that Chubby throw some clams into the iron fry kettle with his potato chips. (Chips themselves were a fairly new invention, from Saratoga, New York.) A week later, on Sunday, July 2, when Mr. Tarr returned, Woodman presented him with a plate of fried clams and some cider on the side.

Woodman's clams are beauties: light gold, not particularly brittle but with a suave crunch to their surface and a velvety interior that is pure pleasure on the tongue. Proprietor Larry Woodman told us that the elegant texture of the crust is due to fresh meal. After the raw clams are dipped in evaporated milk, they are dredged in cornmeal. If the meal isn't regularly sifted, it cakes up and chunks of it stick to the clam. "You want a nice, smooth crust," he said. "You don't want a bead of meal on your clam." On days when the clams run large, they are zestfully clammy, each one a big, juicy mouthful that seafood lovers will adore. Squeamish types who don't want so much clam taste can choose clam strips, an option on almost all eat-in-the-rough menus. Strips, as opposed to "whole belly" clams, are made from sea clams, not steamers, and they have no gooey bellies. They are simply chewy strips of vaguely clam-flavored crispness — fried crust with a soupçon of ocean flavor.

The Holy Grail for clam connoisseurs is the **Clam Box** in Ipswich, a landmark since 1938, built to look just like the trapezoidal pint box in which clams are served: 15 by 15 feet at the bottom, a little wider at the top, and 30 feet high. Clam Box clams are golden blistered squiggles, rich and satisfying, sheathed in a frail corn-flour crust that yearns to blend with the clam inside. They seem nearly weightless compared to most clams, and their taste is melt-away light, too. According to Marina "Chickie" Aggelakis, the proprietor, the secret is ultra-clean oil. (A sign at the order window apologizes for occasional delays that occur when the oil is changed.) The frying medium is a blend of lard and vegetable oil, and the clams are, of course, always local. "You cannot change anything around here," Chickie told us. "Clam eaters like things to stay the same. I know because one time last year my supplier sent me a different brand of corn flour, but I didn't notice the change in packaging. My gardener, who eats here regularly, said, 'Chickie, what have you done? Don't tell me you've changed the recipe!' The next day I went back to my old brand of corn flour."

TOP 3 FRIED CLAMS

1. **Clam Box:** 246 High St.,
   Ipswich, MA
   978-356-9707
   www.ipswichma.com/ipswichma/
   clambox
2. **Clam Shack:** 2 Western Ave.
   (Route 9), Kennebunkport, ME
   207-967-2560
   www.theclamshack.net

3. Woodman's of Essex:
121 Main St., Essex, MA
978-768-6057
www.woodmans.com

Also

Five Islands Lobster Co.: 1447
Five Islands Rd., Georgetown, ME
207-371-2990
www.fiveislandslobster.com
Lenny and Joe's Fish Tale: 1301
Boston Post Rd., Madison, CT
203-245-7289
www.ljfishtale.com
Sea Swirl: 30 Williams Ave.
(Route 1), Mystic, CT
860-536-3452
www.seaswirlofmystic.com

FRIED DOUGH AND DOUGHBOY
Southern New England

Nearly every part of the country has its own way with deep-fried dough, from beignets in New Orleans (page 370) to sopaipillas and Indian fry

Fair food: chewy, sugar-encrusted fried dough

bread in the Southwest (page 356). New England's version is known, cleverly enough, as fried dough.

The great thing about fried dough is getting it just-made and piping hot. That is why it is summer-fair food par excellence, served from food trucks and still glistening with the oil in which it was fried. Fried dough should not be mistaken for Pennsylvania's funnel cakes, now popular at fairs throughout the nation, which differ from fried dough because they are made with unleavened batter rather than with risen yeast dough, and they are crunchier and less chewy.

What is sold throughout the Northeast as fried dough comes in two versions: sweet, spread with melted butter and sprinkled with cinnamon sugar, and savory, painted with Italianate red sauce. Because it is carnival walk-around food, not a lot of restaurants make a specialty of it, which is one reason we treasure **Doogie's** in Newington, Connecticut (the other being its excellent 16-inch monster hot dogs). You can get it sweet or savory at this cheeky drive-in, where a sign on the wall advises, "We're neither slow nor fast. We're half-fast." Doogie's prodigious frying talents are evidenced also in bite-sized mini corn dogs, which our Texas friend Jim Raines praises as being almost as good as those served at the Texas state fair.

Doughboys are a subset of fried dough, spherical and small rather than flat and broad, and they are always sweet. They are a close relation to Portuguese-ancestored *malasadas*, also known as flippers, but are more a side dish than a snack. The spherical fritters of yeasty satisfaction have a nice chew, a faint crispness to their tan skin, and an extra-thick cloak of sugar crystals covering the outside like snowflake iron filings on a magnet. They possess a sweet breadiness that provides exciting equilibrium for almost anything ocean-flavored, whether or not the latter is deep-fried, too; they are especially right alongside that peculiar Rhode Island passion, snail salad (page 62). That's why we recommend eating them at the eponymous eatery **Iggy's Doughboys**, in Warwick, where the snail salad is mighty good, too.

2 TOP FRIED DOUGH SOURCES

Iggy's Doughboys: 889 Oakland Beach Ave., Warwick, RI
401-737-9459
Second location: 1157 Point Judith Rd., Narragansett, RI
401-783-5608
www.iggysdoughboys.com
Doogie's: 2525 Berlin Turnpike, Newington, CT
860-666-6200
See www.doogieshotdogs.com for additional locations.

HOT DOG WAGON
Connecticut

One of us Sterns is such a fanatic when it comes to hot dogs that he dreams about writing a book devoted only to that one subject, listing 500 or so of America's best. When asked what makes his home state of Connecticut great, he can reply "hot dogs" in all honesty, except for the caveat

Get 'em while they're here: An Airstream trailer in Portland, CT, has become a wiener on wheels.

that the answer doesn't respect the state's mother lode of pizza. By any measure, Connecticut is filled with top-tier wieners. Our favorites are Rawley's, Blackie's, and Super Duper Weenie (all discussed on pages 15–16), but respecting the fact that not all readers are quite so wiener-obsessed, we won't sing detailed hosannas to such other worthies as **Capitol Lunch** in New Britain (for the sauce), **Doogie's** in Newington (home of the 16-incher), **Lake Zoar Drive-In** in Stevenson (foot-longs), **Guida's** in Middlefield (10 inches), **JK's** in Danbury (Texas hots), **Mr. Mac's Canteen** in Monroe (fire-breathing chili dogs), and the **Windmill** in Stratford (for brats and kielbasa, too). However, it is important to honor one significant branch of Connecticut wienerdom: the dog wagon. Unlike typical urban hot dog carts, most of which are blah, Connecticut's mobile eateries sparkle with personality, and several have superb hot dogs. It is typical for them to appear on their spot midmorning, then get pulled away after lunch.

The most elusive is **Big Ed's**, which parks in the commuter parking lot next to Chuck's Steak House in Danbury. Tracing its lineage back to the early 1970s, when Big Ed, grandfather of the current proprietor, parked his lunch wagon adjacent to the great Danbury Fair (an annual event that took place where a shopping mall now stands), Big Ed's sells hot dogs and kielbasa in soft buns, available topped with all the usual condiments, including chili, cheese, and sauerkraut, plus Big Ed's cooked onion relish. This is a dark red, hot potion with a sweet, smoky flavor, and it would be good if spread on supermarket bologna. But Big Ed's dogs are superior, so taut in their natural casings that they squeak when teeth attack and spurt a piggy richness for which the sharp taste of onions is a made-in-heaven foil. Big Ed's has no dining facilities other than chest-high counters on the sides of the trailer at which to stand. Most customers eat in their cars. Trash cans are provided. The proprietors go on vacation in winter and take Sunday and Monday off, and sometimes other days, too.

You won't miss **Top Dog** if you are driving along Route 66 in Portland between March and the end of October, Tuesday through Saturday. It is a 1963 Airstream trailer converted into a modern-day Wienermobile, looking like a hot dog in a bun on wheels. (Pulling it is a fully restored Checker cab.) Out the windows of the Wienermobile come plump, snappy franks topped with extraordinary condiments, including slow-cooked sauerkraut and/or Creole relish. Nor is **Carolyn's Weenie Wagon** of Sey-

mour easy to ignore. It, too, is a converted house trailer, not as pop-arty as Top Dog but nonetheless decorated with a charming image of a doghouse out of which flows a never-ending stream of bunned franks. On the car that pulls the trailer, a sign says, DON'T JUST "BEEP." STOP IN AND EAT. Carolyn's forte is sweet and spicy chili sauce. Finally, **Chez Lenard** is a wagon on the sidewalk of Ridgefield's Main Street across from Ballard Park. Its menu lists such gourmet creations as "Le Hot Dog Choucroute Alsacienne" (with sauerkraut and mustard), "Le Hot Dog Excelsior Veneziano" (with Italian peppers and sautéed onions), and the "Logano Suisse" dog, blanketed with cheese fondue. Yes, they sound fancy, and some of the toppings are a cut above, but even with only a line of yellow mustard, they are outstanding all-beef hot dogs with a good garlic kick. The *specialité de la maison* is a "Supreme": mustard, relish (hot or sweet), ketchup, and chopped onions. *Très bon!*

TOP 4 HOT DOG WAGONS

1. **Big Ed's:** 20 Segar St., Danbury, CT
   No phone
   Summer only, Tuesday–Saturday
2. **Chez Lenard:** Main St., Ridgefield, CT
   203-431-1313
   www.chezlenard.com
3. **Top Dog:** Route 66, Portland, CT
   No phone
   March–October, Tuesday–Saturday
4. **Carolyn's Weenie Wagon:** 109 River St., Seymour, CT
   No phone

Capitol Lunch: 510 Main St., New
Britain, CT
860-229-8237

Doogie's: 2525 Berlin Turnpike,
Newington, CT
860-666-6200
See www.doogieshotdogs.com for
additional locations.

Guida's: 484 Meriden Rd.,
Middlefield, CT
860-349-9039
www.guidasrestaurant.com

JK's: 126 South St., Danbury, CT
203-743-4004

Lake Zoar Drive-In: 14
Roosevelt Dr., Stevenson, CT
203-268-8137

Mr. Mac's Canteen: 838 Main
St., Monroe, CT
203-459-9595

Windmill Restaurant: 400
Hollister St., Stratford, CT
203-378-6886

ICE CREAM
Throughout New England

Ice cream in New England deserves
its own special place in these annals.
The region consumes twice as much
per capita as anywhere else. New
England also stakes claim to most of
the great moments in contemporary
ice cream history, from the ingenious
twenty-eight-flavor concept of Howard Johnson, who started in 1925 at
a drugstore in Wollaston, Massachusetts, to the countercultural empire
of Ben Cohen and Jerry Greenfield,
who rode tides of ice cream ardor to
pop-culture fame and fortune with

the superrich, crazy-flavored stuff
they began hand-cranking in 1978 in
a defunct gas station near the University of Vermont in Burlington.

Ice cream is so big in this part of
the world that when an ambitious
team of eaters from Roadfooddigest
.com set out in the summer of 2008
to sample the region's fifty best ice
creams, they were besieged by fans
of at least fifty other celebrated ice
cream parlors that weren't even on
the hit list. Nonetheless, their findings are a gold mine for sweet tooths.
They declared the ice cream at **Tubby's** in Wayne, Maine, "world class,"
and wrote, "Stop what you are doing
and plan a trip right now." Among
Tubby's unique flavors are Tree Hug-
ger, which is maple ice cream speck-

**The custard cone at Connecticut's
Ridgefield Ice Cream Shop tantalizes
with velvety swirls.**

It looks like Carvel, but Ridgefield Ice Cream's similarities to the chain end there.

led with rolled oats, and Cinnamon Trail, cinnamon with raisins, cranberries, coconut shreds, M&Ms, and chocolate chips. Tubby's vanilla ice cream, "smooth and rich without being overly sweet," is crowned magnificently with thin, cocoa-rich fudge sauce. The Roadfood eaters also sang hosannas to **Sundae School** in Dennisport, Massachusetts, for its Bass River Mud, a "combination of solid coffee flavor and abundant mix-ins," and to the idyllic **Buttonwood Farm** in Griswold, Connecticut, for its graham-cracker-flavored ice cream studded with chunks of chocolate-covered graham crackers.

Indian pudding (page 35) is New England's alone, and it is a strange and rare inspiration for ice cream. You will find it every fall at **We-Li-Kit**, a seasonal shack in Abington in northeast Connecticut, where it is redolent of molasses and cream with an earthy corn undertone. The best Indian pudding ice cream — and one of the great ice creams of any flavor — was discovered at out-of-the-way **Shaw's Ridge Farm** in Sanford,

Maine, by our Roadfood eating team, who thought that grainy cornmeal throughout elevated its strong molasses flavor into pantheon status.

You won't find Grape-Nuts ice cream anywhere outside New England, where, like Grape-Nuts pudding, it is a familiar flavor. How and why this came to be, we do not know; but if you want to taste it at its best, and in one of the nicest possible places, go to **Shady Glen** in Manchester, Connecticut, an old-fashioned dairy bar (famous for cheeseburgers; see page 333), where it is as creamy as crème fraîche, with little bits of tan cereal streaking through the white like little shooting stars of whole-grain flavor.

There are exotic and elaborate flavors at the **Big Dipper** at the edge of Waterbury, Connecticut, but as far as we're concerned, only two words need to be spoken when you step to the counter: *toasted almond.* Inspired by the traditional Good Humor bar of the same name but far more delicious, this creamy, nutty stuff has the luxury of marzipan and the euphoria of a sunny summer day. The Big Dipper offers other vivid two-note flavors, including a cinnamon-coffee blend called Cafe Vienna. Buy a cone or cup of whatever size you like; Big Dipper charges by weight (the ice cream's, not yours). Because it is not cloyingly rich, it is the sort of stuff that begs to be a triple-dip fudge sundae. The line stretches far out the door on a pleasant night, and the staff is famously fun to deal with.

In 1976, for the bicentennial parade in Bethlehem, New Hampshire, Bill and Grace Bishop decided to

Two monstrous cones presented by the staff of the Big Dipper in Prospect, CT

hand-crank some ice cream. People loved it and ate all the couple made, so after the festivities were over, the Bishops made more. Four years later they bought a Victorian house across from the three-horse cemetery in Littleton and opened **Bishop's**, now one of the most beloved ice cream parlors in northern New England. Yes, there are some baroque concoctions on the menu, Bishop's Bash in particular (chocolate chips, nuts, and brownie chunks in dark chocolate), but the best flavors here have the carefree quality that ice cream used to have before the era of overwrought amalgams loaded with cookies and candy. Vanilla is cream-white; chocolate is only gently chocolaty and not too serious; coffee is creamy more than caffeinated. Here, too, is the old Yankee favorite Grape-Nuts ice cream, with little nubs of cereal softened to grainy bits of salubrious texture in the smooth ivory custard.

Greater Boston has bragging rights as the city with the best ice cream places, and among these is the historic **Herrell's**, in Cambridge. We say historic not because it is old —

it opened in 1980 — but because its founder, Steve Herrell, had previously opened Steve's Ice Cream, in Somerville, in 1973, and it was at Steve's that the concept of mixing candy and cookies into ice cream was formulated. If you like such flavors as cookies and cream or Heath Bar crunch, you have Steve to thank. Now formally known as smoosh-ins, the extra-added attractions actually seem rather superfluous when you spoon up some of Herrell's unsullied vanilla, a single, perfect confluence of sweet, creamy, and cold.

First the bad news about **Christina's** in Cambridge: seating is severely limited, so it is not uncommon, even in inclement weather, for crowds of Cantabridgians to hover on the sidewalk licking cones and spooning into cups. And it is a nightmare to get here by car; street parking is impossible. Now the good news: burnt sugar ice cream. What a stroke of genius! To combine the luxury of high-butterfat ice cream with the tongue-teasing balancing act of sweet sugar teetering at the edge of bitter-burnt is a pleasure something like great crème brûlée, but cool, refreshing, and vibrant. It is a flavor that stimulates appetite at the same time it sates it, inevitably causing return trips in twenty-minute increments, and finally futile alcoholic-like promises to eat moderately the next time. Burnt sugar is only one of dozens of interesting flavors at this pinnacle of ice cream parlors. Other must-licks include blood peach (in season), saffron, Mexican chocolate, khulfi (cardamom), and banana-cinnamon. **Toscanini's**, also in Cambridge, calls its version of this magic formula burnt caramel, and it is even more intensely flavored, its caramel punch cushioned in a cloud of creaminess. Toscanini's hot fudge sauce is some of the most sophisticated you'll find anywhere, and while you'd never want it atop burnt caramel (which precludes enhancement), it is choco-heaven on the house vanilla.

Believe in the name of rich chocolate, the flagship flavor of **Dr. Mike's**, in Bethel, Connecticut. It is one of the richest dairy dishes this side of butter — creamy and chocolaty beyond the power of prayer. The devilish infusion of cocoa and cream is generally scooped out and planted on a cone or in a cup still fairly hard, presenting major issues for the eater, especially the eater of a cone. You do not want to eat this stuff icy cold. The more it softens, the more its flavor blossoms; it hits maximum cocoa creaminess at the point where it is on the verge of melting. Atop a cone, it is dangerous: the longer you wait for it to reach its peak, the more likely it is to melt onto hands, face, and shirt. And its deep darkness has a way of coloring whatever it hits with the intensity of oil paint. When eating a rich chocolate ice cream cone, even the most dignified adult runs the risk of getting splotched like a chocolate-crazed kid.

Like coffee milk (page 12), coffee ice cream is ubiquitous in Rhode Island. It's rarely espresso-strong, but more like café au lait, with just enough of a caffeinated kick and healthy tan to balance the opulence of cream. **Gray's** coffee ice cream may disappoint caffeine-heads, but for Ocean Staters, it is just-right sweet and creamy with a modest coffee twist. We love to pair a scoop of this gentle-tempered stuff with a scoop of Gray's ginger ice cream, which packs eye-widening bite from bits of fresh gingerroot that dot the cream. Gray's, in Tiverton, is popular and oodles of fun, a quirky combination of ice cream parlor, grocery store, and short-order cafe. Summertime customers eat in their cars in the broad parking lot or at one of a handful of picnic tables with a view of the proprietor's pet llamas.

Open from Mother's Day to Labor Day, **Hodgman's** in New Gloucester, Maine, is the sort of place that calls out all summer to anyone with a sweet tooth and a love for old-fashioned Americana. It is a roadside custard shop offering only basic flavors, vanilla and chocolate plus one special each day. There are no mix-ins, swirls, chunks, chips, cookie dough, or candies desecrating this dairy-pure manna. It's just custard. But oh, what thick and creamy custard it is. We like vanilla best, plain. Nothing is more perfectly satisfying on a warm

The custard ice cream at Hodgman's in New Gloucester, ME, makes a glorious sundae.

Dr. Mike's in Bethel, CT, has some of the richest ice cream in New England.

summer day, whether perched on a cone or served in a cup. You can doll it up if you wish. Hodgman's menu lists sundaes, frappes and floats, banana boats and thunderstorms, hot fudge royals, tin roofs, and tin lizzies. Whole custard pies are also available.

A lot of people we direct to the **Ridgefield Ice Cream Shop** on Route 7 in Connecticut tell us they arrived scratching their heads quizzically, wondering what could be so recommendable about a common Carvel stand. That's what the Ridgefield Ice Cream Shop used to be, and that is exactly what it looks like. However, years ago, proprietor Felix Lechner bought the business from Carvel, keeping the old-fashioned soft-serve ice cream makers. Since then Carvel has gone to manufacturing methods that pump up its product with more air, creating greater volume but dilut-

ing flavor. Lechner never went that route. Using the vintage silver machines that he maintains with parts salvaged from old Carvel stands, he makes what he calls "custard without the egg." Opaque and full-flavored, the velvety creation is robust enough to mound up impossibly high within the store's fine wafer cones. Even a large serving, which rises a full 6 inches above the rim of the cone, is dense enough to grasp a shell of quick-dry dip-top, either chocolate or cherry-flavored. The vanilla is excellent. The chocolate is just about the most perfect chocolate ice cream on the planet: rich enough, but not the least oversweet or overflavored.

The antique hand-cranked, salt-and-ice churners in the windows of **Timothy's** are no longer used to make Bridgeport, Connecticut's best, but the ice cream you'll eat here does have the kind of extreme purity and goodness you'd expect from a farm-churned brand. We adore the elemental Sweet Cream (dulcet white with no flavor other than dairy sweetness) and supercharged Black Rock (French vanilla studded with chocolate-covered almonds), and the Dutch Chocolate is simply the most chocolaty ice cream possible. Waffle cones are made on site in irons behind the counter, and they are broad-mouthed enough to hold multiple scoops dolloped with fudge and whipped cream. Whether such an abundant cone can or should be eaten without utensils is open to debate.

16 GREAT NEW ENGLAND ICE CREAM PARLORS

Be aware that several of the places listed are closed in winter. Call ahead.

New England

1. **Ridgefield Ice Cream Shop:** 680 Danbury Rd., Ridgefield, CT 203-438-3094
2. **Christina's Homemade Ice Cream:** 1255 Cambridge St., Cambridge, MA 617-492-7021
3. **Herrell's:** 15 Dunster St., Cambridge, MA 617-497-2179 See www.herrells.com for other locations.
4. **Toscanini's:** 899 Main St., Cambridge, MA 617-491-5877 www.tosci.com
5. **Buttonwood Farm:** 471 Shetucket Turnpike, Griswold, CT 860-376-4081 www.buttonwoodfarmicecream .com
6. **Big Dipper:** 91 Waterbury Rd., Prospect, CT 203-758-3200
7. **Sundae School:** 381 Lower County Rd., Dennisport, MA 508-394-9122 See www.sundaeschool.com for additional locations.
8. **Tubby's:** 176 Main St., Wayne, ME 207-685-8181 www.tubbysicecream.com
9. **Timothy's:** 2974 Fairfield Ave., Bridgeport, CT 203-366-7496
10. **Dr. Mike's:** 158 Greenwood Ave., Bethel, CT 203-792-4388 Second location: 444 Main St., Monroe, CT 203-452-0499
11. **Hodgman's Frozen Custard:** 1108 Lewiston Rd., New Gloucester, ME 207-926-3553
12. **Shaw's Ridge Farm Ice Cream:** 59 Shaw's Ridge Rd., Sanford, ME 207-324-2510 www.shawsridgefarm.com
13. **Shady Glen:** 840 E. Middle Turnpike, Manchester, CT 860-649-4245 Second location: 360 W. Middle Turnpike, Manchester, CT 860-643-0511
14. **Gray's Ice Cream:** 16 East Rd., Tiverton, RI 401-624-4500 www.graysicecream.com
15. **We-Li-Kit:** 728 Hampton Rd., Abington, CT 860-974-1095
16. **Bishop's:** 183 Cottage St., Littleton, NH 603-444-6039

INDIAN PUDDING
Eastern New England

Served warm with a scoop of ice cream melting into sweet trickles around its edge, Indian pudding is candid Yankee contentment, a menu staple in diners and cafes throughout New England. Upscale restaurants sometimes fancy up the basic formula of cornmeal and molasses with anything from citrus peel to brandy, but such frippery seems insignificant and rather pointless when applied to so elemental a dish, like an earring on an elephant. Indian pudding is nowhere more fundamental than at the communal tables of

A scoop of ice cream rests atop a bowl of Indian pudding at Boston's Durgin-Park.

Durgin-Park, a nineteenth-century eating hall in Boston's Faneuil Hall where the time-honored recipe yields a dessert porridge that is dark brown with substantial gravity, smelling like roasted corn and tasting like the first Thanksgiving. Boston's **Union Oyster House** has been making and serving Indian pudding since 1827, and like Durgin-Park's, its version is a serious dessert lacking any confectionery frivolity.

In Essex, Massachusetts, the **Village Restaurant**, which we discovered on a fried clam hunt, serves a vivid version of the dish, grainy with a powerful molasses kick. At the **Blue Benn Diner**, in Bennington, Vermont, the rugged Indian pudding is available first thing in the morning, where its nature as cornmeal porridge makes it a perfectly reasonable breakfast, especially if the hot samp is drizzled with pouring cream instead of ice cream. Our favorite place in Maine to have Indian pudding is the **Maine Diner** in Wells, which bakes it long

enough and makes it strong enough so it turns a dark red-gold that carries an authoritative molasses kick.

Just to keep the record straight: Indian pudding is *not* a Native American dish adapted by colonist cooks. Its name comes from the fact that early settlers considered virtually anything made with corn to be Indian in nature.

5 BEST INDIAN PUDDINGS

1. **Durgin-Park:** 340 Faneuil Hall Marketplace, Boston, MA 617-227-2038 www.durgin-park.com
2. **Maine Diner:** 2265 Post Rd., Wells, ME 207-646-4441 www.mainediner.com
3. **Union Oyster House:** 41 Union St., Boston, MA 617-227-2750 www.unionoysterhouse.com
4. **Blue Benn Diner:** 318 North St., Bennington, VT 802-442-5140
5. **Village Restaurant:** 55 Main St., Essex, MA 978-768-6400 www.village-essex.com

JONNYCAKES
Rhode Island

If you doubt that Rhode Island is serious about jonnycakes, look at state statutes. A law on the books declares that white cap flint corn, which yields a mere one or two ears per stalk and is too hard to eat on the cob, is the only variety that can be used for true jonnycake meal. Furthermore, the law decrees that *jonnycake* must not be spelled with the letter *h* and the pancakes must not contain either sugar or flour.

Served for breakfast but also as a side dish with lunch, jonnycakes are found in two basic forms in the Ocean State. East of Narragansett Bay, cooks tend to make them broad, dry, and no thicker than flannel. While **Bishop's 4th Street Diner** is equally well known for biscuits and sausage gravy, it is the place to go in Newport for a stack of thin, lace-edged east-of-bay jonnycakes. The thinnest we've ever had are those served at **The Barn** — elegant pancakes as fine as crepes, so tender that you tend to go easy with the edge of your fork lest you bruise the surface when you sever a piece. The Barn is a rustic destination not far from the large granite statue in Adamsville commemorating the Rhode Island Red chicken, which is the official state bird. To drink alongside Barn jonnycakes: the official state beverage, coffee milk (page 12).

Jigger's Diner in East Greenwich serves typical South County 'cakes, which are chubby little disks, scarcely 2 inches wide and at least two fork tines thick, with crunchy brown surfaces sandwiching steamy moist meal within. Their serious earthy texture and unalloyed corn taste are fetchingly anachronous; to eat them is to savor the most fundamental American

---

GINGERBREAD PANCAKES

Since flint corn meal, which legally is the sole correct variety for Rhode Island jonnycakes, is hard to come by and we do not want to encourage lawlessness, we shall not give a recipe. But we would like to share this one for a legendary Jigger's breakfast, gingerbread pancakes. We got it from Carol Shriner, who originally bought the decrepit Jigger's in East Greenwich in 1992 and transformed it into the destination diner it is today.

- 1 cup hot brewed coffee
- 1/2 cup dark brown sugar
- 1 large egg, beaten
- 1/2 stick butter, melted
- 1/2 cup whole wheat flour
- 1/2 cup all-purpose white flour
- 3/4 teaspoon baking soda
- 1/2 teaspoon ground ginger
- 1/2 teaspoon ground cinnamon
- 1/4 teaspoon ground cloves
- 1/4 teaspoon salt
  Applesauce and/or pure maple syrup

Combine the coffee and sugar and mix until the sugar is dissolved. When the coffee is room temperature, combine it with the egg and butter. Add all the dry ingredients and stir to blend.

Ladle the batter onto a hot greased griddle to form 5-inch pancakes. When bubbles appear on the surface of the pancakes, use two spatulas to flip them. Cook through.

Serve with applesauce and/or maple syrup.

MAKES 12 TO 16 PANCAKES; SERVES 4

It's a law: Rhode Island's lacy jonnycakes have to be made with white cap flint corn.

foodstuff. In fact, historians speculate that jonnycakes' name derives from colonial times, when they were known as journey cakes because once cooked, they could be carried on a trip.

Rhode Islanders have laid claim to the pancake-style jonnycake, but up in Weston, Vermont, at the **Bryant House**, an offshoot of the Vermont Country Store, the word *jonnycake* refers to a cornbread loaf, served warm in thick slices and including so much molasses that it resembles anadama bread. We mention this not only because these slices are mighty good (although an altogether different dish), but because the Bryant House also is a great source of such bedrock Yankee fare as Indian pudding (page 35) and crackers and milk (page 13).

3 TOP JONNYCAKES

1. **Jigger's Diner:** 145 Main St., East Greenwich, RI
401-884-5388
2. **The Barn:** 16 Main Rd., Adamsville, RI
401-635-2985

3. **Bishop's 4th Street Diner:** 184 Admiral Kalbfus Rd., Newport, RI
401-847-2069

Also
Bryant House: Main St. (Route 100), Weston, VT
802-824-6287

LOBSTER ROLL
Yankee Shores

A whole lobster requires concentrated effort to eat, but a lobster roll is trouble-free. The best are found at casual places where service is call-your-number brash and facilities are picnic tables. It is the simplest sandwich, basically lobster meat surrounded by bread. The meat can be cool, room temperature, or even slightly warm; it can be mixed with mayonnaise and maybe bits of celery, or possibly with melted butter; there can be heaps of it or merely shreds. The fundamental issue is meat quality. Freshly cooked and only recently extracted from the shell is what you want, and a variety

A hot lobster roll from the Maine Diner in Wells, ME, waiting for butter

Chunks of bunned, fresh lobster meat at Kennebunkport's Clam Shack

of meat is essential: knuckle for tenderness, tail for juiciness, body for maximum flavor. Most lobster rolls are made in a split-top bun, the kind that pulls apart at the top and has flat sides that can be buttered and toasted on a short-order grill, generating a crisp exterior enveloping tender bready insides. Some are served wrapped in wax paper, others in little cardboard boats that tend to squeeze the sides together, like the action of a push-up brassiere, causing the bun to bulge, forcing the meat upward, and making it appear more abundantly endowed than it really is.

Not to beat around the bush, we will start with the best lobster roll on earth, which is served at an extremely humble shack known as **Red's Eats** in Wiscasset, Maine. Red's primacy is a legend among lobster lovers, who flock to it in such numbers (summer only) that the wait in line to get your roll can be an hour. Believe us, it is time well spent. You can count the hunks of lobster in a Red's Eats lobster roll: ten or fifteen great big pearly pieces of claw, tail, and knuckle meat, some so succulent you can hear the

juices ooze when you bite down on them. The management guarantees that each lobster roll contains all the meat from a pound-plus lobster, which is more meat, really, than belongs in the regular-size bun that contains it. The bun is a split-top, toasted to a buttery crispness on the outside, soft and absorbent on the inside, where the meat sits. It plays a crucial role in the roll, especially if you get yours with a cup of drawn butter on the side and pour the butter over the lobster. (Mayonnaise is available in lieu of butter.) All the excess butter soaks into it, along with sweet marine juice, transforming a relatively plain piece of bread into a delirious flavorful companion for the meat.

"Almost like a Downeast version of a deli sandwich" is how Bruce Bilmes and Sue Boyle describe the lobster roll at **Eagle's Nest**, across the Penobscot River from Bangor. Unlike most sources of lobster roll greatness, this place is inland, and unlike all the other excellent lobster rolls we know, Eagle's Nest's is made from bagged lobster meat. But as Bruce and Sue assured us, the meat tastes as fresh-picked as you'll find anywhere — double-mouthful hunks heavy with juice and redolent of ocean flavor.

The motto of **Bob's Clam Hut**, just over the border from New Hampshire in Kittery, Maine, is "Eat Clams," and the clams are swell. The lobster roll also is exemplary, cool and expensive (about $2 more than a fried clam roll), served with twiggy French fries and a couple of pickle slices on a porous paperboard plate. The bun is nice and warm, buttered and grilled until toasty golden brown on both sides; the lobster meat inside is faintly chilled, but not so much that any of the taste has been iced.

It is easy to ignore just how important a role the bun can play in lobster roll satisfaction. The rolls at **Johnny Ad's** in southeastern Connecticut are a reminder. They are the split-top variety, well buttered and cooked on a grill until their outsides get golden brown and crisp. What a perfect holder for buttery piles of lobster meat! In the same neighborhood, and similarly well toasted, the rolls at the **Westbrook Lobster House** in Clinton, Connecticut, deliver veritable mountains of meat.

Although it is all too easy to be sidetracked by the **Maine Diner**'s ambrosial baked lobster pie (page 42), if you are looking for lobster roll excellence, here it is. Actually, here are two: the traditional Maine lobster roll, made with big chunks of knuckle, claw, and plenty of succulent tail meat with mayo in a toasted, grilled bun, and the "hot lobster roll" (originated decades ago in Connecticut), which is unadorned warm lobster meat piled into the toasted bun, accompanied by a cup of drawn butter. "Somebody from Rhode Island suggested the buttered roll many years ago," proprietor Dick Henry said. "But we found that if we served the meat already buttered, the bun fell apart." So you can either pour the butter on the sandwich, risking bun disintegration, or you can simply pick chunks of meat and shreds of toasted bread from the plate and dip them in the cup of butter as you wish. Either way, it's lobster nirvana.

Mabel's Lobster Claw in Ken-

The wait for one of Red's lobster rolls can be more than an hour.

nebunkport, Maine, is sprinkled with celebrity dust. The walls of its cozy wood-paneled dining room are plastered with autographed pictures of many important people who have eaten here in the past half-century, including local householders George and Barbara Bush. It is an old-fashioned summer-resort kind of place: casual and relaxed, staffed by swift waitresses in rubber-soled shoes capable of delivering a lobster treatise if called for: "They'll get cheaper next week because they go into soft-shell. That means you pay less per lobster, but you have to use them right away. They're the lobster lover's choice, from July into November." What about frozen lobster? "Well, you might as well be eating rope!" Mabel's lobster roll verges on swanky, arriving on an actual plate. The meat is juicy, fresh, and copious, nicely complemented by the thinnest possible film of mayonnaise and cushioned by a few leaves of lettuce. Some of the chunks of tail and claw that Mabel's stuffs into the roll are so large that you feel a little embarrassed picking it up and eating it out of hand; a knife and fork seem more suited to the task.

Utensils would be completely wrong at **Jim's Dock** in Jerusalem, Rhode Island, a summer-only shack with deck dining and big beautiful "lobster salad" rolls; but the big surprise, after reading the menu and fearing we'd be getting a little lobster in a lot of mayonnaise, is that Jim's sandwich is nearly all lobster meat — big, succulent sections — and hardly any mayo.

The **Clam Shack** has been a Kennebunkport fixture for three decades, an ebullient little place hardly bigger than a newsstand, with only a few makeshift benches out back to sit on. Customers cluster in the sun, devouring clam baskets, chowder, and lobster rolls standing up. Leaning against the whitewashed bridge rail is a favorite way to dine, too, although you must contend with greedy birds eyeing unattended onion rings (crunchy hoops with luscious warm insides). A posted sign warns BEWARE OF SEAGULLS. THEY LIKE OUR FOOD AS MUCH AS YOU DO. "Many of our lobster rolls

More meat than one bun can hold, plus butter, at Red's Eats

have gone to the Bushes," former proprietor Richard Jacques once told us. "He used to arrive out back in his boat and we'd pass the food down to him. When he became president, the Secret Service started eating here, too. Now they call ahead and come down for two dozen lobster rolls at a time."

When you sink your teeth into a Clam Shack lobster roll, you know instantly you are tasting greatness, on a par with Red's, second only because it is served somewhat unconventionally in a lovely eggy bun. By almost any standard the bun is better than the standard split-top roll, and it makes an especially good companion for lobster meat; but being traditionalists, we think Red's is more right. However, the lobster pieces in a Clam Shack roll are bigger: six, eight, maybe ten big pearlescent chunks of fresh-from-the-shell tail and claw are arranged in the bun; some are so succulent you can hear the juices ooze when you bite them, and each is so big that a single sandwich seems lavish. You have a choice of mayonnaise or butter on this roll; that means that the meat is assembled on the bun and only then is the condiment spooned on. The result is an array of pure pink lobster merely frosted with a dollop of mayonnaise or veiled in a shimmering glaze of melted butter. One July afternoon as we ate from the hood of our car, a lawyer visiting from Idaho polished off a lobster roll and an order of onion rings and stood on the sidewalk announcing to travelers and Kennebunkporters who ambled past, "We've got nothing like this in Boise! Nothing at all!"

9 LOBSTER ROLLS

1. **Red's Eats:** Main and Water Sts., Wiscasset, ME 207-882-6128
2. **Clam Shack:** 2 Western Ave. (Route 9), Kennebunkport, ME 207-967-2560 www.theclamshack.net
3. **Maine Diner:** 2265 Post Rd., Wells, ME 207-646-4441 www.mainediner.com
4. **Mabel's Lobster Claw:** 124 Ocean Ave., Kennebunkport, ME 207-967-2562
5. **Bob's Clam Hut:** 315 U.S. Route 1, Kittery, ME 207-439-4233 www.bobsclamhut.com
6. **Jim's Dock:** 1175 Succotash Rd., Jerusalem, RI 401-783-2050 www.jims-dock.com
7. **Johnny Ad's:** 910 Boston Post Rd., Old Saybrook, CT 860-388-4032
8. **Westbrook Lobster House:** 346 Boston Post Rd., Clinton, CT 860-664-9464 Second location: 300 Church St., Wallingford, CT 203-265-5071 www.westbrooklobster.com
9. **Eagle's Nest:** 1016 N. Main St., Brewer, ME 207-989-7635

LOBSTERMANIA
New England Coast

The two essential ways to enjoy lobster are as part of a shore dinner (page 59) or in a lobster roll (page

Buttery Ritz cracker crumbs cover hunks of lobster in the Maine Diner's pie.

38), but the New England coast offers other novel opportunities to indulge. The most luxurious is lobster pie at the **Maine Diner** in Wells. It doesn't look like much, just a bowl full of dark, greenish brown bread crumbs. But they're way better than bread crumbs; they are Ritz crackers, crumbled fine and moistened with a dash of the sumptuous lobster innards known as tomalley. As soon as your fork sinks through that harmonious flavor duet, you hit pay dirt: jumbo hunks of lobster meat that glisten with butter. The meat is fresh-picked and resilient — whole big pieces of claw and tail glowing with flavor, the moist crumbs on top a perfect foil. There is no better homage to the divine combo of lobster and butter.

If you love BLTs and love lobster rolls, you will think you've died and gone to heaven when you encounter the lobster BLT in Boston's **B&G Oysters**. The combination of hunky lobster salad bound in minimal mayo with thick slices of smoky bacon is the summit of sumptuousness without stepping over the precipice into gouty excess. Bacon and lobster are swank in such different ways, the lobster plump and pearly and sweet-salty like the ocean, the bacon adding waves of crunchiness and chewiness and its very different balance of sweet pork and salt cure. Packed into a fresh ciabatta roll, this is high hedonia with excellent French fries and sweet pickles on the side.

On the subject of lobster excess, mention must be made of the ultimate crustaceous pig-out, at **Custy's** in North Stonington, Connecticut. We're the first to admit that eating here can be gross. Custy's purpose is to serve deluxe food endlessly, lobster being the main attraction. Customers spend days before their visit either fasting or stretching their stomachs (depending on their eating strategy), all for the purpose of ingesting the most they can for the $69.95 fee. For the price of admission, you are free to pillage a 60-foot buffet line that rivals that of any cruise ship, including steak, shrimp, and endless visits to an area called the Lobster Pit, where lobsters are steamed while you watch and served without end. If you prefer your lobster fancy, choose lobster Thermidor, lobster Newburg, baked stuffed lobster, or baked shrimp with lobster stuffing.

3 BEST LOBSTER BLOWOUTS

B&G Oysters: 550 Tremont St., Boston, MA
617-423-0550
www.bandgoysters.com
Maine Diner: 2265 Post Rd.,

Wells, ME
207-646-4441
www.mainediner.com
Custy's: 138 Norwich-Westerly Rd., North Stonington, CT
860-599-1551
www.custys.com

MAPLE DESSERT
Northern New England

Breakfast is maple syrup's table time; swirled with melted butter and running in rivulets off pancakes or pooling in the treads of waffles is where you see it most. Not that there's anything wrong with that — alongside bacon, maple syrup is the top of the morning. But can we talk about maple desserts? New England is rich with them. Here are four you need to eat.

Maple cream pie at the **Wayside Restaurant and Bakery** near Montpelier, Vermont, is a Yankee powerhouse! It isn't dramatic to see — just a modest wedge with an amber filling below a browned crust mottled with sweet cream. The dairy infusion tempers the maple's punch; the flavor

Moody's calibrates the sweetness of its maple walnut pie perfectly.

Luscious maple cream pie, a destination dessert of the Wayside in Montpelier, VT

is intensely woodsy, pure country.

Moody's, a 1930s-era diner that has long been a three-meal-a-day beacon for travelers on Maine's Route 1, is known for all sorts of Downeast specialties; but the legendary item on the menu is maple walnut pie. Alvah Moody told us that the recipe is based on southern-style pecan pie, but because it is made with maple syrup rather than corn syrup, it isn't nearly as sweet. Indeed, if it weren't for the cloud of whipped cream that comes on top, this nutty wedge could almost pass for health food.

The tables at **Polly's Pancake Parlor** in Sugar Hill, New Hampshire, are set with three maple products to spill, sprinkle, or spread across plates of pancakes, waffles, and French toast: syrup, granulated maple sugar, and a special delight called maple spread, which is about the consistency of peanut butter but tremendously maple-sweet. There is a fourth, special-order topping you can get, not only for the usual breakfast entrées but for ice cream as well. It is called maple hur-

MAPLE CREAM PIE

You may want to experiment with grades of syrup in this recipe. People with very refined taste buds tend to prefer clearer Fancy Grade syrup, which makes an ethereal pie. Grade A "Medium Amber," which is darker, yields a more assertive maple cream. Needless to say, you must use 100 percent maple syrup.

    3 large eggs
    3 tablespoons all-purpose flour
    ¼ teaspoon freshly ground black
        pepper
    1½ cups pure maple syrup (see
        above)
    ¾ cup heavy cream

    1 10-inch pie shell, partially baked,
        cool
    Whipped cream

Preheat the oven to 350 degrees. Beat the eggs, adding the flour gradually, then the pepper. While beating, slowly pour in the syrup, then the cream. Pour the filling into the pie shell.

Bake for 40 minutes, or until a toothpick inserted in the center comes out clean. Let the pie cool to room temperature. Serve slices topped with whipped cream. The pie may be refrigerated and served cold or at room temperature.

MAKES ONE 10-INCH PIE

ricane sauce, and it has been a specialty of Polly's since the hurricane of 1938, when the restaurant's founder, "Sugar Bill" Dexter (whose wife was named Polly), found himself with a huge apple windfall that he didn't want to waste. Since the whole point of opening the little pancake parlor in the most scenic part of the White Mountains was to let people know how delicious maple products are, Sugar Bill decided to boil the chunked apples in syrup until the fruit was fully saturated with maple flavor and the syrup had thickened up good. The apple-maple combo is breathtaking, and while it is a sensational topping for ice cream or nearly anything that begs for something sweet, we admit to opening jars of it at home and spooning it up just as it is. Polly's dessert menu offers an opportunity to taste maple pecan cheesecake, a maple sundae, and an airweight froth known as maple Bavarian cream: gelatinized syrup and whipped cream decorated with chopped pecans.

3 MAPLE MECCAS FOR DESSERT

Moody's Diner: 1885 Atlantic Highway (Route 1), Waldoboro, ME 207-832-7785 www.moodysdiner.com

Polly's Pancake Parlor: 672 Route 117, Sugar Hill, NH 603-823-5575 www.pollyspancakeparlor.com

Wayside Restaurant and Bakery: U.S. Route 302, Montpelier, VT 802-223-6611

NEW YORK SYSTEM
Rhode Island

Do not expect to find New York system in New York; it is unique to Rhode Island. The very term is rather ambiguous: New York system is the style of service as well as the product sold, and is usually part of the name of the place that sells it. Here is what New

---

THE MARBLE QUARRIES OF DORSET

When colonists settled in southern Vermont in 1768, they thought they saw vast snowbanks along Dorset Mountain. The white streaks turned out to be marble, and the abundance of it buried under the mountains that surround the Marble Valley became Dorset's endowment through much of the nineteenth century. The town's first quarry, which sent stone to make the

New York Public Library, is now a magical summer swimming hole and picnic area. Trails lead from the side of Route 30 east of town into an otherworldly maze of great white stone blocks that surround pools with a crystalline emerald tint caused by runoff from the marble. When no one is swimming, the water is still, reflecting trees, sky, and rock as clearly as a mirror.
Dorset, Vermont: www.dorsetvt.com

Only in Rhode Island: "New York system" is the local term for little wieners.

New York System, which claims to be the first place in the Ocean State to serve weenies this way, starting in 1927. The configuration here, from the bun up, is a little grilled weenie with squared-off edges (because they are cut rather than tied off), meat sauce, mustard, chopped raw onions, and a sprinkling of celery salt. Locals know them as gaggers, or, as it is properly pronounced, gaggahs.

The other place that lays claim to being the original weenie joint is **Sparky's** in East Providence, which opened in 1915 and calls itself Sparky's Coney Island System. It was at Sparky's that we learned to love this unique little tube steak. Nothing like the brawny beef red hots of Chicago or the garlicky dogs of New York or the crusty fried franks you find in Connecticut and New Jersey, these fingerling weenies, made of beef, veal, and pork, are soft and, alone, bland. But of course nobody in history has ever eaten one alone. The meat sauce on top, which is more a paste than chili, is what delivers the spice, and its pebbly texture, combined with the fleecy softness of the bun, cossets the little pink prize in such a way that it begins to taste delicate and luxurious. This is something we started to discern only after eating a pair (about three bites each). So we had another, but didn't quite nail the flavor. A fourth helped, but it was at the sixth New York system we realized that while no single element of this package is justifiably excellent, the combination is nothing short of addictive.

York system is (or are): little weenies (the term *hot dog* is never used) in little steamy buns dressed with ultra-fine-grind chili sauce, mustard, and onions. It is possible that the "system" element of the moniker derives from the fact that they are made in a systematic way by lining up all the dogs in buns and dressing them assembly-line-style. The lineup may be along a prep area, but the way an old-time counterman does it is to array about a dozen of the dogs from wrist to shoulder, adding chili, mustard, and onions to each with lightning speed. Hence the common local description of New York system dining: "wieners up the arm."

Although the health department frowns on it, they still line them up the arm at Providence's **Original**

Olneyville New York System, also in Providence, is a relative newcomer, opened in 1946 by two brothers who came to New York from Greece in the 1920s (all New York system hot dog places are Greek-run), then moved to Rhode Island, where they joined their family at the Original New York System before opening their own place. We know Rhode Island connoisseurs who consider Olneyville the best. Perhaps our palates aren't yet sophisticated enough, but we thought Sparky's wieners were better balanced. By the way, the thing to drink here, as at any wiener-up-the-arm establishment, is that beloved Rhode Island beverage, coffee milk (page 12). Note also that Olneyville is all set up to ship its New York System Hot Wiener Sauce Spice Mix to mail-order customers.

Wein-O-Rama in Cranston, opened in 1962, differs from most New York system restaurants because it has a full menu, including breakfast, fried seafood, and burgers, and it is so proud of the goodness of its meat sauce topping that nowhere on the menu are its weenies referred to as Coney Islands, a term that suggests hash-house quality. Wein-O-Rama constructs them in the usual way, but as a concession to health department regulations, countermen use a protective sleeve on their arm when they dress them. The sauce here is definitely classier than at any other place we've sampled, actually tasting of beef. Good as it is, though, we're not sure that its quality doesn't in some way detract from the essential greasy-spoon raunchiness that is New York system's heart and soul. This is a difficult and complicated branch of American wienerdom, deserving of further study.

When eating New York system weenies, if coffee milk is not rich enough to drink, ask for a cabinet, either coffee- or vanilla-flavored. *Cabinet* is Rhode Islandese for milk shake.

A QUARTET OF WIENERS UP THE ARM

Olneyville New York System: 20 Plainfield St., Providence, RI 401-621-9500 Second location: 1012 Reservoir Ave., Cranston, RI 401-275-6031 www.olneyvillenysystem.com
Original New York System: 424 Smith St., Providence, RI 401-331-5349
Sparky's Coney Island System: 122 Taunton Ave., East Providence, RI 401-434-9826
Wein-O-Rama: 1009 Oaklawn Ave., Cranston, RI 401-943-4990

PAIN DE CAMPAGNE
Wilton, Connecticut

If you are looking for a slice of bread on which to spread peanut butter or melt cheese in the toaster oven, **Wave Hill** pain de campagne, aka French country bread, could be a big mistake. A slice reveals the loaf to be loaded with air bubbles, most of them small, but a few big enough to form holes that span the depth of even a thick slice, thus allowing anything spread upon the bread to drip right through. But to dip in olive oil, to accompany good cheese, to make sensationally sturdy croutons or a

A chewy slow-rise loaf from Wave Hill Breads in Wilton, CT

but not brittle; the interior, especially when only hours from the oven, holds tremendous spring. When the loaf is sliced, a robust perfume erupts — not the rank smell of sourdough (which this bread is not), nor the tang of yeast (of which this bread has a minimum), but rather the perfume of fields of grain waving in hot sunlight. Rye and spelt berries are milled daily for Wave Hill, energizing the grains' wild yeast and giving the bombs of dough extra lift. The flavor of the three-grain rhapsody is concentrated, so a little should go a long way. However, the bread does not keep well. No problem, because whenever we get near a loaf, it disappears all too fast.

sloppy bruschetta, or just to eat, completely unadorned, there isn't a more satisfying loaf of bread in America. The crust is thick, dark, and chewy

CHOCOLATE TRUFFLE

Of all the taste tests we've ever done, none was so debilitating as the time we set out to determine which chocolatier made the best chocolate truffles. The research took a long time to complete, because after two or three samples of really good ones, appetite was sated and taste buds had become inoperative from the stress of handling so much goodness.

After we sampled over a dozen of the nation's best, there was no question which was the crème de la cocoa. The unequivocal winner: Bridgewater Chocolate. Its hand-rolled truffles' chocolate skin, dusted with fine cocoa powder, offers just the faintest resistance, and inside is silky filling that is unbelievably fresh, indescribably chocolaty, and richer than Croesus. Varieties include milk chocolate, dark chocolate, hazelnut, orange, raspberry, and coffee. Because they are so truly creamy, they need to be kept cool, and while the shelf life is one week, we've never bought a bunch that lasted more than a couple of days.

Bridgewater chocolates are available in local stores, by mail-order, and at the source, a space in a large industrial complex where a picture window provides a view of chocolates being made.

Bridgewater Chocolate: 559 Federal Rd., Brookfield, CT 203-775-2286 www.bridgewaterchocolate.com

Amber waves of grain: Wheat, rye, and spelt are milled daily for Wave Hill.

Wave Hill Breads: 196 Danbury
Rd., Wilton, CT
203-762-9595

PIEROGI, PLACKI, AND GOLABKI
Hartford, Connecticut

Celebrated for superior ice cream, deep-fried hot dogs, and transcendent pizza, Connecticut has a less known but irresistible culinary attraction: great Polish food. From cabbage rolls and Old World cold-cut sandwiches at Danbury's **Beth and Her Alley Deli** to borscht and blintzes at New Britain's **Staropolska**, the state is rich with plain and fancy Polish meals served in restaurants that range from corner cafes to giant function halls. The mother of them all is the **Polish National Home** in Hartford, a massive concrete edifice that looks less like a restaurant than like one of the secret societies around Yale in New Haven. It is a tavern, a restaurant, a clubhouse, and a place to go dancing on weekend nights. Its menu is a Polish primer of utmost excellence.

First-timers and those of indecisive appetite are well served by the Polish plate, which is a sampler of house specialties, each available as a dinner by itself: a kielbasa sausage, a single golabki (stuffed cabbage), and two pierogi dumplings all arrayed around a heap of sauerkraut. The kraut is extraordinary, long-cooked to ultimate tenderness and studded with chunks of sausage, its bright tang an ideal foil for the robust and resilient kielbasa with its deep garlic flavor. Each pierogi is a dollop of cheese-and-potato filling in a steamy soft white dough packet that glistens with onion-laced butter. The supple cabbage wrap of the golabki is painted with sweet tomato glaze. Sunday and Monday you can get fantastic placki (potato pancakes), each an oval about 4 inches long with a crisp-fried, rugged crust that envelops a half-inch ribbon of soft grated potato. Placki are served with sour cream and apple

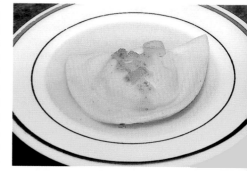

Hartford's Polish National Home serves a dumpling to die for.

sauce and make an agreeable appetizer (if you can restrain yourself and have just one), a companion for any main course, or a satisfying pure-potato meal unto themselves.

To drink with these hearty meals: Krupnik (Polish vodka), Wisniowka (100-proof cherry liqueur), bottles of Okocim beer, or, if you are a minor or a teetotaler, Shirley Temples made with sweet red syrup.

3 PERFECT POLISH MEALS

1. **Polish National Home:** 60 Charter Oak Ave., Hartford, CT 860-247-1784
2. **Staropolska:** 252 Broad St., New Britain, CT 860-612-1711
3. **Beth and Her Alley Deli:** 135 Main St., Danbury, CT 203-743-6818

NATIONAL BESTS

PIZZA

In the not-so-humble opinion of serious devotees, the earth's best pizza is made in New Haven, Connecticut. Foremost among the virtues of New Haven's legendary pizzas is brittle-thin crust, just bulky enough to provide a rewarding chew. Cooked at an extremely high temperature on the brick floor of wood-burning ovens, it sports a puffy edge that is golden brown but occasionally blistered black, and offers profound resilience in every smoky bite. We love **Modern Apizza** because the wait to get in usually is

shorter and its pies consistently rate 9.9 on a scale of 10, but the daddy of them all (since 1923) is **Frank Pepe Pizzeria Napoletana** in the old Italian neighborhood on Wooster Street. As in all of the great New Haven pizzerias, Pepe's pizza men are not sticklers about scraping debris from the oven floor, so your pizza's underside will be speckled with burned grains of semolina and maybe even blotched by an oil spill where another pizza leaked, all of which amplifies the devil-may-care attitude that is part of New Haven pizza's soul.

Pepe's signature is white clam pizza, invented a half-century ago when a clam vendor in an alley near the pizza parlor convinced Frank Pepe that the two of them could make sweet music together. Pepe's clams are always fresh, not canned. They are tender littlenecks — the tinier, the better — that are spread across the pie with just enough of their clear nectar to give the wafer-thin creation a salubrious ocean savor. This is not a cheesy pizza; in fact there is no mozzarella at all, just a scattering of grated sharp pecorino. The

Fresh littleneck clams adorn Pepe's famed white clam pizza in New Haven, CT.

Working the pizza ovens at Pepe's

blistered black," and the undercrust, which is "smudged, greasy, rugged." Only recently did we find out about a house specialty not posted on the menu board: potato pizza. As we understand things, it did not exist in the early days of Wooster Street pizzerias, but several years ago, when Flo, Sal's widow, came back from a visit to Italy, she was inspired to make it a special offering. Potatoes may sound like a strange topping, and we have had pizzas on which they are nothing but that — strange — but on Sally's raunchy, semolina-bottomed, oil-stained, coal-fire-burned-bubble crust, the thin, crisp-edged disks of spud, along with rosemary, oregano, a spritz of oil, and a sprinkle of grated cheese, create as smooth and savory a taste sensation as any pizza pie. Onions are optional, adding sharp-sweet succulence, but don't you dare add any meats or goopy cheeses!

Eddie Martino, who runs **Carminuccio's**, grew up in New Haven eating New Haven pies, so it is not completely shocking to taste one of the roasted garlic pizzas dished out at his inconspicuous pizza house in

bite of the cheese and sweetness of the clams, along with a salvo of minced garlic and spices and a drizzle of oil, make up a topping that does not cover the crust so much as meld with it, creating an expansive vision of golden breadstuff that appears frosted with savory ingredients. The combination of flavors is simple and perfect: yeasty, zesty, and luscious, yet miraculously ethereal.

Then there's **Sally's**, which in many people's minds is the New Haven champ. We love everything about the place (except waiting for a table), especially the crust, which we once described as "glistening, oil-rich,

Garlic-crowned pizza from Carminuccio's in Newtown, CT

Newtown, Connecticut, and recognize you are eating greatness. Carminuccio's merits are a sturdy crust and especially full-flavored vegetables on top. Before going onto the pizza, the vegetables are cooked in a convection oven, sapping crust-threatening moisture and also enhancing the flavor of such toppings as spinach, onions, and tomatoes. Garlic is caramelized by the process, each whole clove turning soft, as all its sharp taste turns tender. Garlic goes well with just about any other topping, but there is no match better than red peppers, which have been roasted to a sunny concentrate as vibrant as sun-dried tomatoes.

Another Connecticut treasure that mustn't be missed is the crazy-crunchy, superthin pizza served at Stamford's **Colony Grill**, a neighborhood bar that has been popular among locals since Prohibition days. Served on battered metal trays, Colony Grill's pizzas are especially irresistible when topped with a peppery olive oil that harmonizes well with sausage from the local butcher.

Pizzeria Lauretano in Bethel, Connecticut, is a worthy destination year-round for the exquisite pies that emerge from the wood-fired oven the owner, Michael Lauretano, got from Italy. Just before the pizza is done and ready to be pulled off the oven's floor, the *pizzaiolo* slides his peel underneath and holds it directly over the smoldering woodpile for a few moments, imparting an exhilarating smoky perfume to the muscular crust. We love the plain garlic pizza — really just a gilded flatbread, heaven for crust lovers — as well as the mighty garlic and broccoli rabe white pizza, but for a

few weeks at the end of summer, one variant deserves all the glory: an off-the-menu special known as the garden pizza. It is topped with thick slices of sunny red and yellow tomatoes fresh off the vine and rounds of summer squash that get baked only long enough to soften slightly, retaining a welcome firmness. They are accompanied by clusters of corn kernels cut straight from the cob and saturated with earthy sweetness, a scattering of tiny champagne grapes which burst like little fruit sparkles, and curls of crisp-edged pancetta, along with a gossamer veil of creamy cheese. Hail to the harvest!

Shame on us for not paying homage to **De Lorenzo's Tomato Pies** before now. This longstanding Trenton, New Jersey, corner eatery doesn't use tomato sauce. It tops thin-crust tomato pies with high-flavored crushed tomatoes plus fennel-spiked clumps of excellent Italian sausage and just enough cheese to make a creamy melody. "The most balanced pizzas around," contend Bruce Boyles and Sue Bilmes, who insisted we give their beloved

The garden pizza at Pizza Lauretano in Bethel, CT, shows off a summer harvest.

the first finger holding down the vortex. Inside the restaurant you can sit down for a whole pie, of which two basic variations are available: fresh mozzarella, with thin pools of creamy sliced cheese spread out within the microthin layer of tomato sauce, and regular mozzarella, on which saltier, slightly oilier shredded cheese is spread evenly all across the surface. The dining room is a special experience because it is presided over by a handsome oil portrait of the Chairman of the Board, Frank Sinatra, who is said to have liked Patsy's so much that he had the pizza flown to him at distant venues around the world.

Ernesto's, a Boston North End institution since the 1980s, also makes a specialty of selling slices as well as whole pizzas. Similar to New Haven pizza, it has a thin crust with a lot of chew. Dozens of varieties are available; we love the one called Old School, which is tomatoes, basil, and grated Romano. Still, our longtime favorite Boston pizza remains **Santarpio's**, not just for the pizza but for the barbecue. Barbecue? In a Boston pizzeria? In this place, *barbecue* means lengths of homemade Italian sausage and skewered hunks of lamb, known as spiedini, cooked over coals on a grate near the front door. Many customers have barbecue as an hors d'oeuvre before plowing into a beautiful, thin-crusted pizza topped with mellow pools of cheese and sweet tomato sauce. The rim is crisp and crunchy, and while the center of the crust tends to soften enough to lead to the heartbreak of cheese slippage, even the softest part has a taste that makes you want to keep on eating, then order more. Although the dining

Frank Sinatra, a fan of Patsy's in Harlem, had the pizza flown around the world to him.

De Lo's a try, having eaten there themselves hundreds of times.

Many New Yorkers grow up deprived of whole pizza pies because they can satisfy the pizza urge at any minute by picking up a slice. The streets of the city teem with little storefronts that sell broad triangles of decent pizza, usually plain but sometimes available with toppings. At **Patsy's,** way uptown in Harlem, the street slice was defined well before World War II, when pizza was virtually unknown to Americans of non-Italian heritage. Today customers of every stripe stand around outside or lean against an open-air counter wolfing down slices of simple, perfect pizza with a fragile crust that bends just enough so the slice can be neatly folded up one-handed, using the middle finger and thumb at the edges,

room is a dimly lit bar with decor that consists mostly of pictures of prize-fighters, the air is positively delicious: a mixed perfume of hot pizza and sizzling barbecue.

Boston's **Excelsior** is top-drawer, pretty fancy. But the combination of two must-eat treats, lobster and pizza, makes it irresistible. The lobster meat is in big hunks, each identifiable as from the claw, knuckle, and tail, densely populating the top of a very thin-crust pie along with soft, sweet cooked onions and garlic. The wood oven delivers a full-flavored crust with wonderful crunchiness and infuses the lobster meat with a savory bite that accentuates the maritime sweetness of the succulent pink meat.

Chicago has a robust pizza culture, with varieties that range from double-crusters, pizza soufflés, and virtual crust-bowls of ingredients to ultra-flatties thinner than a saltine cracker. Its signature is deep-dish pie, as first served there in 1941 at a restaurant called **Pizzeria Uno**. The classic is majestic, its crunchy crust as rich and buttery as a biscuit, its toppings including some of the most distinctive fennel-charged sausage to be found on any pizza, and its sauce big and chunky. (Note: Ignore the Uno's franchises around the country; for the real deal, you must eat deep-dish pizza in Chicago.) An excellent alternative source of Chicago deep-dish is **Original Gino's East**, a dungeon-dark eatery where the sauce is chunks of tomato and sausage is available either crumbled or in patties. There are about three dozen **Lou Malnati's** pizzerias in greater Chicago; the specialty here, too, is classic deep-dish (Lou Malnati

That's *amore!* The big pizza pie at Pizzeria Uno in Chicago.

originally worked at Due's, the sister pizzeria of Uno's), plus a unique item for people on restricted diets as well as sausage hounds: crustless pizza in which the gluten-free crust is in fact made from lean sausage.

Chicago's stuffed pizza is a sub-genre of deep-dish, featuring a tall circumference of flaky dough that shores in gobs of topping, or in this case filling, because a stuffed pizza has both a bottom crust and a top crust. Between them are all the ingredients, and the top crust is spread with tomato sauce. The creation is thick enough to take a full half-hour to cook at **Giordano's,** which claims to have invented it, based on an old-country family recipe for Easter pizza.

Curiously, Old Forge, Pennsylvania, is one of the nation's most passionate pizza enclaves. At least a dozen bars and restaurants specialize in what's known as Old Forge pizza (after the Scranton suburb of that name). It is frequently served double-crusted and is available in some places topped with a full array of breakfast food, including eggs and every omelet ingredient you can name. Even normal-ingredient pizza around here is more American than Mediterranean in character: sunny tomato sauce that is slightly sweet and slightly spicy, cheese that tastes like a mild blend of Italian and American varieties, and crust that is light and chewy from getting cooked in a pan slicked with peanut oil. **Ghigiarelli's** sells it by the tray or slice (slices are rectangular), and although pepperoni and sausage are available, plain is the way to appreciate its simple charms. Across the street from Ghigiarelli's, **Revello's** is known for its meatball topping. **Victory Barbecue** in the nearby town of Wyoming specializes in the fascinating Old Forge subcategory, Polish pizza, which comes with onions and is oily, with a more substantial crust. **Pizza Perfect** serves it Polish-style (with onions unless you specifically refuse them) and offers its rectangular cuts red (no cheese) or white (double-crusted, with no tomato sauce).

Iowa has many well-acknowledged claims to culinary fame, but excellent pizza is not one of them. We're not here to tell you that the pizza served at **Mabe's** in downtown Decorah compares with what you'd get in New Haven, Boston, or New York, but it is something different, and something mighty good. The crust is what makes it special. It is very thin, pale, and crisp, so elegant that it might remind you that Iowa is indeed home to some of the finest pie crusts anywhere. It is definitely a pizza crust, not a pie crust, but there is a textural refinement about it unknown in the brawnier pies of the

Northeast. Although slim, the crust has enough structural integrity to hold a round-the-world deluxe pie of crumbled sausage, pepperoni, mushrooms, onions, tomatoes, and gobs of cheese. As we plowed through one of these super-satisfying giants one evening, a table of cheerleaders sat to one side of us, veritably inhaling square-cut slices by the dozen, and an elderly couple sat to our other side, deciding exactly how many pizzas and with which ingredients they should order to take on the plane when they visit their children, who now live in Phoenix and are homesick for the flavor of Mabe's.

Just when we thought we knew everything about this nation's variety of pizza styles, along came Roadfood.com correspondent Doug Mose to tell us about yet another Iowa pizza, this one unique to the Quad Cities area of Illinois/Iowa along the Mississippi River. At **Frank's**, a locals' Formica-tabled favorite since 1955, a sign advertises "Napoli Pizza," but this dish is much more midwestern than Neapolitan. Frank's pizza sports a bready crust that is somewhat thin but substantial enough to have a perfectly balanced crunch-chew yin-yang. While the usual roster of toppings is available, the one to get is sausage. Rather than being strewn with disks or clumps, Quad City sausage pizzas are completely blanketed with a layer of ground-up Italian sausage bright with fennel. The pies are cut not into triangles or squares but into long strips that make eating easy. This is probably not a dish for pizza elitists, because it is so unlike real Italian pizza and all the exquisite Italianate pizzas of the Northeast, but as a food group unto itself, Quad Cities pizza is an American treat that just may hook you. (Frank's sells and will ship half-baked versions of its pizza to finish in your home oven.)

One other essential American pizza is West Virginia's. Many people are surprised to learn that the Mountaineer State has a large population of people of Italian ancestry and fine Italian-American food that reflects it. Pepperoni rolls (page 187) are one example unique to the state; its pizza is equally distinctive. As made at **DiCarlo's**, a local chain that started in Wheeling in 1949, the pizza is a squared-off slab of medium-thin dough that is put in the oven with only sauce on top. When the tomato-glazed crust reaches the ideal balance between crunch and chew, the baker pulls it out and strews shredded sweet provolone and, if desired, pepperoni slices and peppers on top. Although the crust's heat will melt much of the cheese as the pizza is carried from kitchen to table, the provolone feels more like a mantle than a part of the pie. If you are expecting creamy mozzarella pizza or Neapolitan flatbread, it is disconcerting at first. But as a unique branch of American

A square slice at DiCarlo's in West Virginia delivers the right balance of crunch and chew.

pizzadom, this pie is vital, and as a curious open-face, oven-baked cheese and tomato sandwich, it is beguiling.

If you've eaten barbecue spaghetti (page 132) with pulled pork and barbecue salad topped with sauce rather than dressing along the Mississippi Delta, it will be no great surprise to know that Memphis is the home of barbecue pizza. At **Coletta's Italian Restaurant**, a nice round pie with plenty of mozzarella is topped not with Italian sauce and sausage or pepperoni but with barbecued pork in a zesty cinnabar pit sauce. Weird as it may seem, it works wonderfully, and it is a fitting salute to the unrepressed personality of the once-Italian dish that has become all-American.

Praiseworthy meatless pizza is commonplace, but if you crave a pizza that celebrates vegetables and a vegetarian outlook on life, you need to visit the **Cheeseboard Pizza Collective** in California. Originally branched out from the Cheeseboard Collective, which started selling cheese and bread as one of Berkeley's first collective enterprises in the heady year of 1967, it offers one and only one kind of pizza each day. Let us tell you, these pizzas are on a different plane from those from Domino's and Pizza Hut! On a Saturday in early winter, we tucked into a pie with roasted potatoes, onions, Spanish three-milk Montalban cheese, shiitake mushrooms, herbs, and garlic. The next Tuesday (the place is closed Sunday and Monday) we went back for a topping of olive tapenade, feta cheese, red pepper, onions, and parsley. The exemplary veggies, fresh herbs, and unexpected cheeses are spread across crust that is like a thin disk of garlic bread with a modest crunch. There's no tomato sauce per se, and do not expect gobs of oily mozzarella. This is not American fast-food pizza. Nor is it Italian. It is East Bay, California.

ESSENTIAL PIZZERIAS

1. **Frank Pepe Pizzeria Napoletana:** 157 Wooster St., New Haven, CT
203-865-5762
See www.pepespizzeria.com for additional locations.

2. **Modern Apizza:** 874 State St., New Haven, CT
203-776-5306
www.modernapizza.com

3. **Carminuccio's:** 76 S. Main St., Newtown, CT
203-364-1133
www.carminucciospizza.com

4. **De Lorenzo's Tomato Pies:** 530 Hudson St., Trenton, NJ
609-341-8480
www.delorenzostomatopies.com

5. **Sally's Apizza:** 237 Wooster St., New Haven, CT
203-624-5271
www.sallysapizza.net

6. **Pizzeria Lauretano:** 291 Greenwood Ave., Bethel, CT
203-792-1500

7. **Santarpio's:** 111 Chelsea St., East Boston, MA
617-567-9871
www.santarpiospizza.com

8. **Cheeseboard Pizza Collective:** 1512 Shattuck Ave., Berkeley, CA
510-549-3055
www.cheeseboardcollective.coop

9. **Colony Grill:** 172 Myrtle Ave., Stamford, CT
203-359-2184

10. **Patsy's:** 2287 First Ave., New York, NY
212-534-9783

11. **Pizzeria Uno:** 29 E. Ohio St., Chicago, IL
312-321-1000
www.unos.com

12. **Giordano's:** Various locations in Chicago; see website for specifics.
www.giordanos.com

13. **Original Gino's East:** 633 N. Wells, Chicago, IL
312-943-1124
See www.ginoseast.com for additional locations.

14. **Excelsior:** 272 Boylston St., Boston, MA
617-426-7878
www.excelsiorrestaurant.com

15. **Lou Malnati's:** Various locations in Chicago; see website for specifics.
www.loumalnatis.com

16. **Ernesto's:** 69 Salem St., Boston, MA
617-523-1373
www.ernestosnorthend.com

17. **Ghigiarelli's:** 511 S. Main St., Old Forge, PA
570-457-2652

18. **Pizza Perfect:** 16 Carverton Rd., Trucksville, PA
570-696-2100
www.pizza-perfect.com

19. **Victory Barbecue:** 905 Wyoming Ave., Wyoming, PA
570-693-9963

20. **Revello's:** 502 S. Main St., Old Forge, PA
570-457-9843

21. **Coletta's Italian Restaurant:** 1063 S. Parkway East, Memphis, TN

901-948-7652
Second location: 2840 Appling Rd., Memphis, TN
901-383-1122
www.colettasrestaurant.com
22. **Frank's:** 711 First Ave., Silvis, IL
309-755-8321
23. **DiCarlo's:** Various locations in West Virginia; see website for specifics.
www.dicarlospizza.com
24. **Mabe's Pizza:** 110 W. Water St., Decorah, IA
563-382-4297
See www.mabespizza.com for additional locations.

REAL ITALIAN
Portland, Maine

To call the unique sub of Portland, Maine, a *real* Italian is not adjectival whimsy; Downeast sandwich makers distinguish between a real Italian and a regular Italian. The Italian's origins go back to 1902, when Portland baker Giovanni Amato was convinced by dockworkers to split the long loaves of bread he sold from his street cart and pile them with meats, cheeses, tomatoes, peppers, pickles, onions, and olives. Amato opened a sandwich shop called **Amato's** that became a neighborhood institution and now boasts multiple locations in Maine, Vermont, and New Hampshire, as well as a bakery making the big, soft rolls that are the foundation of the real Italian.

The original sandwich was very much an Italian-*American* creation, anchored by boiled ham and bright orange American cheese. Amato's formula was altered in the 1970s by

Maine's unique sub, the Italian, was created to satisfy dockworkers.

the bakery's new owner, Dominic Reali, who switched out black olives in favor of full-flavored Greeks, added a zestier pickle, and infused the oil with spices. Today's Amato's offers original Italians, double originals (twice as much ham and cheese), "classic Italians" made with Genoa salami, capicola, prosciutto, and provolone, as well as roll-ups, focaccia sandwiches, pizza, and pasta buckets.

The place we like to eat our Italian is **Colucci's Hilltop Superette**, where *real Italian* means salami and provolone — that is, more like a classic Italian but with peppers, tomatoes, onions, and olives added. If you want the original formula of ham and American cheese, you ask the Coluccis for a regular Italian. As proprietor Dick Colucci expertly assembled real ones for us behind the counter of his corner store, he told us that the big issue among those who make them is not lunch meat or seasoning but bread. "A good fresh roll is the key," he counseled, reeling off the names of bakeries known for making the long buns on which Italians are made. (The best one we found is

New England

Micucci's, a grocery that also serves good thick-crust pizza.) Unlike typical sub rolls, an Italian roll is tender and light, something like a gigantic version of the split-top buns in which Yankee wieners are typically served.

Colucci also explained how the layers of salami or ham and cheese form a barrier between the bread and the oily vegetables above, making the sandwich relatively portable and neat-looking. However, as we ate ours off the tailgate of our car outside (there's no seating inside the market), we learned that once that barrier is breached (at first bite), the bread absorbs what's on top and loses its ability to hold anything. The experience is similar to eating a hot buttered lobster roll: midway through, the absorbent bun has transformed from a foundation into just one element among the stuff it originally contained. By the time you near the end of an Italian, the ingredients on the folded-open butcher paper no longer resemble a sandwich at all. They have become a deliciously messy cold-cut salad laced with fluffy tufts of oil-sopped bread.

THE BEST REAL ITALIANS

Colucci's Hilltop Superette: 135 Congress St., Portland, ME
207-774-2279

Also
Amato's: Various locations in New England; see www.amatos.com for specifics.

Rolls
Micucci's Grocery: 45 India St., Portland, ME
207-775-1854

SHORE DINNER
On the Coast

Shore dinner tastes especially right in the summer, outdoors, where sea air rouses appetite and red lobsters shimmer brightly on picnic tables. In southern New England, some of the best lobstercentric blowouts are served forth at **Abbott's Lobster in the Rough** of Noank, Connecticut, which installed invisible netting to keep hungry gulls from snatching tidbits off your plate; **Champlin's Seafood Deck** in Narragansett, Rhode Island (locally loved snail salad, page 62, is the sleeper course); and **Woodman's of Essex**, Massachusetts, where indoor seating has the rollicking feel of an old-time shore dinner hall.

Good as those places are, the ultimate shore dinner experience — just-caught local lobster eaten waterside — is a Maine thing. From **Chauncey Creek Lobster Pier** in Kittery to **Abel's Lobster Pound** in Acadia National Park, picturesque

At Mabel's in Kennebunkport, ME, lobsters and steamers together make one good meal.

Eat your lobster al fresco at the Lobster Shack in Cape Elizabeth, ME.

opportunities to feast abound. The most dramatic of them all, especially when waves are crashing on the rockbound coast, is the **Lobster Shack** in Cape Elizabeth, at Two Lights Park. A restaurant has perched here since the 1920s; the water's-edge setting is spectacular — at the entrance to Casco Bay, framed by a pair of lighthouses. More than a dozen picnic tables are marshaled on a flat patch of sandy land between the takeout counter and huge rocks where the ocean splashes in. When the sea is rough and wind is gusting, a foghorn sounds nearby and a fine mist of salty air blows across your meal, causing hot lobster meat to exude puffs of aromatic steam as you crack claws, vent the tail, and unhinge the back.

About as formal as we like to get on the summer seafood trail is **Mabel's Lobster Claw** in Kennebunkport. Paper place mats explaining how to eat a lobster decorate tables in snug wood booths, sherry-laced lobster Newburg heads the menu, and the lobster roll, heaped with large nuggets of picked meat in a fine film of mayo, is one of the coast's best. Mabel's shore dinner starts with creamy chowder crowded with pieces of clam and potato; then comes a plate crowded with a good-sized lobster perched on a pile of steamers and accompanied by broth and butter. If fudge cake is available, it must not be ignored, but the essential dessert is peanut butter ice cream pie.

Virtually around the corner from Mabel's is the **Clam Shack**, most famous for its lobster roll (page 41) as well as for superlative fried clams (page 24), but also a source for some of the most delicious lobsters anywhere. Boiled in seawater that surges up the Kennebunk River at high tide and is retrieved through a pipe that runs 70 feet down where the channel's current is pure and salty, they pack big fresh flavor with a wicked ocean twist. Tail meat virtually erupts with juice; knuckles are brawny and succulent, claws soft with a saline halo. To say that amenities are minimal is an understatement. The Clam Shack is a shack indeed. Its whole lobsters are boiled and sold from an adjoining store that is also a seafood market and bait and tackle shop. Upon re-

Five Islands' lobsters are brought ashore next to the picnic tables where they are served.

Deep, cold Maine waters produce the sweetest lobsters.

ceiving a cooked lobster, and maybe a half-pound of steamer clams, you must find a place to eat. There are benches on a deck in back and seats facing the sidewalk in front, where fish crates serve as makeshift tables. (Town zoning forbids proper seating here.) Potatoes? Rolls? Corn? Dessert? You are on your own. The store does sell bottles of beer and wine.

Five Islands Lobster Company in Georgetown, between the Kennebec River and Robinhood Cove, is informal, too, and it happens to be the most scenic place we know to indulge in a full shore dinner. Located at the end of the road on a dock from which a couple of dozen lobster boats sail, the dining room is al fresco: picnic tables on the wooden deck overlooking blue waters and five small islands thick with pine trees. The view also includes lobstermen offloading crates of just-trapped lobsters, which, proprietor Chris Butler explains, are so good because the waters they come from are some of the deepest and coldest on the coast. That doesn't explain why the fried clams served here are also among the best anywhere and the dollar-apiece slices of blueberry

cake and brownies are so wonderful. But then, it's always possible we were hypnotized into all-loving ecstasy by the location alone.

9 SUPERIOR SHORE DINNERS

1. **Five Islands Lobster Co.:** 1447 Five Islands Rd., Georgetown, ME
207-371-2990
www.fiveislandslobster.com
2. **Abbott's Lobster in the Rough:** 117 Pearl St., Noank, CT
860-536-7719
www.abbotts-lobster.com
3. **Abel's Lobster Pound:** Sound Dr., Mount Desert, ME
207-276-5827
4. **Chauncey Creek Lobster Pier:** 16 Chauncey Creek Rd., Kittery, ME
207-439-1030
www.chaunceycreek.com
5. **Clam Shack:** 2 Western Ave. (Route 9), Kennebunkport, ME
207-967-3321
www.theclamshack.net
6. **Mabel's Lobster Claw:** 124 Ocean Ave., Kennebunkport, ME
207-967-2562
7. **Woodman's of Essex:** 121 Main St., Essex, MA
978-768-6057
www.woodmans.com
8. **Champlin's Seafood Deck:** 256 Great Island Rd., Narragansett, RI
401-783-3152
www.champlins.com
9. **Lobster Shack:** 225 Two Lights Rd., Cape Elizabeth, ME
207-799-1677
www.lobstershacktwolights.com

SNAIL SALAD
Rhode Island

You'll find something named snail salad only on menus in Rhode Island, where it is about as common as coleslaw is elsewhere. (Neighboring states call it by its Italian name, scungilli salad.) It is a bracing refresher based around thin slices of snail (aka conch or whelk) that are just a wee bit chewy, marinated in olive oil and vinegar. The meaty little pieces with a fine seafoody sweetness are usually tossed with onion, bits of celery, perhaps some olives, and almost always lots and lots of garlic. The snail salad at Cranston's **Mike's Kitchen**, an unlikely source of excellent meals in an inconspicuous VFW post, is the one we recommend most. Turbocharged with little hot peppers, it is a thrilling hors d'oeuvre.

While not nearly as garlicky as most, the snail salad at **Champlin's Seafood Deck** in Narragansett is one of the prettiest versions of the dish, speckled everywhere with crisp, bright vegetables. Actually, the lack of garlic provides greater opportunity to taste the somewhat subtle snail meat, but for us, garlic is a fundamental part of the dish. One of the best-balanced versions — garlicky, but not too — is at **George's of Galilee**, where the thin slices of meat bask in a cool Italian marinade. We don't know of another salad quite so bracing, or so perfect as a cocktail companion.

The least formal and most enjoyable way to eat snail salad is from a Styrofoam clam-shell container at **Iggy's Doughboys** in Narragansett,

Thin slices of snail punctuated by an array of vegetables at Champlin's in Narragansett, RI

which we praise most for its sugared deep-fried dough (page 28) but which offers a super-garlicky, well-oiled array of thin-sliced snail laced with sliced black olives atop a bed of lettuce and tomato, with a lemon wedge to add extra sparkle. It's refreshing and full-flavored — a perfect foil to summertime's fried seafood.

BEST SNAIL SALADS

1. **Mike's Kitchen:** Tabor-Franchi VFW Post 239, 170 Randall St., Cranston, RI
401-946-5320
2. **George's of Galilee:** 250 Sand Hill Cove Rd., Galilee, RI
401-783-2306
www.georgesofgalilee.com
3. **Champlin's Seafood Deck:** 256 Great Island Rd., Narragansett, RI
401-783-3152
www.champlins.com
4. **Iggy's Doughboys:** 1157 Point Judith Rd., Narragansett, RI
401-783-5608
Second location: 889 Oakland Beach Ave., Warwick, RI
401-737-9459
www.iggysdoughboys.com

STEAMED CHEESEBURGER
Central Connecticut

A handful of fresh-ground beef is mashed into a small metal tray, which slides into a steam box, where it is vapor-cooked until insanely juicy but miraculously grease-free. The meat is topped with an oozing blob of melted cheddar that has been prepared in its own separate tray in the steam box. It is set forth upon a fluff-centered hard roll and garnished with a thick slice of crisp raw onion and a schmear of mustard. That is a steamed cheeseburger, unique to central Connecticut.

This strange branch of hamburgerology, in which crustiness is anathema, came into being at the long-gone Jack's Lunch of Middletown back in the 1920s, when steamed food was considered especially healthful by nutrition-conscious people who were starting to worry that anything fried was difficult to digest. We cannot vouch for its nutritional virtue, but it is a regional specialty that is too much fun to ignore.

Quality cheese is a vital component. Moderately aged cheddar is best; when steamed, it transforms into a pearlescent mass viscous enough to seep into every crevice of the meat below but not so runny it escapes the sandwich (although it *will* seriously leak; caution, balance, and many napkins are required). In fact, steamed cheese is so beloved by customers of **O'Rourke's Diner** in Middletown that many order it on things other than hamburgers: hot dogs and slabs of meat loaf and

plates of fried potatoes. Some prefer it alone in a roll, and the dessert connoisseur's choice is hot apple pie covered with a thick draping of it — a marvelous combo.

You can watch exactly how burgers and cheese are steamed at the counter of **Ted's** in Meriden, a little eatshack that has made big steamers its specialty since 1959. Spread before you on a wooden block in the open kitchen are a heap of ground meat

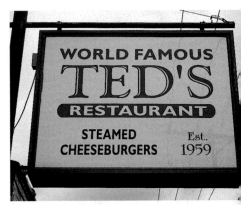

Ted's: a little shack with a big specialty

Cheese oozes seductively out of a steamed cheeseburger from Ted's in Meriden, CT.

ready to be portioned into little metal trays and big blocks of cheddar wait ing to be cut. Every time the steam box is opened for meat and cheese to go in or get pulled out, overwhelm- ing clouds puff out, exuding cheese- burger perfume.

2 BEST STEAMED CHEESEBURGERS

1. **Ted's:** 1044 Broad St., Meriden, CT
   203-237-6660
   www.steamedcheeseburger.com
2. **O'Rourke's Diner:** 728 Main St., Middletown, CT
   860-346-6101
   www.orourkesdiner.com

This way for migraine relief: A giant *Tyrannosaurus rex* guards the entrance to Nature's Art in Oakdale, CT, where you can buy stress-relieving crystals.

NATURE'S ART

You'll have no trouble finding Nature's Art on Connecticut's Route 85. It's just behind the 30-foot concrete *Tyran- nosaurus rex* with glow-in-the-dark eyes. Inside is a museum-quality Fossil Gallery with merchandise that ranges from little leaf imprints to a facsimile of the third largest *Tyran- nosaurus rex* skull ever found. The crystal selection includes sparklers small enough to hang from a rearview mirror as well as glittering sentinels 5 feet tall that are chock-full of luxuri- ant purple amethyst. Throughout the year, Nature's Art hosts workshops in crystal programming, during which a visiting expert helps you pick out the right crystal, then uses her energy to program it so it helps you overcome stress, migraines, or whatever ails you.

People less rigorous in their psychic regimen visit the store and ask if it's okay to stick their aching elbow inside an especially stunning tubular pipe of amethyst on the shelf and absorb its good vibes.

One of the coolest things to buy at Nature's Art is an intact geode. The price, which can rise to over $100 de- pending on size, includes cutting it in half with a diamond saw, a suspense- ful moment that can reveal anything from a "mudball" — one with virtually no crystal formation inside — to a burst of brilliant, fine-quality crystals in rainbow hues. You pay your money and you take your chance.

Nature's Art: 1650 Route 85, Oakdale, CT
860-443-GEMS
www.enaturesart.com

STUFFIE
Southern New England

Inedible whole because it is too big and too tough, the quahog clam packs plenty of meat that is really delicious. So Yankee cooks chop it up for chowder or to make stuffies, which are quahogs scooped out of their shell, chopped, and mixed with bread crumbs, butter, and spices, then packed back in the shell and baked to create a flamboyantly oceanic hors d'oeuvre.

"From an ancient Portuguese recipe," boasts the menu of **Flo's Clam Shack**, just east of Newport, Rhode Island, about its peppery stuffies, which we find go great with Flo's mild-tempered but sweet and clammy clam cakes and a cup of clear-broth chowder. Some of Rhode Island's moistest and most ocean-bright stuffies are sold by a mission-focused restaurant in Newport that calls itself the **Rhode Island Quahog Company**, where the menu offers "fine dining that won't cost you a lot of clams." (RIQC also makes quahog chili.) Baked stuffed quahogs at **George's of Galilee**, which *Narragansett Times* readers have several times elected the state's best, are big and fresh-flavored, nautical and earthy at the same time, the standout on a full-bore baked seafood platter that also includes scrod, scallops, stuffed blue crab, stuffed shrimp, and steamed littlenecks and mussels.

Although stuffies belong more to Rhode Island than to anywhere else, the best ones we've ever eaten are in Massachusetts, at **Margue-**rite's in Westport, a friendly little town cafe known also for fried clams, billi-bi (creamy mussel soup), and chicken pie. Marguerite's mixes the bits of full-flavored quahog with pepper-hot linguiça sausage, sweet onion, green and red pepper, and just enough bread to hold it all together. It's a magical seafood stuffing, so well liked that the management is accustomed to takeout orders of stuffies by the dozen for people who need them for a party at home.

BEST STUFFIES

1. **Marguerite's:** 778 Main Rd., Westport, MA
508-636-3040
www.margueritesrestaurant.com

2. **Rhode Island Quahog Co.:** 250 Thames St., Newport, RI
401-848-2330
www.riquahogco.com

3. **Flo's Clam Shack:** 4 Wave Ave., Middletown, RI
401-847-8141
www.flosclamshack.net

4. **George's of Galilee:** 250 Sand Hill Cove Rd., Galilee, RI
401-783-2306
www.georgesofgalilee.com

SUMMER SAUSAGE SANDWICH
Danbury, Connecticut

Karl Ehmer is a familiar name to sandwich lovers in the Northeast. Beginning as a butcher shop in New York City in the 1940s, Ehmer's is now a small chain of stores as well as a brand name for cold cuts sold by groceries from Massachusetts to Florida. We cannot vouch for the other places, but we can tell you that the little Karl Ehmer shop at the bottom of Federal Road in Danbury, Connecticut, is a source of rare and wonderful sandwiches. Meat is not cut on the premises, but this place has the feel of an old neighborhood butcher shop. German music plays on the radio; Gabrielle Freundt, the nice woman at the counter, has a charming Old World mien (and accent), and the variety of salamis, sausages, and head cheeses on the shelves is vast. Meats and cheeses for sandwiches are sliced to order, and as good as they are, it is the German bread that puts Ehmer sandwiches over the top — dense rye with real character, hand-cut into broad slices that make each sandwich the size of two. We are especially fond of summer sausage, sliced thin and piled high, with Swiss or muenster cheese and maybe some spicy German mustard.

There are no dining facilities at Karl Ehmer. Service is takeout only.

Karl Ehmer: 6 Federal Rd.,
    Danbury, CT
    203-744-3950

TURKEY DINNER
Meredith, New Hampshire

Okay, so the Pilgrims did not eat turkey and mashed potatoes at the first Thanksgiving. So maybe it is not appropriate to name turkey dinner as a New England specialty. But hey, we are the last people to let historical fact stand between appetite and primeval turkey dinner. Since opening as a twelve-seat restaurant in 1954, the now-cavernous **Hart's Turkey Farm** has served its year-round Thanksgiving in three plate sizes, the largest piled with over a pound of hot-off-the-bird white and dark meat (or just white, if you pay extra), plus moist, sage-scented stuffing, mashed potatoes, gravy, cranberry sauce, rolls and butter. Cutting-edge this menu is not, but if you are a culinary pop-classicist of the American persuasion, there is no meal in the land more completely perfect. It starts with vivid carrot relish and saltines, the relish available from Hart's online store. Dessert? Apple pie, of course!

Hart's Turkey Farm: 233 Daniel
    Webster Highway, Meredith, NH
    603-279-6212
    Second location: 21 Front St.,
    Manchester, NH
    603-669-3333
    www.hartsturkeyfarm.com

WHOOPIE PIE
Maine

Imagine an Oreo cookie as big as a hamburger bun filled with a thick layer of sweet white faux cream, its chocolate disks soft and fudgy and so moist that it is impossible to grasp the thing, no matter how gingerly, without getting your fingers smudged with cake. The dilemma every eater faces is that the urge to lick cake off fingers immediately competes with the urge to lick cream from all around the edge before taking a first bite.

A sandwich of pure satisfaction

When the trademarked Whoopie! Pie was introduced in 1928 by the Berwick Cake Company (which three years before had created the Devil Dog), Eddie Cantor was starring in a Boston musical called *Whoopee.* During the performance, the chocolate pies were tossed into the audience as Cantor sang the hit song "Makin' Whoopee!" No one knows for sure whether it was the cake or the musical that was named first and inspired the other. The Berwick Bakery was in Roxbury, Massachusetts, but somehow Maine has become the place where the whoopie pie thrives as the semiofficial picnic-table snack and shore dinner dessert.

Big, soft, chocolaty whoopie pies are always available at the hugely picturesque lobster pound known as **Harraseeket Lunch and Lobster** in Freeport. At least 4 inches across and nearly as tall, loaded with sweet white stuff and yet surprisingly lightweight, this dessert has chocolate parts that are devilishly dark, and it is so frag-

ile that it is a challenge to remove it from its plastic wrap without tearing it apart. It is a great conclusion to one of Maine's premier waterside picnics — lobster, steamers, and corn on the cob, with no utensils but nutcracker and pick to excavate the lobster's meat.

When you develop a whoopie pie craving anywhere outside of Maine, there is a solution: **Labadie's Bakery** in Lewiston, which claims to have been making "the original (not a copy) Maine Whoopie Pie" since 1925. Labadie's makes standard whoopie pies as well as pies filled with peanut butter creme and white whoopies made from vanilla cake. It also makes an 8-pound whoopie pie that will serve twenty-plus people. All these products are available by mail.

Isamax Snacks sells whoopie pies at its bakeries in Gardiner, near the junction of I-95 and I-295, but is mostly a mail-order business with a slick online order procedure. Isamax's "wicked whoopies" are available dipped in chocolate (known as a whoop-de-doo), made with red velvet cake instead of regular devil's food, and filled with flavors that range from mint and maple to pumpkin and peanut butter. Another mail-order source is **Cranberry Island Kitchen** in Cumberland, just north of Portland, which makes what it calls "gourmet whoopie pies," meaning that the filling is genuinely creamy and they come in such sophisticated flavors as Cointreau, rum, espresso, and champagne. Using free-range chicken eggs, spring water, organic vanilla, and so on, Cranberry Island makes a ritzy dessert — in half-circle

Whoopie pie cake ribboned with
marshmallow-light icing

shape rather than full circle — costing about four times more than a
typical convenience-store whoopie
pie. But it is in a class by itself. In the
summer of 2008, **Bob's Clam Hut** in
Kittery was selling Cranberry Island
whoopies for $3.95 apiece. If you
plan to eat one at Bob's, we suggest
you secure it at the same time you order the meal that precedes it. Because
real cream is used, the pies are kept
refrigerated. They need time for their
temperature to rise; their flavor flowers as they lose their chill.

GREAT WHOOPIE PIES

Cranberry Island Kitchen: 7B
Corey Rd., Cumberland, ME
207-829-5200
www.cranberryislandkitchen.com

Labadie's Bakery: 22 Haley St.,
Lewiston, ME
207-582-0620
www.labadiesbakery.com

Isamax Snacks: 5 Mechanic St.,
Gardiner, ME
877-447-2629
Second location: 621 Maine Ave.,
Farmingdale, ME
207-622-8860
www.wickedwhoopies.com

**Harraseeket Lunch and
Lobster:** Town Landing, Main St.
South, Freeport, ME
207-865-3535

Bob's Clam Hut: 315 U.S. Route 1,
Kittery, ME
207-439-4233
www.bobsclamhut.com

Thrift inspired Becky Rand's whoopie
pie cake.

WHOOPIE PIE CAKE

While it is possible to make whoopie pies at home, we find it much more satisfying to make whoopie pie cake. This is a recipe from Becky Rand, proprietor of Becky's Diner on Hobson's Wharf in Portland. She told us she was inspired to make it not only by the popularity of whoopie pies along the Maine coast, but by a recipe for low-cost icing she found while browsing through a World War II cookbook that was written to help housewives deal with food rationing. She calls it "poor man's icing," and its marshmallow texture gives it the plebeian character that whoopie pie demands.

CAKE

    2 sticks margarine, softened
    2 cups sugar
2¼ cups all-purpose flour
    1 teaspoon baking soda
    1 teaspoon salt
1¼ cups buttermilk
    3 large eggs, at room temperature
    9 tablespoons cocoa powder

ICING

    2 cups whole milk
 ¾ cup all-purpose flour
    2 cups sugar
    1 stick butter, softened
    1 tablespoon vanilla extract
    1 cup solid vegetable shortening, at room temperature

Preheat the oven to 350 degrees. Grease two 9-inch round cake pans.

FOR THE CAKE: Beat together the margarine and sugar. Add the flour, baking soda, and salt. Mix slowly, then gradually add the buttermilk. Beat for a full 2 minutes. Add the eggs, then gradually add the cocoa. Beat for another 2 minutes, stopping occasionally to scrape down the sides of the bowl. Pour the batter into the prepared pans and bake for about 40 minutes, until the center springs back when gently pushed. Cool the cake layers for 5 minutes, then remove them from the pans and cool them completely on a wire rack.

FOR THE ICING: Pour the milk into a saucepan over medium heat. Gradually whisk in the flour until a thick paste forms. Do not scorch! Remove the pan from the stove and cool the paste in the refrigerator.

In a bowl, mix the sugar, butter, vanilla, and shortening. Add the cooled paste. Whip for at least 3 minutes, until creamy.

TO ASSEMBLE: Put one cake layer on a cake plate and frost. Top with the second layer and frost the top and sides.

MAKES ONE 2-LAYER 9-INCH CAKE

Becky's Diner: 390 Commercial St., Portland, ME
207-773-7070
www.beckysdiner.com

MID ATLANTIC

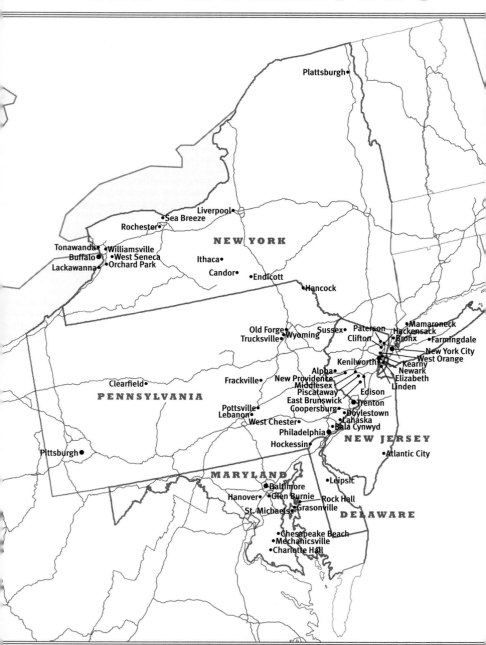

Plattsburgh•

NEW YORK

Liverpool•
•Sea Breeze
Rochester•
Tonawanda• •Williamsville
Buffalo• •West Seneca
Lackawanna• •Orchard Park
Ithaca•
Candor•
•Endicott
•Hancock

Old Forge• Sussex• Paterson• •Mamaroneck
Trucksville• •Wyoming Clifton• Hackensack
•Bronx •Farmingdale
Kenilworth• New York City
•West Orange
•Kearny
Newark
Alpha• Elizabeth
Clearfield• Frackville• New Providence• Linden
Middlesex•
Piscataway• Edison
East Brunswick •Trenton
Coopersburg• •Doylestown
Pottsville• •Lahaska
Lebanon• •Bala Cynwyd
West Chester•
Philadelphia•
Hockessin• **NEW JERSEY**

Pittsburgh• •Atlantic City

PENNSYLVANIA

MARYLAND
•Leipsic
•Baltimore
Hanover• •Glen Burnie
St. Michaels• Rock Hall
•Grasonville
DELAWARE
•Chesapeake Beach
•Mechanicsville
•Charlotte Hall

BEEF ON WECK
Greater Buffalo, New York

Buffalo roast beef is beautiful. A 40-pound center-cut round, draped with suet and seasoned with salt and pepper, is cooked until the outside turns dark and glistens with juice while the interior stays vivid red. It is a firm hunk of food that jiggles when it is moved around on the butcher block next to the bar in the dining room of Buffalo's premier beef house, **Schwabl's.** As the carver plants a fork in the top and his knife glides easily into the center, slices settle onto the carving board like soft petals of a great crimson rose. The warm meat is assembled in a mass about an inch tall on the bottom half of a unique hard roll that is known in western New York State as a kummelweck.

From the German *kummel,* meaning "caraway seed," a kummelweck, or simply weck, is shaped like a kaiser roll but crowned with a diadem of seeds and coarse salt so abundant that it crunches audibly when bitten.

When in Buffalo, roam into Schwabl's for the best roast beef.

It has an extraordinarily fine crumb, with a light texture crucial to cushion but not compete with the gentle feel of the sliced beef. Its top half is customarily immersed in pan juice just long enough for it to start to soften before it is set atop the sandwich.

According to Charlie Roesch, proprietor of **Charlie the Butcher's Kitchen** out near the Buffalo airport, it was beer that inspired the invention of beef on weck. He believes that sometime in the 1880s a now-forgotten local tavern owner (perhaps a Schwabl) decided to offer a sandwich that would induce a powerful thirst in his patrons. He had plenty of coarse salt on hand for the pretzels he served, so he painted a mixture of the salt and caraway seeds on some hard rolls, cooked a roast, sliced it thin, and piled the meat inside the rolls. As in any self-respecting Buffalo beef house, Charlie slices his roasts by hand, on the counter at the front of the restaurant. "To have your meat carved by a real butcher is special," Charlie says. "Some people come in here who have never seen that."

Eckl's Beef & Weck Restaurant is another of Buffalo's longstanding shrines to red meat, in business since 1934 in a building that used to be a brewery tavern. Proprietor Dale Eckl likes to point out that a proper roll is every bit as significant as good beef in making the city's cherished sandwich so special. "It is surprisingly difficult to maintain the kummelweck," he says. "You can't ship them or store them because they stale so fast and the salt crust will break down if it is exposed to humidity." Eckl is also passionate about horseradish, the beef

A kummelweck roll spangled with caraway and salt cushions roast beef.

on weck eater's preferred condiment. "The hotter, the better!" he says. "I get mine from a Jewish man in Buffalo who gets the roots from Mexico and grinds it fresh." Eckl's beef is singular, sliced as thin as prosciutto and piled extra-high. "You have to *shave* that roast," Dale Eckl maintains. "It has so much good flavor, but it is going to be tough if it's cut too thick."

The beef at **Steve's Pig & Ox Roast** is not the rose-red slices typical of Buffalo but thicker slices of cooked-through meat that is as moist and tender as Grandma's pot roast. Bruce Bilmes and Sue Boyle, who tipped us off to this neighborhood roaster-cafe, warned that unless you specifically ask for a kummelweck roll, sandwiches are served on regular buns. At $5 each — for pork, lamb, and turkey as well as beef — these mountainous sandwiches are a great beef on weck bargain, available with Buffalo's beloved loganberry juice to drink and magnificent servings of French fries.

Laughlin's calls itself a bistro, a term that would never apply to any of the Nickel City's old-line beef houses. But there is no faulting the elegant, carved-to-order roast beef piled generously into sandwiches, which for the saltphobe are also available on regular kaiser rolls. **Buffalo Brewpub**, which offers nearly three dozen beers on tap, seasons its roast with house-made ale that adds a clever sour twist to the brawn of the meat. Those with limited appetites who want to taste two Buffalo specialties on one dish can get a sampler platter of six wings — mild, medium, hot, or BBQ — along with a mini beef on weck.

SIX BEST BEEF ON WECKS

1. **Schwabl's:** 789 Center Rd., West Seneca, NY
   716-674-9821
   www.schwabls.com

2. **Charlie the Butcher's Kitchen:** 1065 Wehrle Dr., Buffalo, NY
   716-633-8330
   See www.charliethebutcher.com for additional locations.

3. **Steve's Pig & Ox Roast:** 951 Ridge Rd., Lackawanna, NY
   716-824-8601

4. **Eckl's Beef & Weck Restaurant:** 4936 Ellicott Rd., Orchard Park, NY
   716-662-2262

5. **Laughlin's:** 333 Franklin, Buffalo, NY
   716-842-6700
   www.laughlinsrestaurant.com

6. **Buffalo Brewpub:** 6861 Main St., Williamsville, NY
   716-632-0552
   www.buffalobrewpub.com

Mid Atlantic

PARKSIDE CANDY

One of Buffalo's least-touted culinary assets is its plethora of great candy stores, of which Parkside Candy is a leading light. Like a grand old movie palace, it is a 1927 sanctuary of architectural wonder with a domed ceiling, soft recessed lighting, and a series of vending windows around the circumference of the room where creams and chews, truffles and cordials, clusters, dixies, and barks are displayed and sold. The counters are spaced by ornate carved columns and mirrors, and in the center of the room are little ice-cream-parlor tables where you can order from a menu of fountain delights that range from frappes, parfaits, and sundaes to the lovers' indulgence "Old Granada Special" — eight scoops of ice cream, four toppings, and two varieties of toasted nut under a mountain of whipped cream, served with two spoons.

Parkside Candy: 3208 Main St., Buffalo, NY
716-833-7540
See www.parksidecandy.com for additional locations.

BIALY
New York City

Bagels are everywhere, but bialys are unique to kosher-style bakeries and delis. It is rare to find a good one outside New York, and in New York, one place has set the benchmark since 1936: **Kossar's Bialys**. A bialy is about the same size as a bagel and of similar shape, except that where a bagel's hole would be, the bialy has a thin web of dough inlaid with a paste made of minced onion. As the bialy bakes, the onion nearly chars, weeping bits of flavor into the bread. Whereas bagels have slick skin (because they are boiled), the skin of a bialy has a grippier matte finish. The fate of most bialys is to get toasted and buttered or schmeared with cream cheese, which is a good thing, but there is nothing quite as wonderful as the absolutely fresh ones you'll find at Kossar's, maybe still hot and not yet toasted. Brick-oven baked, a Kossar's bialy has a handsome tan exterior that is more leathery than crisp; it is chewy but lightweight and fragile to the touch. It's delicious as is; when toasted, it turns crisp and the heat draws savory perfume from its onions.

Kossar's Bialys: 367 Grand St., New York, NY
877-424-2597
www.kossarsbialys.com

BISCOTTI
Pittsburgh, Pennsylvania

Larry Lagattuta makes over two dozen flavors of large, hand-cut biscotti, including classic anise-almond and black pepper–walnut as well as white chocolate with macadamia

The biscotti from Pittsburgh's Enrico bakery are made fresh each morning.

biscotti is an Italian word meaning "twice-baked": first as a loaf, then as cookies cut from the loaf.)

On the subject of fresh, if ever you walk into Enrico Biscotti and the macaroons are warm from the oven, buy some and eat them right away! Macaroons are a regular part of the repertoire but not always available. Indeed, other than biscotti, the inventory at Enrico cannot be predicted. Some days you will find sweet coconut macaroons; other days there might be Italian cornmeal cake or scones.

Enrico Biscotti Co.: 2022 Penn Ave., Pittsburgh, PA
412-281-2602
Second location: 665 Washington Rd., Lebanon, PA
412-563-0311
www.enricobiscotti.com

nuts. They have a good crunch, but it is not because they are stale, for after the crunch comes a deep, delicious mouthful of full-bodied pastry. For dunking into coffee or eating as a snack, **Enrico Biscotti Company** biscotti are a revelation if all you know are the dry ones that come packaged in plastic. In the world of baking, freshness rules, and early in the morning here in Pittsburgh, the biscotti are only hours out of their second bake in the oven. (Larry explained to us that

BREAD-BAKING SCHOOL

Once a month, Larry Lagattuta of Enrico Biscotti Company offers a three-hour class for twenty people who want to learn how to bake bread. During the class, students are treated to a full Lagatutta-cooked meal, including the bread he makes during class, concluding with macaroons. For further information, visit the store's website.

CANNOLI
New York

Cannoli at the **Arthur Avenue Baking Company** in the Bronx are filled when ordered, which is perhaps one minute before you crush into the parchment-fragile pastry shell with your teeth and savor the ricotta inside. To underline the pure creaminess of the filling, you might want to have it speckled with a cocoa hailstorm in the form of little bits of dark chocolate, and on the side of this elegant piece of food, the bakery's good cappuccino is well-nigh perfect. You will watch your cannoli filled just down the street at **Madonia Brothers Bakery**, too, where they pipe in so much filling that it wants to spill

Crispy cannoli from the Bronx's Arthur Avenue, filled with ricotta and served pronto

out the ends of the crunchy pastry tube. Madonia's ricotta is a notch less sweet than most, and maybe even denser, and for these reasons tastes the richest of all.

Why do we say cannoli are essential eats in New York? Because even though they are found on Italian menus everywhere, most bakeries and restaurants fill them in advance. A cannoli stuffed an hour ago is almost as sad as an oyster opened an hour ago. It has lost its charm. The shell's crunch is gone; the dairy freshness of the ricotta has dissipated or, worse, been frozen to death.

The Arthur Avenue cannoli are classics. For something exciting and different, have dessert after your fine Italian meal at the Greenwich Village spot called **Gusto Ristorante e Bar Americano**. The shells for these fingerling cannoli (three to an order) are ultra-crisp mocha-flavored pastry sheaths that enclose silky cheese flavored with orange and cinnamon, the exposed white ends dipped in chocolate and pistachio nuts.

THE CANNOLI TRIO

Arthur Avenue Baking Co.:
   2413 Arthur Ave., Bronx, NY
   718-365-8860
Madonia Brothers Bakery:
   2348 Arthur Ave., Bronx, NY
   718-295-5573
**Gusto Ristorante e Bar
   Americano:** 60 Greenwich Ave.,
   New York, NY
   212-924-8000
   www.gustonyc.com

CHEESE STEAK
Philadelphia

Once many years ago, and again only recently, we set out to eat every cheese steak in and around Philadelphia and decide which was best. We hit the big-name places in the Italian Market, which, generally speaking, are more about reputation than about deliciousness, and we visited little-known ones to which we had been clued in by their devoted fans. Both times one restaurant was the standout: **Mama's Pizzeria**, an unlikely neighborhood storefront in

Roast pork and broccoli rabe, the noteworthy combination at Philly's Tony Luke's

the suburb of Bala Cynwyd, far from the bustle of the market. Mama's steak's extraordinary culinary refinement tests the proletarian nature of a street-food sandwich most commonly made from stringy beef and Cheez Whiz. Chef Paul Castellucci's beef is thin-sliced, lean, and scarlet, hitting the hot griddle in clumps that get hacked to smithereens with a trowel until browned, at which point he applies a great mound of what looks like shredded mozzarella but is in fact a proprietary mix that, incredibly, does not stick to the hot iron surface. The beef and cheese are worked over together so thoroughly that you barely see cheese in the finished product, but its luxury saturates every bite. The onions are not cooked on the grill along with the beef, which is the customary way to do it. Instead, Castellucci sautés them separately to the exact point where they tip from sharp to sweet and crisp to limp. They are added after the great loose log of meat and cheese is hoisted from the griddle into the jaws of a length of muscular Italian bread. Long hot peppers, roasted in Mama's pizza oven, add brilliant red and jade green as well as exclamatory heat to the earthy combo.

"The perfect balance of flavors and textures" is how Bruce Bilmes and Sue Boyle describe the cheese steak at **Steve's Prince of Steaks** in northeast Philadelphia, where the steak is thin-sliced rather than chopped. They noted that you tend to get less meat in a Steve's steak than in some of the overstuffed ones, but if that is a problem, you can pay $2.30 extra for double meat.

The single greatest sandwich at **Tony Luke's** is roast pork, piled in shreds and chunks inside a fine long hero roll along with sautéed broccoli rabe. The limp greens, cooked with plenty of garlic, carry a faintly bitter chlorophyll nature that dramatically accentuates the pork, giving this utterly informal sandwich a broad-spectrum taste that is as grand as that of any four-star fine-dining entrée. Essential as the roast pork may be, no cheese steak honor roll would be complete without Tony Luke's: tender, juice-dripping petals of beef ("cut daily," the menu assures) heaped

MÜTTER MUSEUM

While we adore the Mütter Museum, we recommend you tour it long before or well after your cheese-steak-eating expedition around Philadelphia. For one thing, food is not allowed. For another, the exhibits are not exactly an appetizer. Here you will see the body of a woman who turned to soap after she was buried, a face rotted by syphilis, the smashed skull of a murder victim, an ovarian cyst the size of a honeydew melon, and, our personal favorite, a megacolon — the largest known human colon, removed from the twenty-nine-year-old man it killed.
Mütter Museum of the College of Physicians of Philadelphia: 19 S. 22nd St., Philadelphia, PA
215-563-3737
www.collphyphil.org

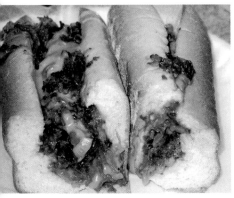

Lorenzo's Pizza turns out some of the best Philly cheese steaks in the city.

ach sautéed with pepper and garlic. John's cheese steaks also are among the city's best, which John Bucci, Jr., attributes to the fact that every sandwich is made from scratch, starting with a clean griddle, raw beef, and raw onions. Each sandwich holds two thirds of a pound of meat so luscious that it verges on lascivious, layered with five slices of cheese (unless you ask for extra cheese: five slices). There is so much stuff that the griddle man tears out some of the good roll's soft insides to make room. Like Luke's, John's has no indoor seating. Dining is at picnic tables.

into a sturdy roll, and dolloped with the requisite Cheez Whiz. Variations include pizza steak with sauce, pepperoni cheese steak, and a plain steak without cheese.

The roast pork sandwich at **John's Roast Pork** in the old shipyards neighborhood is right up there with Tony Luke's, especially when piled into a sturdy, seeded Carangi Baking Company roll with clumps of spin-

One of the best-tasting but least famous steaks in town is at **Lorenzo's Pizza**, a corner storefront not far from the market, where it is a joy to watch the sandwiches made to order. It starts when a few thin slices of steak are laid on the grill. As they begin to cook, the chef hacks them into hash along with onions that turn soft and weep flavor into the beef as they cook. The hash is formed into

HOT WITH LONG HOTS

Many savvy Philadelphians include Johnny's Hots on the short list of essential cheese steak sources; and while Johnny's steak looks nice, it is the namesake hot sausage that must be eaten at this stand-up, al fresco joint in Philadelphia's old Fishtown. As firmly packed as a D.C. half smoke (page 165), Johnny's hot is breathtaking pepper-orange and comes in an extremely buff bun with your choice of condiments. Philadelphia's uniquely zesty slaw, known as pepper hash, is a good pairing, especially with mustard, but the really great companion is what's known in local sandwich shops as long hots — roasted peppers with a fiery bite that sings high-pitch harmony alongside the sausage.

Johnny's Hots: 1234 N. Delaware Ave., Philadelphia, PA
215-423-2280
www.johnnyshots.com

a tubular heap perfectly fitted to be shoveled into a torpedo roll. At this point slices of provolone or a couple of ladles of Whiz are added. The meat and cheese meld together and are stuffed into a fine long roll.

Jim's Steaks is a handsome art deco eatery that claims to be the second oldest cheese steak shop in town (after Pat's, which originated the idea back in the 1930s). Of all the old big-name cheese steak shops, it is the one worth visiting. Jim's steaks — the meat for which is sliced while you watch from the long line of customers waiting to get one — are hacked into fine smithereens with onions and get piled on top of cheese if you order American or provolone or smothered with cheese if you go for Whiz. They are not huge sandwiches. Nevertheless, we were stunned by a plaque on the wall, seen during a 2007 visit, that honored "Humble" Bob Shoudt for his achievement of eating thirteen sandwiches in one hour.

BEST CHEESE STEAKS

1. **Mama's Pizzeria:** 426 Belmont Ave., Bala Cynwyd, PA 610-664-4757 www.mamaspizzeria.com
2. **John's Roast Pork:** 14 E. Snyder Ave., South Philadelphia, PA 215-463-1951 www.johnsroastpork.com
3. **Tony Luke's Old Philly Style Sandwiches:** 39 E. Oregon Ave., Philadelphia, PA 215-551-5725 www.tonylukes.com
4. **Jim's Steaks:** 400 South St., Philadelphia, PA 215-928-1911
5. **Lorenzo's Pizza:** 900 Christian St., Philadelphia, PA 215-922-2540
6. **Steve's Prince of Steaks:** 7200 Bustleton Ave., Philadelphia, PA 215-338-0985 See www.stevesprinceofsteaks .com for additional locations.

CORNELL CHICKEN
New York

Popular throughout New York's southern tier and served at outdoor picnics, in supermarket parking lots, and at church suppers as well as in a few restaurants, Cornell chicken is the creation of Professor Robert Baker, who developed a marinade and/or basting sauce back in the 1950s that is a tomato-free vinaigrette enriched with eggs and shot through with poultry spice. Slow-cooked over charcoal, the chicken comes off the grill with a golden glaze, its skin delivering a salty punch in a plush glove. (Cornell chicken was just one of Dr. Baker's creations. He also invented

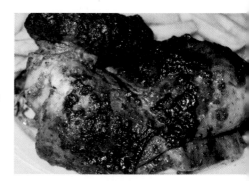

Egg, not tomato, in the marinade gives Cornell chicken a golden sheen.

chicken nuggets, chicken hot dogs, and turkey ham. Known as the "Edison of the Poultry Industry," he was inducted into the American Poultry Hall of Fame in 2004.)

Many cooks in New York have their own twist on the formula, but Phil Card, who opened **Phil's Chicken House** in Endicott in the mid-1960s, explained the time-honored way to do it: "We baste our chickens on the rotisserie every seven to ten minutes for two hours." Although the technique made Phil's a thriving business, Mr. Card was not entirely happy with his success. "We can never franchise this," he lamented. "You can't do it

---

CORNELL CHICKEN MARINADE

1 large egg
1 cup vegetable oil
2 cups cider vinegar
3 tablespoons salt
1 tablespoon poultry seasoning
1 teaspoon freshly ground
    black pepper

Beat the egg well in a medium bowl. Whisk in all the remaining ingredients. Set aside about a cup of the sauce to use for basting the chicken as it cooks.

Place patted-dry chicken parts in a shallow dish and coat them with the remaining sauce. Cover the dish and refrigerate the chicken for 24 hours.

MAKES ENOUGH TO MARINATE 2 CHICKENS

---

on a timer. The chickens are different sizes, and the rotisserie runs hotter some days. You need a cook who knows how to look at chicken and knows when and how to baste it. Years ago the Boston Market people came here and visited us to learn, but they walked out in frustration. 'You're too complicated for us,' they told me."

One of the most alluring sources of Cornell chicken along Route 96 was the half-drum open cooker maintained by grill man Jim Campoli in the parking lot of Metro's Restaurant, north of Owego. We can't guarantee he'll be there if you drive by — his hours have been Saturdays only, between May and September — but if he is, you must stop. Jim sops sizzling halves of chicken with barbecue sauce and serves them with salt-roasted potatoes and bacon-and-brown-sugar beans. There is no dining room; customers carry meals to tables at the miniature golf course next to the parking lot. We watched Jim use a long-handled sponge mop to press vast amounts of sauce onto the grilling chicken, and as the sauce and chicken juices dripped down onto coals, the air filled with so much aromatic smoke that our camera didn't know where to autofocus. Alternately basting and using tongs to rearrange the birds on the grate, Jim said, "This is my theory on the Cornell chicken recipe: When our body gets thirsty, we need to drink. So it is with chicken. When it cooks over coals, it needs marinade. It is thirsty chicken and will drink all the marinade you can give. Then, when you eat it, the meat gives back the flavor."

We're not quite sure if **Jim's BBQ**

Near Ithaca, Jim Kurtz serves up chicken to friends and passersby in his backyard.

Chicken, thirty minutes' drive south of Ithaca, is a restaurant or an ad hoc picnic in the proprietor's backyard, but for the past ten years, starting around Mother's Day, Jim Kurtz has been cooking and serving Cornell chicken five days a week to friends and passersby. Up front by Foundry Street there is a small house trailer, at the door of which you place your order (whole or half chicken or, on some occasions, pork ribs). The dining area is a cluster of covered wooden tables on a gravel patio in the yard. C&W music plays from a radio located somewhere above the trio of avocado-green refrigerators in which Mr. Kurtz keeps extra salads. While accommodations are informal, they are shipshape. Every wooden table is impeccably arranged with matching salt and pepper shakers, a supply of toothpicks, a stock of moist towelettes, and a glass jar of cellophane-wrapped red and green mints for after-chicken refreshment. All this is designed to maximize enjoyment of what must be called Platonic picnic chicken — glazed mahogany brown, easy to pick

up, and so tender that pulling meat from any part is easy, every fiber virtually drenched with rich chicken fat and the tang of its marinade.

MUST-EAT
CORNELL CHICKEN

Jim's BBQ Chicken: 20 Foundry St., Candor, NY
607-659-4181
Phil's Chicken House: 1208 Maine Highway, Endicott, NY
607-748-6855
www.philschickenhouse.com

CRAB CAKE
Baltimore

Along with whole crabs, which require some expenditure of energy to eat, most Chesapeake Bay restaurants also offer crab soup and crab cakes. The latter are one of those local dishes that cooks and fanciers take seriously enough to compare and contrast and argue about. **Faidley Seafood**, which started in the seafood business in 1886 and is now a fixture of Baltimore's Lexington Market, has been making crab cakes at or near the top of every taste-off for as long as anyone can recall. They are without question the lumpiest, which is a wonderful thing, because the lumps are sweet pieces of Chesapeake Bay crab seasoned with Old Bay bound together by so little filler that there seems to be none. Made by hand and grilled to order at the Faidley stand in the temptatious market, the cakes appear to be single units, but when prodded with a fork, they immediately fall into piles of crabmeat. Pieces from the inside

A whopping fresh Chesapeake crab cake, crisped to perfection

are cream-soft and glisten with moisture; pieces from the outside develop a golden crunch that only accentuates the inherent buttery richness of the meat.

Faidley crab cakes are especially notable because they are available not only at the Lexington Market on disposable plates but also by mail-order. Delivery is next-day only, for these crab cakes are made and shipped fresh, never frozen. They are available already cooked, ready to be warmed in a frying pan or microwave, or uncooked so you can fry, broil, or bake them to taste.

Faidley Seafood: Lexington Market, 203 N. Paca, Baltimore, MD 410-727-4898 www.faidleyscrabcakes.com

CRAB FEAST
Maryland and Delaware

Newspaper tablecloths, paper-towel napkins, dozens of hard-shell crabs radiating peppery spice — this ritual meal, a banquet unique to mid-Atlantic shores, is a godawful mess.

Once the crabs are dumped onto the paper tablecloth, it is the eater's job to retrieve the meat by using pick and mallet. Oh, what delicious meat it is! Soft and sweet yet laced with spice, it is as addictive as food can be. At **Seaside Restaurant and Crab House**, just east of BWI Airport, a boisterous place that is always crowded and always heaps of fun, you buy the crustaceans by the dozen and toss shells and debris into paper bags on the floor. The only proper beverage is cold beer on tap and plenty of it.

The **Crab Claw** in St. Michaels started in the mid-twentieth century as a wholesale crab business and has now become a destination for crab lovers, who arrive by boat as well as by car. Some come to take away bushels full of crabs for waterside picnics; many come to sit at the Crab Claw tables with rolled-up sleeves and dig in. The dining room clatters with the sounds of hammering, cracking, and slurping, which are a crab feast's happy tune. Written instructions are provided, telling exactly how to extract meat from a cooked hard-shell crab.

Like the Crab Claw, Gunning's started modestly, as a Baltimore bar. It grew huge and about ten years ago moved from the city to Hanover and renamed itself **Gunning's Seafood Restaurant**, reflecting the fact that it has a big menu of everything oceanic. (It is open year-round, but crab feasts are served only when the blue crabs are in season, usually from April through November.) Gunning's is especially known for its deep-fried pepper rings, whose faint sugary sweetness add a unique twist to the big marine feast.

We particularly love eating crabs off the brown paper tablecloths at **Copsey's**, because this place never grew into a huge eating hall. It has the feel of a local joint, which is what it is: a combination crab house, seafood market, liquor store, and gathering place for the Mechanicsville Optimist Club. It is a great place to eat big meaty crab cakes, pounds of peel-them-yourself

Napkins required: a mess o' blue crabs slathered with peppery spices

steamed shrimp (infused with the same peppery orange spice mix that is used on the crabs), and raw oysters by the dozen. Many regular patrons come to eat fried chicken dinners; they are apparently that jaded about their superb local seafood.

Sambo's, a big crabcentric tavern with a view of crab boats coming in along the slow-moving Leipsic River in Delaware, has great crab cakes as well as fried (or grilled) seafood, but it's the kicking-fresh blue crabs crusted with Old Bay seasoning that are its claim to fame. It really is a tavern and therefore not a place to take the kiddies — sloppy, slurpy, messy eating can be enjoyed by adults, too.

5 TOP CRAB FEASTS

1. **Sambo's Tavern:** 280 Front St., Leipsic, DE
302-674-9724

Mid Atlantic

JOUSTING TOURNAMENT

The oldest jousting tournament in the United States, an every-August event at Old St. Joseph's Mission Church in Cordova, Maryland, began in 1868. Unlike medieval jousting, in which the point was to poke a rider off his horse as violently as possible, this sport involves spearing a tiny ring on the end of a lance while galloping — about as easy as trying to thread a needle while surfboarding. In 1917 an attempt was made to modernize the proceedings by substituting automobiles for horses. Jousters perched on running

boards with lances poised, but the twentieth-century version of the sport was a flop, and the tournament soon dumped Model T's and returned to single-horsepower rides. The jousting tournament includes a public dinner of barbecued chicken, country ham, and beaten biscuits, with a mint julep or two for refreshment. For details, and to find out about other jousts in Maryland (where jousting is the official state sport), visit www.national jousting.com.

Old St. Joseph's Joust: 13209 Church Lane, Cordova, MD
First weekend in August

Maryland is crab country.

2. **Seaside Restaurant and Crab House:** 224 Crain Highway North, Glen Burnie, MD
410-760-2200
www.theseasiderestaurant.com

3. **Gunning's Seafood Restaurant:** 7304 Parkway Dr., Hanover, MD
410-712-9404
www.gunningsonline.com

4. **Crab Claw:** Route 33 West, Navy Point, St. Michaels, MD
410-745-2900
www.thecrabclaw.com (March through November)

5. **Copsey's Seafood:** 28976 Three Notch Rd., Mechanicsville, MD
301-884-4235

CRUMB CAKE
New Jersey and New York

Pastry eaters in New York and New Jersey tend to get blasé about crumb cake. Delis and coffee shops throughout the region sell cut squares of it wrapped in cellophane, piled up near the cash register and ready to become a lapful of streusel as you juggle cake and to-go coffee while driving to work. Entenmann's bakery makes its own version of the mid-Atlantic bakery specialty, known as Ultimate Crumb Cake, which is quite all right for supermarket pastry. It is hard to say whether Entenmann's version has become less ultimate over the years or whether our standards have elevated, but now when we want the best crumb cake ever — truly the ultimate — we go to Hackensack, New Jersey, for a big square of what the **B&W Bakery** calls heavy crumb cake.

Bruce Bilmes and Sue Boyle, who originally pointed us to this more-than-sixty-year-old landmark bakery, called it "crumb cake that just cries out for a pot of coffee and a lazy morning." What sets it apart is the ratio of crumb to cake, at least two to one — far more crumb than cake. The cake is soft and just a little bit sweet, primarily a pallet for a crunchy, buttery stratum of endless crumbs dusted with powdered sugar.

If you are an expatriate who has come to realize that the crumb cake you grew up with simply does not

The ultimate crumb cake fairly begs for a pot of coffee.

exist anywhere else, or if you live far away and want to have a pastry experience to remember, check out **Hahn's Old Fashioned Cake Company**, which is all set up to mail-order a beauty. It isn't as outrageously crumby as B&W's, but the streusel topping, consisting of what Hahn's calls "extra large handmade crumbs," has vivid brown-sugar intensity that pairs very well with the buttery cake that supports it.

2 CRUMBIEST CRUMB CAKES

B&W Bakery: 614 Main St.,
Hackensack, NJ
201-342-5577
www.bwbakerynj.com
Hahn's Old Fashioned Cake Co.: 75 Allen Blvd., Farmingdale, NY
631-249-3456
www.crumbcake.net

DEEP-FRIED DOG
New Jersey and New York

If you like your wiener with skin so crisp it crunches, charbroiling is good. But deep-frying is bliss. Boiling franks in oil is common practice in New Jersey, which is a hotbed of hot dog fanaticism and categorical justification for thinking of the East as the nation's tube steak treasury.

Rippers are hot dogs that earned their nickname because **Rutt's Hut** in Clifton boils them in oil until their skins split. The cooking method turns the pork and beef links rugged, dark, and chewy on the outside while the interior remains soft and

juicy. (Weenie wimps can order an in-and-outer, which spends only a short time in the oil and remains soft and pink. Hopeless hard-core fried-dog hounds ask for cremators, which means well done and almost thoroughly browned, crunchy and extra-intense.) Rutt's fans are legion, and nearly all have their rippers topped with spicy relish, made from onions and finely chopped carrots and cabbage. No hot dog lover can say his life is complete until he has dined at Rutt's off a paper plate at a counter with a view of the parking lot.

The **Hot Grill**, also in Clifton, calls its franks Texas wieners. Within ninety seconds of the counterman calling back "Two, all the way!" (it would be ridiculous to get only one), they appear on the empty tray that has been readied at the counter. They are seated in too-short buns, their skin wrinkled and chewy and piled with chili that is a little sweet and a little spicy, plus finely chopped raw

Rippers from Rutt's Hut in Clifton, NJ, are boiled in oil until their skins split.

onions and mustard. On the side you can get French fries topped with gravy, chili, molten cheese, or any combination of the three.

Hot dog historians believe that Texas wieners (or, as they are frequently spelled hereabouts, weiners) were invented in Paterson, New Jersey, three quarters of a century ago by John Patrellis, who devised a spicy meat sauce that he thought was reminiscent of what Texans eat. In fact it is much more Greek than Texan, but the Lone Star moniker has stuck, and today at hot dog joints throughout the East *Texas* suggests a chili dog. The classic New Jersey version is served by **Libby's Lunch**, a 1936-vintage dog house in Paterson that doles them out topped with mustard, chopped onions, and sauce. Good as the spicy chili sauce is (you can buy it by the pint), it is the hot dog itself that makes this a memorable eating experience. Its insides are tender and succulent, while the exterior is blistered and chewy because of its hot-oil bath. Extra-large dogs (and cheese dogs) are available, but we believe the original size works best. A pair of these tube steaks with a side of crisp French fries blanketed with gravy is a grand plate of food: true New Jersey, and uniquely American.

"If you haven't had one, you ain't livin'," wrote Roadfood.com Insider Aleswench about a **Charlie's Pool**

PAPAYA KING

We don't think the hot dogs served at Papaya King are the world's best (as myriad fans do), but it would be a big hole in this book to omit them. There is a similar (but unaffiliated) Gray's Papaya King on the West Side, one in New Jersey, and a few others around the city, but here we refer to the original on Manhattan's Upper East Side, which opened in 1932 as, oddly enough, a health-food juice stand boasting that it sold "nature's own revitalizer." Soon frankfurters were added to the menu, primarily to please a large German population in the neighborhood, and it is the franks that make the place worth a visit. They are slim and taut and reverberate with garlic. A neon sign in the window boasts that they are "tastier than filet mignon," which is a correct statement if tastier means *more* taste. A pair of these dogs is something you will be tasting long after you've consumed them. Lightly grilled, they develop a few darkened splotches on their coral-orange surface but are never crunch-crusted or burned. They come in toasted buns, the purpose of which, other than to hold the dog, is to provide a bland background for the wieners' pyrotechnics. Available toppings include chili, cheese, New York stewed onions, grilled onions, raw onions, sauerkraut, relish, and coleslaw. Only mustard is essential.

Papaya King: 179 E. 86th St., New York, NY
212-369-0648
www.papayaking.com

Rutt's Hut needs no filigree to provide a great eating experience.

Room hot dog topped with Grandma Fencz's sauce. Although the Kunzler-brand pork and beef dog is not technically deep-fried, the oil in the skillet is deep enough for it to qualify. The skillet is on a stove in a tiny kitchen in John Fencz's old wood-frame house west of Newark, which used to be a barbershop and a jail and now has a single table to eat at. Fencz snugs his muscular hot dogs into soft steamed buns, then sends them into the culinary stratosphere with an application of a thick sweet-and-sour onion-tomato sauce prepared exactly according to specs set down by Grandma Fencz. The Hungarian-accented sauce is not incendiary, but it has real bite, and although it comes on top of a bargain weenie, it has refined complexity that reveals the skills of an accomplished cook. Grandma Fencz originally served her sauced hot dogs in 1925 so the boys playing pool at her place would have something to eat. The only possible improvement on this high-class pool-room dog is to order a "mealy,"

which adds chopped raw onions and hot peppers to the concoction.

Although New York City is best known for "dirty water dogs" sold from street carts, as well as the tubular filet mignon hot dogs of Papaya King (page 86) and kosher franks at Katz's (page 97) and elsewhere, it also has an impressive downtown take on the deep-fried tube steak. **Crif Dogs**, a claustrophobically little eatery below street level, fries the dogs up and sells them topped with chili, wrapped with bacon, and even heaped with Korean kimchee. Deep-frying gives them serious chew and intensifies the flavor. For people who are, for whatever reason, unable to choose what kind of hot dog they want, Crif's sells "stoner packs," which are groups of items selected by the staff for customers too dazed to decide for themselves.

Walter's Hot Dog Stand weenies are not deep-fried and so perhaps deserve an entire listing of their own, but no discussion of the mid Atlantic's essential hot dogs would be complete without their mention. Years ago, when *Gourmet* magazine asked us to name the ten best wieners in the nation, Walter's, in Mamaroneck, New York, headed the list.

Papaya King, begun in 1932 as a health-food stand, is now famous for franks.

Mid Atlantic

Maybe there are some that are better, maybe not; but we wouldn't roll in our graves if that proclamation were inscribed on our headstones. Beef-pork-veal franks made exclusively for Walter's, as they have been since 1919, are bisected lengthwise and cooked on a grill coated with secret-formula sauce. It's a buttery sauce with an ineffable spice that insinuates flavor into the cut-flat surface of the weenie and gives it crunch that is a joy to bite, especially inside a soft bun that has been toasted on an adjacent grill. Some customers ask for their hot dog well done and therefore crisper than usual (not a bad idea), and others get a double dog, but however you like it, please apply mustard. It is Walter's own, coarse-grained and dotted with pickle bits.

NEW JERSEY'S FINEST DEEP-FRIED DOGS

1. **Rutt's Hut:** 417 River Rd., Clifton, NJ
973-779-8615
2. **Charlie's Pool Room:** 1122 East Blvd., Alpha, NJ
908-454-1364
3. **Walter's Hot Dog Stand:** 937 Palmer Ave., Mamaroneck, NY
No phone
www.waltershotdogs.com
4. **Hot Grill:** 669 Lexington Ave., Clifton, NJ
973-772-6000
www.thehotgrill.com
5. **Libby's Lunch:** 98 McBride Ave., Paterson, NJ
973-278-8718
6. **Crif Dogs:** 113 St. Marks Place, New York, NY
212-614-2728

GARBAGE PLATE
Rochester, New York

Invented by diner man Alex Tahou during the Great Depression, the garbage plate was originally known as hots and potots, *hots* being the upstate New York term for hot dogs. Alex's son Nick renamed the hash-house symphony and became a local legend as the proprietor of his eponymous late-hours cafe, **Nick Tahou Hots.** Even at Nick Tahou's, there was never one single way to make a garbage plate, but as the name suggests, it necessarily includes heaps of all kinds of stuff. Typical ingredients include (but are not limited to) a pair of Texas hot wieners, hamburgers (with or without cheese), Italian sausage, or steak, plus baked beans and home-fried potatoes, a scoop of cool macaroni salad, a dollop of spicy chili sauce, a squirt or two of mustard, and a sprinkle of chopped raw onions. Garbage plates are served on extra-heavy disposable cardboard plates, accompanied by a bottle of ketchup,

Everything but the kitchen sink: the garbage plate at Nick Tahou's in Rochester

extra hot sauce, and white bread with butter.

Tahou's signature dish became such a chowhound favorite over the years that other entrepreneurs around town started making and serving the same thing. Today more than fifty Rochester-area restaurants serve their own versions. But because Nick's son Alex trademarked the name Garbage Plate in 1992, the others go by such names as Dumpster Plate, Trash Plate, Messy Plate, Sloppy Plate, Rubbish Plate, and Plat de Refuse. We'll stick with the source, and while we have sampled a few others in the area, we certainly haven't tried them all; frankly, doing so in hopes of one day ranking every garbage plate

in upstate New York makes even our appetites blush. Further complicating any reasoned rating system is the contention of most connoisseurs that a garbage plate cannot fully be appreciated until after midnight, while drunk.

Nick Tahou Hots: 320 W. Main St., Rochester, NY
585-436-0184
www.garbageplate.com

GRIBENES
New York City

Schmaltz, or rendered chicken fat, is to Jewish cooking what olive oil is to Italian: its soul. *Gribenes,* a Yiddish

E. VOGEL BOOTS

If you want or need the very best bespoke footwear in the East, riding boots in particular, Vogel's is the place to go. It opened for business in 1879 and still makes boots and shoes the old-fashioned way. To listen to the Vogels describe their occupation, they are less shoe salesmen than practitioners to whom customers bring aching arches and spindleshank calves and stand in their socks or stockings, with pants or skirts hiked to the knee, to have their foot problems solved. The Vogels told us that custom shoemaking is a challenge, because no two feet are alike and because everybody has a different idea of how a shoe should fit. Women like their shoes tighter; European feet are stronger; Japanese

feet require extra toe room.

The Vogels are quite sure that founder Egidius Vogel was the first to make a low-cut shoe in an age of high-buttoned styles around the end of the nineteenth century. Today most of Vogel's business is riding boots, which are known to horsemen around the world as the very best. But not everyone who buys a pair is an equestrian. Dean Vogel once told us about an order from a religious guru who needed custom-fitted boots for his chronically frostbitten feet, a condition he got while trekking across mountains in Tibet.

E. Vogel: 19 Howard St., New York, NY
212-925-2460
www.vogelboots.com

word that means "scraps," are the leftovers from rendering the fat. They are squiggles and nibbles of skin along with tiny shreds of onion that have in effect been deep-fried in chicken fat. The skin is miraculously succulent, both chewy and melty, transmogrifying from physical foodstuff into intangible flavor that floods taste buds with golden opulence. The onion bits char in the fat, their sweet, smoky crunch adding tease to the orgiastic chicken-fat inundation. You will get a bowl of gribenes when you sit down for a meal at the **2nd Avenue Deli**. They are fine to munch on and nearly impossible to stop eating. However, you should stop eating them, because they are more intense than they seem and will soon overwhelm the appetite. And you definitely want appetite remaining for 2nd Avenue's pastrami, matzoh brei, and chopped liver. (There is no better complement for a chopped liver sandwich than a sprinkling of gribenes.)

Note that the 2nd Avenue Deli actually is no longer on Second Avenue. The old location closed in 2006, and this one opened in 2008. The food remains a New York deli paradigm.

2nd Avenue Deli: 162 E. 33rd St.,
New York, NY
212-689-9000
www.2ndavedeli.com

HOT TRUCK
Ithaca, New York

Like so many great food inventions, Ithaca's hot truck began as the solution to a problem. The problem was that Bob Petrillose's food truck, now called **Hot Truck**, once known as Johnny's Pizza on Wheels, sold excellent whole pizza straight from its ovens, but most Cornell students couldn't afford an entire one. They came for a slice or two. But singles need to be reheated when ordered. The result: soggy pizza. According to Albert Smith, who bought the food truck from Petrillose in 2000 and whose son Michael now operates it, "Bob was from the old school. He believed pizza is something you serve hot enough to burn your mouth."

Petrillose's solution was what he called Poor Man's Pizza, or PMP in hot truck lingo, also known as a pizza sub. Every pizza sub was made to order, served crisp and piping hot. The invention became a campus sensation, as much a part of college life as the Bell Tower and Taughannock Falls.

Hot truck, the food, is baked open-faced on a length of French bread, then folded over into the familiar tubular hero formation. It is served in configurations with names that can seem as obscure as Navajo. A suicide, or sui (pronounced *sooey,* like the pig call), got its name because it is piled with a murderous quantity of ground sausage, pepperoni, and mushrooms on a bed of tomato sauce under a mound of melted mozzarella. G&G means grease and garden — that is, mayo and lettuce. A high-carbon sub is one that is run through the oven twice so the edges of the dense bread turn black and its crust starts to flake. If Hot Truck is not serving, you can always get the sandwich at the **Shortstop Deli**.

Ithaca folklore says that one of the students who assisted Petrillose in

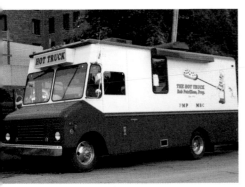

Ithaca's Hot Truck, helping poor college students stay well fed for less

the truck's early days took the idea to Cleveland and sold it to Stouffer's, begetting French Bread Pizza. In fact, Stouffer's VP of manufacturing in 1962, when the company introduced frozen prepared foods, was Cornell Hotel School graduate C. Alan Mac-Donald; the French Bread Pizzas were launched twelve years later, in 1974.

HOT TRUCK & SON

Hot Truck: 635 Stewart Ave., West
   Campus, Ithaca, NY
   607-273-1111
   Serves only during the school
   year, every night from about 10
Shortstop Deli: 203 W. Seneca
   St., Ithaca, NY
   607-273-1030
   Always open
   www.shortstopdeli.com

JEWISH APPLE CAKE
Pennsylvania

Jewish apple cake is a dense coffee cake laced with soft apple slivers that makes a can't-stop-eating pastry with coffee at breakfast and a welcome nosh at any time of day. The apples have a cinnamon bite, and the spicy cake is moist and rich even though it contains no butter at all. It's the sort of snack that, while perfectly edible with a fork, makes us want to pull off hunks by hand, lick apple syrup from our fingers, and dunk pieces into coffee. We assume it got its name because of its lack of dairy products, making it an acceptably kosher dessert with either a meat or a dairy meal. But it is not by any means exclusively Jewish. In fact, it's non-Jews who refer to it as Jewish apple cake. To Jewish cooks, it's just plain apple cake. Tom and Jennifer Levkulic of Pennsylvania coal country's **Dutch Kitchen**, which is the only restaurant we know that regularly serves it, both recall it as part of their families' culinary heritage, which includes Lithuanian, Lebanese, and Pennsylvania Dutch recipes but nothing specifically Jewish.

While more a home dish than a restaurant one, Jewish apple cake is frequently found in bakeries and at food markets in eastern Pennsylvania. In Lahaska, the **Town Crier Bakery** tops it with a drizzle of sweet frosting. In Philadelphia, the **Night Kitchen**, best known for its huge, sticky, nutty cinnamon-bun cakes sized for six, bakes an apple-dense version (a day's advance order is required). Out in the country at Lisa Urffer's Coopersburg family farm, formally named **Pappy's Orchard & Lisa's Kitchen**, you can buy the homiest possible Jewish apple cake, made using apples from their own trees (which go into apple butter, applesauce, apple dumplings, and cider). Lisa's bakery also is a great source for whoopie pies (page 66) and sticky buns.

NONDENOMINATIONAL JEWISH APPLE CAKE

1. **Dutch Kitchen:** 433 S. Lehigh Ave., Frackville, PA
   570-874-3265
   www.dutchkitchen.com
2. **Pappy's Orchard & Lisa's Kitchen:** 2576 Cassel Rd., Coopersburg, PA
   610-462-2734
3. **Night Kitchen:** 7725 Germantown Ave., Philadelphia, PA
   215-248-9235
   Second location: 45 E. State St., Doylestown, PA
   215-348-9775
   www.nightkitchenbakery.com
4. **Town Crier Bakery:** 29 Peddler's Lane, Lahaska, PA
   215-794-9910
   www.shoptowncrierbakery.com

For all its richness, Jewish apple cake has no butter.

An overstuffed omelet at Jo Jo's in Pittsburgh awaits pickup.

JO JO SPECIAL
Pittsburgh, Pennsylvania

If you have the appetite of a Pittsburgh Steeler, most of whom are regular customers of **Jo Jo's Restaurant**, consider tackling a Jo Jo Special. It is in principle an omelet made with a mere three eggs. Folded inside the three-egg cake are an immeasurable amount of peppers, onions, mushrooms, provolone and American cheese, bacon and/or sausage and/or ham, plus a spatula-load of hot fried potatoes. The special is delectable evidence for our assertion that cheap eats in Pittsburgh are uniquely multifarious — single dishes or sandwiches that contain far more than their fair share of wide-ranging ingredients. A single Jo Jo Special is so impossibly overstuffed that unless you have the appetite of a 3-4 nose tackle, it is definitely a meal for two.

Jo Jo's Restaurant: 110 24th St., Pittsburgh, PA
412-261-0280
Although its motto is "Breakfast Served All Day, Every Day," Jo Jo's

is open only from 11 p.m. until noon. The schedule is made to jibe with that of truck drivers who haul produce up from the South, arriving at the nearby Pittsburgh Produce Market shortly after midnight.

MATZOH BALL SOUP
New York City and Environs

Chicken soup is known as Jewish penicillin for its curative powers; add a matzoh ball or two and you have a wonderful drug. At the **Carnegie Deli**, across from Carnegie Hall, a serving comes with two balls that are soft and bland and fluffy, well complemented by broth that is cock-a-doodle-doo salty. At **Café Edison**, on 47th Street, just sniffing the rich yellow broth is guaranteed to make anyone feel hale and hearty. The big soft spheres of matzoh fall apart when you go at them with a spoon, making little dumplings in the soup below. Known to its fans as the Polish Tea Room, Café Edison is a bastion of such other Old World pleasures as beet borscht and cheese blintzes.

Deli delight: Matzoh ball soup is good for your health and good for your mood.

One of New York's best matzoh ball soups is actually on the other side of the Hudson River, in Edison, New Jersey, at **Harold's New York Deli**. Although Harold's is best known for its outrageously large sandwiches, the soup has a soothing taste and aroma that are better than homemade. Both cups and bowls are available, but if you really need a lot of medicine, you can order a 60-ounce bowl, recommended for two people, and extra matzoh balls for $3.95 each.

3 MOST SALUBRIOUS MATZOH BALL SOUPS

1. **Café Edison:** 228 W. 47th St., New York, NY 212-840-5000 www.edisonhotelnyc.com
2. **Harold's New York Deli:** 3050 Woodbridge Ave., Edison, NJ 732-661-9100 www.haroldsfamousdeli.com
3. **Carnegie Deli:** 854 Seventh Ave., New York, NY 212-757-2245 or 800-334-5606 www.carnegiedeli.com

MICHIGAN
Clinton County, New York

Chili dog taxonomy is bewildering. Coney Islands are found throughout the Midwest, but there is nothing like them in Coney Island. Texas wieners are pretty much limited to New Jersey and unheard of in Texas. And the Michigan? Don't look for it in Michigan. The small, porky frank bedded in a soft-as-a-cloud bun and topped with mustard, onions, and a sauce made from a little tomato, a

Why is it called a Michigan? Don't ask.

lot of spices, and finely ground beef is unique to New York: the north country between the Adirondacks and Lake Champlain, primarily in Plattsburgh.

Why is it called a Michigan? "No clue!" exclaimed the waitress at **Gus' Red Hots**, a full-service Plattsburgh restaurant that started as a hot dog stand in 1951. Gus's menu boasts, and we quote, "just about everything, including their famous 'Michigan red hot,' which they invite you to try while dining." One Michigan costs $2.25 and is presented in a cardboard boat. It is a piggy-pink wiener in a split-top bun, topped with dark orange chili sauce in which the meat is sandy smithereens. The heft of the sauce contrasts with the fluffy bun and fatty frank, and while each separate ingredient is inarguably inglorious, the combo has charisma, especially when topped with a streak of yellow mustard and a scattering of crisp chopped raw onions.

A writer in the *Plattsburgh Press-Republican* once claimed that the Michigan owes its name to a short-order cook who came to Clinton County from Detroit by way of Coney Island. At **Clare & Carl's Hot Dog Stand**, the oldest extant red-hot stand in the city (since 1943), a story from the *Plattsburgh Daily Press* posted on the wall credits the term to a Michigander named Eula Otis who came to work for Clare Warn in the early days and went around to area restaurants saying, "I'm from Michigan. Would you like to try one of our chili dogs?" The state's name clung to the hot dog topped with Warn's sauce, which she had invented because New York–style hot dogs with mustard and sauerkraut weren't selling well at her stand. The Michigan became a local passion, served at summertime stands, in grocery stores, and even in the cafeteria at the Champlain Valley Physicians Hospital Medical Center.

Clare & Carl's presents its Michigans in a tender bun that is similar to the traditional New England split-top but is thicker at the bottom and closed at both ends, forming a trough to shore in the sloppy topping. The chili is thick with minced meat enthusiastically spiced, not at all sweet and just barely hot. It is intriguing and addictive, but there are Michigan connoisseurs who contend that the greatest of all sauces was the one made at Nitzi's, a vanished eatery on the other side of Lake Shore Road that used to compete with Clare & Carl's.

McSweeney's is a relative newcomer, opened in 1991, still spanking-clean and tidy. While it features car-hop service and an inside counter, there are comfortable tables, too, and its Michigans cost $1.95. The menu calls them red hots, but our waitress assured us that they are indeed Michigans. She also recounted the bun crisis of 2002, when long buns became unavailable, thus wreaking havoc on the eating habits of those who order their Michigans with buried onions. "Buried means underneath the weenie," she said. "That makes the weenie stick up above the bun and the sauce will fall off." McSweeney's sauce is flecked with pepper, which kindles a nice glow on the tongue. The whole package is substantial enough that Michigans come with a fork. Looking around the dining room and at people eating off trays hung on car windows, we discovered that most customers forgo the utensil. A few people we observed had perfected a technique of hoisting the entire cardboard boat to chin level with one hand, then using the other hand to ease the Michigan from boat to mouth, bite by bite.

NEW YORK'S 3 GREAT MICHIGANS

1. **Clare & Carl's Hot Dog Stand:** 4727 Lake Shore Rd., Plattsburgh, NY 518-561-1163
2. **McSweeney's Red Hots:** 535 N. Margaret St., Plattsburgh, NY 518-562-9309 See www.mcsweeneysredhots .com for additional locations.
3. **Gus' Red Hots:** 3 Cumberland Head Rd., Plattsburgh, NY 518-561-3711

NEWARK HOT DOG
Newark, New Jersey

Of the nation's eminent franks, none is more cornucopic than the Ital-

ian hot dog of Newark, New Jersey. A Newark double (the only way to go) starts with one half of a round loaf of fresh, chewy-crusted Italian bread. Like a muffaletta loaf, it must be tough enough to remain intact when wrapped around oily foods. The half-circle of bread is squeezed open to become a pocket like a huge, spongy pita. Into the pocket go a pair of all-beef hot dogs fried in hot fat until crunch-crusted, a heap of onions and peppers sautéed until limp, and a handful of crisp-fried potato chunks. Each ingredient is forked directly from the frying caldron into the sandwich, which is why the bread needs oomph — to absorb drippings from the garlicky dogs and sweet vegetables. Options include mustard, marinara sauce, fire-hot onion relish,

James Racioppi of Jimmy Buff's shows off a Newark double, created by his grandparents.

Mid Atlantic

and — are you ready? — ketchup. When you consider the fried potatoes that are an essential element of the sandwich, the ketchup, which is generally anathema on hot dogs, makes some kind of sense.

A good handful of sandwich shops in and around Newark specialize in Italian hot dogs. The bread is similar at all of them, bought from neighborhood bakeries, where it is known as pizza bread; and the hot dogs are slim, all-beef tubes that are always deep-fried; but each place has its own signature. **Charlie's Famous Italian Hot Dogs** in Kenilworth piles in peppers but serves fried potatoes on the side. **Dickie Dee's Pizza** in the old North Ward deep-fries everything in the same oil. **Jimmy Buff's** separately deep-fries the hot dog and the potatoes but sautés the peppers and onions. **Tommy's Italian Sausage and Hot Dogs** in Elizabeth is also well known for its sausage sandwich and for vegetarian versions of the Newark hot dog (!): fried spuds with a tangle of onions and peppers stuffed into the round loaf, hold the frankfurters. Potatoes are available alone, too, served as a side dish in a cup.

The genealogy of the Italian hot dog is debatable, but James Racioppi, proprietor of Jimmy Buff's, believes it was his grandparents, James and Mary Racioppi, who started it at their home. Mr. Racioppi says, "My grandfather played cards there every week. My grandmother served sandwiches to him and his associates. After a while people started coming just to eat, so in 1932 they opened a store at Fourteenth and Ninth to sell the sandwiches. That was the beginning."

As for the name of the store, Mr. Racioppi explains: "My grandfather Jimmy was an excellent card player. He was known for his talent to bluff, but with their Italian accents, they used to call him Jimmy Buff."

NEWARK HOT DOG HIERARCHY

1. **Jimmy Buff's:** 60 Washington St., West Orange, NJ 973-325-9897 See www.jimmybuff.com for additional locations.
2. **Charlie's Famous Italian Hot Dogs:** 18 S. Michigan Ave., Kenilworth, NJ 908-241-2627
3. **Tommy's Italian Sausage and Hot Dogs:** 900 Second Ave., Elizabeth, NJ 908-351-9831
4. **Dickie Dee's Pizza:** 380 Bloomfield Ave., Newark, NJ 973-483-9396

OCTOPUS SALAD
New York City

We got hooked on the Cuban sandwiches, oxtail, and hypersonic espresso at **Margon** right away. But it took a few visits to this minuscule Latino eatery just off Times Square in New York to try the octopus salad. It was love at first bite. Actually, love at first sight. It is a beautiful mix of tender flaps of octopus with a confetti of green olives and red peppers, all glistening with garlicky oil. Cool and refreshing, it comes appetizer-sized or in a big bowl that makes a welcome lunch on a hot summer day.

Tasty tentacles, olives, and peppers star in an octopus salad at Times Square's Margon.

Margon: 136 W. 46th St., New York, NY
212-354-5013

PASTRAMI SANDWICH
New York City

Pastrami is the most voluptuous of delicatessen meats, and while it is found in nearly any deli, the best is in New York (plus Ann Arbor, Michigan, where **Zingerman's Deli** makes peerless pastrami). New York delis offer exquisite meat, cured and smoked by experts, served with all the fixin's that only a vintage Jewish restaurant can offer, including hard-crusted, tender rye bread and pickles as sour as the beleaguered waiters who schlep the thick crockery plates of food from the meat counter to the tables. New York has many Jewish delis that do it right, some strictly kosher (no dairy products are served), some "kosher-style," which refers to an open kitchen area behind a long

glass counter where smoked fish are displayed and meats sliced.

The oldest — since 1888 — is **Katz's** of the Lower East Side. The inside of this eccentric culinary landmark is a confusing cacophony of shouted orders and clattering carving knives, all swirling through a high-ceilinged eating hall festooned with odoriferous garlicky salamis and pictures of happy celebrity customers ranging from the comics Jerry Lewis and Henny Youngman to Rudy Giuliani. The pastrami is cut by hand, and each brick-red, glistening moist hunk is rimmed black, redolent of garlic, smoke, and pickling spices, as savory as food can be. Aside from the delicious taste and the fact that the meat is hand-cut, one thing that sets Katz's apart from most of New York's pastrami shrines is that the sandwich is merely large, not insanely enormous. The 12 ounces of pastrami between slices of rye make it feasible actually to hoist half a sandwich from plate to mouth with minimal fallout. Likewise, the esteemed **Barney Greengrass** of the Upper West Side

Katz's in New York City hand-cuts sobering portions of juicy pastrami.

portions its excellent pastrami generously, but not comically so.

The automatic slicer at midtown's **Carnegie Deli** does a fine job of creating a steaming-hot jumble of long flaps, little nuggets, chewy morsels, and supple shreds, all so fatty that your fingers glisten as you pick. And pick you will, for Carnegie sandwiches are piled too high to hoist and eat. To accompany this plate of luscious meat and bread, the Carnegie supplies perfect puckery accouterments — half-sour and sour dills and pickled green tomatoes. The bright red pastrami at the legendary **2nd Avenue Deli** is also heaped so heavily on bread that the sandwich is barely pick-up-able. It tends to have a mild personality, more smoky than spicy, and unless you say otherwise, it comes plenty fatty.

The tallest of all pastrami sandwiches, sandwiches that are crazily overloaded with meat, are made at **Harold's New York Deli** in Edison, New Jersey. Harold Jaffe, who used to work at the Carnegie, offers it three ways: regular, lean, and juicy, the last a nutritionally correct word for fatty. Regular is just right by us. We agree with Bruce Bilmes and Sue Boyles that Harold's pastrami is New York's best, even if it is in New Jersey. They describe it as having a "hauntingly smoky flavor and a steamy melting

BELGIAN WAFFLE

Most Belgian waffles you find in American restaurants are gross, *Belgian* a code word meaning thick and doughy. Wafels & Dinges, a bright yellow food truck that parks in Manhattan and occasionally in Brooklyn, is a convincing argument that a real Belgian waffle (spelled *wafel*) can be one of life's culinary joys. Two kinds are available: the Brussels waffle, which is crisp and elegant, cooked to order so you get it steaming hot, and the Liège waffle, which is soft, chewy, and dotted with sugar pearls that melt into veins of caramelized sweetness. Either one of these waffles, eaten plain, is a fine sidewalk snack (presented in a cardboard boat), but note that the name of the truck is Wafels & Dinges; the second word is Flemish slang for "stuff."

The stuff available to top a wafel includes Nutella, dulce de leche, maple syrup, strawberries, whipped cream, and, best of all, Belgian chocolate fudge made by waffle man Thomas DeGeest.

DeGeest is a man on a mission. Having grown up in Belgium eating good waffles, he was perpetually disappointed by the ones he found when he came to America. So in 2007 he quit his corporate job, bought a truck, and outfitted it with waffle irons, creating one of New York's finest street foods.

Wafels & Dinges: 866-429-7329 www.wafelsanddinges.com Wafels & Dinges' location is fluid. To be sure of locating it, check the blog on the Wafels & Dinges website.

texture." To go with the sandwich, Harold's offers the world's largest help-yourself pickle bar.

5 TOP PASTRAMIS

1. **Harold's New York Deli:**
   3050 Woodbridge Ave., Edison, NJ
   732-661-9100
   Second location: 195 Route 18 South, East Brunswick, NJ
   732-246-7505
   www.haroldsfamousdeli.com
2. **Katz's:** 205 E. Houston St., New York, NY
   212-254-2246
   www.katzdeli.com
3. **Carnegie Deli:** 854 Seventh Ave., New York, NY
   212-757-2245
   Carnegie Deli sells its pastrami via mail . . . in 75-pound increments.
   www.carnegiedeli.com
4. **2nd Avenue Deli:**
   162 E. 33rd St., New York, NY
   212-689-9000
   www.2ndavedeli.com

5. **Barney Greengrass:** 541 Amsterdam Ave., New York, NY
   212-724-4707
   www.barneygreengrass.com

Also
Zingerman's Delicatessen:
   422 Detroit St., Ann Arbor, MI
   734-663-3354
   www.zingermansdeli.com
   Zingerman's sells its pastrami by mail and is an excellent mail-order source of classic Jewish rye bread, better than any in New York.

PRIMANTI'S SANDWICH
Pittsburgh, Pennsylvania

For people who work in the Pittsburgh produce market and truckers who haul vegetables up from the South, as well as for those who are insomniacs, early risers, or closing-time party animals coming out of Strip clubs (that's clubs on the Strip, not clubs where ecdysiasts perform), **Primanti Bros.** is the only game in town. It is known for amazing Dagwoods, which are a kill-or-cure approach to wee-hour cookery in which all the components of a sandwich meal, including a great double fistful of delicious French-fried potatoes as well as coleslaw, tomatoes, and any other necessary garnishes, are heaped between thick slices of French bread along with your meat, eggs, and/or cheese of choice. Double-egg-and-pastrami with cheese is a longtime favorite among Primanti veterans, as are roast beef, cheese steaks, and kielbasa. An extra egg or extra cheese

A beacon for truckers and other night owls, Primanti's satisfies rig-sized appetites.

on any sandwich will set you back 50 cents.

Legend says that the idea of including the fries inside the sandwich came about to make life easy for truck drivers whose rigs were idling outside and who had no time to spare picking up a sandwich, putting it down, then nibbling on a French fry, then back to the sandwich, etc. We're a bit dubious, as the mishmash, everything-goes style of meal assemblage is true throughout much of Pittsburgh, even where truckers do not eat. Whatever its origin, a Primanti's sandwich is a joy to remember — especially if you have it at three o'clock in the morning.

Primanti Bros.: 46 18th St.,
Pittsburgh, PA
412-263-2142
See www.primantibrothers.com
for additional locations.

RYE BREAD
New York City

You don't come across too many loaves like **Orwasher's** traditional Jewish rye these days, not even in otherwise good Jewish delis, where first-rate meat is all too often sandwiched in flabby bread. Made from a starter that dates back to 1916, Orwasher's rye is fine-textured and springy and delivers a wave of intoxicating rye berry flavor; its crust is brown-gold and shiny, with an incalculable number of little facets, and, although very thin, a significant contrast to the inside. What sheer pleasure it is to tear into a slice, or, better yet, a whole unsliced loaf, or, best of all, two thick slices sandwiching good pastrami,

Orwasher's distinctive loaves have been made the same way since 1916.

chopped liver, or brisket. You can buy the rye plain, packed with caraway seeds, or laced with onions. The roster of great loaves at this East Side institution also includes black pumpernickel, raisin pumpernickel (invented here), marble rye, crisp-crusted potato rounds, cakelike cinnamon-raisin, and of course egg-rich challah. Breadbaskets in some of New York's finest restaurants are stocked from Orwasher's brick ovens.

Orwasher's: 308 E. 78th St., New
York, NY
212-288-6569
www.orwasherbakery.com

SALT PEANUTS
New York City

Count on getting the best salted peanuts you ever ate in New York City. Danny Meyer, the remarkable restaurateur who has made a point of tasting his way west of the Hudson River and south of the Battery, found these unbelievably crunchy, well-salted goobers in North Carolina at the First Methodist Men's Club of Mt. Olive. He gets them shipped to his urban smoke parlor, **Blue Smoke**, where they are bar food that makes even a nondrinker crave cold beer to accompany them. They are large, but not freakishly so, and pale yellow (skinless), and the pleasure of hearing them crack between your teeth is almost as ecstatic as the creamy flavor that erupts when you chew them.

Blue Smoke: 116 E. 27th St.,
New York, NY
212-447-7733
www.bluesmoke.com

SHOOFLY PIE
Pennsylvania

Eastern Pennsylvania's shoofly pie is a legacy of Amish cooks, for whom electric-powered refrigerators are taboo. There are several explanations for the name, the weirdest being that its crumbly top vaguely resembles the texture of a cauliflower and *shoofly* is a corruption of the French word *choufleur,* meaning cauliflower. We think it's more logical to consider that someone in the family had to spend time shooing flies away from the supersweet molasses-and-brown-sugar pie until it was served.

It's on menus throughout eastern Pennsylvania farmland; the best place for a taste test is the **Reading Terminal Market**, Philadelphia's cornucopic food bazaar. Among the RTM places that have it, usually only on weekends, is **Fisher's Soft Pretzels**, where girls in farmhouse garb sell broad slices ready to eat on paper plates (there are tables in the terminal). Before sitting down, it is essential that you also get coffee or water. Shoofly pie is sweet and crumbly enough to demand liquid refreshment at least every few bites. **Beiler's Bakery** is another RTM source, not only for shoofly pie but also for excellent sticky buns and apple fritters. For shoofly pie in the ultimate rural

COAL CANDY

There is only one place we know where children are happy to get lumps of coal in their stockings at Christmas: Pottsville, Pennsylvania, an old mining town where coal is a good thing. Coal candy, that is. The unique confection, formally known as Black Diamonds, was invented by Catherine Mootz in the 1950s. It is intensely anise-flavored, black, and oily, made in hard, irregular chunks that come packaged in miniature buckets with a small hammer for smashing the chunks into bite-sized pieces. At Christmas, Mootz Candies sells stockings already filled with it.

Mootz Candies: 220 S. Centre
St., Pottsville, PA
570-622-4480
Second location: Fairlane Village
Mall, Route 61, Pottsville, PA
No phone
www.mootzcandies.com

An Amish legacy, shoofly pie is molasses-and-brown-sugar sweet.

context, **Pappy's Orchard & Lisa's Kitchen** in Coopersburg, south of Bethlehem, can't be beat. Made with huge-flavored blackstrap molasses, dense and heavy and immensely satisfying, Lisa Urffer's shoofly demands cups of her made-on-premises apple cider to wash it down.

The **Dutch Kitchen** in Schuylkill County makes two kinds of shoofly pie: the familiar ooey-gooey, crumble-topped pie, known as "wet bottom," and a cakelike "dry bottom" shoofly pie, which is the same idea without the moist, dark ribbon of sweetness at its heart — more like a big hunk of coffee cake.

SUPER SHOOFLY PIES

1. **Pappy's Orchard & Lisa's Kitchen:** 2576 Cassel Rd., Coopersburg, PA
610-462-2734
2. **Dutch Kitchen:**
433 S. Lehigh Ave., Frackville, PA
570-874-3265
www.dutchkitchen.com
3. **Beiler's Bakery:** in the Reading Terminal Market
215-351-0735

DUTCH KITCHEN SHOOFLY PIE

1½ cups all-purpose flour
¼ teaspoon salt
1 cup dark brown sugar
¼ cup solid vegetable shortening, at room temperature
½ teaspoon baking soda
½ cup hot water
½ cup molasses
1 unbaked 8-inch pie crust

Preheat the oven to 450 degrees. Make the crumbs by combining the flour, salt, brown sugar, and shortening in a medium bowl. Mix with your hands until it is crumbly.

Make the syrup by combining the baking soda, hot water, and molasses in another bowl.

Reserve 1 cup of the crumbs. Add the rest of the crumbs to the syrup mixture and stir gently. Pour this into the unbaked pie crust and sprinkle the top with the remaining cup of crumbs.

Bake for 10 minutes. Lower the heat to 350 degrees and bake for 30 minutes longer, or until the filling doesn't jiggle.

MAKES ONE 8-INCH PIE

4. **Fisher's Soft Pretzels:** in the Reading Terminal Market
   215-592-8510
5. **Reading Terminal Market:**
   51 N. 12th St., Philadelphia, PA
   215-922-2317
   www.readingterminalmarket.org

SLAMMER
Pittsburgh, Pennsylvania

Pittsburgh is a city of outlandish sandwiches; chipped chopped ham is the one that most Pittsburghers consider their own. Devised in the 1930s at **Isaly's**, a local chain of dairy stores known to the world as the original home of the Klondike Bar, chipped chopped ham is shaved see-through thin and piled high on bread. It is customarily served warm and is frequently glazed with barbecue sauce, but its finest self is in a sandwich created by Tom Weisbecker at the West View Isaly's. Known as the Slammer to honor the criminals who pass through the magistrate's office across the highway, it is a fresh roll enclosing a great clump of chipped chopped ham that has been grilled with sweet onions. It's a simple sandwich, improvable only, perhaps, by the addition of mustard.

Chipped chopped ham from Isaly's — which local folklore says is an acronym for I Shall Always Love You — is available in grocery stories in Pennsylvania, Ohio, Maryland, Indiana, New York, and West Virginia or by mail-order.

Isaly's: 448 Perry Highway, Pittsburgh, PA
   412-931-9994
   www.isalys.com

SMOKED EEL
Hancock, New York

If you are traveling along Highway 17 through Hancock, New York, you must get off the road and find **Delaware Delicacies**, even if you don't love to eat eels. This smokehouse deep in the woods is one of the great roadside culinary attractions anywhere, primarily because of its stewardship by Ray Turner, who surely is the world's greatest admirer of the *Anguilla rostrata*. Yes, it's slimy and it has an ugly face. But is it delicious? Is it nutritious? "It is good groceries!" Mr. Turner proclaims.

His account of the lifestyle of the snake-shaped fish is inspirational. "Your androgynous species, like the salmon," he scoffs, "they travel by rote back to where they were spawned. The eel migrates to where the water tastes best. It has an acute olfactory system, with two sets of nostrils, and can smell a few parts per million when it wants to look for brackish water. The male likes hanging back

Ray Turner smokes improbably delicious eel in Hancock, NY.

Stop in for a bite if you're in the neighborhood.

along the coast farther south, but the female, she likes fresh water. She will stay here and grow for years. Do you know you can read the age of an eel, just like a tree, by counting the rings on the stones in its head? After maybe twelve years she will reach sexual maturity, and when the drive hits to go down to the Sargasso Sea, look out, here she comes."

When she comes, Mr. Turner is ready and waiting. He has been an eeler on the Delaware River for more than a quarter-century, and he speaks of the migration with joy. "Once the weir is built in July, we'll catch maybe one or two a day from those who live in these waters," he says. "In August and September it will grow to double digits. Then one night in September, when the moon is full and there has been a good rain, we will start to see the large black females. It is about to happen." As he describes it, spotting the first big females in the weir is as awesome as seeing a couple of longhorns in a bedded herd rise to their feet — the signal of an impending slithery stampede. In the first good night he will trap more than one thousand eels, which is about half of the whole season's catch.

He kills them by dousing them with salt, then he scrubs away the slime by putting five or six dozen in a cement mixer with #2 stone. "They come out clean as you or I," he says. "I wash them, I rinse them, then I gut them, slicing upwards with my spoon." Mr. Turner shows us the tool he has made from an ordinary kitchen spoon to remove the blood groove with a fast swoop. It is sharp on the sides and has stubby tines at the tip like a grapefruit spoon. "Then I weigh them, bag them, and freeze them."

Before he started freezing his catch, Mr. Turner generally ran out of eel by midwinter. Now he manages to hold on to some nearly all year, and in the process of evening his inventory flow, he discovered that freezing actually changes the way the eel fat renders. It is true that eel lovers welcome the luscious texture of the meat, but it is so oily that some of the excess must be drained away. "The fat seems to break down and extract better," Mr. Turner says. "Freezing improves them. That's a strange thing to say about a fish, but this is one strange fish."

When thawed, they are soaked in honeyed brine, hung by the tail so the oil can drain out, then smoked over applewood. The result is meat that is easily shoveled off the bone in soft hunks. It is dark and full-flavored, glowingly haloed by the smoke.

As much as Mr. Turner delights in catching mature females on their way south, he disapproves of nabbing eels earlier in their life cycle, as they float north with the currents. Eating the young ones, known to epicures as glass eels, is bad for the health of the species, he maintains. With avuncular affection for the little critters, he asks, "Do you know that when an eel is born, it looks like a willow leaf? It's that fragile. Aristotle believed that an eel grew from a single horsehair dropped in the water. So little is known about them — it's a shame."

What really bends Ray Turner out of shape is people's unfounded aversion to the eel. "It is a cross the eel must bear," he says. "People think of it as a snake, which it is not. I guarantee you will find eel good to eat, if only you can get over the eww! factor."

Delaware Delicacies Smoke House: 63 Wheeler St., Hancock, NY 607-637-4443

SMOKED STURGEON
New York City

Barney Greengrass is an Upper West Side luncheonette that has reigned as the "sturgeon king" since 1908. Although sturgeon probably is best known as a source of caviar, when insinuated with a whisper of wood smoke, the meat of the big fish is itself a rare delicacy, veined with threads of melt-in-the-mouth fat and yet not at all fishy, each cool white slice firm and moist. Have it on a sandwich between slices of superb rye bread or on a toasted bagel or as part of a smoked fish platter along with silky pink Nova Scotia salmon and whitefish. Like its roe, sturgeon really is a luxury dish. Last we looked, a sandwich was about $20, and the three-fish platter was just shy of $50.

One other great thing to eat at one of the Greengrass family's Formica-topped tables is scrambled eggs studded with nuggets of Nova Scotia salmon and laced with caramelized onions that perfume the air.

Barney Greengrass: 541 Amsterdam Ave., New York, NY 212-724-4707 www.barneygreengrass.com

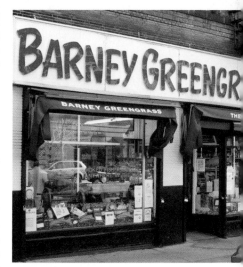

Greengrass's luncheonette in New York City has reigned supreme in smoked fish since 1908.

Mid Atlantic

SOFT PRETZEL
Philadelphia

Street-food fans of the East are accustomed to seeing carts that sell big soft pretzels, and while most of the carts warm them up before serving, infusing them with a rather pleasant smoky taste, the sad fact is that about 98 percent of the ones you'll get are pretty old and far from the bakery where they were made. (We won't even get into the cloying grotesqueries that pass as soft pretzels in airports and malls.) While there are times when even a somewhat stale soft pretzel can hit the spot, if you want a great one, fresh and chewy, with a slick, tough skin and steamy cake insides, hot from the oven, the place to go is Philadelphia, which has two primary sources.

While a single pretzel from the **Center City Pretzel Company** is big enough to be a nice snack, you

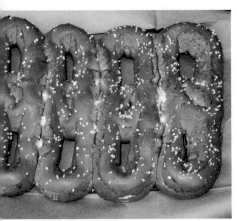

Bet you can't eat just one: offerings from Philly's Center City Pretzel Company.

will regret buying only one if you eat it the way it should be eaten, on the stroll. It's such a significant piece of food that by the time it's been consumed, you will be too far away from the Washington Avenue bakery to return easily for a second. But you will want a second. That's why we recommend buying four when you stop in. The quartet will still be stuck together from the oven, their traditional pretzel shape somewhat compressed, making the set of them look like quadruple figure-8 stitches in some doughy knitting project.

"The Good Ones" is the motto of **Philadelphia Soft Pretzels**, which wants to distinguish itself from lesser, similarly named pretzel bakeries around town. Like Center City, it is primarily a wholesale operation, hand-twisting more than 25,000 pretzels every day. Walk-in customers are welcome to buy them by the piece or bag and avail themselves of a counter where various kinds of mustard are available from pump jars and squeeze bottles. Delaware Valley culinary savants Bruce Bilmes and Sue Boyle wrote that while they are fans of all kinds of exotic mustards, the one place they demand the plain yellow stuff is on a soft pretzel, "a bright yellow squiggle tracing its full serpentine length."

In our experience, "the Good Ones" have a slightly slicker surface than Center City's pretzels, but honestly, the differences between the two are microscopic. Their similarities — warmth, freshness, and a certain brackish tang that some attribute to the crappy Philadelphia water in which they are boiled before being baked — put them in the highest tier of street snacks. If you are any kind of bread lover, the pleasure of sinking your teeth into one of these beauties, feeling the occasional crackle of coarse salt that dots the outside, is one of life's unmitigated joys.

PHILADELPHIA SOFT PRETZELS AT THE SOURCES

Center City Pretzel Co.: 816-18 Washington Ave., Philadelphia, PA 215-463-5664
Philadelphia Soft Pretzels: 4315 N. 3rd St., Philadelphia, PA 215-324-4315
www.philasoftpretzels.net

STUFFED HAM
St. Mary's County, Maryland

Stuffed ham is one of the best-tasting and least-known regional specialties in America. If you want to eat some, you must travel down the western shore of the Chesapeake Bay nearly as far south as you can go in Maryland into St. Mary's County. The dish exists nowhere else but in this ancient spit of land defined by complicated coves and creeks, where gulls and ospreys glide overhead and the air smells of the sea. A layered serving of sweet pink meat with spiced greens, it is the mainstay of countless church

Mid Atlantic

CHESAPEAKE BAY FRIED OYSTERS

A fabulous fringe benefit of finding a church supper at which stuffed ham stars is that the menu also will likely feature fried oysters from the Chesapeake Bay. It's local tradition to pair them up at a celebratory meal — a natural duo of surf 'n' turf or, in this case, swine 'n' brine. But even if there's no ham involved, it behooves eaters to know that throughout southern Maryland and up and down the Delmarva Peninsula, fried oysters from the Chesapeake Bay are as beloved as blue crabs. They are good-sized fellas, very delicious when buttered and roasted in the shell, but they are at their ocean-sweet peak when lightly breaded in cornmeal and fried. They cook very quickly; the coat crisps, and

the oyster itself — known affectionately as white gold — is warmed only enough for its saltwater succulence to erupt on your tongue at first bite.

3 TOP-OF-THE-LINE FRIED OYSTER SOURCES

1. **Waterman's Crab House:** 21055 Sharp St., Rock Hall, MD 410-639-2261 www.watermanscrabhouse.com
2. **The Narrows:** 3023 Kent Narrows Way South, Grasonville, MD 410-827-8113 www.thenarrowsrestaurant.com
3. **Beach Cove Restaurant & Lounge:** 8416 Bayside Rd., Chesapeake Beach, MD 301-855-0025 www.beachcoverestaurant.com

Tender ham with a stuffing of spicy greens, the specialty of the southern Maryland shore

suppers and firemen's balls from autumn into spring.

Stuffed ham's seasonal appearance dates back to the days of the autumn hog slaughter, when plantation slaves were given the hog's head, which they made more appealing by stuffing it with such late-crop produce as kale, turnip tops, wild watercress, or collards and mustard greens. The harmony of pork and greens was so good that the concept went high on the hog, from head to ham. Stuffed ham is served in slices that resemble piggy braciole with alternating ribbons of meat and filling. It's rare to find it

WOODSIDE FARM CREAMERY

If you like ice cream and find yourself heading south to Maryland for ham and crabs or north to Philadelphia for street-food sandwiches and pretzels, take a detour into the Delaware countryside and find Woodside Farm. Jim Mitchell, whose family started the outfit in 1796, points to his herd of grazing Jersey dairy cows and boasts, "Two weeks ago, our ice cream was grass." As produced in the creamery adjacent to the milking parlor, his ice cream is more cream-sweet than sugar-sweet. Low overrun (minimal added air) creates such density that when the ice cream melts, it's more like crème fraîche than spilled milk. The butterfat content is about 15 percent, varying slightly depending how the cows' grass is growing, placing it high on the richness scale. But unlike many

high-butterfat, super-premium brands, which can assume such overwhelming intensity after a scoop or two that even ice cream fanatics begin to slow their attack, this stuff tastes positively salubrious. The genuinely farm-fresh flavors range from chocolate and coffee to pumpkin pecan and butter brickle toffee as well as such summer treats as peach, strawberry, black raspberry, and black cherry. Our personal favorite is African vanilla, which is pure and creamy with a flavor you want to call vanilla squared. Spooned up just slightly softened, unadorned by any topping whatever, it is a bowl of bovinity cum divinity.

Woodside Farm Creamery:
1310 Little Baltimore Rd.,
Hockessin, DE
302-239-9847
www.woodsidefarmcreamery.com

in restaurants, although a few places between the Potomac and Patuxent rivers serve it in the cool months. **St. Mary's Landing**, a tavern frequented by locals who come to drink and play Keno as well as to eat, has it on the menu year-round.

"You know, you don't just heat and cut a stuffed ham!" our St. Mary's Landing waitress, Peggy, announced with some hauteur, spotting us as tenderfeet who scarcely knew a city ham from its country cousin when we came in one morning to try it. When we showed interest, she eagerly gave us the lowdown on a culinary subject dear to her heart. "You must *shock* that ham, plunge it into ice to stop the cooking right away," she declared. "Then you refrigerate it so you can serve it good and cool. Believe me, that's the way you want it." Stuffed ham is almost always served cool, although the menu says, "We'll serve it warm if you ask." Peggy explained to us that heat messes up the flavor of the dish; when it's cool, you get a good, clear taste of sweet ham and the tonic greens it has been boiled with.

St. Mary's Landing: Route 5, Charlotte Hall, MD 301-884-3287

SUBMARINE SANDWICH
Delaware Valley

It is fun to muse on the crazy aliases of the sub (grinder, bomber, hoagie, blimp, zep, wedge) as well as on its genealogy and its countless incarnations around the nation, from the Key West Cuban to SoCal's French dip.

And it's also fun to do a taste-off to compare the best. Most issues of origin and taxonomy are up for grabs, but these two things are certain: the tubular, multi-ingredient hero attains perfection in New Jersey, and those made at the **White House Sub Shop** in Atlantic City are the paradigm.

It's not only the superior bread, delivered six or seven times daily from a bakery across the street, or the first-rate cold cuts from Philadelphia, or the Jersey tomatoes (in summer) that make White House subs the ne plus ultra of overstuffed hero sandwiches. It is the art of sandwich building, which is a simple kitchen task, like roasting a chicken or cooking an omelet, that can be done pretty well by almost anybody but will produce something transcendent when conducted by a master.

If you sit at the short counter or wait in line for a sub to go, you can watch the half-dozen White House sandwich makers work — a hypnotic scene that is cold-cut poetry in motion. The men who slice the bread

Sandwichery becomes choreography at Atlantic City's White House Sub Shop.

and array the filling work in a voluble fugue state, chattering among themselves and with customers as they slice and reach and grab around each other in a free-form ballet of bread and meat and cheese. When making a regular sub, which consists of cotechino, capicola, Genoa salami, provolone cheese, lettuce, tomatoes, onions, hot peppers, and oil, or a special (same ingredients but twice as much), they use the back of their big knife blade to fold over the meats and cheeses inside the bread, so instead of being piled up densely, the cold cuts become a serpentine pile that allows the unctuous luxury of the cotechino and the zest of the capicola to swirl together in the interstices and welcomes juice from the hot peppers and the obligatory spritz of oil to seep in among them all.

Tom LaRocca, a White House employee for some fifty years, disabused us of the notion that subs were named after the ships of the silent service during World War II. "Atlantic City said *submarine* long before this place opened [in 1946]," he said, contending that the length of bread used to make the sandwich was always known as a sub. "Because it is not a full-sized loaf. It is subsized." Philadelphians call the same sort of sandwich a hoagie, one explanation for which is that Italian shipworkers at the city's shipyard, known as Hog Island during the First World War, brought effulgent lunches that became known as Hog Island sandwiches, a term that eventually morphed into *hoagie*. Most sandwich shop menus in the city offer both cheese steaks and hoagie cheese steaks, the latter including let-

FORMICA BROS. BAKERY

White House subs would not be superior if it weren't for the superior bread they are built on. For that, you can thank the aquifer below the New Jersey Pinelands. The Formica (say For-*mee*-ka) Bros. Bakery mixes Pinelands water with brewer's yeast and flour, then proofs the dough three times before baking. The result: a loaf with a crumb that is sturdy, crust that is firm, and flavor that is a welcoming bready tableau for anything with which the White House can adorn it. The Formica family has perfected the formula since Grandpa Francesco and his wife,

Rosa, opened their resort-town bakery in 1919. During the Second World War, when fuel for home stoves was rationed, residents of the Ducktown neighborhood of Atlantic City came to cook their meals in Formica's coal ovens, which did not shut down until 1988, when a modern oven was installed. Frank Formica lamented the change he had to make, joking with us, "If I go to hell for any reason, it will be for knocking down that old oven."
Formica Bros. Bakery: 2310 Arctic Ave., Atlantic City, NJ 609-344-2732 www.formicabrosbakery.com

Mid Atlantic

tuce and tomato along with steak and cheese, but the classic Italian hoagie, as splendidly constructed at **Mama's Pizzeria** in the Philadelphia suburb of Bala Cynwyd, is strata of capicola, salami, and provolone with chopped iceberg lettuce, sliced tomatoes, and raw onions, a good drizzle of oil, and, optionally, some of Mama's roasted peppers, either the sweet ones or the fiery long hots. We also recommend the excellent Italian hoagies in the Roxborough neighborhood of Philadelphia at **Dalessandro's**, known too for mountainous cheese steaks in the freshest possible bread. In this always-crowded corner diner, counters are arrayed with at least six different garnishments to accentuate the cold cuts: hot peppers, superhot pepper hash, sweet peppers, yellow peppers, cherry peppers, and pickle chips.

3 TERRIFIC SUBS

1. **White House Sub Shop:** 2301 Arctic Ave., Atlantic City, NJ 609-345-1564
2. **Mama's Pizzeria:** 426 Belmont Ave., Bala Cynwyd, PA 610-664-4757 www.mamaspizzeria.com
3. **Dalessandro's Steaks:** 600 Wendover St., Philadelphia, PA 215-482-5407

TAYLOR HAM
New Jersey

Taylor ham, which is what Spam would be if it went to the gym on a regular basis, is a big, coarse-textured sausage that arrives in burlap and is sliced thin like bologna — but not too thin — and pan-fried like bacon. Also known as pork roll, it was invented in New Jersey in 1856, and that is where it has stayed. Few outsiders have ever heard of it, but it is the unofficial state sandwich, and to those who grew up eating Taylor ham, it is a wanton comfort food that no high-on-the-hog pork can match. While you will sometimes find it used as lunch meat, or even as a burger topping (think bacon cheeseburger), its true raison d'être is breakfast. Glistening pink hot off the grill, golden brown in a few splotches, bubbled up in the center, and crisp at its edge, which has been scored all around so it doesn't curl up completely, it is a superb side dish for eggs or, better yet, packaged in a hard roll with egg and cheese (known in diner slang as a Triple Bypass). Taylor ham gushes the kind of flavor that makes a morning meal extravagant. Indeed, a single slice supplies 26 percent of the fat recommended in a normal daily diet.

Three slices are packed into breakfast sandwiches made at **White Rose System** in Linden, which Roadfood

White Rose in Linden, NJ, is famous for Taylor ham, a big-flavored sausage.

authorities Bruce Bilmes and Sue Boyles declared to be the source of the state's best. Along with the melty-rich fried pork are a couple of eggs cooked as runny or as firm as you require and heat-softened orange cheese. The "complete" version also includes large sections of cooked-soft home-fried potatoes. (The New Jersey proclivity for including fried potatoes in a sandwich is a topic for further investigation. See also the Newark Hot Dog, page 95.) And if you are really, really hungry, you can have an extra measure of all these ingredients layered into a long roll, supplying the average eater with nutrients for the next forty-eight hours.

Johnny's Deli in New Providence respects Taylor ham by listing it on the breakfast sandwich menu as a "classic Trenton pork roll." (Do not confuse with Trenton brand pork roll, which is a more mildly seasoned version of Taylor brand.) With a couple of eggs and a slice of cheese, it is known as the Porker.

As good as it is for breakfast, or as a lunch-meat sandwich (try the **Pot Belly Deli** in Sussex or **Jimmy John's Pipin Hot Sandwiches** in

West Chester, Pennsylvania, where it comes on a nice club roll), Taylor ham is one of those reckless splurges that goes well with drinks, especially if you've already had a few. A good place to enjoy the ham in that manner is **Cahoots**, in Middlesex, a bar and burger joint where the pork is sliced extra-thick and piled into a bun with cheese, creating a supersalty sandwich that demands more beer.

Note that **Relli's Deli** in Piscataway invites customers to call in orders for as many pounds of Taylor ham as they need, available sliced or cooked. Relli's suggests, "If you're heading away on vacation and you want to stock up on pork roll to take to friends and family, call ahead."

TAYLOR HAM HONOR ROLL

1. **White Rose System:** 1301 E. Elizabeth Ave., Linden, NJ 908-486-9651
2. **Pot Belly Deli:** 52 Main St., Sussex, NJ 973-702-2322
3. **Johnny's Deli & Catering:** 76 Marion Ave., New Providence, NJ 908-464-2787 www.johnnysdeli.com
4. **Jimmy John's Pipin Hot Sandwiches:** 1507 Wilmington Pike, West Chester, PA 610-459-3083
5. **Relli's Deli:** 177 Stelton Rd., Piscataway, NJ 732-752-9838; for pork roll orders, call 866-4NJ-PORK www.rellisdeli.com
6. **Cahoots:** 624 Lincoln Blvd., Middlesex, NJ 732-469-3455

Breakfast of champions: Taylor ham coupled with eggs and cheese

WHITE HOT AND RED HOT
Upstate New York

You cannot drive far in western New York without noticing that this is serious hot dog country, where the primary partition is between white hots and red hots. Although it resembles a weisswurst, the beloved white hot, found mostly around Rochester and Syracuse, is all-American, especially as served by the Lake Ontario shore at **Don's Original**, dolloped with chili. Not like chili you'd eat from a bowl, this dog dressing is more a spicy fine-grind meat sauce devoid of tomatoes. Nor is the white hot much like a normal hot dog. While some regional white hots include veal, Don's uses Zweigle brand sausages, which are nothing but pork. In fact they are known to Flower City fans as porkers, and they are significantly oinkier and plumper than red hots, which are referred to in this area as Texas hots. The whites are something like a natural-casing bratwurst, but they are split lengthwise before getting grilled. A complete white hot will also be topped with mustard and chopped raw onions.

You'll find white hots in Rochester, but the frankfurter to eat farther west is a red hot off the grill at **Ted's** of Tonawanda. Ted's cooks them over charcoal. While they are cooking, the grill man worries them on the grate enough to rip, tear, and bruise them, thus allowing maximum pungent smoke flavor to invade the meat contained in their flame-burnished skin. Smoky dogs indeed! The Sahlens brand red hots, available regular, foot-long, and jumbo, are dressed in powerful, peppery hot sauce and at their best sided by hard-crusted onion rings. The locally favored beverage to accompany a grilled red hot is loganberry-flavored bug juice. (Ted's has several branches in greater Buffalo and one in Tempe, Arizona.)

In Syracuse, **Heid's of Liverpool**, which began in 1886, long before hot dogs existed, completely confuses the issue by offering white hot dogs containing veal, which are called Coneys (but bear no resemblance to Coney Island hot dogs elsewhere) and red hots, here known as German franks. The grilled Coneys have tremendous mouthfeel and are called snappies for their taut skin. Long ago, the only available condiment was mustard, but since John and Randall Parker started running Heid's back in 1995, the topping choices have expanded to include chili, onions, and ketchup.

BLUE-RIBBON WHITE HOTS AND RED HOTS

1. **Ted's Jumbo Red Hots:** 2312 Sheridan Dr., Tonawanda, NY 716-834-6287 See www.tedsonline.com for additional locations.
2. **Don's Original:** 4900 Culver Rd., Sea Breeze, NY 585-323-1177 See www.donsoriginal.com for additional locations.
3. **Heid's of Liverpool:** 305 Oswego St., Liverpool. NY 315-451-0786 www.heidsofliverpool.com

SOUTH

Plantation Grill- Charleston - coconut cake

ALABAMA
Banana Pudding: Birmingham, 117
Barbecue Ribs: Mobile and Tuscaloosa, 124
Dixie Dog: Mobile, 155
Fried Crab Claws: Gulf Shores, Mobile, and Spanish Fort, 161
Pulled Pork: Mobile, 196
Streak o' Lean: Tuscaloosa, 201
West Indies Salad: Mobile and Theodore, 208

ARKANSAS
Barbecue Beans: Hot Springs, 119
Barbecue Ribs: Hot Springs, 124
French Fries: Hot Springs, 247
Hamburger: Scott, 328
Tamale: Lake Village, 203

FLORIDA
Barbecue Ribs: West Palm Beach, 124
Catfish: Orange Park, 143
Conch Chowder: Fort Lauderdale, 151
Cuban Sandwich: Miami Beach and Tampa, 150
Datil Peppers: St. Augustine, 152
Fried Shrimp: Atlantic Beach, Ponte Vedra Beach, and St. Augustine, 162
Key Lime Pie: Big Pine Key, Key West, and Miami Beach, 173
Media Noche: West Palm Beach, 181
Pancakes: Key West, 402
Perloo: St. Augustine, 189
Rock Shrimp: Titusville, 198
Smoked Mullet: South Pasadena, 198
Stone Crab: Marathon and Miami Beach, 200

GEORGIA
Barbecue Ribs: Atlanta, 124
Biscuits: Conyers, Gainesville, and Jefferson, 134
Boardinghouse Meal: Dahlonega and Dillard, 137
Boiled Peanuts: Hawkinsville, 138
Brunswick Stew: Atlanta, 141
Dixie Dog: Atlanta, Columbus, and Macon, 155
Lemon Icebox Pie: Atlanta, 175
Peach Cobbler: Fort Valley, 184
Streak o' Lean: Atlanta, 201

Sweet Tea: Fayetteville and Social Circle, 202
Vidalia Onions: Vidalia, 157

KENTUCKY
Barbecue Beans: Henderson, 119
Burgoo: Louisville and Owensboro, 142
Chess Pie: Louisville, 145
Dutch Apple Pie: Louisville, 158
Five-Way Chili: Alexandria, 243
Hot Fried Chicken: Henderson and Sturgis, 169
Mint Julep: Louisville, 143
Mutton Belt: Henderson, Owensboro, and Waverly, 182
Red Velvet Cake: Louisville, 196
Sweet Tea: Louisville, 202

LOUISIANA
Beignets: Breaux Bridge and New Orleans, 370
Boudin Sausage: Baton Rouge, Jennings, and Port Barre, 140
Catfish: Pass Manchac, 143
Crawfish: Basile, Breaux Bridge, Henderson, Mamou, and New Iberia, 147
Crawfish au Gratin: Lafayette, 148
Gateau Sirop: Breaux Bridge and Lafayette, 164
Hansen's Sno-Bliz: New Orleans, 193
Louisiana Meat Pie: Basile, Breaux Bridge, and Natchitoches, 178
Oreille de Cochon: Breaux Bridge, 184
Pancakes: Lafayette, 402
Po Boy, Oyster Loaf, Muffaletta: Arabi and New Orleans, 192
Red Velvet Cake: Lafayette, 196
Smothered Cabbage: New Iberia, 199

MISSISSIPPI
Banana Pudding: Jackson, 117
Barbecue Pork Sandwich: Clarksdale and Southaven, 121
Boardinghouse Meal: McComb, 137
Chess Pie: Jackson, 145
Fried Shrimp: Clarksdale, 164
Hamburger: Holly Springs, 328
Lemon Icebox Pie: Greenwood, 175
Tamale: Clarksdale, Greenville, Rosedale, and Vicksburg, 203

South

Lexington VA -
Southern Inn
at 37 Main St

NORTH CAROLINA

Barbecue Slaw: Charlotte, Gastonia, Greensboro, Wilson, and Windsor, 130
Biscuits: Asheville and Chapel Hill, 134
Brunswick Stew: Chapel Hill, 141
Chess Pie: Cary, 145
Dixie Dog: Raleigh, 155
Hamburger: Charlotte, 328
Hot Fried Chicken: Cleveland, 169
Hushpuppies: Chapel Hill, Greensboro, and Shelby, 171
Lexington Barbecue: Lexington, 177
Peach Ice Cream: Lilesville, 185
Pimento Cheese: Charlotte, 191
Steamed Oysters: Garner and Williamston, 199
Sweet Tea: Charlotte, Greensboro, and Huntersville, 202
Whole-Hog Barbecue: Ayden and Goldsboro, 210

SOUTH CAROLINA

Biscuits: Charleston, 134
Boiled Peanuts: Pocataligo and Yemassee, 138
Creamy Grits: Charleston and Columbia, 149
Fish Head Stew: Mount Pleasant, 159
Flounder: Charleston, 160
French Fries: Spartanburg, 247
Fried Shrimp: Charleston, 163
Hushpuppies: Folly Island, 171
Lima Beans: Charleston, Mount Pleasant, and North Charleston, 178
Peach Cobbler: Abbeville, 184
Perloo: Charleston, Mount Pleasant, and North Charleston, 189
Pimento Cheese: Charleston and Columbia, 191
Red Velvet Cake: Charleston, 196
Steamed Oysters: Folly Island, 199
Sweet Tea: Mount Pleasant and Spartanburg, 202

TENNESSEE

Banana Pudding: Nashville, 117
Barbecue Beans: Bluff City, 119
Barbecue Pork Sandwich: Memphis, 121
Barbecue Ribs: Germantown and Memphis, 124
Barbecue Spaghetti: Memphis, 132
Biscuits: Nashville, 134
Boardinghouse Meal: Lynchburg, 137

Catfish: Nashville, 143
Chess Pie: Nashville, 145
Chipburger: Greeneville, 146
French Fries: Bluff City, 247
Hot Fish Sandwich: Nashville, 167
Hot Fried Chicken: Nashville, 169
Lemon Icebox Pie: Chattanooga, Memphis, and Nashville, 175
Meat and Three: Nashville, 180
Pancakes: Nashville, 402
Pimento Cheese: Franklin and Memphis, 191
Pizza: Memphis, 50
Red Velvet Cake: Knoxville, 196
Tamale: Memphis, 203

VIRGINIA

Banana Pudding: Galax, 117
Box Lunch: Richmond, 166
Dip Dog: Marion, 154
Half Smoke: Arlington, 165
Peanut Pie: Wakefield, 185
Peanut Soup: Middletown, New Market, and Surry, 185
Virginia Ham: Culpeper, Fulks Run, New Market, Portsmouth, Richmond, Roanoke, Smithfield, Williamsburg, and Wolftown, 206

WASHINGTON, D.C.

Half Smoke: 165

WEST VIRGINIA

Dixie Dog: Clarksburg, Huntington, and Webster Springs, 155
Italian Bread: Clarksburg, 189
Pepperoni Roll: Clarksburg and Fairmont, 187
Pizza: Wheeling, 50

BANANA PUDDING
Heart of Dixie

Of all the South's soothing desserts, none is quite so palliative as banana pudding, or, as aficionados of comfort food know it, 'naner pudding. When Elvis secluded himself at Graceland in search of peace and serenity, it was his favorite sweet, an essential element in the repertoire of all who cooked for the King. It is the right finish for any meal of meat and three (page 180), especially welcome as the denouement following salty country ham. It is exactly perfect after super-savory fried chicken like that served at Jackson, Mississippi's **Two Sisters' Kitchen**, which sets the banana pudding bar. Loaded with perfectly ripe pieces of banana and vanilla wafer parts that range from crunchy to soft, Two Sisters' banana pudding is tropical and creamy. It is not always available at this estimable soul-food restaurant in an old neighborhood house north of downtown

Elvis's favorite: Custard, vanilla cookies, bananas, and meringue meld in 'naner pudding.

Jackson, but that's all right. When banana pudding isn't on the menu, your choices will likely be bread pudding with whiskey sauce or fruit cobbler, both of which are out of this world.

Meat-and-three restaurants in Tennessee can always be depended on for banana pudding. It is at its best at **Arnold's Country Kitchen** in Nashville, but it is not necessarily an easy choice. Pure and fresh and tender as the banana pudding is, Arnold's chess pie, available with or without meringue on top, is some of the best anywhere (page 145). Likewise, it would be a crime to visit Nashville's **Sylvan Park** and not eat one of the legendary meringue pies, caramel pie, or chess pie, but the banana pudding is irresistible: baby-food tender, a delicate dance of custard, soft cookie, bananas, and streaks of meringue.

Cliff Strutz, who is one of the most ambitious and discriminating omnivores we know, declared the banana pudding at **Niki's West** in Birmingham, Alabama, "the best I have ever had." While it was the vegetables that wowed us on our first visit to this big cafeteria near the truckers' terminal, we returned to reexamine dessert, and my, oh, my, was Cliff ever right. The coconut cream pie is one of the creamiest ever, and the banana pudding is smooth and caramel-rich, virtually all of its cookies softened into tender grain.

When spicy barbecue leaves your tongue aglow, few desserts are as appreciated as a cool serving of banana pudding. The **Galax Smokehouse**, which bills its fare as "Texas-size portions of Memphis style BBQ in the heart of a mountain town in

South

FOR AMBITIOUS COOKS:
LOVELESS CAFE'S BANANA PUDDING

CUSTARD
- ½ cup cornstarch
- 1 quart whole milk
- 12 large egg yolks
- ¼ vanilla bean, split and seeds scraped out
- 1¼ cups sugar

NILLA WAFERS
- 1 cup plus 2 tablespoons sugar
- 4 large eggs
- 2⅓ cups all-purpose flour

- 4–6 ripe bananas
  Whipped cream

FOR THE CUSTARD: Place the cornstarch in a bowl. Add enough of the milk to dissolve it completely. Add the egg yolks to the cornstarch and whisk thoroughly. Set aside.

Place the vanilla bean and sugar in a heavy-bottomed stainless steel pot. Add the remaining milk and bring to a boil, stirring to prevent scorching. When the milk is boiling, reduce the heat slightly to prevent it from boiling over the sides of the pot. Remove the vanilla bean. With a small ladle, whisk a small amount of milk into the egg-yolk mix. Repeat this step until one third of the milk is mixed into the eggs. Whisk the egg yolks into the remaining boiling milk and return to a boil while you continue to whisk. The mix will thicken quickly. Continue whisking for 1 minute.

Remove from the heat and pour the custard into a heatproof dish. Press plastic wrap onto the surface and refrigerate to cool.

FOR THE WAFERS: Lightly oil a cookie sheet and preheat the oven to 375 degrees. Place 1 cup of the sugar and the eggs in a stainless steel bowl and whisk them together. Place the bowl over simmering water and whisk until the sugar dissolves and the eggs are slightly warmed. Immediately pour into a bowl and beat on high with an electric mixer until the mixture forms mounds when you lift the beaters out. Sift the flour over the egg mixture in several batches, folding it in gently.

Using a piping bag with a straight tip, pipe the mixture onto the cookie sheet into cookies the size of a quarter. Sprinkle them with the remaining 2 tablespoons sugar and bake for 10 to 12 minutes, or until golden. Cool on a rack.

To assemble, spread a small amount of the custard in a decorative glass dish. Top with a layer of sliced fresh bananas. Top with a layer of custard, then a layer of cookies. Spread enough custard over this to create a smooth surface and repeat the layers until the dish is filled, ending with a layer of custard. Wrap well and allow to sit overnight in the refrigerator. Before serving, decorate with whipped cream, remaining cookies, and banana slices.

SERVES 12

Virginia" and serves everything from smoked hot dogs to racks of ribs with five different kinds of sauce to embellish them, makes a beaut. It is smooth and so seductively banana-intense that you might guess it is laced with some sort of banana liqueur. Perhaps it is. The house policy is that if you guess its secret ingredients, you get it for free.

Other than bananas, the common denominator of all banana puddings is Nilla Wafer cookies. Alissa Huntsman, pastry chef at Nashville's **Loveless Cafe**, told us she never liked banana pudding because most versions she found used canned pudding, plus she's no fan of Nabisco cookies. So when the management of the Loveless told her they needed to put banana pudding on the menu, she devised her own recipe, even for the cookies that are part of it. The pudding itself is ultimate banana-cream luxury; the wafers are pure cookie, without a hint of ersatz chemical flavoring. While there are many fine banana puddings throughout the mid-South, the Loveless version, made strictly from scratch, is in a class by itself.

TOP BANANA PUDDINGS

1. **Two Sisters' Kitchen:** 707 N. Congress St., Jackson, MS
   601-353-1180
2. **Arnold's Country Kitchen:** 605 Eighth Ave. South, Nashville, TN
   615-256-4455
3. **Loveless Cafe:** 8400 Highway 100, Nashville, TN
   615-646-9700
   www.lovelesscafe.com
4. **Sylvan Park:** 4502 Murphy Rd., Nashville, TN
   615-292-9275
5. **Niki's West:** 233 Finley Ave. West, Birmingham, AL
   205-252-5751
   www.nikiswest.com
6. **Galax Smokehouse:** 101 N. Main St., Galax, VA
   276-236-1000
   www.thegalaxsmokehouse.com

BARBECUE BEANS
Smoke Pit Country

Baked beans are a good thing; barbecue beans are better. **Stubby's Bar-B-Que** in Hot Springs, Arkansas, calls them Pot-O-Beans — a crock full of smoky-sweet beans liberally larded with pig-fat-dripping hunks of pit-smoked meat baked into a thick gravy of dark red, woo-hoo-spicy sauce. They are great on the side of ribs and especially welcome as the ultimate garnish for one of Stubby's oversized pit-baked potatoes, its soft insides loaded also with chopped pork, slaw, and sauce.

Side dish, sandwich, or garnish: barbecue beans from Thomason's in Henderson, KY

Nobody goes to the **Ridgewood Barbecue** for beans. It is pork shoulder — slow-cooked in a smokehouse adjacent to the restaurant, sliced, then heated on the grill, brushed with sauce, and piled into sandwiches — that has put this mid-twentieth-century east Tennessee barbecue at the top of so many travelers' all-time fave lists. It is that very pork that infuses the beans with smoky savoriness. An optional side dish, they come in a little crockery bean pot, the firm, leguminous heft of each one sent into a fourth dimension of deliciousness

The smokehouse at Ridgewood Barbecue in Bluff City, TN: unlikely site of some of the best pork shoulder in Tennessee

CARBO'S POLICE MUSEUM

Buford Pusser, the club-wielding Tennessee folk hero whose battle against corruption was depicted in the *Walking Tall* movies, was shot by enemies eight times, stabbed seven times, and run over once. His jaw was blown off in an ambush (which killed his wife) in 1967. But he kept on fighting the bad guys until one fatal day in 1974. After being featured in the Jaycees' Dunking Barrel at the McNairy County Fair, Pusser sat in the front seat of his maroon Corvette eating two pork sandwiches and a fried fish sandwich from Coleman's Bar-B-Q. He sped off toward home along U.S. 64 at 100 mph, zooming past his daughter Dwana, also heading for home. At the crest of a hill, Pusser lost control. The car left the road, slammed into a red clay embankment, exploded, and burned.

As Pusser lay on the ground with a broken neck, Dwana approached and is said to have cried, "Daddy's dead this time!"

The surreal death car, which is now a black charcoal mass that resembles licorice drippings on a steel frame, is the highlight of some five thousand artifacts on display at Carbo's Police Museum, dedicated to all police officers who have died in the line of duty. Other Pusser memorabilia include his sheriff's desk, his size 14D shoes, and items from the movies about his life. The museum's collection also includes badges, guns, and uniforms from around the world, as well as a death mask of John Dillinger that is among the best anywhere, according to the death mask aficionado we know.

Carbo's Police Museum: 311 Parkway, Pigeon Forge, TN 865-453-1358

by all the shreds of meat that populate the pot and seem virtually to melt into pure flavor. The pork-and-bean duet attains perfect pitch cosseted in Ridgewood's vibrant, spicy-sweet sauce.

At the 2007 Taste of Henderson (Kentucky) Barbecue, which kicks off the annual W. C. Handy Blues and Barbecue Festival, the surprise hit on the smoky menu was a bean sandwich from **Thomason's**. A bean sandwich is an odd duck in the culinary repertoire of most Americans (other than old-time Bostonians, who make bean sandwiches on brown bread), but to those who know Thomason's beans, it was not such a surprise. These are some of the most meat-laden beans in western Kentucky, bound in a moist, highly spiced emulsion, but not so drippy that they don't make a suitable sandwich filling. The beans are tender but not mushy, bright with the flavor of Thomason's superb sauce (known in this region as dip), and meat is laced among them so liberally that the starch redundancy of bread with legumes never occurs to a palate overwhelmed with joy.

BEST BEANS

1. **Thomason's Barbecue:**
   701 Atkinson St., Henderson, KY
   270-826-0654
2. **Ridgewood Barbecue:**
   900 Elizabethton Highway (Old Route 19 East), Bluff City, TN
   423-538-7543
3. **Stubby's Bar-B-Que:** 3024 Central Ave., Hot Springs, AR
   800-36-SAUCE or 501-624-1552
   www.stubbysbbq.com

BARBECUE PORK SANDWICH
Memphis and the Mississippi Delta

The pig sandwich, as it is popularly known, was first constructed by Leonard Heuberger of **Leonard's Pit Barbecue** in Memphis in 1922. Mr. Heuberger's idea was to pile shreds of sauced smoked pork shoulder onto a bun and top the pork with coleslaw. Warm meat/cool slaw, spicy/creamy, piggy/veggie: The pig sandwich is a mesmerizing confluence of opposites, a yin/yang combination that is now popular throughout much of the South. Leonard's longtime motto is "Mr. Brown Goes to Town," a reference to the difference between inside and outside meat, explained to us by a waitress here many years ago: "Mr. Brown was the term used for brown-meat barbecue. It is the outside of the shoulder, which gets chewy from the sauce and the smoke in the pit.

A neon pig strides jauntily over Leonard's Pit Barbecue in Memphis.

The inside part of the roast, which is moist but has very little barbecue flavor, is known as Miss White. People in Memphis used to ask for plates and sandwiches of Mr. Brown and Miss White." "To go to town" was Mr. Heuberger's way of suggesting that customers grab a sandwich before they got on the (now defunct) streetcar nearby to head downtown. Leonard's pork is classic and world-class, made of finely chopped cabbage and mixed with sauce that delivers a mustard kick. The slaw is a sharp contrast to the sweet tenderness of the meat it tops.

As in most Memphis pork parlors, you will not be asked if you want slaw on your extraordinarily delicious sandwich at the extremely humble **Payne's**. It's automatic. When you order one, a sufficient amount of meat is heated, then vigorously chopped on a wooden block and piled on a bun, mixed with your choice of hot or mild sauce. Atop the pork goes

Defying easy eating, Payne's pig sandwich overflows with pork, slaw, and sauce.

pickly-sweet slaw. Available in normal and jumbo sizes, the sandwich is wrapped in wax paper and held together with toothpicks, although it is well-nigh impossible to eat in a traditional manner. You can try to pick it up in one or two hands and bring the whole thing to your mouth, but chopped pork will spill, sauce will drip, and slaw will scatter. Eventually you will be picking up meat, slaw, and sauce-sopped bun with two fingers as if each were a dainty (albeit outrageously messy) canapé.

The pig sandwich at **Interstate Bar-B-Que** is in the Memphis pantheon: shoulder meat, oozing juice and dripping sauce, piled into a bun with cool slaw. The bun melds with the wet ingredients, and you will be licking a good portion of the pandemonious pork off your fingers. At the counter of **A&R Bar-B-Que**, customers are serenaded by a blissful smokehouse lullaby: *chop chop chop* on the cutting board as hickory-cooked pork gets hacked into mottled shreds and pieces for plates and sandwiches. It occurred to us as we plowed through an A&R jumbo that the slaw in a Memphis barbecue sandwich is as important for its texture as for its taste. The cabbage provides such nice little bits of crunch among the velvety heap of pork.

In all truth, the tastiest item on the menu of the **Cozy Corner** is barbecued Cornish game hen, with fragile, burnished skin and unspeakably tender meat. Cozy Corner spareribs, glazed with sauce, pack a huge flavor punch; baby backs have meat that slides off the bone if you look at it hard. Great as all those things are, the

This small Oklahoma chain trademarked the term *pig sandwich*.

single item we return to again and again is an iconoclastic variant of the pig sandwich built around a thick-cut disk of pit-perfumed bologna, its skin slightly crisp, its edges dark, its inside luscious beyond all measure. Dollop this with hot, cinnabar-red barbecue sauce and ease it into a bun under a pile of sweet, fine-cut coleslaw. The result is a sandwich that is ignominious compared to pulled pork, but irresistible and guaranteed to satisfy anyone's desire for maximum oink.

One of the most impressive pig sandwiches is due south of Memphis along Highway 61 in Clarksdale, Mississippi, at **Abe's**. The Big Abe sandwich is a lofty double-decker loaded with a good half-pound of pork that has been slow-cooked in pecan wood smoke, then sliced and heated on the griddle. While on the griddle, the meat is hacked into a rugged hash that is crunchy at its edges but mostly velvet-soft. Veiled in Abe's sensational sauce, which is a precarious balance of pepper, sugar, and spices, the great piles of pork are complemented by a

layer of crunchy-cool slaw. The whole package, sweet, hot, porky, bursting with spice and dripping juice, is the most satisfying pork sandwich in the Mississippi Delta.

Although the pig sandwich is historically more a mid-South thing, at its best in Tennessee and North Carolina, it attains a kind of irreverent perfection at **Van's Pig Stand**, a five-unit Oklahoma chain that started in 1928 and has actually trademarked the term *pig sandwich*. Van's version is unique in that the pork is not actually topped with coleslaw; instead, it is heaped with a fine slawlike relish that does a hot tango with chunky pork pulled from shoulders that have been slow-cooked over hot coals to exquisite tenderness.

6 + 1 GREAT BARBECUE PORK SANDWICHES

1. **Payne's:** 1762 Lamar Ave., Memphis, TN
901-272-1523
Second location: 1393 Elvis Presley Blvd., Memphis, TN
2. **A&R Bar-B-Que:** 1802 Elvis Presley Blvd., Memphis, TN
901-774-7444
See www.aandrbbq.com for additional locations.
3. **Cozy Corner Restaurant:** 745 N. Parkway, Memphis, TN
901-527-9158
4. **Leonard's Pit Barbecue:** 5465 Fox Plaza Dr., Memphis, TN
901-360-1963
www.leonardsbarbecue.com
5. **Abe's Bar-B-Que:** 616 N. State St., Clarksdale, MS
662-624-9947
www.abesbbq.com

South

6. Interstate Bar-B-Que:
2265 S. Third St., Memphis, TN
901-775-2304
Second location: 150 W. Stateline
Rd., Southaven, MS
662-393-5699
www.interstatebarbecue.com

Also

Van's Pig Stand: 717 E. Highland
St., Shawnee, OK
405-273-8704
See www.pigstands.com for
additional locations.

GRACELAND

The biggest attraction in Memphis, and the most visited home in America after the White House, Graceland is a destination for pilgrims from around the world. Elvis fans come to commune with the King of Rock and Roll in the place he bought when he got rich and famous . . . and the place where he died and is buried. Graceland is an exuberant home, full of the E-man's artifacts and rich with his over-the-top personality. Tours include a viewing of his grave in the Meditation Garden, a walk past the pink Cadillac he bought for his mother (even though she didn't drive), and, of course, a visit to the fur-covered Jungle Room.

Graceland: 3734 Elvis Presley
Blvd., Memphis, TN
800-238-2000 or
901-332-3322
www.elvis.com/graceland

NATIONAL BESTS

BARBECUE RIBS

Ribs are the ultimate finger food — or, more accurately, fist food, because a big bone loaded with meat requires a seriously sturdy grip. Utensils are irrelevant; stacks of napkins are essential. The first Rule of Rib is roll up your sleeves; its corollary, avoid wearing silk, suede, or any other fabric you don't want sauce, spice, or glistening pork juice to decorate. While some cities are famous as rib meccas — Memphis, Chicago, and St. Louis come to mind — many of the nation's great ribberies are in unexpected places and off the beaten path.

Memphis has the messiest ribs of all. Known as wet ribs, the beauties dished out at the **Cozy Corner** are laden with meat that squirts succulence when bitten, and they are glazed with a drippy red sauce that is a little sweet and a lot peppery and so delicious that you will grab a spongy white bun to mop the last of it from the plate. At the eastern edge of the city, the **Germantown Commissary** serves slabs that are less wet because the sauce bakes into the meat, infusing the hickory-scented pork with a kaleidoscopic shot of spice. And downtown at **Charles Vergo's Rendezvous**, the specialty is dry ribs, which are dry-rubbed and charcoal-broiled rather than pit-cooked. The result: Racks are sauce-free but enveloped in a sandy halo of shockingly intense, paprika-colored spice that sings wild harmony with the supertender meat.

The insanely spicy ribs at Charles Vergo's Rendezvous in Memphis are dry-rubbed and charcoal-broiled.

The South, where pork rules, is home to more than its fair share of the nation's top rib joints, foremost among them the vintage Hot Springs, Arkansas, roadhouse **McClard's**. This happy, always-crowded diner has been perfecting the art of barbecue since 1928, when a customer at the family's trailer park offered a recipe for sauce in lieu of payment of his bill. The sauce mixes with chopped pork deliriously well, but the supreme dish in the house — and one of the best plates of barbecue anywhere in the U.S.A. — is a rib and fry combo: a rack of meaty bones with crusty edges and succulent insides completely covered with a serving of honey-toned French fried potatoes. Eating such a meal is a chaotic task that demands nimble fingers and countless napkins. The process of picking up a few fries every time you heft a rib soon becomes an art unto itself, and the flavor of the moist, sweet meat close to the bone is simply beyond description. The sauce on the ribs will gradually set your tongue aglow, which is why McClard's cool, finely chopped

coleslaw is such a perfect side dish.

In Alabama, the most famous bone depot is **Dreamland** in Tuscaloosa (with offspring throughout the state), a monomaniacal restaurant where the entire menu is ribs, potato chips, and banana pudding, plus beer, tea, and soft drinks. Down in Mobile, the go-to place is the **Brick Pit** (see page 196 for pulled pork), where smoke-blackened ribs are so gentled by their long tenure in the pit that the lightest finger pressure causes pieces of meat to slide off the bone.

Devotees of **Tom's Place**, which was Boca Raton, Florida's premier barbecue shack for some thirty years, panicked when the old establishment on Federal Highway was shuttered a few years ago. But the family-run restaurant has been reborn in bigger quarters in West Palm Beach, still featuring a panoply of soul food, from collard greens to sweet potato pie, headlined by mighty, tangy-sauced St. Louis–style ribs. (St. Louis–style means bones with no gristle or membrane, just a succulent sheath of meat crusted with sauce.) Baby backs are also available — good and chewy — and if you have a hard time committing to a single entrée, "Tom's Feast" is a multitreat meal of ribs, pulled pork, and fried chicken, plus baby backs if desired.

No heart-of-Dixie roster is complete without a salute to **Harold's**, an Atlanta institution where long, lovely slabs are laden with an embarrassment of meat that has a sauce glaze the color of an autumn sunset. On the side come squares of gritty-textured cornbread and a small bowl of Brunswick stew loaded with shreds of pulled pork, corn kernels, and tomato.

South

Seductively sauced slabs at Harold's, an Atlanta institution

Although it is a stark building in a bedraggled neighborhood, Harold's is a welcoming place. Its wood-paneled walls are hung with earnest religious homilies, including this one above the door to the rear dining room: "God has time to listen if you have time to pray."

Most of Texas disses pig in favor of beef, but Houston has a couple of places where the spareribs are world-class. They're called "lean ribs" at **Goode Company Texas Bar-B-Q**, and a lingering spell over smoldering green wood inundates the pork fibers with a deliriously smoky aura. On the side at Goode Co.: how about thick slices of just-baked jalapeño cheese bread? Another Texas rib source not to be missed is in Elgin, a Hill Country town best known for beef sausage links (page 339) and oak-smoked brisket. At **Crosstown BBQ**, you'll also find beautiful ribs that are served unsauced, all the better to emphasize their crunchy crust and the juicy thick ribbons of meat within. Oklahoma is another big-beef state, but it is home to a necessary stop on any rib-rack quest: **Van's Pig Stand** in Shawnee.

Van's ribs are muscular, but the slightest tooth pressure releases cascades of sweet, piggy juice; their exterior is crusted with glaze; and Van's Curly-Q fries are a spuddy tangle that pairs perfectly with pork.

For anyone who intends to eat America's greatest ribs, the cities of the Midwest are essential stops on the tour. Chicago in particular has a thriving rib culture that the local eating community loves to rate and rank. For years the upscale steak house named **Carson's**, which has two branches in the city, has been the leader in baby backs. They are served as half slabs or foot-and-a-half-long whole slabs partnered with dark, sweet sauce that is slow-baked deep into them from the start. By the time they've basked in smoke long enough, the meat has absorbed the spiciness and sweetness of the sauce, and they are sensuously sticky, their meat threaded with come-hither wood-fire perfume, glistening with veins of lubricating fat. The ribs are so rich they demand an equally sumptuous companion, which Carson's supplies in the form of several four-star potato options: big bakers and twice-baked,

Yielding to pressure, ribs from Van's in Shawnee, OK, spurt porcine juices.

skins and French fries, and, best of all, au gratin potatoes that are not the least bit goopy but rather shawled with cheddar cheese and flecked with grated onions.

For rib eaters who love the act of worrying the last shreds of meat from the bone, Chicago's South Side is the place to go. We shan't cast aspersions on baby backs, which can be delicious and are as easy to eat as an Iowa pork chop, but we do believe that spareribs, at their best, are more satisfying. Yes, they can be difficult — too chewy, more bone than meat, or sometimes desiccated — but gnawing on great ones is an experience more soulful than that delivered by any other part of the pig. The original **Leon's** (since 1941) delivers spareribs that are big and brawny, dripping juice as soon as your teeth cut down below the crust. The pork is sweet and tender of spirit, infused with but not overwhelmed by the taste of smoke. The ribs are so nicely cooked that you can easily pull individual bones off the rack, providing yourself a dozen good mouthfuls of porcine paradise per bone. Some Leon's fans leave their ribs plain. We wouldn't want them without a generous application of sauce. Hot sauce, please (mild also is available). It teases from the meat nuances of flavor you otherwise might not know. In turn, the pork is a cushion that gives the heat of the sauce a pleasurable sting instead of a painful one. Leon's dishes out slabs and half slabs in cardboard boats, ribs at the bottom. On top of the ribs come a mess of crinkle-cut French fries, which by the time you open up the package have virtually meshed with the sauce to become a kind of starchy, greasy glaze.

The takeout window at Leon's in Chicago is sleek, stylish, and bulletproof.

South

On top of the fries is a sheet of wax paper, and on top of that two slices of clean, spongy white bread. You would not want this bread for any other meal, but as a salve between bouts with barbecue, it's the right stuff.

Rib tips are a low-cost menu staple of soul-food barbecues in many midwestern cities. They can be some trouble, demanding vigorous tooth-and-tongue work to get to their good parts. But the work is worth it, because tips are luxuriously laced with fat and therefore more flavorful and juicier than baby backs or even spareribs. (They are in fact the tips from spareribs.) At their best, as made by Mack Sevier of Chicago's **Uncle John's** (formerly of Barbara Ann's, page 226), they yield little nuggets of meat that are dizzyingly swirled with the potent flavors of hickory and oak smoke. Inevitable cartilaginous areas deliver tides of flavor when well sucked and gnawed. Mr. Sevier's sauce is fetching but in our opinion actually detracts from the extravagant porky goodness of the meat itself.

The late Arthur Bryant, "the King of Ribs," juggles orders.

Kansas City is famous for all kinds of barbecue — beef and mutton as well as pork. **Arthur Bryant's** is the best-known source; in fact the late Mr. Bryant once anointed himself "King of Ribs." These racks are extraordinarily juicy with crisp edges, and the wicked orange barbecue sauce is liquid dynamite. Sauce is hugely important at Bryant's, as at most barbecue parlors throughout the Midwest. Whereas Texans abjure it and eastern North Carolinians are at best suspicious of anything more than vinegar and peppers, sauce is what makes so many urban barbecue parlors so great. Not that they don't make beautiful meat; it's just that their meat tastes incomplete without sauce. Even brisket, a totally nonsauced meat in much of the Southwest, gets better when you add some of Arthur Bryant's magic potion. The late Mr. Bryant was in fact originally a Texan, and while his brisket is Hill Country delicious, it tends to be drier than its Lone Star forebears. Add that sauce, however, and you've got one of this nation's miracle foods. It is really good-looking sauce, nothing

like ketchupy interiors — slightly gritty, speckled with spices, and packed with enough paprika and cayenne pepper to kindle taste-buds brushfires. It's thick stuff; Mr. Bryant once told us that he frequently enjoyed it with no meat whatsoever, simply as a dip for slices of supermarket white bread. We'll take ours painted on his restaurant's excellent brisket, ribs, mutton, or hot links, thank you very much. (At today's Bryant's, tables are outfitted with two variants: sweet, and rich and spicy. We prefer the latter, but the former is no weak sister.)

Since eating ribs is an utterly informal affair, it makes sense that some of the most wonderful places to enjoy them are out in the country — way, way out. And a little wacky, too. Consider, for example, the self-proclaimed "9th Wonder of the World," **Curtis's Barbecue** of Putney, Vermont. Curtis Tuff's summer-only place isn't really a restaurant; it is more a picnic. Place your order at the window of one of the blue-painted schoolbuses that are

Smoldering ribs at Curtis's in Putney, VT, prove that great barbecue isn't limited to the South.

permanently anchored in the meadow. When you have paid and it is ready, you will be directed to a stack of cardboard cartons that are useful for toting the disposable plates full of food to a table. Dine al fresco, then toss your trash in a can and be on your way. Tuff's ribs are cooked so the meat pulls off in big, succulent mouthfuls that virtually burst with piggy flavor. We are especially fond of the house mascot, Isabel, whom we met when she was a little pink piglet. Isabel has become a gigantic sow whom Mr. Tuff refers to as "the boss," and who occasionally waddles from picnic table to picnic table, grunting for a handout. Pork ribs are her favorite.

BEST BARBECUE RIBS

1. **McClard's Bar-B-Q:** 505 Albert Pike Rd., Hot Springs, AR 501-623-9665 or 866-622-5293 www.mcclards.com
2. **Cozy Corner Restaurant:** 745 N. Parkway, Memphis, TN 901-527-9158
3. **Van's Pig Stand:** 717 E. Highland St., Shawnee, OK 405-273-8704 See www.pigstands.com for additional locations.
4. **Brick Pit:** 5456 Old Shell Rd., Mobile, AL 251-343-0001 www.brickpit.com
5. **Dreamland Bar-B-Que:** 5535 Fifteenth Ave. East, Tuscaloosa, AL 205-758-8135 www.dreamlandbbq.com
6. **Leon's Bar-B-Que:** 1158 W. 59th St., Chicago, IL 773-778-7828 Multiple locations.

7. **Uncle John's BBQ:** 337 E. 69th St., Chicago, IL 773-892-1233 Takeout only.
8. **Arthur Bryant's BBQ:** 1727 Brooklyn Ave., Kansas City, MO 816-231-1123 See www.arthurbryantsbbq.com for additional locations.
9. **Carson's:** 612 N. Wells St., Chicago, IL 312-280-9200 Second location: 200 N. Waukegan Rd., Deerfield, IL 847-374-8500
10. **Crosstown BBQ:** 202 S. Avenue C, Elgin, TX 512-281-5994
11. **Germantown Commissary:** 2290 S. Germantown, Germantown, TN 901-754-5540
12. **Goode Co. Texas Bar-B-Q:** 5109 Kirby Dr., Houston, TX 713-522-2530 See www.goodecompany.com for additional locations.
13. **Harold's Barbecue:** 171 McDonough Blvd. SE, Atlanta, GA 404-627-9268
14. **Curtis's Barbecue:** Route 5, Putney, VT 802-387-5474 Summers only.
15. **Tom's Place:** 1225 Palm Beach Lakes Blvd., West Palm Beach, FL 561-832-8774 www.tomsplaceforribs.com
16. **Charles Vergo's Rendezvous:** 52 S. Second St., Memphis, TN 901-523-2746 www.hogsfly.com

South

SCHWAB'S

Schwab's is a time-burnished dry goods store in Memphis that smells great: a blend of cotton fabrics, simple soaps, inexpensive perfume, and worn wood fixtures. Because of its age, it attracts tourists who come to marvel at its creaking floor and its immense inventory of odd, outdated merchandise. But a good number of customers are still Memphians who trust the old family business just as their fathers and grandfathers did. They come for size 74 overalls or trolley garters, Lover's Moon perfume, Big Gals knee-length panties, gents' stingy-brim porkpie hats, plumbing supplies, walking sticks, and coffee-table Bibles with squishy white leatherette binding. The store motto is "If you can't find it at Schwab's, you're better off without it."

Abraham Schwab founded the store in 1876, and it was during the reign of his three sons in the 1920s that the inventory expanded to include voodoo talismans. "We used to sell incense to the fish joints around here that stunk," Mr. Schwab (third generation) told us many years ago. "They said, 'Don't you have oil to go with the incense?' So my uncle sent to Chicago for scented oils. He didn't have any idea what they were used for — he just thought to make a place smell nice, to take the fish odor away. Ever since then we have sold incense, oils, and candles for casting and removing spells."

Schwab delighted in showing us the D.U.M.E. candle, which is black wax inside a tall-boy glass cylinder with blank lines on the outside where you can write the names of people you hate. "This is the candle of last resort," he explained, chuckling. "D.U.M.E. means 'Death unto My Enemies.' It's my bestseller." Other practical candles and room sprays sold at Schwab's include Law Stay Away, Pay Me Now!, I Can You Can't, and the ever-popular Come to Me.

Schwab's: 163 Beale St., Memphis, TN 901-523-9782

BARBECUE SLAW
North Carolina

Coleslaw is an essential part of nearly every North Carolina barbecue meal, and it varies dramatically in character — sweet or tangy, fine or coarse, hot or not. Mustard slaw, made with dry and prepared mustard as well as mayonnaise, is the most distinctively Carolinian variant, because it is reminiscent of the hallowed barbecue at the dearly departed Bob Melton's place in Rocky Mount. Melton died in 1958, but his restaurant lived on long enough for us to eat there when we first hit the road and thereby develop both respect and craving for eastern North Carolina's unique style of whole-hog barbecue. We fell in love with mustard slaw at Melton's, and we were thrilled to discover that it is part of every plate at **Bill Spoon's** in

The slaw at Parker's in Wilson, NC, has a kiss of sweet and a mustardy bite.

Charlotte. The late Mr. Spoon learned the ways of the pit from John Skinner, who was at one time employed by Bob Melton, and those ways, slaw included, now are upheld by Bill's grandson, Steve.

Bright yellow mustard slaw is not ubiquitous in eastern North Carolina, where you'll find as many that use only mayonnaise; nor is it exclusive — we've had something similar served, as "poolroom slaw," in Alabama. But at Bill Spoon's you can see why it's become part of local food lore. The sharply seasoned heap of crisp, finely chopped cabbage offers a counterweight to soft and exquisitely smoky pork, and it is a welcome participant at a perfect party of barbecue, Brunswick stew, and crisp, tubular hushpuppies.

The slaw at **Parker's** in Wilson, one of the biggest pork parlors in the state, has a sunny hue like mustard slaw and does, it seems, have a bit of a mustard bite. But it is sweeter and lighter, chopped so fine that it's almost creamy. It's a good balance for the crunchy nature of Parker's other signature side dishes, hushpuppies and

long, crisp-edged sticks of cornbread.

As far as we've been able to determine, there aren't clear regional boundaries between fine-cut and coarse-cut or sweet and tart. In general, the slaw will be hotter in the area around Lexington and creamier to the east, where the pork tends to sing a higher note on the pepper scale. But most barbecuists have their own way. There is no way quite as distinctive as that of the venerable **Stamey's** of Greensboro. Stamey's pork is tradition itself — finely chopped, with a slight vinegar-pepper aura — and the hushpuppies are somewhat eccentric, shaped like shrimp, but the coleslaw is atomic. On a sandwich in a bun or occupying one third of a partitioned heavy cardboard plate, it has a hot-sauce zing that adds brilliant panache to the classic North Carolina feast.

The freshest coleslaw we've ever had is at **Bunn's**, a charming little place in a former Windsor gas station, where we dined at the counter while looking out the window at a truck loaded with cabbages that had just pulled up to supply the kitchen. The slaw really did taste like it had been cut and mixed just moments before being plated with pulled pork and lovely squares of thin cornbread with a serious chew.

The strangest coleslaw in the state is that served at **R.O.'s** in Gastonia. In fact, it stretches the definition of slaw. Yes, it is made from cabbage, and yes, it accompanies plates of minced pork and hushpuppies and is packed into barbecue sandwiches. But it is also an ingredient to use in meat loaf or as a sauce for cocktail shrimp, a hamburger condiment, and

A converted gas station, Bunn's is an essential pit stop for fresh slaw.

a dip for chips or crudités, as well as something so intriguingly spicy that when we nab a container (available in local markets or by mail), we sometimes just put it into a saucer and mop it up with a soft roll. The recipe dates back to the 1940s, when Robert Osy Black opened his restaurant and added his wife Pearl's specialty condiment to the menu. Bearing little resemblance to the crunchy green stuff most people think of as coleslaw, it is dark red, sweet with pickle juice, and a little bit peppery, with a consistency more like that of thick soup than salad. Roadfood explorers Chris Ayers and Amy Briesch, who pointed us to R.O.'s, noted also that the restaurant's beverage repertoire includes house-made Cherry-Lemon Sun Drop, which tastes to us like a cross between Mountain Dew and Hawaiian Punch. Note also that R.O.'s offers carhop service, with meals served at your vehicle's window.

5 SUPERB SLAWS

1. **Bunn's Barbecue:** 127 N. King St., Windsor, NC
   252-794-2274

2. **Bill Spoon's Barbecue:** 5524 South Blvd., Charlotte, NC
   704-525-8865
3. **Stamey's:** 2206 High Point Rd., Greensboro, NC
   336-299-9888
   Second location: 2812 Battleground Ave. (U.S. Route 220 North), Greensboro, NC
   336-288-9275
   www.stameys.com
4. **R.O.'s Barbecue:** 1318 Gaston Ave., Gastonia, NC
   704-866-8143
   www.rosbbq.com/whole.htm
5. **Parker's Barbecue:** 2514 U.S. Highway 301 South, Wilson, NC
   252-237-0972

BARBECUE SPAGHETTI
Memphis, Tennessee

Why not? If you've got some delicious barbecue sauce, why not use it in lieu of ordinary tomato sauce to dress your hot noodles? It should come as no surprise that the place where this practice is most common is Memphis, Tennessee, home also to barbecue pizza and barbecue salad, not to mention some pretty fair barbecued pork. At several of the city's top smoke shacks, you'll find spaghetti listed alongside whatever meats get barbecued. At **A&R Bar-B-Que**, where the kitchen offers ribs both dry (crusted with spice mix) and wet (glazed with sauce), barbecue spaghetti is part of an extensive repertoire that goes way beyond ribs: pulled pork, catfish, hot tamales, and — a dish we've seen nowhere else other than state fairs in

Use your noodle: barbecue spaghetti at the Cozy Corner in Memphis.

The pasta part of the equation is both a vehicle to get sauce to mouth and a soft-flavored carbo contrast for especially aggressive sauce. In other words, the barbecue spaghetti at the **Cozy Corner** is terrific! The sauce at this little gem of a smoke pit is so vivid that it needs balance. You can dunk white bread in it; nothing wrong with that. Pork is a great medium, of course, and coleslaw included with pork in the pig sandwich offers contrasting crunch, but there is no canvas quite as plain and perfect as cooked-soft noodles to accentuate the pepper-hot, slightly sweet, one-two punch of Cozy Corner sauce. It is thick enough to cling well to the spaghetti, making every forkful a mighty mouthful.

the Midwest — meatballs on sticks. The sauce is kaleidoscopically spiced and laced with shreds of smoky meat — frankly, so good that it would be praiseworthy if it was served on slices of shirt cardboard.

CHAMPION'S PHARMACY

Are you in need of Black Stallion tabs, an herbal alternative to Viagra? Cat's Claw Capsules to treat gout? Hot Flash Tablets, Father John Cold Medicine, or Dr. Pure's Golden Metal Discover? Go to Champion's Pharmacy, just up the road from Graceland, and you can get the cures as well as pharmacological advice from Dr. Charles A. Champion himself, a compounding pharmacist with over half a century of experience. Dr. Champion has something for every complaint, real or imagined, from FDA-approved drugs to vintage herbal elixers. "The young pharmacists do not know about the old remedies," he told us.

Many of the products sold at the store are available by mail-order, and the website includes "Grandma's old-fashioned remedies" for ailments ranging from poison ivy to varicose veins, but there is no substitute for visiting in person. Dr. Champion and his pharmacist daughter, Carol, give the kind of personal attention that scarcely exists in modern drugstores. Furthermore, upon entering the store, each customer trips a switch that starts a scratchy recording of Dr. Champion exalting some particular cure with all the enthusiasm of a carnival barker.

Champion's Pharmacy: 2369 Elvis Presley Blvd., Memphis, TN 901-948-6622 www.theherbalman.com

A&R Bar-B-Que: 1802 Elvis
  Presley Blvd., Memphis, TN
  901-774-7444
  See www.aandrbbq.com for
  additional locations.
Cozy Corner Restaurant: 745
  N. Parkway, Memphis, TN
  901-527-9158

BISCUITS
Throughout the South

Carol Fay Ellison has been mixing
up buttermilk biscuits at Nashville's
Loveless Cafe for thirty years.

Owen Webb's Snack Shack northwest of Augusta, Georgia, deserves extremely honorable mention for chili dogs and slaw burgers, but its biscuit is the blue-ribbon champ. Warm from the oven, with a knobby golden surface that offers muted resistance before yielding to offer up fluffy insides, this just might be the definitive biscuit of the South. Eating it plain is a pure sensation; it is plush enough to make even butter seem superficial, but such sandwiched ingredients as sausage, steak, egg, and cheese are all at home. The photocopied menu that you receive with a slip of paper bearing your order number cautions that the biscuits are available only early, starting at 9 a.m., until they are gone, which can be as soon as 11.

The best destiny for a biscuit from **Mamie's Kitchen Biscuits** in Conyers is to be pulled into two circular, gold-topped halves so it can sandwich a slice or two of country ham grilled until its rim of fat becomes translucent amber and the brick-red surface starts to turn crisp. It is a stunning harmony of two dramatically disparate ingredients: complex, zesty cured country ham and a biscuit eager to absorb the ham's savory drippings. Mamie's proprietor, Jack Howard, explained why his biscuits are so good: "We don't roll them with a rolling pin; we don't cut them with a can; we don't make them from a recipe." He lifted a hot one off its paper plate and cupped it in one hand, using a deft twist of his other hand to separate its wavy top and raise it like a Tiffany jeweler showing what's inside a ring box. A buttermilk-scented cloud of steam wafted up. "This is what you call a scratch biscuit," he continued. "It is made from nothing but White Lily flour, buttermilk, and lard. *Pure, refined* lard," he emphasized.

Biscuits reign at the **Sunrise Biscuit Kitchen** of Chapel Hill, North Carolina, where everything is delivered out the drive-through window because there are no seats, indoors or out. You can have a classic egg-bacon-cheese combo, streak o' lean (bacon on steroids), or an exemplary ham biscuit. The star of the show, we think, is a chicken biscuit, which is altogether different. Crisp-fried chicken, lacking the cured-meat drama of bacon or ham, offers the soulful opulence of meat that fairly drips with the savor of fat, the bird encased in a golden crust so luscious that it seems quite literally to melt in the mouth.

Chef Robert Stehling of Charleston's **Hominy Grill** attributes the goodness of his biscuits to the South's low-gluten red winter wheat, which begets fluffiness. The large mile-highs he serves are shockingly lightweight, slightly crisp on the top and bottom, fine and fleecy inside. Made with butter, vegetable shortening, and enough lard to add intemperate savor, they make breakfast meat almost irrelevant. However, Hominy Grill's housemade sausage begs to be sandwiched in one, and there are few meals more overwhelmingly hedonistic than the Big Nasty — a biscuit cut in half and loaded with a fried chicken cutlet, sausage gravy, and cheddar cheese.

For a classic supper (or lunch or breakfast) of country ham and/or fried chicken, the **Loveless Cafe** has been a Nashville destination for more than half a century. The menu's constant has always been little biscuits. The recipe for the ones you eat today is essentially the same as that originally used by Annie Loveless back in the 1950s, passed along to the next owners, Cordell and Stella Maynard, then to Donna McCabe, whose chief biscuit maker, Carol Fay Ellison, has been mixing, rolling, and cutting them every day for some thirty years. They are small, steamy biscuits with a quiet buttermilk tang, and they always come to the table warm (the basket is replenished as needed throughout the meal). To adorn them, in addition to cream gravy, redeye gravy, sorghum, and honey, the kitchen provides beakers of its own preserves — sunny-flavored peach and seriously indigo blackberry. A spoonful of these stunning preserves on a warm biscuit is one of the great flavors in all Tennessee, and the ideal counterbalance for a serving of powerhouse country ham.

As their name suggests, cat head biscuits are big and rugged-textured on the outside, no matter how smooth within. At the breakfast buffet of the **Longstreet Cafe** in Gainesville, Georgia, you can get a nice-sized cat enclosing country ham, sausage, fried chicken, or a ten-

Rugged country ham and fluffy biscuit: the classic southern breakfast combo

South

Chicken meets biscuit in loving union at the Sunrise Biscuit Kitchen in Chapel Hill, NC.

derloin. Best of all, for the sum of 93 cents, is the plain and pure "butter biscuit." In the mountains of western North Carolina, **Tomato Jam** serves tawny whole-grain cat head biscuits either plain or topped with smooth milk gravy or pork sausage gravy (or even vegan sausage gravy!). Or you can buy a Tomato Jam cat plain, which means hot enough from the oven to allow sweet, fruity tomato jam to swirl into the biscuit's fluff along with rivers of melting butter.

Finally, here's a must-eat biscuit that is pure Tarheel but happens to be in Portland, Oregon. As the name of the place suggests, **Pine State** makes biscuits like they do in North Carolina, the home of proprietors Kevin Atchley, Brian Snyder, and Walt Alexander. Making their reputation at a stand in the Portland Farmers Market, these guys developed such a following that the wait in line to get one of their biscuits could be longer than a half-hour. In 2008 they finally opened a breakfast/lunch cafe for sit-down biscuit indulgence. While the cream-top biscuits themselves are superior — oven-hot, fluffy-centered, just a little bit tangy — the Pine State lure is all the stuff you can get inside. That can be as familiar as egg and cheese, pimento cheese, or apple butter, or as intriguing as the combo known as the McIsley, which includes fried chicken, sweet pickles, mustard, and honey. The grand poobah of biscuits is the Reggie Deluxe: fried chicken, smoky bacon, an egg, cheddar cheese, and gravy. Incredibly, this can be picked up and eaten like an ordinary sandwich.

THE MAGNIFICENT 7 BEST BISCUITS

1. **Owen Webb's Snack Shack:** 627 Lee St., Jefferson, GA
   706-367-9066
2. **Mamie's Kitchen Biscuits:** 1295 N. Main St. NW, Conyers, GA
   770-922-0131
   Other locations in Georgia
3. **Hominy Grill:** 207 Rutledge Ave., Charleston, SC
   843-937-0930
   www.hominygrill.com
4. **Longstreet Cafe:** 1043 Riverside Terrace, Gainesville, GA
   770-287-0820
   www.longstreetcafe.com
5. **Tomato Jam Cafe:** 379 Biltmore Ave., Asheville, NC
   828-253-0570
   www.tomatojamcafe.com
6. **Loveless Cafe:** 8400 Highway 100, Nashville, TN
   615-646-9700
   www.lovelesscafe.com
7. **Sunrise Biscuit Kitchen:** 1305 E. Franklin, Chapel Hill, NC
   919-933-1324

Also

Pine State Biscuits: 3640 S.E. Belmont St., Portland, OR 503-236-3346 www.pinestatebiscuits.com

BOARDINGHOUSE MEAL
Old South

We are not talking about a big salad bar or all-you-can-eat buffet here. "Boardinghouse meal" means that everything is set out on the dining table on platters and in bowls. Friends, family, and strangers reach, pass, and grab for what they want. It is vital to come to such a meal with a big appetite; it would be wrong to practice moderation.

It was in 1915 at the late Mendenhall Hotel in Mendenhall, Mississippi, that a new twist was added to the old-time boardinghouse feeding formula: revolving tables. About a dozen chairs are arrayed at the circumference of a round table. In the middle is a big lazy Susan, on which are marshaled bowls and platters of everything the kitchen has cooked that day. Such service not only makes it easy to get to what you want without too rude an exercise of boardinghouse reach; it encourages social niceties such as braking the table if it is spinning too fast for an elderly neighbor to help herself to what she wants or taking the initiative to spin the rutabagas toward a diner who has eaten all the ones on his plate.

The Mendenhall closed about a dozen years ago, but revolving tables are still the modus operandi at the Dinner Bell in McComb. For $11 ($12 Friday and Saturday, $13 Sunday), you maintain possession of your seat and are welcome to keep the lazy Susan spinning for as long as you are hungry. It's not just the gimmick that makes dining here essential. The food, made by cooks who have been in this kitchen their whole working lives, is the embodiment of southern comfort, from such familiar items as chicken and dumplings and sweet potato casserole to the house specialty, fried eggplant.

At the **Smith House** in Dahlonega, Georgia, the communal tables are crowded with fried chicken, baked ham, and roast beef plus a dozen vegetables, including such specialties as chestnut soufflé, finely chopped collard greens, and fried okra with see-through-thin crust. Plus oven-warm yeast rolls and tender cornbread muffins. Also up in the north Georgia hills you will find the **Dillard House**, where the one thing they never run

The Dinner Bell in McComb, MS, where lazy Susans make boardinghouse reach unnecessary

South

out of is fried chicken. Country ham, prime rib, and barbecue chicken are the other entrées, almost always available. But it's the ever-changing roster of vegetables that keeps us going back. You never know exactly what they will be at any point in the meal, since bowls of new ones take the place of those that are eaten up, but we guarantee that these are not spartan health-food veggies. They are lavish, ultra-flavored, stars-and-bars Dixie vegetables such as acorn squash soufflé loaded with coconut and raisins, creamy vanilla-scented yams streaked with mini marshmallows, and limp-leaf collard greens pungent with the smack of a salty ham bone. The one dessert that must be eaten is Georgia peach cobbler.

At one point in its recent history, **Miss Mary Bobo's Boarding House** was available only to people who toured the Jack Daniel's distillery in Lynchburg, Tennessee. It has since gone public and is far from the modest boardinghouse Mary Bobo opened in 1908 in what had been the Salmon Hotel. Now run by Lynne Tolley, a great-grandniece of Jack Daniel himself, it has become a major mid-Tennessee attraction, so popular that reservations need to be made weeks, sometimes months, in advance. Still, once you find yourself waiting on the porch of the old columned mansion, you are transported to a charming and hospitable dining experience that is probably much the same as it was a hundred years ago. There is no telling what you'll get to eat, because it is different every day. Fried chicken is a likely entrée, or maybe chicken pie. Vegetables are de-termined by what is fresh. Count on tomato relish in tomato season and fresh corn by midsummer. And count also on macaroni and cheese, which belongs on the saints' table, served in the cooking bowl so that the top center is chewy and you have to scrape to get the crisp edges into the mix with the soupier, cheesier middle. One thing you can be sure of is great dessert, such as Tipsy Bread Pudding, so named because it is dabbed with a high-proof cloud of Jack Daniel's–enhanced whipped cream.

BEST BOARDINGHOUSE BIG FEEDS

1. **Dinner Bell:** 229 Fifth Ave., McComb, MS
   601-684-4883
   www.thedinnerbell.net
2. **Miss Mary Bobo's Boarding House:** 295 Main St., Lynchburg, TN
   931-759-7394
   Please do not call between 11 a.m. and 2 p.m., when lunch is served.
3. **Smith House:** 84 S. Chestatee St., Dahlonega, GA
   706-867-7000
   www.smithhouse.com
4. **Dillard House:** 1158 Franklin St., Dillard, GA
   800-541-0671 or 706-746-5348
   www.dillardhouse.com

BOILED PEANUTS
Dixie Highways

Available from spring to late autumn, sold at roadside stands throughout the Carolinas and much of the Deep South, the boiled peanut is a forceful reminder that peanuts are in fact not nuts but legumes. Always eaten warm, usually while you are standing up or in the car with an open window out of which shells can be tossed, they do not crack. After several hours in boiling salted water (preferably over a fire), the shell peels away from the softened green peanut inside, which has fairly blossomed with fresh-dug flavor. While vendors sell Cajun-flavored and barbecue-flavored boiled peanuts, we highly recommend that the novice start with plain ones. For most people who know only roasted peanuts, that first taste is puzzling, but it is easy to become so addicted that you, too, will one day be dropping a handful into your bottle of RC Cola for a true country cocktail.

If you don't stop for boiled peanuts, you've missed one of the South's great food finds.

On occasion you will find boiled peanuts served as freebies in a bar or restaurant, but the right and proper place to buy and eat them is by the side of the road, preferably from a shack or open-air stand that cooks them on the spot. (Freshness is a top priority; old, cold ones are unacceptable.) **Hardy Farms**, which calls its homegrown goobers "the country caviar," has several locations in and around south-central Georgia that are open from summer into autumn, and Hardy will mail its product if you are willing to foot the bill for second-day delivery. Available varieties include Georgia jumbos, hot and spicy jumbos, fresh green peanuts ready to boil, and boiled peanut pouches that supposedly have an unopened shelf life of three years.

Carolina Cider Company in South Carolina's Lowcountry has a nice mail-order catalog of pickles,

sauces, green tomato relish, benne wafers, pecans, and stone-ground grits, but the best reason for coming to one of the two branches of the store, other than to drink fresh-pressed peach cider, is to eat boiled peanuts; and they do not sell them by mail. Just-boiled and still hot is the only way you'll get them here, either regular or Cajun-spiced. Of special note are rocking chairs on the front porch — an ideal location for sipping and snacking.

PEANUT STOPS

Hardy Farms Peanuts:
341 Eastman Rd. (Route 2), Hawkinsville, GA
888-368-NUTS or 478-783-3044
Check www.hardyfarmspeanuts.com for the location of peanut stands.

Carolina Cider Company:
81 Charleston Highway, Yemassee, SC
843-846-1899
Second location: 1398 Kings Highway, Pocataligo, SC
843-726-4477
www.carolinaciderco.com

South

BOUDIN SAUSAGE
Cajun Louisiana

Boudin sausage is a Cajun cook's call to glory, so intense a passion among southern Louisianians that it has inspired www.boudinlink.com, a website entirely devoted to rating butchers who make it. The basic formula is simple — rice, pork, and spices packed into a natural casing — but the adventurous eater will find infinite differences among butchers' links. While andouille sausage tends to get more glory from some Cajun food fans for its high spice quotient, boudin's charms are about subtlety. Is the pork mashed smooth or chopped rugged? Is the texture of the meat complemented by bits of green onion? Do the individual pieces of rice retain their granular integrity? Is the casing easily breakable, or does it have too much give? Is the sausage dry or fatty, hot or mild, plump or skinny? Is it bright red with paprika or nearly black from an infusion of blood (boudin noir)?

Waiting for the first bite, three golden-fried boudin balls

Boudin is common in butcher shops, gas stations, and small groceries but rare in restaurants. Our longtime favorite is **Boudin King** in Jennings, which has declared itself the Boudin Capital of the World. The title is owed in no small part to the late Ellis Cormier, known as the Boudin King of swamp country fairs and food festivals, who started this modest drive-in business in 1975. The sausages are sold in large links, mild or spicy, for eating at the restaurant or taking home. Caution: Even the mild boudin packs a punch; spicy is sinus-draining. Either kind is porky, powerful food, best enjoyed in the company of such other good menu items as smoky gumbo, crisp-fried catfish, and fried crawfish, as well as freshly made hogshead cheese.

The moist innards of a boudin ball from Bourque's Supermarket

Jerry Lee's Kwik Stop is a small convenience store that makes the best boudin in Baton Rouge. Each link is a long fellow with little bits of onion and a rumble of spices punctuating rice and coarse-ground pork that is succulent but not greasy, all packed into a thick, tight skin that is a joy to sever. Jerry Lee's has no place to eat. It is not uncommon to see people standing by their cars in the parking lot, unwrapping the sausage, and eating it right there.

Most boudin devotees eat the link and nothing but the link, but you have not lived until you have sunk your teeth into a boudin ball made at **Bourque's Supermarket** in Port Barre. The small sphere is made of all the elements of sausage but battered and fried rather than packed into casing. Its surface has a crunch so forthright that it is a shock when your teeth crack through the skin and plunge into the soft sausage mash within. Audibly moist, unbearably savory, creamy-flavored at first but with a superspicy afterburn, each ball is two big bites. Being a grocery store rather than a restaurant, Bourque's sells most of its boudin balls to take home and reheat, but you can buy them warm at the butcher's counter in back and devour a half-dozen while shopping in this Cajun food wonderland.

Browsing along the aisles munching warm boudin balls, we were reminded that a grocery store can be as vivid a reflection of local taste as a restaurant, especially in this part of Louisiana. Shelves hold store-made roux, tasso ham, bags of cracklin's, giant jars of hog lard, and plenty of chicory coffee. The butcher's case includes such awesome ickies as chicken hearts, hog jowls, a variety of tripe, and one especially fearsome-looking heap of animal protein labeled "beef bouille." We asked the butcher what it was. "Are you sure you want to know?" He grinned at us. We gulped and nodded. "Oh, it's not really that bad," he said. "It's liver, kidney, sweetbreads, and hearts. For when you make your sausage."

BEST BOUDIN

1. **Jerry Lee's Kwik Stop:** 12181 Greenwell Springs Rd., Baton Rouge, LA
225-272-0739
2. **Boudin King:** 906 W. Division St., Jennings, LA
337-824-6593
3. **Bourque's Supermarket:** 581 Saizan Ave., Port Barre, LA
337-585-6261
www.bourquespecialties.com

BRUNSWICK STEW
Georgia and North Carolina

Virginia, North Carolina, and Georgia all claim to be the birthplace of Brunswick stew, which traditionally is a hunter's gallimaufry of whatever critters could be caught along with

A salubrious mélange of barbecued pork and vegetables, Harold's Brunswick stew in Atlanta tempts the spoon.

whatever vegetables were available at the time. We've never (knowingly) had one made with squirrel. In modern times shredded barbecued pork tends to be the meat of choice, sometimes accompanied by barbecued chicken, the pit-cooked meats adding strong smoky character. Tomatoes are always part of the mix; lima beans and corn kernels are common. **Fox Bros. Bar-B-Q** in Atlanta sells an iconoclastic appetizer of Tater Tots smothered with Brunswick stew and melted cheese, which seems like the kind of thing we'd like to have at dawn after an all-night binge. But the best classic B-stew in town is that served at the respected barbecue parlor called **Harold's**. As a meal unto itself or as the companion to ribs or pulled pork, Harold's stew is authoritative. Fork-thick with a tangle of meat, it has vegetable sweetness that is quietly accentuated by a distant vinegar bite. Grab a square of Harold's cornbread to crumble on top.

Twice a year in Chapel Hill, North Carolina, there's a grand opportunity to have Brunswick stew cooked the old-fashioned way — over a fire outdoors in big bubbling caldrons. It's part of the **Mount Carmel Baptist Church**'s barbecue fund-raiser, held in May and October.

IMPORTANT BRUNSWICK STEWS

1. **Harold's Barbecue:** 171 McDonough Blvd. SE, Atlanta, GA 404-627-9268
2. **Fox Bros. Bar-B-Q:** 1238 Dekalb Ave., Atlanta, GA 404-577-4030 www.foxbrosbbq.com

Also
Mount Carmel Baptist Church: 2016 Mount Carmel Church Rd., Chapel Hill, NC 919-933-8565 www.mount-carmel-baptist.org May and October barbecues; call for dates.

BURGOO
Western Kentucky

Kentucky food lore says burgoo traditionally was made from whatever small animals a hunter could catch, and that it got its name when a Civil War cook with a speech impediment tried to say *bird stew*. Who knows? The fact is that if you come to western Kentucky, burgoo is essential any time of year . . . but especially when there's a brisk nip in the air or when it's Derby Day in Louisville, where burgoo is as much a part of culinary tradition as the mint julep. Served in all the local barbecue parlors, burgoo is a thick vegetable soup/stew anchored by pork and chicken and the local's favorite pit-cooked meat,

The best place to savor spicy, meaty Kentucky burgoo is George's in Owensboro.

mutton (page 182). It is stick-to-the-ribs satisfying, and it packs the eye-widening spice onslaught of Creole gumbo. The best place to savor it is the modest booth-and-table lunchroom called **George's**, located in Owensboro, a northwest Kentucky city just across the Ohio River from Indiana. Owensboro may or may not be the barbecue capital of the world that it claims to be, but it is without a doubt the burgoo capital.

Many of the grand dining rooms around Louisville offer burgoo, especially at Derby time, but we are happy to recommend having it any time of year at a four-outlet city chain known as **Mark's Feed Store**. Available by the cup or bowl, and especially right beside a barbecue sandwich — perhaps Mark's "world's largest bar-b-q sandwich," built around a pound of pork — this burgoo, loaded with meat and vegetables in a thick hot-pepper stock, is almost shockingly aromatic, so fine to sniff that it risks eclipsing the good red-sauced Q.

2 BURGOOS

George's Bar-B-Q: 1362 E. 4th St., Owensboro, KY 270-926-9276

Mark's Feed Store: 11422 Shelbyville Rd., Louisville, KY 502-244-0140 See www.marksfeedstore.com for additional locations.

CATFISH
South and Plains

South

Josie Middendorf opened **Middendorf's** in 1934 and created the dish that has become its trademark. "Catfish is now popular and trendy," said

MINT JULEP

Mint julep is the official drink of Kentucky Derby Day, during which the crowd consumes more than 100,000 of them. While it is a virtual necessity for watching the race and while Churchill Downs is the right and proper place to drink one, at any other time of year we recommend a visit to the Old Seelbach Bar, which has been around for over one hundred years and has been restored to its Victorian glory. The Seelbach has a mind-boggling collection of rare and pricey bourbons, and serves its juleps in a shiny metal cup so icy that you will leave fingerprints in the frost on the side when you hoist it and try to get your lips to the cup's rim through a jungle of mint leaves. While many bars and restaurants make theirs from an insipid mix (just add bourbon and ice, or in some cases simply ice; the bourbon's already mixed in), the Seelbach concocts its juleps from scratch: muddled mint, sugar, and good bourbon. It is a truly intoxicating taste of Kentucky.

Old Seelbach Bar: in the Seelbach Hilton Hotel, 500 Fourth St., Louisville, KY 502-585-3200 www.seelbachhilton.com

Middendorf's in Manchac, LA, elevates the lowly catfish to greatness.

Joey Lamonte, who married Josie's granddaughter, Sue. "Back then, you didn't want to talk about it. Trout was the premium catch. Catfish was a low, lowly food. She didn't even call it catfish on the menu. It was 'the Middendorf Special.' They ate it when they came down from Hammond or up from New Orleans to party in Manchac." The special looks nothing like the more familiar whole catfish, or even a standard-sized catfish fillet. Cut into ultra-thin strips, breaded in cornmeal, and fried, it is a tangle of crunchy curlicues and bows like pale gold bunting piled high on a plate. The ribbons of white meat are startlingly moist, their catfish flavor cushioned by the envelope of crust to become mudpuppy in a minor key. You eat thin catfish by hand, and once you pluck that first piece, there is no stopping until the plate is empty.

Whole catfish aren't nearly as easy to eat, but if you are looking for the most succulence per forkful, they are the only way to go, and the premier place to indulge in them is **Whitey's Fish Camp** in Orange Park, Flor-

ida. Whitey's serves all you can eat — whole fish (headless) encased in a cornmeal shell so you have to pick and pluck your way through the skeleton to get all the juice-dripping meat. Whitey's catfish are wild-caught, not farm-raised, meaning they are laden with flavor. It is possible to ask for very small ones, which experienced eaters devour in their entirety, bones along with flesh, leaving only tailfins and backbone.

In one way, the catfish fillets at **Bolton's Spicy Chicken & Fish** in Nashville are far easier to eat than the whole ones at a classic fish camp, but in another way, Bolton's cats are murder. While the fillets eliminate meat-extrication and bone-avoidance issues, they are the hot fish so beloved in Nashville (page 167), which means their sandy coats are liberally splotched with vivid red hot-hot-hot sauce. We venerate the trinity of moist white meat that drips sweet fresh-water flavor, sandy seasoned crust, and nuclear sauce, especially when sided by Bolton's goopy mac 'n' cheese and porky collard greens.

Hushpuppies and fried onions cozy up to fried cats at White River Fish Market in Tulsa, OK.

Two other shovelhead beacons, farther afield: **White River Fish Market** in Tulsa (Oklahoma is serious catfish country), where light gold fillets are accompanied by gorgeously crunchy spherical hushpuppies; and **Surfside Club** in Omaha, Nebraska, where, instead of hushpuppies, a basketful of hot corn fritters starts the meal, along with honey to squirt on them. Surfside's cats are whole and headless, encased in fragile crust, accompanied by steak fries, lemon wedge, and tartar sauce.

The divinity of chess pie lies in its simplicity.

NOT-TO-MISS CATFISH

1. **Middendorf's:** U.S. Highway 51 North, Pass Manchac, LA
   985-386-6666
   www.middendorfsrestaurant.com
2. **Bolton's Spicy Chicken & Fish:** 624 Main St., Nashville, TN
   615-254-8015
3. **Surfside Club:** 14445 N. River Dr., Omaha, NE
   402-451-9642
4. **White River Fish Market & Seafood Restaurant:** 1708 N. Sheridan, Tulsa, OK
   918-835-1910
   www.whiteriverfishmarket.com
5. **Whitey's Fish Camp:** 2032 County Road 220, Orange Park, FL
   904-269-4198
   www.whiteysfishcamp.com

CHESS PIE
Everywhere Southern

Chess pie is seldom spectacular. By nature it is basic, and by some accounts that is how it got its name. When asked what kind of pie was coming from the oven, a long-forgotten cook is supposed to have shrugged and said, "Nothing special. Jus' pie." Or maybe it's descended from English cheese pie. On the same family tree as such arcane Dixie desserts as Jefferson Davis pie and transparent pie, its bedrock recipe calls for eggs, a little cornmeal (not flour), butter, and sugar (mostly white, but usually brown, too), sometimes with a few drops of vanilla and often a teaspoon of vinegar added to give a twang. While cooks build fancier creations on this foundation — chocolate pecan chess pie, almond amaretto chess pie, for example — there is unimprovable magic in a pie that is so absolutely simple and completely satisfying. Meat-and-three restaurants (page 180) frequently have it on the menu.

Examine a picture-perfect slice as served at **Arnold's Country Kitchen** in Nashville. Atop a flaky crust is a thick ribbon of filling baked to the point that it has jelled together into a bright yellow curd, its top browned and a little bit chewy from its time in the oven. That toothsome top is why we are not fans of chess pie capped

South

Delectable lemon chess pie, fresh out of Sylvan Park's oven in Nashville

with whipped topping or meringue, both of which eclipse the good texture. The taste? Eggs plus butter plus sugar is a formula for sweet-tooth satisfaction that is baby-food primal, especially if you arrive early in the lunch hour and the pie is still a little warm.

Adding lemon to the formula is welcome gilt for this lily, for its tartness is a superb balance for the pie's sugar soul. At the **Once in a Blue Moon Bakery & Café** in Cary, North Carolina, the big dilemma is choosing between the tart-sweet perfection of lemon chess and the sweet-tart perfection of the bakery's Key lime pie.

Some of the tried-and-true sources for superb chess pie in the mid-South include the **Homemade Ice Cream and Pie Kitchen**, where you can have lemon chess, chocolate chess, or plain chess; the **Elite** of Jackson, Mississippi, where our friends Bruce Bilmes and Sue Boyle describe the lemon chess pie as tasting "almost like sweetened and lemoned butter in a flaky crust"; and **Sylvan Park** in Nashville, where the unadorned and unadulterated chess pie is so moist

you can hear it bubble when a fork plunges through it and the brown-top baked-sugar crust is as crisp as the top of a crème brûlée.

5 TOP CHESS PIES

1. **Arnold's Country Kitchen:** 605 Eighth Ave. South, Nashville, TN
615-256-4455
2. **Sylvan Park:** 4502 Murphy Rd., Nashville, TN
615-292-9275
3. **Homemade Ice Cream and Pie Kitchen:** 2525 Bardstown Rd., Louisville, KY
502-459-8184
See www.piekitchen.com for additional locations.
4. **Once in a Blue Moon Bakery & Café:** 115-G W. Chatham St., Cary, NC
919-319-6554
www.bluemoonbakery.com
5. **Elite Restaurant:** 141 E. Capitol St., Jackson, MS
601-352-5606

CHIPBURGER
Greeneville, Tennessee

Pittsburghers consider chipped ham their own, and with good reason (see the Slammer, page 103), but the chipburger of Greeneville, Tennessee, demands attention. Created in the late 1940s by Sonny Paxton at his Big Top eatery, it is a bun filled with pink petals of ham sliced so thin you can see through them. In a story written by regional food sage Fred Sauceman at GoTriCities.com, Mr. Paxton's son Keith (who opened the **Little Top**

Drive-Thru in 1986) recalls that his father jury-rigged a slicer using a fly-wheel and a washing-machine motor and honed the parts to cut the ham superthin. The result is a feathery sweetness with none of the mass of thick slices. Chipburgers come on buns, preferably with Swiss or American cheese (a cheese chipper), and the ham is also available in a club sandwich.

Little Top has a handful of seats, but most business is via the drive-through.

Little Top Drive-Thru: 507 N. Main St., Greeneville, TN 423-639-9800

CRAWFISH
Acadian Louisiana

Breaux Bridge is the crawfish capital of the nation, hosting an annual fais do-do the first weekend in May, when the good eats include crawfish-based jambalaya, étouffée, po boys, egg rolls, and enchiladas (www.bbcraw fest.com). **Poche's Market**, a humble plate-lunch convenience store we discovered while hunting andouille sausage (there's none better than here), boils up some 50 tons of craw-dads starting in the spring. While simply spiced and boiled is the best way to savor their buttery luxury, it's a special treat to sink your teeth into Poche's magnificent smoked tasso and crawfish boudin sausages, the flavors of ham and crawdad saturating rice inside the casing.

Looking for a truly authentic crawfish eating experience? That will be found to the max at **Guiding**

Star in New Iberia, where the tables are spread with newspapers in lieu of cloths to catch the inevitable debris from picking meat and sucking heads of crawfish infused with the flavor of Tabasco peppers. **D.I.'s**, an obscure roadhouse in Basile to which we were directed by Major George McNeil of the Sulphur, Louisiana, police department, is another real-deal destination where the crawfish come from the kitchen piled onto big round beer trays, and where the live Cajun music starts every night at 7.

We have a soft spot for Chef Lionel Robin, because many years ago, when we were new to the food of southern Louisiana, it was he who explained a lot of it to us, and for sure, crawfish isn't all this guy knows (or cooks). But it is his passion, available nine different ways at his fine-dining restaurant, **Robin's**: fried, boiled, stewed, stuffed into green peppers, rolled into boulettes (similar to meatballs), made into meatballs, cooked in a pastry crust, in gumbo, and in bisque. A crawfish dinner gets most of them, starting with

At D.I.'s, a roadhouse in Basile, LA, the crawfish platter comes with live Cajun music.

bisque, then moving on to boiled and fried ones, boulettes, a crawfish-stuffed pepper, and a superior pie in which the little crustaceans share space with vegetables and plenty of garlic in a translucent-thin crust. Étouffée, served over rice, is the crowning glory of this feast, complex and smoky, with that special crawdad taste that is at once swampy-rich and exhilarating. For dessert, Tabasco ice cream!

The number of excellent crawfish places in Acadiana is fathomless, but we cannot leave this subject without

Chef Lionel Robin of Robin's in Henderson, LA, exercising his passion for crawfish

CRAWFISH AU GRATIN

The kitchen repertoire at Don's in Lafayette is a primer of south Louisiana food: remoulade, bisque, gumbo, shrimp, oysters, and crawfish all kinds of ways. The best thing Don's makes, and a dish that's relatively hard to find in other Cajun restaurants, is crawfish au gratin, a plump casserole of fatty tail meat submerged in cheese sauce with insistent but not overwhelming spice vibrations. Normally you get it as part of a crawfish dinner, but we prefer to coax an order from the kitchen for use as a topping for broiled flounder, tilapia, or catfish, or as the creamy completion for shrimp and oysters en brochette.

Don's Seafood & Steakhouse: 301 E. Vermillion St., Lafayette, LA 337-235-3551 www.donsdowntown.com

recommending a visit to **Carl's** in Mamou. It always seems the mudbugs at Carl's are meatier and sweeter-fleshed than anywhere else, perhaps because this is one place where spices are applied prudently, allowing all the full-fat opulence of the meat fairly to glow as it emerges from the shell.

5 CRAWFISH DESTINATIONS

1. **Carl's Seafood & Steak:** 427 Sixth St., Mamou, LA 337-468-2330
2. **Robin's:** 1409 Henderson Highway, Henderson, LA 337-228-7594
3. **Guiding Star:** 4404 Highway 90 West, New Iberia, LA 337-365-9113

4. **Poche's Market and Restaurant:** 3015-A Main Highway, Breaux Bridge, LA 800-3-POCHES or 337-332-2108 www.pochesmarket.com

5. **D.I.'s Cajun Restaurant:** 6561 Evangeline Highway, Basile, LA 337-432-5141 www.discajunrestaurant.biz

Creamy grits enriched with cheddar make a plush bed for shrimp in a classic South Carolina dinner.

CREAMY GRITS
Charleston, South Carolina

Primarily a specialty of the Lowcountry, creamy grits are long-cooked, not with water but with butter and milk, producing a plush pabulum that verges on the gravity of polenta. Usually made from coarse-ground grits, the dish is a compelling paradox of rugged maize that is custard-lush, plain grain that has become some-

⁂ **SERPENTARIUM**

Less than an hour outside Charleston, on Edisto Island, is a place where you can see snakes, 'gators, and turtles in habitats that approximate nature. The Serpentarium was opened in 1999 by native Edistonians Ted and Heyward Clamp, brothers who seem truly to love wildlife and have provided as happy a captivity for their collection as possible: "Alligators and turtles swim and play in large ponds in our outdoor gardens while other reptiles bask in the large, indoor solarium." Serpentarium literature invites guests to "walk, crawl, slither, swim, or drive" to come for a visit.

Beyond the Serpentarium, Edisto Island is a rare peaceable kingdom. Because its palmetto-shaded beach is the nesting place for endangered loggerhead turtles from May through autumn, disruptive activities are forbidden; terrapin harassment is punishable by a fine, and waterfront residents must keep lights off or drapes drawn after dark so the shoreline remains tranquil enough for the 300-pound terrapins to drag themselves onto the sand and lay their eggs in peace. A citizen-volunteer "Turtle Patrol" keeps a lookout for unleashed dogs who might disturb the nests.

Serpentarium: 1374 Highway 174, Edisto Island, SC 843-869-1171 www.edistoserpentarium.com Open from May 1 to Labor Day

South

MAIL-ORDER GRITS

Anson Mills of Columbia, South Carolina, opened in 1998 with the purpose of growing and milling heirloom corn, rice, and wheat that harkened back to the Old South but had become virtually extinct. The first product that the miller, Glenn Roberts, sold was grits made from Carolina Gourdseed white corn. Today Anson Mills is a thriving outfit, all set up to take mail-orders for what it calls antebellum coarse grits (white or yellow) as well as quick grits and whole hominy corn kernels, plus a wide selection of meal, wheat flour, rice, oats, and buckwheat.

Anson Mills: 1922-C Gervais St., Columbia, SC
803-467-4122
www.ansonmills.com

Dinnertime creamy grits are an inspired bed for a school of grilled shrimp crusted with barbecue sauce and topped with melted cheese and pieces of apple-smoked bacon at the elegant Lowcountry citadel **82 Queen**. The diversity of ingredients makes for an endlessly opulent plate of spice and comfort. Chef Brad Jones also uses them as the foundation layer for a sparkler of a meal of pesto-crusted mahimahi with fried green tomatoes.

GREAT CREAMY GRITS

1. **Hominy Grill:** 207 Rutledge Ave., Charleston, SC
   843-937-0930
   www.hominygrill.com
2. **82 Queen:** 82 Queen St., Charleston, SC
   843-723-7591
   www.82queen.com

thing outrageously rich. Whereas ordinary grits are mostly a bland breakfast starch, creamy ones are good for three meals a day. Indeed, one of the memorable dishes at the true-South **Hominy Grill** in Charleston is an equally good breakfast, lunch, or supper: atop a bed of sunshine-yellow creamy grits further enriched with cheddar cheese is a circle of hot-peppered shrimp strewn with a confetti of chewy bacon and sautéed green onions and mushrooms. Chef Robert Stehling notes with some pride that he uses only stone-ground flint-corn grits from the Old Mill of Guilford in Oak Ridge, North Carolina — his family's source when he was growing up.

CUBAN SANDWICH
Florida

There are many Cuban sandwiches in Florida, and many opinions about exactly which ingredients one should

The Cuban, Florida's claim to sandwich fame, is said to have been invented in Tampa.

contain, the primary point of contention being Genoa salami. Most Cubans in Tampa, where it is said the sandwich was invented, include Genoa salami. Most in Miami do not. We are in no position to proclaim which is correct, nor would we call one better than the other, except to say that there is something pretty darn wonderful about the way salami's garlicky fat oozes out as the sandwich is heated and lends its flavor to the whole package.

There is no salami in the sandwich dished out at **Las Olas Cafe**, a low-priced South Beach cafeteria that makes a Miami version with ingredients that each defines goodness: hunks of fall-apart-tender roast pork, a firm slab of ham, a layer of Swiss cheese, plenty of puckery pickles, and mustard, all heaped into fresh buttered Cuban bread. Grilled long enough in the sandwich press known as a *plancha* for all the ingredients to

Roast pork, ham, puckery pickles, and oozy Swiss cheese in Cuban bread

sound a single, sensational chord of flavor, this is unquestionably among the greats.

Aficionados may want to excommunicate us for admitting that our favorite Cuban sandwich is at **Carmine's Seventh Avenue**, in Tampa's Ybor City, because Carmine's 9-incher includes lettuce and tomato as well as mayonnaise —heresy in Cuban canons. But there is no denying the way the cheese and meats meld perfectly when the sandwich is slathered with

CONCH CHOWDER

Ernie's menu declares, "Conch Is King," and its chowder is regal: potent stuff, vividly peppered, thick with sweet bits of nicely clammy conch and chopped vegetables, with sherry available to add a whole other layer of intoxicant to the heady Caribbean classic. It is hearty enough to be a meal or, in a smaller portion, a sturdy companion to one of Ernie's fine barbecue sandwiches, constructed on thick-sliced Bimini bread and accompanied by a bowl of barbecue sauce

for dipping. Even if you don't have a sandwich, get some of that bread to go with the chowder. It looks pretty much like white bread but is dense and nearly cakelike, with alluring sweetness that partners nicely with the briny flavor of mollusk. Conch fritters and conch salad are also featured on Ernie's menu.

Ernie's Bar-b-que & Lounge:
1843 S. Federal Highway, Fort Lauderdale, FL
954-523-8636

butter and gets cooked and pressed in the *plancha* until steaming hot. The pork-and-cheese alchemy is dazzling, as is the range of textures, from gooey to chewy and tender to crisp. The bread is real Cuban bread, lighter inside and more fragile than French and Italian loaves, and the sandwich is cut on a dramatic diagonal, as tradition demands. And talk about sacrilege (but a mighty tasty one): Carmine's Seventh Avenue offers a vegetarian Cuban of cheese, roasted peppers, onions, mushrooms, lettuce, tomato, and pickles.

2 TOP CUBANS

Carmine's Seventh Avenue: 1802 E. Seventh Ave., Tampa, FL 813-248-3834

Las Olas Cafe: 644 Sixth St., Miami Beach, FL 305-534-9333

DATIL PEPPERS
St. Augustine, Florida

One of the most circumscribed of all local foods, Minorcan clam chowder looks like Manhattan clam chowder, and a first taste confirms the resemblance. But as you spoon up more, a glow starts at the back of the throat, and after a few mouthfuls the sensation gets hot and begins to roll forward. Midway through a bowl, your tongue is on fire and your lips feel like they might go numb. Chopped clams, shreds of tomato, corn kernels, and hunks of potato ride a slow-rolling capsicum wave that swells with sweet-tart citrus zest. The heat and the pungency come from datil pep-

pers, which, like their close botanical relative the habanero, feel like they blossom in your mouth — a completely different sensation from fiery peppers that shock or stab.

There is no Minorcan chowder on the island of Minorca, nor anywhere else we know other than Florida's northeast coast, where almost all of the world's datil peppers are grown. The peppers arrived in the late eighteenth century in the hands of Minorcans who came to work the once-ubiquitous indigo fields and finally settled in St. Augustine. They probably picked up the New World peppers in Cuba, as there are none in Spain, and while you won't find an eatery devoted to Minorcan cuisine, datil pepper–charged food is served in restaurants throughout the city.

Barnacle Bill's is known for lush-crusted fried shrimp, which can be ordered with attitude in the form of powdered datil peppers added to the batter. The restaurant's founder, Chris Way, created the first successful line

Originally imported from the Caribbean by Minorcans, datil peppers pack a slow-burning punch.

Datil-laced sauce and vinegar at
O'Steen's cafe in St. Augustine, FL

Chanel St. Clair, proprietor of **Hot Stuff Mon**, a small peppercentric shop in the city's historic downtown, contends that the unique charm of datils is that heat doesn't overwhelm flavor. She notes that the most prolific use of them is not in restaurants but in homes, where it is customary to serve an hors d'oeuvre of crackers spread with cream cheese dolloped with locally made pepper jelly, and where powdered datil pepper, marketed as Lust Dust, is many cooks' secret spice. Among her shelves of sauces, rubs, and preserves are packets of seeds for people to grow their own. "It is a backyard crop," she says, pointing out that even the few commercial growers are small-scale and that producers of the city's best hot sauce maintain private fields. "That can be a problem if you run out of peppers, because no one else will sell you theirs. The crops are small enough that everybody holds on to what they grow." Local folklore says they are so precious that growers use alligators as sentinels to guard their crop. "It is a personal pepper," Ms. St. Clair concludes.

Excellent clam chowder is the prelude to a seafood banquet at the extremely colorful **Salt Water Cowboy's**, a restaurant designed to look like a salt-marsh fish camp from a hundred years ago. Sunset over the marshes and the intercoastal waterway is a spectacular setting for two-alarm chowder loaded with tender nuggets of clam followed by fresh-caught Gulf or Atlantic fish or such deep-fried cracker specialties as 'gator tail, catfish, cooter (turtle), and frogs' legs.

of commercial datil pepper products, the Dat'l Do-It brand, in the 1980s, after he noticed that customers were stealing the homemade sauce he put on tables. The restaurant also makes chicken wings plastered with buttery barbecue sauce that smolders with datil power. When our waiter noticed how much we were enjoying the chewy-skinned drumettes and bows, he reached up behind the ship's-prow podium at the front of the restaurant to bring us a fresh bottle of Devil Drops. "Now, this is hah-ot," he intoned; and sure enough, a few datil droplets, in which the peppers are combined with lime juice, mango, and passion fruit, sound reveille that feels hotter than Tabasco and yet in a beguiling Caribbean way is also breezy and refreshing.

The Minorcan clam chowder of Florida's northeast coast tastes deceptively innocent at first bite.

The best Minorcan chowder in town is served at **O'Steen's**, a no-frills cafe with about a dozen tables and a six-stool counter. O'Steen's chowder is loaded with clams and radiates the datil's fruity potency. By the end of a bowl, every taste bud is at attention, ready to fully appreciate some of the north coast's finest shrimp. "Have you been here before?" the waitress asks as she sets down a plate of them. When we say no, she points out that the French fries are underneath the shrimp and that the plastic ramekin on the plate holds the kitchen's special pink sauce for dipping. She then hoists a Grolsch beer bottle. "And this is the datil pepper sauce we make. Don't start with it alone. Mix it with the pink." O'Steen's datil sauce is hot and fragrant, and even when prudently blended with the pink sauce engenders that distinctive back-of-the-throat roar that rumbles forward with inexorable titillation. The waitress suggests decorating the day's vegetable, field peas, with datil pepper vinegar set out on the counter

next to the sauce; it's an ideal match for the fatback-flavored legumes. For everything else, O'Steen's translucent red datil sauce becomes essential. As we clear space on the plate, we pour out a big puddle of it in which to dip shrimp, hushpuppies, French fries, cornbread, and biscuits.

DATIL-CHARGED MENUS

1. **O'Steen's:** 205 Anastasia Blvd., St. Augustine, FL
   904-829-6974
2. **Salt Water Cowboy's:** 299 Dondanville Rd., St. Augustine, FL
   904-471-2332
   www.saltwatercowboys.com
3. **Barnacle Bill's:** 14 Castillo Dr., St. Augustine, FL
   904-824-3663
   Second location: 451 A1A Beach Blvd., St. Augustine, FL
   904-471-2434
   www.barnaclebillsonline.com

For sauces, spices, and hot ingredients of all varieties
Hot Stuff Mon: 34½ Treasury St., St. Augustine, FL
   904-824-4944

DIP DOG
Marion, Virginia

A dip dog looks like a corn dog, but it is not. The batter isn't doughy at all. It is light and crisp, less like a hushpuppy or fritter and more like the crunchy envelope around onion rings (another great thing to order at the **Dip Dog**). The weenie is bright red and unctuous, small enough (and cheap enough, at a little over $1) for a quartet to be right for a decent appetite. Pulled hot from the fry kettle, a dip dog is painted with unusually mild, bright yellow mustard. The combination of blubbery dog, crisp crust, and smooth mustard is proletarian perfection. The dogs are served on paper boats and loaded into brown paper bags. Dining is in-car or at a handful of picnic tables.

Dip Dog: Highway 11 West, Marion, VA

276-783-2698

www.dipdogs.net

DIXIE DOG
Dixie

Compared to barbecue, hot dogs are second-class citizens in the world of southern Roadfood. Not to diss Q, which deserves its exaltation, but it's high time Dixie weenies got their due.

The place to start is West Virginia, which has a hot dog culture as flourishing as that of New Jersey or Chicago, its star the spicy little frank served at **Stewart's** in Huntington. Hot dogs here are incomplete without chili, a dense, barely beefy hash that is known not as chili but as sauce. And while slaw is an option, it is also essential. Stewart's slaw is sweet with a pickly punch, just creamy and cool enough to sing dramatic harmony with the dog and sauce, all of them loaded into a steamed-soft bun. Ritual demands measures of chopped raw onions and yellow mustard to complete the slaw dog picture. Slaw dogs are popular throughout the South; their exact provenance is lost in time, but there

are some who claim Huntington as their birthplace. Stewart's opened in 1932 as a root beer stand, with popcorn the only food on its menu. The next year, proprietor Gertrude Mandt developed a chili sauce and started serving hot dogs.

Given slaw's importance in West Virginia, it is no mere aside to say that the best slaw in the state is the one that crowns dogs at **Hazelett's Triple H Drive Inn** in Huntington. It is cream-rich, tangy, and full of good crunch. It sits on a wiener that is bedded on top of the sauce in a spongy little bun. The sauce is on the bottom, too, at **Frostop Drive Inn,** heralded by a giant root beer mug on its roof. Frostop dogs are boiled, the beefy chili spiked with cumin, the coleslaw especially zesty, if overly messy. Frostop features instantaneous carhop service. **Custard Stand** beef chili is sold in grocery stores throughout the state and is so satisfying that the Webster Springs restaurant, which has outdoor picnic seating only, offers it as a meal unto itself as well as topping for its traditional West Virginia hot dogs.

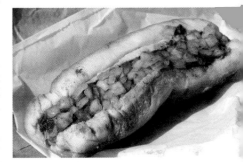

A Dixie dog comes with varying combinations of dense beefy sauce, slaw, and onions.

Ritzy's in Clarksburg, WV, drew on the knowledge of the area's immigrants to devise the best dog.

John Selario, known in Clarksburg as Hot Dog John, tells us that "a hot dog without chili is not a hot dog!" The proprietor of the hot dog mecca **Ritzy Lunch** explains, "Clarksburg is an important hot dog town. There are so many immigrants and sons and daughters of immigrants — Greeks and Italians, mostly — that when we spice up our chili, we know how to do it right." Ritzy Lunch hot dogs are pretty puppies that come nestled deep inside a steamed bun and topped with a zesty ground-beef sauce that is gently peppered and earthy-flavored.

A scrambled dog, unique to Georgia, is topped with chili completely unlike the finely ground stuff in West Virginia. It contains beans as well as coarse-chopped raw onion and transforms a little weenie into a huge-flavored snack. At **Dinglewood Pharmacy** in Columbus, the chili is augmented by ketchup and mustard, dill pickle slices, and a handful of oys-

ter crackers, making this meal into a major chord in which the hot dog is but a single oinky note.

The world's largest drive-in, the **Varsity** of Atlanta, has a hot dog lingo all its own. Naked means plain. Heavyweight means a double order of chili. Yankee means a yellow streak of mustard. Sideways means onions on the side. A regular C is topped with chili, mustard, and ketchup. A naked Varsity hot dog is a modest critter — a little pink tube steak served in a soft bun (unless you order a Mary Brown, which is bunless on a paper plate). It begs to be dolled up, the prime adornment being chili. Varsity chili isn't necessarily something you would want to eat plain as an entrée, but somehow when it and the dog are joined, fast-food magic happens. It is a finely pulverized brew, not too spicy but with a beefy heftiness that perfectly complements the frivolity of the dog. Chili dogs are served with a big stripe of yellow mustard running across the top of their chili blanket, a welcome condiment with a sunny punch. "A couple of chili dogs a day keep you young," said Frank Gordy, who named his original hot dog stand The Varsity in 1928 because he believed college students from nearby Georgia Tech would appreciate simple food served cheap and fast.

Perhaps someone, at some point in history, has ordered a **Nu-Way** weiner plain, but "all the way" is the only way to go: a proprietary red link that is grilled and bedded in a soft bun, topped with mustard, onions, and a fine-grained chili with barbecue-sauce zing. While not absolutely essential, whole-hog treatment demands creamy coleslaw on top to create a dramatic spectrum of sweet and hot. This delightful indulgence was first dished out in a shoebox-shaped restaurant with instantaneous service, now the flagship of a dozen Nu-Ways in the Macon area. The original Nu-Way was established in 1916 by James Mallis and, being that old, is another contender as birth mother of the slaw dog. Far from a gourmet sausage, the Nu-Way weiner (purposely spelled *ei* rather than *ie*) is slim and snappy and, with chili, a hot and spicy contrast to the slaw. An alternative way to enjoy it is on a scrambled dog platter, which tops the dog with chili sauce and beans. Also notable: extra-thick chocolate malts and soft drinks served over Nu-Way's "flaky ice."

It has been nearly seven decades since George and Mary Charles opened the **Roast Grill**, a little downtown Raleigh, North Carolina, dog house where the motto is "We burn 'em for you." That means that the hot dogs are cooked on a grill until their skin begins to blister. Exactly how blistered is up to each customer. Degree of burn is one of a very limited number of choices here, the other being condiments: mustard, onions, chili, or coleslaw. We like them all, especially the combo of slaw (which is tangy, not sweet) on top of soulful chili, which adds an irresistible one-two punch to a nearly blackened hot dog. Beyond those four toppings, few decisions need to be made. There are no potato chips or side dishes, no tea, and

VIDALIA ONIONS

If you have a sweet tooth and happen to be around Macon, Georgia, at the end of April, you're in luck. Head southeast along Interstate 16 about 100 miles and you will find the town of Vidalia, home of the annual two-day Vidalia Onion Festival. Declared Georgia's official state vegetable in 1990, these big, crisp alliums have just a hint of sharp pungency and are so sweet that you can slice them thick, place them between a couple of pieces of soft white bread, add salt, pepper, and mayonnaise, and achieve sandwich ecstasy. They're even good eaten out of hand like an apple. And oooeee, are they delicious made into onion rings, of which there are an abundance

at the festival. Events include a cook-off and an onion-eating contest, plus, of course, the crowning of a local girl who is sweet enough to be the onion queen.

Fresh onions can be ordered from the Vidalia Onion Factory & Gift Shop in boxes of 10, 25, and 40 pounds. They're best ordered in April and May, but supplies may last until fall. Jams and jellies are also available.

Vidalia Onion Factory & Gift Shop: 3309 E. First St., Vidalia, GA
912-526-3466 or 800-227-ONION
www.vidaliaonionfactory.com
Information about the festival is at the City of Vidalia website: www.vidaliaga.com.

no coffee except during the annual Christmas parade. The entire menu, not counting candy, gum, and cigarettes, is hot dogs, soda, and beer, plus pound cake and baklava. The hot dogs are presented on wax paper. There are no plates, and no need for utensils.

Frankfurter purists, skip this paragraph and move on. South Alabamians put ketchup on their hot dogs — a boner in most places, a criminal act in Chicago, New York, and Coney Island shops throughout the land. But talk to any wiener lover who grew up in Mobile and you will see eyes mist with nostalgia for the unique joy of their hometown hot dog as dished out by street vendors during Mardi Gras and as served at the **Dew Drop Inn** year-round. This folksy wood-paneled cafe is the city's oldest restaurant and the place where original proprietor George Widney introduced hot dogs to southern Alabama in 1924. They are bright red steamed franks of medium size, and the presentation is a work of art. They come in toasted buns, topped with cool sauerkraut and a layer of warm, beefy chili with spicy-sweet zest that elevates the simple dog to something irresistible. Standard condiments include mustard and pickles as well as ketchup. Aesthetes order them upside-down (the dog sits atop the condiments), and others like them "shaved" (without kraut).

TOP 10 DIXIE DOGS

1. **Nu-Way:** 430 Cotton Ave., Macon, GA
   478-743-1368
   See www.nu-wayweiners.com for additional locations.

2. **Roast Grill:** 7 S. West St., Raleigh, NC
   919-832-8282
   www.roastgrill.com

3. **Ritzy Lunch:** 456 W. Pike St., Clarksburg, WV
   304-622-3600

4. **Stewart's Original Hot Dogs:** 2445 Fifth Ave., Huntington, WV
   304-529-DOGS
   See www.stewartshotdogs.com for additional locations.

5. **Hazelett's Triple H Drive Inn:** 4450 Fifth Street Rd. (WV Route 152), Huntington, WV
   304-696-9863

6. **Custard Stand:** 364 Webster Rd., Webster Springs, WV
   304-847-7774
   www.custardstand.com

7. **Frostop Drive Inn:** 1449 Hal Greer Blvd., Huntington, WV
   304-523-6851

8. **Dew Drop Inn:** 1808 Old Shell Rd., Mobile, AL
   251-473-7872

9. **Varsity Drive-In:** 61 North Ave., Atlanta, GA
   404-881-1706
   See www.thevarsity.com for additional locations.

10. **Dinglewood Pharmacy:** 1939 Wynnton Rd., Columbus, GA
    706-322-0616

DUTCH APPLE PIE
Louisville, Kentucky

Caramel and apples were meant to be together, and not only on a stick. Among the several dozen supreme sweets made at Louisville's **Home-**

Any hour is right for a slice of Dutch apple caramel-crusted pie.

made Ice Cream and Pie Kitchen is caramel Dutch apple pie. It is configured by spreading a thick layer of golden caramel frosting right across the apple pie's flaky top crust. The cinnamon-spiced pie is terrific to begin with, but it soars when the buttery suavity of caramel is part of every bite. It provides a cushiony dairy richness similar to an à la mode treatment, but should you wish to go all

the way, you can order caramel Dutch apple pie served warm and ask for a scoop of the restaurant's own vanilla ice cream on top. The melting cream, caramel, spiced apples, and fragile crust swirl together in an ecstasy that could solve all the problems of the world.

Homemade Ice Cream and Pie Kitchen: 2525 Bardstown Rd., Louisville, KY 502-459-8184 See www.piekitchen.com for additional locations.

FISH HEAD STEW
Mount Pleasant, South Carolina

Most gumbos pale in comparison to the amazing fish head stew made by Charlotte Jenkins at her **Gullah Cuisine** restaurant in Mount Pleasant. Okra, tomatoes, and hot peppers

South

SWEETGRASS BASKETS

Gullah Cuisine's decor includes finely woven baskets, the likes of which have been sold at roadside stands in Mount Pleasant since Highway 17 was paved in the 1930s. Grass-weaving along the coast goes far back to the days of the slaves, who brought the craft with them from West Africa. Traditionally made from long-bladed sweetgrass, bulrush, longleaf pine needles, and palmetto leaves in soft shades of green, tan, and yellow, the baskets are

sensuously curving objets d'art as well as being strong and practical. In the old days, big sturdy ones were used to collect vegetables and grains in the field; some were made to winnow rice; smaller ones, made from the softer grasses, became serving trays and sewing boxes.

You can buy sweetgrass baskets by mail at www.edistosweetgrassbaskets .com. Grown from a basket stand on Edisto Island, this company also sells handmade birdhouses.

South Carolina's Gullah food has deep roots in African coastal traditions.

Gullah Cuisine: 1717 Highway 17 North, Mount Pleasant, SC 843-881-9076 www.gullahcuisine.com

FLOUNDER
Charleston, South Carolina

Flounder is common. Wild-caught flounder from the southeastern coast, as served in and around Charleston, is uncommonly wonderful. For one thing, the presentation is huge — you will get one whole (headless) fish larger than a dinner plate; for another, the meat is ethereal. Broiled right, it is bright white and beads with moisture, flaking into pieces with flavor as pure as an ocean breeze. Flounder is the most popular dish in the house at **Hyman's Seafood**, a sprawling restaurant with a vast, mostly fish menu, which lists it as "crispy flounder." It weighs more than a pound, and it arrives with its flesh scored in a diamond pattern. Broiling causes it to firm up and contract, forming a geometric pattern of bite-sized nuggets

galore are cooked together with shreds of tender meat picked from fresh grouper heads. The flavor of the fish is big and bright and as fresh as a sea breeze, and yet its presence is so much more refined than that of a fillet or fish steak. You almost want to call it sweet, especially when it is suspended in the powerful broth spiked with cayenne peppers and bay leaves' vegetable jolt.

Fish head stew is just one item on the endlessly wonderful menu of Gullah's modest dining room, where you can also get classic Creole gumbo that is thickened with okra and dizzyingly spiced. Gullah food, the legacy of sea-island-dwelling African-Americans who were so isolated that they developed their own culture and cuisine, shares glory here with such exemplary regional icons as fried chicken (some of the best anywhere), barbecued pork, and big, limp collard leaves lolling in their liquor along with chunks of ham and ham bone.

The crispy broiled flounder at Hyman's in Charleston, SC, is scored for easy eating.

of meat arrayed neatly atop the skeleton. With the slightest upward pressure of a fork slid underneath, each piece comes easily away from the bone. Its edges are crisp and slightly chewy, its interior a moist mouthful of sweet sea satisfaction. The fish is complemented by Hyman's peppery sweet chutney.

Apricot shallot sauce is what makes the crisp-fried whole flounder at **Anson** compelling. The sunny-sweet sauce, along with sesame coleslaw, draws maximum attention to the pure white goodness of the fish, which is firm and filling. To make a full Lowcountry feast of it, you can start with an exemplary mint julep (which some say was invented in Charleston) and a bowl of she-crab soup sparkling with sherry poured on top. For dessert, try a see-through-thin benne-almond basket filled with ice cream.

2 FANTASTIC FLOUNDERS

Anson: 12 Anson St., Charleston, SC
843-577-0551
www.ansonrestaurant.com
Hyman's Seafood: 215 Meeting St., Charleston, SC
843-723-6000
www.hymanseafood.com

FRIED CRAB CLAWS
Greater Mobile, Alabama

About the size of a Buffalo chicken wing, the fried crab claw is every bit as habit-forming. With its pink pincer a perfect handle sticking out from the breaded part, it is a one-handed

If you don't like exquisite fried food, don't come here.

snack and demands a bit of dental dexterity to get all the sweet marine meat and spicy crust that envelops it. You won't find ones better than those served at **Nan-Sea's**, a Mobile seafood landmark that got knocked out of commission by Hurricane Katrina but recently was reborn in a safer, if somewhat less scenic, location. What's great about Nan-Sea's claws is that the batter encasing the meat isn't at all doughy. It is brittle and seems almost to evaporate on the tongue as you retrieve nuggets of pearly crab. Nan-Sea's is notable for the excellence of all its fried seafood, including shrimp and oysters. Its gumbo is effulgent, and it, too, contains a good measure of succulent little claws.

The goofy but great **Wintzell's Oyster House** will sell you sautéed crab claws as well as fried ones, and while the combo of crab and butter has much to recommend it, we find the breading of fried ones an essential luxury. Note also the topnotch version of West Indies salad (page 208). If you are allergic to fried food as well as butter, you have our sympathy, but also a recommendation to try the blue crab claws at the **Original Oyster House** in Spanish Fort, where you have the option of getting them steamed. To be honest, we've never tried them that way, but we can tell you that the fried ones, each a nice little drumstick mouthful of crunchy gold breading with just enough juicy crab below the crust, are among the city's best.

MOBILE'S BEST CRAB CLAWS

1. **Nan-Sea's:** 650 Cody Rd. South, Mobile, AL
   251-342-1353
2. **Original Oyster House:** 3733 Battleship Parkway, Spanish Fort, AL
   251-626-2188
   Second location: 701 Highway 59, Bayou Village, Gulf Shores, AL
   251-948-2445
   www.originaloysterhouse.com
3. **Wintzell's Oyster House:** 605 Dauphin St., Mobile, AL
   251-432-4605
   See www.wintzellsoysterhouse .com for additional locations.

FRIED SHRIMP
Florida

Fried shrimp are everywhere, but the best fried shrimp are on the northeast coast of Florida, which claims to be the birthplace of commercial shrimping. The exact variety you'll get here varies with the seasons and is a complicated roll call of white, brown, pink, rock, and wild ocean labels, a nomenclature we cannot pretend to comprehend. What makes a Florida coast shrimp extraordinary is not its size — it is smaller than a Pacific prawn and bigger than a Myrtle Beach mini — but its freshness. Caught in cold Atlantic waters, instantly iced, and brought ashore at Mayport (in Jacksonville), the best shrimp in this region are characterized by firm flesh and mellow ocean flavor, and while you'll find them broiled, stuffed, and baked, fried is the right way to go.

Lulu's Waterfront Grille in Ponte Vedra Beach calls them "1st Coast Shrimp." Medium-sized, firm-fleshed, sweet, and juicy, they are prepared in the traditional local way, which is butterflied, enrobed in thin batter, and fried until the crust turns light gold and is as elegant as tempura. Lulu's serves them with sides of tropical slaw and superbly crusty hushpuppies.

Talk about a no-frills cafe! **O'Steen's** in St. Augustine takes no reservations, accepts no credit cards, serves no cocktails, wine, or beer, and has no cloths on its tables. This twelve-table, short-counter shrimp lover's shrine is so popular that there always is a wait, even at 11:30 a.m.

At Singleton's Seafood Shack in Atlantic Beach, FL, shrimp are brought direct from shore to kitchen to plate.

and 5 p.m. An antiques mall on the other side of the parking lot invites O'Steen's customers to shop in the meanwhile, and a sign outside its door promises, "Hear names on the speaker inside . . . Enjoy the shrimp." Available by the 9, 12, 18, or 24, they are medium-sized and each perfectly butterflied to resemble the lines inside the circle of a peace symbol. Sheathed in a crunchy veil, their muscular pink flesh packs nutty luxury that gets delirious when dipped in house-made pink sauce and datil pepper sauce. **Barnacle Bill's** also features St. Augustine's hot datil pepper sauce on its tables (see page 152) and offers its local shrimp fried in regular batter as well as batter with attitude in the form of hot datil pepper powder added to the mix.

Outside Singleton's, the boat that caught your meal

If you are an eater who likes to dine near the source, the place to eat Florida shrimp is **Singleton's Seafood Shack**, the screened porch of which looks out over the harbor where Atlantic Beach's fishing fleet docks and where shrimp are brought ashore. A ramshackle eatery of utmost leisure

South

DAVE'S CARRY-OUT

The cooks of coastal South Carolina tend to be accomplished fryers. Combined with a prolific ocean bounty, that talent makes for magnificent fried shrimp. Case in point: Dave's Carry-Out, where Charlestonians in the know go for Styrofoam boxes full of just-fried schools of them long into the wee hours of the morning when everything else in town has closed. Dave's shrimp are breaded one by one before going into the hot oil. They emerge packed in a pale gold veil of crunch that is thin enough to show the taut pink meat within. French fries cooked in the same savory oil are an excellent companion.

Dave's moved to its current spic-and-span location a couple of years ago from famously disheveled quarters where, local food savant Peter Wilborn recalled, if you parked your car in one particular place on the street near the exhaust fans, then went in to wait for an order (a good half-hour or more on busy nights), you would come back to a vehicle so infused with fumes that it smelled like shrimp oil for days. The current Dave's does have a few chairs that are used mostly by customers to wait for their carry-out orders to be readied. There is no table service.

Dave's Carry-Out: 42 Morris St., Charleston, SC 843-577-7943

(Styrofoam plates, plastic utensils), its broad Dixie menu ranges from slaw dogs to collard greens and a full Gulf Coast seafood repertoire, with shrimp the star. Singleton's shrimp are crisp-crusted and sumptuous.

FIRST COAST
FRIED SHRIMP

1. **O'Steen's:** 205 Anastasia Blvd., St. Augustine, FL
   904-829-6974
2. **Lulu's Waterfront Grille:** 301 Roscoe Blvd. North, Ponte Vedra Beach, FL
   904-285-0139
   www.luluswaterfrontgrille.com
3. **Singleton's Seafood Shack:** 4728 Ocean St., Atlantic Beach, FL
   904-246-4442
4. **Barnacle Bill's:** 14 Castillo Dr., St. Augustine, FL
   904-824-3663
   Second location: 451 A1A Beach Blvd., St. Augustine, FL
   904-471-2434
   www.barnaclebillsonline.com

GATEAU SIROP
Acadian Louisiana

There may be a French cognate for *gateau sirop,* but in our book this syrup cake is pure Acadiana. You won't find it in other regions, and we've yet to see it on a menu even in New Orleans, but head into the swamps, where sugarcane is harvested and good cooking is a way of life, and you will find it served in town cafes as well as fine-dining restaurants. Like a moist gingerbread cake redolent of cloves, it is presented at **Prejean's** in Lafayette crowned with Frangelica cream sauce, which is a nice foil for the smoky cane syrup that sweetens it. Gateau sirop at **Café des Amis**, an everyday party in Breaux Bridge, adds crunchy roasted pecans to the formula and offers the cake with chocolate or vanilla ice cream, either of which we feel is counterproductive. This spicy *gateau* is so moist and rich that ice cream is only a distraction.

BIG BUTTERFLIED SHRIMP

In the heart of the Mississippi Delta, Ramon's serves some of the most awe-inspiring fried shrimp anywhere. They are tremendously meaty, their firm pink flesh heavy with juice, and they are as big as moon pies, butterflied so that each one is a several-bite proposition. Their crust is dark, shatteringly crisp, and only thick enough to contribute a slight bready cushion to the shellfish within. After Ramon's garlicky green salad and an appetizer of mighty fine onion rings, a large order of these shrimp is daunting. "We were taking bets in the kitchen if y'all would be able to finish," a waitress admitted when, dispossessed of all appetite, we left two of our giant dozen uneaten on the plate.

Ramon's: 535 Oakhurst St., Clarksdale, MS
662-624-9230

Topped with nuts at Café des Amis, Acadian gateau sirop gets exceptional moistness from sugarcane syrup.

2 GLORIOUS GATEAU SIROPS

Café des Amis: 140 E. Bridge St., Breaux Bridge, LA
337-507-3398
www.cafedesamis.com
Prejean's: 3480 N.E. Evangeline Throughway (I-49 North), Lafayette, LA
337-896-3247
www.prejeans.com

HALF SMOKE
Washington, D.C.

The District of Columbia has one food specialty that is its alone. That's the half smoke, a very plump sausage link that sizzles on a hot griddle until its skin turns snapping crisp, then gets bunned like a hot dog. Its pedigree is hard to track down, and no one can say for sure whether its name comes from the fact that it is only lightly smoked (halfway) or because it is a half-and-half mix of beef and pork or because in some hash houses it is split in half before getting griddled. You'll find half smokes sold at street-corner carts throughout D.C.; the oldest extant restaurant serving it is **Weenie Beenie**, which once sprouted a small local chain but is now the single, original place in Arlington, Virginia. Weenie Beenie splits its sausages and grills them so the inside gets crusty. Lunchtime half smokes come dressed with chili, mustard, onions, and relish; breakfast half smokes are matched with a fried egg and a slice of bright orange cheese.

The half smoke at **Ben's Chili Bowl** is luscious beyond description,

Ben Ali outside Ben's Chili Bowl, a D.C. landmark established in 1958

South

The name *half smoke* may come from the lazy smoking method or the equal mix of beef and pork.

wonderful all alone in a steamed-soft bun or topped only with a line of mustard. The ultimate rendition is ribboned with yellow mustard, sprinkled with a few crisp chopped onions, and buried under a spill of Ben's thick, peppery chili: the transcendent chili dog. (Chili is also available alone in a bowl, on a burger, or spread across a plate of French fries with or without melted cheese.) Ben's half smokes are presented in a red plastic basket along with potato chips, and they find their denouement in an oh-so-mellow slice of sweet potato layer cake.

Historically and by nature, the half smoke is plebeian. Cheap eats. Street food. But it had to happen: the upscale half smoke. In Penn Quarter at **PS7's**, where chef Peter Smith is described as someone "born with an instinct to take experiences and turn them into flavors and creations," we were served a trio of pe-

BOX LUNCH

There is nothing singularly spectacular about the meal you get at Sally Bell's except for its immunity to anything modern. Sally Bell's serves the exact lunch it served a half-century ago, which is probably much the same one that polite Virginians ate a hundred years ago. There are two salads from which to choose: macaroni, which is fine, and spicy-sweet potato salad laced with onions, which is memorable. Of the eleven kinds of sandwiches, we seldom can resist pimento cheese (page 191), but we have not regretted chicken salad (on a roll rather than white bread), cream cheese and olive (talk about a bygone taste!), and thin-cut Smithfield ham. As for cupcakes, there's no beating the orange-and-lemon, its icing sprinkled with little bits of citrus confetti. All the elements are neatly packaged in a cardboard lunch box lined with wax paper.

Note: Among its other charms of yesteryear, Sally Bell's offers beaten biscuits, which are not the typical southern fluffy-centered biscuit but more like a cracker, hard and crisp. Also try spongy-sweet Sally Lunn muffins and lemon chess pie.

Sally Bell's: 708 W. Grace St., Richmond, VA
804-644-2838
www.sallybellskitchen.com

THE NEWSEUM

We cannot guarantee you will see the Unabomber's shack if you visit Washington's Newseum. Last we heard, Mr. Kaczynski, the social critic, mathematician, and homegrown terrorist, was suing to have his 10-by-12-foot residence, formerly of Lincoln, Montana, removed from display. It was brought to D.C. as part of an exhibit commemorating the FBI's most newsworthy stories; other artifacts include the electric chair in which the Lindbergh baby kidnapper Bruno Hauptmann fried and the jacket Patty Hearst wore when she and the Symbionese Liberation Army did their bank job. (The FBI exhibit is scheduled to close in mid-2009 anyway).

What you will see in what bills itself as the "world's most interactive museum" are galleries devoted to the Berlin Wall and its fall, the terrorist attacks of 9/11, journalists who have died on the job, and Pulitzer Prize–winning news photos. The interactive aspect of the place that is the most fun is "How to Be a TV Reporter," in which you can pay to stand with a microphone in front of a blue screen that makes it look like you are addressing the camera with a weather map, a sports event, or some newsworthy location behind you. Your presentation is captured on tape, which you can then submit to the museum in hopes of joining the Be a TV Reporter Hall of Fame.

The Newseum: 555 Pennsylvania Ave. NW, Washington, DC
888-639-7386
www.newseum.org

South

---

tite cherrywood-smoked half smokes anointed with Danish smoked salt and Banyuls-scented pommes frites. Not a bad snack, but perhaps not as interesting as the lounge menu's tuna tartare sliders.

HALF SMOKE HONOR ROLL

Ben's Chili Bowl: 1213 U St. NW, Washington, DC
202-667-0909
www.benschilibowl.com

Weenie Beenie: 2680 S. Shirlington Rd., Arlington, VA
703-671-6661

PS7's: 777 I St. NW, Washington, DC
202-742-8550
www.ps7restaurant.com

HOT FISH SANDWICH
Nashville, Tennessee

Hot fish sandwiches, which are served warm, temperature-wise, and hot on the Scoville scale, which measures spiciness, are a staple at soul-food restaurants throughout the South, but the tradition is strongest in Nashville. Dozens of shacks, stands, and drive-throughs sell them, usually along with a repertoire of fried chicken and not-hot catfish.

The biggest one in town, and also the best, is the Giant King, specialty of **Eastside Fish**, a small storefront with exactly one table for eating in and a window for takeout orders. The

Big, juicy, and crisp cornmeal-fried whiting fillets at Eastside Fish in Nashville

Giant King is a pair of whiting fillets, each at least a half-pound, dredged in seasoned cornmeal and crisp-fried, then sandwiched between four slices of supermarket white bread. The fish is moist and delicate, its brittle crust mottled with four-alarm Louisiana hot sauce and festooned with crunchy raw onion, dill pickle chips, and smooth yellow mustard.

Donald "Bo" Boatright, who started Eastside Fish in 2003, grew up eating hot fish sandwiches as part of what he calls "summer nights of fun" — evenings when neighbors gather to play cards and to eat hearty. Standard companions for hot fish are bread, hushpuppies, coleslaw, and, strangely enough, meat-sauced spaghetti. When he opened his shop, Boatright's goal was to set a benchmark for hot fish: bigger, juicier, crisper, and just-right hot. "As long as anybody has been living here in Nashville, there has never been a sandwich this big before," he boasts. "We did not invent the wheel. We improved it."

There is serious rivalry among Nashville's hot fish restaurants, especially between Eastside Fish and a newcomer that calls itself **King Fish**, a name Boatright sees as an infringement of his own royal title. "We are the kings of fish," he insists. "Let the people decide." King Fish offers grilled fish (unheard of in the old-time places), and it claims to be king not only of fish but of chicken, too. We found its hot whiting pretty mild but loved the fried catfish. At **Bolton's Spicy Chicken & Fish** (see page 144), the whiting is so fiery that you'll hear spontaneous yelps at tables in the tiny dining room as customers' tongues light up a few moments after the first bite. Another highly respected hot fish sandwich destination is **Joe's Bar-B-Que & Fish**, which we once declared to be the "world's slowest fast-food restaurant," because each fish sandwich is fried and assembled to order, and given that each order must be placed from your car (there is no indoor seating or order counter), the wait can be excruciating. But, oh, is it ever

At Bolton's in Nashville, the spicy whiting causes yelps of painful ecstasy.

worth it when the sandwich with its steaming hot, supercrunchy fillets is delivered. **White's Fish & Bar-B-Cue**, in a parking lot off to the side of a gas station (always an inviting location), makes mighty fine sweet-sauced barbecued pork as well as a lusciously fresh-from-the-fryer hot fish sandwich.

HOT FISH SANDWICH RANKING

1. **Eastside Fish:** 2617 Gallatin Pike, Nashville, TN
   615-227-8388
   www.eastsidefish.com
2. **Bolton's Spicy Chicken & Fish:** 624 Main St., Nashville, TN
   615-254-8015
3. **Joe's Bar-B-Que & Fish:** 3716 Clarksville Pike, Nashville, TN
   615-259-1505
   www.joesbarbq.com
4. **White's Fish & Bar-B-Cue:** 730 McFerrin Ave., Nashville, TN
   615-226-4722
5. **King Fish:** 708 Monroe Ave., Nashville, TN
   615-242-5700

HOT FRIED CHICKEN
Mid-South

There is fried chicken, which can be crunchy-chewy-juicy bliss, and there is hot fried chicken, which just might make you swoon, not only because it is dizzyingly delicious but because it is thermonuclear. Hot chicken isn't as prevalent in the mid-South as hot fish (page 167), but it tends to be significantly hotter. And just so there's no misunderstanding: We are not

The secret to Bon-Ton's chicken is a power-packed marinade.

talking Fahrenheit, we are talking hair-raising, sweat-inducing, tongue-tingling pepper hot. At Nashville's premier hot chicken place, **Prince's Hot Chicken Shack**, it is sold mild, medium, hot, and very hot. Hot had us gasping for breath and made our lips glow for hours after lunch. What's particularly interesting about its heat is that it does not emanate from the sauce that clings to every piece; it penetrates down to the bone and quite literally oozes from the pieces of chicken so delectably that the blah white bread included in each order, saturated with spices and chicken juice, is delicious. There is plenty of flavor, too, in the skin that envelops every piece; it is chewy stuff, even richer than bacon, a joy that will have your taste buds singing hallelujah.

What spicy food lover wouldn't be drawn to the Nashville restaurant named **400 Degrees Soul Food and More**, where hotness of the chicken is specified in digital increments by the hundred? The hottest, 400-degree chicken, is very different from Prince's, in that the heat is severely concentrated in a sandy coating that does cling to the skin but also easily rubs off. We know people who swear by this 400-alarm stuff; we prefer Prince's more fully saturated hot-grease variety.

Keaton's in Cleveland, North Carolina, calls its hot chicken barbecued, but it isn't. After being fried to a golden crisp, the parts are dipped in simmering barbecue sauce just long enough for the skin and the meat to suck in the sauce's hot-pepper zest. Keaton's sauce (which can be bought by the bottle) is hot, complex, endlessly intriguing, described in restaurant literature as capturing "the 'taste' of all walks of life." Keaton's says, and

Prince's Hot Chicken Shack in Nashville tortures and titillates taste buds.

we quote, "Your taste buds have never had it Soooooooooooooo Good!" When dipped in this sauce, the chicken retains its outside crunchiness, but the skin becomes extra-chewy and will pull away in glistening ribbons from insides that are saturated with flavor. These breasts and thighs and wings are breathtaking; they belong to a food group separate and apart from either fried or barbecued.

That part of western Kentucky where Colonel Sanders got his start has a handful of places that specialize in a style of fried chicken that isn't really so pepper hot as it is ferociously seasoned. When you order bird at **Coach's Corner** in Sturgis, the girl at the counter will warn you that you're going to have to wait a good twenty-five minutes. Without heat lamps to keep it warm, every piece of Coach's chicken comes hot from the fryer with a fine golden crust, infused with the vividly salty marinade in which the chicken has been soaked before getting fried. A 1954-vintage eatery that was once a drive-in, Coach's uses a recipe known locally as Colonel Jim's, the same recipe used up in Henderson at **Mr. D's**, which remains a full-menu drive-in. But Mr. D's is even spicier, its crust so intense that your eyes might water.

Henderson's **Bon-Ton Mini Mart** serves the best version of this style of chicken, and in our estimation one of the best fried chickens anywhere. Bon-Ton pieces are suffused with a power-packed marinade of cayenne and garlic that penetrates every fiber of the meat; they are encased in a dark, brittle crust nearly as salty as a potato

The spice level in Mr. D's chicken in Henderson, KY, is something to crow about.

amazing fried chicken and the rapturous necessity of devouring every morsel of it.

GREAT HOT FRIED CHICKEN

1. **Keaton's:** 17365 Cool Springs Rd., Cleveland, NC
704-278-1619
www.keatonsoriginalbbq.com
2. **Bon-Ton Mini Mart:** 2036 Madison St., Henderson, KY
270-826-1207
3. **Prince's Hot Chicken Shack:** 123 Ewing Dr., Nashville, TN
615-226-9442
4. **Coach's Corner:** 9178 U.S. Highway 60 West, Sturgis, KY
270-333-4317
5. **Mr. D's:** 1435 S. Green St., Henderson, KY
270-826-2505
6. **400 Degrees Soul Food and More:** 2012 Clarksville Highway, Nashville, TN
615-244-4467

chip. Dark or light, they deliver a taste thrill like no other. Donna King, who was there when Bill Koch developed the recipe back in the 1960s, recalls, "When he first started making it, it was really, really hot. People would cry when they ate it . . . but they liked it and wanted more! He finally got the cayenne pepper down to where it was supposed to be, and I guess we sold a million pieces of chicken." To most of those who have never tasted it, a first bite of Bon-Ton chicken is astonishing. Like aged country ham, it seems too intense: spicy, salty, crunchy all at once. But as tongue-shock settles, taste buds crave more, and after a few bites, one's whole world very quickly shrinks to nothing other than this

HUSHPUPPIES
The South, Wherever Fried Meals Are Sold

The traveling trencherman will meet all shapes and sizes of hushpuppy in the South: big spheres, tidy tubes, and curliques. Usually they are a plebeian dish, but there are wicked-good sophisticated ones, too, like the exclamatory jalapeño cheddar nuggets at chef Bill Smith's **Crooks Corner** in Chapel Hill, North Carolina, where they are an hors d'oeuvre served a dozen at a time, handsomely

South

marshaled in a circle around a dish of very spicy cocktail sauce.

Hushpuppies used to be exclusively a fried-fish companion, but ever since pork Zeus Warner Stamey started serving them at his smoke pit, **Stamey's**, in Greensboro, in the 1950s, they have become a fundamental element of barbecue trays through much of central and eastern North Carolina. Following Stamey's style, pups in this region tend to be more tubular than spherical. Among the best are the brittle-crisp, sandy-coated cylinders dished out at the estimable **Bridges Barbecue Lodge** in Shelby (Alston Bridges apprenticed with Mr. Stamey).

Some of the strangest-shaped variants are made by Travis Hocutt at his **Hocutt's Carolina Barbecue.** Hocutt's actually is in Ohio, but Travis uses a recipe he got from his North Carolina grandmother, creating squiggly hushpups as different from one another as are snowflakes: little balls, twists, knots, ovals, hearts, and nuggets, small enough so that there is a good, solid crunch to every bite but big enough that each one also delivers the creamy cornmeal goodness that's inside. All alone, they'd be cause for celebration, but Hocutt sides them with warm butter, honey butter, and molasses butter for dipping, bite by bite. It is very hard to say which of the three is the best, but we assure you that it is a supreme pleasure of Buckeye State dining to try to resolve that issue.

Hushpuppies might be the last thing on the minds of most customers who come with the single purpose of eating pecks and bushels of steamed oysters at **Bowens Island Restaurant** in Folly Island, South Carolina (page 199). But we assure you, they are first-rate. Made from a recipe perfected by the late May Bowen, they are large, irregular spheres with dark crust that crunches brutally when your teeth attack. The inside is buttercup yellow and nearly as tender as angel cake, and they are, for their size, remarkably light. Proprietor Robert Barber (Mrs. Bowen's grandson) attributes their goodness to the fact that his grandmother's recipe calls for the batter to be cured a spell before frying. Uncured batter, he explains, causes a hushpuppy to blow up and suck in oil.

5 BLUE-RIBBON HUSHPUPPIES

1. **Bowens Island Restaurant:** 1870 Bowens Island Rd., Folly Island, SC
843-795-2757
www.bowensislandrestaurant.com
2. **Hocutt's Carolina Barbecue & Seafood Buffet:** 56080 National Rd., Bridgeport, OH
740-633-2710
3. **Crook's Corner:** 610 W. Franklin St., Chapel Hill, NC
919-929-7643
www.crookscorner.com
4. **Bridges Barbecue Lodge:** 2000 E. Dixon Blvd., Shelby, NC
704-482-8567
5. **Stamey's:** 2206 High Point Rd., Greensboro, NC
336-299-9888
Second location: 2812 Battleground Ave. (U.S. Route 220 North), Greensboro, NC
336-288-9275
www.stameys.com

KEY LIME PIE
Florida

Because Key limes are too fragile to ship and store by the truckload, they are not a supermarket staple. Residents of the Florida Keys, where they grow, refer to them as a "dooryard fruit" because they grow fairly wild in people's backyards, just outside their doors. Their juice is brilliantly tart; when combined with sweetened condensed milk, the flavor creates a taste-bud teeter-totter of sugary opulence and citrus sourness that is Key lime pie's magic.

Dependable sources for Key limes are rare and prized by cooks. Chef Doug Shook of **Louie's Backyard** restaurant in Key West reveals only the first name of his supplier — Doris — and says that she makes it her business to know which yards have the good Key lime trees. Wherever their exact origin, these primo limes are the basis for a pie that we consider the best. It is not outrageously different, for the basic ingredients of Key lime pie are (or

At Louie's in Key West, the key limes come from neighboring yards.

ought to be) immutable: sweetened condensed milk, lime juice, and egg yolks. It is the crust that makes Louie's transcendent. Instead of the usual crumbled graham crackers, pastry chef Niall Bowen uses gingersnaps. The result is a crunch that is spicy enough to seem almost hot, a marvelous foil for the cool, creamy lime filling that sits upon it. Louie's serves its pie topped with a raspberry coulis, a handful of blueberries, a big half strawberry, and a dollop of whipped cream — Parrot-head heaven!

Even at Louie's, which prides itself on the freshest ingredients closest to the earth and ocean, canned milk is essential. This culinary law dates back to the years after the Civil War, when Bahamian settlers in the Keys, having limited access to fresh dairy products, made pies with canned milk along with juice of their native limes or sour oranges (another dooryard fruit), plus egg yolks for extra richness.

Key West Key Lime Pie Company is not a restaurant but a business devoted exclusively to making and selling pies. These are ultra-smooth ones with vigorous lime spunk, made from a family recipe

Louie's Key lime pie, a transcendent sweet-and-sour blend of lime and condensed milk

that is generations old. You can get a single slice here for an instant-gratification snack, or you can buy a whole pie, ready to take home and slice. Frozen pies are available to carry on long trips, and no matter where you are in the United States, you can have one delivered via overnight carrier.

Because Key lime pie can be light and bracing, it has become an especially popular dessert at high-end restaurants where people eat large. At **Harry Caray's Italian Steakhouse** in Chicago, it's bliss to top off a meal of prime sirloin strip and Vesuvio potatoes with Key lime pie built on a crust that includes finely chopped walnuts and a dash of cinnamon. **Joe's Stone Crab** of Miami Beach sells Key lime cake as well as a version

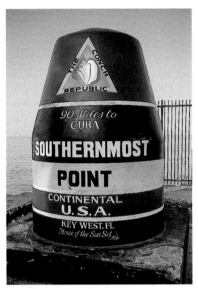

Photo op: the 9,000-pound monument at Key West

SOUTHERNMOST

The intersection of Whitehead and South Street, between South Beach and Fort Taylor in Key West, Florida, 75 miles from the Dry Tortugas, is the southernmost point in the continental United States. It overlooks the Atlantic Ocean and is designated by a 9,000-pound concrete monument resembling a black, red, and yellow buoy. From dawn until long after dusk, visitors stand on this spot to have their pictures taken. Before the heavyweight marker was installed, there was just a driftwood sign underneath the corner cork tree; actually, there were countless such signs, one after another. Souvenir hunters kept stealing them,

and so finally the immovable buoy was installed.

Along the street near the buoy, vendors sell conch shells, seashell lamps, key rings, sponges, and refrigerator magnets that commemorate a visit to this notable spot. On adjoining streets are dozens of businesses and tourist attractions that boast of being southernmost: southernmost motel, southernmost coffee roaster, southernmost pharmacy, southernmost nail salon, southernmost hairdresser, and southernmost one-hour photo lab. Even a medical practice bills itself as Southernmost Foot & Ankle Specialists, the website for which is www .painfulfoot.com.

of Key lime pie declared by the *Miami Herald* to be "the paradigm." At **La Bodeguita del Medio** in Palo Alto, California, silky Key lime pie is the natural conclusion to a white-table-cloth Cuban meal of pork chops and garlic mashed potatoes. The swankiest version we've found is that served at **Quinn's** in Miami Beach: its graham-cracker crust is buttery beyond belief; its one-two punch of sweet and tart is dazzling; and the plate comes fes-tooned with berries, Chantilly cream, and raspberry coulis.

A cool wedge of lemon icebox pie topped with whipped cream from the Crystal Grill in Greenwood, MS

Early in the twentieth century, Key lime groves thrived throughout the Keys, but after a 1926 hurricane wiped them out, they were not replanted. Since then the lime has remained an elusive citrus legend — although Key lime pie has been formally recognized as the official state pie of Florida.

FLORIDA'S GREAT KEY LIME PIES

1. **Louie's Backyard:** 700 Waddell Ave., Key West, FL
305-294-1061
www.louiesbackyard.com
2. **Key West Key Lime Pie Co.:** 225 Key Deer Blvd., Big Pine Key, FL
305-872-7400 or 877-822-PIES
www.keywestkeylimepieco.com
3. **Joe's Stone Crab:** 11 Washington Ave., Miami Beach, FL
305-673-0365
www.joesstonecrab.com
Joe's is closed in August and September.
4. **Quinn's:** 640 Ocean Dr., Miami Beach, FL
305-673-6400
www.quinnsmiami.com

Also

Harry Caray's Italian Steakhouse: 33 W. Kinzie St., Chicago, IL
312-828-0966 or 773-HOLYCOW
See www.harrycarays.com for additional locations.

La Bodeguita del Medio: 463 N. California Ave., Palo Alto, CA
650-326-7762
www.labodeguita.com

LEMON ICEBOX PIE
Below the Mason-Dixon Line

Like iced tea, lemon icebox pie is a passion in locales where the weather gets oppressively hot. A cool wedge of this custard-smooth indulgence seems especially right after a high-octane meal of smoky barbecue or spicy fried chicken, and it is a famil-iar presence on menus of meat-and-three eateries throughout the South. In Nashville, at the **Elliston Place Soda Shop**, it is an uncomplicated wedge that fully expresses the pie's basic personality, a balancing act between lemon and cream. Likewise, at the vegetable-centric **Cupboard** in Memphis, it arrives with no topping at all, just cool sunny-yellow curd on a sweet crumble crust. The Cupboard pie is a virtual twin to Key lime pie, which makes sense considering that the recipes, both of which call for sweetened condensed milk, are the same except for the choice of juice.

The **Crystal Grill** in Greenwood,

ALLUVIAN HOTEL

The Alluvian is outfitted with the sort of amenities you would expect in a four-star hotel in San Francisco or Chicago: feather beds in every room, a luxurious spa across the street, and a legendary restaurant, Giardina's, specializing in up-to-date versions of Deep South classics. A vintage hostelry originally refurbished so Viking range distributors would have a place to stay when they came to visit headquarters, it has become a destination for anyone who seeks to enjoy the sweet luxury of Old South hospitality and New South style. If cooking is your game, talk to the Alluvian concierge about signing up for Viking Cooking School classes, many packages for which include weekend stays at the hotel.

Alluvian Hotel:
318 Howard St.,
Greenwood, MS
866-600-5201 or
662-453-2114
www.thealluvian.com

Mississippi, enhances the formula with a sumptuous ribbon of cream topping, which, although not nearly as awe-inspiring as the restaurant's high-rise meringues, adds another smooth white element to the magnificent balance. In Chattanooga, the lunch-only cafe **Zarzour's** makes the balmiest version, just barely tart and nonassertively sweet: sheer comfort.

The best lemon icebox pie on the planet is served at a mid-twentieth-century blue-collar diner in Atlanta called the **Silver Skillet**. It is as smooth as a triangle of yellow custard, but thicker and more substantial, quite sweet but also significantly tart, at once luxurious and refreshing. Supplies are extremely limited — sometimes just one pie is made each day — so it is often gobbled up midmorning by breakfast eaters who enjoy it after a meal of country ham and redeye gravy.

5 MOST FORKWORTHY LEMON ICEBOX PIES

1. **Silver Skillet:** 200 14th St., Atlanta, GA
   404-874-1388
   www.thesilverskillet.com
2. **Elliston Place Soda Shop:** 2111 Elliston Place, Nashville, TN
   615-327-1090
3. **Crystal Grill:** 423 Carrollton Ave., Greenwood, MS
   662-453-6530
4. **Cupboard:** 1400 Union Ave., Memphis, TN
   901-276-8015
5. **Zarzour's Café:** 1627 Rossville Ave., Chattanooga, TN
   423-266-0424

LEXINGTON BARBECUE
North Carolina

Last we looked, Lexington, North Carolina, had a population of fewer than 20,000 people and over a dozen barbecue parlors to serve them. To smoke-pit fans, the meat made here is the *grand cru* of barbecue, and Lexington isn't just a place, it is a style: hog shoulders cooked over hardwood coals (no charcoal, gas fire, or electric heat), then chopped or sliced, barely sauced, and served with coleslaw and hushpuppies.

Lexington's **Bar-B-Q Center** offers its extraordinarily juicy pork sliced, chopped, or coarse-chopped. Sandwiches are heaped with a bright red cabbage slaw flavored with apple cider vinegar and powered by hot sauce. The sauce isn't so hot at **Lexington Barbecue #1**, which many consider to be the definitive barbecue not just of Lexington or of North Carolina but of our solar system. The shoulders loll in the smoke of hickory and oak coals; the ambrosial pork they yield is shredded into a jumble of pieces that vary from melting soft (from the inside) to crisply cooked (from the "bark," or exterior). The hacked meat gets just enough sauce to coax out its full flavor and is served on a bun with slaw or in a small yellow cardboard boat with slaw in the other half. Like the meat, the slaw is flavored with a vinegar/sweet red barbecue sauce. As part of the platter, you get crunch-crusted hushpuppies with creamy insides.

JR CIGAR

If you are a cigar smoker on a budget, you likely know about JR Cigar, whose prolific mail-order business offers top brands at low prices. What you might not know is that JR has three retail outlets in North Carolina (although, curiously, it began as a cigar store in New York City). While one cavernous, humid sanctorum inside the Burlington location is devoted to smokes, all around it is a football-field-sized showroom of extremely cheap name-brand merchandise, ranging from perfume and jewelry to Western boots and patio umbrellas. Of special note is JR's vast NASCAR collection: jackets, hats, mugs, and bric-a-brac honoring the track's top drivers, current and past.

JR Cigar: 2589 Eric Lane, Burlington, NC
336-222-1300
www.jrburlington.com

Perhaps the ultimate barbecue to be found in this, or any, galaxy, at North Carolina's Lexington Barbecue #1

TOP 2 LEXINGTON BARBECUES

1. **Lexington Barbecue #1:** 10 Highway 29-70 South, Lexington, NC
910-249-9814
2. **Bar-B-Q Center:** 900 N. Main St., Lexington, NC
336-248-4633
www.barbecuecenter.com

LIMA BEANS
South Carolina

Must-eat lima beans? Yes, indeed, if you happen to be in Charleston, South Carolina, where that stark listing on the menu of the city's soulfood cafes doesn't mean a bowl of bland legumes. Far from it. Even if you ask for your limas plain at **Bertha's Kitchen** or **Ernie's** or the **H&R Sweet Shop**, the butter-soft school of khaki-colored pods is laced with pork, the flavor of which has transformed them from mere vegetables into sheer indulgence. As a side dish, they're a revelation. As a meal — served with a surfeit of neck bones loaded with dark-pink hunks of ham and pig tails so rich they make bacon seem austere — they are a triumphant treasure of the Lowcountry, rich and satisfying beyond measure, yet little known to outsiders. Robert Stehling of the esteemed Hominy Grill (page 150), who likes the limas at Bertha's, exclaimed to us that he couldn't figure out how these kitchens could afford to include so much meat in a meal that generally costs about $7, including cornbread, plus sweet tea.

LIMA BEANS OF THE GODS

1. **Ernie's:** 64 Spring St., Charleston, SC
843-723-8591
2. **Bertha's Kitchen:** 2332 Meeting Street Rd., North Charleston, SC
843-554-6519
3. **H&R Sweet Shop:** 102 Royall Ave., Mount Pleasant, SC
843-884-2118

LOUISIANA MEAT PIE
Acadiana

A semicircular pastry pocket about the size of a taco with a rugged crimp around its edges, the Natchitoches version of a Louisiana meat pie has a golden crust that is brittle and crunchy near the crimp, pliant near its mounded center. Inside the flaky sheaf is a good-sized portion of deftly seasoned ground beef, moist enough to make gravy irrelevant. Spicy but not fire-hot, complex and succulent,

Hunks of pork transform pillowy limas into sheer indulgence.

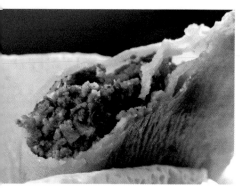

Spiced with nuance, the Louisiana meat pie, once a Christmas treat, offers old-fashioned satisfaction.

it is an honest piece of food that satisfies in an old-fashioned way. At **Lasyone's Meat Pie Restaurant**, you can have one for breakfast, accompanied by eggs and hash browns, but most customers come at midday to get a pair of them for lunch, with dirty rice on the side, darkened with plenty of gizzards and topped with zesty gravy.

"I cannot explain for certain how meat pies first came to this place," says James Lasyone, who suspects that it might have happened in the nineteenth century when Natchitoches — the oldest settlement in the Louisiana Purchase, founded in 1714 — was a thriving trade center and outfitting point for settlers heading west. By the mid-twentieth century, however, street-corner pie vendors were fading into history. Lasyone, who had grown up as a sharecropper's son out in the country and had enjoyed the pies when his family came to town, became the butcher at a grocery store on Second Street. When he wanted a meat pie, he knew which ladies to call. "Some were white, some were

black," he remembers. "But there weren't many of them left." In the mid-1960s, he began experimenting with recipes to make his own pies. He sold some over the butcher's counter at the store, then in 1967 he opened his restaurant in a minuscule retail space near the meat market. It has since become a southern food landmark.

Meat pies, which used to be a traditional Acadian Christmastime treat, are one of Louisiana's least-touted specialties. They certainly are overshadowed by the excellent crawfish at **D.I.'s** in Basile, but their beefy authority paves the way for a platter of boiled and fried crawdads, frogs' legs, flounder, and shrimp. D.I.'s meat pies are little two-bite crescents, served in a basket with a couple of dipping sauces. We've also enjoyed rich, vividly spiced meat pies from **Champagne's Breaux Bridge Bakery**. There is no place to sit and eat in this bakery in the heart of crawfish country, but you can get your pie heated up, and it is wieldy enough to handle easily in the car.

If you love pie and you love meat, try this portable meal from Champagne's in Breaux Bridge, LA.

South

A TRIO OF
LOUISIANA MEAT PIES

1. **Lasyone's Meat Pie Restaurant:** 622 Second St., Natchitoches, LA
   318-352-3353
   www.lasyones.com
2. **Champagne's Breaux Bridge Bakery:** 105 S. Poydras, Breaux Bridge, LA
   337-332-1117
3. **D.I.'s Cajun Restaurant:** 6561 Evangeline Highway, Basile, LA
   337-432-5141
   www.discajunrestaurant.biz

MEAT AND THREE
Nashville, Tennessee

The southern cafe term *meat and three* is direct and on the level, referring to a style of service by which you pick one meat from the day's selection of three to six choices and three vegetables from a daily list that is twelve or more items long. The "vegetable"

At Arnold's in Nashville, the service is cafeteria-style, and the food is beautiful.

selection in most meat-and-three cafes includes such nontonic items as Jell-O, macaroni and cheese, and spaghetti. It is possible to get meat and two or meat and one, and even meat and three without the meat, meaning an all-vegetable plate of three or four selections. Cornbread almost always comes on the side, and the proper libation is sweet tea.

While meat and three is popular throughout the mid-South, in Nashville it has a pulse-quickening effect, like the word *barbecue* in Memphis — a seductive incantation to lovers of paper-napkin cuisine, a phrase that holds the promise of glorious vittles served with utmost informality. It isn't easy deciding which of some dozen places in the Music City offers the quintessential meat-and-three experience, but you won't go wrong if you head straight for **Ron's BBQ and Fish**, a fairly new and completely boring-looking storefront with some of the best fried chicken, fried catfish, and fried whiting in a town full of superlative examples of all of them. Each of Ron's sides is paradigmatic: creamy mac 'n' cheese (with crusty squiggles from the top mixed in), green beans saturated with pork flavor, pot-liquor-dripping turnip greens, and on the side of everything, knobby hunks of hot-water cornbread.

Other contenders for Nashville's top rank include **Silver Sands**, a soul-food cafeteria that is also famous for its ham and/or pork chop breakfasts, and **Sylvan Park**, best known for its superb pies and puddings. And who could not love **Arnold's**? Service is cafeteria-style, tables are shared by strangers when the place is

The daily specials at a meat and three, where mac and cheese counts as a vegetable

NASHVILLE'S TOP 4
MEAT AND THREES

1. **Arnold's Country Kitchen:** 605 Eighth Ave. South, Nashville, TN
615-256-4455
2. **Ron's BBQ and Fish:** 2689 Murfreesboro Rd., Nashville, TN
615-361-8993
www.ronsbbq.com
3. **Sylvan Park:** 4502 Murphy Rd., Nashville, TN
615-292-9275
4. **Silver Sands:** 937 Locklayer St., Nashville, TN
615-742-1652

South

crowded (it always is), and the food is beautiful. Not beautiful in a glossy-magazine sense, but beautiful the way plate lunch ought to be: messy, colorful, bread-crumb-crusted, cheese-dripping, hog-jowl-flavored soulful. The meats include moist and mighty meat loaf, exemplary fried chicken, pulled pork, and catfish; among the side dishes that cannot be ignored are greens, squash casserole, and most especially that distinguished vegetable macaroni and cheese. Two kinds of cornbread are available, both essential: muffins and skillet-cooked cakes, the latter especially useful for mopping gravy, sopping the liquor under porky green beans, and dipping into the creamy emulsion in which black-eyed peas are suspended.

Did we mention Arnold's pies? We have raved enough, but suffice it to say that good pie is a foregone conclusion to any decent meat-and-three experience, and that Arnold's chess pie (page 145) is the best we've ever tasted.

MEDIA NOCHE
Florida

Media noche means "midnight," which traditionally is when this unique variant of the Cuban sandwich (page 150) is the snack of choice. It is suitable for late-late night because it is somewhat lighter than a dinner-sized Cuban . . . but only somewhat. The ingredients are the same — roast pork, ham, and Swiss cheese — but instead of a hearty Cuban loaf, sweet eggy bread serves as the base. When steamed and grilled so the ingredients meld, the sweet bread develops a light crunch that is completely different from the chewier nature of the traditional baguette. **Havana** serves it from a round-the-clock walk-up window but also in its full-service, sit-down restaurant, which boasts a vast traditional Cuban menu, from white bean soup on Sunday to guanabana milk shakes and A-1 café con leche. The media noche and classic Cuban are supplemented by an "Especial de West Palm Beach," a similar Dagwood but with a full deck of ham, turkey, Swiss cheese, bacon, lettuce, and tomato. Note: Pickles are almost everywhere a standard Cuban sandwich ingredient, but they must be requested at Havana.

Havana: 6801 S. Dixie Highway,
West Palm Beach, FL
561-547-9799
www.havanacubanfood.com

MUTTON BELT
Western Kentucky

Mutton is king of the pit west of Louisville, Kentucky. It is strong and smoky with flavor that is bigger than pork's, bigger even than beef's. It isn't pepper-sharp, and the old ewe tang is significantly mollified by all the time it spends enveloped in smoke from smoldering coals, but still it is meat with a knockout punch. Owensboro, which likes to think of itself as the

West of Louisville, mutton is king of the pit.

At the Moonlite in Owensboro, KY, customers clap when barbecued mutton emerges from the kitchen.

barbecue capital of the world, is home of the **Moonlite Bar-B-Q Inn,** a huge restaurant with a mutton-centric menu. It is possible to order from a menu at the Moonlite, but the endless buffet, which also includes pit-cooked pork and beef plus ham biscuits, a dozen side dishes, and a dozen excellent pies for dessert, is irresistible. Here customers returning for second and third helpings stand and admire the 'cue out loud, cheering and clapping when new trays are brought forth from the kitchen. As at nearby **George's,** the Moonlite's mutton comes chopped, sliced, and as ribs, sauced or "off the pit" (unsauced). In most mutton restaurants, you have your choice of a sandwich, a tray (with pickle, onion, and bread), or a platter (plus beans and coleslaw). One of the lesser-known but essential mutton sources is in the nearby town of Henderson: **Thomason's Barbecue,** where the meat is so tender that it falls apart like pot roast. Thomason's is also notable for superb barbecue beans (page 121) and bottled "dip," which is barbecue sauce as thin as au jus.

Louis Hatchett, the biographer of Duncan Hines and an infallible tipster for western Kentucky eats, referred to the town of Waverly as "the western edge of barbecued muttonland." In this dot-on-the-map destination, **Peak Brothers** has been the smokehouse star since 1948, only recently rebuilt after a devastating fire in 2006. Here is the place to eat chipped (that's like chopped, but more so) sandwiches of mutton on rye with raw onion and pickle slices. Peak Brothers' mutton is moist and mellow, with none of the rank bite typical of mature lamb elsewhere.

The most painful interview we ever conducted was in Peak Brothers' old kitchen with Tony Willett, who has tended smoked meats here since the early 1970s. The pit door was open, and he was busy throwing spice on pork ribs, peeling skin off hams, and turning briskets and hunks of lamb on the grate. Hellish heat and blinding puffs of smoke emanating from the pit didn't bother him at all, but our eyes teared, our glasses fogged, and our lungs resisted taking in the cloudy air. The fumes of burning wood and cooking meats were penetrating. "When I get home, my wife makes me stay outside until I take off my clothes," Willett confided. "When I walk into a store, you can hear people say, 'Here comes Peak Brothers.'"

Willett starts his fire at 3 a.m., first with ash, white oak, and red oak, then finally tossing on hickory logs. "The main purpose of cooking is to tenderize," he said. "And to keep the meat from drying out." Everything he cooks gets vigorously poked with a long fork each time he turns it, and on alternate turns he slathers it with a mix of vinegar, water, and top-secret spices, a process he calls dipping. He explained that dipping is essential for full flavor because when hot meat is poked, it wants to draw in the spices. "Anybody can barbecue," he declared, "just so long as they know how to dip."

TOP 4 MUTTON SOURCES

1. **Peak Brothers Bar-B-Que Restaurant:** 5363 U.S. Highway 60 East, Waverly, KY 502-389-0267
2. **Moonlite Bar-B-Q Inn:** 2840 W. Parrish Ave., Owensboro, KY 800-322-8939 or 270-684-8143 www.moonlite.com
3. **Thomason's Barbecue:** 701 Atkinson St., Henderson, KY 270-826-0654
4. **George's Bar-B-Q:** 1362 E. 4th St., Owensboro, KY 270-926-9276

When it comes to barbecue, mutton is tenderer than pot roast and bigger-flavored than beef or pork.

OREILLE DE COCHON
Breaux Bridge, Louisiana

Named because it resembles a pig's ear, oreille de cochon is a breakfast pastry served at the quintessential Cajun country eatery **Café des Amis**. To us it resembles a hound's ear more than a pig's. It is a long strip of light-weight fried dough that is available either plain, which means blanketed with powdered sugar, or stuffed with rich and spicy boudin sausage, also well sugared. The latter is a meal unto itself, and a thrilling stretch of the taste buds from piggy filling to sweet coat. Substantial as the sausage filling is, it in no way detracts from the fine flakiness of the pastry ear that encloses it.

AN OREILLE TO HAIL

Café des Amis: 140 E. Bridge St., Breaux Bridge, LA
337-507-3398
www.cafedesamis.com

A Cajun "pig's ear" envelops spicy-sweet boudin sausage in a deep-fried pastry showered with powdered sugar.

PEACH COBBLER
Georgia and South Carolina

The **Peachtree Café** at Fort Valley, Georgia's Lane Packing Company, which farms over 2,500 acres of peach trees, has a pleasant menu of barbecue, sandwiches, and salads, but we have never tried any of those. Dessert is too compelling, especially during peach season, when over two dozen different varieties are ripening on company trees. Peach muffins and peach soft-serve ice cream with bits of fruit in it are swell, as are pecan pie and butter pecan ice cream made from Lane Company nuts. But what knocks our socks off is peach cobbler. A common dessert throughout the South, cobbler is seldom really bad, but neither is it often very good. Lane's is outstanding. Big hunks of peach are cooked only enough to soften but not so much they get mushy or lose their bright sunshine flavor; their presence overwhelms that of the pastry, which exists only to offer nice contrasting toothsomeness and a measure of sweetness to balance the peachiness that dominates.

The peachiest peach cobbler into which we've ever plunged a utensil is that made at the **Belmont Inn**, a Victorian hostelry on the square in Abbeville, South Carolina. The lattice crust on top is boulangerie-fine; the peach slurry it covers bursts with fruit flavor (laced with peach schnapps), and it is topped with peach ice cream and peach-flavored whipped cream.

PEACH ICE CREAM

Have you ever eaten a WinBlo, Sweet Sue, China Pearl, or Flame Prince? They are just a few of the varieties of peach grown by **Pee Dee Orchards**, whose farmstand in Lilesville, North Carolina, is open from mid-May to mid-October. There is no fruit more overwhelmingly sunny than a peach picked ripe off the tree, but if you are an ice cream lover, you need to lick some Pee Dee's ice cream. It is peachier than a peach itself, with all the added pleasure of creamy coolness: a summer snack par excellence.

Pee Dee Orchards: 11279 U.S. Highway 74 East, Lilesville, NC 704-848-4801

2 ESSENTIAL PEACH COBBLERS

1. **Peachtree Café at the Lane Packing Company:** Highway 96 East and 50 Lane Road, Fort Valley, GA 800-27-PEACH or 478-825-3362 www.lanepacking.com
2. **Belmont Inn:** 104 E. Pickens St., Abbeville, SC 864-459-9625

PEANUT PIE
Wakefield, Virginia

It would be possible to consider peanut pie a poor man's version of pecan pie, because the two are similar,

but if you are a peanut connoisseur, peanut pie at the **Virginia Diner** is second to none. It is a modest-looking wedge, extremely peanutty on top, with a thin amber ribbon separating a blanket of chopped goobers from the crust. It is not gooey-sweet; in fact it is more earthy than syrupy, accenting the unique non-nut soul of the peanut. It comes from the kitchen warm, which is the best possible temperature for full peanut enjoyment, and it has a small dollop of whipped cream on top. A scoop of vanilla ice cream is a welcome companion.

It is stark reality that not all peanuts are equal. Far, far from it. Some peanuts are small and wizened. This pie's goodness is due in large part to the fact that it is made with large, meaty Virginia peanuts roasted to blistery perfection. At the diner, and through the diner's website, these nuts are available salted or not, butter-toasted, spiced, and chocolate-covered.

Virginia Diner: 408 Country Dr. North, Wakefield, VA 888-VADINER or 757-899-3106 www.vadiner.com

PEANUT SOUP
Virginia

Known to some as Tuskegee soup, after the university where George Washington Carver conducted his famous experiments that turned peanuts into everything from tile flooring to peanut butter, peanut soup is a specialty of ham houses and cafes as well as swank restaurants throughout Virginia, especially around Williamsburg. It is a dish that can seem sophisticated or plain, and that serves well as the companion for a sandwich at lunch or as the first course of an elaborate dinner.

Surry County, in which the **Surrey House** is located (please don't ask about the different spellings), is peanut country. Historically, the local hogs ate peanuts, giving their flesh extra richness that would eventually come to define Smithfield ham. Government meddling and overregulation of ham producers has pretty much done away with true Smithfield ham, but the crunch of those good peanuts can still be savored in Surrey House peanut soup. Chicken broth mixed with cream, liberally sprinkled with nuts, and prudently spiced makes for a charmingly old-fashioned bowl of earthy succor. The high-end **Wayside Inn** of Middletown includes creamy, velvet-smooth "colonial peanut soup" in its Old Dominion repertoire (along with spoonbread), but the version we consider just about perfect is the one you'll have at the **Southern Kitchen**, a modest town lunchroom not far from I-81 in New Market. This soup is milky more than creamy, nutty-flavored but not rich like liquid peanut butter, and laced with a fetching onion sweetness. It is an ideal prelude for a dinner of Virginia country ham or crisp-crusted fried chicken.

PEANUT SOUP

Our recipe for peanut soup is based on the kind they serve at the Southern Kitchen: buttery-rich but not creamy. If you want to convert it into a major rib-sticker, stir in a cup of cream or condensed milk at the very end of the cooking process, just before serving. Or, to give it a streak of distinctive luxury, lace each serving with a shot of sherry just before garnishing with peanuts.

   ½ stick butter
   ¾ cup diced celery
   ¾ cup diced green onions
   6 cups chicken stock
   4 teaspoons all-purpose flour
   ¾ cup creamy peanut butter
   1 cup heavy cream (optional)
   6 tablespoons chopped salted
      peanuts

Melt the butter in a saucepan over low heat. Add the celery and onions. Cook, stirring occasionally, until they are tender but not brown. Stir in the chicken stock, bring it to a boil, and boil for 1 minute. Strain the soup and return it to the saucepan. Cool to room temperature.

Mix the flour with just enough cool water to form a paste. Whisk the paste into the broth. Blend in the peanut butter. Simmer slowly for 15 minutes, stirring occasionally. Add the cream, if desired, just before removing the soup from the heat.

Serve hot. Garnish each serving with a tablespoon of chopped salted peanuts.

SERVES 6

In New Market, VA, a sign points the way to peanut soup perfection.

3 FINE PEANUT SOUPS

1. **Southern Kitchen:** 9576 S. Congress St., New Market, VA 540-740-3514
2. **Wayside Inn:** 7783 Main St., Middletown, VA 540-869-1797 or 877-869-1797 www.alongthewayside.com
3. **Surrey House:** 11865 Rolfe Highway, Surry, VA 757-294-3389 www.surreyhouserestaurant.com

PEPPERONI ROLL
West Virginia

A sheaf of pencil-thin twigs of pepperoni folded inside a tube of yeast dough that is risen and then baked: that's a pepperoni roll, the savory snack of choice throughout north-central West Virginia. A cooked roll is a wieldy handful about 6 inches long that resembles the border of a thick pizza. Inside its crust, the resilient red sticks of meat occupy a tight tunnel, the bottom of which has been moistened by their hot-oil seepage, while the sides and top remain soft and fluffy.

It has been claimed that the pepperoni roll was originally designed in 1927 at the **Country Club Bakery** in Fairmont as a handy snack for miners. Today's Country Club pepperoni rolls are tidy little pockets of lightweight bread enclosing three or four chewy pepperoni sticks. **Colasessano's** in Fairmont makes pepperoni rolls that are too big to be carried. They are in fact less like the classic enclosed roll and more like a hot pepperoni grinder in a cut-open loaf, gobbed with sauce and melted cheese.

The most delicious ones we've found are as handy to eat out of hand as a dinner roll. They are made at **Tomaro's**, a vintage neighborhood bakery (since 1914) in the old Elk Point section of Clarksburg. There

A popular snack, pepperoni rolls may have come into being as a quick bite for West Virginia miners.

South

is no place to sit and eat in this tiny store with shelves holding the oven-hot loaves of hard-crust bread, so we dined standing up on the sidewalk. Midmorning, our pepperoni rolls were still so warm that the simple combination of spicy meat, its oozing oil, and the yeasty, just-baked bread was insanely opulent. Mini rolls, a soulful equivalent of cocktail-frank pigs in blankets, were less overwhelming but addictive all day, until the dozen we bought were gone. While Tomaro's doesn't have a formal mail-order business, the business is accustomed to entreaties from Clarksburg expatriates to please, please pack some up and ship them.

Gothic shop of horrors: the West Virginia Penitentiary, now a tourist attraction

A ROLL CALL OF WEST VIRGINIA PEPPERONI ROLLS

1. **Tomaro's Bakery:** 411 N. 4th St., Clarksburg, WV
   304-622-0691
2. **Country Club Bakery:** 1211 Country Club Rd., Fairmont, WV
   304-363-5690
3. **Colasessano's Pizza and Pepperoni Rolls:** 506 Pennsylvania Ave., Fairmont, WV
   304-363-9713
   www.colasessanos.com

WEST VIRGINIA PENITENTIARY

One of the scariest tourist attractions anywhere is the old West Virginia State Penitentiary in Moundsville. The horrifically somber Gothic stone edifice, where hippie killer Charles Manson and his mother were incarcerated (at separate times), was built by convict labor decades ago and was decommissioned in 1995 after the state supreme court deemed tenancy of its small cells to be cruel and unusual punishment. But souvenir T-shirts are available, and tours include a view of the electric chair in which criminals were juiced. The chair is especially interesting because instead of ordering one from whoever manufactured electric chairs at the time, the West Virginia prison authorities sent a team of convicts over to the Ohio pen to study its chair so they could come back and build one for themselves — at a cost much lower than that of a new one.

West Virginia Penitentiary: 818 Jefferson Ave., Moundsville, WV
304-845-6200
www.wvpentours.com

South

TOMARO'S BREAD

If you are a fan of firm-crusted loaves of Italian bread, you need to eat one from Tomaro's in Clarksburg, West Virginia. The old bakery delivers to area grocery stores, but customers who demand that their bread be absolutely fresh come to the source. What amazing loaves! Regulars know to ask for theirs with either a regular crust or a hard crust; even the regular crust has a brawny chew. Serious crust lovers get the loaf that is here known as a "hard crust baked," meaning the same dough is baked longer, directly on the hearth. The bread emerges with an exterior as brittle as a bread stick (but silk-tender inside). Fredda Martin, Tomaro's sales manager, told us that some old-timers ask for extra-hard crust baked, the outside of which feels like hardtack. "The hard-crust lovers are fading," she advised. "New customers like it softer. And the soft does last longer." Fredda reminded us that Tomaro's motto isn't just clever wordplay. It's good advice, especially regarding hard crust loaves: "Eat Tomaro's Bread Today."

PERLOO
Lowcountry

In true gallimaufrian spirit, many Lowcountry dishes that contain many different ingredients go by the name of perloo. Or perlau. Or pilaw, pilau, or pilaf. Call it what you will, the common denominator is rice, and the common history is cooks making something big and bountiful out of what they happened to have on hand.

Charleston's citadel of easygoing but just-right Lowcountry cooking, the **Hominy Grill**, makes what it calls purloo — an energetically spiced rice casserole loaded with chicken, sausage, and shrimp — as well as the soft-tempered dish known as country captain, which is white-meat chicken in spicy tomato sauce ladled over aromatic rice. Just north of the city in Mount Pleasant at **Gullah Cuisine**, an African-American gloss on the concept is known as Gullah rice, an eye-opening dish that reminds us of gumbo but without the liquid — shrimp, spicy sausage disks, and chicken shreds all mixed together with rice that has been so intensely infused with spice that it has turned mahogany brown. Its flavor is big

The perloo at Gullah Cuisine in Mount Pleasant, SC, tastes like an intensified gumbo.

Hominy Grill in Charleston, home to the region's best Lowcountry cooking

and dignified, and it is the perfect example of a meal with modest origins that has assumed a regal aura. The offering at **82 Queen**, Charleston's most deluxe purveyor of Lowcountry cuisine, is known as Frogmore stew (also called Beaufort stew and Lowcountry boil): smoked sausage, shrimp, corn, nuggets of okra, and red potatoes, all mixed together in a tomato-sauce base. Although Frogmore stew supposedly was conceived as a shrimpers' way to use leftovers, 82 Queen's version, accompanied by slabs of grilled sourdough bread, is virtually aristocratic.

Down in St. Augustine, Florida, while looking for Minorcan clam chowder (page 152), we came across chicken pilau as the daily special while sitting at the counter of **Schooner's Seafood House**. "This here pilau is good but needs a kick in the you-know-what," suggested a cologne-scented fatso in beltless high-pocket slacks and a torso-hugging, no-iron shortsleeve shirt. He threw his tie back over one shoulder and poured a thick coat of dark red datil pepper

MIDDLETON PLACE PLANTATION

About a half-hour northwest of Charleston, the plantation home of Henry Middleton, president of the First Continental Congress, can be a whole day's diversion. Its sweeping green terraces, gardens, and manmade lakes are magnificent and impeccably maintained. Attractions include Eliza's House, a freedman's dwelling that shows what life was like for African-Americans who stayed on the plantation after the Civil War, and the plantation stable yards, where farriers, potters, carpenters, and weavers demonstrate their eighteenth-century skills. Trail rides are available from the Equestrian Center, and the Middleton Place restaurant features such traditional Lowcountry fare as she-crab soup and Huguenot torte.

Middleton Place Plantation:
4300 Ashley River Rd.,
Charleston, SC
843-556-6020
www.middletonplace.org

sauce over the old-time coastal casserole of chicken and rice, then forked into it with a madman's glee. Pilau proved to be a welcoming tableau for the fiery sauce, which transformed it from palliative comfort food into a meal so exhilarating that a cool piece of Key lime pie became a necessary conclusion.

4 FINE PERLOOS

1. **Gullah Cuisine:** 1717 Highway 17 North, Mount Pleasant, SC
843-881-9076
www.gullahcuisine.com
2. **Hominy Grill:** 207 Rutledge Ave., Charleston, SC
843-937-0930
www.hominygrill.com
3. **82 Queen:** 82 Queen St., Charleston, SC
843-723-7591
www.82queen.com
4. **Schooner's Seafood House:** 3560 N. Ponce De Leon Blvd., St. Augustine, FL
904-826-0233
www.schooners-seafood.com

PIMENTO CHEESE
The Well-Bred South

Other regions of the country scarcely think about pimento cheese. In the South, it is an obsession — as a topping for cheeseburgers, as a dip, and as the star of a supercharged sandwich. Perhaps *supercharged* is not quite the right term, for the pimiento is the mildest of peppers (zero on the Scoville scale, which is used to measure hotness), and in its basic form, pimento cheese — southerners drop the i — is simply orange American cheese dotted with bits of red for the sake of appearance. There is no pimento cheese sandwich more polite than what is served at the charming old **Woman's Exchange of Memphis**, where it is presented in quarters, crustless, as a garnish for the chicken salad plate. **Merridee's Breadbasket**, a hometown restaurant and bakery in Franklin, Tennessee, mixes mild grated cheddar cheese with dots of red pepper, relish, and mayonnaise and layers it between wheaty slices of Merridee's oven-fresh white bread. The tender bread and balmy cheese, layered with a crisp leaf or two of lettuce, is quiet contentment. Outside of Franklin, in a bucolic countryside of horse farms and two-lane roads, the **Henpeck Market** amplifies the formula by weaving rugged shreds of jack and cheddar with hot horseradish and peppery seasonings. The zesty spread is good on plain white bread, better when the bread is buttered and grilled, best with slices of bacon and tomato added.

The Henpeck Market in Franklin, TN, amplifies the pimento cheese formula with jack, cheddar, and horseradish.

South

Magnolia's rendition of pimento cheese makes this simple classic classier.

The sign at **Magnolia's** in Charleston, South Carolina, says UPTOWN DOWN SOUTH, and true to that mission statement, its pimento cheese is pretty fancy stuff. Served as an appetizer, it is a mound of finely chopped sharp cheese mixed with pimiento and enough green olive bits to give it an inviting pucker. It is surrounded by triangles of salt-spangled flatbread that are so thin and crisp that you need to be careful not to crush and splinter them when spreading on the chunky cheese.

Southern cooks are fond of using pimento cheese on hamburgers, a custom we first encountered at the late, lamented Ruby Seahorse Grill on Edisto Island. At Charlotte, North Carolina's delightfully disreputable late-night beer-and-burger hangout, the **Penguin Drive-In**, melted pimento cheese atop the jumbo hamburger known as the Full Blown Hemi makes it into what customers call the Full Blown Pimp. The most beloved pimento cheese beacon in South Carolina is Columbia's **Rockaway Athletic Club**, a restaurant without a sign (everybody just knows where it

is), where the pimento cheeseburger is a large, craggy patty on a beautiful, glossy-skinned bakery bun completely smothered with drippy, goopy cheese with just enough pepper and spice to remind you of the pimientos' presence.

6 OUTSTANDING PIMENTO CHEESES

1. **Henpeck Market:** 1268 Lewisburg Pike, Franklin, TN
615-794-7518
www.henpeckmarket.com
2. **Magnolia's:** 185 E. Bay St., Charleston, SC
843-577-7771
www.magnolias-blossom-cypress .com
3. **Merridee's Breadbasket:** 110 Fourth Ave. South, Franklin, TN
615-790-3755
www.merridees.com
4. **Penguin Drive-In,** 1921 Commonwealth Ave., Charlotte, NC
704-375-6959
5. **Woman's Exchange of Memphis:** 88 Racine St., Memphis, TN
901-327-5681
www.womans-exchange.com
6. **Rockaway Athletic Club:** 2719 Rosewood Dr., Columbia, SC
803-256-1075

PO BOY, OYSTER LOAF, MUFFALETTA
New Orleans

Along with the Delaware Valley, New Orleans vies for bragging rights as the source of the nation's biggest va-

Biggest of the big: the New Orleans po boy, one of the wonders of the sandwich world

riety of really big sandwiches, foremost among them the po boy. And the good news is that none of the Big Easy's top sandwich shops were put out of commission by Katrina. We have long been on record favoring **Domilise's**, and we shall not retract our faith in the corner sandwich store, for its fully dressed hot smoked sausage and gravy po boy is one of the wonders of the sandwich world. But let's also consider **Johnny's**. Of the forty-five different po boys on Johnny's menu, including a two-sausage, ground-beef bonanza called the Judge Bossetta Special and cold cuts and hot meats and fried seafood of all kinds, the one that wins our attention every time is roast beef — arguably a Creole signature dish. We can say with certainty that all of Johnny's sandwiches are pretty wonderful, even the one filled quite monomaniacally with French fries(!), because they are built on long lengths of fluffy-centered French bread. The bread is particularly companionable for roast beef, able to absorb and hold all the flavorful juices that characterize the garlicky, deeply seasoned beefs that are a pride of Creole cooks. If you're

South

HANSEN'S SNO-BLIZ
New Orleans is best known for food that is hot and spicy. Hansen's Sno-Bliz is cool and soothing. It was here that the shaved ice machine was invented, in 1939. You may have had a fast-food Slurpee or similar palate-refresher that combines ice and syrup, but Hansen's is something else. Its machine, now seventy years old, makes ice that is neither crushed nor crystals but more like newly fallen snow. Flavored syrups are added in layers, so you taste them all the way to the bottom of the cup, and per the recommendation of Stephen Rushmore, who directed us to this bracing snack shack, we get ours with condensed milk on top, adding richness to refreshment.
Hansen's Sno-Bliz: 4801
    Tchoupitoulas St.,
    New Orleans, LA
    504-891-9788
    www.snobliz.com
    Hansen's is open in the summer
    from approximately 1 p.m. to 7
    p.m. every day except Monday.

lucky, the sandwich makers will have some debris (that's the scraps and nuggets and burned ends from the cutting board) to pile in with the well-done slices. Traditional condiments for a fully dressed roast beef po boy are lettuce, tomato, mayonnaise, and pickle. Hot sauce is an option also worth considering.

The immaculate Casamento's in New Orleans fries sparkling-fresh oysters and tucks them into po boys.

AUDUBON INSECTARIUM

Hot, damp, and disheveled, New Orleans has been an insect asylum going back at least to the yellow fever epidemic of 1847. But it was not until 2008 that the city's most populous group was duly honored with the opening of the largest bug museum in the nation, the Audubon Insectarium. Here is an ode to entymology in all its glory and ghastliness, from a walk-in Japanese garden of living butterflies to a single jar filled with 400,000 dead termites. Visitors are invited to eat a chocolate-covered cricket and to watch dung beetles eat dung. Despite the museum's contention that insects add "intrigue, color, texture, and majesty to our world," its sponsors include the DA Exterminating company and Terminix. The museum's catchphrase is "You'll be infested with fun."

Audubon Insectarium: 423 Canal St., New Orleans, LA 800-744-7394 or 504-581-4629

At the **Parkway Bakery & Tavern**, debris is not called debris, just gravy, but it is so substantial that a po boy of only gravy, at about half the price of a full-bore roast beef sandwich, is hugely beefy and fully satisfying. If you are really hungry, we suggest the unlikely surf-and-turf po boy, which includes not only roast beef and gravy but a large school of fried shrimp that magically retain their crisp crust despite the bovine onslaught. Another not-to-be-missed roast beef po boy is served at the deliciously divey **Parasol's Restaurant and Bar** in the city's Irish Channel, where the long-cooked beef, supersaturated with gravy, becomes clumps and shreds as tender as the finest pulled pork.

The oyster loaf is a close relative of the po boy, featuring fried oysters. Note that name: *loaf.* Indeed, to call it a sandwich is to stretch the definition of the word, because an oyster loaf is one entire normal-sized loaf of bread into which are heaped countless hot-from-the-oil fried oysters. There is no better setting in which to savor one of these ultra–big boys than **Casamento's**, a spanking-clean neighborhood oyster bar that closes for a long summer vacation when oysters are not at their peak. Casamento's loads a couple of dozen ocean-sweet fried oysters, bursting with marine flavor, between two big slabs of what locals know as pan bread, like the top and bottom halves of a good-sized loaf of white bread, which has been slightly toasted so it has a buttery, crisp crunch to its skin. A total-oyster feast for two would be twenty-four just-opened raw ones on the half shell followed by a full-sized oyster loaf accompanied, of course, by cold Dixie or Abita Amber beer.

Central Grocery lays claim to inventing the muffaletta, a New Orleans sandwich on a circular loaf of chewy bread that is sliced horizontally, like a yeasty flying saucer. The cold cuts stacked on the bottom half include salami, ham, and provolone; they are topped with a spicy mélange of chopped green and black olives fragrant with anchovies and garlic; the bread is generously sprinkled with olive oil; and the whole package is cut in quarters — each a modest serving for one — and wrapped in paper so you can carry it away. We do love the original sandwich, but we also need to salute the more commodious **Napoleon House**, a historic eighteenth-century, full-menu French Quarter lounge that serves quarters, halves, and wholes

and adds pastrami and Swiss cheese to the mix, then — iconoclastically — heats the sandwich, creating a truly heroic variation. And out in St. Bernard Parish, **Arabi Food Store** offers not only classic muffs but also laudable hot dog and hot chili po boys.

MUST-EAT NEW ORLEANS SANDWICHES

1. **Domilise's Sandwich Shop and Bar:** 5240 Annunciation St., New Orleans, LA 504-899-9126
2. **Parkway Bakery & Tavern:** 538 Hagen Ave., New Orleans, LA 504-482-3047 www.parkwaybakeryandtavern nola.com
3. **Johnny's Po Boys:** 511 St. Louis St., New Orleans, LA 504-524-8129
4. **Casamento's Restaurant:** 4330 Magazine St., New Orleans, LA 504-895-9761 www.casamentosrestaurant.com
5. **Parasol's Restaurant and Bar:** 2533 Constance St., New Orleans, LA 504-897-5413 www.parasols.com
6. **Central Grocery:** 923 Decatur St., New Orleans, LA 504-523-1620
7. **Arabi Food Store:** 650 Friscoville Ave., Arabi, LA 504-277-2333
8. **Napoleon House:** 500 Chartres St., New Orleans, LA 504-524-9752 www.napoleonhouse.com

South

PULLED PORK
Mobile, Alabama

There are good reasons to chop up barbecued pork (it mixes well with sauce) as well as to slice it (for a sizzle on the griddle), but the ultimate way to turn a hunk of cooked pig into a plate of edible ecstasy is to use your hands and pull pieces away, carefully separating chunks and shreds from any excess fat. The resulting hodgepodge of large and small pieces, some butter-soft, others chewier, is perhaps more fork-friendly than sandwich-suited, but even if it does tend to tumble from the bun, pulled pork is the most fun for an adventuresome tongue. It is found on barbecue menus everywhere, but the one place to which we want to direct your attention is the **Brick Pit** of Mobile, Alabama. Brick Pit butts loll for some thirty hours in the haze of smoldering pecan and hickory wood as their fat oozes flavor into every fiber of the meat. They are not basted, spiced, or seasoned in any way; their virtue is a simple concord of smoke and swine. When pulled into a pile, each shred, as unique as a snowflake, is exquisitely moist and radiant with flavor. The Brick Pit serves it undressed, which is the way it should be — it needs to be tasted in its pure and perfect form — but accompanies it with a dark, intriguing sauce (regular or spicy-sweet) that adds its own beautiful chimes to the symphonic satisfaction of superior barbecue.

THE SOUTH'S BEST PULLED PORK

Brick Pit: 5456 Old Shell Rd., Mobile, AL
251-343-0001
www.brickpit.com

Pulled pork at the Brick Pit in Mobile, AL, spends thirty hours over pecan and hickory wood attaining perfection.

RED VELVET CAKE
Throughout the South

Red velvet cake once was found on menus and in community cookbooks from everywhere. In the mid-twentieth century, it became almost exclusively southern, and then rare even in the South, but in recent years, it has made a comeback. Like cupcakes, its charm has a big kitsch quotient that makes it every bit as comfortable on trendy menus as in humble cafes. In fact, some of the most delicious red velvet cake comes in the form of sophisticated cupcakes at the suave new **Sugar Bakeshop** in Charleston, South Carolina, where each moist cake is slathered with frosting when ordered.

Moist, light, and pleasantly chocolaty, red velvet cake owes its vivid hue to food coloring.

For strangers to this culinary curiosity, we must explain that red velvet cake really is scarlet. It usually contains cocoa and has a chocolate taste, but its hue has nothing to do with flavor and everything to do with an astonishingly large measure of food coloring.

Homemade Ice Cream and Pie Kitchen of Louisville serves a classic: blood-red, moist, and pleasantly chocolaty. At **Prejean's** in Cajun country, it comes ribboned with drizzles of chocolate syrup and garnished with berries and whipped cream, the icing insanely sweet. And if you are looking for the most, and most buttery, cream cheese frosting, you need to head west to **Lo-Lo's Chicken and Waffles**, a soul-food beacon in Phoenix, Arizona.

It's always fun to see red velvet cake in diners, meat and threes (page 180), and soul-food cafes, but to be honest, we never fully appreciated it until we had the one served at **Regas**, Knoxville's fine-dining beacon since

1919. It is chocolaty but without devil's-food force — more reminiscent of fine Swiss milk chocolate magically transformed into the tenderest of cakes. Nearly a half-inch of frosting separates three tall layers, and the swirled frosting on top is sprinkled with a confetti of pink coconut shreds. It's even better with a scoop of the kitchen's homemade vanilla ice cream alongside. (Regas is not your typical Sterns recommendation. It is expensive and relatively formal. The radiantly beefy prime rib is what we hope for in a high-end meal, and the house's unique spinach-strawberry salad heaped with crumbled gorgonzola is a welcome eye-opener.)

**EXEMPLARY
RED VELVET CAKES**

1. **Regas:** 318 N. Gay St., Knoxville, TN
865-63-REGAS
www.thechophouse.com

The siren sign of Prejean's in Lafayette, LA, where red velvet cake is a signature dish.

2. **Sugar Bakeshop:** 59½ Cannon St., Charleston, SC
843-579-2891
www.sugarbake.com

3. **Homemade Ice Cream and Pie Kitchen:** 2525 Bardstown Rd., Louisville, KY
502-459-8184
See www.piekitchen.com for additional locations.

4. **Lo-Lo's Chicken and Waffles:** 10 W. Yuma St., Phoenix, AZ
602-340-1304
www.loloschickenandwaffles.com

5. **Prejean's:** 3480 N.E. Evangeline Throughway (I-49 North), Lafayette, LA
337-896-3247
www.prejeans.com

ROCK SHRIMP
Titusville, Florida

Rodney Thompson, founder of **Dixie Crossroads Seafood Restaurant**, is the man who figured out how to make rock shrimp something great to eat. It was in the early 1970s and he was at the helm of a trawler he had built as a shrimp boat, but he was getting nowhere trying to net the always-popular tender-shelled brown shrimp. Encouraged by the captain of a research vessel who directed him 20 miles east of Melbourne, Thompson dropped his nets into the deep water and came up with half a ton of rock shrimp, once considered worthless because of their shells, which are as hard as a lobster's. "If you can figure out how to sell those peanuts," the captain said, "you'll be a millionaire!" Thompson shipped them to the Fulton Fish Market in New York City ... where they spoiled because no one knew what to do with the seemingly impenetrable oddities. He thought they could be steamed in the shell like Maryland crabs, but even after steaming, they were every bit as tough to crack as a crab, and there was too little meat in each to make the effort worthwhile. Thompson's daughter Laurilee had an idea: split the shrimp first, butter them, then put them under a broiler still in the shell. The results, extracted from the shell, were grand, as sweet and luxurious as Maine lobster, inspiring Thompson to invent a high-speed machine that splits and cleans rock shrimp. In 1983 he opened the Dixie Crossroads with his wild ocean shrimp as the menu headliner. You can have them fried or steamed, rolled in coconut, filled with crabmeat stuffing, or wrapped in bacon, but plain old broiled is best.

Dixie Crossroads Seafood Restaurant: 1475 Garden St., Titusville, FL
321-268-5000
www.dixiecrossroads.com

SMOKED MULLET
Florida

Although it sometimes is known as Biloxi bacon, smoked mullet is a Florida thing. Throughout the panhandle and around Tampa Bay, you will find it on restaurant menus and along the byways in little shops and at roadside stands. Since 1948 the place to sit down and eat it is an open-air joint by St. Pete Beach called **Ted Peters Famous Smoked Fish**, where the menu also features smoked mahi-mahi, smoked salmon, and smoked mackerel, stupendously good smoked fish spread, as well as worthy cheeseburgers and essential potato salad. The mullet, netted locally in shallow-draft bird-dog boats, starts as a very oily fish. But when it is long-smoked over red oak, its oils evaporate and infuse the heavy flesh with richness as forceful as that of a macadamia nut, and not the least bit fishy. Sided by a bunch of crackers, it is the archetypal cracker feast. (Attention, fishermen: If you bring your own catch, Ted Peters will smoke it for $1.50 per pound.)

Ted Peters Famous Smoked Fish: 1350 Pasadena Ave. South, South Pasadena, FL 727-381-7931

SMOTHERED CABBAGE
New Iberia, Louisiana

Please pay attention, even if you think you don't like cabbage. What Brenda Placide serves in her out-of-the-way soul-food diner in southernmost Acadiana bears no resemblance to the stark, smelly, and strangely bland leaf that many of us learned to abhor as part of school lunch, or perhaps in a prison cafeteria. **Brenda's** cabbage is smothered, meaning sautéed for a long time with an Independence Day fireworks show of Cajun spices. It is so luxurious that the small shreds of cabbage actually remind us more of cooked bacon fat than of a healthful herbaceous crucifer. To balance such tenderness, the cabbage is larded with disks of muscular sausage that deliv-ers its own volley of pepper heat and swampland spice and sweet pork perfume. It makes all kinds of sense that New Iberia is just 7 miles north of Avery Island, where Tabasco peppers grow.

Brenda's Dine In & Take Out: 411 W. Pershing St., New Iberia, LA 337-367-0868

STEAMED OYSTERS
The Carolinas

Fastidious epicures, keep your distance from a Lowcountry oyster roast, where bivalves are steamed over an open fire just long enough for the shells to begin to open. It is a one-utensil meal, that utensil being a knife, which the eater uses to pry the shell fully apart, then sever the meat and finally convey that meat to mouth. At **Bowens**

Abandon preconceptions, all ye who enter here. At her New Iberia soul-food diner, Brenda Placide presides over sensational smothered cabbage.

Island outside of Charleston, the devil-may-care ritual has been going on since 1946, when May and Jimmy Bowen started serving oysters to the public at their fish camp.

To call the facilities informal is a hilarious understatement. Garden shovels are used to bring cooked oysters to tables, which have big holes in the center with garbage cans underneath so diners can toss shells as they eat. These are some of the ugliest oysters anywhere, their gnarled outer surface caked with pluff, which is the silt that clings to them when they are harvested. Unlike pretty oysters presented by the dozen on the half shell, these come in clusters — three, six, or more of them all stuck together in a clump of shells on which you need to find openings to pry apart and retrieve meat. They are a little salty and marine-sweet, mild enough to be maddeningly addictive. Buy them by the tray or on an all-you-can-eat basis.

At **Sunny Side**, you can have oysters any way you like, so long as you like them steamed. What you get is a peck (a quarter bushel) or a half peck of just-steamed Stumpy Point bivalves served with drawn butter and Sunny Side's hot cocktail sauce. That's the way it has been at this single-purpose eatery since it opened in 1935. Actually, there's more than oysters. Shrimp, scallops, and crab legs are also available, also steamed. In fact, Sunny Side boasts of not having any kitchen whatsoever other than its steamer out back, from which the oysters are brought to be shucked, served, and eaten at the horseshoe-shaped bar. They are meaty, salty critters, well cushioned by a dip in butter and given exclamatory potency by the sauce, which is poured from silver pitchers. Forget hushpuppies, slaw, and French fries. The only available side dish is broccoli — steamed, of course!

SENSATIONAL STEAMED OYSTERS

Bowens Island Restaurant: 1870 Bowens Island Rd., Folly Island, SC
843-795-2757
www.bowensislandrestaurant.com

Sunny Side Oyster Bar: 1102 Washington St., Williamston, NC
252-792-3416
Second location: Sunny Side Too Oyster Bar, 111 W. Main St., Garner, NC
919-662-7994

STONE CRAB
South Florida

The most famous place to eat stone crabs is the unambiguously named **Joe's Stone Crab** of Miami Beach. They are impeccable; claws only, of course, ranging in size from a serving of mediums about 3 or 4 inches long to jumbos like a big turkey drumstick. Their coral-pink shells are packed with meat of intense ocean taste even sweeter than that of perfectly cooked lobster. Their serving temperature is balmy, coaxing all the flavor out, and they can be improved only by a dainty dip into Joe's creamy mustard sauce.

Joe's gets its crabs from **Keys Fisheries** on Marathon, so if you are traveling along the Overseas Highway and want them fresh off the boat, inscribe this jolly place on your hit list. The experience of dining here is completely different from the one at Joe's, where inevitably you will wait in line (no reservations are taken) and pay top dollar (Damon Runyon once joked that stone crabs are sold by the karat), but the claws cannot be faulted. And in contrast to ordering from one of Joe's formally attired waitstaff, the process of getting crabs at Keys Fisheries is purposely silly. The custom is to place your order at a counter and give the order-taker a celebrity name, not yours, to call out when it's ready. Plates and utensils are disposable, dining is virtually outdoors (with plastic sheeting to keep out wind and rain, if necessary), and the view is fishing boats coming or going and a nightly ooh-and-ahh sunset. The menu is replete with local seafood dishes, from conch chowder to Key West pink shrimp; many devotees swear by the lobster Reuben, a locally loved grilled sandwich of lobster meat, Swiss cheese, sauerkraut, and Thousand Islands dressing on rye. But it's stone crabs you want. Nowhere will you find them cheaper or more perfectly fresh.

2 TOP STONE CRABS

Keys Fisheries: 3502 Gulf View Ave., Marathon, FL
305-743-4353
www.keysfisheries.com
Joe's Stone Crab: 11 Washington Ave., Miami Beach, FL
305-673-0365
www.joesstonecrab.com
Joe's is closed in August and September.

STREAK O' LEAN
Deep South

Once a familiar farmhouse dish, streak o' lean has virtually disappeared from the American cook's repertoire, and that's a shame, because it is one incredible plate of food. If you like your bacon well fatted and thick enough to have a crust that encases a thin ribbon of pig meat, you will love this ribbon of salt-cured fatback. And if you are an aficionado of no-nonsense blue-plate diners, you will especially enjoy eating it at **Bobby & June's Kountry Kitchen** in Atlanta. There is no way the cost of a meal will reach into the double digits at this big-city bastion of good ol' country cookin'. Lunch plates can be swell, but breakfast is the meal to have. Buttermilk biscuits are big and beautiful, and you can get them with an order of streak o' lean, which is semitranslucent bacon fat with just a few wisps of pink lean running through it. The biscuit will most likely still be oven-hot, so this über-bacon will quite literally melt right into it.

For about a half a century, streak o' lean has been the main breakfast attraction at the **Waysider** restaurant in Tuscaloosa, Alabama. Four crisp-fried slabs, each a good quarter-inch thick, arrive on the plate — with gravy and biscuits, of course. Words cannot convey the overwhelming sumptuousness of this dish, which for bacon lovers is a spiritual event. It is quintessential bacon, bacon squared, bacon to the nth degree, with its chewy, lean veins of meat striating a strip of amber fat that we want to call lascivious — a piece of food transformed into utter, unadulterated flavor.

2 MEMORABLE STREAKS O' LEAN

1. **Waysider:** 1512 Greensboro Ave., Tuscaloosa, AL
205-345-8239
2. **Bobby & June's Kountry Kitchen:** 375 14th St. NW, Atlanta, GA
404-876-3872

SWEET TEA
Dixie

Forget the Mason-Dixon Line and red state/blue state taxonomy. The most definitive partition of the United States is between those places that serve sweet tea (the South) and those that serve sugarless tea (everywhere else). To a stern Yankee, the first taste of true sweet tea can seem like pure glucose, but in Dixie and west into Texas, it is nothing short of eau de vie. It is best drunk from a tall, widemouth glass with clear fresh ice cubes or heaps of crushed ice. Lots and lots of ice, always lots of ice. There is no way to describe just how welcome sweet tea can be alongside barbecue, salty country ham, spicy fried chicken, or just about any meat-and-three meal (page 180) that features porky, well-seasoned vegetables. It quenches thirst, replenishes verve and vitality, and stimulates appetite for a nice hot supper.

No one in history has drunk one single glass of sweet tea. It is customary for a restaurant to provide each table with a pitcher to pour refills as

Sweet tea, as vital to a southern meal as a napkin

needed, or at least for a waitress to patrol the dining room topping off glasses. And never is it presented as a small portion. At such classic southern eateries as **Melear's Barbecue** in Fayetteville, Georgia, **Stamey's** in Greensboro, North Carolina, **Lupie's** in Charlotte, and **Mike Linnig's** fish camp in Louisville, it comes not in a normal-sized glass but in a tankard or a Mason jar, or a tumbler or a goblet holding at least a pint and sometimes a quart.

The differences among sweet teas have more to do with strength and freshness than with dramatic flavor innovations. The tea at **Gullah Cuisine**, north of Charleston, South Carolina, stands out because it is sweetened with honey. At the **Blue Willow Inn** of Social Circle, Georgia, where it is lovingly referred to as "the champagne of the South," the kitchen's admonition is to serve tea that is "strong and just a little too sweet." The **Beacon Drive-In** of Spartanburg, South Carolina, boasts of serving "the great drive-in tea of the South — generously sweetened, laced with a touch of lemon, served over a pack of shaved ice. We sell more tea than any other single restaurant in the U.S.A.!"

EXEMPLARY SWEET TEAS

1. **Beacon Drive-In:** 255 John B. White Sr. Blvd., Spartanburg, SC 864-585-9387 www.beacondrivein.com
2. **Blue Willow Inn:** 294 N. Cherokee Rd., Social Circle, GA 770-464-2131 www.bluewillowinn.com
3. **Gullah Cuisine:** 1717 Highway 17 North, Mount Pleasant, SC 843-881-9076 www.gullahcuisine.com
4. **Lupie's Café:** 2718 Monroe Rd., Charlotte, NC 704-374-1232 Second location: 101-A Old Statesville Rd., Huntersville, NC 704-948-3959 www.lupiescafe.com
5. **Melear's Barbecue:** Highway 85, Fayetteville, GA 770-461-7180 www.melearspitcookedbarbecue.com
6. **Stamey's:** 2206 High Point Rd., Greensboro, NC 336-299-9888 Second location: 2812 Battleground Ave. (U.S. Route 220 North), Greensboro, NC 336-288-9275 www.stameys.com
7. **Mike Linnig's:** 9308 Cane Run Rd., Louisville, KY 502-937-9888 www.mikelinnigsrestaurant.com

TAMALE
Mississippi River Valley

Highway 61 leads south out of Memphis into cotton country, where the blues were born. There are wonderful things to eat in this land of heartache set to slide guitar, most of them widely known icons of Dixie soul: barbecue, catfish, and vegetables aplenty. But few people outside the region know about its most prevalent dish, the hot tamale. Between the **A&R Bar-B-Que** just down the street from Graceland and **Solly's Hot Tamales** in Vicksburg, countless men and women, black and white, sell their steamy corn-husk packets from street-corner carts, back porches, tamale-only shops, pork parlors, and steak houses. Tamales are eaten standing up by hand or at a table with a fork; they are a snack, an hors d'oeuvre, and a meal; they are served plain, wrapped in butcher paper, or on a plate topped with chili; you buy them tied up with string by threes and packed into large coffee cans that hold exactly three dozen.

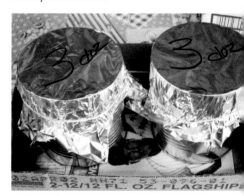

Coffee cans full of mouthwatering tamales, a Mississippi River tradition

South

We have long sought a logical historical or cultural explanation for tamales' ubiquity along the Mississippi River, and we have actually found several. Nearly every tamale person has a good story to tell about how this particular dish got so popular in this particular place. And every one of those stories is different! Even tamale makers who have no idea why tamales are a Mississippi River valley passion agree that the tradition stretches back in time nearly as far as the blues.

CAT HEAD DELTA BLUES & FOLK ART

In the heart of old Clarksdale, an amazing store on old Delta Avenue is a resource for anything you need to know about life in this part of Mississippi. Cat Head stocks hard-to-find recordings, local folk art, and roots-music publications, and it is the instigator of the annual Juke Joint Festival. While we were stocking up on a Son House CD and a biography of Ike Turner (both men Clarksdale natives), proprietor Roger Stolle gave us a thorough rundown of where to find great regional eats in the area, ranging from tamales and barbecue to fried chicken livers and spaghetti.

Cat Head Delta Blues & Folk Art: 252 Delta Ave., Clarksdale, MS
662-624-5992
www.cathead.biz

Folklore designates the crossroads of Highways 61 and 49 in Clarksdale, Mississippi, as the spot where Robert Johnson sold his soul to the Devil in exchange for music mastery. In 1924, when Johnson was thirteen, Abraham Davis began selling sandwiches in Clarksdale. He opened **Abe's Bar-B-Que** at the infamous crossroads in 1937, and today his grandson Pat Davis runs the place, which is known for pecan-smoked pork and hot tamales. Served three to an order, with or without chili on top, Abe's tamales are packed into cayenne-red husks, their yellow cornmeal moist with drippings from a mixture of beef and pork. The recipe is Abe's, unchanged. "No doubt Granddaddy got it from someone in town," Pat suggests, reminding us that Abe had come to the United States from Lebanon, where tamales aren't a big part of the culinary mix. Why Abe thought they would sell well in his barbecue place is a head-scratcher. "There were no

From Graceland to Vicksburg, steamy corn-husk tamales are sold from street carts and porches and at steak houses.

Mexican restaurants here then," Pat says. "And as far as I know, not many Mexicans."

While we were browsing in Clarksdale at Cat Head Delta Blues & Folk Art (see page 204), we talked tamale with proprietors Scott and Jennifer Stolle, who pointed us to their favorite source, the **White Front Café** over on Highway 1 in Rosedale. Jennifer also apprised us of the cracker issue. When served tamales at Abe's, we had been given a plate full of saltines on the side, and the waitress had said, "I'll bring you more if you need them." Her offer meant nothing to us

Succulent beyond measure, the tamales at Rhoda's in Lake Village, AR, claim divine inspiration.

South

DELTA BLUES MUSEUM

It is staggering to count how many of the great blues musicians have come from the Mississippi Delta, Clarksdale in particular. To honor them and their music, the Delta Blues Museum, located in the town's old train terminal, features a guitar gallery of great instruments and specific exhibits dedicated to such native-son giants as B.B. King, Robert Johnson, Son House, Bessie Smith, and Big Mama Thornton. It also houses the Muddy Waters Cabin, the small wood-frame shack in which Muddy was raised in the 1920s and 1930s.

Delta Blues Museum:
1 Blues Alley, Clarksdale, MS
662-627-6820
www.deltabluesmuseum.org

until Jennifer told us that many tamale eaters insist on scooping bites of filling from their husk and putting them on crackers, adding crunch to the otherwise mealy food.

Doe's Eat Place is known by devoted carnivores for serving some of America's most delicious steaks, in the back room/kitchen of a dilapidated former grocery store on Greenville's once notoriously wicked Nelson Street. The improbable restaurant, in which customers sit adjacent to the stove where French fries sizzle in big iron skillets, is the source of some 450 dozen tamales per week. Most are packed in coffee cans to go — three dozen per can — but many are served as appetizers to precede heavyweight sirloins and porterhouses. We spoke with "Little Doe" Signa at the grill in the parlor where he makes the steaks, and over the sputter of beef in the roaring heat of the grill, he told us that it was his parents, "Big Doe" and Mamie Signa, who started the tamale tradition in their grocery store back in 1941, simply because it was a good way to make a little cheap beef go a long way. Steamed in parchment rather than corn husks, Doe's tamales are fine-textured and luxuriously oily. A basketful of plastic-wrapped cracker two-packs is provided.

Across the Mississippi River from Greenville, in Lake Village, Arkansas, we visited with Rhoda and James Adams, who run **Rhoda's Famous Hot Tamales**. James believes that the region's tamale tradition goes back to the late 1940s and a man known as Hot Tamale Charlie. "When I was a boy living in the country, I used to come to Lake Village and watch him sell his tamales out on the street from a bicycle wagon," he recalls. "They were fifty cents a dozen. People bought them from his stacked-full lard can. When he opened up that can, the aroma would knock you down with goodness." Rhoda's tamales are succulent beyond measure, luminous with spice that made our lips tingle until noon. What's her secret? "Chicken," she explains. "I add it to the beef." This is not random parts of chicken, certainly not mild white meat. Rhoda uses only thighs, including skin — "all but the gristle," she jokes — thus infusing her tamales with the flavor that gives so much soul food its soulfulness: chicken fat. She says she learned the recipe from an Oklahoma woman many years ago, but if you ask Rhoda, it isn't the chicken that makes the difference; it is God. She points to the blue T-shirt she's wearing, which says, "When praises go up, blessings come down."

6 TOP TAMALES

1. **Rhoda's Famous Hot Tamales:** 714 St. Mary St., Lake Village, AR 870-265-3108

2. **White Front Café:** 902 Main St. (Route 1), Rosedale, MS 662-759-3842
3. **Doe's Eat Place:** 502 Nelson St., Greenville, MS 662-334-3315 See www.doeseatplace.com for additional locations.
4. **Abe's Bar-B-Q:** 616 N. State St., Clarksdale, MS 601-624-9947 www.abesbbq.com
5. **A&R Bar-B-Que:** 1802 Elvis Presley Blvd., Memphis, TN 901-774-7444 See www.aandrbbq.com for additional locations.
6. **Solly's Hot Tamales:** 1921 Washington St., Vicksburg, MS 601-636-2020

VIRGINIA HAM
Virginia

A country ham smells strong. It is extremely salty and a tough chew. It costs three times as much as a canned one, and if you order it by mail, it will arrive covered with mold in a burlap sack. Sound good? It is! Like aged veined cheese, sourdough bread, and fine old Bordeaux, country ham arouses the strange allure of flavors that teeter on the refined side of rot.

Although the process of curing pork is centuries old, the term *country ham* did not exist until the middle of the twentieth century, when it first was used to describe cured hams (both smoked and unsmoked) produced in rural locations as diverse as Vermont, Georgia, and, of course, Virginia. Virginia's hams are the

Wafer-thin slices of Virginia ham luxuriate in redeye gravy; biscuits are essential.

most celebrated and, to the taste of many connoisseurs, the most aristocratic. Supposedly, Jamestown settlers watched Native Americans cure venison and applied the technique to wild hogs. The state legislature formally defined Smithfield ham in 1926 (not coincidentally, the same year Hormel started offering ham in cans) as a ham cured and aged in the town of Smithfield, made only from hogs fattened on Virginia peanuts. The peanut precondition, which hard-core traditionalists maintain was what made Smithfield ham meat especially luxurious, was dropped in 1966, but even today only hams from Smithfield can bear the label.

What makes that one so swell? Salt-cured for six or more months and smoked over applewood and/or oak and hickory for flavor, it is long and lean (but encased in fat), dark red, and so deliriously packed with flavor that to slice it thicker than a lettuce leaf is obscene. The **Genuine Smithfield Ham Shoppe** sells them in burlap ready to cook or al-

ready cooked and ready to heat. This purveyor, with two retail outlets and a large mail-order business, even has hams cured a mere three to six months, resulting in a less pungent salty smack. Generally speaking, the longer the cure, the more intense the flavor. To a ham fancier, a ham cured for a couple of years or more is the *grand cru* of pig meat.

Country ham is part of the South's iconic breakfast: eggs and biscuits accompanied by a slab or two that has been sizzled on a griddle or in an iron frying pan until the rim of fat turns translucent amber and the red meat glistens and is blotched with burn marks from the grill, frequently accompanied by redeye gravy made from ham drippings and black coffee. Such fine Old Dominion ham is served at New Market's **Southern Kitchen** and at Roanoke's **Roanoker** (which bills its as "wafer sliced"). The wallop of ham makes it eminently suitable as a flavor agent or companion to milder foods, for example as an add-in to crab Norfolk, a traditional Tidewater dish in which Chesapeake Bay crabmeat is sautéed in plenty of butter. Another logical place for high-octane ham is peanut soup. The swanky **Lemaire** restaurant in Richmond's Jefferson Hotel laces its creamed nuts and sharp green onions with a measure of silky country ham from Madison County's **Kite's Hams**. (Jim Kite is renowned as perhaps the best producer in the state. He makes so few, however, that you need to contact him well in advance if you want to get one for yourself. Another excellent source of country ham, which also sells sausage, side meat for flavoring vegetables, and even ham biscuits, ready to eat, is **Calhoun's Country Hams** in Culpeper. Tom Calhoun is known for hams that are somewhat less salty than the classic version and that virtually drip with flavor.)

Our favorite place to shop in person for a Virginia ham is in the Shenandoah Valley at the old **Fulks Run Grocery**, where Turner Ham House hams are on display wrapped in cheesecloth and unceremoniously piled up in shopping carts arrayed in the aisles of the wood-floored market. Turner hams add sugar to the curing process, thus mitigating the punch of salt.

Saltiness is no liability to the ham purist; the older the ham and the saltier it is, the greater its value. Case in point: the Owen Gwaltney's ham on display at the **Isle of Wight Museum** in Smithfield. It is a wizened, mold-encrusted hog hindquarter cured in 1902 and not once refrigerated since then. Museum curators refer to it as the world's oldest edible ham.

VIRGINIA HAM AT ITS FINEST

1. **Kite's Hams:** 3957 Wolftown Hood Rd., Wolftown, VA
540-948-4742
2. **Calhoun's Country Hams:** 219 S. East St., Culpeper, VA
540-825-8319 or 877-825-8319
www.calhounhams.com
3. **Fulks Run Grocery:** 11441 Brocks Gap Rd., Fulks Run, VA
540-896-7487
www.turnerhams.com
4. **Lemaire:** in the Jefferson Hotel, 101 W. Franklin St., Richmond, VA

800-424-8014 or 804-788-8000
www.jeffersonhotel.com
5. **Smithfield Collection:** PO Box 250, Portsmouth, VA
800-628-2242
www.smithfieldcollection.com
6. **Southern Kitchen:** 9576 S. Congress St., New Market, VA
540-740-3514
7. **Roanoker Restaurant:** 2522 Colonial Ave. SW, Roanoke, VA
540-344-7746
www.theroanokerrestaurant.com
8. **Genuine Smithfield Ham Shoppe:** 224 Main St., Smithfield, VA
757-357-1798
Second location: 421 Prince George St., Williamsburg, VA
757-258-8604
www.smithfieldhams.com

Also
Isle of Wight Museum: 103 Main St., Smithfield, VA
757-357-7459

WEST INDIES SALAD
Mobile Bay

Years ago we met Bill Bayley, who claimed to have invented West Indies salad back in the late 1940s, when, as steward of a ship docked in the Cayman Islands, he cooked up some lobsters and marinated their meat in the only other ingredients he had available: oil, vinegar, salt, pepper, and chopped sweet onion. When he opened a restaurant in Mobile a few years later, he remembered how good the dish was and decided to put it

Few seafood restaurants in Mobile Bay would dare leave West Indies salad with fresh crabmeat off the menu.

on his menu. However, no lobsters were available, so he substituted crab. West Indies salad was a hit and is now found on menus throughout the Mobile Bay area. The late Mr. Bayley, who is said also to have invented fried crab claws, was an extremely colorful gent, never without a fat stogie clamped in his mouth, and we shall not forget his watchwords: "If you ain't et West Indies salad, you ain't et Mobile." Although he is gone, as is the original restaurant, today's **Bayley's** — still known to locals as Bayley's Corner — continues to serve the dishes he invented, as well as superb fish and grits and gumbo.

There are few seafood restaurants around Mobile Bay that do not offer West Indies salad. At **Wintzell's Oyster House**, it is axiomatic, so pure you want to call it creamy, with only minimal seasonings and a lemon wedge, available by the cup as an ap-

petizer and by the half-pound as a big hors d'oeuvre or supper. We also like it at **Banana Docks Cafe**, where the competitive sweetnesses of blue crab and Vidalia onion bits are moderated by puckery vinaigrette dressing.

3 GREAT WEST INDIES SALADS

1. **Wintzell's Oyster House:** 605 Dauphin St., Mobile, AL 251-432-4605 See www.wintzellsoysterhouse .com for additional locations.

WEST INDIES SALAD

1 pound fresh lump crabmeat, picked clean
2/3 cup chopped sweet onion
1/4 cup light salad oil
1/3 cup cider vinegar
1/2 teaspoon freshly ground black pepper
1/2 teaspoon salt
1/2 cup crushed ice
    Paprika and chopped fresh parsley
    Saltine crackers

Make alternating layers of crabmeat and onion in a 1- to 2-quart Mason jar or a bowl. Combine the oil and vinegar, pepper, and salt and pour it over the crabmeat. Top the crabmeat with the crushed ice. Cover and refrigerate for 24 hours. Serve dusted with paprika and garnished with parsley, accompanied by saltines.

SERVES 4 TO 6 AS AN APPETIZER

South

Wintzell's in Mobile draws kudos for West Indies salad, sold by the half-pound.

2. **Bayley's Carry Out Seafood:** 10805 Dauphin Island Parkway, Theodore, AL 251-973-1572
3. **Banana Docks Cafe:** 36 Hillcrest Rd., Mobile, AL 251-342-2775 www.bananadockscafe.net

WHOLE-HOG BARBECUE
North Carolina

The barbecue of eastern North Carolina tastes great, but before you enjoy eating it, you will smell it and you will hear it. The air surrounding each of the region's top pits is so heavily per-fumed with the scent of halved hogs sizzling on a grate, their fat dripping onto white-hot hardwood coals, that your hair, your clothes, and your car will glow with the sweet aroma for hours after you leave. Inside the restaurant, there is no music and conversation is hushed. One steady sound sets a cadence, not continuously, but as a punctuating on-and-off rhythm for as long as customers are coming in. It is the thump of heavy cleavers hacking up large sections of cooked meat on a rock maple butcher block. The beat is ubiquitous at barbecues where whole hogs are cooked, and often it emanates from an out-of-sight kitchen.

At the **Skylight Inn** in Ayden, the kitchen is not hidden so the sound is louder and you see the beautiful sight of barbecue being made. Enter the building and step up to the counter to place an order. Like an altar in a church, it is front and center, and all congregants come to it first. Here stands James Howell, just behind a large pass-through window, working at the cutting block, a cleaver in each

North Carolina's glorious trio: barbecued pork, a slab of cornbread, and cole slaw

hand, whacking at the meat. This table is the sanctum sanctorum, where cooked pig becomes North Carolina's signature smokehouse meal. Periodically, Mr. Howell puts the blades down and reaches back for a bottle of vinegar or Texas hot sauce to splash onto the pork, and he shakes on salt and pepper straight from the carton. Nothing is measured out and there are no secret ingredients. When he's got a moist, steaming heap of five or six pounds that are the texture of coarse hash, he uses both cleavers to shovel it forward through the window onto an adjoining butcher block in the preparation area toward the counter. Here servers assemble trays and sandwiches. Sandwiches, which include coleslaw, are wrapped in wax paper. Trays full of meat are topped with a square of cornbread.

The union of smoke and pork is a subtle flavor, enhanced but not the least bit overwhelmed by the addition of vinegar and hot sauce as the meat is chopped. What's striking about whole-hog barbecue is its texture. Along with velvet-soft shreds from the interior of the flesh are chewy strips from the outside as well as shockingly crunchy nuggets of skin. The cooked skin is insanely succulent, and its firmness gives this meat edible drama that is lacking in barbecue made only from upscale hams or shoulders.

"Each pig part has its own different flavor," pit master Wilber Shirley once said. "They're all good, but all together they're true barbecue." The fame of Mr. Shirley's restaurant, **Wilber's Barbecue** in Goldsboro, has been spread by pilots who take off from nearby Seymour Johnson

Cleavers thud sweetly at the Skylight Inn in Ayden, NC. Nothing is measured, and there are no secret ingredients.

Air Force Base, but even if Wilber's weren't at the end of the runway, its reputation could never have remained merely local. This place is world-class! Since 1962, when Wilber stoked the oak coals in old-fashioned pits, it has been known for whole-hog barbecue long-cooked until it is as soft as a sigh. The sweetness of the chopped pork is laced with the indescribably appetizing tang of hardwood smoke and a judicious measure of hot sauce and vinegar. It comes with excellent Brunswick stew and squiggly hushpuppies. Wilber's serves until about 9 o'clock each night or until all the meat is gone, at which point a sign is hung on the door announcing, "Out of Barbecue!"

THE WORLD'S BEST WHOLE-HOG BARBECUES

1. **Skylight Inn:** 1501 S. Lee St., Ayden, NC
   252-746-4113
2. **Wilber's Barbecue:** 4172 U.S. Highway 70 East, Goldsboro, NC
   919-778-5218

MIDWEST

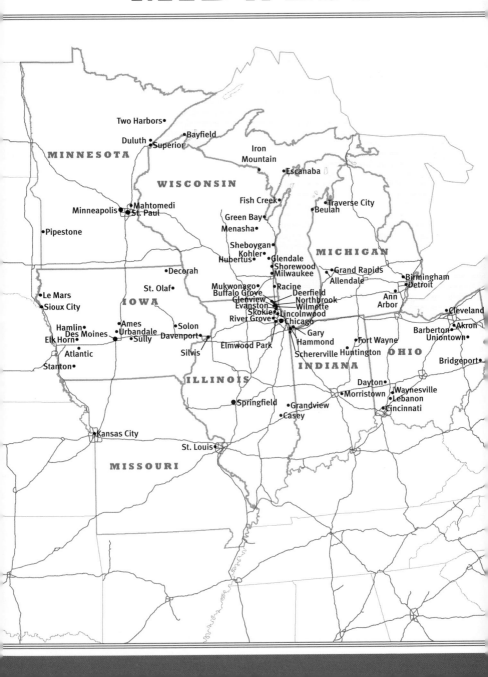

ILLINOIS

INDIANA

IOWA

MICHIGAN

MINNESOTA

MISSOURI

OHIO

APPLE FRITTER
Chicago

Old Fashioned Donuts' apple fritters are shockingly huge and plenty weighty (what would be the point of a fritter lite?), but the dough has the quality of being puffed up rather than ballasted by its time in hot oil. Gnarled and knobby, they have abundant surface area thickly crusted with a sugar glaze that ranges from crunchy to tender, and they are loaded with nuggets of apple suspended in cinnamon goo. While we've never eaten one still hot from the big vat of bubbling oil behind the counter, those we have devoured always taste fresh and are never grease-sodden.

We are particularly fond of Old Fashioned Donuts because fritters are among life's continual disappointments. So many look good but taste bad. The fact that they are an especially indulgent foodstuff — little more than grease, sugar, dough, and

Freighted with apples, the huge fritters at Chicago's Old Fashioned Donuts are worth the calorie extravaganza.

perhaps a soupçon of fruit — makes eating a bad one particularly disheartening. What a waste of appetite!

As you might guess, the doughnuts in this extremely humble shop on the far South Side are special, too. Look for blueberry doughnuts in the summer and caramel maple anytime.

Old Fashioned Donuts: 11248 S. Michigan Ave., Chicago, IL 773-995-7420

APPLE PIE BAKED IN A BAG
Mukwonago, Wisconsin

With crust like a butter cookie blanketing a dense apple pack of firm Ida Red crescents bound in thick syrup, the apple pie at the **Elegant Farmer** just might be America's best. The crust is so brittle that when pressed with the edge of a fork, it makes a cracking sound; grains of cinnamon sugar bounce off the surface as it shatters. Where the top and bottom crusts meet at the circumference, a knotty cord of dough can be pinched away in bite-sized nuggets impregnated with enough seepage of fruit filling that they have become chewy.

While there is nothing eccentric or innovative about the product — it is basic apple pie — how it's baked is unusual: inside a brown paper bag. This allows the juices of the fruit to simmer, mellowing its tang. When the pie is mostly baked, a large hole is cut in the top of the paper bag, which makes the crust get hard. The bags in which the pies are baked (and sold) are blotched with dampness drawn from within. At this huge produce

The Elegant Farmer in Mukwonago, WI, sells apple pies baked in a bag.

No gimmick, the brown paper bag allows the apple juices to simmer.

market and informal cafe in Wisconsin farm country, you can buy pie by the piece to eat at a casual table or whole to take home. Bag-baked pies also include apple-peach, apple-rhubarb, and apple with caramel.

Elegant Farmer: 1545 Main St., Mukwonago, WI
262-363-6770
www.elegantfarmer.com

BENNY WEIKER
Le Mars, Iowa

Sioux City once had a thriving stockyard, the foremost legacy of which is **Archie's Waeside**, source of corn-fed prime beef the likes of which has virtually vanished from all but the most expensive restaurants, here available at about half-price. Archie's dry-ages sides of beef up to three weeks, so the meat's fibers shed moisture while they absorb the luxury of profuse marbling to become steaks that resonate with brawny character. No cut is more handsome than the Benny Weiker, a filet mignon named for a good customer who used to be a Sioux City cattle buyer. It is an 18-ounce filet mignon that rises a good 4 inches above the plate, its exterior dark and firm, the inside radiant pink and bulging with juice. A steak knife virtually falls through the

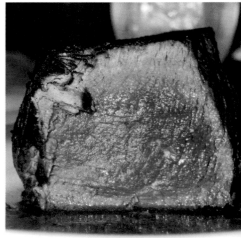

At Archie's Waeside in Le Mars, IA, filet mignon delivers big-beef satisfaction.

big hunk of beef with little more effort than gravity itself, and unlike so many filet mignons, which are tender but elusive, this one delivers big-beef satisfaction. It is graded prime, and it delivers a protein punch that feels utterly rejuvenating.

Archie's Waeside: 224 Fourth Ave. NE, Le Mars, IA
712-546-7011

HISTORIC AUTO ATTRACTIONS

Of the bounty of automobile museums we've visited in America, from the humble Wilbur's Old Cars Edsel Museum of Muskogee, Oklahoma, to the flabbergasting Auto Collections of Las Vegas, where most exhibits are for sale (at prices that can hit seven figures), no place is more fun than Wayne Lensing's Historic Auto Attractions, just south of the Wisconsin-Illinois border. As a collector, Mr. Lensing has a diverse catalogue that ranges from a piece of the Porsche in which James Dean died to Joseph Stalin's bulletproof limousine, plus all kinds of things in some way related to the motorcade in which President John F. Kennedy was assassinated. These include the Secret Service car that was directly behind the car in which JFK was riding, the ambulance in which Lee Harvey Oswald was taken away after Jack Ruby shot him, and a window from the Texas School Book Depository, taken from near the window where Oswald shot the president. When you look through, you see a miniature re-creation of the motorcade.

What's great about this museum is its free-association philosophy. With cars at the nucleus, exhibits branch out with no inhibition. Here's a Lincoln that Elvis Presley owned; why not also display one of his shirts and a pair of glasses he scrunched into a tangle when he got angry? Orbiting around the JFK motorcade stuff are eighteen of Jackie Kennedy's dresses ("The Clothes of Camelot"), a pen the president used to sign the nuclear test ban treaty, a golf ball inscribed "Mr. President," and a piece of picket fence from the grassy knoll behind which a second assassin may have hidden.

Many exhibits have no auto logic whatsoever, but, hey, it's one man's museum, and this is a man of promethean curiosity: a collection of taxidermized North American animals, John Dillinger's death mask, a Superman outfit worn by Christopher Reeve, and Marilyn Monroe's nightgown.

Historic Auto Attractions: 13825 Metric Dr., Roscoe, IL
815-389-7917 or 815-544-3147
www.historicautoattractions.com

Also
Wilbur's Old Cars Edsel Museum: 3010 N. Main St., Muskogee, OK
918-683-4475
Auto Collections: 3535 Las Vegas Blvd. South, Las Vegas, NV
702-794-3174
www.autocollections.com

BONED AND BUTTERED PERCH
Northern Indiana

Great Lakes perch are firm little sweeties that remain intact as their skin crisps in a frying pan and becomes a translucent envelope around the fine meat. Six or ten make one serving. It is traditional for restaurants to offer them whole or boned, plain from the skillet or drizzled with melted butter. Any way you choose to have it, this is one of the heartland's delights. Although the flesh is compact, it flakes into tiny segments with a tantalizing dainty texture. Drawn butter wants to seep into its crevices, but even if you get it without butter and merely apply a squeeze of lemon, the fish is intrinsically luscious. Juicy and clean on the tongue, it is an eating experience that makes us think of summer breezes, wooded shorelines, and the sizzle of a day's catch over a crackling campfire.

An Amish dry goods store, Gohn Brothers in Middlebury, IN, shuns fashion with a passion.

Whole or boned, buttered or not, there's nothing sweeter than a meal of lake perch.

For all its outdoorsy flavor, a perch meal in northern Indiana has customarily been quite formal, a night of gastronomic indulgence that seems in some ways lavish yet has all the joie de vivre of a neighborhood picnic. **Teibel's** of Schererville serves perch on thick china spread across soft tablecloths in majestic dining rooms designed to accommodate sybarites. The joy of supper here includes not only the sublime fish but the ritual banquet in which it stars. Relishes are the way to start: coleslaw, pickled beets, cottage cheese. Old-school customers drink old-school highballs: neat martinis with olives, sweet manhattans with maraschino cherries, Tom Collinses, and Rob Roys. Teibel's began as a twelve-stool fried chicken diner in 1930, and family-style fried chicken, made from Grandma Teibel's recipe brought from Austria, is still a major draw.

Pictures near the entrance of the **Beach Cafe** show the city of Gary back when the south shore of Lake

Michigan was still a fisherman's paradise, and the menu at this half-century-old restaurant, while now including steak and chicken, is all about perch, served in half-pound portions, either boned and buttered or de Jonghe–style (page 283). A single portion is a great pile of tender pieces oh-so-lightly breaded and glistening with butter. Briefly fried, the fillets emit little puffs of buttery steam when you separate forkfuls of meat; there is simply nothing fresher-tasting.

The Cav, as longtime patrons refer to the **Cavalier Inn** in Hammond, offers a Friday fish fry and buttered perch every night, but it is most beloved to local Poles as a source of potato pancakes, golumbki (stuffed cabbage), kielbasa, and some of the most buttery, tender handmade pierogi you will ever eat.

GOHN BROTHERS

At Gohn Brothers of Middlebury, Indiana, all the latest styles are shunned with a passion. The inventory of this Main Street dry goods store is virtually identical to what George Gohn sold when he opened for business in Hoosier farm country over a hundred years ago. There is never anything unconventional or exciting available, which is just the way the clientele likes it. The majority of them are Amish people who know just what they want, which is precisely what they wanted last year and what their ancestors wanted generations ago.

The Plain People arrive at Gohn Brothers in horse-drawn buggies, and when they buy something, they pay cash. Cars and credit cards, like rhinestones and gay new hats, are nothing but distractions from a godly life. Men wear drill denim overshirts and broadfall work pants. Zippers are considered a concession to indolence, so trousers have button-front barn doors. The men's jackets have no outside pockets, buttons, or collars, all of which suggest the frippery of military uniforms, which these pacifists especially abhor. Bright colors are scorned; nearly everything Amish people wear is black, navy, gray, or white.

If your sartorial ideal is duds that will endure, Gohn Brothers is a wonderland. Here you will find rugged work pants, ladies' service-weight hose with seams on the legs and clocks on the ankles, infants' pure cotton cloth diapers with pins to match, and colossal boots guaranteed to keep your feet warm at 80 degrees below. While a majority of customers shop here to obey a religious edict, plenty of other working people and farmers, as well as a handful of fashion outriders, come to this heartland reliquary in search of overalls, shoes, hats, and underwear that might best be described as Platonic garments — perfect forms, unaffected by the vagaries of the material world.

Gohn Brothers: 105 S. Main St., Middlebury, IN
800-595-0031 or 574-825-2400
www.gohnbrothers.com

Midwest

JOHN DILLINGER MUSEUM

The delightfully frenzied John Dillinger Museum uses the motto "Crime doesn't pay" to reassure visitors that it does not exist to celebrate one of America's most notorious bad guys. The stated purpose is to glorify crime fighting, not crime, and to that end we learn about the birth of the FBI and advances in crime-fighting technology via wax-figure exhibits and forensic memorabilia that show what happens to people who flout the law. For all the tsk-tsking, it is hard not to get a naughty thrill from seeing the bloodied "death trousers" Dillinger was wearing when G-men gunned him down, as well as the lucky (not!) rabbit's foot he carried. The museum does not address either of the persistent urban legends about Dillinger: (a) that it was not really he who was killed outside the Biograph Theater on July 22, 1934, and (b) that he was endowed with an extra-large penis, which FBI director J. Edgar Hoover kept in a glass jar as a postmortem souvenir.

John Dillinger Museum: Indiana Welcome Center, 7770 Corinne Dr., Hammond, IN 219-989-7979 www.dillingermuseum.com

---

BONED AND BUTTERED PERCH TRIUMVIRATE

1. **Teibel's Family Restaurant:** 1775 Route 41, Schererville, IN 219-865-2000 www.teibels.com
2. **Beach Cafe:** 903 N. Shelby St., Gary, IN 219-938-9890 www.millerbeachcafe.com
3. **Cavalier Inn:** 735 Gostlin St., Hammond, IN 219-933-9314 www.cavalierinn.net

---

BREADED STEAK
South Side Chicago

Breaded steak is street food that was once popular on Chicago's South Side but is now fairly hard to find. The biggest and one of the best is constructed at **Freddie's Pizza**, where a pounded-thin sheet of beef is breaded and deep-fried, then coiled up and stuffed into a foot-long roll with mozzarella and hot giardiniera relish and virtually soaked with red gravy (tomato sauce). It is not knife-and-fork-friendly, so it must be picked up, which guarantees that you will wind up with hands that look like a MASH unit surgeon's. The breaded steak at **Uncle Johnny's Grocery and Deli** isn't as sloppy, but it is the premier incarnation. Pan-fried after being mallet-tenderized, each order is tended as carefully as if it were a $50 porterhouse, resulting in a piece of meat that is as yielding as filet mignon encased in a seasoned crust. With mozzarella and sweet peppers and a judicious application of gravy, it is everything a breaded steak sand-wich ought to be.

Ricobene's is a one-stop shop for great versions of most of Chicago's quick-eats specialties, including breaded lake perch, aromatic lengths of Italian sausage, Italian beef, and superthick pizzas glazed with crushed tomatoes. Its breaded steak is a beaut, garnished with fried hot peppers and shredded mozzarella and a bright red splotch of sauce. Here is a meal — no, two meals — in a heroically chewy Italian roll, demanding undivided attention from its eater as well as a large stack of napkins on the side. And do not forget: Ricobene's French fries are not to be missed (page 248).

BEST BREADED STEAKS

1. **Uncle Johnny's Grocery and Deli:** 500 W. 32nd St., Chicago, IL
312-225-6111
2. **Freddie's Pizza & Sandwiches:** 701 W. 31st St., Chicago, IL
312-808-0147
www.freddieson31st.com

At Ricobene's in Chicago, the breaded steaks require two hands and a stack of napkins.

3. **Ricobene's:** 252 W. 26th St., Chicago, IL
312-225-5555
See www.ricobenesfamoussteaks.com for additional locations.

BUTTER BURGER
Milwaukee

Wisconsin cooks take every opportunity to showcase cheese, custard, cream, and butter. The butter burger at **Solly's Grille** is a heady example. It is a modest patty of good beef, cooked through, served on a bun that is quite literally soaked with melted butter. Not margarine, not flavored oil: pure, dairy-rich butter. Words cannot describe the wanton opulence of hoisting this burger from plate to mouth and seeing the pool of melted butter that remains on the plate, as well as feeling it run in hot rivers down your chin, fingers, and wrist. North of downtown at the edge of Lincoln Park, Solly's is fun, a place where seating is at a pair of horseshoe counters and the beverage of choice, even in below-zero Great Lakes weather, is a fresh banana malt.

North of Milwaukee at the uppermost tip of Lake Winnebago, **Mihm's Charcoal Grill** offers one of the best butter burgers you can eat, cooked over charcoal, but we need to caution you that it is not listed on the menu as a hamburger. Yes, there are burgers on the menu, and they're fine, but the item you want to eat is a ground steak sandwich, maybe even a double-ground steak sandwich. At Mihm's, you can specify light butter if you don't want it sopped. Here a traditional chocolate malt is the preferred libation.

Before you go on a Dairy State custard binge at the great Leon's drive-in (page 237), you definitely should have a hamburger across the street at **Mazo's Fine Foods**. Made from beef that is trimmed and ground daily in the kitchen and grilled in gobs of butter, Mazo's 6-ounce hamburgers, while not especially thick, are tremendously juicy, and the combination of all that oozing beef gravy and swirling butter is divine, if not exactly kosher.

Culver's started as a single store in Sauk City and has become a big chain with restaurants in seventeen states. Despite our aversion to cookie-cutter franchises, we cannot deny the excellence of Culver's butter burgers. They are freshly made and abundantly buttery, available with cheese and/or bacon and with milk shakes (made from Culver's good custard) on the side.

Sopped with butter and oozing cheeses, Solly's burger is total dairy decadence.

Sobelman's, a corner bar that began as a Schlitz tavern, does not officially sell a butter burger, but its Sobelman Burger is butter-rich enough: a crusty, juice-laden quarter-pound of beef shoveled into a buttery, shiny-domed bun with three kinds of cheese, grilled onions, and jalapeño peppers. It is listed on the menu also in a double-patty version, and big eaters go for the S.O.B., which is four burgers, with cheese and bacon atop every one, stacked into a multilayered bun.

BUTTERIEST BUTTER BURGERS

1. **Solly's Grille:** 4629 N. Port Washington Rd., Milwaukee, WI 414-332-8808
2. **Mihm's Charcoal Grill:** 342 Chute St., Menasha, WI 920-722-0306 www.mihmscharcoalgrill.com
3. **Culver's:** Multiple locations; see www.culvers.com for details.

⭐ BEST BLOODY MARY

Outlandish as the towering S.O.B. is, Sobelman's bloody Mary puts it in the shade. Served in a Mason jar, this well-spiced vodka delivery system is nearly as much a meal as the S.O.B. Burgeoning from the top of the jar is a cornucopia of celery, olives, cheeses, a beef stick, an asparagus stalk, a shrimp, a radish, and a cocktail onion. It is served in the traditional Milwaukee tavern way, with a short beer on the side as a chaser.

4. **Mazo's Fine Foods:** 3146 S. 27th St., Milwaukee, WI
414-671-2118
5. **Sobelman's Pub and Grill:** 1900 W. St. Paul Ave., Milwaukee, WI
414-931-1919
www.milwaukeesbestburgers.com

CHEESE CURDS
Wisconsin and Michigan

Cheese curds, which are about the size of a walnut, are nuggets of cheddar with an agreeable rubbery resilience not unlike that of fresh mozzarella. Yellow or white, plain or flavored, they are a country-pure delectation known for a high-pitched squeak as your teeth attack them. Freshness is everything; within twelve hours of a package being opened, the squeak will diminish and ultimately disappear, leaving cheese-curd ecstasy only a memory. You can buy curds with freshness sealed in the package at any grocery store in Wisconsin, but the best likelihood of finding great ones is at a creamery or cheese store.

Beer-battered and deep-fried, cheese curds transform from salubrious farm food into profligate snacks. Frying turns the cheese melty inside its crisp, seasoned coat, and the result is a pop-in-the-mouth savory that is ideal tavern food for beer drinkers and an immensely popular munchable at fairs throughout the upper Midwest's dairyland. Although fried cheese curds are the veritable state snack of Wisconsin, and definitely the side dish you want with your butter burger at **Mihm's**, the best ones we ever ate are at **Zingerman's Roadhouse**, in Ann Arbor, Michigan. Zingerman's doesn't always have them, but when it does, they come fresh from Theresa, Wisconsin, and are battered with Wisconsin's Sprecher's ale. They are served with jalapeño-heated cool ranch dressing.

Midwest

MUSEUM OF HISTORIC TORTURE DEVICES

Here's a place to visit with the whole fam damily if you are vacationing in the Wisconsin Dells. The Museum of Historic Torture Devices is a ghoulish collection of miscellaneous reminders of humankind's depravity, but displayed with a tip of the hat to the exhibits' educational value. Things you will see include John Wayne Gacy memorabilia (he was Illinois's serial-killer clown), racks and skull crushers from the Inquisition, whips, chains, and an autographed picture of the Three Stooges (presumably because of their sadistic brand of comedy). Visitors can pay $1 to mock-electrocute themselves. The house catchphrase: "Nothing is more frightening than human history."

Museum of Historic Torture Devices: 740 Eddy St., Wisconsin Dells, WI
608-254-2439
www.dellstorturemuseum.com

A dairy country favorite, cheese curds should be so fresh they squeak.

2 CHEESE CURD SOURCES

1. **Zingerman's Roadhouse:**
   2501 Jackson Ave., Ann Arbor, MI
   734-663-FOOD
   www.zingermansroadhouse.com
2. **Mihm's Charcoal Grill:** 342
   Chute St., Menasha, WI
   920-722-0306
   www.mihmscharcoalgrill.com

At www.eatcurds.com, a downloadable map lists 28 sources for cheese curds around Wisconsin.

CHERRY PIE
Northern Michigan

Northern Michigan is cherry country, where orchards form a landscape that is fluffy pink in the spring with hills of blossoming cherry trees, and starting in June, roadside stands sell bags of washed cherries ready to enjoy while you drive. Most of us eat cherries cool, but these roadside fruits tend to get a little warm in the summer sun, so when your teeth snap through their taut maroon skins, unspeakably sensuous warm nectar floods your tongue. It's easy to understand why a happy life is described as a bowlful of cherries.

A first-rate cherry pie is more than happy and delicious. It has mystique; it is fresh, bright, and innocent. It is the purest of pies, in the sense that *cherry* means virginal. Taste a piece of pie at the **Cherry Hut** and your tongue knows the charisma of the cherry even if words are inadequate to express it. What's striking about northern Michigan's favorite summer fruit is that whether you eat it raw or in a pie, sweetness is its secondary quality. It is sweet, but more than sweet, it is tart and exciting. Like all the region's distinguished pie places, the Cherry Hut makes its

The Cherry Hut in Beulah, MI, uses only just-picked local cherries in its first-rate pies.

pies from "five-plus-one" cherries, which are tart ones harvested from local trees just after the sweet cherries ripen. They are pitted and put up in 5-pound batches with 1 pound of sugar poured on each batch. Andy Case, the Cherry Hut's proprietor, advises, "You never want to use sweet cherries in a pie. A sweet cherry is good for eating, but when it is cooked, it turns dull. Five-plus-ones pack the flavor."

Some 18 tons of five-plus-ones are used each week in the Cherry Hut kitchen, where up to 500 pies

Tart cherries and lard in the crust are two secrets of the Cherry Hut's pie.

are handmade, one by one, every day from Memorial Day through leaf season in mid-October. From a sidewalk promenade at the side of the building, visitors can look into the kitchen and watch the process. The 6-pound tins are drained in a big colander. (Drippings are combined with lemon juice to make salubrious cherryade.) The fruit is mixed with a bit of flour, and a pound of the mixture is hefted into an uncooked circle of pie dough in an 8-inch pie pan. The dough is made from the same recipe used at the Cherry Hut since it opened in 1922, which demands pure lard for flavor and flakiness. A second circle of dough is laid over the cherries and pressed around the edges firmly enough to separate any excess, which falls onto the cutting board to be rerolled for the next batch of bottoms. Finally, the edges are pinched all around to seal together top and bottom. The assembled pie is chilled for a few hours — cooling makes it brown better and inhibits the cherry juice from overflowing as it bakes. Before it goes in the oven for 45 minutes, the pie is brushed with milk and

FRISKE ORCHARDS

Northern Michigan's best-known fruit is cherries, but apples are big, too — a fact you will appreciate when you open the door of the apple room at Friske Orchards. The place is crowded with baskets and bags full of countless varieties, and the air is saturated with apple intensity that, while unfermented, is positively intoxicating. You can buy them by the bushel or singly for eating out of hand. Better still, step to the bakery area and get yourself a piece of caramel apple pie à la mode to eat at one of Friske's tables. Or a warm apple dumpling. Or a piece of apple cake.

Friske Orchards: 10743
U.S. 31 North, Ellsworth, MI
888-968-3554 or
231-599-2604
www.friske.com

Midwest

an *X* is cut across it, giving steam a place to escape and transforming the 8-inch circle into four quarters, each one a serving. Three out of four slices are ordered à la mode.

Cherry Hut: 216 N. Michigan Ave., Beulah, MI

231-882-4431

www.cherryhutproducts.com

CHICAGO HOT LINK
Chicago

Seasoned with sage, red pepper, and fennel, hot pork links come with barbecue sauce.

Chicago hot links are only distant relations of Texas sausages that go by the same name (page 339). Nor are they anything like Windy City red hots (page 275), for they are pork, not beef; they are fatter and they are fattier, saturated with savory juices, and they are shot through with sage, red pepper, and fennel, which bring them close to the taste of a breakfast sausage. Furthermore, they are customarily served with barbecue sauce. At **Barbara Ann's BBQ**, a four-star carryout joint adjoining a dramati-cally less-than-four-star motel, those in the know ask for a mix of hot and mild sauce, the pungency of which is a perfect foil for links that have licked up the smoke of smoldering hickory and cherrywood. Ask for them well done and you get a little less juice but more crunch and chew.

While Barbara Ann's are impossible to beat, the hot links at **Lem's**, a South Side favorite for decades, are essential, too. They are somewhat more muscular and not quite as spicy, and Lem's sauce is kaleidoscopic. Lem's ribs, by the way, are right up there with Leon's (page 127) — some say even better.

Both places are takeout only. Business is conducted via pass-throughs in bulletproof glass.

On Chicago's South Side, business at Lem's takes place through bulletproof glass.

TOP HOT LINKS

1. **Barbara Ann's BBQ:** 7617 S. Cottage Grove Ave., Chicago, IL 773-651-5300
2. **Lem's BBQ House:** 311 E. 75th St., Chicago, IL 773-994-2428

CHICAGO MIX
Chicago

Chicago is home of the best caramel corn on earth. It is called Caramel-Crisp, a name trademarked by **Garrett Popcorn Shops**, of which there are five in the city, and now two in New York. One thing that makes it good is that it is always served hot. As you wait your turn in line, you can see (and smell) it being air-popped in a great copper kettle that resembles a superload washing machine. As the kettle rotates, it gets filled with kernels, then disgorges popped corn. The hot corn is mixed with caramel and dumped into troughs, where a clerk worries it with two large scoops, ensuring that the hot caramel corn doesn't clump into pieces larger than three or four popped kernels.

CaramelCrisp is riotously buttery-tasting, and its caramel coat is crisp but not brittle. The flavor is earthy and serious, nearly burned in character, and downright addictive. In addition to caramel corn, Garrett's makes CheeseCorn, which is equally buttery and ultra-cheesy. In fact, unless you wear gloves, it is not possible to eat CheeseCorn without having your fingers turn bright orange from the cheese that coats and infuses the hot popped kernels. Even knowing the mess that inevitably results, including orange stains on jeans and jackets, lips and chins, we cannot stop eating it once we start. The vivid cheese immeasurably enhances the starchy corn flavor of the puffy kernels, making a savory snack that is almost unimprovable.

Seriously addictive, Garrett's popcorn crackles with buttery, caramely, cheesy flavor.

But it can get better. Instead of ordering either CaramelCrisp or Cheese-Corn, you can ask for a mix, also known as a Chicago mix. The clerk fills a bag half full with caramel corn, then tops it off with CheeseCorn and shakes it. The combo (which stains fingers only half as badly) is a giant taste sensation that seems to cover the whole spectrum of what a tongue can appreciate: salty, sweet, buttery, earthy, crisp, and chewy. Frankly, even a mini-mix, which is a mere 8 ounces, exhausts our ability to eat anything else for hours.

Garrett Popcorn Shops: Multiple locations; see www .garrettpopcorn.com for specifics.

CHICKEN VESUVIO
Chicago

The word *seductive* only hints at the aromatic power of a plate of chicken Vesuvio, a spellbinding meal that dates back to the 1920s and a Chicago restaurant named Vesuvio's. While Windy City cooks have sixteen angles

Midwest

on the exact way to do it, the center-piece always is bone-in chicken pieces sautéed to a point where they are encased in a dark, red-gold crust of lush skin that slides from the meat as the meat slides off its bone. The chicken is served on a plate heaped up with wedges of potato sautéed in a bath of white wine, garlic, olive oil, and spices until they are as soft as mashed inside but with crunchy edges.

Seekers of off-the-radar eateries will love having chicken Vesuvio at **Il Vicinato** in old (not tourist-trod) Little Italy. You can order white or dark meat, on or off the bone, and while Vesuvio is itself not purely Italian, the dining experience in this checked-tablecloth, pine-paneled neighborhood place is as purely Italian-American as can be, including a fabulous antipasto salad and meat ravioli. **Francesco's Hole in the Wall**, a well-known nonsecret among the Chicago culinarati, features such true hole-in-the-wall policies as low prices, no reservations, no credit cards, and no personal checks. It is also home to what many consider to be Chicagoland's perfect chicken Vesuvio: bone-in pieces spangled with herbs and bits of garlic and big wedges of cooked-soft potato on a dish of savory garlic butter.

CHICKEN VESUVIO

½ cup all-purpose flour
½ teaspoon salt
½ teaspoon freshly ground black pepper
½ teaspoon dried thyme
½ teaspoon dried rosemary
1 teaspoon dried oregano
1 3-pound chicken, rinsed and patted dry, cut into 8 pieces
Olive oil for frying
4 baking potatoes, unpeeled, cut lengthwise into eighths, soaked in ice water
⅓ cup chopped fresh parsley
4–8 garlic cloves, minced (to taste)
1 cup dry white wine
1 cup cooked green peas

Preheat the oven to 350 degrees. Mix together the flour and seasonings. Lightly dredge the chicken in the mixture.

Heat about ½ inch olive oil in a large, heavy skillet to 360 degrees. Fry the chicken pieces a few at a time (don't crowd the pan) until well browned, turning once or twice and allowing 15 to 18 minutes per batch. Drain the chicken on paper towels.

Pat the potatoes dry, then add them to the skillet of hot oil. Cook until golden brown all over. Remove and drain on paper towels. Pour off all but ¼ inch of fat from the pan.

Return the chicken parts and the potatoes to the skillet, crowding them in as necessary. Sprinkle with the chopped parsley and minced garlic and pour the wine over them. Bake, uncovered, for 20 to 25 minutes. Strew the peas over the dish before serving.

SERVES 4

At the **Rosebud**, where the decor includes an oil painting of Frank Sinatra with a microphone in one hand and a highball in the other, you can order an incongruously stylish chicken Vesuvio — a lone boneless breast and two pieces of potato in the center of a too-large plate instead of the usual tumble of white-and-dark, skin-on, bone-in chicken parts with piles of potato that totally eclipse a plate. Although **Ricobene's** has been known for its bodacious breaded steak sandwich since 1946 (page 221), we recently discovered its delectable Vesuvio Italian Classic sandwich, which is a crisp, garlicky breaded cutlet dressed with onions, lettuce, tomato, and mayo stuffed into a length of Italian bread — a quick-eats version of the knife-and-fork meal.

Gene & Georgetti, rightfully known for its peerless steaks, also happens to make superb Vesuvio that reminds us of the folktale that the dish was named because it looks like

Chicago's Gene & Georgetti, known for great steaks and chicken Vesuvio

A high-rising chicken Vesuvio perches on potato wedges sautéed in buttery garlic and white wine.

Mount Vesuvius — a lofty volcanic jumble of crusty potatoes and glistening sections of chicken rising up from a pool of the garlic-tinged white wine in which they have been cooked. The skin on the chicken, plastered with herbs and permeated with savory chicken fat, peels off the pieces of meat like strips of crisp-fried bacon.

The Vesuvio way of doing things is a passion at **Harry Caray's**, which was opened in 1987 by the sportscaster known as the voice of the Chicago Cubs (and which boasts a phone number honoring his most famous exclamation: 773-HOLYCOW). In this festive, brick-walled dining hall, patronized by Windy City celebs, sports stars, tourists, and discriminating devotees of prime beef, you can get any steak in the house served Vesuvio style, as well as archetypal chicken Vesuvio and the less soulful boneless white-meat Vesuvio. The menu warns that the old-time version takes thirty minutes to prepare,

Midwest

and when you apply silverware to it, you understand why. Several pieces of chicken are sautéed, then baked, to utmost succulence. Are they tender? Forget about it! The dark meat in particular sets new standards for chicken tenderness. Spilled across this powerfully seasoned hodgepodge of food and aromatic pan juice is a handful of green peas, more for color than for taste. Steaks Vesuvio are grilled to order in a traditional manner, then smothered with potatoes and peas that have been given the white wine, herb, and garlic treatment.

CHICAGO'S BEST CHICKEN VESUVIOS

1. **Harry Caray's Italian Steakhouse:** 33 W. Kinzie St., Chicago, IL
   312-828-0966 or 773-HOLYCOW
   See www.harrycarays.com for additional locations.
2. **Gene & Georgetti:** 500 N. Franklin St., Chicago, IL
   312-527-3718
   www.geneandgeorgetti.com
3. **Francesco's Hole in the Wall:** 254 Skokie Blvd., Northbrook, IL
   847-272-0155
4. **Il Vicinato Ristorante:** 2435 S. Western Ave., Chicago, IL
   773-927-5444
5. **Rosebud:** 1500 W. Taylor St., Chicago, IL
   312-942-1117
   www.rosebudrestaurant.com
6. **Ricobene's:** 252 W. 26th St., Chicago, IL
   312-225-5555
   See www.ricobenesfamoussteaks.com for additional locations.

CINNAMON ROLL
Minnesota and Iowa

Is it a sin to conflate cinnamon rolls and caramel rolls? While the latter are by definition stickier, we contend that the two pastries are fundamentally alike in shape, size, and carb appeal.

Iowa is the nation's great cinnamon roll state, where many restaurants and town cafes make big, swirly-sweet hot ones every morning, but the very best version is over the north border in Minneapolis, at **Hell's Kitchen**. This superior sweet roll, the recipe for which chef Mitch Omer gives credit to his father, is a hefty swirl of tender dough topped with plenty of caramel glaze and a spill of roasted pecans. The dough is not the buttery, croissantlike stuff that makes many of the nation's top buns such delicate delicacies; rather, it is soft and pillowy, and hence more absorbent. That's the way it needs to be, because as soon as you press down with your fork edge and separate a bite, you want to mop it through the caramel that has spilled off the roll onto its plate. It is nearly

At Hell's Kitchen in Minneapolis, caramel sauce saturates a cinnamon roll sprinkled with pecans.

as thin as pancake syrup and at least as buttery as it is sweet. While pushing the mouthful through the caramel, you need to gather up as many chunks of nut as you can, for it is the nuts that elevate an mmm-good roll to omigod! status. They are broken coarsely enough to embody fresh nut-meat luxury within a roasted-crisp skin, and they are sprinkled with a few grains of coarse salt. Therein lies the magic. The occasional ping of a salt crystal in a sea of buttery caramel gives the glaze a dramatic vibrancy beyond anything that is purely sweet

The cinnamon roll at Gus Balon's in Tucson takes the cake.

or salty. It is the same flavor alchemy that prevails in those wonderful little caramel candies from Brittany, but here delivered on a grand scale.

One more supreme Twin Cities caramel roll is the supersticky one made by **Bread & Chocolate** of St. Paul. Catty-corner to its parent restaurant, the estimable Cafe Latté, this happy morning bakery makes them as delicate as a croissant — maybe it is croissant dough — so they have a fine, crisp bite and tend to fall into countless little flakes of pastry on the plate. Garlanded with crisp pecans and sheathed in amber glaze, these are perhaps the most elegant sweet rolls in the Midwest.

We love the **Coffee Cup** in Sully, Iowa, mostly because it is a quintessential Midwest town cafe where the locals go every morning and where such loves as pork chops and cream pie are always on the menu. While its cinnamon bun is by no mean's Iowa's largest, it is a beautiful little specimen, especially early in the morning, when it's still warm from the oven and the thin sugar glaze remains a tender veil over the rolled sweet dough.

TUCSON'S SUPERIOR CINNAMON ROLL

We are sorry to break the news to the good cooks of Iowa (where cinnamon rolls are a statewide passion), but Gus Balon's cinnamon roll in Tucson takes the cake. It is high, wide, and handsome, about the size of half a loaf of sandwich bread, swirled with veins of sweet cinnamon sugar and frosted on top. It fills a plate, and while it does come with utensils, the sensible (and sensual) way to eat one is to tear off big soft pieces by hand and use the knife to slather on butter. Because the roll comes warm from the baking pan, the butter melts and melds with the cinnamon, making hot-bun syrup too good to be true.

Gus Balon's: 6027 E. 22nd
   St., Tucson, AZ
   520-747-7788

Midwest

Size is a big deal among cinnamon roll aficionados, and if you are looking for the biggest, head west to Loveland, Colorado, where **Johnson's Corner** serves a shockingly large roll that has become a legend among truckers and travelers. It is the size of a dinner plate and arrives at the table warm and smothered with sweet syrupy icing, accompanied by buttery spread. It's definitely the most number of calories for the least amount of money ($2.25). On the other hand, if you are looking for class more than calories, head down to Denver and the **Duffeyroll Cafe**, where the spiral, cinnamon-plastered Duffeyroll sets high pastry standards for light weight and crispness. While flavored frosting is available, it should be a misdemeanor to ask for it. The unfrosted roll is unimprovable; a less-is-more phenomenon worthy of Mies van der Rohe.

For a really huge roll that's super-goopy and memorably delicious, the place to go is one of the six **Machine Shed** restaurants in the heartland. If we tell you that the Machine Shed is a carefully crafted theme restaurant, you might think that the rolls' girth is some sort of gimmick, but there is nothing at all disingenuous about these magnificent mountains of bakery freshness. (In fact, we love pretty much all of the Machine Shed menu, including its spectacular Iowa pork chops, page 259; despite its rustic theme, it is nothing at all like a cloying Cracker Barrel.) The rolls, which really are better described as loaves, are made from extremely tender dough that is just barely sweet, all the better to be a medium for torrents of amber-brown sugar and butter glaze and a copious mantle of real buttercream frosting. If that design isn't quite indulgent enough, you can get a caramel sticky bun, which is basically the same idea but way stickier, or a pecan caramel sticky bun, completely encased in nutmeats.

As large as a plate, Johnson's cinnamon roll in Loveland, CO, lives up to its legend.

TOP 4 CINNAMON ROLLS

1. **Hell's Kitchen:** 80 S. 9th St., Minneapolis, MN
   612-332-4700
   Second location: 310 Lake Ave. South, Duluth, MN
   218-727-1620
   www.hellskitcheninc.com
2. **Bread & Chocolate:** 867 Grand Ave., St. Paul, MN
   651-228-1017
   www.cafelatte.com
3. **Machine Shed:** 11151 Hickman Rd., Urbandale, IA
   515-270-6818
   See www.machineshed.com for additional locations.

4. Coffee Cup Café: 616 4th St.,
   Sully, IA
   641-594-3765

Also

Johnson's Corner: 2842 S.E.
   Frontage Rd., Loveland, CO
   970-667-2069
   www.johnsonscorner.com
Duffeyroll Cafe: 1290 S. Pearl
   St., Denver, CO
   303-753-9177
   www.duffeyrolls.com

CONEY ISLAND
Ubiquitous

Coney Islands — chili-topped weenies — were named for the Brooklyn Beach resort where the hot dog
was invented, in 1867, when butcher
Charles Feltman first put a sausage
in a bun. However, the Coneys sold
today nearly everywhere west of the
Delaware River, especially throughout the Midwest, bear little resemblance to anything served in New
York. While Coneys vary from place
to place, their single common denominator is chili dressing, which
was never part of the boardwalk formula. The Coney Island's formidable
beef topping with a sweet-hot twang
has a marked Greek accent — virtually all Coney restaurants were started
by Greek immigrants, many of whom
passed through New York on their
way west — but hot dog historians
get tied up in knots trying to explain
exactly how a Macedonian gloss on a
Tex-Mex dish became an emblem of
hot dogs named for New York.

   Thankfully, we are not historians.

The little weenies of the Tulsa, OK,
chain offer a nostalgic taste of history.

Our job simply is to pinpoint the
top Coney Islands in the land. It's no
small task, but there is only one place
to start, and that is Detroit. Nowhere
is the passion for them more intense
than at an adjoining pair of rival
storefront Detroit doggeries known
as **American Coney Island** and
Lafayette Coney Island, each with
its fanatic supporters. The two outfits serve dogs that might look pretty
much alike to the casual observer and,
frankly, taste pretty much alike to
us: little snappy-skin red weenies in
steamy soft white buns topped with
chili, raw onions, and mustard. These
are not aristocratic sausages like you
find on the other side of Lake Michigan, in Chicago and Milwaukee. Far
from it: they are cheap-tasting. But
we mean that with all respect; when
the craving strikes for a brace of them,
no prime filet mignon can satisfy it.
"Forget that Nathan's crap from the
East!" one Lafayette fan wrote to us a

Midwest

Haystacks of cheddar cover plump onion-laced, chili-sauced Coneys.

while back, proclaiming the Detroit Coney to be the king of all weenies.

It's not called a Coney at **Yesterdog** in Grand Rapids' Eastown, but the similarities are too big to ignore. Dressed by the dozen on pizza peels, the modest-sized wieners are traditionally topped with ketchup and mustard, chili, and finely chopped pickles. The Ultradog adds cheese to the mix; a Killer dog also includes sauerkraut; and there is even a Veggie version, which is cheese, kraut, onions, pickles, ketchup, and mustard loaded into a spongy little bun without a hot dog. Grand Rapids' **Grand Coney** serves a more traditional version, which it dubs "Detroit style": chili, mustard, and onions on a grilled natural-casing, all-beef Koegel hot dog (made in Flint) in a fleecy bun. Variations include the Grand, topped with cheddar cheese and jalapeño peppers, and the Loose, which is a wienerless bun filled with chili beef, mustard, and onions. Typical of

Coney shops everywhere, both Yesterdog and Grand Coney keep hours that reflect the Coney's unique attraction to gastronomic hedonists. Yesterdog is open Monday through Saturday from 10:30 a.m. to 2:30 a.m.; Grand Coney is open around the clock Thursday through Sunday.

We first came across **Coney Island Wiener House** looking for loosemeats (page 266) in Sioux City, Iowa. But given the name of the place, it behooved us to sample the Coney dogs, and we are glad we did. These bitesized pups get a nice surface crackle from time spent cooking on the grill, and the meat sauce on top is surprisingly mild — a good contrast, along with the little bun, to all the flavor fireworks in other ingredients. Sioux City also is home to the **Milwaukee Wiener House**, which boasts that it has served over 10 million and offers a Bow Wow (that's a double) and a Barker (with sauerkraut).

According to John Johnson, proprietor and chef at **Camp Washington Chili** in Cincinnati, the only proper side dish for a plate of fiveway chili is a brace of Coney Island chili dogs. Coneys are the secondtier specialty of every chili parlor in town, and they are topped with the same extra-spicy meat sauce that is used to blanket noodles on a plate of five-way (page 243). As on the chili, a great fluffy fistful of finely grated cheese on top is practically essential as the right creamy counterpoint.

A Main Street storefront in Fort Wayne, Indiana, formally known as the **Famous Coney Island Wiener Stand**, established in 1914, has built its reputation on the classic Greek-

American frankfurter: a modest-sized bright and blubbery pink weenie nestled in a soft bun and topped with fine-grind Coney sauce that has a fetching peppery sweetness. Everyone here orders a Coney with Coney sauce, although technically it is optional, as are mustard and chopped raw onions, also de rigueur. As is correct in all Coney Island shops, seating is at counter stools, many of which offer a nice view of hot dog assemblage. It's nearly the same configuration at the **Coney Island Lunch Room** in Grand Island, Nebraska, where a great old sign depicting a chili- and onion-topped hot dog extends over the sidewalk. Serving classic Coneys since 1933, this tiny storefront is also known for milk shakes.

The greatest-looking source is the **Coney Island Hot Dog Stand** in Bailey, Colorado. Originally built in Denver in 1966 and finally relocated in 2007 to the banks of the South Platte River, it is a diner shaped like a hot dog, its exterior painted red, yellow, green, and beige (weenie, mustard, relish, bun). No attempt is made to depict chili, which is in fact an optional topping here. Expect to wait quite a while for your food, and accommodations inside the 42-foot-long dog are only a few booths and tables. While the hot dog is not itself the most delicious in the land, the experience of eating here is roadside America par excellence.

Oklahoma is especially rich in classic Coneys. In addition to the amazing Coney slaw dogs sold in all of El Reno's onion-fried burger joints (page 350), it has a small chain of **Coney I-Lander** shops, which, in our opinion, perfectly deliver the cheap-eats ecstasy that is the Coney's soul. Piggly little weenies, two or three bites each, are bedded in steamed-soft buns and dressed with great panache and blinding speed behind the counter. The chili is intense, chocolate brown, very finely ground, slightly sweet, and slightly hot. Shredded cheese, pepper sauce, and cayenne pepper are optional; onions are essential.

TOP CONEY ISLANDS

1. **American Coney Island:** 114 W. Lafayette Blvd., Detroit, MI 313-961-7758 www.americanconeyisland.com

And

   Lafayette Coney Island: 118 W. Lafayette Blvd., Detroit, MI 313-964-8198
2. **Yesterdog:** 1505 Wealthy St. SE, Grand Rapids, MI 616-336-0746 www.yesterdog.com
3. **Camp Washington Chili Parlor:** 3005 Colerain Ave., Cincinnati, OH 513-541-0061 www.campwashingtonchili.com
4. **Coney I-Lander:** 7462 E. Admiral Place, Tulsa, OK 918-836-2336 Other locations in Oklahoma.
5. **Milwaukee Wiener House:** 309 Pearl St., Sioux City, IA 712-277-3449
6. **Grand Coney:** 809 Michigan St. NE, Grand Rapids, MI 616-776-5580 Second location: 6101 Lake Michigan Dr., Allendale, MI 616-895-9999

Midwest

7. Coney Island Wiener House: 510 Nebraska St., Sioux City, IA
712-258-7479
Second location: 3013 Hamilton Blvd. at the Marketplace, Sioux City, IA
712-258-6756

8. Coney Island Lunch Room: 104 E. 3rd St., Grand Island, NE
308-382-7155

9. Fort Wayne's Famous Coney Island Wiener Stand: 131 W. Main St., Fort Wayne, IN
219-424-2997

10. Coney Island Hot Dog Stand: 10 Old Stagecoach Rd., Bailey, CO
303-838-4210

CORNED BEEF SANDWICH
Illinois and Wisconsin

At Manny's in Chicago, a six-inch mound of fragile slices of corned beef renders bread almost irrelevant.

There are many praiseworthy corned beef sandwiches in this country, including the hand-sliced jumbos at Katz's in New York and the thick-sliced classics at Shapiro's in Indianapolis and D.Z. Akins in San Diego. We believe the best are in Milwaukee and Chicago. **Jake's Deli** in Milwaukee, a relic that has been around since 1935, when the neighborhood was mostly Jewish, offers an amazing sandwich-eating experience. The original proprietor, Reuben Cohen, sold the place to Jake, who sold it to Michael Kassof's dad in 1967, and now Michael runs it — the last Jewish business in a neighborhood that is mostly African-American. But superlative corned beef is a crosscultural infatuation, and when the restaurant opens at 10 a.m., the line of people waiting to eat corned beef is as heterogeneous as Milwaukee itself.

No automatic meat slicers are used. Michael Kassof hand-cuts the beef, a process he says is necessary because the seasoned briskets are cooked so long and become so fragile that they would disintegrate if cut by machine. There is no corned beef anywhere in America so rapturously luscious. A bit of its taste secret is that each hunk of brisket is sprinkled with paprika just before getting sliced, but the flavor penetration also comes from the fact that a dozen or more briskets are boiled together, their pot becoming a slurry of spice and beef flavor that reinsinuates itself into the fibers of the meat. Slices come medium-thick and are piled into slick-crusted, Milwaukee-made seeded rye from the Miller Bakery. Only one condiment is available. (Hint: It is not mayonnaise or ketchup.) Dill pickles served on the side are made here, too. And of course the beverage of choice is the classic deli drink, Dr. Brown's soda, preferably celery-flavored.

People accustomed to corned beef sandwiches everywhere else are shocked when they go to Chicago. Throughout the city and suburbs, the custom is not to slice the beef thick but to shave it as thin as possible. You'd think it would dry out that way, and we suppose that if it sat around a while, it would; but at **Manny's Cafeteria & Delicatessen** at the west edge of the Loop, it is such a popular item that scarcely seconds tick by as it is sliced, sandwiched, plated, carried to a table, and devoured. It is warm and sparkles with beads of moisture, and because of its diaphanous thin-ness, it is implausibly tender when piled 6 inches high on rye.

There is one and only one side dish to have with a Manny's corned beef sandwich, and that is a latke (or two). Manny's potato pancakes are ovoid and hard-crusted but tender inside, made by plopping the batter into an iron skillet of bubbling oil, then using a spoon to flatten the cake and form ridges in the top as it turns golden brown. Served hot, with sour cream or applesauce on the side, three or four of them would make a fine pure-potato meal. In Manny's cafeteria line, plates are set up and ready to go with a corned beef sandwich and a latke by its side.

2 GREAT MIDWESTERN CORNED BEEF SANDWICHES

Jake's Deli: 1634 W. North Ave., Milwaukee, WI
414-562-1272
Manny's Cafeteria & Delicatessen: 1141 S. Jefferson St., Chicago, IL
312-939-2855
www.mannysdeli.com

Jake's Deli in Milwaukee, around since 1935, now draws a cross-cultural crowd.

CUSTARD
Wisconsin and Missouri

If you think of custard as the commonly found franchised soft-serve fare pumped full of air, you need to eat custard in Wisconsin. Step up to the counter at **Leon's** in Milwaukee and order a cup of vanilla. It is dense and smooth. There are no mix-ins and no silly flavors. Custard is scientifically not as rich as ice cream (about

10 percent butterfat, as opposed to ice cream's 12 to 18 percent), but it tastes even more luxurious. Beyond Leon's pure vanilla custard, we highly recommend a chocolate sundae. That comes topped with some of the most delicious toasted nuts on the planet: pecan halves with a resounding crunch, a salty punch, and an earthy flavor that helps accentuate the heavenly clarity of the custard itself.

Leon's is especially noteworthy not just for its superior custard but for its ambiance, which is true and pure (not retro) American drive-in doo-wop: garish neon signage, a broad parking lot (no formal seating whatsoever), and weekend hours until midnight (it used to stay open later, but a city ordinance now cuts it off at 12).

Milwaukee's oldest custard stand, since 1938, is **Gilles Frozen Custard**, but a newcomer might find getting the right stuff confusing. Because of business deals too complicated for us to understand, the Gilles custard sold in stores and supermarkets is not in any way connected with what you'll get freshly made at the stand. The stand's custard is top-drawer stuff, pure and velvet-smooth, available plain or in super-duper fancy sundaes such as the Lalapalooza, the Bananarama, and the Zombie.

Kopp's has three locations around Cream City (which, amazingly, is a nickname derived not from dairy's dominance but from the cream-colored clay used to make the bricks for so many old Milwaukee buildings). Kopp's custard menu is baroque, with two different flavors of the day, every day of the year. These range from rum and Coke to butter brickle and cookie dough to Kona Coco Mac (that last one a mix of Kona coffee, coconut, and macadamia nuts). While you can get any flavor all by itself, Kopp's makes a specialty of sundaes so elaborate that it offers architectural diagrams pointing out various ingredients and their place in the sundae's structure. A blueprint for the staggering Kopp's Special shows pineapple and raspberry sauces, sliced bananas, hot fudge, toasted pecans, and a cherry on top.

No salute to midwestern custard would be complete without recognition of the legendary **Ted Drewes** of St. Louis. Ted's signature dish is a "concrete," the name of which has been appropriated by many of the region's custard shops that want to brag about how thick their product is. In our experience, Ted Drewes still makes the best — a milk shake that is presented out the window of the stand in an upside-down paper cup with a straw and a spoon planted in custard so thick that the utensils stay anchored and nothing drips out.

Never fluffy, never puffy, the dense vanilla custard of Leon's in Milwaukee supports luxurious add-ons.

Kopp's in Glendale, WI, serves sundaes so elaborate they occasionally need diagrams.

Gradually, it will melt as it warms, but it never melts too much. This fine custard is strapping.

Once you've sampled a pure concrete, available in flavors that include Abaco mocha, tart cherry, caramel, cookie dough, and hot fudge, it is time to move on to a Drewes specialty dessert, available as either a sundae or a concrete (not a huge difference between the two). The Dutchman's Delight is made with chocolate, butterscotch, and pecans; Terramizzou combines chocolate and pistachio nuts; an All Shook Up concrete includes peanut butter and bananas; and a Sin Sunday is made with tart cherries and hot fudge.

Ted Drewes is too quality-focused ever to have franchised, but there are two locations in St. Louis. Both sell wreaths and Christmas trees at holiday time.

TOP CUSTARDS

1. **Ted Drewes:** 4224 S. Grand
   Blvd., St. Louis, MO
   314-352-7376
   Second location: 6726 Chippewa,
   St. Louis, MO
   314-481-2652
   www.teddrewes.com
   Closed December and January

BUREK

A burek is a plate-wide circular plateau about 3 inches high made of phyllo leaves layered with beef, cheese, or a cheese and spinach mix that is slow-baked until the phyllo is brittle gold around the top and sides, its buttery see-through layers permeated with flavors of the filling within. It is warm, luxurious, just a bit spicy, and overwhelmingly satisfying. A burek is considered an appetizer, but if so, it is an appetizer for four. As made at Three Brothers, it is too large even to be a meal for a single person of normal appetite. Also, be aware that it is not fast food. Cooking one takes a good forty-five minutes, so unless you intend to spend time sipping wine or beer at leisure (a wonderful idea in this vintage cafe, which opened in 1897 as a Schlitz brewery tavern and is now handsomely spare, with quiet Old World charm), call ahead and ask the management to get your burek in the oven before you arrive.

Three Brothers: 2414 S. St. Clair
St., Milwaukee, WI
414-481-7530

Midwest

2. **Leon's Frozen Custard Drive-In:** 3131 S. 27th, Milwaukee, WI
414-383-1784

3. **Kopp's Frozen Custard:** 5373 N. Port Washington Rd., Glendale, WI
404-961-1393
See www.kopps.com for additional locations.

4. **Gilles Frozen Custard:** 7515 W. Bluemound Rd., Milwaukee, WI
414-453-4875
www.gillesfrozencustard.com

An otherworldly tableau of eggs, sweet-and-sour dressing, and iceberg, Dutch lettuce is unique to central Iowa.

DUTCH LETTUCE
Sully, Iowa

A culinary verity: the primary reason to visit the **Coffee Cup Café** is to eat pie. Banana cream, cherry-berry, hot peach: Any of these would deserve a place on our roster of things that need to get eaten. But estimable pies can be found in many places; Dutch

---

PELLA BOLOGNA

If the word *bologna* conjures up an image of perfectly circular pale pink slices of lunch meat found in grocers' cases and an insipid taste that is not much more than salted fat, we've got some real bologna for you to try. A Pella town specialty brought by Dutch settlers over 150 years ago, this is a real sausage made of rugged-textured beef, flamboyantly spiced, packed into a horseshoe-shaped ring, and smoked over hickory. The best place we know to eat it is at a stand called the Wooden Shoe on the grand concourse of the annual Iowa State Fair. Here the servers cut a quarter from a hot ring, pierce it with a stick, and hand it over so you can eat it on the stroll. What's especially fun about getting a bologna-sicle at the Wooden Shoe is that you can also purchase a Dutch letter here for dessert. Dutch letters are another Pella specialty: flaky pastries made in alphabet shapes and filled with a stripe of almond paste. When we got one of each, the man tending the bolognas behind the counter called out, "Dandy meal! Good combination!"

Iowa State Fair: Des Moines, IA (August); or year-round from www.ulrichsmeatmarket.com

lettuce, as far as we've been able to discern, is unique to central Iowa. We have found several recipes in locally published cookbooks but only one Dutch lettuce served in a restaurant. That's the Coffee Cup in Sully, just a half-hour's drive from Pella, which has a big population with Dutch ancestry (it is home of Dutch letters and Pella bologna).

Dutch lettuce is nothing like any salad you'll find on either coast, or, for that matter, anywhere outside of Midwest farmland, where it and similar ingenuous salads are a staple. The common denominators of all Dutch lettuces are hard-boiled eggs, bacon, sweet-and-sour dressing, and, of course, lettuce. The Coffee Cup's is cool, its dressing spiced with mustard, which makes it an especially good companion to pork tenderloin or baked ham. The following recipe, adapted from a mimeographed sheet we picked up long, long ago, is for a hot version of the dish, a Dutch-named version of that other midwestern favorite that we have yet to find on any restaurant menu, wilted lettuce.

Coffee Cup Café: 616 4th St., Sully, IA 641-594-3765

DUTCH LETTUCE

- 1 large egg yolk, beaten
- 2 tablespoons sugar
- 5 tablespoons cider vinegar
- 1 tablespoon butter
- 1 tablespoon all-purpose flour
- 5 tablespoons water
- 6 strips bacon, cooked but not until crisp, cut into small pieces
- 5 cups coarsely chopped lettuce (preferably a crisp lettuce such as iceberg or romaine)
- ½ cup chopped sweet onion
- 4 hard-cooked eggs, sliced

Beat the egg yolk with the sugar and 2 tablespoons vinegar in a medium bowl. Set aside.

In a small saucepan over medium heat, make a roux by melting the butter and thoroughly blending in the flour. Add 2 tablespoons water.

Stirring constantly, turn up the heat to bring it to a low boil. Pour just a bit of this mixture into the egg yolk mixture, stirring vigorously, then add the egg yolk mixture back into the saucepan and bring to a low boil. Remove from the heat, stir in the remaining 3 tablespoons vinegar and 3 tablespoons water, and add the bacon.

Spread one third of the lettuce in a broad serving dish. Top with half the chopped onion, then add half the hot dressing. Add another one third of the lettuce and the other half of the chopped onion. Top with more hot dressing. Arrange the slices of hard-cooked egg and the remaining lettuce on the dressing and top with some of the remaining dressing (or all, if you like it really goopy).

SERVES 4 TO 6

Midwest

FISH BOIL
Door County, Wisconsin

Never was there an ickier name for so delicious a ritual. The fish boil, which is not an eruption of piscatorial scales, is a way of cooking Great Lakes whitefish unique to the slim peninsula of Door County, Wisconsin, which juts into Lake Michigan east of Menominee and north of Sturgeon Bay. Fish steaks and red potatoes are gathered in separate nets to bubble in a big iron caldron over crackling hardwood. When the boilmaster decrees the food nearly done, he tosses a pint of kerosene straight into the fire. Flames shoot up, engulfing the cook pot and instantly jacking up the heat. In the flash of the blaze, the heavily salted water boils over and splashes down onto the inferno, nearly dousing it.

The big bang that signals the end of a fish boil isn't only for dramatic effect. It ensures the taste of the whitefish. As explained to us long ago by Russ Ostrand, who was boilmas-

ter at the **White Gull Inn** for thirty years, a ratio of 1 pound of salt for every 2 gallons of water in the pot creates a buoyancy that makes ingredients want to float. As the fish cooks in a net, its oils rise and hover at the surface. The volcanic upsurge at the moment of the boil-over forces all the oils and impurities to cascade out over the edge, leaving nothing in the boiling water but clean-flavored fish steaks and potatoes.

Timing is crucial. Once the water in the caldron hits a rolling boil, the potatoes go into the pot, along with half the total salt. Onlookers gasp: Surely this is going to be the saltiest meal ever served. The potatoes cook for twenty minutes, during which hungry customers gather around the fire on the patio, drinking beer or cider. Accordion music is an essential part of the ceremony. Russ Ostrand used to wear both hats — cook and musician — and explained that he started playing the accordion because if he didn't, people would get bored just staring at a pot over a fire. At the twenty-minute mark, the fish is added to the caldron along with the rest of the salt. Eight or nine minutes later, when the fish tests done, not quite breaking apart under its own weight, the kerosene conflagration signals that it's time to eat.

For those of us who arrive skeptical about the flavor potential of boiled fish, not to mention vastly oversalted boiled fish, this true-Wisconsin meal is stunning. The thick hunks of whitefish remind us of lobster: milk-moist, dense, and fine-textured. Incredibly, their elusive freshwater sweetness is just barely haloed by the presence

Flames shoot into the night at a Wisconsin fish boil, signaling that the caldron is almost ready.

Freshwater goodness: Great Lakes whitefish and red potatoes, straight from the kettle

White Gull Inn: 4225 Main St., Fish Creek, WI 920-868-3517 www.whitegullinn.com Fish boils are three times a night on Wednesday, Friday, Saturday, and Sunday throughout the summer. Reservations well in advance are almost always necessary.

FIVE-WAY CHILI
Cincinnati, Ohio

of salt. At the White Gull Inn, when the flames have subsided, you go indoors and are given a plate crowded with a brace of fish steaks along with potatoes (which imbibe only a bit more of the salt), and then you have the opportunity to drench the whole shebang with ladlefuls of melted Badger State butter, or to sprinkle it with lemon and pepper if you prefer. (Most chefs in Door County include onions that get boiled along with the potatoes, but the White Gull Inn contends that the alliums overpower the subtle flavor of freshwater fish.) As accompaniments, every table gets a help-yourself bowl of coleslaw and a variety of seasonal sweet breads — blueberry in the summer, pumpkin and apple in the fall — as well as Swedish limpa rye. If you want second helpings of anything, just ask. The required dessert is house-baked cherry pie à la mode. Door County is one of the nation's primary sources of tart Montmorency cherries, which make the best pie.

Cincinnati is a city bewitched by chili. At least a hundred joints in town make a specialty of it. And we do mean *joints,* for chili Cincinnati-style tends to be one rude plate of food, best eaten off a Formica counter under humming fluorescent lights after midnight in the company of other devout chiliheads.

Bearing no resemblance to a Texas "bowl of red" (page 314), it is called five-way because there are five separate layers in its full configuration. On a thick oval plate that has enough inward slope so ingredients list toward the center, a base is created from a heap of glistening limp spaghetti noodles; they are topped by a deliriously spiced sauce of finely ground beef, then beans, then raw onions, and finally a fluffy crown of shredded cheddar cheese. Oyster crackers are offered as a garnish.

A true melting-pot specialty, Cincinnati chili was invented by John and Athanas Kiradjieff, two brothers from Greece who came to New York

Midwest

in 1920 and spent a couple of years selling hot dogs in lower Manhattan. To the Kiradjieffs' taste, plain wieners were bland, so they concocted a chili-sauce topping for the tube steaks, using a rainbow of spices from the old-country kitchen, including such heady flavors as cinnamon, cardamom, turmeric, and even perhaps unsweetened chocolate. (We say *perhaps* because the Kiradjieff recipe, like every Cincinnati chili-parlor recipe, is as secret as the launch code for America's ICBM fleet.) When the brothers moved to Cincinnati in 1922 and opened a small cafe on Vine Street next to the Empress Theater, they sold not only chili-topped "Coney Island style" hot dogs but also chili ladled onto noodles. Onions, a customary hot dog garnish, were a natural element of the new dish, and

it is believed that a customer suggested adding a layer of kidney beans. At some point in history, a halo of Wisconsin cheddar cheese became the fifth and final layer.

The Kiradjieffs' parlor, known as **Empress Chili**, thrived and multiplied, and soon some of its employ-

Goetta, fried pork-shoulder loaf mixed with oats, is an essential breakfast item at Hathaway's in Cincinnati.

GOETTA

Goetta (rhymes with feta) is not unique to chili parlors; it is served in cafes and diners throughout Cincinnati, and it is every bit as much a Queen City icon as five-way chili. A distant cognate of Pennsylvania scrapple, it is a loaf of pork shoulder mixed with steel-cut oats — the traditional Low German cook's way of stretching a minimum amount of meat to feed a maximum number of people. The loaf is cut into slices and fried in butter to melt-in-the-mouth tenderness. It is a welcome companion for eggs, waffles, and pancakes. Usually we are too distracted by chili, Coneys, and double-deckers

to sample it at Camp Washington, but it is irresistible at Hathaway's Coffee Shop, where it goes particularly well with cinnamon-accented French toast, which arrives dusted with powdered sugar and topped with a glob of butter large enough to melt over all four slices. Hathaway's itself is a trip back in time: a bustling urban coffee shop snuggled in the Carew Arcade, complete with uniformed waitresses who pad around the room refilling coffee cups as required.

Hathaway's Coffee Shop: 441 Vine St., Cincinnati, OH 513-621-1332

ees struck out on their own to open competitive eateries. Among these were the Lambrinides family, who started **Skyline Chili**, now a huge local chain, and Pete and Harry Vidas of the much-esteemed **Chili Time**. "Just about anyone who makes and sells chili in Cincinnati either worked for the Kiradjieffs, got their idea from our family, adapted our recipe, or were inspired by them," declares Ed Kiradjieff, son of founder John.

Every Cincinnatian has a favorite parlor, and the serious aficionados can tell you the exact day of the week and hour of the day when their cho-

Cincinnati's Camp Washington, a landmark for chili hounds

GREEN BAY CHILI

In 1913, "Chili John" Isaac devised a recipe for ground round cooked with a fusillade of spices. His recipe was superhot, but served at his little Green Bay eatplace, in concert with spaghetti noodles, beans, and cheese, it became part of a well-balanced plate of food. Architectonically similar to Cincinnati chili but known throughout Wisconsin as Green Bay–style chili, it is especially noteworthy because it was the inspiration for oyster crackers. Chili John is the man who originally convinced cracker manufacturers to make little crackers to fit better in the spoons he used as part of his chili service.

Chili John's: 519 S. Military Ave., Green Bay, WI 920-494-4624 www.chilijohns.com

sen concoction is at its peak. They'll debate whether Skyline chili is spicier than Empress, or whether Chili Time's blend is more atomic than the **Blue Ash** brand. Ourselves, we've never had a plate of chili in this city that we didn't like, but when we crave the very best, there is just one place to go: **Camp Washington Chili Parlor**, where the five-way is piled high and handsome. This wonderful, one-of-a-kind hash house, named after its neighborhood (which was a Civil War encampment), is a true landmark for chili hounds, featuring all the proper ambiance, including sports trophies displayed above the counter and great vats of bubbling chili in back. The air smells of onions and spices, and by midmorning the counter and tables are packed with cheap-eats fans, who fork their way into plates of five-way

Midwest

FIVE-WAY CHILI

No self-respecting Cincinnati chili chef shares his secrets. John Johnson told us that the spice mix he and his wife make is kept above the kitchen in a locked vault. In the morning, just before the chili is brewed, Johnson slips upstairs and comes down with a brown paper bag full of the potent seasonings.

The following recipe is one we devised based on much trial and error and detailed instructions that we secured by sending a dollar to a lady over the border in Kentucky, who advertised in the back of a midwestern housewife's magazine that she knew how to make the real thing. It works for us, and closely approximates some of the city's best brews. But feel free to fiddle and fuss to your own taste, and if you are missing cardamom or coriander, substitute something else. Five-way practically demands that you reinvent the recipe and make it your own.

1 pound ground beef
2 medium onions, chopped
2 garlic cloves, minced
1 cup thick barbecue sauce
$\frac{1}{2}$ cup water
$\frac{1}{2}$ ounce unsweetened chocolate, grated
1 tablespoon chili powder
1 teaspoon freshly ground black pepper
$\frac{1}{4}$ teaspoon ground cumin
$\frac{1}{4}$ teaspoon turmeric
$\frac{1}{4}$ teaspoon ground allspice
$\frac{1}{4}$ teaspoon ground cinnamon
$\frac{1}{4}$ teaspoon ground cloves
$\frac{1}{4}$ teaspoon ground coriander
$\frac{1}{4}$ teaspoon ground cardamom
$\frac{1}{2}$ teaspoon salt
Tomato juice, as needed
9 ounces spaghetti, cooked and lightly buttered
1 16-ounce can kidney beans, drained and heated
1 pound cheddar cheese, finely shredded
Oyster crackers

Brown the meat in a Dutch oven with half the chopped onion and the garlic, stirring well to break up the meat. (Set the remaining onion aside to top the chili when it's done.) Drain any fat from the pan. Add the barbecue sauce and water and bring to a boil. Add the chocolate, spices, and salt. Cover the pan and reduce the heat to low. Simmer for 30 minutes, stirring occasionally. The chili will thicken as it cooks. Add tomato juice as necessary to create a brew that ladles up easily. Allow the chili to rest for at least 30 minutes in a covered pan at room temperature. Reheat over medium heat until warmed through. (The chili can be refrigerated for up to 5 days and reheated to serve.)

To make each plate, put down a layer of spaghetti, top it with hot chili, then a few beans, then the reserved chopped onions to taste. Pat on the cheese so the chili's heat begins to melt it. Serve with oyster crackers.

SERVES 4

and heft Coneys (little weenies topped with chili and cheese) and mile-high double-decker sandwiches.

Chef John Johnson, who started working for his uncles at Camp Washington in 1951 and is said to have actually improved their (top-secret) formula, makes his chili using lean beef that is finely ground on the premises and brewed in batches of 60 gallons each day. It is dark and meaty, exuberantly spiced but not painfully hot, and thick enough to blend perfectly with the tender noodles onto which it is ladled. Add beans, onions, and cheese and you've got one of this nation's most distinctive regional plates of food. It is served twenty-four hours a day, every day, with the exception of the hours from 4 a.m. on Sunday to 5 a.m. on Monday, when the parlor is closed. But Monday at dawn, a line begins to form at the locked door: hungry Cincinnatians eager to fork

into a morning plate of five-way and start the week right.

4 ESSENTIAL CINCINNATI CHILI PARLORS

1. **Camp Washington Chili Parlor:** 3005 Colerain Ave., Cincinnati, OH
513-541-0061
www.campwashingtonchili.com
2. **Blue Ash Chili:** 9565 Kenwood Rd., Cincinnati, OH
513-984-6107
www.blueashchili.com
3. **Chili Time:** 4727 Vine St., Cincinnati, OH
513-641-1130
4. **Empress Chili:** 8340 Vine St., Cincinnati, OH
512-761-5599
Two other locations:
7934 Alexandria Pike, Alexandria, KY
859-635-5900
5675 Rapid Run Rd., Cincinnati, OH
513-922-6669

Also
Skyline Chili: See www .skylinechili.com for locations.

Chef John Johnson at Camp Washington happily shows off his chili kettle but keeps his spice mix locked in a vault.

NATIONAL BESTS

FRENCH FRIES

Like humans, French fries come in all shapes and sizes. The slender, honey-brown twigs served at **Swanky Frank's** in Norwalk, Connecticut, are every bit as beautiful as the fat, creamy

Midwest

Skinny fries at Swanky Frank's in Norwalk, CT

steak fries at the **Wolf Lodge Inn** in Coeur d'Alene, Idaho, and Spokane, Washington.

Attractive French fries are dressed in so many different ways. Throughout much of Rhode Island as well as at the **Argyle** in Kearny, New Jersey, where the thick spud logs that accompany fried fish are known by their Brit moniker, chips, a spritz of malt vinegar is de rigueur; at **Murphy's Steak House** in Bartlesville, Oklahoma, thick brown gravy is the condiment of choice; **Hires Big H** of Salt Lake City offers a pink sauce like French dressing; and at **Mustard's Last Stand** in Evanston,

Fries blanketed with gravy at Murphy's Steak House in Bartlesville, OK

Illinois, where ketchup is anathema on hot dogs, it is the obligatory dip for French fries.

Presentation is critical. Partly this has to do with beauty. What potato lover's heart doesn't skip a beat upon sighting a heap of crunch-crusted spuds under a twinkling halo of just-sprinkled salt? It's awfully cozy to see your French fries nestled in a basket along with a cheeseburger (as at **Hodad's** in Ocean Beach, California) or fried chicken (as at **Maddox Drive-In** of Brigham City, Utah).

Beyond appearance, proper plating ensures textural integrity. There is no potato abuse more heinous than enclosing French fries in a stifling Styrofoam takeout container, where they steam soft. On the other hand, a semiporous paper bag just may be the ideal delivery system. As at many of Chicago's best street-food eat-shacks, **Ricobene's** loads just-cooked potatoes into a brown bag that opens at your table (or on your dashboard) like a cornucopia. The first few that fall out are brittle, and as you eat your way deep into the bag, you discover some at the core that have softened in their center but retain crusty edges. The greatest of all fry bags — and some would say the greatest of all French fries, period — are those served at Pittsburgh's **Essie's Original Hot Dog Shop**, known to devotees as the Big O, where sizes range from small to the $7-plus extra-large, a potato orgy for four.

Southern barbecues use potatoes as dressing for a pork plate. At the **Beacon Drive-In** of Spartanburg, South Carolina, Pork-a-Plenty is a mound of smoked meat virtually eclipsed by a tangle of French fries and onion rings. Similar tactics are used at the **Ridgewood Barbecue** of Bluff City, Tennessee, where the French fries are especially dark gold, and at **McClard's Bar-B-Q** of Hot Springs, Arkansas, where they top slabs of hickory-cooked ribs. As you dig into these platters with fork or fingers, the meat, sauce, and potatoes mingle in wanton rapture. At **Mariscos Chihuahua** in Tucson, the pattern is reversed: shrimp *endiablados,* bathed in peppery glaze, are served *on top* of French fries, their four-alarm sauce seeping down into the crusty potatoes and infusing them with heat and flavor.

Of all the pleasures of the French fry (other than putting it in one's mouth), none is so satisfying as watching a basketful emerge from hot oil, steamy and glistening. At the counter of **Super Duper Weenie** in Fairfield, Connecticut, you see them cooked and drained, then you watch each order being piled into its cardboard boat and dusted with pepper along with salt. That nip of pepper seems minor but makes Super

A shower of black pepper brings fries alive at Super Duper Weenie in Fairfield, CT.

Duper Weenie's fries super-duper in their own right. In our book, the only hot-dog-companion potatoes even more delicious than these are the duck-fat French fries at Chicago's **Hot Doug's**, which bills itself as "the sausage superstore and encased meat emporium." Duck-fat French fries are dark and extra-crisp, just about the most dissolute way to fry a spud, and while most places that serve them are upwardly mobile, from the **Duck Fat Restaurant** in Portland, Maine, to the **Crow Bar and Kitchen**, a California gastropub, they are unbeatable companions for a fully dressed Chicago all-beef red hot (page 275), of which Hot Doug's is one of the city's top purveyors. (They are available only Fridays and Saturdays; the rest of the week, Hot Doug's regular French fries, which are fresh-cut, are superb.)

The most delicious French fries in America are available only twelve days a year, in Minneapolis, at the **Minnesota State Fair** at the end of August.

Midwest

At McClard's in Hot Springs, AR, fries crown slabs of hickory-smoked ribs.

Dozens of different food booths sell them all around the fairgrounds, in sizes that range from a modest 32-ounce container to an 88-ounce bucket. It is hard to say exactly why these fries taste so swoonfully swell. Perhaps it's the atmosphere: children screaming with glee on the midway rides, the appetizing smells of hot corn dogs and pork-chops-on-a-stick wafting through the air, the sheer joy of being at a huge state fair where nutritional priggishness holds no sway. Or perhaps their goodness comes from how utterly fresh they are. In the back of every stand are piled-up bushels of potatoes, skin still on. You can watch them get swiftly peeled and fried in clean oil, and the lines to buy them are always so long that the instant they emerge from the oil they are scooped into a cardboard container, ready to be salted (or spritzed with malt vinegar) and eaten while still dangerously hot. Each serving contains a few savory bits and tips of potato cooked to a dark gold crunch; the majority of pieces are thin-cut square logs that are crisp on the outside, but sensuously creamy just underneath the burnished crust. With or without ketchup for dipping, alongside a foot-long hot dog or all by themselves, Minnesota State Fair potatoes are fried-food perfection, rivaled only by the midway's magnificent onion rings . . . But fried O-rings are another story altogether.

BEST FRENCH FRIES

1. **Hot Doug's:** 3324 N. California, Chicago, IL
   773-279-9550
   www.hotdougs.com
2. **Super Duper Weenie:** 306 Black Rock Turnpike, Fairfield, CT
   203-334-DOGS
   www.superduperweenie.com
3. **Minnesota State Fair:** 1265 N. Snelling Ave., St. Paul, MN
   651-288-4310
   www.mnstatefair.org
4. **McClard's Bar-B-Q:** 505 Albert Pike, Hot Springs, AR
   501-623-9665 or 866-622-5293
   www.mcclards.com
5. **Ridgewood Barbecue:** 900 Elizabethton Highway (Old Route 19 East), Bluff City, TN
   423-538-7543
6. **Ricobene's:** 252 W. 26th St., Chicago, IL
   312-225-5555
   See www.ricobenesfamoussteaks.com for additional locations.
7. **Essie's Original Hot Dog Shop:** 3901 Forbes Ave., Pittsburgh, PA
   412-621-7388
8. **Mustard's Last Stand:** 1613 Central St., Evanston, IL
   847-864-2700
9. **Duck Fat Restaurant:** 43 Middle St., Portland, ME
   207-774-8080
   www.duckfat.com
10. **Crow Bar and Kitchen:** 2325 E. Coast Highway, Corona del Mar, CA
    949-675-0070
    www.thecrowbarcdm.com
11. **Hodad's:** 5010 Newport Ave., Ocean Beach, CA
    619-224-4623
    www.hodadies.com
12. **Beacon Drive-In:** 255 John B. White Sr. Blvd., Spartanburg, SC
    864-585-9387
    www.beacondrivein.com

13. **Swanky Frank's:** 182 Connecticut Ave., Norwalk, CT
    203-853-3647
14. **Maddox Drive Inn:** 1900 S. Highway 89, Brigham City, UT
    435-723-5603
15. **Argyle Fish & Chip Restaurant:** 212 Kearny Ave., Kearny, NJ
    201-991-3900
16. **Mariscos Chihuahua:** 2902 E. 22nd St., Tucson, AZ
    520-326-1529
    Multiple locations in Tucson.
17. **Wolf Lodge Inn:** 11741 E. Frontage Rd., Coeur d'Alene, ID
    208-664-6665
    Second location: 104 S. Freya St., Spokane, WA
    509-535-8975
    www.wolflodgerestaurants.com
18. **Murphy's Steak House:** 1625 S.W. Frank Phillips Blvd., Bartlesville, OK
    918-336-4789
19. **Hires Big H:** 425 S. 700 East, Salt Lake City, UT
    801-364-4582
    See www.hiresbigh.com for additional locations.

FRIDAY FISH FRY
Milwaukee

Imagine a vast triangle with points in Buffalo, Cincinnati, and Grand Forks, North Dakota. This is the fish-fry zone. Throughout the central Northland in city taverns, American Legion halls, and woodland supper clubs, Friday night is all about fish and beer. Not all who enjoy the weekly custom are Catholic, although the old canon

law against eating meat on Fridays is certainly how it started. Fish-fry culture thrives in cities with big Catholic populations and communities that maintain strong European ethnic identity. Foremost among them is Milwaukee, where the ritual is so much a part of life that it is rare to find a restaurant that does *not* dedicate Friday night to it. Whether you spend Friday night in a traditional Jewish deli or the Pottawattamie Indian casino, you'll be having fish and beer.

At **Serb Hall**, fish fries are the only meal regularly served, and only on Fridays. The scale of the place is stunning. It is a chandelier-crowned eating stadium with a capacity of 1,086 at hundreds of four-tops and dozens of big-party tables. Nevertheless, arrive anytime after 6 p.m. and you will wait in line. The fish of choice is what's called Icelandic cod, thin-crusted blocks of soft white meat served in a plastic basket with French fries, tart coleslaw, and rye bread on the side. A much-loved destination for schnitzels and sausages as well as a Friday fish fry every day of the week is the **Historic Turner Restaurant** in an 1883 city landmark building. For a fun, family-style fish fry that includes entertainment by the Brew House Polka Kings with their squeezebox tunes, the place to go is **Lakefront Palm Garden**, where you can get cod, perch, or bluegill or tilapia that is baked, not fried. Tours of the adjoining brewery are part of the evening's fun.

McBob's Pub & Grill is a Central City bar that attracts a boisterous after-work crowd and where the fish

Midwest

The meaty fried grouper from McBob's in Milwaukee comes with oniony potato pancakes.

fry comes in three configurations: a single serving of perch, walleye, or grouper, a combo of perch and walleye, or a super combo of all three. The walleye is light and ephemeral; the grouper is mild, with a sweet oily flavor. The perch is snowy white. Fanned out under the fish are sensational potato pancakes laced with onion and packing full spuddy flavor. The libation of choice is a shot and a beer.

The preferred upscale fish to fry in Milwaukee is perch, a clean-fleshed lake denizen known for its freshwater sweetness. All the swankier fish-fry places offer it; at **Jack Pandl's Whitefish Bay Inn**, otherwise celebrated as a daily source of broiled Lake Superior whitefish and *schaum torte* (baked meringue) dessert, Friday's perch come three to a plate, each whole one split into a pair of connected fillets. Crisp-skinned potato pancakes sing nice harmony with the fish's golden crust. The po-

tato pancakes at **Polonez** are as thin as a dime and lace-edged; they pack a sour-creamy wallop that makes perch seem all the sweeter. (Good as that meal is, even on Friday it would be a sin to visit this immaculate Old World eating hall and not also have the butter-glistening pierogi and the hunter's stew known as *bigos,* packed with ham and sausage . . . and of course finish things off with a *digestif* of plum-flavored *sliwowica.*)

Our buddies Jessica Zierten and Brad Warsh, both lifelong Milwaukeeans, insisted that any significant exploration of the city's fish fries needed to include a visit to their favorite tavern in the Riverwest neighborhood, **Klinger's East**. The swinging door opens onto concrete stairs that lead up and inside. "These five steps take you to northern Wisconsin," Brad declared as we came in off the sidewalk late one Friday night. He said he was reminded of summer places far from the lights of Milwau-

The tradition of Friday night fish fries began in cities with large European and Catholic populations.

kee every time he stepped up into the beery air. It is so dim that we saw nothing other than a few neon window signs when we walked in; ambient light at our table under a corner television seemed to go from noonbright to twilight and back again as the TV's image flickered light and dark. The Klinger's East fish fry is either cod or smelt, the latter a springtime fish that is small and crunchy and so hugely flavorful that none but serious fish lovers need consider ordering them.

Milwaukee's Serb Hall seats more than a thousand for the fish fry.

THE GREAT MILWAUKEE FISH FRIES

1. **McBob's Pub & Grill:** 4919 W. North Ave., Milwaukee, WI 414-871-5050
2. **Polonez:** 4016 S. Packard Ave., Milwaukee, WI 414-482-0080
3. **Jack Pandl's Whitefish Bay Inn:** 1319 E. Henry Clay St., Milwaukee, WI 414-969-3800 www.jackpandls.com
4. **Serb Hall:** 5101 W. Oklahoma Ave., Milwaukee, WI 414-545-6030 www.serbhall.com
5. **Historic Turner Restaurant:** 1034 N. 4th St., Milwaukee, WI 414-276-4844 www.historicturner.com
6. **Klinger's East:** 920 E. Locust, Milwaukee, WI 414-263-2424
7. **Lakefront Palm Garden:** 1872 N. Commerce St., Milwaukee, WI 414-273-8300 www.cafevecchio.com

FRIED CHICKEN DINNER
Midwest

Chicken dinner is universal, and superior examples can be found from the Blackstone Valley of New England (page 5) to **Chicken on the Way** in Calgary, Alberta, but when it comes to full-bore, family-style, groaning-board feeds, the Midwest is the place to go.

With crust that magically crunches into disembodied pure chicken-fat flavor and young-fryer meat that slides from the bone and glistens with golden juice, skillet-fried chicken is the crème de la crème. The **Kopper Kettle Inn** of southern Indiana dishes it out, along with bowls full of whipped potatoes, green beans, buttered corn, dinner rolls, and, the coup de grâce, pan-drippin' cream gravy that serves as a dip for chicken pieces and dinner rolls and as a coronation

Midwest

Stroud's in Kansas City, MO, makes the best chicken dinner in America.

gown for those whipped potatoes. We recommend the Kopper Kettle among the many great fried chicken dinners of southern Indiana not only for its good food, but for ultra-feminine Victorian ambiance like nowhere else. The building, which started as a grain elevator, then became a tavern, then a tearoom, consists of count-less rooms added on over the years, each with its own name: the Music Room, the Crystal Room, and so on. Each table in each room has its own name too: the French Window, the Yellow Tulip, the Dresden. Pink voile curtains shimmer at the windows, candelabra grace the larger tables, and among the antiques and bric-a-brac are tasteful objets d'art with the female form as subject: a bas-relief nude above the fireplace, a statuette of Aphrodite running so fast that her toga blows away from her shapely body. Waitresses echo the artistic im-ages, dressed in outfits that might be called Early American Milkmaid, with mop caps and thigh-high skirts over thick petticoats.

At the restaurants of Barberton, Ohio (at the edge of Akron), fried chicken is the center of a ritual feast that also includes a timbale of tart coleslaw, good French fries, and a bowl of spicy tomato-rice hot sauce that is positively addictive. Barberton chicken is not like other fried chicken. Cooked in lard, it has a shimmering red-gold crust, and it differs from or-dinary fast-food fried chicken both in the dripping moistness its coat encases and in its shape. It is cut the old-fashioned way into wing, drum-ette, breast, leg, thigh, and back, an economical technique left over from Depression days, when cooks tried to maximize the number of pieces they could get from one chicken. When you sink your teeth into a piece, you may find meat where you don't ex-pect it or not enough meat where you want it (in the back), but all chicken lovers will deeply appreciate the Bar-berton experience. (Roadfood.com's Bruce Bilmes pointed out that Bar-berton chicken bears a close resem-blance to chicken served at northern Indiana's Teibel's, page 218, which uses a recipe brought by Grandma Teibel from Austria.) **Belgrade Gar-dens**, open since 1933, is the original source of the Barberton banquet, the concept of which was imported by the Topalsky family, who emigrated from Serbia early in the twentieth century. You can get white or dark meat or a combination or a plate of nothing but legs, thighs, backs, wings, or tenders. Each is available small, medium, and large.

Frankly, we'd have a hard time choosing the absolute best of all the stellar fried chickens in this book from the likes of Keaton's (page 170) and Prince's Hot Chicken Shack (page 169), not to mention the important chicken meccas of Pittsburg, Kansas (page 308), and Henderson, Kentucky (page 170). All great places, all worth trying. But if you are looking for the most effulgent chicken *dinner* in the land, there is only one place to go: **Stroud's** of Kansas City, Missouri. Here is chicken pan-fried to supreme succulence, plus pan-dripping gravy, fluffy mashed potatoes, buttery-sweet cinnamon rolls, and even superb chicken soup with homemade noodles and juicy shreds of thigh meat. Tablecloths are red-checked, and meals are served family-style in voluminous bowls meant for passing among friends and family. Stroud's location on Oak Ridge Drive lacks the tumbledown charm of the original restaurant that Mrs. Stroud opened in the 1930s on the location of the family fireworks stand, but in some ways the new place is even better: a sprawling frontier farmhouse with dining tables overlooking green

Stroud's serves family-style in a farmhouse overlooking the idyllic countryside.

grass on the rolling countryside. If there's a chicken dinner hall in heaven, we expect it to be just like this.

ULTIMATE FRIED CHICKEN DINNERS

1. **Stroud's:** 5410 N.E. Oak Ridge Dr., Kansas City, MO
816-454-9600
Second location: 4200 Shawnee Mission Parkway, Fairway, KS
913-262-8500
www.stroudsrestaurant.com

2. **Belgrade Gardens:** 401 E. State St., Barberton, OH
330-745-0113
Second location: 3476 Massillon Rd., Uniontown, OH
330-896-3396

3. **Kopper Kettle Inn:** 135 W. Main St., Morristown, IN
765-763-6767
www.kopperkettle.com

Also
Chicken on the Way:
1443 Kensington Rd. NW, Calgary, AB, Canada
403-283-5545

The shimmering sunset-gold crust of Barberton chicken comes from frying it in lard.

Midwest

FRUITS-OF-THE-FOREST PIE
Wisconsin

A dozen fruits-of-the-forest pies are made and sold each day at the 130-year-old monastery at the Holy Hill Shrine a half-hour northwest of Milwaukee. The pie contains slices of al dente sweet apple and a vivid scarlet mélange of spring rhubarb and berries. Very yummy filling! However, it's the crust that will knock your socks off. As you put a knife to the pie and press down, you will hear it crunch, then shatter and give way. Waves of brittle crust above the filling glisten with sugar crystals and veins of the fruits' juices that have seeped up through the cracks and around the edge, now adhering as little chewy seams of baked fruit essence. The bottom crust remains flaky under its load of fruit and adds a faint hint of cinnamon to the mix. In the never-ending quest to determine which state de-

Fruits of monastic living, from the Holy Hill Cafe in Hubertus, WI

serves the crown as America's premier pie source, this pie helps keep Wisconsin among the frontrunners.

Located in an unbelievably picturesque setting high on a hill in the Wisconsin countryside, the **Holy Hill Cafe**, also known as the Old Monastery Inn Cafe, happens to be a motherlode of comfort-food lunch served cafeteria-style, including chicken noodle soup, meat loaf with mashed potatoes, green bean casserole, and fresh-baked breads and muffins.

Holy Hill Cafe: 1525 Carmel Rd., Hubertus, WI
262-628-4295
www.cateringbyfrank.com and
www.holyhill.com

GOOEY BUTTER CAKE
St. Louis, Missouri

"The perfect Tupperware Party food" is how *St. Louis Post-Dispatch* food editor Judith Evans once described the local bakery specialty known as gooey butter cake. Legend says it was created in the 1930s, when a now-forgotten cook mixed the wrong ingredients for a cake but decided to bake it anyway. The result — a low-rise pastry with a tender crust around the edge and a moist center that is custard-soft — has become a St. Louis passion and a hallmark of the city's best bakeries. It is the signature dish of **Park Avenue Coffee**, which boasts that it makes sixty-four different varieties (not including the heart-shaped one sold for Valentine's Day). About a dozen are available on any one day, and as much as we are intrigued by blueberry and peanut butter, it's the traditional gooey butter cake that we like best. It's the butteriest.

Park Avenue Coffee: 1919 Park
Ave., St. Louis, MO
314-621-4020
www.parkavenuecoffee.com

HOPPEL POPPEL
Milwaukee

If you are looking for a really big breakfast in Wisconsin or Iowa, find a place that serves hoppel poppel. We first came across this mighty meal-in-a-skillet at breakfast in Iowa's Amana Colonies, where it had been entrenched by Lutheran separatists who probably needed a multicalorie breakfast before plowing fields all day. It is a staple of community cookbooks (where it sometimes is titled hoffel poffel) but pretty hard to find in restaurants, except in and around Milwaukee, where there are two outstanding versions. At **Jo's Cafe,** you can sit at the counter opposite the grill and watch it assembled — better yet, smell it as it cooks. The aroma starts getting good when onions are mixed with a mound of chunky home-fried potatoes on the griddle. A few eggs are vigorously stirred in, then nuggets of salami that send garlic perfume clouds into the air. Melted cheese on top is optional. The only reason we would suggest not getting hoppel poppel for breakfast at Jo's is that the diner's thin-cut hash browns are even more delicious than the home fries. Cooked in a flat patty until brittle-crisp, they, too, are available enveloped in melted cheese.

Benji's is a Jewish-style delicatessen that lists hoppel poppel on its menu between a corned beef omelet and fried kreplach (little dumplings). While definitely neither religiously kosher nor traditionally Jewish, it is labeled the Benji's Special. You can

MATZOH BREI

Like hoppel poppel, matzoh brei is a skillet egg breakfast, but traditionally Jewish and somewhere on the egg-dish spectrum between Tex-Mex migas and French toast. The basic idea is to scramble small pieces of the unleavened bread known as matzoh into eggs, then cook the mixture in a pan of butter. The ratio of matzoh to egg makes a huge difference in the nature of the dish. Is it basically an egg recipe with a hint of texture from a few bits of matzoh? Or is it all about the crunch of matzoh, with just enough egg mixed in so the matzoh can be fried? Benji's in Shorewood, Wisconsin, is a good place to decide how you like it, because the kitchen offers it both ways, scrambled and pancake-style. We like scrambled, in which the matzoh pieces are softened just enough so that there is no disturbing brittleness, but they do provide the kind of textural poise that no other bread or cracker could deliver. Cooked in lots and lots of good Wisconsin butter, this is a plateful of comfort, deli-style.

Hoppel poppel started as a rib-sticking breakfast for Lutheran farmers.

have regular hoppel poppel, which is a dramatic sweep of butter-soft browned potatoes, chewy chunks of salami, and creamy scrambled eggs, or you can kick it up by choosing super hoppel poppel, which adds green peppers, mushrooms, and melted cheese.

HOPPEL POPPELS

1. **Jo's Café:** 3519 W. Silver Spring Dr., Milwaukee, WI
414-461-0210
2. **Benji's Deli:** 4156 N. Oakland Ave., Shorewood, WI
414-332-7777

HORSESHOE
Springfield, Illinois

Shoes are common on tables in Springfield, Illinois, but no one eats them elsewhere. Known formally as a horseshoe, Springfield's signature dish is a huge, messy, open-faced hot sandwich made in countless configurations. At breakfast time you can get

one with eggs, cream gravy or cheese sauce, and hash browns. Lunch and supper shoes are piled up with hamburgers, pork tenderloins, fried chicken, whitefish, or just about any other main course you'd find on the menu of a diner or pub.

Kurt Ritz of **Ritz's Cafe** explains how they got their name. "The scattered potatoes looked like shoeing nails. A slice of ham laid on toast was the shape of a horseshoe, and the plate was an anvil." Ritz, whose cafe and **Ritz's Li'l Fryer** serve shoes for breakfast and lunch, doesn't know how the basic ham-and-cheese open-faced hot sandwich formula became what is perhaps the most massive single-dish meal in the nation, bearing no resemblance to a horse's footwear. As the standard topping for its breakfast shoes, Ritz's cooks up hash browns that are thick and chunky with an abundance of crisp surface area — definitely the way to go.

There are no shoes better or bigger than those at **D&J Cafe**, where the morning version can include sausage,

The horseshoe of Springfield, IL, a giant open-faced sandwich of shredded potatoes, eggs, and toast

fried eggs, hash browns, and a half-and-half layout of gravy and cheese. One is enough food for three or four normal appetites — a big savory mound almost fully enclosed by a red-gold net of fried shredded potatoes, with yolks of eggs seeping creamy gold protein throughout. White toast at the very bottom, turned soft by the time a fork excavates its way that far down, is a reminder of normalcy on a plate of otherwise unbridled plebeian opulence.

CHOICE SPRINGFIELD HORSESHOES

1. **D&J Cafe:** 915 W. Laurel St., Springfield, IL
   217-753-1708
2. **Ritz's Cafe:** 700 W. Jefferson St., Springfield, IL
   217-523-7680
3. **Ritz's Li'l Fryer:** 2148 N. Grand Ave. East, Grandview, IL
   217-528-0862

IOWA PORK CHOP
Iowa

In Iowa, the term *pork chop* has a different meaning than it does in most other places, where it refers to a modest triangle of meat about as thick as a slice of Wonder Bread and, sadly, sometimes as chewy as a dog toy. In fact, food-conscious citizens of the Hawkeye State rarely say the words *pork chop* without preceding them with the modifier *Iowa*. An Iowa pork chop is a grand and special cut, more prized than porterhouse is in beef country. First off, it is as thick as a cylinder of filet mignon, but of course it is broader by a factor of four, reminding us of a whole rack of lamb. The **Machine Shed** outside Des Moines calls it a double-cut chop, noting that it looks more like a pork roast. The inside spurts and sputters as a knife glides down

Midwest

SPRINGFIELD CHILLI

In 1993 the Illinois legislature declared Springfield to be the "Chilli Capital of the Civilized Universe," the double-*l* spelling of the word ordained by force of senate resolution. Strangely, most of the restaurants that serve chili in Springfield now spell it with only one *l*, but it is nonetheless a chili with character all its own. As made at Joe Rogers' since 1945, it is a fully customizable dish, the beans and meat cooked separately. The most basic variant is simply meat or beans. You can have chili with no beans or extra beans, no meat or extra meat. Customers specify whether or not they want extra oil or if they want the grease skimmed, and what degree of heat they prefer from five grades that range from mild to hot and the ultra-hot JR Special, known to regulars as firebrand. (Those who survive a bowl of JR get their names posted on the wall.)

Joe Rogers' Original Recipe Chili Parlor: 820 S. 9th St., Springfield, IL
217-522-3722
www.joerogerschili.com

through the caramel-colored exterior and into the vast lode of meat. It comes topped with extremely savory pan gravy, which is less for the chop itself, which needs nothing but eager taste buds to attain its destiny, than for the great reef of mashed potatoes that accompany the chop on its plate. To complete the bigger-than-life experience, have banana cream pie or chocolate layer cake for dessert. Each is enough for three or four travelers, or for one person who needs to remedy the multithousand-calorie deficit created by a day of farming.

The **Iowa State Fair** is a bonanza of eats of all kinds, but the single obligatory thing to have is the Iowa pork chop served in the Pork Producers' Tent. It is a big boy well over an inch thick and approximately 1 pound, and if skinny supermarket flaps of meat are your idea of a pork chop, this glistening Gargantua, hot off the grate, is a revelation, like eating a prime T-bone after a lifetime of

nothing but cube steaks. Utensils are flimsy plastic, but anything heavier would seem brutal on a chop so tender. The men who cook the chops on grills outside the tent wear aprons that boast of "the other white meat," but no other meat we know, white or red, has such fathomless succulence.

Even though Iowa is Pork Chop Central, if you are in search of maximum pig on a plate, you cannot ignore Casey, Illinois, and the 1-pound pork chop at **Richards Farm Restaurant**. This hunk of oink is slow-roasted until its white flesh glistens with juice, then broiled in a tangy tomato sauce that gives its edges a bacony crispness and seeps a certain sweetness into the meat. Purchase of a chop (or any other entrée) grants you access to a cornucopic farmland salad bar, and in autumn Richards' menu features that southern Midwest delicacy: persimmon pudding.

IOWA'S BEST PORK CHOPS

1. **Machine Shed:** 11151 Hickman Rd., Urbandale, IA
   515-270-6818
   See www.machineshed.com for additional locations.
2. **Iowa State Fair:** Mid-August at the Iowa State Fairgrounds, E. 30th St. and E. University Ave., Des Moines, IA
   800-545-FAIR
   www.iowastatefair.com

Also
Richards Farm Restaurant:
   607 N.E. 13th St., Casey, IL
   217-932-5300
   www.richardsfarm.com

An Iowa pork chop as served at the Machine Shed in Urbandale

ITALIAN BEEF
Chicago

Street food is déclassé, but in Chicago it is not disrespected. In fact, Italian beef, the prince of Chicago street foods, is so cherished that restaurants are specifically designed for eating it. These brash canteens have no tables; accommodations are waist-high counters where you stand and unwrap your sandwich and then eat leaning forward so that dripping juices hit Formica rather than lap or shoes. The counters not only divert the inevitable spillage that oozes from one of the juiciest sandwiches on earth; they provide diners with quality time to admire the meal. While Italian beef is quick and cheap, it is not slapdash fare to be consumed while walking. You wouldn't want to do anything while enjoying it other than contemplate its excellence.

A Near West Side invention with only vague antecedents in the old country, Italian beef is a mountain of roast beef shaved so thin that it is as tender as hash. It is never served on a plate, but always in a sturdy torpedo roll, and it is rarely served plain; garnishes and gravy are essential. Probably the best place to learn about Italian beef, and certainly one of the best places to eat one, is **Mr. Beef**. Directly across the street from the Scala Packing Company, which supplies roast beef to many of the top beef stands in Chicago, Mr. Beef in fact was owned by Scala into the 1980s. Its counter affords a fine view of how a sandwich is assembled. Needless to say, each one is made to order; an Italian beef sim-

Street food: Chicago's Mr. Beef is one of the best places to enjoy an Italian beef.

ply cannot be assembled in advance. The beef is retrieved with tongs from a pan of garlicky natural gravy and loaded into a chewy torpedo of Italian bread.

That's just the foundation. Italian beef isn't only about great beef and bread. You'll have a plethora of options, and here is the lingo you need to know to select them:

Big beef = extra-large sandwich

Double-dipped = the whole sandwich gets dipped in gravy after being assembled

Dry = the sandwich maker lets excess juice drip off the beef before he puts it in the bread

With hot = a request for giardiniera atop the beef

Sweet = a request for roasted green peppers

Combo (or **half and half**) = a sandwich that contains both beef and sausage

According to the Pacelli brothers of **Al's #1 Italian Beef** in Chicago's Little Italy, it was their grandfather, Tony

Ferreri, who conceived the mighty sandwich during the Great Depression. "He and my uncle Al were doodlers," Chris Pacelli remembers. "Forever trying something new. Tony used to drive a coach along the streets and sell his sandwiches in the hospitals. All the doctors knew him. So one day he decides to shave his beef, thin as you could cut it with a knife, and with a little gravy to soften the bread,

An Italian beef from Al's, whose founder is said to have invented the sandwich

and everybody wanted some. In 1938 my uncle and my father opened a beef stand to sell it on the sidewalk. They sold beef in its juices in sandwiches, and they cooked sausages over charcoal. There were no tables, no place to sit down; people ate all along the street. In those times in this neighborhood, every day was a food festival."

When Tony Ferreri's friends and associates saw how well his enterprise was doing, they opened their own beef eateries in and around Little Italy, and during the years after World War II, Italian beef stands became part of the Chicago landscape. Not all places cooked their own. For the last half-century, a majority of Italian beef restaurants have procured their meat and gravy from Scala. (While Scala beef is excellent, not every stand that serves it has the expertise to steep it properly and to construct a first-rate sandwich.)

ITALIAN LEMONADE

Italian beef always leaves us with a powerful hankering for something sweet, cool, and refreshing. The solution to that problem is directly across the street from Al's: Mario's. The Italian lemonade Mario's makes is crushed ice saturated with slightly sweetened lemon juice. As the ice melts, you can suck the cold, tart liquid from the bottom of the cup, and you can eat the less lemony ice from the top with the white plastic spoon provided. The ingredients are not pure

and homogenized. Included in the cup will be bits of pith and rind. Lemon can be drunk pure or used as the base for all sorts of other flavors, including piña colada, chocolate, pineapple, banana, mixed fruit, and, at summer's end, fresh peach. Italian lemonade is a warm-weather drink. Mario's closes in the winter.

Mario's Italian Lemonade:
1068 W. Taylor St., Chicago, IL
Closed from mid-September
through early May

Mr. Beef's Italian "with hot": giardiniera garnishing garlicky beef

The sign above **Johnnie's Beef** in Elmwood Park says "charcoal broiled," which refers to the tight-skinned sausage that you can get alone in a roll or packed underneath a heap of what we consider to be the ideal beef — moist, tender, infused with garlic but in a motherly, inoffensive way. While both the beef and the sausage are superlative, we are especially fond of Johnnie's giardiniera, spicy enough to make you absolutely need a big cup of Johnnie's Italian lemon ice to salve your tongue.

TOP ITALIAN BEEFS

1. **Al's #1 Italian Beef:** 1079 W. Taylor St., Chicago, IL 312-226-4017 See www.alsbeef.com for additional locations.
2. **Mr. Beef:** 666 N. Orleans St., Chicago, IL 312-337-8500
3. **Johnnie's Beef:** 7500 W. North Ave., Elmwood Park, IL 708-452-6000

KILLER BROWNIE
Akron, Ohio

We've come across a number of places that sell what they call killer brownies, but that term is trademarked by **West Point Market**, which invented the idea of ultra-super-duper-death-by-chocolate brownies over a quarter-century ago. Made from batter that is good and chewy and incomprehensibly fudgy, studded with chocolate chips and chopped walnuts, and layered with thick caramel, a single original Killer Brownie contains a lifetime of sweet-tooth pleasure. In addition to originals, the West Point Market bakery turns out killer blondies, peanut butter krazies, chocolate raspberry suicides, and killers without nuts, each of which is definitive.

This grocery store is well worth a visit even if you aren't a chocoholic. It boasts of being "a market like no other," and you can take that to the bank. Originally opened seventy years ago, it has become a food shopper's paradise, with a vast array of hard-to-find domestic and imported products, a beautiful seafood market,

Midwest

The aptly named Killer Brownie, fudgy and layered with caramel

BUZZARD SUNDAY

If you travel a half-hour northwest of Akron on March 15, look up to the sky while approaching the town of Hinckley. Every year on that precise date, for no scientifically determined reason, buzzards fly home toward their roost in the town park. They stay throughout the summer, flying around hunting carrion, and while the bald-headed, black-winged carnivores are not nearly as pretty as Capistrano's swallows, they have provided Hinckley with a mascot and an annual celebration day of their own — the first Sunday after the birds arrive. Citizens elect a Buzzard Queen (human) and host a pancake breakfast, and visitors can buy buzzard-themed T-shirts, bumper stickers, and cookies made in the birds' image.

Cleveland columnist Joe Newman wrote this ode to the buzzards' visit:

The buzzards of Hinckley are back on their ledges,
All ugly and wrinkly, their eyes glowing pinkly, they perch in the hedges,
Their feathers unruly, their beaks dripping cruelly, repulsive and drooly,
Their claws bloody wedges with flesh on the edges.

---

a prime butcher shop, a florist, a chocolatier, and a kitchenware department. Ceilings are low, lighting is soft, room tone is quiet. To shop here is to visit a refined culinary boutique — nothing like a trip through the garish supermarket.

And the very good news for those not traveling to Akron is that the market is all set up to mail-order brownies to wherever the pinnacle of chocolate indulgence is required.

West Point Market: 1711 W. Market St., Akron, OH
330-864-2151
www.westpointmarket.com

KRINGLE
Racine, Wisconsin

It used to be that Racine, Wisconsin, was the only place to get kringle, and although we have seen more and more of it in other locations over the past several years, Racine is still the right and proper city in which to eat it. Brought to America by Danish settlers along the southwestern shore of Lake Michigan over a century ago, a kringle indeed is a Danish pastry, but taken to extremes. Imagine the Danish of your dreams formed into a great circle nearly as large as a spare tire, made of the finest flaky butter-layered dough (known as *weinerbrod*), stuffed with fruit preserves, cheese, or chopped nuts and baked, and topped with sweet buttercream frosting or a clear sugar glaze. A slice is one of the world's great coffee companions, and there are at least three different bakeries in Racine that make a specialty of it.

Honestly, we couldn't tell the difference between Racine's kringle sources if we were eating blindfolded, but remove the blindfolds and we would recognize one made by **Larsen's Bakery** because it is bigger than the others. We also like Larsen's because it usually offers little samples of different kinds of kringle arrayed on the counter. The classics are almond, pecan, and raspberry; in addition to these, Larsen's makes almond macaroon, chocolate, date, apricot, apple, and a spectacular turtle kringle that is iced with chocolate and filled with rum-flavored caramel. One other reason for favoring Larsen's is its fritters: big, holeless doughnuts with crunchy skin and lusciously cakey insides. In comparison to a kringle, it's cloddish, but for maximum pastry avoirdupois, it's a must.

According to **O&H Danish Bakery**, kringles as brought by Danish immigrants were shaped like pretzels and always filled with almond paste. Today's oval or round shape came about because it makes the kringle easier to slice and serve. And the single filling has expanded exponentially. In fact, you can join O&H's Kringle Club and receive a different flavor every month for a year, from cream cheese in January to pecan in December.

While O&H is big business, with two large, modern establishments, **Bendtsen's** remains a charming little bakeshop, its kringle a bit more irregular than the others, a fact the bakery's website attributes to its being "the last authentic hand-made kringle in Racine." Bendtsen's is still in the same family that started it in 1934, and if you treasure chitchat with the staff, such as advice about how to butter a kringle while it's still warm, this is the place to go.

King of all Danish pastries, the kringle

Since discovering kringle many years ago, we have found it impossible to drive by Racine without stopping for a ring to eat in the car (sloppily — this is *not* hand food). Our ritual is to buy one fruit kringle and one turtle kringle or nut kringle and alternate between the two of them on our way around Lake Michigan.

TOP 3 KRINGLES

1. **Bendtsen's Bakery:** 3200 Washington Ave., Racine, WI 262-633-0365 www.bendtsensbakery.com
2. **Larsen's Bakery:** 3311 Washington Ave., Racine, WI 262-633-4298 www.larsenskringle.com
3. **O&H Danish Bakery:** 1841 Douglas Ave., Racine, WI 262-637-8895 or 866-637-8895 Second location: 4006 Durand Ave., Racine, WI 262-554-1311 or 866-554-1311 www.ohdanishbakery.com

Midwest

LOOSEMEATS
Iowa

A loosemeats is a Siouxland sloppy Joe but without slop: ground beef that is cooked loose — unpattied — and seasoned and drained but sauceless. The pebbly beef holds together nearly as well as sticky rice when gathered up and positioned on the bottom half of a burger bun. It is customarily dressed with pickle, mustard, and a slice of cheese — a remix of the cheeseburger with fragmented harmony. Like grits, it is a food spoken of with singular/plural ambivalence. Usually one sandwich is *a* loosemeats; a batch in the kitchen or a bowlful without the bun *are* loosemeats.

Arguably the most beloved fast food in northwest Iowa, loosemeats appears on very few menus. That is because it is listed by one of its several aliases, which include tavern, Big

A loosemeats from Bob's in Le Mars, IA: ground beef browned, strained, and pressure-cooked with spices

T, Charlie Boy, and Tastee. History-minded loosemeats connoisseurs like the term *tavern* because that is what it was called when David Heglin first served it in 1924 at a twenty-five-seat Sioux City restaurant called Ye Old Tavern. It was a time when many Americans worried about the ill ef-

BING CANDY

Svelte, cherry-flavored nougat is the heart of the Twin Bing, the original Bing, and the King Bing. Introduced in 1923 (the birth year also of Butterfinger and Milky Way) to celebrate the Palmer Candy Company's forty-fifth anniversary, the Bing is a free-form sphere with a heavy coat of chocolate and chopped nuts. Originally the Bing was a single lump available in pineapple, vanilla, maple, and cherry flavors. Over the years cherry became the flagship, and 1973 marked the birth of the Twin Bing — two lumps joined in a form that resembles an amoeba about to split. The King Bing, a triple-lump candy, was introduced in 1986. The combination of cherry, chocolate, and nuts is beyond reproach, and while the Bing is far from artisan chocolate, there is relentless appeal to its ingenuous sweetness. Bings are available via mail-order.

Palmer Candy Shoppe: 2600 Highway 75 North, Sioux City, IA 712-258-7790 www.palmercandy.com

fects of frying meat. Steaming was a popular alternative, so Heglin's steamed beef sandwiches were a sort of health food. In 1934 Abe Kaled bought Ye Old Tavern, changed its name to Ye Olde Tavern, and tinkered with the formula for ground beef on a bun. By the time Ye Olde Tavern closed in 1971, the sandwich had become a local favorite, served at fundraisers, church suppers, and virtually every drive-in restaurant and bar throughout the counties of Sioux, Plymouth, Cherokee, and Woodbury.

A loosemeats is especially well suited to be bar food because it is always presented as it was at Ye Olde Tavern: wrapped in wax paper, never on a plate. At Sioux City's **Miles Inn**, where the sandwich is called a Charlie Boy (after Charlie Miles, son of founder John Miles, the bricklayer

Sioux City's Tastee Inn & Out, a classic drive-in serving loosemeats, not burgers

who built the inn in 1925), it is the only food you can buy other than Beer Nuts and potato chips. Sitting at the bar, you have a view of the steam box in which the meat is kept and of Charlie Boys being assembled as you drink beer from a frosted goblet. The wax paper in which they are presented unfolds to become a dropcloth for catching meat that falls out as they are eaten. Miles Inn's Charlie Boys are small and addictive, their finely ground meat so soft and gently seasoned that it hits the tongue as smooth as cream.

Tastee Inn & Out, just around the corner from Miles Inn, calls its loosemeats sandwich a Tastee and also sells Tastee meat to go at $3.99 per pound. Tastee is a classic American drive-in in every way except for the fact that it doesn't serve hamburgers. Opened by the Calligan family in 1955, Tastee has become nearly as famous for onion chips as for seasoned beef. Chips are like rings, but made from large sections of a petaled onion that retain sweet vegetable crunch inside their crust. As for the Tastee, it has a zing we want to call tomato-like, except for the fact that every loosemeats cook unconditionally abjures tomatoes.

"Tomatoes? No way!" says Myles Kass of **Bob's Drive-Inn** when we try to pry loose the recipe. "You know how when you eat a sloppy Joe you get that orange ring around your mouth?" He grins, using a spoon to stir a batch of ready-to-serve loosemeats. He lifts the spoon to show that it is clean and tomato-free — no orange whatever. "We brown the ground beef; we strain it; we pressure-cook it in the sauce, then we strain it again.

At Sioux City's Miles Inn, loosemeats is the only food offered.

That's why it has so little fat and so much flavor."

Although Siouxland is the birthplace of loosemeats, you will find them all over the state of Iowa and beyond, at **Maid-Rite**, a franchised sandwich shop that first started serving them in 1926 and now has some seventy outlets. The Maid-Rite menu includes Cheese-Rites, Chili-Rites, Bacon-Rites, Taco-Rites, BBQ-Rites, and Mega-Rites, as well as salads that include the pebbled beef and bowls filled with nothing but. While they lack the ambiance of the northwest Iowa one-of-a-kind joints, we've never had a bad Maid-Rite, the motto of which is "Too Good to Be a Patty."

BEST LOOSEMEATS

1. **Miles Inn:** 2622 Leech Ave., Sioux City, IA
   712-276-9825
2. **Bob's Drive-Inn:** Highway 75 South, Le Mars, IA
   712-546-5445
3. **Tastee Inn & Out:** 2610 Gordon Dr., Sioux City, IA
   712-255-0857

Also
Maid-Rite: Multiple locations; see www.maid-rite.com for specifics.

MAHNOMIN PORRIDGE
Minnesota

Hell's Kitchen chef Mitch Omer says he got the idea for Mahnomin porridge while reading the Lewis and Clark diaries, in which the explorers described a Cree Indian dish based on the region's hand-parched wild rice. To the native Minnesota grain he adds enough cream to give it a thick, oatmeal-like consistency; then he flavors it with roasted hazelnuts, dried berries, and warm maple syrup. Can you say, "Ooo-eee, that tastes good"? It is comfort food, sure enough, but such an unusual set of textures and flavors that it wakes up pleasure cen-

Hazelnuts, dried berries, and maple syrup flavor Minnesota's native wild rice in a traditional porridge.

ters of taste rather than lulls them asleep. It is deeply satisfying, fascinating, and just plain delicious.

Hell's Kitchen: 80 S. 9th St.,
Minneapolis, MN
612-332-4700
Second location: 310 Lake Ave.
South, Duluth, MN
218-727-1620
www.hellskitcheninc.com

OLD POTATOES
Skokie, Illinois

What an outstanding idea! Nuggets, shreds, bits, and pieces of home fries from the **Patty's Diner** grill are gathered together and deep-fried until they are mostly crunch, with just a few soft creamy areas at the center of the biggest pieces of potato. They are vigorously peppered and as addictive as potato chips but far plusher. Ham is the obligatory companion at Patty's — handsome pink slices cut off the bone and piled into breakfast sandwiches, served on the side of eggs, and chunked to become a brawny hash with onions and potatoes. Old potatoes are great not only at breakfast but along with Patty's first-rate hamburgers and meat loaf at lunch.

Patty's Diner: 3358 Main St.,
Skokie, IL
847-675-4274

ONION LOAF
Chicagoland

Tony Roma's chain of ribberies borrowed the concept and Outback's blooming onion seems to be an at-

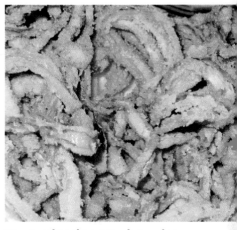

Disentangling the crusty skeins of an onion loaf takes persistent tugging.

tempt to improve upon it, but neither of these corporate creations can compare to the goodness of the original onion loaf at **Hackney's**. Thin and thick hoops of sweet Spanish onion are dipped in batter, then crammed into a fry basket so that as they cook, they meld together into a brick of hot onion threaded with veins of crunchy gold batter. There is no way to serve or eat one of these things politely. It requires pulling and tugging with a fork to get some off the serving platter, and as you pull, shards of melting-tender batter fall onto plate and table, demanding immediate attention. Glistening fingers are an inevitable consequence. Hackney's onion loaf is the designated companion for the house's football-sized hamburgers, preferably served on dark rye bread.

Hackney's: 1241 Harms Rd.,
Glenview, IL
847-724-5577
See www.hackneys.net for
additional locations.

Midwest

PASTY
Michigan's Upper Peninsula

Until eclipsed by homogeneous fast food sold at national franchises, the pasty (say *pass*-tee) was the favorite quick meal of the Northland: folded-over, enclosed pastry pockets packed with spiced seasoned beef (or sometimes beef and pork). The word *hearty* was invented to describe it. Originally eaten by immigrant Cornish miners, who were as tough as mules and therefore nicknamed Cousin Jacks (after the mule's donkey sire, aka jack), the pasties were made by their wives, called Cousin Jennies, who packed them for lunch so the men could heat them up on the end of a shovel held over a headlamp candle.

Chunks of beef, potato, onion, and rutabaga in a flaky crust make up the pasty, originally a Cornish miners' snack.

"It's Not a U.P. Vacation Without a Pasty" says the sign outside **Dobber's**, which has been the Upper Peninsula's bastion of traditional pasties for over a quarter-century. Traditional means a three-quarter-pound boatload of beef, potato chunks, onion, and rutabaga surrounded by a sturdy crust. This is hugely satisfying food, more rib-sticking than spicy, with an old-fashioned clarity of flavors that evokes rugged frontier fare without adornment or frippery. Dobber's offers only three variations on the fundamental theme: a chicken pasty, a vegetarian pasty in which cheddar cheese takes the place of beef or chicken, and mini pasties suitable for taking home and heating up as hors d'oeuvres.

Cousin Jenny's is a modern cafeteria that serves pasties for both breakfast and lunch. The breakfast pasties, known as bobbies, are completely self-contained pastry pillows of eggs, bacon or sausage, hash browns, and cheese, and while they can be picked up and eaten by hand, they're hefty and drippy and so stuffed that a knife and fork make good sense. Lunch pasties definitely need utensils, especially if served with gravy. They are listed on the menu as "Gourmet Pasties," but the steak pasty is the traditional configuration, filled with beef, potatoes, onion, and rutabaga. You can get a meatless seven-vegetable pasty with cream and cheese, and novelty pasties, such as Italian (with pizza sauce and pepperoni) and German (Swiss cheese, ham, and sauerkraut in a rye-flavored crust), are always available.

Before you fork into the celebrated pies at **Betty's Pies** on the north shore of Lake Superior, you can have what seems to us to be a classic pasty — a rather mildly spiced chunky hash of cubed roast beef, rutabaga, potatoes, carrots, and onions in a frail pastry crust. Definitely fork food!

The beverage you want to accompany a pasty is either home-brewed beer or a Detroit-made Vernor's ginger ale.

TOP-RANKED PASTIES

1. **Dobber's Pasties:** 1402 S. Stephenson Ave., Iron Mountain, MI
   906-774-9323
   Second location: 827 N. Lincoln Rd., Escanaba, MI
   906-786-1880
   www.dobberspasties.com
2. **Cousin Jenny's Gourmet Cornish:** 129 S. Union, Traverse City, MI
   231-941-7821
3. **Betty's Pies:** 1633 Highway 61, Two Harbors, MN
   218-834-3367
   Second location: 700 Wildwood Rd., Mahtomedi, MN
   651-777-6728
   www.bettyspies.com

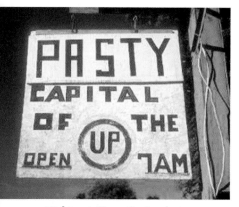

Michigan's Upper Peninsula serves pasties with pride.

Too good for bread: the handmade peanut butter at Hell's Kitchen in Minneapolis

PEANUT BUTTER
Minnesota

If you like peanut butter that is nothing more than peanuts turned to paste, please turn the page. **Hell's Kitchen** peanut butter is to plain peanut butter what a pitcher of great hot fudge is to a scattering of cocoa nibs: the most advanced, ingenious, extreme, decadent, variegated amplification of something that begins simple. The nuts are roasted enough to acquire a smoky kick. They are coarse-ground to be extraordinarily chunky, some pieces probably a good eighth of a peanut, and yet with enough smooth nut emulsion that the stuff is loose and drippy when at room temperature. To the nuts, chef Mitch Omer adds something sweet — honey or brown sugar, we guess — but only enough to leaven the legume's earthy essence, not actually making it sweet. And probably clarified butter or some other oil, because it is so extraordinarily richer-tasting than anything that contains only peanuts. Hell's Kitchen offers jars

Midwest

of it, along with homemade jam, to accompany breakfast breads, and it is available via mail-order. We limit how much we keep around the house because it is one of those staples that vanishes all too quickly, on sandwiches or crackers, off the end of a spoon or fingertip.

Hell's Kitchen: 80 S. 9th St.,
Minneapolis, MN
612-332-4700
Second location: 310 Lake Ave. South, Duluth, MN
218-727-1620
www.hellskitcheninc.com

PIE SHAKE
Minnesota

In the last half-century, **Betty's Pies** has earned a sterling reputation for its pies: fruit-filled with crisp crusts, cream pies as rich as cheesecake, a five-layer chocolate extravaganza, and Great Lakes Crunch, which is five kinds of fruit packed under a streusel-rich top crust. Only recently a new item was added to the menu: the pie shake. It sounds crazy, and it is, but believe us, it works. One entire slice of pie is heaped into a blender along with ice cream and milk. Whirled long enough to get relatively smooth, the thick drink is pie à la mode in a tall glass.

Although any of Betty's excellent pies can be selected for a pie shake, the waitress will strongly advise against choosing fruit pie with its crunchy crust, because the result is too grainy. But banana cream and chocolate cream and French cherry cream and Key lime all blend beautifully into a

miraculous, if ridiculous, ultimate indulgence for pie lovers. Even the smoothest cream pie will present problems to someone trying to suck up the shake with a straw, which inevitably gets clogged with bits of crust and nuggets of banana or cherry.

Betty's Pies: 1633 Highway 61,
Two Harbors, MN
218-834-3367
Second location: 700 Wildwood Rd., Mahtomedi, MN
651-777-6728
www.bettyspies.com

PLAYBOY STEAK
Kansas City, Missouri

Jess & Jim's is a vegetarian's vision of hell. Open the front door and you are accosted by the booming aroma of sizzling meat, which for carnivores is a hunger supercharger. If you order the Playboy strip steak (named because many years ago the men's magazine exalted it), you will not just smell it; you will hear it even before you see it, for it comes to the table sputtering hot on a metal platter. It is an extra-broad and extra-

Not just another pretty steak: the Playboy at Jess & Jim's in Kansas City, MO

thick pound-and-a-half sirloin with a dark charred crust and a wildly delicious ribbon of amber fat all along one edge. Is the meat tender? Not that much. No, this is not a steak for those who gauge beef's goodness by how little tooth pressure is required. You will chew this big boy — not too strenuously, that's for sure, for it is free of gristle and by no means tough. But you will chew it. And if your teeth are fairly well anchored in your jaws, you will love chewing it, for it fairly erupts with flavor under pressure. It isn't even overly juicy, but somehow its dense fibers give unbelievable amounts of beefitude per forkful. There is only one right side dish for a steak like this: Jess & Jim's pound-plus twice-baked potato, filled with unconscionable quantities of bacon, cheese, butter, and sour cream.

Jess & Jim's Steak House: 517 E. 135th St., Kansas City, MO 816-941-9499 or 816-942-2959 www.jessandjims.com

Eden Alley's open-faced sandwich: no cheese combo more flavorful or more garlicky

ULTIMATE GARLIC GRILLED CHEESE

As culinary extremists, we are drawn to any food that someone declares the ultimate, so as garlic lovers as well as fans of the grilled cheese sandwich, how could we not want to love Eden Alley's ultimate garlic grilled cheese? This open-faced knockout is a thick slab of sturdy garlic bread spread with chile cumin aïoli, layered with pickles, onions, and tomatoes, then topped with cheddar, mozzarella, blue, and Parmesan cheese and baked until bubbly. Its garlic punch is tremendous — you will find plump, perfumy cloves buried underneath the melted cheeses — and the garlic toast at the bottom is chewy and full-flavored.

The haymaker sandwich is dished out at a vegetarian restaurant named Eden Alley on the lower level of the Unity Temple in Country Club Plaza, where it shares space with a New Age book and chachka store. No doubt Kansas City is a place to indulge in meat — steak, barbecue, fried chicken — but if you like garlic, you need to visit Eden Alley. As an accompanying libation, we recommend a glass of watermelon mania: melon juice combined with the juice of Granny Smith apples, carrots, and lemons. For dessert, how about a lavender chocolate chip cookie?

Eden Alley Café: 707 W. 47th, Kansas City, MO 816-561-5415 www.edenalley.com

Midwest

POLISH BOY
Cleveland, Ohio

Hot Sauce Williams Barbecue on Carnegie Road is a pink and blue eatery with a big smoker out back. It's the source of brilliant fried chicken and wings, but the reason we direct you here is for the unique Cleveland sandwich known as a Polish boy. The main ingredient is a massive length of juice-spurting kielbasa. It is packed into a bun along with sweet coleslaw, accompanied by French fries, and the whole huge heap of food is sopped with radiant barbecue sauce. You might think utensils would come in handy, but experienced customers easily eat it by hand, rolling up sleeves, leaning forward to avoid drippage, and using sheaves of napkins. All food at Hot Sauce Williams comes wrapped and ready to go. There is a fetching sweetness to the sauce in the sandwich, but if you need something really sweet, have banana pudding for dessert.

An excellent alternative source of Polish boys as well as superior wings and soulful barbecue is **Freddie's Southern Style Rib House.** In our experience, Freddie's kielbasa is bigger and not quite as superjuicy, with its crisper skin verging on charred (not necessarily a bad thing!). Fries come inside the bun, and the hot sauce will drizzle out of the sandwich and onto your lap even more freely.

CLEVELAND'S PREEMINENT POLISH BOYS

1. **Hot Sauce Williams Barbecue:** 7815 Carnegie Ave., Cleveland, OH
216-391-2230
Two other locations: 12310 Superior Ave., Cleveland, OH
216-249-0710
3770 Lee Rd., Cleveland, OH
216-921-4704
2. **Freddie's Southern Style Rib House:** 1431 St. Clair Ave. NE, Cleveland, OH
216-575-1750

Kielbasa to go at Hot Sauce Williams Barbecue in Cleveland, OH

PRETZEL SANDWICH
St. Louis, Missouri

Soft pretzels are not unique to St. Louis, but we'll match those made by **Gus'** every morning against any city's. They are hand-twisted from a recipe that goes back to 1920, when St. Louis was full of pretzel shops. Gus' is the one remaining, known for a dough with delicious inherent salinity even before coarse salt is affixed. The texture below a slick, dark exterior is a delight for those of us who love to chew good bread: soft, but with muscular resilience. At 50 cents apiece, Gus' pretzels are a terrific bargain snack. We love them plain, and they are available with cups of mustard or honey mustard and/or melted cheese for dipping, but the most sensational incarnation is as a pretzel sandwich. That is Gus' good pretzel dough wrapped around a hot dog, a German sausage, or an Italian sausage — a dandy self-enclosed meal that demands a few mugs of beer on the side.

In fact, Gus' is just down the street from the Anheuser-Busch brewery. It has no tables or counter; business is all takeout, for eating at home, in the car, or on the sidewalk. Frozen cooked pretzels are available, as are bags of "Bake UR Owns."

Gus' Pretzel Shop: 1820 Arsenal
St., St. Louis, MO
314-664-4010

Fluky's, the rumored mother of Chicago's red hot

RED HOT
Chicago Area

Chicago's premier street food is the hot dog, known to devotees as a red hot. No ordinary frank, the Chicago red hot's claims to glory are manifold. In all the topnotch dog houses, the sausage itself is all beef, long and slim, dense-textured, and with a garlic kick. Whether skinless or packed in a natural casing (you'll find both), it is steamed until taut enough for a first bite to erupt with savory juices on the tongue. Also of paramount importance is the bun. Expect a Windy City red hot to be nestled in a gentle-flavored pocket of fleecy bread, prefera-

bly one from Rosen's Bakery spangled with poppy seeds across its tan outsides. The bun serves as a handy mitt and naturally plays a secondary note beneath the meat within, providing a soft environment that is absolutely necessary for full appreciation of the spicy red hot and its condiments.

While many people define a Chicago hot dog by a surfeit of condiments, **Gene & Jude's** defies that definition. Dressing for this dog is minimal — only mustard, onions, piccalilli, and little sport peppers (like Tabasco peppers). No baroque additions of pickle, tomato, cheese, chili; not even celery salt, as is customary at most of the highly respected Chicago dog houses. According to Chicago tipster Glen Stepanovic, Gene & Jude's represents the way Chicago hot dogs were served before the fancier toppings took hold. Also classically Chicagoan are the dining facilities: no tables, just a counter at the rim of the room, to which you take

Midwest

your wrapped hot dog to eat standing up. Gene & Jude's serves a natural-casing, all-beef Vienna dog boiled to a point of such supreme, bursting plumpness that when your teeth first attack, the sound of its skin snapping will be alarming. It's garlicky, but not too much so, dense and full-flavored. Now for the exclamation point: Before getting wrapped in wax paper by the staff, your bunned and dressed single (or preferably double) dog is piled with a generous portion of some of Chicago's best French fries, dark brown and crunchy in some places, creamy-spuddy in others, made from potatoes that are peeled, cut, and fried right behind the counter where the hot dogs are assembled. The whole package, in the opinion of one Stern (the one raised in Chicago), is nothing less than the Perfect Food.

Gene & Jude's aside, condiments are an essential part of the Chicago red-hot experience. Bright yellow mustard and dark green piccalilli are the basics, but at an esteemed place like the ultra-sassy **Wiener's Circle**, the available folderol also includes sport peppers, raw onions, sliced tomato, bun-length pickle spears, and a dusting of celery salt. In Chicago, when you ask for your dog "dragged through the garden" (with the works), only the sport peppers are considered optional, and don't dare ask for ketchup — on a Chicago hot dog, it is taboo. As at many of the better joints, the Wiener's Circle makes regular steamed dogs, which are smooth and firm, as well as charcoal-cooked dogs, which develop a crackling crust over flames on a grate. If it's a char dog you crave, the best place to have that is

Poochie's, where the frank is significantly scarified before getting cooked so that maximum surface area blisters and blackens and turns crunchy.

Frankfurter historians believe the Chicago red hot as we know it was first configured at **Fluky's**, now a small chain of modern cafeteria-style hot doggeries where they know exactly how to pile on the condiments, and where the Polish sausage — denser and oozier than a red hot — is superb. Of course Fluky's makes chili dogs and cheese dogs like nearly every other place in town, but it is the only restaurant we know that also offers short, tubular lengths of hot dog–shaped gum (cinnamon-flavored) for chewing after the meal!

Some of the other top dogs around town include those served at **Wolfy's** (especially the lusciously blackened Polishes), the fine old original **Byron's Hot Dog Haus** (where the motto on the wall reads "Thee Hot Dog"), and **Superdawg**, where a pair of 10-foot statues of a male and female hot dog in leopardskin togas guard the roof and where meals come packed in a little box that announces, "Your Superdawg lounges inside contentedly cushioned in Superfries, comfortably attired in mustard, relish, onion, pickle, and hot pepper." Superdawg is also noteworthy because it continues to offer carhop service.

The taut, garlicky, all-beef hot dogs that are the basis of Chicago's red-hot culture are made by the Vienna Beef Company, which happens to run the **Vienna Beef Cafe** out of its factory. Step up to the hot dog counter and order the archetype: wiener steamed to bursting plumpness, the tenderest

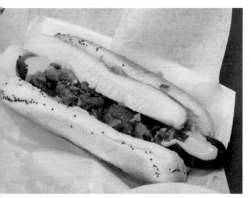

Poochie's charcoal-kissed red hot

possible poppy-seed roll, crisp pickle spears, fresh-cut tomatoes, brilliantly spicy-sweet piccalilli. Even the bright yellow mustard tastes like it was made that morning. And if by some strange happenstance you come here not wanting a red hot, the cafe also cooks up such other top-of-the-line Vienna Beef products as Polish sausages (grilled to delirious juiciness) and a "3XL" corned beef sandwich guaranteed to contain 9 ounces of steamy, brick-red beef.

Silly names (often with a canine theme) are a fundamental part of hot dog culture in Chicago, a good example of which is **Mustard's Last Stand** in Evanston, north of the city, where stools against the wall counter are emblazoned with pictures of fully dressed hot dogs. The house motto is "Catch-up to Mustard's," and they actually do keep ketchup behind the counter for those who need it on their hot dogs, as opposed to using it properly, to dress French fries. As a test — and only a test — we requested some on a red hot. "Really?" asked the counterman. "Are

you sure?" When we told him we were only kidding, he beamed with relief and took extra care arranging the condiments on our wiener like a horn of plenty.

9 TOP-RANKED CHICAGO RED HOTS

1. **Vienna Beef Cafe:** 2501 N. Damen Ave., Chicago, IL
773-435-2277
www.viennabeef.com
2. **Poochie's Hot Dogs:** 3832 W. Dempster, Skokie, IL
847-673-0100
3. **Wiener's Circle:** 2622 N. Clark St., Chicago, IL
773-477-7444
4. **Gene & Jude's Red Hot Stand:** 2720 N. River Rd., River Grove, IL
708-452-7634
5. **Superdawg Drive-In:** 6363 N. Milwaukee Ave., Chicago, IL
773-763-0660
www.superdawg.com
6. **Wolfy's:** 2734 W. Peterson Ave., Chicago, IL
773-743-0207
7. **Byron's Hot Dog Haus:** 1017 W. Irving Park Rd., Chicago, IL
773-281-7474
See www.byronshotdogs.com for additional locations.
8. **Fluky's:** 1038 Weiland Rd., Buffalo Grove, IL
847-229-0833
Second location: 3333 W. Touhy Ave., Lincolnwood, IL
847-677-7726
www.flukys.com
9. **Mustard's Last Stand:** 1613 Central St., Evanston, IL
847-864-2700

Midwest

ST. LOUIS–STYLE RIBS
Missouri

St. Louis–style ribs are long, thin spareribs trimmed of all extraneous matter to be nothing but meat on bone, and the place to know them as they should be known is the legendary **C&K Barbecue**, a takeout-only stand that has long been the Gateway City's premier source of smoked meat. C&K makes ribs bathed in thin, addictive sauce that is hot enough to clear your sinuses. But ribs are not the whole story at C&K. Proud of serving every part of the pig "from the rooter to the tooter," this soulful destination makes a specialty of snoots, which are pig proboscides sliced into wieldy cutlets, then baked until crusty. They have a good crunch to their exterior, inside of which is something more like fat than meat. Not that there's anything wrong with that — what's better than hot pig fat? — but alone on a plate, snoots are overwhelming, like a pound of *cuchifritos* in every bite. That's where C&K's thick red sauce springs into action. The hot stuff especially adds tang and a pepper punch that are a miracle pick-me-up for snoots, transforming something low on the hog into a barbecue parlor delicacy.

While we are on the subject of interesting pig parts, it behooves us to mention ears, which are at their finest at both C&K and another favorite soul-food eatery, **Niecie's** in Kansas City. Ears come in sandwiches and on plates with beans and potato salad on the side. Their flavor is good and piggy, and unlike snoots, which metamorphose into something that resembles processed food, ears look just like ears. They are boiled, not baked and fried, and achieve a gelatinous texture reminiscent of big pointy slabs of streak o' lean (page 201).

2 BEST RIBS AND EARS

C&K Barbecue: 4390 Jennings Station Rd., St. Louis, MO 314-385-8100
Niecie's: 5932 Prospect, Kansas City, MO 816-921-5990
Second location: 8686 E. 63rd St., Kansas City, MO 816-358-8100

ST. PAUL
St. Louis, Missouri

St. Louis has a lot of interesting culinary specialties, from toasted ravioli (page 291) to gooey butter cake (page 256), but the oddest of them all, and one so reprobate that no St. Louis food authority or cultural historian owns up to knowing anything about it, is the St. Paul sandwich. You will find it on the menu of virtually every takeout chop suey parlor in town. (And St. Louis has plenty such eateries, which, by the way, are the source of such darn good passé Chinese-American meals as chop suey and chow mein, made in a wok when ordered.) Even if its origins are unfathomable and its name is a mystery, the oddball St. Paul is something every curious eater should try at least once. At **Wong's Inn**, it is a thick patty of egg foo yong cooked to your specifications with diced pork, ham, chicken, beef, shrimp, or just vegetables, placed between two pieces of soft white bread and dressed with lettuce, tomato, pickle, and mayonnaise. A slab of American cheese is optional, generally costing about 25 cents more than the average $2 tariff for a St. Paul.

Wong's Inn: 2666 S. Big Bend
Blvd., St. Louis, MO
314-647-1176
Also at countless other Chinese
restaurants throughout the city

SAUERKRAUT BALL
Akron, Ohio

The fried sauerkraut ball is one of Akron's great inventions.

When the Akron (Ohio) Aeros played the Portland (Maine) Sea Dogs for the AA Eastern League baseball championship in 2006, Jim Cohen, the mayor of Portland, was prepared to send Akron's mayor, Don Plusquellic, a passel of Maine lobsters if his team lost. But the Sea Dogs won, and so Mayor Plusquellic sent Mayor Cohen a bunch of sauerkraut balls. Among the things to which Akron proudly has given birth, including synthetic rubber, mass-produced marbles, and Alcoholics Anonymous, the sauerkraut ball remains a mystery. The story of its genesis is lost. But Akron's culinary community is adamant about its local roots. Surely no other place claims it, and we've yet to find one anywhere outside the Buckeye State.

You can count on having sauerkraut balls anytime at the **Golden Lamb**, a fine old restaurant in Leb-anon, Ohio, where they come as hors d'oeuvres: eight golf ball–sized spheres, fried dark brown and arrayed around a ramekin of cocktail sauce. But the most enjoyable chance to eat them is at the **Ohio Sauerkraut Festival** in Waynesville, held the second weekend in October. They are served on picks, hot from the fryer, their skin dark, tough, and chewy, the inside a moist and spicy mélange of ham, pork, and sauerkraut. In addition to the balls, taste opportunities at the fair include kraut pizza, kraut doughnuts, kraut ice cream, and some really fine plates of bratwurst and kraut.

**WHERE TO EAT
SAUERKRAUT BALLS**

Golden Lamb: 27 S. Broadway,
Lebanon, OH
513-932-5065
www.goldenlamb.com

Midwest

DR. BOB'S HOME

Alcoholics Anonymous started in Akron, Ohio, in 1935, when Bill Wilson, a stock trader from New York, met Akronite Bob Smith, a rectal surgeon, and the two dipsomaniacs realized that by sharing their stories with each other and with other alcoholics, they could stay away from a drink. Many of the first members of AA were sobered up at Dr. Bob's house on Ardmore Street, where they were taken upstairs to what was known as the "surrender room" because they were required to get on their knees and ask God for help. Today Dr. Bob's Home is a magnet for twelve-steppers from around the world, who are taken on tours that show the surrender room, the bathtub to which detoxing drunks were rushed when they needed to throw up, and secret places in which the pre-sober doctor hid liquor bottles.

Dr. Bob's Home: 855 Ardmore
  Ave., Akron, OH
  330-864-1935
  www.drbobs.com

Ohio Sauerkraut Festival:
  Waynesville, OH
  513-897-8855
  www.sauerkrautfestival.com

For further information and a line on wholesale connoisseur sauerkraut balls, as well as habanero balls, contact
Or Derv Foods: 53 S. Maple St.,
  Akron, OH
  330-376-9411
  www.ordervfoods.com

SHEBOYGAN BRAT
Sheboygan, Wisconsin

"My dears, everything we make is charcoaled except the BLTs and the egg salad," the waitress informed us when we asked about the specialties at the **Charcoal Inn**, a luncheonette on the south side of Sheboygan, Wisconsin. She pointed to a grill behind the counter where flames were licking up above the grate, and where sputtering Sheboygan brats were sending their pork sausage sweetness into the air. (*Brat,* short for *bratwurst,* rhymes with *hot.*)

Sheboygan brats are link sausages 4 to 6 inches long made of pork or a combination of beef and pork. In recent years, some of the town's butchers have developed chicken brats and turkey brats as light alternatives to the succulent originals, and during deer season, venison brats are popular in hunters' homes. Whatever they are made from, Sheboygan brats share a unique flavor that usually comes from two things: being immersed in beer at some point during their preparation and getting cooked over coals. Some bratmeisters boil the sausages in a brew of pilsner and onions and merely finish them over hot coals; others steep them cold, then do all their cooking on the grill. According

A tangle of onions and pickles complements a Sheboygan brat.

to **Miesfeld's Meat Market**'s Chuck Miesfeld, a third-generation sausage maker and many times grand champion in the Wisconsin Association of Meat Processors' bratwurst judging contest, the sausages should be grilled over coals with no adornment whatsoever. He says beer is what you drink with them, not what you cook them in.

Despite differing ingredients and diverse recipes, all Sheboygan brats are served in a similar manner. It is impossible to think of one presented in any way other than as the heart of a hard-roll sandwich. In fact, it is almost impossible to think of *one*, presented in any way, for the vast majority of brats are eaten in tandem, two to a sandwich. "Double brat, with the works" is the Sheboyganite's call to glory.

The waitress at the Charcoal Inn offered her observations about what *the works* means: "People in Sheboygan like everything they eat with pickle, mustard, and onions, and butter oozing out on every side." Brat enthusiasts may add ketchup or delete the pickles or choose fried onions over raw ones, but every Sheboygan

hot meat sandwich — brat, burger, or butterflied pork chop — drips butter. At a cinder-block diner named **Schulz's**, where the char-cooked brats are patties rather than links, the waitress concluded that we were alien weirdos when we asked for a double with nothing on it so we could study the texture of the patties. "Not even butter?" she asked, wide-eyed.

A Charcoal Inn double brat is brought to the table without a plate. It is wrapped in wax paper, which you unfold and use as a drop cloth to catch dripping condiments. Each of the brats is split and flattened before getting grilled, which makes for an easily stacked sandwich. Thick and resilient but thoroughly tooth-tender, they are as luscious as sausage can be, oozing a delectable blend of meat juice and pure melted butter.

The roll on which a brat is served is as meaningful as the sausage itself. Sheboygan bakeries specialize in both brat rolls and hard rolls. The former resemble hot dog buns and are designed to hold a single brat; the latter are moderate-sized circular buns, suited to the more popular double-wide sandwich. Both types of rolls are tender inside so they can sop up large amounts of butter. Their tan surface has a supple leathery texture, never brittle or crusty, that makes it easy to grip and transforms the bun into a kind of mitt for holding on to all its ingredients. **City Bakery**'s are the best: light and fluffy, but steamed as they bake in the brick-floored hearth so they develop the distinctive durable exterior that makes them tough enough to hold two brats and the works.

Midwest

Sheboygan brats are not unique to sleeves-up eateries. You can enjoy good ones at **Rupp's Downtown**, a city-center, fine-dining restaurant known for plush steaks (butter-basted, of course!) and authentic sauerbraten. The local sausages are made into a handsome meal at **Horse and Plow**, a restaurant at the American Club resort in nearby Kohler, where plump, thin-skinned brats are presented in high style on an actual plate with all the other sandwich components, including a bottle of Grey Poupon mustard on the side.

Sheboygan's aficionados think about brats as much as Memphians about ribs or New Mexicans about chiles. Fanciers can spot the difference between a Henry Poth brat and a Miesfeld brat at twenty paces. Many years ago, at a now-vanished corner neighborhood bar named Tiny's, we spent a long lunch hour listening to an exquisite colloquy about the virtues of City Bakery hard rolls compared to those made by **Johnston's Bakery**. (Debaters considered brat rolls, for singles, unworthy of discussion.) The mania goes public in early August, when the Jaycees sponsor Bratwurst Day, which features a brat-eating contest and a parade featuring a truck hauling Johnsonville Foods' 16-ton Big Taste Grill, the world's largest mobile cooker. In recent years there has been talk around town about establishing a brat museum in an old building that had been the Heinecke Meat Market since the 1870s. "Here in Sheboygan we have raised the lowly sausage to a level of prominence," one museum booster told the *Sheboygan Press*, which reported that exhibits being considered were "Weber Grills I Have Known," "The First Sheboygan Brat," and "From Cave Man to Present — Outdoor Cooking." So far the brat museum is only a hope and a dream . . . as are plans for a sister museum devoted to the Sheboygan hard roll.

TOP BRATS

Charcoal Inn: 1313 S. Eighth St., Sheboygan, WI
920-458-6988
Second location: 1637 Geele Ave., Sheboygan, WI
920-458-1147

Horse and Plow: American Club, 441 Highland Dr., Kohler, WI
920-457-8888

Miesfeld's Meat Market: 4811 Venture Dr., Sheboygan, WI
920-565-6328
www.miesfelds.com

Rupp's Downtown: 925 N. Eighth St., Sheboygan, WI
920-459-8155

Schulz's Restaurant: 1644 Calumet Dr., Sheboygan, WI
920-452-1880

BRAT ROLL BAKERIES

City Bakery: 1102 Michigan Ave., Sheboygan, WI
920-457-4493

Johnston's Bakery: 1227 Superior Ave., Sheboygan, WI
920-458-3342

BRATS BY MAIL

Sheboygan Bratwurst Co.: PO Box 276, 1138 Jefferson Ave., Sheboygan, WI
888-966-6966 or 920-208-7787
www.bratwurst.net

SHRIMP DE JONGHE
Chicago

Many of us who grew up along Lake Michigan's southwest shore take shrimp de Jonghe for granted, and we might even forget it if we move away to eat through other towns and exotic new cuisines. But returning to Chicago and inhaling its sweet sherry-garlic aroma is like sniffing the seductive perfume of a long-lost love. Curiously, it is virtually invisible on the regional-food radar that tends to target such other Windy City specialties as red hots (page 275) and Italian beef (page 261), but it remains a menu staple that any hungry visitor needs to know.

About ten years ago in the fine old **Cape Cod Room** of the Drake Hotel, we had a shrimp de Jonghe epiphany that reminded us that food culture is a reflection not only of social history but of personal history, too. Ensconced in the dimly lit, Downeast-decorated dining room with its red-checked tablecloths and anachronous menu of Thermidors and Newburgs and Dover sole to die for, we eavesdropped on the adjacent booth as a man said, "I don't know how it happened. I just don't know. I must be the luckiest man in Chicago." Glasses clinked and he toasted his wife on the occasion of their forty-ninth anniversary. At this moment, the aroma of sherry and garlic began to fill the air as two piping-hot casseroles arrived at their table. "Shrimp de Jonghe!" the man tenderly exclaimed, as if greeting a beloved grandparent, explaining to the waiter that this had been their anniversary meal since the day he and his wife were married in 1950.

In fact, shrimp de Jonghe tastes far earlier than 1950. Its quaint and captivating formula of toasted bread crumbs, sweet sherry, butter, and garlic, laced with rosemary and thyme, all blanketing a cluster of taut-bodied shrimp baked in a casserole so the edge gets a lovely brown crust, sends our gastronomic fantasies back to the heyday of the chafing dish, shrimp wiggle, and first-edition Fannie Farmer. Historians have been unable to document its exact provenance convincingly, but the best explanation we know comes from Nancy Buckley, the granddaughter of Pierre "Papa" de Jonghe. As Nancy tells the tale, Pierre, along with three brothers and three sisters, opened the de Jonghe restaurant at the Columbian Exposition and moved from there to Monroe Street in downtown Chicago. It was at their restaurant that shrimp de Jonghe was created, by Pierre or perhaps by Pierre and his chef, Emil Zehr. Mr. Zehr's son, a professional accordionist, wrote to us several years ago to say he was quite certain it was his father who invented it, a possibility Nancy Buckley allows. In any case, the start of Prohibition caused the de Jonghe family to sell the restaurant (with no wine for cooking, what was the point?), which finally closed sometime in the 1930s. Despite the temporary unavailability of sherry, shrimp de Jonghe lived on.

Nonclassic versions of the dish abound. **Carson's**, home of the city's champion baby back ribs (page 126), adds cheese to the formula. **Myron &**

Phil's does a magnificent traditional version (as appetizer or entrée) and offers scallops, lobster, scrod, walleye, perch, and salmon prepared de Jonghe style. You can even have your steak or lamb chops blanketed with intoxicating de Jonghe butter.

Gene & Georgetti, the city's finest fortress of steak, makes a divine, if dramatically eccentric, version of the dish that is not a baked casserole. It is a broad, deep plate that holds a golden pool of herbed garlic butter laced with crumbs so soft they have become tiny supple shreds of flavor. In this pool wade a spill of huge pink shrimp. You can cut the shrimp into bite-sized pieces with a fork and knife, but you also need a spoon, or plenty of G&G's stout Italian bread for mopping all that garlic butter. Also on the menu, at twice the price of a 2-pound porterhouse steak, is lobster de Jonghe, which is a veritable seascape of plump white hunks of sweet tail meat cosseted in the luminous pool of juice. For this dish, so rich it is dizzying, we call upon an overused food-writer adjective that in this case seems appropriate: decadent!

CHICAGO'S BEST SHRIMP DE JONGHE

1. **Gene & Georgetti:** 500 N. Franklin St., Chicago, IL
   312-527-3718
   www.geneandgeorgetti.com
2. **Cape Cod Room:** 140 E. Walton Place (in the Drake Hotel), Chicago, IL
   312-787-2200
   www.thedrakehotel.com
3. **Myron & Phil's:** 3900 W. Devon Ave., Lincolnwood, IL

847-677-6663
www.myronandphil.com

4. **Carson's:** 612 N. Wells St., Chicago, IL
   800-438-7427 or 312-280-9200
   www.ribs.com

SILVER-BUTTER-KNIFE STEAK
Minneapolis, Minnesota

Rippling pink drapes hang heavy on the walls of **Murray's,** a plush Minneapolis supper club where a spritely piano-violin duo serenades the room with "Polonaise," "Bali Hai" from *South Pacific,* or "Happy Birthday," as weekend customers' moods require. Murray's lavish menu includes such regional exotica as a walleye and wild rice spring roll, but "butter-knife steaks" have been the beacon for generations of Twin Citians who crowd the white-clothed tables to eat hearty and toast life's good moments. Murray's silver-butter-knife sirloin (for two) and golden-butter-knife porterhouse (for three) are blackened, roast-sized hunks of beef that arrive whole from the kitchen and are sliced tableside into thick cuts that are tender, but so substantial that you may indeed decide to use the knife that is part of each place setting's battery. Because the steak is so immense, sliced pieces offer an appealing textural range from juicy center to seasoned crust. Alongside Murray's steaks come au gratin potatoes or French fries, an assortment of interesting-shaped dinner rolls, a salad, and a basket of garlic toast. The toast, which is put on the table when you first sit down, is wick-

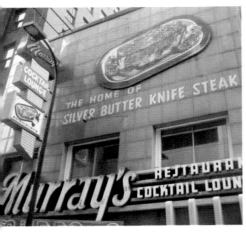

At Murray's, Minnesotans celebrate the good times with immense blackened steaks.

you. She must have loved us, as our table of six went through three baskets one evening while laying waste to approximately 8 pounds of golden-butter-knife porterhouse.

Murray's: 26 S. 6th St.,
Minneapolis, MN
612-339-0909
www.murraysrestaurant.com

edly buttery, so lush that it seems to melt when you bite into it. Nothing goes better with cocktails. For years, the word around town was that once all your toast was eaten, the basket was replenished only if your waitress liked

SLINGER
St. Louis, Missouri

The slinger, a St. Louis version of the Rochester, New York, garbage plate (page 88), is an eye-opening meal, generally eaten in the morning, either in the wee hours after the night before or bright and early for those in search of serious fortification for the day. It consists of a pair of cheeseburgers sided by griddle-cooked American fried potatoes, topped with a couple of sunny-side-up eggs

BUTTER-SCULPTURE EXHIBIT

If you go to Murray's for a silver-butter-knife steak at the end of August, you have the opportunity to visit what may be the most delicious state fair — Minnesota's, known not only for the most things on sticks (from bananas Foster to walleye pike) and world-class French fries (page 249), but also for the best butter-sculpture exhibit in dairy country. Motifs include public buildings and dairy cattle, plus likenesses of all twelve contestants in the

Princess Kay of the Milky Way contest, whom fairgoers can watch posing in the refrigerated, glass-walled studio. And by the way, the medium used is not some aberrant buttery tallow or yak butter; it is edible, blue-ribbon, farm-fresh butter, regularly tastetested by juries of dairymen and always plied in studios kept at a steady 38 degrees.

Minnesota State Fair: 1265
Snelling Ave. North, St. Paul, MN
651-288-4400
www.mnstatefair.org

A raft of two cheeseburgers, fried potatoes, chili, and cheese, the St. Louis slinger is not for the faint of appetite.

and completely blanketed with chili, then garnished with grated cheese and chopped raw onions. As served at **O.T. Hodge**, which claims to have invented the concept, the chili is a no-bean diner classic — thick, meaty, not ferociously spiced — available also on platters of chili mac (atop spaghetti noodles) and mac à la mode (atop noodles and eggs).

Although O.T. Hodge dates back to the World's Fair of 1904, the slinger did not appear on its menus until the early 1970s. Historians suggest that in fact slingers may have been part of St. Louis's reprobate gastronomy long before that, as a kill-or-cure diner/tavern meal for people who had drunk too much and needed to sober up late at night. Slinger variations you will find around town substitute sausage patties or Spam for the burgers and

sausage gravy for the chili.

Even if it didn't serve an exemplary slinger, we'd feel kindly toward the **Eat-Rite Diner** for its motto alone: "Eat Rite or Don't Eat at All." It's a twelve-stool urban hash house along old Route 66, open around the clock and permeated with the aroma of things sizzling on the griddle. Eat-Rite's slinger is a layered dish of crusty fried potatoes, cheese, chili, and eggs, including your choice of ham, bacon, sausage, hamburger, or T-bone steak. At $6.25, it vies for the prize of the dish providing maximum calories for minimum cost, but if even that's too much, hot dogs and hamburgers are available for about $1.40 each.

Pack your Rolaids if you plan to eat large at **Big Ed's Chili Mac's Diner**, a former O.T. Hodge shop, where the chili is hot and oily, available plain, with beans, on top of spaghetti or tamales, and as the crown of a slinger, which here is a couple of cheeseburgers, fried potatoes, and an egg.

Among the most uncouth of meals, the slinger shows a classier side at the **South City Diner**, where the morning menu also includes vegetarian eggs Benedict and espresso, and you can accompany supper with cocktails or wine by the glass and bottle. Not that there's anything pretentious about the slinger (or, for that matter, about this friendly neighborhood diner), but the chili isn't quite as unctuous as that of a typical St. Louis hash house. The cheese is cheddar rather than American, and the accompanying toast is whole wheat.

Connelly's Goody Goody Diner's version of a slinger is known as the Wilbur, the difference being that

Goody Goody's excludes the burgers. It is a mammoth omelet filled with peppers, onions, tomatoes, and home-fried potatoes and blanketed with chili, then shredded cheese — a soulful meal, profoundly satisfying. It's the chili that does the trick — a moderately spiced concoction laced with plenty of meat, also available plain in a bowl or as chili mac on noodles. Usually chili mac comes garnished with a mass of shredded cheddar cheese — unless you order chili mac à la mode, which in St. Louis means a crown of two fried eggs.

THE GREAT ST. LOUIS SLINGERS

1. **South City Diner:** 3139 S. Grand Blvd., St. Louis, MO 314-772-6100
2. **Connelly's Goody Goody Diner:** 5900 Natural Bridge Ave., St. Louis, MO 314-383-3333 www.goodygoodydiner.com
3. **Eat-Rite Diner:** 622 Chouteau Ave., St. Louis, MO 314-621-9621 Second location: 5513 S. Lindbergh Blvd., St. Louis, MO 314-842-1514
4. **O.T. Hodge Chile Parlor:** 1622 S. Jefferson Ave., St. Louis, MO 314-772-1215 www.othodge.com
5. **Big Ed's Chili Mac's Diner:** 510 Pine, St. Louis, MO 314-421-9040 Second location: 3523 N. Broadway, St. Louis, MO 314-342-9562

All but unknown elsewhere, sour cream raisin pie is one of the heartland's great desserts.

SOUR CREAM RAISIN PIE
Midwest Dairyland

Sour cream raisin pie is all about a precarious balance of elements: sweet custard and sour cream; intense raisins and airy meringue; flaky crust and silky filling. A cafe menu staple throughout Wisconsin, Minnesota, and Iowa, where dairy riches are cause for celebratory desserts, it is especially right after a substantial meal of hot beef or pork chops, but it's also ideal as a pie-break snack at any time of day or night. **Lange's Cafe**, in Pipestone, Minnesota, open twenty-four hours every day, makes one that is creamy and sweet with a sharp sour-cream edge that makes its sweetness all the more potent. The meringue is a puffy cloud of sugar; the crust is the melt-in-the-mouth kind, so good that we found ourselves hunting stray little slivers on emptied plates, gathering them up by pressing down with our forks' tines.

Midwest

We missed out on sour cream raisin pie the first time we visited the 24/7 **Crystal Cafe** truck stop in South Sioux City, Nebraska, because it was morning and the pie wasn't ready yet. But the high quality of our caramel sweet roll ensured that we would return. We're glad we did, because this is one of the great sour cream raisin pies of the heartland, its golden, raisin-studded body deeply satisfying and perfectly complemented by the tall white meringue on top.

The buffest sour cream raisin pie we've ever slid a fork into is that served at the **Farmer's Kitchen** in western Iowa. The meringue is twice as tall as the filling, but the filling is so creamy-thick and packed with raisins that all the meringue simply melts into a halo around it. What a suitably frothy conclusion to one of the Farmer's Kitchen's mighty tenderloins!

SUPERLATIVE SOUR CREAM RAISIN PIES

1. **Lange's Cafe:** 110 Eighth Ave. SE, Pipestone, MN 507-825-4488
2. **Farmer's Kitchen:** 319 Walnut St., Atlantic, IA 712-243-2898
3. **Crystal Cafe:** 4601 Dakota Ave., South Sioux City, NE 402-494-5471

SUGAR PIE
Farm Country

Sugar pie is a heartland staple that is brown-sugar sweet, cream-and-butter rich, flavored with a dash of vanilla and a sprinkle of nutmeg. There is

In classic Shaker tradition, sugar pie makes the most of simple ingredients.

scarcely more to it. But the sum total, nestled in a fragile, flaky crust, transcends rudimentary ingredients to become quintessential luxury. Baked in a very hot oven until the layered (not stirred) ingredients coalesce into velvety amber custard, the pie is believed to have come from the kitchens of nineteenth-century Shakers. It is an everyday dessert at the **Golden Lamb**, an inn established in 1803 and dedicated to the preservation of such hospitable traditions as a relish tray of put-by produce, roast pork loin with sage dressing, and, in addition to the Shaker sugar pie, a twin-layer chocolate stack pie that includes an extra stratum of crust in the center, allowing for twice the filling.

Golden Lamb: 27 S. Broadway, Lebanon, OH 513-932-5065 www.goldenlamb.com

TENDERLOIN
Iowa

When you ask for tenderloin in a lower Midwest cafe, drive-in, or diner, you will get a slice of boneless pork loin that has been pounded flat, breaded, fried to a crisp, planted in a bun, and dressed with mustard and pickle, maybe lettuce and tomato. Experts assess tenderloins not only by taste but by girth. The smallest are large, protruding maybe an inch past the circumference of the bun; the biggest are so freakishly wide that it is impossible for even the longest-fingered hands to grasp the bun and pick it up like a normal sandwich.

Where is the best place to eat a tenderloin? Iowa, which loves pork more than any other state, is prime territory. Des Moines boasts **Smitty's Tenderloin Shop**, which claims to be "Home of the REAL Whopper," and the reference is not to hamburgers. The whopper here is called the King Tenderloin. Available in small or large (small is large; large is huge), this fantastic piece of pork is delivered on an ordinary burger bun, the bun irrelevant except as a method for keeping condiments adjacent to the center section of the cutlet and as a mitt to hoist the vast disk from plate to mouth. It's an exemplary tenderloin, the inside a soft and flavorful ribbon

Pounded, breaded, and fried to a crisp, pork loin reaches its apotheosis in Iowa.

of succulence, the crust brittle and luscious.

In 2007, **Larsen's Pub** in Elk Horn won the Iowa Pork Producers Association award for the best breaded tenderloin in the state. That is a very big deal, like making the best barbecue in Memphis or the best fried clams in New England. Larsen's pounds its pork extra-wide. It is nearly a half-pound, extending beyond the bun in all directions, but not so far that you can't pick it up handily. Its crunch-to-chew balance is ideal. The 2004 tenderloin champ was **Darrell's Place** in Hamlin, which is noteworthy because its tenderloin is significantly thicker than most and its crust is thinner and flaky more than brittle. Definitely the juiciest possible version of the dish, it actually spurts when you sink your teeth into it.

A sign over the door of **Joensy's Restaurant** in Solon announces that it is "Home of the BIGGEST & BEST Pork Tenderloin in Iowa." We're not sure about that, but we do believe it is one of the two widest — ridiculously so, extending inches beyond the bun in all directions. The other widest one is that served at **St. Olaf Tavern** — 1 full pound, stretching out like a full-sized pizza, eclipsing not only the bottom of its bun but the very plate on which it arrives. It must be said that both Joensy's and St. Olaf's tenderloins are not just big; they are delicious: hand-breaded, expertly fried, crisp-crusted, and bacon rich.

Historians believe that the tenderloin was first served to the public not in Iowa (where a claim has been made that it was invented by eastern Europeans trying to re-create schnit-

Nick's in Huntington, IN, started the tenderloin tradition in 1904.

zels with pork rather than veal) but in Indiana, in the town of Huntington (home of former vice president Dan Quayle). Nick Frienstein started frying breaded pork cutlets in 1904 to sell in sandwiches from a street cart in town; four years later he opened

Nick's Kitchen. The method of preparation was changed one winter shortly after Nick moved to the cafe, when his brother Jake suffered such severe frostbite that he lost his fingers. Jake, whose job it was to bread the slices of pork, found that his stumps made good tools for pounding the meat to make it tender. Since then, all tenderloins are either beaten tender (with a wooden hammer) or run through a mechanical tenderizer, or both.

Now run by Jean Anne Bailey, whose father owned the town cafe starting in 1969, Nick's Kitchen lists its tenderloin on the menu with a challenge that's ironic considering its culinary history: "Bet You Need Both Hands." Two hands are barely adequate for hoisting the colossal sandwich, which is built around a wavy circle of audibly crunchy pork that extends a good 2 to 3 inches beyond

NICK'S KITCHEN'S DESSERTS

While it is rightly best known for its tenderloin, Nick's Kitchen also happens to be a major Midwest dessert destination. "My father served frozen pies," proprietor Jean Anne Bailey says. "I knew I wanted something better." Made using a hand-me-down dough recipe that incorporates a bit of corn syrup, her fruit pies have a flaky crust that evaporates on the tongue, melding with brilliant-flavored rhubarb or black raspberries; the butterscotch pie, which she learned to cook from

her grandmother, is more buttery than sweet, nothing at all like cloying pies made from pudding filling. Jean Anne's apple dumpling is magnificent — a bowl full of heartland warmth that vents fruity, aromatic steam under the large scoop of fast-melting vanilla ice cream plopped on top. As the dumpling bakes, juices bubble up around the gnarled circumference, forming an amber glaze that clings to the edges of the fine pastry dough and offers a cidery, fruity foretaste of the apples that lie below.

the circumference of a 5-inch bun, virtually eclipsing its plate. Soaked in buttermilk, which gives a tangy twist to the meat's sweetness, and tightly encased in rugged cracker crumbs (not the more typical finely ground cracker meal), the lode of pork inside the crust fairly drips with moisture.

5 ESSENTIAL IOWA TENDERLOINS (+1)

1. **Larsen's Pub:** 4206 Main St., Elk Horn, IA
712-764-4052
2. **St. Olaf Tavern:** 106 S. Main St., St. Olaf, IA
563-783-7723
3. **Darrell's Place:** 4010 1st St., Hamlin, IA
712-563-3922
4. **Smitty's Tenderloin Shop:** 1401 S.W. Army Post Rd., Des Moines, IA
515-287-4742
5. **Joensy's Restaurant:** 101 W. Main, Solon, IA
319-624-2914
See www.joensys.com for additional locations.

Also

Nick's Kitchen: 506 N. Jefferson St., Huntington, IN
260-356-6618
www.nickskitchen.net

TOASTED RAVIOLI
St. Louis, Missouri

Toasted ravioli, once a specialty unique to the Italian restaurants of the Hill neighborhood in St. Louis, now appear even on the menu of the Olive Garden. Their popularity makes sense. They are great bar food and an easy snack or hors d'oeuvre to eat with either fork or fingers. The term *toasted* isn't right, because these pasta pockets, filled with a spiced hash of meat and cheese and vegetables, are rolled in seasoned bread crumbs and, unlike traditional ravioli, are deep-fried until the envelope of pasta becomes a savory crust.

There are none quite so perfect as the golden bite-sized beauties at **Charlie Gitto's**, one of the top fine-dining Italian restaurants in town. Gitto's is located at the address of the late Angelo's, where restaurant folklore says the dish was invented in the late 1940s when a chef accidentally dropped ravioli into a pan of bread crumbs and decided to fry them rather than boil them. Gitto's t-ravs are handmade using homemade dough and a vivid filling of beef, veal, onions, celery, carrots, spinach, eggs, and Parmesan cheese, all pulverized in a meat grinder. They arrive at the table crisp and chewy, with a sandy seasoned crust and a bowl of cocktail sauce for dipping.
Charlie Gitto's: 5226 Shaw Ave., St. Louis, MO
314-772-8898
www.charliegittos.com

TURTLE SUNDAE
Chicago

The turtle-configured ice cream sundae is especially popular in the Midwest. In our opinion, Chicago soda fountains display the highest turtle consciousness — their fudge is the

Midwest

Swirls of fudge and caramel layer a tall pecan-crowned turtle sundae.

strawberries and about a half-dozen different toppings. The cost: $50.

Margie's Candies: 1960 N. Western Ave., Chicago, IL 773-384-1035
Second location: 1813 W. Montrose Ave., Chicago, IL 773-348-0400

WHITEFISH
Northern Midwest

Whitefish is a staple of cheese-curd shacks and smokehouses throughout the upper Midwest as well as of Jewish delis everywhere, but the opulence of smokehouse whitefish bears little resemblance to the refined flavor of fish that has been caught that morning in the deep, cold waters of Lake Superior, cleaned and filleted, then broiled on a cedar plank. The wood below imparts a whiff of woodsy smoke taste to the sparkling white meat, the freshwater clarity of which is something you want to call sweet. But it is sweet-water sweetness, nothing like sugar.

There is something especially good about savoring the north-country catch at **Maggie's** in the old lakeshore village of Bayfield in northernmost Wisconsin, where the twenty-two Apostle Islands punctuate a horizon of enamel-blue sky and steel-gray waters. In addition to fillets, Maggie's usually offers a Friday night special of a headless but otherwise whole whitefish with all its bones, skin, and fins. It is sautéed in a pan full of butter, and even if you've never faced a whole fish like this, getting all the meat is a snap.

fudgiest, the caramel warm and buttery, the pecans toasted crisp. As proof of this contention, we offer **Margie's**, a 1921 neighborhood candy store and ice cream parlor, where the sundae is presented as a tall glass full of vanilla ice cream topped with hot caramel and nuts, with a good-sized pitcher of hot fudge on the side. The fudge is dark and bittersweet, and to see it swirl with the caramel and nuts and softening ice cream is rapturous. If you are really hungry, Margie's offers a fifteen-scoop version of the turtle sundae.

If you are really, really, really hungry, or if you go to Margie's as a party of six, eight, ten, or twelve people, you might also consider ordering the Royal George sundae. That's twenty-five scoops of ice cream with bananas and

Maggie's in Bayfield, WI, is the place to savor pristine whitefish fillets.

The waitstaff will show you how to peel back the skin, then start at the top and easily separate moist forkfuls from the bone. The flavor of whole whitefish is not significantly different from that of those which are filleted and broiled or sautéed, but the presentation adds fish-camp fun to the dining experience.

Whitefish is common on Great Lakes menus, but whitefish livers are rare. Because it takes a lot of fish to gather a small amount of livers — they're about the size of a quarter, and a dinner might include fifteen or twenty — mongers who sell to local restaurants and markets traditionally have thrown them away. But old-time fishermen have long considered them a delicacy, and in recent years, as northernmost Wisconsin's fishing villages have become a popular destination for nature-loving travelers, livers have begun to appear on the menus of plain and fancy restaurants. Maggie's serves the best we've had, rolled in spiced flour and sautéed with peppers, onions, and mushrooms until the outsides have a bit of crunch and the insides turn meltingly soft. Like whitefish flesh, they have a pure, mellow flavor that is creamy and sweet and not nearly as visceral as a mammal organ.

Looking for the best smoked whitefish? Located in the DeWitt-Seitz Marketplace in Duluth's gentrifying Canal Park, **Northern Waters Smokehaus** doesn't look like a gold mine as you walk past. But if your nose is operational, it's impossible to ignore. Smoldering maple wood, infusing fish from Lake Superior and beyond with a great-outdoors perfume, is a siren call that will stop you in your tracks. Inside, whole whitefish, a good 2 feet long, lie ready to be wrapped and taken home (or shipped). Delicate as it is, whitefish was spawned to smoke. Its dense, pure-white meat sucks in plenty of smoke piquancy but is flavorful enough not to be overwhelmed by it. We love having a big, buttery hunk of it on a plate and teasing off bite-sized flakes with the tines of a fork, adding, perhaps, only the smallest dab of horseradish mayo as a garnish.

EXEMPLARY WHITEFISH

Maggie's: 257 Manypenny Ave., Bayfield, WI
715-779-5641
www.maggies-bayfield.com

Northern Waters Smokehaus: 394 Lake Ave. South, Suite 106, Duluth, MN
218-724-7307
www.nwsmokehaus.com
Whole fish, smoked meats, and gift boxes are available via mail-order.

Midwest

SOUTHWEST

ARIZONA

Carne Adovada: Mesa and Scottsdale, 302
Carne Seca: Tucson, 304
Cheese Crisp: Tucson, 306
Chicken and Waffles: Phoenix, 307
Chile Relleno: Tucson, 312
Chimichanga: Mesa and Tucson, 317
Cinnamon Roll: Tucson, 230
Coctel de Elote: Phoenix and Tucson, 319
French Fries: Tucson, 247
Green Corn Tamale: Tucson, 327
Horchata: Tucson, 338
Huevos Rancheros: Tucson, 342
Pico de Gallo: Tucson, 355
Red Velvet Cake: Phoenix, 196
Sonoran Hot Dog: Tucson, 356
Tamale Pie: Tucson, 358
Topopo Salad: Scottsdale and Tucson, 362

COLORADO

Chocolate Almond Butter Toffee: Grand Junction, 318
Cinnamon Roll: Denver and Loveland, 230
Coney Island: Bailey, 233
Hamburger: Colorado Springs, 328
Testicles: Denver, 360

KANSAS

Chicken Dinner Road: Pittsburg, 308
Chili Con Carne: Kansas City, Overland Park, and Topeka, 314
Fried Chicken Dinner: Fairway, 253
Garlic Salad: Wichita, 324
Hamburger: Salina, 328
Valomilk: Merriam, 363

NEW MEXICO

Carne Adovada: Albuquerque, Chimayó, and Santa Fe, 302
Chile Relleno: La Mesa, 312
Frito Pie: El Rito, Española, and Santa Fe, 320
Green Chile Cheeseburger: Española, San Antonio, and Santa Fe, 324
Horchata: Albuquerque, 338
Huevos Rancheros: Albuquerque and Las Cruces, 342
Pancakes: Santa Fe, 402
Sopaipilla: Chimayó, El Rito, Las Cruces, and Santa Fe, 356
Tamale Pie: Albuquerque and Taos, 358

OKLAHOMA

Barbecue Pork Sandwich: Shawnee, 121
Barbecue Ribs: Shawnee, 124
Beef Burrito: Ponca City, 301
Beef Jerky: Clinton, 305
Catfish: Tulsa, 143
Coney Island: Tulsa, 233
French Fries: Bartlesville, 247
Horchata: Tulsa, 338
Migas: Oklahoma City, 347
Onion-Fried Burger: El Reno, 350
Testicles: Krebs, McAlester, and Oklahoma City, 360

TEXAS

Barbecue Ribs: Elgin and Houston, 124
Beef Barbecue: Driftwood, Lexington, Lockhart, Luling, Taylor, and Tioga, 296
Breakfast Taco: Buda, 350
Chicken-Fried Steak: Austin, Bandera, Dallas, Houston, and Johnson City, 309
Chile Relleno: Dallas and El Paso, 312
Chili Con Carne: Austin, Canutillo, Grapevine, Houston, and Lockhart, 314
Frito Pie: Amarillo, Dallas, and Irving, 320
Hamburger: Fort Worth and Houston, 328
Hot Guts: East Bernard, Elgin, Lockhart, Luling, and Taylor, 339
Huevos Rancheros: El Paso, 342
King Ranch Casserole: Georgetown and Houston, 344
Kolache: Austin, La Grange, and West, 345
Migas: Austin, Bee Cave, Georgetown, and Houston, 347
Nachos Jorge: Houston, 349
Pecan Pie: Georgetown, Kyle, and Round Top, 354
Sonny Bryan's Sandwich: Dallas, 298
Testicles: Tioga, 360

BEEF BARBECUE
Central Texas

How juicy can beef be? The answer is found in the barbecue belt of central Texas, a wedge of prairie east of I-35 and north of I-10, where brisket, prime rib, and beef sausage are cooked in the haze of oak smoke slowly enough to baste themselves. Not much fat drips out; the fire is so low that it cooks in. The fibers of the meat absorb all the fat's flavor, giving the beef tremendous heft. Even

Basking for hours in wood smoke turns brisket at Louie Mueller's in Taylor, TX, buttery.

FLEA MARKET AND FINDS

While the barbecues of central Texas tend to be shockingly stark, the region is rich in opportunities for collectors and browsers of art, antiques, and crafts. Myriad small communities feature artisans' studios and jumble shops. East of Lockhart, Round Top, which started as a backyard flea market and now draws merchants and buyers from all over the United States, hosts huge antiques fairs in January, April, June, and October. Round Top also happens to be the home of Royer's Round Top Café (page 354).

Round Top Antiques Fair:
475 N. Highway 37, Round Top, TX
512-237-4747
www.roundtoptexasantiques.com

the dark-crusted rim of brisket fairly drips with protein potency, and the outer, less pink circumference of a slice of prime rib radiates the earthy perfume of burning wood.

Originally evolved early in the twentieth century, when butchers decided to smoke unsold and unwanted cuts of beef and serve them at makeshift tables in the back rooms of their meat markets, Texas barbecues are secret-seeming places where amenities are minimal. Order meat by the pound. It is cut, weighed, and slapped down on a sheet of pink butcher paper, along with a stack of soft white bread. Plates are extraneous, as are forks. As for side dishes beyond bread or saltines, don't expect more than onion, pickle, jalapeños, and maybe beans. Sandwiches are unheard of. Barbecue sauce? Some places have it, some don't; in the best of them, sauce is inconsequential. Meat is all that matters, and this meat doesn't need it.

A half-century ago, *Dallas News* columnist Frank X. Tolbert wrote that Taylor, Texas, "has more barbecue places . . . than any town of ten thousand that I know about." Tolbert cited **Louie Mueller's** as the best of them. Opened in 1949, Mueller's seems ancient, located on a side street and fronted by a raised sidewalk shaded by a broad awning. Housed in a big hall that was once a school gymnasium but now has peeling-paint walls that have been exposed to smoke for so long that they have become the color of tobacco, it has a churchlike ambiance, so dark it appears to be lit by candles. Even the business cards tacked up on the wall under a neon beer sign have turned brown. Mueller's brisket is celestial. As the inherently fatty cut of cow basks in wood smoke, its marbling melts and turns the once-tough cut recklessly tender, more like warm butter than beefsteak. Its exterior, blackened by time in the pit, has some crunch and an even more concentrated flavor; fibers that are still laced with fat quite literally melt on your tongue.

Uncharacteristically (for Texas), the **City Market** in Luling makes significant barbecue sauce — a spice-speckled, dark orange emulsion reminiscent of Arthur Bryant's (page 128), so coveted by customers that signs on the wall above every booth implore "Please Leave Sauce Bottles on Tables." Luling's sausage rings are superb (page 341); slabs of pork ribs, usually an afterthought in Texas barbecue parlors, are laden with glistening tender meat, and the brisket is positively lascivious, heaped onto butcher paper that is soon splotched with its juices. Luling City Market has no plates, and if you want a utensil, grab a plastic knife from the cigar box near the cash register. Few people do. Messy as it is, Texas barbecue is finger food. It is a meal to feel as well as to taste.

The most inaccessible excellent barbecue in Texas is that served at a shack called **Snow's BBQ** in Lexington. It is hard to get because Snow's is open only one day a week — actually a half-day, on Saturday from about 8 a.m. until the meat runs out, which can be before noon. There's a full smoke-pit menu, including ribs, sauce-brushed chicken, pork steak, and pork butt. Brisket is the star: melting-tender, its juicy fibers invigorated by a powerful infusion of soft smoke flavor. Opened in 2003, Snow's was little known until 2008, when *Texas Monthly* declared it the best barbecue in the state, anointing pitmaster Tootsie Tomanetz a genius. Tootsie, now seventy-five, has been smoke-cooking meat since 1967. The rest of the week, when she is not cooking barbecue, she is a custodian in the local school district.

While it is north of Dallas, far from heart-of-Texas barbecue country, **Clark's Outpost** in Tioga (Gene Autry's hometown) belongs on any

In Texas, one word says it all.

Texas barbecue is finger food.

short list of the best beef barbecues on earth. This legendary smokehouse surrounded by quarterhorse farms cooks briskets in a haze of smoldering green hickory and pecan wood at 175 degrees for a few hours, then at a superslow 150 degrees for three days more. Nothing is put onto the beef as it cooks — no seasonings, no sauces, no marinade. The result is beef and smoke laced together in an exquisite harmony that words cannot convey. Rimmed with a crust of smoky black, each slice is so supple that the gentlest fork pressure separates a mouthful. The warm barbecue sauce, supplied on the side in Grolsch beer bottles, is dark, spicy, and provocatively sweet. Clark's menu goes beyond the primitive basics of a classic Texas pit, offering such country-style side dishes as crisp-fried okra, jalapeño-spiked black-eyed peas, and a marvelous oddity, French-fried corn on the cob. Lengths of corn, unbattered and unadorned, are dipped in hot oil for a minute or so, just long enough for the kernels to cook and begin to caramelize. The result is corn that is quite soft, with a mere veil of a crust, and astoundingly sweet. Each piece is served with blacksmith's nails stuck in its ends to serve as holders.

SONNY BRYAN'S SANDWICH

The classic barbecues of central Texas tend not to offer sandwiches. If you need one, you make your own with the stack of white bread provided. But at Sonny Bryan's in Dallas, a sandwich is the way to go: brisket, bathed for hours in a lazy veil of hickory smoke until it verges on disintegration, is so juicy that no sauce is required. However, Sonny's sauce is a beautiful thing spread on the meat in its broad, plain bun: opaque red with a tang made to complement a booming protein punch.

Dating back to 1910, when Elias Bryan opened a smoke shack in Oak Cliff, Sonny Bryan's is now a small chain in the Dallas area and a well-known tourist attraction. We most enjoy the oldest of the restaurants, on Inwood Road, where dining accommodations include awkward but irresistibly charming school-desk seating.
Sonny Bryan's Smokehouse: 2202 Inwood Rd., Dallas, TX 214-357-7120
See www.sonnybryans.com for additional locations.

In Driftwood, southwest of Austin, the **Salt Lick** is without doubt the biggest barbecue place in Texas, and while it has far more amenities than most — a printed menu! waiter service! food served on actual plates! — its slow-smoked meats are the real thing. All meats come sauced, which is unusual in Texas but welcome here because sauce is the Salt Lick's greatest virtue — a sweet glaze with spice and tang so inviting that we find ourselves dipping white bread in it just to get more. The Salt Lick's sausage, equal parts pork and beef, is juice-oozing succulent, and the ribs are a huge amount of meat that ranges from tender at the bone to crusty-chewy burned ends.

With four estimable pits, Lockhart, population 11,000, is indisputably the state's barbecue capital, making it something like Mecca's Kaaba: the heart of the heart. **Black's** is somewhat unusual in that it offers such niceties as hard-boiled eggs stuck on toothpicks, little garden salads in bowls, and cobbler for dessert. You can even have the man behind the counter put your meat into a sandwich and your sandwich on a plate! Not only that, the dining room has decor, in the form of game trophies and pictures of the high school football team, on its knotty pine walls. Such small luxuries, so atypical of the great Texas pits, have no bearing on Black's ribs, the meat of which pulls so easily off the bone, or its brisket slices, bisected by an ethereal ribbon of translucent fat that leaches flavor into every smoky fiber of the meat. We once asked Edgar Black if he uses a special kind of wood or secret sea-

Smitty's in Lockhart, TX: literally the most atmospheric restaurant in America

sonings to make his barbecue so intense. "Twelve hours is the secret," he told us. "Twelve hours over post-oak wood. Cook your brisket long enough and it will make you weep."

Kreuz (rhymes with *lights*) technically is the oldest barbecue business in Lockhart, opened over a hundred years ago just off the town square. In 1948 Charles Kreuz sold the business to the Schmidt family, but about a dozen years ago a feud split the Schmidts and sent the Kreuz Market out to a big new building on the highway. The modern Kreuz is an immense roadside dining barn with all the charm of an airplane hangar, but there is no denying that its fatty — okay, we'll say "well-marbled" — slabs of pit-cooked prime rib are among the most carnivorously satisfying foodstuffs on earth. Despite modern facilities, Kreuz has maintained pit-cook tradition: a limited menu that is meat, bread, and condiments (and you can get an ice cream cone at a separate counter), and tote-your-own service from a ferociously hot pit where meat is sliced to order and sold by the pound.

Located where Kreuz began, **Smitty's** is the most atmospheric restaurant in America. Literally. Eye-stinging clouds rise from open wood fires around the indoor pit, so that it's finally a relief to gather your food in its butcher paper and take it to a table in the air-conditioned dining room with its institutional seafoam-green walls. Smitty's atmosphere also is an intangible sense of the past that hits like a sudden dizzy spell when you walk in from South Commerce Street. Out of the sunlight, a dim, time-burnished eating hall is outfitted with rows of wooden benches facing the walls for eating brisket and sausage side by side in reverential silence rather than at tables that promote conversation.

The ultimate in luxury: glistening brisket, hot from the pit

The room is no longer in use for anything but passage to the pit, giving it the feel of a hushed exhibit of indigenous Texas foodways in a museum of culinary history. When we first came upon this place in the 1970s, the benches were outfitted every 10 feet or so with sharp knives attached by chains so that diners could use the blades to cut their meat but not steal them or stab anyone.

Smitty's menu, posted on the wall, is meat by weight. Choices include lean beef (shoulder) and fat beef (brisket), super-succulent sausage (page 340), and boneless prime rib. That last one has got to be the ultimate in smokehouse luxury: cut to order (extra-thick, please), rosy pink in its center, saturated with juice, and yet handsomely lean, laced with smoke tang and giddy with carnivorous energy.

THE FOREMOST HEART-OF-TEXAS BARBECUES

1. Louie Mueller Barbecue:
206 W. 2nd, Taylor, TX
512-352-6206
www.louiemuellerbarbecue.com

Louie Mueller's in Taylor, TX: an ancient, churchlike ambiance for barbecue worshippers

2. **Clark's Outpost:** 101 Highway 377, Tioga, TX
940-437-2414
www.clarksoutpost.com
3. **Smitty's Market:** 208 S. Commerce St., Lockhart, TX
512-398-9344
www.smittysmarket.com
4. **Black's Barbecue:** 215 N. Main St., Lockhart, TX
512-398-2712
www.blacksbbq.com
5. **Snow's BBQ:** 516 Main St., Lexington, TX
979-773-4640
www.snowsbbq.com
Open only on Saturday, 8 a.m. until sold out. To place an order during the week, call 979-542-8189.
6. **City Market:** 633 E. Davis St. Luling, TX
830-875-9019
7. **Kreuz Market:** 619 N. Colorado St., Lockhart, TX
512-398-2361
www.kreuzmarket.com
8. **Salt Lick:** 18001 FM 1826, Driftwood, TX
512-858-4959
www.saltlickbbq.com

BEEF BURRITO
Ponca City, Oklahoma

There are excellent burritos from coast to coast, but if you like yours with a hot pepper kick, the one you must eat is in Ponca City, Oklahoma. It is listed on the menu with the warning "Only for the Brave," and what is so unusual about it is that the extreme heat isn't sprinkled on or folded in; it resides in the fibers of

Near a small airport in Ponca City, OK, Enrique's cooks up a fiery beef burrito.

the meat. Like the intensely flavored carne seca of Sonoran cuisine (page 304), the beef in Ponca City has been marinated prior to grilling and is super-saturated with flavor, chewy but also unbelievably moist. It is available with additional green peppers, which add crunch, as well as beans, guacamole, and cheese. Frankly, we find all but the peppers superfluous. You don't want anything to distract you from your focus on the delicious meat in its warm flour tortilla wrapping.

This sensational burrito is available only on Friday and Saturday nights, when it is the specialty of an unlikely restaurant located at the outskirts of town in the sleepy, low-slung cinder-block terminal of a one-runway airport. **Enrique's** is the airport's only place to eat, and from its counter and tables you can sometimes see small planes landing or taking off during mealtime. Beyond its essential burrito, Enrique's is known to private plane pilots throughout the Southwest for its *pollo loco* chicken soup, handmade tortilla chips, and sopaipillas hot from the fry kettle. Breakfast is served only the

Southwest

first Saturday of every month, when Enrique's hosts a pancake fly-in.

Enrique's: 2213 N. Waverly St.,
  Suite 3, Ponca City, OK
  580-762-5507
  www.enriquesrestaurant.com
  Burritos available only on Friday
  and Saturday nights

CARNE ADOVADA
New Mexico

Here is a dish that celebrates pepper power. Carne adovada — pork marinated in liquefied chiles until it absorbs both their flavor and their heat — can be as humble as the tamales made at a roadside stand called **Leona's Restaurante** in Chimayó. Leona sparingly laces shreds of pork into the cornmeal masa that is the tamale's essence, adding fire to the earthy corn and creating a duo that is especially good to eat under the blue sky of the Sangre de Christo mountain range. Or it can be a romantic banquet, as served in that same mountain range at the patio tables of **Rancho de Chimayó**, to the serenade of mariachis in the flicker of candlelight at dusk. Here carne adovada is the definitive Native Foods meal, the chunks of meat turned tender from their long marinade and glistening fiery red. On the side is a mound of posole (hominy corn), mild little lumps of tenderness to soothe the tongue. And to drink? How about a Chimayó cocktail made with gold tequila and cider squeezed from high mountain apples?

The great bargain carne adovada — no less delicious for its $1.99 price — is a burrito at the **Frontier** in Al-buquerque. It doesn't contain any extras, just chile-infused meat intense enough to turn the tortilla that wraps it the color of sunset. An unusual version is served at **Papa Felipe's Mexican Restaurant**, a big restaurant and banquet hall in Albuquerque, where the pork is sopped with a marinade of green chiles, giving it unique vegetable potency. It's great as a green tamale pie, baked in sweet corn masa and laced with cheese. Another Albuquerque hot spot is **Sadie's**, where you can have a carne adovada stacked enchilada, made with white or blue cornmeal tortillas and available strewn with pumpkin seeds.

While most carne adovada appears as lunch or supper, the eating of fiery pork is every bit as much a morning custom for many New Mexicans. Evidence of that fact is breakfast at the **Horseman's Haven Café**, an improbable eatery adjoining a filling station at the western end of Cerrillos Road in Santa Fe. Operated by the Romero family since 1981, this extremely modest cafe, with its short counter and half-dozen little

At Albuquerque's Frontier, a burrito of carne adovada, pork marinated in chiles, costs just $1.99.

booths and its delirious decor of all-equine art (statuettes, paintings, and plaques), has inspired decades of buzz for its superb breakfast burritos loaded with eggs and bacon and topped with cheese and chiles and its gorgeous carne adovada accompanied by eggs, potatoes, and a warm homemade tortilla for mopping the last of the marinade.

Although it is a New Mexican thing, one of the hottest adovadas with which you'll ever ignite your tongue is found in Mesa, Arizona, at **Blue Adobe**, which bills itself as a Santa Fe grill. It is ember-red, and chiles seem to saturate every fiber of the tender pork. The warm flour tortillas — a Sonoran Desert touch

Dogs lounge in the shade in Taos, NM.

— are welcome heat dampers, as are pinto beans and rice.

CARNE ADOVADA HOT LIST

1. **Rancho de Chimayó:** Santa Fe County Road 98 (State Route 520), Chimayó, NM 505-351-4444 or 505-984-2100 www.ranchodechimayo.com

2. **Horseman's Haven Café:** 4354 Cerrillos Rd., Santa Fe, NM 505-471-5420

3. **Frontier Restaurant:** 2400 Central SE, Albuquerque, NM 505-266-0550 www.frontierrestaurant.com

4. **Leona's Restaurante:** 4 Medina Lane, Chimayó, NM 505-351-4569 www.leonasrestaurante.com

5. **Sadie's of New Mexico:** 6230 4th St. NW, Albuquerque, NM 505-345-5339 www.sadiessalsa.com

6. **Papa Felipe's Mexican Restaurant:** 9800 Menaul Blvd. NE, Albuquerque, NM 505-292-8877 www.papafelipes.com

TAOS PUEBLO

Believed to have been built about a millennium ago, Taos Pueblo was one of the enchanted cities of Cíbola seen by the Spanish explorers of the sixteenth century. It is the oldest continuously inhabited community in the United States: a thriving settlement of terraced multifamily homes made of mud bricks and reached via wood-and-hemp ladders. Guests are welcome, but photography is limited, as is access to the private areas of the sprawling community of 150 Pueblo Indians.

Taos Pueblo: Highway 68, Taos, NM 575-758-1028 www.taospueblo.com

Southwest

Also

Blue Adobe Grille: 144 N. Country Club, Mesa, AZ 480-962-1000 Second location: 10885 N. Frank Lloyd Wright Blvd., Scottsdale, AZ 480-314-0550 www.blueadobegrille.com

CARNE SECA
Tucson, Arizona

Do you know the plastic-wrapped beef sticks sold in convenience stores? Please forget about them. Have you had beef jerky from a vendor at a flea market or a gun show? Erase its taste from your memory bank. Dried beef ought not to be a plug of shoe leather chemically treated to remind you of beef and smoke. At its best — and here we are thinking of the carne seca made at **El Charro** in Tucson — it is meat that has blossomed: glistening mahogany and exploding with flavor, dry and yet vigorously succulent, rugged and pure pleasure to chew.

El Charro's recipe for carne seca is a family secret, but it is no mystery how it is dried. Monica Flin, who opened the landmark restaurant in 1922, used to hang strips of beef on a clothesline in a storage shed; today the Flores family takes advantage of the desert sun and hoists strips of marinated thin-sliced tenderloin up above the patio off El Charro's south-facing roof. The beef is held in a metal cage that keeps it safe from vultures but leaves it in the open air to dry for several hours. Suspended on ropes and pulleys, the cage sways above the patio, wafting the perfume of lemon and garlic into the Arizona air. The infusion of the marinade and

10,000 WAVES

A unique place to pamper your body and heighten your spirit, this New Age spa offers steamy saunas, reflexological healing, underwater *watsu* massages, massages by certified masters, four-hand massages, organic facials, herbal wraps, and super-premium baths with "heated cooling berths" (cooler than the water, warmer than the air). Billing itself as "a Japanese hot spring resort, adobestyle," it is an only-in-New-Mexico way to relax for a few hours or a day — or a dreamy vacation in one of thirteen serene suites.

10,000 Waves: 3451 Hyde Park Rd., Santa Fe, NM 505-992-5025 www.tenthousandwaves.com

El Torero in Tucson sets off the intense flavor of its carne seca with a bright, juicy salad.

the caress of a clean desert breeze transform it from something merely meaty into an eating experience that is wild and profound. After it is air-dried, carne seca is shredded, spiced, sautéed, and generally served in concert with sweet onions, hot chiles, and tomatoes, or as the fanciest top-

BEEF JERKY

Beef jerky is the most familiar form of carne seca, and a good chaw unless you are dentally challenged. Jigg's Smoke House on old Route 66 in Oklahoma makes some of the toughest, and we mean that in the nicest way. Slices of loin as big as a handkerchief are desiccated in a dry mix of brown sugar, garlic, and cayenne pepper, then slow-smoked over coarse-ground hickory sawdust for up to twenty-four hours. The result? Gnarled burnt-sienna-colored patches that are a resounding harmony of beef, pepper, and smoke. Chew, chew, chew: The waves of flavor are relentless. Accommodations in the weatherbeaten Okie shack include a front porch, where you can sit in the shade, and construction spool tables opposite the butcher counter inside, where the paneled walls feature portraits of the meat-eating heroes John Wayne, Bob Wills, and Marty Robbins. Mesquite-cooked barbecue, tender as warm butter, is also available.

Jigg's Smoke House is not set up to ship its dried beef. That is one reason we highly recommend getting in touch with Green Light Jerky Company in California. They not only mail it, they offer the opportunity to join the Jerky Junkies Club, members of which receive a different flavor of jerky every

A taste of the Old West, the gnaw-worthy jerky of Jigg's in Clinton, OK, is best enjoyed on the front porch.

month of the year. Green Light is big into its jerky's being nutritionally virtuous: no nitrates, no food coloring, nothing that is bad for you. The classic jerky is flavored with slightly sweet, slightly hot peppers; there are super-hot chipotle jerkies, and one, named PRD, seasoned with rosemary, thyme, and horseradish, that is alleged to taste like a prime rib dinner. While you probably won't confuse PRD with a real slice of prime rib, it is some of the most full-flavored jerky we've ever savored.

Green Light Jerky Co.:
Redwood City, CA
www.greenlightjerky.com
Jigg's Smoke House: Exit 62 off
I-40, Clinton, OK
580-323-5641
www.jiggssmokehouse.com

Southwest

ping for a *tostada grande*, a crisp foot-and-a-half-wide tortilla blanketed with molten cheese and strewn with green chiles, guacamole, and *refritos* (refried beans), served *en pedestal* and sometimes colloquially known as Mexican pizza.

Carne seca is a natural filling for tacos, which are available three ways at Tucson's **La Indita**, which means "little Indian woman" and serves south-of-the-border food with a Native American twist. There are soft Tarascan tacos (*Tarascan* means American Indian–Mexican), which make a handy wrap and whose steamy corn flavor beautifully envelops the meat; there are fried-crisp ones; and there is an Indian taco, served open-faced on a round of fry bread. One of the dandiest uses for carne seca is in a topopo salad (page 362), especially the one made at **El Torero** in south Tucson, where a great conical mound of lettuce, vegetables, and logs of hard cheese is packed with chewy shreds of it. The greenness of the salad only amplifies the dark intensity of the beef, making a dramatic plate of food.

CARNE SECA AT ITS BEST

1. **El Charro Café:** 311 N. Court Ave., Tucson, AZ
   520-622-1922
   See www.elcharrocafe.com for additional locations.
2. **La Indita Restaurant Mexicano:** 622 N. Fourth Ave., Tucson, AZ
   520-792-0523
3. **El Torero Restaurant:** 231 E. 26th St., Tucson, AZ
   520-622-9534

CHEESE CRISP
Arizona

Sometimes known as Mexican pizza, the cheese crisp is a broad circular tortilla that is baked with such minimal adornment as melted cheese and a scattering of *cebillitos* (green onions), or as dressy as a full-meal medley of green chiles, guacamole, refried beans, and carne seca. Generally the plain cheese-topped ones are served as appetizers before a full meal. They are wafer-thin, brittle, and customarily presented on a silver pedestal that enables those at far ends of the table to reach a piece.

The cheese crisp is a staple in nearly all of southern Arizona's Mexican eateries, and it's hard to find a bad one, but if you are looking for the most extraordinary incarnation, **Blanco Tacos + Tequila** is the place to go. A snazzy "contemporary Mexican" place in a strip mall up on Skyline Drive, BT+T boasts a broad selection of exotic margaritas and tequilas and meal prices that can top $25. Its *queso* crisp menu is headlined by an amazing one webbed with a combination of Oaxaca, Asadero, and manchego cheeses on top of which is sparkly pico de gallo, chunks of avocado, and — ready for this? — braised short ribs. The rib meat oozes dark beef flavor and is more tender than the accompanying ripe avocado. It is supposed to be an appetizer, and it might well be for a couple or three people, but this mighty circle will challenge any single appetite. Another *blanco queso* crisp not to be missed is chipotle shrimp and corn.

WHEAT FLOUR TORTILLAS

Carlotta Flores of Tucson's El Charro Café tells us that southern Arizona took to the flour tortilla because wheat thrived in the area's mild winters. Farmers found that they could grow two crops per year. "So while elsewhere in the New World corn remained king, Tucson became the hometown of the flour tortilla," she says. Carlotta notes that as farming methods improved, corn regained its place in the Tucson diet, and now corn tortillas are popular as well, but Tucson's passion for the giant wheat tortilla remains unique.

Blanco Tacos + Tequila: La Encantada Center, 2905 E. Skyline Dr., Suite 246, Tucson, AZ 520-232-1007 www.foxrestaurantconcepts.com/blanco.html

CHICKEN AND WAFFLES
Soul-Food Restaurants

Syrup or gravy, that is the question. The other question is, how did the once-popular waffle become pancakes' lonely alternate on breakfast menus, rarely appearing at any other meal? Waffles used to serve as the bed for all sorts of chafing-dish meals, from shrimp wiggle to beef tips. Alice Foote McDougal, who ran a coffee shop in New York's Grand Central

Not just for breakfast: In soul-food restaurants, waffles star as a crunchy escort for all sorts of dishes.

Station early in the twentieth century, titled her memoir *Coffee and Waffles,* and it contains all sorts of clever ideas for serving waffles at lunch and supper and tea. They had already declined in favor by 1964, when the appearance of Belgian waffles at the world's fair and their subsequent proliferation sounded a thin-waffle death knell virtually everywhere except the ever-present highway-exit Waffle House.

The one place you will still find waffles in a starring role is soul-food restaurants, where they become an eggy trivet for pieces of fried chicken. We love the immense crusty wings doled out at **Niecie's** in Kansas City, Missouri, and it's hard to resist the funky old L.A. charm of **Roscoe's House of Chicken and Waffles** in Hollywood and Long Beach, but the best version of the dish we know is at **Lo-Lo's Chicken and Waffles** in Phoenix. The waffles have a nice crunch, but not so much as to detract from their steamy insides, and they come gobbed with a sphere of

Come on in to Niecie's in Kansas City, MO, for a heap of chicken and waffles.

CHICKEN DINNER ROAD
Pittsburg, Kansas

You cannot really say you have eaten your way around the U.S.A. until you have stopped for a meal or two on Chicken Dinner Road in Pittsburg, Kansas. Formally known as 600th Avenue, far from anything and everywhere, the country lane features two gargantuan restaurants serving nearly identical meals. Both **Chicken Mary's** and **Chicken Annie's** date back to the hard times of the 1930s. In 1934, after Annie's husband lost a leg in a mine accident, she opened a little restaurant to make ends meet. A few years after that, Mary's husband had to quit work, too, because of a bad heart. She saw how well her neighbor was doing and opened Chicken Mary's less than a mile away.

sweet butter, sided by pieces of beautifully fried chicken (your choice of parts), and furnished with a pitcher of syrup. Waffles are available smothered with gravy and sweet onions, too, but somehow, believe it or not, the syrup makes much more sense.

EXEMPLARY CHICKEN AND WAFFLES

1. **Lo-Lo's Chicken and Waffles:** 10 W. Yuma St., Phoenix, AZ
   602-340-1304
   www.loloschickenandwaffles.com
2. **Roscoe's House of Chicken and Waffles:** 5006 W. Pico Blvd., Los Angeles, CA
   323-934-4405
   See www.roscoeschicken andwaffles.com for additional locations.
3. **Niecie's:** 5932 Prospect, Kansas City, MO
   816-921-5990
   Second location: 8686 E. 63rd St., Kansas City, MO
   816-358-8100

Chicken Annie's in Pittsburg, KS, began in the 1930s when Annie's husband lost a leg.

Chicken Mary's features an identical meal of deep-fried chicken and German side dishes.

The meals at both places are family-style feasts built around deep-fried chicken that is preferably sided by German potato salad and German coleslaw and most definitely preceded by delightfully crisp, tangled-up onion rings. The chicken is opulent, arriving at the table glistening with grease and girdled with chewy, fat-rich skin. You can have whatever parts of the bird you like in whatever quantity: dark meat, white meat, wings, and backs, even an appetizer of livers, gizzards, and hearts.

2 EQUALLY PERFECT CHICKEN DINNERS

Chicken Annie's: 1143 600th Ave., Pittsburg, KS 620-231-9460

Chicken Mary's: 1133 E. 600th Ave., Pittsburg, KS 620-231-9510

CHICKEN-FRIED STEAK
Texas Hill Country

The best chicken-fried steak in all of Texas? We say it's at **Hoover's Cooking** in Austin, and we are not alone in that contention. After the 2008 Roadfood.com tour of central Texas, it was agreed by all serious eaters who tried it that Hoover's is tops. It is not particularly huge; there is room on the broad, unbreakable plate for two or three of the kitchen's superbly soulful vegetables: mashed potatoes, macaroni and cheese, black-eyed peas, porky mustard greens, fried okra, or jalapeño-spiked creamed spinach. The gravy is wonderful (we ask for extra to blanket the mashed potatoes) — true pan gravy made with flavorful drippings and sharply peppered. The steak has a crisp golden crust so rich that it virtually melts into liquid luxury.

Bandera's **OST** (short for Old Spanish Trail) serves a chicken-fried steak to inscribe on the Texas honor roll: a pounded-tender slice of steak encased in batter and deep-fried, the result a tantalizing balance of crunchiness and tenderness, topped with gravy that is cream-soft but pepper sharp. The ribbon of beef inside glistens with juice, and the crust cracks when bitten. OST serves its lovely cutlet for lunch and supper, but we like it best as part of the plentiful Cowboy Breakfast, where it is accompanied by potatoes, refried beans or

Southwest

FRIED CHICKEN

This dish comes pretty close to what you will get in Pittsburg, Kansas. It's utterly basic. Fry with lard and it soars.

1½ cups all-purpose flour
1 tablespoon kosher salt
1 teaspoon freshly ground black pepper
½ teaspoon cayenne pepper
1 tablespoon margarine, melted
1 large egg, beaten
¾–1 cup flat beer
2 pounds chicken (in parts), washed and patted dry
Vegetable oil for deep-frying, or, if you dare, lard

Mix the flour, salt, peppers, margarine, and egg in a large bowl. Add enough beer to make a thick paste. Spread the paste over the chicken parts and turn the chicken to coat. Cover and refrigerate for 2 to 3 hours or overnight.

Heat oil in a deep fryer or large skillet to 365 degrees. Fry the chicken pieces, a few at a time, for 15 to 20 minutes, or until golden brown. Be sure to move the pieces around in the oil so they don't stick, but turn and handle them carefully so the coating doesn't break. Drain on brown paper bags or paper towels.

SERVES 4

grits, biscuits, a couple of eggs, and, needless to say, plenty of peppery cream gravy.

A sign over the door of the **Hill Country Cupboard** in Johnson City announces that it serves the world's best chicken-fried steak (NEARLY THREE DOZEN SOLD, it boasts). Two sizes are available: regular and large,

Hoover's in Austin makes the best chicken-fried steak in all of Texas.

the latter as big as its plate. Neither requires a knife; a fork will sever golden brown crust that is rich and well spiced, a perfect complement to the tender beef inside. Alongside the slab of crusty protein comes a great glob of skin-on mashed potatoes, and thick white gravy blankets the whole shebang.

The **Ozona Bar and Grill** of Dallas offers a fascinating twist on the classic formula, a configuration connoisseurs know as "cowboy style": Instead of cream gravy, the fried cutlet is topped with true-Tex, no-bean chili. If you love a crunchy crust, this is not a good idea, since the chili quickly sogs out the crust, but the powerful beef flavor of Ozona's CFS is in fact beautifully complemented by the bright (but not too hot) chili and shreds of cheese melted on top. (Suggestion:

Order your chili on the side and dunk the steak into it forkful by forkful, thus retaining the crust's crispness. This tactic is also good for classically presented chicken-fried steak, which can suffer from its gravy blanket.)

While there are plenty of bad chicken-fried steaks to be eaten along the highways of the Southwest, after you've eaten one of these great ones, you'll find it easy to understand why so many Texans consider it the state's unofficial iconic dish. No excuses need be made for the one served at **Ouisie's Table**, a Houston home-cooking cafe with a raised culinary consciousness. The batter is severely crunchy, the beef is juicy, and the milk gravy is speckled with hot black pepper. Ouisie's also offers chicken-fried venison dressed up with sides of corn pudding, risotto, and superb biscuits that beg to be pushed through gravy on the plate.

TEXAS CHICKEN-FRIED STEAK AT ITS FINEST

1. **Hoover's Cooking:** 2002 Manor Rd., Austin, TX 512-479-5006 www.hooverscooking.com
2. **OST Restaurant:** 305 Main St., Bandera, TX 830-796-3836
3. **Ouisie's Table:** 3939 San Felipe Dr., Houston, TX 713-528-2264
4. **Hill Country Cupboard:** 101 S. U.S. Highway 281, Johnson City, TX 830-868-4625
5. **Ozona Bar and Grill:** 4615 Greenville Ave., Dallas, TX 214-265-9105

RIDING THE HILL COUNTRY

Guest ranches around Bandera, Texas, offer many ways to relish the West, from inert meditation — poolside margaritas at the Silver Spur, with a view of Saddleback Mountain — to all-day golf and/or all-day trail rides. The place we like to stay for full appreciation of cowboy culture is the Dixie Dude Ranch, a working cattle outfit since 1901 and a dudes' haven since 1937. When you hit the trail through Dixie's 725 acres, you will likely encounter sho-'nuff browsing longhorn cattle, and if you opt for an overnight horseback ride, you will make camp in a tepee, chow down from a chuck wagon, and have a twilight serenade by cowboy balladeers (occasionally accompanied by feral coyotes). The smell of strong coffee and baking biscuits is your alarm clock, and the open-air excursion concludes at a slow trot through magnificent Hill Country vistas and back to the ranch for lunch.

Dixie Dude Ranch: PO Box 548, Bandera, TX 800-395-YALL or 830-796-7771 www.dixieduderanch.com

Silver Spur: 9266 Bandera Creek Rd., Bandera, TX 830-796-3037 www.silverspur-ranch.com

Southwest

CHILE RELLENO
Throughout the Southwest

Fire-roasted, cheese-stuffed green chiles prepare to meet their maker.

Chiles rellenos is a Mexican-menu standard all across the nation, but only in the Southwest, where the chile pod is sacrosanct, does it sing hallelujah. The strapping capsicum-vegetable punch packed in the thick walls of a good roasted chile is what makes the dish something more than just a lot of melted cheese and crisp breading. Roasted to bring out its sun-earth essence, the long green chile **Chope's** in La Mesa, New Mexico, uses to make its rellenos is just barely peppery enough to make your tongue tingle. It is encased in a fragile batter with minimal crispiness and arrives on its plate unsauced, all the better to showcase not only the elemental flavors of chile and cheese but also the great span of textures from the outside's crunch to the chile's meaty flesh to the molten cheese within.

Chope's, which is a planters' cafe in the heart of the Mesilla Valley's chile fields, gets its year's supply of chiles, about 3 tons, during the autumn harvest from a farmer who, the proprietor Cecilia Benavides Yanez says, "knows what we like — not too hot, not too mild. He plants it, grows it, picks it, then takes it to a man outside Las Cruces who roasts it." While the local peppers are delicious in Chope's unsauced rellenos, their spirit glows in the puree that is made in the kitchen each Monday. Mrs. Yanez stems, seeds, soaks, and blends whole red ones to create a thick opaque vermilion liquid with flavor as clear as fruit nectar's, and fairly hot — the kind of lip-sear-ing hot that any restaurant outside New Mexico would warn customers about. When you paint this onto the skin of one of Chope's rellenos, you create a dish with flavor like liquid sunshine and fireworks heat like the Fourth of July.

Along the Rio Grande just over the state line in El Paso, you have the opportunity to watch the creation of beautiful chiles rellenos from a counter seat at the **H&H Car Wash and Coffee Shop**. In this tiny diner with an open kitchen just across the counter, trays of long greens are stuffed with cheese, then dipped one by one into a big metal bowl filled with batter that is the texture of whipped cream. The covered pods are then eased into boiling oil, where the foamy coating turns into a crisp gold cloud that holds the pod, which is still al dente when it is retrieved from the oil. The hot relleno is set on a plate and topped with a thick blanket of chunky salsa.

H&H salsa, like the chile itself, is hugely flavorful but relatively mild. If you want it hot — very, very hot —

you need to request some of the chile de arból salsa made by the waitress Artemisa. At 15,000 to 30,000 units on the Scoville scale (which measures chiles' hotness), the chili de arból is exclamatory. It's a familiar bright red little pod (although it has a distinctly green flavor), used whole as a flavoring agent in seasoned vinegars and oils and in its dry form to make the wreaths so common on homes in northern New Mexico. Because of its sharp, cayennelike heat, the chile de arból (the name of which literally translates as "tree chile," for its woody stem) is used judiciously in soups and chili stew. But in Artemisa's salsa it is not used judiciously, and the result is a smoky heat that makes your tongue feel phosphorescent. Spoon some of this over the crisp coat of an H&H relleno and you have an edible fireball!

The ouch factor tends to be less in Arizona's Mexican food repertoire, and the rellenos at **Mi Nidito** in south Tucson are proof that flammability is only an option in a good chile relleno. Made from al dente peppers as friendly as a balmy desert evening, these beauties have only enough

In the heart of chile country, Chope's in La Mesa, NM, goes through three tons of peppers each year.

Vibrant salsa tops a chile relleno at H&H Car Wash in El Paso, TX.

cheese to underscore their pure vegetable goodness.

Frying a chile relleno is the normal way to cook the stuffed peppers in most cafes throughout Texas and New Mexico, but at its worst, frying can be cloddish, turning the chile into mush and adding nothing but fatty weight to the dish. Rellenos at **Avila's** in Dallas are something else. They are baked rather than fried, and they are available with fillings other than mere cheese. Without the fried blanket around them, these stuffed peppers have a spritely quality even when filled with ground beef or, on request, shreds of juice-heavy brisket. The chile is a not-too-hot poblano that retains some muscle in its walls. It comes atop a pool of bright red tomato sauce, draped with a thin coat of melted cheese, and it is accompanied by pico de gallo.

Avila's notwithstanding, most chiles rellenos are meatless, but at **La Cabañita** in Glendale, California, the cooks make a relleno that really celebrates vegetables, a roasted (not fried) poblano pepper stuffed with black beans and rice or with corn kernels and diced zucchini in a buttery sauce. Most iconoclastic and intriguing of all are La Cabañita's chiles en Nogales — poblanos stuffed with ground beef, chopped nuts, and raisins, not fried but blanketed with cream-sweet gravy.

SUPERB CHILES RELLENOS

1. **H&H Car Wash and Coffee Shop:** 701 E. Yandell Dr., El Paso, TX
   915-533-1144
2. **Chope's:** 16165 S. Highway 28, La Mesa, NM
   575-233-3420
3. **Avila's Mexican Restaurant:** 4714 Maple Ave., Dallas, TX
   214-520-2700
4. **La Cabañita:** 3447 N. Verdugo Rd., Glendale, CA
   818-957-2711
5. **Mi Nidito:** 1813 S. Fourth Ave., Tucson, AZ
   520-622-5081

CHILI CON CARNE
Texas ... and Kansas

Incredibly, chili in its classic form, as chili con carne, is something of a rarity in diners and cafes throughout Texas. Plenty of places offer dolled-up chili or chili made with ground beef (a minor crime against the traditional recipe, which calls for chunks of beef) and even chili that includes beans (a felony), but if you are looking for what Texans call a bowl of red, head for the **Little Diner** outside El Paso. The proprietor, Lourdes Pearson, buys her

The Little Diner's fiesty and vivid variations, yours in Canutillo, TX

chiles over the border in New Mexico at harvesttime and uses them to create a stunning bright red chili that surrounds tender shreds of beef with the flavor of concentrated southwestern sunshine and the heat of the famously flat Llano Estacato of northwest Texas. You can have the magnificent dish the traditional way, in a bowl, with tortillas on the side for mopping the last of it, or, even better, as the stuffing of one of Lourdes's lovely, crisp-skinned cornmeal pockets, known as gorditas.

With a menu of burgers, fajitas, tacos, and burritos, **Texas Chili Parlor** in Austin is a primer in Tex-Mex cuisine, and as its name suggests, chili is the star. Available in heat increments from ! (whew) to !!! (ouch), it is a fundamental foodstuff that is deeply satisfying all alone or on top of enchiladas, hot dogs, and hamburgers. Don't tell purists, but Texas Chili Parlor also offers chili that includes Elgin sausage and beans. Even **Tolbert's Restaurant** in Grapevine, Texas, makes what it bills as "North of the Border" chili, including pinto beans. We've never tried that, but we can tell you that Tolbert's "Original Texas

Red" is mighty good, even if Frank X. Tolbert, author of the definitive chili bible, *A Bowl of Red,* might raise an eyebrow over the cheese and onions that are part of the package. (The restaurant is run by his daughter.)

While the **Avalon Diner** in Houston uses coarse-ground beef instead of chunks, its chili tastes right: not too hot despite its incendiary red color, thick enough for a fork but without a bean in sight, and served drugstore-style, which means blanketed with melted cheese shreds and chopped raw onion. About the thickest chili we've found in Texas is that served at the great barbecue **Black's** in Lockhart: just a crowd of cumin- and pepper-spiced ground beef, so unctuous that it invites you to dip in forkfuls of white bread to sop up the flavor.

Texas chiliheads tend to be persnickety about the exact, correct recipe for their venerated dish, but the rest of the Southwest is full of restaurants that play with the formula and create bowls of chili that may not be true to the dish's historical roots as sold in the San Antonio Market in the nineteenth

Big portions of burnt, meaty ends from the barbecue make the Woodyard's chili superb.

century but are memorably delicious. One of the strangest and, to our taste buds, most haunting such creations is burnt-end chili at the **Woodyard** in Kansas City, Kansas. The sustaining plateful of hearty, bean-choked chili is combined with a large portion of burnt-end barbecue. Burnt ends, also known as brownies, are the most concentrated form of barbecue, where the most flavor resides and the most intense chewing satisfaction is found. All by themselves, they can be too, too much, the savory equivalent of an overlarge slice of flourless chocolate cake. But pair burnt ends with the chili's starchy multibean quietude and you have a mighty bowl full of satisfaction. Almost as beguiling as the flavor poise of this ingenious dish is its textural range, which includes nuggets of meat that are velvety and some that are crunchy-crisp. Available condiments are chopped red onion, sliced jalapeños, grated cheese, corn chips, and sour cream, but we suggest

A mighty bowl of satisfaction at the Woodyard in Kansas City, KS

Southwest

In Topeka, KS, Charlie Porubsky hots up his chili with four-alarm horseradish pickles.

that such festooneries only detract from the inspired combo of chili and barbecue.

Less like familiar styles of chili and more like western Iowa's loosemeats (page 266), the chili at **Fritz's**, also in Kansas, is listed on the menu as chili meat, and that is exactly what it is: no more, no less. Most people ask for beans with it, but if you want something spicy, it's your job to transform the plate of pebbly, spiced ground beef into your own version of chili. Peppered vinegar and chili powder are set out at the counter and on tables. Cheese (60 cents), chopped onions (15 cents), jalapeños (20 cents),

pickles (30 cents), and ketchup (10 cents) are also available, and the plain chili beef can be ordered as a topping for hamburgers and hot dogs.

West of Kansas City in Topeka, **C. W. Porubsky Grocery** serves a one-alarm chili that is elevated into the pantheon by a unique garnish: four-alarm horseradish pickles. Between October and March (chili season), Charlie Porubsky will grind some 80 pounds of chuck in the morning and cook it up with a judicious measure of chili powder and other spices, then add the meat to a battered old pot of simmering beans. Dished out in a disposable bowl, it is a very satisfying lunch for under $5. Add the pickles and your hair will stand on end. They are dills cut into big-bite-sized pieces and steeped in brine with hot horseradish, Tabasco sauce, and powdered mustard. The result is a boldface, large-font, screaming-red exclamation point for that gentle dish of protein and starch. The beef-bean-pickle combo is like no other chili we've tasted: meaty thick and shot through with a devilish pucker that leaves careless novices gasping for air after a couple of mouthfuls.

SOUTHWEST'S TOP CHILIS

1. **Little Diner:** 7209 7th St., Canutillo, TX
   915-877-2176
   www.littlediner.com
2. **Tolbert's Restaurant:** 423 S. Main St., Grapevine, TX
   817-421-4888
   www.tolbertsrestaurant.com
3. **Woodyard Bar-B-Que:** 3001 Merriam Lane, Kansas City, KS
   913-362-8000

4. **Black's Barbecue:** 215 N. Main St., Lockhart, TX
   512-398-2712
   www.blacksbbq.com
5. **Texas Chili Parlor:**
   1409 Lavaca St., Austin, TX
   512-472-2828
6. **Avalon Diner:**
   2417 Westheimer Rd.,
   Houston, TX
   713-527-8900
   Second location:
   12810 S.W. Freeway,
   Houston, TX
   281-240-0213
   www.avalondiner.com
7. **C. W. Porubsky Grocery and Meats:** 508 N.E. Sardou Ave., Topeka, KS
   785-234-5788
8. **Fritz's Chili:** 6737 W. 75th St., Overland Park, KS
   913-381-3543

CHIMICHANGA
Mesa and Tucson, Arizona

What a dramatic moment when the food cart rolls out from the kitchen at **Mi Nidito** with a table's worth of smoking-hot chimichangas on board! Since each is nearly the size of a coffee can, a quartet of them looks like statuary as much as food. When you sever the crisp-fried tortilla wrap and excavate, the Mexican aromas are intoxicating. Mi Nidito, once a little taqueria and now the go-to place for visiting celebrities, offers its chimis loaded with red or green chile sauce, carne seca, cheese, beans, or combinations thereof. The only bad thing about getting a chimichanga for supper is that it is big enough to preclude also ordering tacos, tostadas, rellenos, enchiladas,

PAUL BOND BOOTS

South of Tucson in the border town of Nogales, you will find the best boot-maker in the land. Paul Bond, who celebrated his ninetieth birthday a few years ago, no longer plies leather, but most days you will find him in the bootery, still presiding over a spacious wonderland of footwear that exudes the delicious smell of tanned leather and rings with the soft thud of hammers nailing soles. While some boots are ready-made and available to buy on the spot, most of what comes from here is bespoke. Paul or one of his heirs will guide you through piles of available skins, from barn-work tough to Saturday-night plush, as well as consult about such seductive issues as inlaid brands or monograms, toe shape, and stitch pattern. We must warn you, though: Once you've gone this route, you will never be happy with ordinary boots again. And all other kinds of shoes suddenly become very boring. Prices range from $500 for off-the-shelf work boots to $5,000 for all-alligator showstoppers.

Paul Bond Boot Co.: 915 W. Paul Bond Dr., Nogales, AZ
520-281-0512
www.paulbondboots.com

Southwest

and tamales, all of which Mi Nidito makes in exemplary fashion.

The history of **El Charro** restaurant says that founder Monica Flin accidentally dropped a stuffed burrito into a vat of sizzling oil, then christened the mistake *chimichanga*, which translates as "thingamajig." Whatever the chimi's beginning, El Charro serves some of the best and definitely the biggest in the form of the "USA Today Chimichanga," named to honor the newspaper that declared the restaurant's carne seca (page 304) one of the best fifty plates in America. This battleship is about twice as expensive and three times as big as an ordinary (quite large) chimi, and it comes loaded with guacamole, salsa, cheese, rice, beans, and sour cream in addition to a full measure of carne seca. Cleverly, El Charro deals with the size dilemma by offering mini chimis as appetizers. You'll also find minis, sold by threes and sixes, on the appetizer menu at the venerable **Casa Molina**, which sells full-sized ones with your choice from among three meats — ground, shredded, and carne seca — plus vegetarian chimis ballasted with beans.

What's most impressive about the chimi served at **Mangos** in Mesa is not the size but the shell. It is crisp but with enough chewiness to make it a major player in every bite, and it is deeply flavorful all by itself. Sided by good guacamole and sour cream, packed with tender pork and green or red chile sauce, this is one of the best dishes in greater Phoenix.

CHOICEST CHIMICHANGAS

1. **El Charro Café:** 311 N. Court Ave., Tucson, AZ

520-622-1922
See www.elcharrocafe.com for additional locations.
2. **Mi Nidito:** 1813 S. Fourth Ave., Tucson, AZ
520-622-5081
3. **Mangos Café and Mexican Bakery:** 44 W. Main St., Mesa, AZ
480-464-5700
4. **Casa Molina:** 6225 E. Speedway Blvd., Tucson, AZ
520-886-5468
www.casamolina.com

CHOCOLATE ALMOND BUTTER TOFFEE
Colorado

If you are a toffee hound, it is likely you already know about **Enstrom's**, which has been making the world's most delicious chocolate almond butter toffee since the 1930s, when Chet Enstrom, the soda jerk at a Colorado Springs ice cream shop, created it. If you don't know about it but have a sweet tooth, get some now! No other toffee can compare. Sweet and buttery, it is hard but not really brittle, so that when you sink your teeth through the dusting of ground almonds and sheath of milky chocolate that enclose it, the confection feels supple, on the easy side of crunchiness. Made with pure Colorado butter, it must be kept cool and can be stored in the freezer. Many have been the times, desperate for a chaw, we have broken off chunks that are still frozen solid, swooning as they melt in the mouth.

Enstrom's: 701 Colorado Ave.,
   Grand Junction, CO
   970-683-1000
   See www.enstrom.com for
   additional locations.
   Toffee is available by mail-order.

COCTEL DE ELOTE
Southern Arizona

Coctel de elote, meaning "corn cocktail," is definitely not a cocktail, nor is it soup or stew. Whatever its classification, it is a dish to reckon with when you visit Tucson in search of Mexican food treasures. There's a basic version at **Los Pollos Raspados**, where it is little more than cut

The Virgin of Guadalupe, patron saint of Mexico and the Southwest

THE VIRGIN OF GUADALUPE

Throughout the Southwest, but especially in south Tucson, the Virgin of Guadalupe is everywhere. Nuestra Señora de Guadalupe, who has come to represent Mexican pride, is a popular tattoo for limbs or entire backs or fronts; her image adorns low-riding custom cars and pickup truck mud flaps; there are Virgin T-shirts, key rings, glow-in-the-dark statuettes, rosary boxes, and coffee mugs. In 2007, when Miss Mexico competed in the Miss Universe Pageant, she planned to wear a dress with an image of the Virgin of Guadalupe on the front (but was dissuaded because it had a picture of a man facing a firing squad on the back).

Images of the Virgin of Guadalupe show her with roses. This depiction dates back to the 1500s, when a man named Juan Diego Cuauhtlatoatzin was walking in Mexico and saw an apparition of the Virgin Mary, who asked him to build a church in her honor. The Virgin told the humble man to go to the bishop of Mexico City, which he did twice. Each time he was rebuffed. On the third trip, the Virgin appeared again and instructed Juan Diego to take wild roses. He found these roses growing at the exact spot where she had appeared and took them to the bishop. The bishop saw that an image of the Virgin Mary was imprinted on the man's cloak, in which he had wrapped the roses. The bishop then believed.

Southwest

Pico de Gallo in Tucson offers homespun coctel de elote: warm sweet corn, melted cheese, hot chili, and lime.

A TRIO OF COCTELS DE ELOTE

1. **Taqueria Pico de Gallo:** 2618 S. Sixth Ave., Tucson, AZ 520-623-8775
2. **Los Pollos Raspados:** 2618 S. Sixth Ave., Tucson, AZ 520-903-1403
3. **Oasis Raspados:** 6629 S. Central Ave., Phoenix, AZ 602-305-6806 Second location: 1617 N. 32nd St., Phoenix, AZ 602-267-9174

corn, chili powder, and lime, but we like it best as served at **Pico de Gallo**, a little taqueria run by the Delgado family. Using a recipe passed down by Grandma Delgado, it is a homespun jumble of warm sweet corn kernels, drifts of soft melted cheese, hot chili, and lime. You scoop it up with a plastic spoon like some electrically spiced chowder that combines the earthiness of corn with the zest of lime and pepper. Most people get it as an hors d'oeuvre before a plate of Pico de Gallo's estimable tacos, but a big Styrofoam cup full of *coctel de elote,* all alone, will satisfy a healthy appetite.

Best known for its hot-weather relief in the form of *raspados* (fruit ices not unlike snow cones) made with fresh fruits and, if desired, ice cream, **Oasis Raspados** of Phoenix is armed for cooler weather, too, in the form of a buttery corn cocktail to which mayonnaise is added on request. When last we checked, the proprietor of this *raspados* stand (there are many throughout southern Arizona) was planning to fortify the menu with Sonoran hot dogs (page 356).

FRITO PIE
New Mexico and Texas

"We feel it is time for Santa Fe to stop pretending that Frito pie was created there," wrote Joyce Sáenz Harris in the *Dallas Morning News.* "Historically and culturally, Texas *owns* this dish, baby." We won't debate provenance with Joyce, who knows more than a thing or two about southwestern food, but we will point out that she herself observed that the "prettiest Frito pie ever seen" is served at Santa Fe's oldest restaurant (since 1918), the **Plaza**. And while it is somewhat iconoclastic — *not* served inside a Fritos bag, as is traditional; *not* containing chili con carne — it is the Frito pie to eat if you are planning to eat only one. Using zesty strips of carne asada instead of soupy chili, it combines the meat with pinto beans, shredded cheese, a vivid green chile sauce, lettuce, tomato, onion, and, of course, ribbons of Fritos. Whereas the chips soften in classic Frito pies, they maintain their salty, earthy crunch at the Plaza.

Joyce's assertion notwithstanding, many culinary historians do believe that the Frito pie was invented in Santa Fe at the lunch counter of the old Woolworth's, which has become the **Five & Dime General Store**, at the corner of the Plaza. Teresa Hernandez, who came to Santa Fe from Madrid, New Mexico, about sixty years ago, told us she had always enjoyed the way local drive-ins served their chili: in a paper cup on a bed of shredded lettuce, garnished with a handful of Frito chips. "When I came to work at Woolworth's, I thought maybe we could make a different kind of Frito dish," she recalled. "My idea was to eliminate the lettuce and to use the Fritos on the bottom." Rather than serving it in a paper cup, she ladled the chili directly onto the chips in a slit-open Fritos bag. That's just the way it is done today. Mild and meaty red chili is ladled into an opened "Big Grab" bag of corn chips, then shredded cheese is spread across the top. The chili is hot enough to begin to

El Farolito in El Rito, NM, a must for ravishing Frito pie

melt the cheese, and by the time you plant a plastic fork, the cheese is molten. The chips below start to soften, retaining only the echo of a crunch. Chopped onions and sliced jalapeños are offered as a garnish. It's a pleasure to stand at the counter and fork into a Frito pie, but these Big Grab meals are indeed portable, and it is entirely possible to eat one on the stroll in the Plaza, as generations of Santa Feans have done.

"You've had the Frito pie at Woolworth's on the Plaza?" asks Dominic Trujillo of a tiny diner called **El Farolito**, far off the beaten path in the one-street town of El Rito, northwest of the capital. "Ours blows it away!" El Farolito serves its version in a bowl, and it is ravishing: A massive layer of beefy red chili garnished with shredded cheese, lettuce, and tomato completely blankets a foundation of salty corn chips — the whole food pyramid in a single bowl! Beyond the persuasive combination of flavors, the magic here is the textures of the dish. The Fritos soften but retain a ghostly crunch. Dominic tells us that some customers who get their pies to

Woolworth's in Santa Fe, the birthplace of Frito pie, is still a general store.

Southwest

go have the corn chips packed separately so they don't get too soft by the time dinner is ready to eat.

At the **Atomic Grill**, a tiny cafe just off the Plaza, a bowl of Atomic Frito Pie gets its nuclear charge from green chili (not the usual red), plus jalapeño slices all over the melted cheese on top, which also is scattered with carrot sticks, chopped tomatoes, and sliced onions. Frito pie is by definition plebeian, and there is none more down-to-earth than that served at the **Stop and Eat Drive-In** up in Española. At this roadside attraction (which offers no seating at all, inside or out), the Frito pie is served in a plastic cup and is almost more like tortilla soup than pie, the corn chips lolling in viscous, *muy piquante* red

North of some of the best hiking in the Southwest towers the largest cross in the Northern Hemisphere.

chili and softening into streaks of earthy grain. Curiously, it is served without shredded cheese on top.

If indeed Frito pie was invented in Texas, the great moment might have

THE BIG CROSS AND PALO DURO CANYON

If you are heading toward the Golden Light Cafe from the Oklahoma side, you won't need a map to find the town of Groom, about 40 miles east of Amarillo. It is extremely well marked by the largest cross in the Northern Hemisphere, 190 feet tall. Whatever your religious belief, this is one awesome roadside attraction. To the south is an amazing detour for a day or many days. The Palo Duro Canyon is a vast rainbow-hued rock formation with a floor of grassland, where well over a century ago cattleman Charles Goodnight fattened longhorns for the legendary trail drives north. Today the 25,000-acre parkland paradise is a destination for horseback riders and hikers in search of trails or wild backcountry. The winding 16-mile road through the canyon is one of the most beautiful drives in the Southwest. Admission to the park is $4 per person; overnight facilities include backpacking campsites, equestrian campsites, and "primitive areas" with no restrooms or shower facilities. You also can sleep in one of two 1930s cabins perched on the rim of the canyon, now renovated and modernized ($110 per night). For details and reservations, call 512-389-8900.

Palo Duro Canyon State Park: 11450 Park Road 5, Canyon, TX 806-488-2227 www.paloducocanyon.com

occurred at the **Golden Light Cafe**, which opened in 1946 and is Amarillo's oldest restaurant. On its Route 66 menu of burgers and chili is a listing for Flagstaff Pie — a plate of Fritos topped with red chili and shredded cheese and garnished with lettuce and tomato. It is strange to eat Frito pie off an actual, nondisposable plate, but don't worry that something uppity is going on. The Golden Light is as down-home as cafes get, adjoining the Golden Light Cantina, a venue for drinking beer and listening to live music performed by Texas Red Dirt music bands.

Although **Tillman's Roadhouse** in Dallas bills itself as a come-as-you-are eatery, most meals cost well over $20, making it something more than a chili parlor. One of the cheapest entrées on the menu is about the most deluxe Frito pie we've ever seen, made with venison chili that includes wild mushrooms. It is so polite that a bag of extra Fritos is included on the side, allowing diners to add crunch when needed.

The rarest version of the dish is found at the town pharmacy in Irving, **Big State Drug**, where yeomanly drugstore chili comes in a bowl laced with only a handful of chips and well adorned with cheese and chopped raw onions. You can have a nice lunch-counter hamburger any day at this time-machine eatery from 1948, but Frito pie is made only on Thursday, and only in the winter.

8 GREAT FRITO PIES

1. **Plaza Café:** 54 Lincoln Ave., Santa Fe, NM
   505-982-1664
   www.thefamousplazacafe.com
2. **Five & Dime General Store:** 58 E. San Francisco St., Santa Fe, NM
   505-992-1800
   www.fiveanddimegs.com
3. **El Farolito:** 1212 Main St., El Rito, NM
   575-581-9509
4. **Golden Light Cafe:** 2908 S.W. 6th, Amarillo, TX
   806-374-9237
   www.goldenlightcafe.com
5. **Big State Drug:** 100 E. Irving Blvd., Irving, TX
   972-254-1521
   www.bigstatedrug.com
6. **Atomic Grill:** 103 E. Water St., Santa Fe, NM
   505-820-2866
   www.theatomicgrill.com
7. **Stop and Eat Drive-In:** 110 S. Paseo de Onate, Española, NM
   505-753-7400

Eat Santa Fe's Frito pie — red chili on corn chips covered with molten cheese — right from the bag at the Five & Dime.

Southwest

8. Tillman's Roadhouse:
324 W. 7th St., Dallas, TX
214-942-0988
www.tillmansroadhouse.com

GARLIC SALAD
Wichita, Kansas

Doc's is a steak house, and the steaks are a tremendous bargain, but its website is named www.garlicsalad .com, offering a clue to the real specialty of the house. Although made of lettuce, the salad feels more like coleslaw. Other than a dusting of paprika on top, it looks ordinary — finely chopped, slightly creamy — but at first bite you know you have forked into something different. Garlic predominates. It's not insanely garlicky, unless you order a double or triple garlic salad, and it is tempered by the plain leaves of lettuce on which it sits, but the presence of the stinking rose is undeniable and very aromatic. Doc's will sell garlic salad to go but warns that it will wilt after only a short time. Fresh is the way to have it, prior to a well-marbled rib eye.

Doc's Steak House: 1515 N. Broadway, Wichita, KS
316-264-4735
www.garlicsalad.com

GREEN CHILE CHEESEBURGER
New Mexico

It's the perfect storm of hamburgerology: a big palm of char-cooked beef, a luxurious mantle of oozing orange cheese, and a throbbing mound of

The fire-licked green chile cheeseburger at Bert's Burger Bowl in Santa Fe

ferociously hot, flame-roasted New Mexican green chiles, all heaped into a bun, preferably with raw onion, chopped lettuce, sliced tomato, and pickle chips. The place you must eat a green chile cheeseburger is the **Owl Bar**, a drinker's haven in the small town of San Antonio, not far from White Sands, where some of the first atom-bomb tests were conducted over a half-century ago. It is said that the GCCB was invented here for nuclear scientists who used to come for a truly explosive meal after a day of detonating megatons, but the Owl Bar's burger isn't just hot. It is beautiful and delicious: a crisp-edged, gnarled patty of juicy beef covered with fiery chopped green chiles, the chiles in turn topped with a slice of cheese that melts into them and the crevices of the hamburger.

As pilgrims on the road of reprobate gastronomy, we've come upon all sorts of green chile cheeseburgers at drive-ins and truck stops of the Southwest, but all the great ones are made in New Mexico, where chile is a passion. In the Mesilla Valley of the south, where most long green chiles grow, hamburgers are frequently draped with whole pods that have been roasted, peeled, and seeded. At the Owl Bar and north, the custom is to chop the chiles. In and around Santa Fe, the art of making GCCBs reaches its apotheosis, and not just in bars, dives, and dime-store dining areas. They turn up on some of the most respected menus in town; even stylish chefs try their hand at updating the straightforward sandwich recipe. The formula is so prevalent in the Capital City that **La Plazuela**, the restaurant at the old La Fonda Hotel on the Plaza, lists its palate-pleasing combo of beef, cheese, and green peppers as a "Santa Fe style" hamburger. You can get a tasteful redaction of it in the Dragon Room Lounge of Rosalea Murphy's venerable **Pink Adobe** restaurant, where a handsome grilled chopped sirloin patty is available with green chile relish, and an even fancier one at **Geronimo**, a restaurant on Canyon Road that offers a smoked Black Angus rib-eye burger with Gruyère cheese and Anaheim chile–pineapple salsa.

The **Blue Corn Café** in the Plaza Mercado attempts to solve the fundamental problem of constructing a sandwich out of such messy stuff by offering its GCCBs wrapped in a large flour tortilla rather than between the halves of a bun. It makes a neat pack-

CAFE PASQUAL'S

You cannot say you have eaten your way around Santa Fe unless you've been to Cafe Pasqual's. Three meals a day are served, each exemplary, but it's breakfast we like best, and pancakes in particular. This is a city of pancake excellence, including blue corn cakes dotted with piñon nuts at the Tecolote Café and blueberry buckwheat cakes with thick strips of smoked bacon at the Inn of the Anasazi. Cafe Pasqual's makes whole wheat pancakes so feather-light that a stack with a pitcher of real maple syrup might even leave room to sample one of the kitchen's other sensational breakfasts, which include banana-wrapped *tamales dulce,* chunky corned beef hash, five-grain hot cereal, and honey/whole wheat French toast. On the side, coffee is good, but so is dizzyingly spicy Mexican hot chocolate, topped with freshly grated cinnamon.

Cafe Pasqual's: 121 Don Gaspar Ave., Santa Fe, NM 800-722-7672 or 505-983-9340 www.pasquals.com

Inn of the Anasazi: 113 Washington Ave., Santa Fe, NM 505-988-3030 www.innoftheanasazi.com

Tecolote Café: 1203 Cerrillos Rd., Santa Fe, NM 505-988-1362 www.tecolotecafe.com

Southwest

age on the plate — nothing oozing out — but once you bite into it, cheese runs, carrying chopped green chiles in the molten flow. The hamburger is terrific, a half-pound of beef that drips juice from its crust; the cheeses (yellow and white intermingled) are creamy; and the chile, not ferociously hot, is redolent of sunny days and clean air. The soft tortilla lacks the absorbent qualities of the more traditional spongy burger bun, but its wheaty taste and pliant texture add welcome variety to the mix.

The classic GCCB experience tends to be a walk on the wild side of culinary life. Or, in the case of the **Stop and Eat** up in Española, it is a *drive* on the wild side. This old-time drive-in on the town's main drag serves not only swell little GCCBs and two-patty "jumbo twin" GCCBs, but green chile hot dogs, too — a subject for further study. The burgers are the glistening little patties you expect at a drive-in, and the green chile is 3.75-alarm H-O-T. In the evenings, half the fun of Stop and Eat is people- (and car-)

The Owl Bar in San Antonio, NM, invented its atomic chile cheeseburger to satisfy the appetites of nuclear scientists.

watching. The clientele includes a large number of local low-riders in their chromed and tassled V-8 cruisers with fuzzy shag-rug dashboards that serve as informal dinner tables.

Some of the cheapest GCCBs in Santa Fe, and all the more likable for their cut-rate surroundings, are those served at **Bert's Burger Bowl** (which also lays claim to inventing them). Bert's cooks broad, flat patties of beef on a grate over charcoal, from which flames lick up and flavor not only the meat but also the slices of cheese laid upon it and the big dollop of fiery green chile mounded on the cheese from a bucket near the fire. Bert's burgers come fully dressed with mustard, pickle, lettuce, onion, and tomato. As they eat, experienced customers, who dine under umbrellas on a patio overlooking Guadalupe Street, gradually peel back the wax paper in which the sandwich is wrapped, thus avoiding too much spillage.

The GCCBs we like best, for intrinsic flavor as well as for the roadhouse milieu of the joint that serves them, are found way out on Old Las Vegas Highway southeast of town, at **Bobcat Bite**. At first look it appears to be a dilapidated roadhouse, an impression reinforced when you pull into the rock-and-pothole parking lot around the low-slung 1950s-vintage adobe cafe. And yet when you enter the little shoebox dining room and admire the polished wood on the five tables and the tidy nine-seat counter built of log-cabin lumber, you realize this place is immaculate, so natty that it seems more like a highway hash house from a postwar Hollywood film noir than a restaurant of the real

Surpassingly large, the chile cheeseburger at Santa Fe's Bobcat Bite comes with fried spuds or chips.

world. The menu is simplicity itself — steaks, chops, sandwiches, chili in the winter, and a superb green chile cheeseburger year-round. Like everything else about this singular place, the presentation of the GCCB is impeccable and precise and a little eccentric. In a plastic basket lined with yellow wax paper, the jumbo burger arrives displayed on a bun bottom that rests on a bed of potato chips. On top of the meat, instead of the usual chile-on-cheese configuration, cheese is melted over the chile, the two elements melding into one. Hidden beneath the bun top, which also rests on the potato chips, are tomato slices and lettuce. It is barely possible to put everything together and eat it with two big fists. The meat in this GCCB is extraordinarily tasty — high-quality beef, a full inch thick — complemented but not overwhelmed by chile that is tangy more than hot.

MUST-EAT GREEN CHILE CHEESEBURGERS

1. **Bobcat Bite:** 420 Old Las Vegas Highway, Santa Fe, NM 505-983-5319 www.bobcatbite.com
2. **Owl Bar Café and Steakhouse:** 77 U.S. Highway 380, San Antonio, NM 575-835-9946
3. **Bert's Burger Bowl:** 235 N. Guadalupe St., Santa Fe, NM 505-982-0215
4. **La Plazuela:** in La Fonda Hotel, 100 E. San Francisco St., Santa Fe, NM 800-523-5002 or 505-982-5511 www.lafondasantafe.com
5. **Blue Corn Café and Brewery:** 133 Water St., Santa Fe, NM 505-984-1800 Second location: 4056 Cerrillos Rd., #G, Santa Fe, NM 505-438-1800 www.bluecorncafe.com
6. **Geronimo:** 724 Canyon Rd., Santa Fe, NM 505-982-1500 www.geronimorestaurant.com
7. **Stop and Eat Drive-In:** 110 S. Paseo de Onate, Española, NM 505-753-7400
8. **Pink Adobe:** 406 Old Santa Fe Trail, Santa Fe, NM 505-983-7712 www.thepinkadobe.com

GREEN CORN TAMALE
Tucson, Arizona

Summer is green tamale time in the Southwest. Fresh sweet corn, picked when still slightly green, is used to make packets that look like regular tamales but bear a sunny cereal fla-

Southwest

vor that is smoother and deeper than that of ripened corn. The kernels are transformed into firm, moist masa, with plenty remaining intact, and mixed with lard, roasted chiles, and cheese. They are packed into a fresh husk, well wrapped, and steamed until all the combined ingredients become a fused tube from which the husk peels back easily. Forked up or scooped out with a saltine, this is true melt-in-the-mouth food.

Lerua's, which competes with El Charro (page 304) for the title of Arizona's oldest restaurant, opened in 1922 and remains a small place with only a handful of tables. It is known also for excellent guacamole, but the time you must give it a try is early summer, when the free-standing sign announcing that green corn tamales are in season is set up on East Broadway.

Casa Molina, which has been around for only about sixty years, also puts green corn tamales on the menu in the summer, and this is the place to go if you are looking to eat off a complete Sonoran Mexican menu, from chimichangas and wieldy mini chimis to a carne seca topopo salad (page 362).

2 GREAT
GREEN CORN TAMALES

1. **Casa Molina:** 6225 E. Speedway Blvd., Tucson, AZ 520-886-5468 www.casamolina.com
2. **Lerua's Fine Mexican Food:** 2005 E. Broadway, Tucson, AZ 520-624-0322

NATIONAL BESTS

HAMBURGER

Hot dog loyalty is local. New York, Chicago, Detroit, Tucson: Each has its own distinctive way with wieners. But favorite hamburgers transcend place. They tend not to be regional in character — with such notable exceptions as New Mexico's green chile cheeseburger (page 324), Oklahoma's onion-fried burger (page 350), central Connecticut's steamed cheeseburger (page 63), and Wisconsin's butter burger (page 221). Large and small, plain and fancy, great hamburgers are everywhere. Here is our exegesis of the nation's best.

The most deluxe hamburgers generally are found in steak houses, but, as at the famous 21 Club, they tend to stretch the definition of the term to its breaking point, primarily because they are so big that they must be eaten with a fork. Nor shall we bother with elitist hamburgers, such as the one filled with foie gras served at DB Bistro Moderne in New York. In our book, an essential characteristic of any worthy hamburger is that it is democratic in spirit, accessible to all, and doesn't cost an arm and a leg.

That said, we need to begin with a fairly high-end steak house that makes what just may be the biggest-flavored hamburger anywhere. Not many places butcher their own meat, grind the trimmings, and blend their own ground beef as does the estimable **Pine Club** of Dayton, Ohio, which, although best known for ravishing steaks, makes a spectacular hamburger by mixing aged

America's emblem

prime sirloin, tenderloin, and dry-aged lamb. Broiled medium-rare, it is not overly oozy, but the hefty half-pounder reverberates with knockout meat power. Regulars have it with melting clods of blue cheese on top and an Anchor Steam beer on the side.

The hamburgers people fall in love with tend to be proletarian eats, their natural habitats being the drive-in, the roadside stand, and the old-fashioned lunch counter. Lunch-counter burgers are unique not only because of their location — the drugstore, soda fountain, or variety store — but because they share a single quality: lack of extremism. Not too thin, not too fat, neither spartan nor gobbed with anything exotic. The ideal incarnation, as served at Houston's **Avalon Diner** (attached to the Avalon Drug Co.), is somewhere between 3 and 4 inches in diameter and less than a half-inch thick. Its crust has crunch; its interior is juicy enough to imprint the bun but not oozy; it is cooked through, with only the faintest hint of pink inside. All alone it might be boring, but in full lunch-counter dress — topped with melted cheese and

accompanied by sliced tomato, crisp lettuce leaves, mustard, mayonnaise, onion, and pickle — and packed into a bun whose insides have been grilled in butter, it is an American classic.

A whole book can (and should) be devoted to pub burgers, but in our experience, one pub's burger stands above all others. That's the one you'll get at **R. F. O'Sullivan & Son**, a watering hole in Somerville, Massachusetts. Actually, we shouldn't say the *one* you'll get, for the menu lists a few dozen versions topped with all kinds of cheeses, bacon, onion, peppers, salsa, even sausage. Without considering condiment or garnish, these are superior measures of meat, so thick — a good 2 inches — that they cook for at least fifteen minutes on the charcoal grill, inhaling maximum smoky flavor and remaining succulent enough to demand that you tuck a napkin in your shirt collar before the first bite triggers a geyser of beefy juices.

Stella's, near Omaha, serves another fine pub burger. It is not as outsized as O'Sullivan's, nor are all the optional variants available, but one of these hand-pattied beauts on a big, round-topped bun with the standard complement of cheese, lettuce, tomato, onion, mustard, ketchup, and pickle is a thing of humble beauty. How humble? The cost is $4.50. It comes on a broad square of paper rather than a plate.

If you are looking for a hamburger that is really big and also bunned, the way any self-respecting hamburger ought to be delivered, the place to go is **Denny's Beer Barrel Pub** in Clearfield, Pennsylvania. Denny's everyday menu lists hamburgers that are 2 and 3

Southwest

The burger at Cotham's Mercantile in Arkansas's Grand Prairie is a foot wide.

pounds, as well as special-order ones that weigh in at 6, 15, and 50 pounds, for which the buns are custom-baked. In October 2008, Brad Sciullo became the first person ever to consume an entire 15-pounder — 20.2 pounds with bun and toppings. It took him 4 hours and 39 minutes. If dozens of pounds of meat seem daunting, you might want to try the relatively modest "hubcap hamburger" at a funky lunchroom called **Cotham's Mercantile** in Arkansas's Grand Prairie. It is a circle of cooked ground beef about a foot in diameter that comes in a bun that nearly fits, dressed with a salad's worth of mustard, lettuce, tomato slices, pickles, and hoops of onion. **Conway's Red Top** of Colorado Springs boasts of its hamburger, "One's a meal," and like the hubcap burger, this giant is perfectly proportioned, looking just right in its well-fitted bun. The outrageous size is obvious only when you see it in human hands, which in contrast look like those of a tiny doll. Although longhorn-wide, a Red Top

hamburger is not superthick, meaning it maintains the honest, oily smack of a good lunch-counter hamburger.

For seekers of maximum height rather than width or weight as the hamburger Holy Grail, three destinations are essential. First is the **Penguin** of Charlotte, North Carolina, where the Full Blown Hemi is an outlandish pile of three one-third-pound patties available southern-style, with chili, mustard, onions, coleslaw, bacon, and pimento cheese. The burgers themselves are super: thick, craggy patties oozing juice — a beef bonanza, protein forever. Amazingly, although the meat is monumental, the condiments copious, and the bun normal-sized, the mighty hemi is wieldy enough to pick up and eat without significant spillage. Less ambitious appetites can have a Big Block Burger (two patties) or a one-patty Small Block.

The **Anchor Bar** on the shore of Lake Superior is also known for its

On Lake Superior, the Anchor Bar's Gallybuster boasts a mountain of meat.

triple-decker, known as the Gally-buster. "This is what you call the meat loaf between the bun, hon," said the waitress when she delivered one to our table. It is indeed a mountain of food: three one-third-pound patties of beef layered with melted cheese and piled with caramelized onions. These sinfully oily hamburgers have tremendous bar-burger appeal. There is little else of note on the menu other than excellent French fries and a long list of porters, ales, bocks, and lagers to drink.

We believe that the best of all triples is served by a Houston lunchroom at the **Lankford Grocery and Market**, located in a former icehouse. "It's hard to keep a straight face when someone thinks they are going to eat one of those," said the waiter, grinning, when we ordered a triple-meat bacon cheeseburger. It's not that there is too much food — it's only about a pound of meat — but the three patties, cheese, bacon, and condiments are impossibly hard to manage. The taller-than-it-is-wide sandwich can barely be lifted with two hands, and at the slightest pressure of jaws or fingers, the ingredients start to slip and slide. Even if you can get the thing from its wax paper wrap to your face, there is no way a hinged human jaw can embrace any significant portion of it. We consulted with the staff, as well as with customers at nearby tables who were enjoying the presentation of the triple, and they all said that the only way to go at it was with fingers, knife, and fork, tearing off portions bit by bit. We need to note that it isn't only size that makes Lankford's hamburger essential. The burgers themselves are wonderful, each patty a gnarled, uneven circle

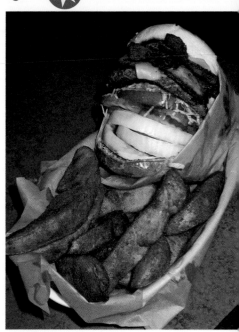

Hodad's tidy burger package: The paper is there for a reason.

with crunch to its crust and juices that erupt the moment that crust is severed. It is deliciously beefy — not an effete gourmet burger, but neither a skinny lunch-counter patty.

No hamburger is more heroic to eat, or more delicious, than the one served by **Hodad's** of Ocean Beach, California. The proprietor, Mike Hardin, whose parents paid $600 for the place in 1973 when it was a snack shack on the beach, explains precisely how one is constructed. Mayonnaise is spread on the bun bottom, then mustard. Atop the mustard go several crunchy hoops of raw onion, onto which is piped ketchup, whose fruitiness deactivates the sting of the onion. The ketchup is covered with a sheaf of pickle slices;

The flamboyant interior of Hodad's in Ocean Beach, CA

their puckery tang balances the sweetness below. Onto the pickles are piled thick slices of beefsteak tomato, echoing the ketchup; then comes a large ball of shredded lettuce. The grilled hamburger patty is set on the tower of condiments so its drippings seep down through them. (Above this layer, cheese and bacon are popular options.) Finally, the bun top is applied, making one strapping sandwich. It is enclosed in yellow wax paper in such a way that approximately one third is exposed and the rest is snugly wrapped. "That paper is your burger trough," Hardin advised. "We tell people, 'Do not take the paper off! It is there for a purpose.'" The purpose is to keep the immense thing from disintegrating. Mike pointed around the dining room at veteran customers wolfing down not merely huge hamburgers but doubles, which are an insanely larger bun, larger patty, and larger larder of toppings all in one package. He noted that experts all eat their Hodad's hamburgers the same way. Grasping it by the paper-covered part, they gingerly rotate it

around within the wrapper, and most important of all, they never let go of it once they hoist it from the plastic-weave basket in which it is served. "Eat your onion rings and French fries first. Drink your milk shake. Do whatever else you have to do," Mike says. "Then pick up your hamburger." We did notice that the big kahunas of Hodad's tables — those with literally very large hands — were able to keep a semi-wrapped double bacon cheeseburger secure in one mitt while they plucked French fries with the other. But barneys who don't focus on keeping it together risk epic burger wipeout.

You'll have no problem hoisting a squeezeburger at Sacramento's **Squeeze Inn,** although it looks more like a work of art than lunch. Not a fancy-food work of art but hash-house art, for sure. Onto a handsome, hand-pattied one-third-pound circle of grilling beef the short-order cook piles a double fistful of shredded cheese. The heat of the meat and the grill around it causes the cheese to melt and flow like heavy lava out beyond the edges of the hamburger it covers. When it hits the grill it sizzles and starts to cook seriously. By the time the burgermeister lifts it off the metal, the circumference of the cheese has become dark gold and brittle-crisp, while an inner aura closer to the meat is good and chewy and pliable enough to be bent upward like the petals of a flower, and, of course, the cheese that has remained on top is creamy smooth. The cheese spill is so extensive and the ring of hardened, chewy cheese that circles the burger so broad that when the meat is bunned, a short-fingered person might have trouble picking it up like a normal sandwich. It's that long a reach from the outside of the cheese ring to the bun.

A similar beauteous cheeseburger has been the specialty of a Connecticut dairy bar called **Shady Glen** for over half a century. Long before hifalutin chefs started wowing modern gastronomes with food that is as dramatically beautiful as it is tasty, Shady Glen was transforming ordinary cheeseburgers into edible sculptures. Made of regular American cheese and slim patties of 90 percent lean beef like those that anyone can buy at the market, the dazzling burgers are created by laying the sliced cheese on the grilling meat patty so that the edges of the cheese grill too. As the hot cheese begins to toughen, the cook flips up its still-pliant corners and curls them above the meat. The parts that have been bent upward offer a luxurious chewy-cheese texture as well as toasty edges that are crisp enough to break. It adds up to a cheeseburger that is a textural delight as well as a thing of beauty.

Louis' Lunch in New Haven, CT, purports to have invented the hamburger in 1895.

The inordinate number of burgers on this list from Connecticut is not because it's our home state. Connecticut really is cheeseburger paradise, plus it is home to **Louis' Lunch**, which claims to have invented the hamburger in 1895, when Louis Lassen decided not to waste steak trimmings at his lunchwagon but to ball them up and fry them. Today hamburgers are served on toast, because when Lassen began serving them, there was no such thing as a hamburger bun. Louis's grandson, Ken, whose grandson now operates Louis' Lunch, told us his version of hamburger history with an entirely straight face: When the Tartars ravaged Europe, they killed cattle, butchered them, and put cuts of meat under their saddles as they rode north, thus creating steak tartare, the meat pulverized by galloping and flavored by the horses' sweat. When, finally, the Tartars arrived in Hamburg, they stayed a spell and decided to cook the meat that had been ground up under their saddles, and thus it was in Hamburg that the first hamburger was cooked.

An edible basket of toasted cheese cradles a burger at Shady Glen in Manchester, CT.

Southwest

It was Ken's grandfather's genius to sandwich the meat patty in toast so it became edible without utensils, even portable. The Lassen family still cooks its burgers in a delightfully old-fashioned metal broiler that suspends the meat between two heat sources so the fat drips off as the patty cooks. The result is a sphere with big-beef taste, available with or without onions, on plain toast or toast spread with Velveeta cheese. You also can get sliced tomato, but ketchup is not allowed at Louis' Lunch.

Connecticut is also home to a couple of compelling summer-only hamburgers: the made-to-order, craggy, dark-crusted, juice-dripping orbs that get loaded into elegant buns at **Harry's Place** in Colchester, and the flatter ones (also cooked exactly as ordered) at the shockingly inconspicuous **Clamp's** in New Milford, the business card of which reads, "No Sign, No Address, No Phone, Just Good Food." If you like grilled onions, Clamp's might become your favorite burger

Sweet onions tumble from the bun at Clamp's in New Milford, CT.

on earth. Here they are cooked until soft and caramel-sweet, to become a cheeseburger's best friend. And on the subject of good-weather eats, we also salute the laudable **Shake Shack** in New York's Madison Square Park, where you can have your grill-pressed but still juicy cheeseburger on a buttery potato roll and accompanied by a masterfully made St. Louis–style concrete (page 238). It is open year-round, but picnic-style service always reminds us of summer, even when the temperature is freezing.

A lot of good burgers come from grocery stores or former grocery stores, the two shining examples being **Kincaid's** in Fort Worth and **Phillips** in the Mississippi Delta. Kincaid's was merely a corner grocery store until one day in 1954 when the butcher decided to grind up some leftover chuck steak and turn it into great big hamburgers. Customers raved, and soon thereafter space was cleared along the grocery shelves for people to eat burgers and drink a soda pop while standing up in the aisles at lunchtime. Eventually tables were added, and now Kincaid's is known for its lean and lovely charred half-pound burger, served with lettuce, tomato, and condiments inside a capacious bun. The hamburger is presented wrapped in wax paper that becomes a handy drop cloth for all the juices that inevitably squirt out as you heft it in two hands.

Phillips's burger comes wrapped in yellow wax paper inside a bag for easy toting, and when you peel back the wrapping, particularly on a half-pound Super-Deluxe, it is a vision of burger pulchritude. Cooked on a hot grill, the thick patty has a crunch to its nearly blackened skin. Inside, the meat is smooth-textured and super-juicy. There has long been speculation about why Phillips's hamburgers are so delicious, but when asked for details, the cooks say only that the recipe has been handed down since 1948, when Mr. and Mrs. Phillips took over the grocery store. Some time ago a rumor went around Holly Springs that the trick was to mix the meat with peanut butter, which was categorically denied. Frankly, we wouldn't even hazard a guess as to these burgers' secret. To us, they taste like freshly ground meat with enough seasoning to bring out their natural protein relish. Our honest suspicion is that the mystery is not any stealthy spice or condiment at all, but every Mississippian's favorite ingredient — tradition. Phillips's hamburgers are cooked on the same grill that has been used since 1948. Over half a century of sizzling meat has seasoned that grill with character that no mere foodstuff could beget.

So much for multiple-layer burgers, heavy burgers, and tall burgers. All true burger hounds know what is yet to be honored: the smallest of all burgers, known as a slider. Once considered the most ignoble branch of hamburger cookery, sliders have become trendy in recent years, and it is not unusual to find the little meat divots served as butlered hors d'oeuvres at cocktail parties and on menus in expensive taverns. As tasty as a gourmet slider may be, its soul is déclassé, which is why we cannot think of a more suitable place to eat sliders than **Hunter House Hamburgers** in Birmingham, Michigan. Topped with onions and pickles and, if desired, cheese, and

served on steamy little buns, they are slightly bigger than White Castle's, but small enough for four to six to make a meal.

A bit bigger than slider-sized, at 1.6 ounces each, the hamburgers served at Ann Arbor's **Krazy Jim's Blimpy Burger** are a bit too seditious to fit any mold. It is a terrible faux pas to get a single one in a bun; you must get two or three or go for what's known as a Quint. They're swell patties in a greasy-spoon way, but what makes them especially fun is Krazy Jim's uncontested boast that it offers 2,147,483,648 variations. After naming the number of patties you want, you decide on the roll: kaiser, regular, or onion. Cheese? Choose from among cheddar, Swiss, provolone, American, blue, and feta. Then: any extras with your meat? These include fried eggs, bacon, salami, grilled onions, banana peppers, sautéed mushrooms, olives (black or green), ranch dressing, tomatoes, and extra cheese. Finally, when everything else is settled, give the list of condiments you want applied. Minutes later, a beautifully built hamburger will arrive.

Since nobody eats just one or three, the heart-of-Kansas **Cozy Inn** offers a value meal of six hamburgers, a bag of potato chips, and a cold can of soda, currently priced at $5.93. To many loyal customers, a Cozy is the definition of a slider. For one thing, it claims the high moral ground by refusing to offer cheese. These burgers are pure! You can even order them plain, without pickles, but that would be a big mistake, as the deuce of dills in the bun actually outweighs the meat and contributes significantly to

Southwest

the Cozy Inn magic. And it theoretically would be possible to ask for no onions, but that would be nothing less than insane, as the flavor and the smell of onions are as much a component of the little sandwiches as the beef itself. Plus the slippery pucker of the pickles and onions is a foil that teases all possible beefy flavors from the rugged little hamburger. All this is not to denigrate the importance of the bun, which is as modest as a little tuft of bread can be, but its absorbency is vital and its blandness is the wrapper that this patty package needs.

Finally, a trio of Northwest hamburgers that must be inscribed on every eater's life list. The first is the Huddy Burger, which is the one and only thing on the menu of **Hudson's** in Coeur d'Alene, Idaho. There are no side dishes at all — no French fries, no chips, no slaw, no garnishes. The choices you will make are whether you want double cheese and whether you want both, *both* meaning pickle and onion. The burger itself is a lunch-counter masterwork, a little bit crusty with lots of beef flavor in its juices. When Todd Hudson gets an order (which he does about every five seconds during lunch), he grabs a fistful of beef, forms it into a patty, and slaps it on the grill. As burgers cook, he uses a sharp knife to form little clusters of sliced onion and pickle to go atop them; to watch him bun the burger with the condiments is a study in short-order dexterity. When you receive your hamburger at the counter, you have another choice to make: hot mustard or hot ketchup. These are said to date back to the Great Depression, when they were concocted extra-spicy as a

way to keep customers from consuming too much of them.

Rocky's Burger Bus hamburgers are particularly handsome: broader than the bun, cooked through but astonishingly succulent, with charred black outsides as flavorful as bacon. A single is a big sandwich. A double is a meat orgy. When we asked Jim Rockwell, the proprietor of Rocky's Burger Bus, what makes his hamburgers taste so good, he had a two-word answer: "Alberta beef!" Each is hand-pattied extra-thick and slow-cooked on the grill. French fries are cut and cooked to order. This is amazing attention to detail, considering that Rocky's really is nothing more than a bus from the 1960s that appears to have long ago run aground in an industrial park at the southeastern edge of Calgary, in Canada. Order your food by stepping up on a metal grate at the window near what used to be the driver's seat. (By local ordinance, Rockwell must be able to drive the bus away with twenty-four hours' notice. That would be an amazing feat, considering how deeply ensconced in silt it is.) Order your burgers and fries, then wait a while. This is

Step up to order the extra-thick hamburger made with Alberta beef at Rocky's in Calgary, Canada.

not fast food, and when things get busy — as they do at lunch, when battered pickups and Mercedes fight for parking space in the adjoining prairie grass — French fry production runs far behind demand. Dining facilities are a few picnic tables painted red to match the bus.

We almost never recommend eating at a chain restaurant, but for the bacon blue-cheese burger at **Burgerville**, a Pacific Northwest chain with dozens of locations, we gladly make an exception. At these drive-ins, $5 buys you an aristocratic hamburger. Nothing about it is mundane. The beef, from hormone-free, antibiotic-free Oregon cattle, is saturated with protein savor; the cheese is Rogue River valley blue that melts into a velvety cloak with a thick-veined tang, and the bacon, secured from an Oregon smokehouse, radiates peppery zest. It adds up to a Fourth of July fireworks explosion of flavor and a bacon cheeseburger especially wonderful to eat when accompanied by Burgerville's sweet potato French fries with marshmallow–brown sugar dipping sauce and a fresh peach milk shake.

ESSENTIAL HAMBURGERS

1. **Hodad's:** 5010 Newport Ave., Ocean Beach, CA
   619-224-4623
2. **Pine Club:** 1926 Brown St., Dayton, OH
   937-228-7463
   www.thepineclub.com
3. **R. F. O'Sullivan & Son:** 282 Beacon St., Somerville, MA
   617-492-7773
   www.rf-osullivan.com
4. **Lankford Grocery and Market:** 88 Dennis St., Houston, TX
   713-522-9555
5. **Louis' Lunch:** 261-263 Crown St., New Haven, CT
   203-562-5507
   www.louislunch.com
6. **Shake Shack:** Southeast corner of Madison Square Park, New York, NY
   212-889-6600
   www.shakeshacknyc.com
7. **Harry's Place:** 104 Broadway St., Colchester, CT
   860-537-2410
   www.harrysplace.biz
8. **Hudson's Hamburgers:** 207 Sherman Ave., Coeur d'Alene, ID
   208-664-5444
9. **Rocky's Burger Bus:** 1120 46th Ave. SE, Calgary, AB, Canada
   403-243-0405
10. **Clamp's Hamburger Stand:** Route 202, New Milford, CT
    No phone; summer only
11. **Squeeze Inn:** 7918 Fruitridge Rd., Sacramento, CA
    916-386-8599
12. **Shady Glen Dairy Store:** 840 E. Middle Turnpike, Manchester, CT
    860-649-4245
    Second location:
    360 W. Middle Turnpike, Manchester, CT
    860-648-0511
13. **Penguin Drive-In:** 1921 Commonwealth Ave., Charlotte, NC
    704-375-6959
14. **Krazy Jim's Blimpy Burger:** 551 S. Division St., Ann Arbor, MI
    734-663-4590
    www.blimpyburger.com

Southwest

15. **Cozy Inn:** 108 N. 7th St., Salina, KS
785-825-2699
www.cozyburger.com

16. **Denny's Beer Barrel Pub:** 1452 Woodland Rd., Clearfield, PA
814-765-7190

17. **Kincaid's:** 4901 Camp Bowie Blvd., Fort Worth, TX
817-732-2881

18. **Phillips Grocery:** 541 E. Van Dorn Ave., Holly Springs, MS
601-252-4671

19. **Avalon Diner:** 2417 Westheimer Rd., Houston, TX
713-527-8900
www.avalondiner.com
Second location:
12810 S. W. Freeway, Houston, TX
281-240-0213

20. **Anchor Bar:** 413 Tower Ave., Superior, WI
715-394-9747
www.anchorbar.freeservers.com

21. **Hunter House Hamburgers:** 35075 Woodward Ave., Birmingham, MI
248-646-7121

22. **Cotham's Mercantile and Restaurant:** 5301 Highway 161 South, Scott, AR
501-961-9284
www.cothams.com

23. **Burgerville:** 7401 E. Mill Plain Blvd., Vancouver, WA
360-694-4971
See www.burgerville.com for other locations in the Pacific Northwest.

24. **Stella's Hamburgers:** 106 Galvin Rd. South, Bellevue, NE
402-291-6088

25. **Conway's Red Top:** 1520 S. Nevada Ave., Colorado Springs, CO

719-633-2444
See www.conwaysredtop.com for additional locations.

HORCHATA
Southwest

Anyone who eats in the Mexican restaurants of the American Southwest will come across plenty of *horchata,* the refreshing Latino rice milk beverage that varies from skim-milk thin to milk-shake rich. We could drink it all day at south Tucson's **Pico de Gallo**, where it is milky enough to gulp and yet creamy enough to salve a chile-ravaged tongue, and where the traditional cinnamon on top seems chunkier than usual and extra-spicy. **Teresa's Mosaic Cafe** (which serves marvelous Oaxacan chicken in brown sauce) makes a classic version, with finer cinnamon on top, as does **El Norteño**, Albuquerque's home of meals that are true Mex, not Tex-Mex or New Mex. **Cancun**, in Tulsa, uses no cinnamon, and its *horchata* is thin, more like rice wine than rice milk, and significantly less sweet than most, all of which makes it eminently drinkable alongside such mighty thirst-inducers as *camarones a la diabla* (devilishly hot shrimp) and chile-sopped superburritos.

While *horchata* is most common in the Southwest, California's Mexican restaurants are the source of some superb versions. San Francisco's **El Metate**, which has four-star carnitas burritos and exemplary fish tacos (page 385), serves *horchata* that is not the least bit sugary but more an ode

Horchata, **a Latino rice milk drink, salves the chile-ravaged tongue.**

3. **Teresa's Mosaic Cafe:** 2455 N. Silverbell Rd., Tucson, AZ 520-624-4512
4. **El Metate Restaurant:** 2406 Bryant St., San Francisco, CA 415-641-7209
5. **Cancun:** 705 S. Lewis Ave., Tulsa, OK 918-583-8089
6. **El Norteño:** 6416 Zuni Rd. SE, Albuquerque, NM 505-256-1431 www.elnorteno.com

to the rich flavor of rice itself. The most extraordinary version we have found is served at **Guelaguetza** in Los Angeles. At this Oaxacan eatery and market, where English isn't yet a second language and where the *mole negro* is justly famous, the *horchata* isn't just rice milk flavored with cinnamon and vanilla. It sports chopped almonds, cantaloupe, and aromatic sweet cactus juice, all of which transform a simple refresher into a potable event — hands down, the queen of *horchatas.*

Note to really adventurous eaters: Guelaguetza's menu lists empanadas stuffed with roasted grasshoppers. If you try one, let us know how it tastes!

6 DELICIOUS HORCHATAS

1. **Guelaguetza:** 3337½ W. 8th St., Los Angeles, CA 213-427-0601 See www.guelaguetzarestaurante.com for additional locations.
2. **Taqueria Pico de Gallo:** 2618 S. Sixth Ave., Tucson, AZ 520-623-8775

HOT GUTS
Central Texas

Peppered, coarse-ground beef is packed into pork gut that is porous enough to suck in the flavor of burning wood as the sausage cooks but so impenetrable that no juice leaks out. Whereas Texas brisket, ribs, and mutton laze on the grate in the pit for hours, link and ring sausages — which Texas food writer Frank X. Tolbert dubbed hot guts — swell up as fast as the flue on one end of the pit draws smoke from the fire at the other, maintaining a temperature of about 250 degrees. When they are done, the casing has transformed from a translucent membrane into a chewy, wrinkled coat and the inside is ready to burst forth with flavor.

The **Southside Market** knows a thing or two about charcuterie. It has been Elgin's butcher shop since 1882. Although it moved from downtown to modern quarters on the highway sixteen years ago, it remains one of a handful of regional pits that feature bull-meat sausage that is cooked,

Southwest

Treat the coarse beef sausage of Smitty's in Lockhart, TX, like a champagne bottle about to pop.

served, and eaten primordially. Step inside and the tallowy sweet smell of beef steeping in the smolder of live-oak wood thickens the air as it surely did when Texas barbecue began over a century ago as the meat markets' way of making use of unsold and unwanted cuts. This particular smoke-pit smell, unique to Texas and a Pavlovian appetizer for barbecue aficionados, is a signal to everyone you meet after eating that you have been to one of meat's hallowed shrines. It will cling to your clothes and hair all day.

A Southside Market link is about a quarter-pound and a foot long, its orange skin dotted with pepper flecks. As the counterman assembles the food — which can be ordered by weight or plate — he cuts each one nine tenths of the way through in four places so it holds together but can be pulled into segments easily. Sauce is available, and it has a beguiling tang that perks up brisket; but the squishy succulence of Elgin links makes sauce redundant. Preferred side dishes are

raw onion slices, pickles, and a hunk of orange cheese. Elginites start eating hot sausage and brisket every day at 8 a.m.

Louie Mueller in Taylor is a magnet for devotees of smoke cooking, maybe the most beloved barbecue parlor in the state (see beef barbecue, page 297). "I've got one sausage left," says assistant pit boss Lance Kirkpatrick when we arrive for lunch at 1 p.m. "We'll take it!" we exclaim, feeling mighty lucky. The last link from the pit, which Kirkpatrick delivers by hand directly to the sheet of butcher paper that lines our tray, sports a leathery, crackle-textured skin and glows with salt-and-pepper zest. Some juice spills out when the sausage is bitten, but it isn't nearly as plump and oozy as a traditional Texas hot link. "You got the short end of the stick," Kirkpatrick jokes. "I've been worrying that link all day. But I'll tell you what. We have people who come in and ask for it just like that. You know, 'one of those nasty old ones from the corner of the pit.'" Sublime as the juicy links are, there is something to be said for these well-done sausages, known to pit men as dry links because so much fat has been rendered out of them. Extra time on the grate diminishes the wanton hedonism of the sausage and concentrates its flavor into an edible epigram of beef, pepper, and smoke.

Composed of 85 percent beef and 15 percent pork, the sausage ring of **Smitty's** in Lockhart has got to be the juiciest in Texas. It is so succulent that if you plan to snap it into two pieces, you must treat it like a bottle of champagne with a cork about to pop. Use two hands and significant pressure and be certain to push outward. When the casing has reached the breaking point, it bursts. Juice erupts and will splatter your face and shirt if it is not aimed away from you, preferably downward toward the table rather than at the person sitting opposite. By the time a ring is halfway dispatched, the butcher paper underneath it will be pooled with drippings of such beefy baritone depth, sparkling with the bite of red and black pepper, that it seems the best idea in the world to sop it up with creamy white slices of Butter-Krust bread. You want a stack of bread slices also because they are much handier than napkins. Every time you pick one up, you automatically blot fingers glistening with sausage grease.

East Bernard, in the greater orbit of Houston, is far from heart-of-Texas barbecue country, but if you are a pit-smoked sausage lover, you need to know about **Vincek's Smokehouse** (including Vincek's bakery, where you can get some fine kolaches; see

The Southside Market in Elgin, TX, has been making and smoking hot guts since 1882.

page 345). Not too far from the wide assortment of summer sausages, jerkies, bacons, and hams in the butcher case is a small area where tables are covered with red-checked plastic. Step up to the window in the corner and tell the man what you want. The pork ribs are massively meaty, the chicken is embarrassingly juicy, and the sausages, which are pork and beef and a hailstorm of black pepper, are as succulent as they come, with a sharp snap to casings that hold cascades of juice ready to run.

Even when the long communal tables of the **City Market** in Luling are crowded and a dozen conversations are in full sway all around, you cannot help but hear the crunch and snap as diners' teeth bite into the unbelievably taut casings of all-beef sausage rings. These horseshoe-shaped, string-tied guts are a lean, rugged grind with only the echo of pepper laced through their mineral-rich tautness. As is true of all the great sausage shrines of central Texas, you fetch your own meal at this Houston eatery. Venture into an enclosed back room where the smoke haze is dense and the temperature is about that of Hades. Tell one of the pit men how many sausage rings you want and how much brisket he should slice to accompany them, and he arranges the selection on a couple of sheets of pink butcher paper, along with slices of the soft white bread that is ubiquitous in southwestern smoke parlors. Eyeing us as out-of-towners but not wanting to embarrass us among the crowd of locals getting lunch, our man tactfully demonstrates how to keep the butcher paper wrapped around the

Southwest

meal as we prepare to carry it out to a table. Big men exit the pit room carrying their pounds of meat swaddled in paper with the extreme care they might give a newborn baby.

1. **Smitty's Market:** 208 S. Commerce St., Lockhart, TX 512-398-9344 www.smittysmarket.com
2. **Louie Mueller Barbecue:** 206 W. 2nd St., Taylor, TX 512-352-6206 www.louiemuellerbarbecue.com
3. **City Market:** 633 E. Davis St. Luling, TX 830-875-9019
4. **Vincek's Smokehouse:** Highway 60, East Bernard, TX 979-335-7921
5. **Southside Market and Barbeque:** 1212 Highway 290 East, Elgin, TX 512-285-3407 www.southsidemarket.com

HUEVOS RANCHEROS
Arizona, New Mexico, and Texas

Huevos rancheros are simple: eggs and salsa with tortillas. Cheese is a frequent addition, melted on the eggs, as are *refritos* (refried beans) on the side. Excellence is seldom a matter of exceptional ingredients and more about the just-right cooking of every element. On a perfect plate, which you will find at **Teresa's Mosaic Cafe** in Tucson, the eggs are sunny-side up, their whites pure and their yellows radiant, butter glisten-

ing across their surface. Between eggs and plate is a soft tortilla heated on the grill just enough for its edges to have begun to crisp but retaining a chewy resilience and the absorbency to be a perfect mop for running yolk. The salsa is chunky and chile-charged; the cheese is warm, smooth, and rich. The sum of it all: perfect breakfast.

Albuquerque's **Frontier** is known for many good things: being open around the clock, instantaneous counter service, a vast collection of art depicting John Wayne, gigantic cinnamon rolls, green chile cheeseburgers, and beautiful burritos, but the huevos rancheros at breakfast steal the show. That's partly because the Frontier offers them smothered not just with salsa but with chili, turning them into a dish more like chilaquiles than basic huevos. And some fine chili it is — green chili, radiating full vegetable taste. Spilled all over the eggs and laced with thick veins of melted cheese, it is gorgeous

A glorious mess: The huevos of Minneapolis's Hell's Kitchen includes salsa, three cheeses, black beans, scrambled eggs, and hash browns.

stuff . . . but difficult to eat with even a fork or spoon. That is where Frontier's flour tortillas come into play, and it is these tortillas that make this huevos rancheros–eating experience sensational. Are they freshly made? Look to the left of the order counter and you will see a primitive assembly line where a single cook sends flattened bombs of flour into a flame roaster and pulls out platewide, light tan cooked tortillas that are presented on their own paper plate, still too hot to handle. They are slightly puffy but have a gratifying chew and honest grain flavor. Nothing is simpler: wheat flour and water and fire's effect on them. You might call them plain-tasting, but if warmth and freshness and purity are important, these are essential. Torn-off strips of this warm tortilla are the utensil God intended us to use for shoveling up the chili, cheese, and eggs on a plate of Frontier huevos rancheros.

Some of the best scenery along old Route 66 in Albuquerque is the view from a stool at the lunch counter of **Duran Central Pharmacy** as you watch your huevos rancheros being made from scratch. And we do mean scratch. Wooden dowels are used to roll out rounds of dough into broad beige circles that are then cooked on the grill in plain sight, each flatbread blistering golden brown. Meanwhile, watch the eggs bubble in a butter puddle and get plated in the traditional way, on a corn tortilla, then topped not with salsa but with radiant red chili. What's a better way to start the day than by dipping a griddle-hot flour tortilla brushed with butter into bright yellow yolk and fiery chili?

At Albuquerque's Frontier, huevos smothered with chili steal the show.

It is strange to recommend the huevos rancheros at El Paso's **H&H Car Wash and Coffee Shop**, which we also like for its blindingly hot chile de arból salsa (page 312), but the fact is that a plate of these eggs is one of the gentlest-tempered breakfasts you'll encounter in the Southwest. If you've been on a chile-eating binge, what a fine sop this is! Unlike other versions of the dish, these eggs come smothered with gravy — gossamer stuff that seems little more than butter and milk and maybe some mild cheese. Flecks of red and green pepper decorate the plate, but they are mild ones. The eggs sit on a soft tortilla and are further mollified by mounds of smooth, lard-rich *refritos* and starchy disks of griddle-fried potato which share the plate.

If you need your huevos hot, we recommend a visit to **Nellie's** in Las Cruces, the heart of chile-growing country. The proprietor, Danny Ray Hernandez, Nellie's son, offers traditional huevos rancheros with the brilliant seven-pepper salsa he makes, as well as such incendiary variations on the theme as chile-eggs, in which

Southwest

red and/or green chiles take the place of salsa, and a superhot huevos à la mexicana, which is eggs scrambled with jalapeños.

Parenthetically, mention must be made of the huevos rancheros cooked by chef Mitch Omer at **Hell's Kitchen** in Minneapolis. Far from the nation's great lode of Tex-Mex food, Mitch has created an outlandish gloss on the dish with no regard to tradition. It's got all the ingredients and then some, more in casserole form than as a plate of different things. Mounded high on a tortilla is a baked mesa of spicy black beans and crisp-fried hash-brown potatoes, scrambled eggs, three cheeses, salsa, and sour cream — a dish so formidable that you might want to consider a trowel rather than a fork as the suitable eating tool.

Nellie's in Las Cruces, NM, serves traditional huevos with seven-pepper salsa.

SOUTHWEST'S TOP HUEVOS RANCHEROS (+ 1)

1. **Teresa's Mosaic Cafe:** 2455 N. Silverbell Rd., Tucson, AZ 520-624-4512
2. **Frontier Restaurant:** 2400 Central SE, Albuquerque, NM 505-266-0550 www.frontierrestaurant.com
3. **Duran Central Pharmacy:** 1815 Central Ave. NW, Albuquerque, NM 800-842-5005 or 505-247-4141
4. **Nellie's Café:** 1226 W. Hadley, Las Cruces, NM 505-524-9982
5. **H&H Car Wash and Coffee Shop:** 701 E. Yandell Dr., El Paso, TX 915-533-1144

Also
Hell's Kitchen: 89 S. 9th St., Minneapolis, MN 612-332-4700 Second location: 310 Lake Ave. South, Duluth, MN 218-727-1620 www.hellskitcheninc.com

KING RANCH CASSEROLE
Texas

Not all Texas signature dishes are four-alarm, beefcentric, supersmoked, deep-fried, or sugar-sweet. King Ranch casserole is polite and tender and mild. It is said that there are as many recipes for it as there are Lone Star cooks. The basic elements are canned soup, cheese, tortillas (flour,

The politely traditional chicken casserole of the Lone Star State soothes the soul.

corn, or just chips), and chicken. Ro-Tel brand tomatoes or low-heat chopped green chiles are common.

How a chicken casserole got named for a famous cattle ranch is anybody's guess. Ubiquitous in Texas Junior League cookbooks and once common on the menus of tearooms where ladies lunch (when ladies used to lunch in tearooms), it is today a staple of school lunch cafeterias as well as of Texas-themed caterers. We once went to a party in Houston where King Ranch casserole was the featured attraction at the buffet table, catered by **Buffalo Grille**. It was a modern gloss on the dish, lacking the canned soup and featuring pieces of chicken that had actually been grilled. The Buffalo Grille does not offer King Ranch casserole on its regular menu, but you can order King Ranch spinach enchiladas with cilantro cream sauce.

The one place we highly recommend eating King Ranch casserole (other than in the home of someone's mother) is Georgetown's **Monument Cafe**. It's a lunch special not on the menu every day, but we lucked out on our last visit and finally understood why Texas traditionalists love it so. Our waitress guaranteed that it was "just like home," and while its beige hue is dotted with red bits of pimiento, it is in no way exciting, disturbing, or challenging. Here is an all's-well-with-the-world meal guaranteed to make you feel better even if you didn't feel ill to begin with.

WHERE TO EAT KING RANCH CASSEROLE

1. **Monument Cafe:** 1953 S. Austin Ave., Georgetown, TX 512-930-9586 www.themonumentcafe.com
2. **Buffalo Grille:** 3116 Bissonnet, Houston, TX 713-661-3663 Second location: 1301 S. Voss Rd., Houston, TX 713-784-3663 www.thebuffalogrille.com

KOLACHE
Texas

In central Texas, kolaches outrank doughnuts. Just north of Waco, the small town of West, known for clarity's sake as West Comma Texas, is the state's kolache capital, where the **Czech Stop**, the **Ole Czech Bakery**, and the **Village Bakery** make little square pastries that hold an open-faced dollop of fruit in a center indent rimmed by a puffy pillow of supple dough.

It looks vaguely like the Danish you get for breakfast in any diner, but a really good kolache feels and tastes

Southwest

like a Danish transfigured by charm school. It is so exquisitely tender that a too-eager grip will compress it from a square into a blob. All the good kolache places serve what they make usually within hours of baking it. "Kolache are sold warm from the oven," assures the movable-letter sign above the counter at the Village Bakery, a shop with three small tables and one circular ten-seat seminar table that hosts an ad hoc community kaffeeklatsch throughout most mornings. The coffee drinkers gasped as if they were watching fireworks when we sat at their table and pulled a kolache apart so that a cloud of steam puffed upward. They had directed us to try apricot and prune, intriguing dour fillings that proved to be scarcely as sweet as the dough itself. They're the flavors favored by old-timers, as are poppy seed and cottage cheese. Tourists tend to favor fruitier versions — apple, strawberry, blueberry — as well as those made with cream cheese.

Fruit and cheese kolaches are Old World standards; the Village Bakery added a Tex-American turn to tradition in the early 1950s, when baker Wendell Montgomery, worrying that his big loaves of sausage bread weren't selling well, asked his mother-in-law to come up with a snack-sized version that included the sausage links that are another passion of eastern Europeans who settled the heart of Texas. Her creation was a gloss on Czech *klobasniki,* which are customarily made with ground sausage. Purists still refer to them as that, or possibly as pigs in blankets, reserving the term *kolache* for those filled with fruit, cheese, or poppy seeds. Sa-

vory *klobasnikis* have become a staple of kolache bakeries throughout the state. The Village Bakery makes regular and hot sausage versions, the latter marked by two slits in the top of the bun, and you'll find bakeries that add cheese and jalapeño peppers and even sauerkraut, too.

The widest variety we found was at the **Kolache Factory**, a thirty-three-store Texas chain with outposts in Colorado, Missouri, Indiana, and Kansas. At the Austin store on Lamar Boulevard, we ordered and ate from batches carried forth from the kitchen that were still too hot to handle: classic fruit and cream cheese for under a dollar and utterly Americanized meal-in-one kolaches where the sweet dough encloses pockets of bacon, egg, and cheese.

As with any baked pastry, the fresher the kolache, the better. "Of course it's best the first day," says Phillip Weikel of **Weikel's Bakery** in La Grange, who says he has had a customer pay $80 for overnight air

A collection of kolaches: The beloved puffy pastries of Czech origin outsell doughnuts in Texas.

Peaches and cheese fill a kolache made at Weikel's in La Grange, TX.

shipping of $10 worth of kolaches. But ground service for his mail-order kolaches works, too. Weikel's dough defies going stale; it stays light, moist, and soft for four or five days, a feat he attributes not to unique ingredients and certainly not to preservatives, but to the way it is made and handled. "That's the secret that separates us from bakeries that buy kolache mix in fifty-pound bags — tenderness," he says. "Tenderness now and tenderness tomorrow."

No kolaches anywhere are more intriguing than Weikel's little apricot rectangles, in which the fruit's sunny-sour smack accentuates the yeasty sweetness of the pastry cloud around it, and there are few snacks as authoritative as the *klobasnikis,* with their dramatic harmony of supremely tender golden dough around a vigorously chewy beef sausage from the meat market over in Schulenburg. Weikel's Bakery is in the back of a gas station convenience store; you could walk in for a Coke and a beef stick and not notice that there is something extraordinary to eat here. However, one big hint outside lets travelers know they have found a special place. The sign that rises high above the building and the gas pumps reads, WEIKEL'S BAKERY — WE GOT'CHA KOLACHE.

TOP KOLACHES

1. **Weikel's Bakery:** 2247 W. State Highway 71, La Grange, TX 979-968-9413 www.weikels.com Weikel's is set up for mail-order.
2. **Village Bakery:** 108 E. Oak St., West, TX 254-826-5151
3. **Czech Stop:** 105 N. College St., West, TX 254-826-5316 www.czechstop.com
4. **Ole Czech Bakery:** 511 W. Oak St., West, TX 254-826-3307
5. **Kolache Factory:** 3706 N. Lamar Blvd., Austin, TX 512-467-2253 See www.kolachefactory.com for additional locations.

MIGAS
Texas and Oklahoma

Migas is a textural fun ride of eggs whipped into fluffy curds, tortilla strips that range from crunchy to cornbread-soft, chewy nuggets of sweet sausage, chunks of tomato, and a cloak of rich molten cheese. A Lone Star cognate of the midwestern hoppel poppel (page 257) and Jewish matzoh brei (page 257), migas has

Southwest

to some degree been eclipsed by the rise of the breakfast taco; it is a hearty meal that requires a fork rather than an eat-on-the-run snack.

Migas means "crumbs" in Spanish, and traditional Iberian migas is made with crumbly day-old bread. It seems logical that the migas found in the American Southwest is a Tex-Mex descendant of true-Mex chilaquiles, a casserole of hot peppers, salsa, tortilla strips, and cheese topped with fried eggs, the best version of which we've found at Houston's **Lankford Grocery**. With its concrete floor and "how're ya' doin', hon?" service, this extremely colorful former icehouse is best known for its flabbergasting triple cheeseburger (page 331), but the migas is classic, as is the morning beverage regular customers wash it down with: cold bottles of Shiner bock. Another Houston migas shrine is the **Avalon Diner**, attached to the Avalon Drug Co., where the kitchen makes migas with tostada chips sided by grits and where dieters can get *migas blanco*, made with six egg whites instead of whole eggs and available with oatmeal instead of grits.

Two breakfast/lunch eateries in Austin vie for migas eminence. If quantity is the measure, **Juan in a Million** wins. You will pay extra for cheese (well worth it), but even cheeseless, Juan's heap of eggs scrambled with onions, tomatoes, and tortilla chips is a mighty meal, sided by *refritos* (refried beans), fried potatoes, and flour tortillas. Juan also offers more moderately sized migas breakfast tacos for about $2 each. An Austin favorite for decades, **Cisco's** plate of migas is close to what we consider

Sunny sight: migas — fluffily scrambled eggs with tortilla strips, cheese, tomato, and sausage

perfection: tomatoes, onions, and crisp tortilla chips scrambled into a fluff of sunny yellow eggs and available with a good-sized slice of fajita meat, which is marinated and grilled skirt steak. It's your job to slice fork-sized pieces of the steak, an inspired companion for the traditional migas ingredients. Warning: Do not have a bite of Cisco's buttery, crunch-crusted biscuits. They are so good you will eat way too many and have no room for your migas and fajitas.

While we seldom can resist chicken-fried steak and oven-hot, pecan-studded coffee cake at the **Monument Cafe** north of Austin, migas must also be part of every breakfast in this way-better-than-you-think-it's-going-to-be, three-meals-a-day eatery. The menu boasts of "yard eggs," which means they come from free-range chickens, and sure enough, there is something especially sun-shiny about the buttery yellow eggs scrambled with cheese, diced tomatoes, and small ribbons of tortilla that variously soften and turn crisp, depending on where they are in the pan. On the side come peppered bacon or sausage, salsa to seriously raise the temperature, warm square biscuits, and hash browns. OJ is squeezed to order. You'll also get fresh juice with your breakfast up in Oklahoma City at the estimable **Classen Grill**, where superb migas is served with a brace of soft flour tortillas to use as a handy mitt for picking up mouthfuls if you get bored with a fork.

Migas' legendary ability to cure hangovers is second only to that of *menudo* (tripe and hominy stew), and it tastes especially salubrious when plenty of hot jalapeño peppers are added to the mix. So it is at **Rosie's**, a cantina west of Austin that specializes in breakfast tacos. All the usual egg-meat-potato combos are available, but the choice variant is the migas taco, made with a surfeit of cheese and all the peppers you desire. What's great is the delicious disparity between the soft tortilla that wraps the taco and the wickedly crisp, see-through-thin sheaves of fried tortilla within.

The Classen Grill in Oklahoma City serves superb migas, a traditional cure for a hangover.

BEST MIGAS

1. **Monument Cafe:** 1953 S. Austin Ave., Georgetown, TX
512-930-9586
www.themonumentcafe.com
2. **Classen Grill:** 5124 Classen Circle, Oklahoma City, OK
405-842-0428
www.classengrill.com
3. **Cisco's Restaurant Bakery & Bar:** 1511 E. 6th St., Austin, TX
512-478-2420
4. **Lankford Grocery and Market:** 88 Dennis St., Houston, TX
713-522-9555
5. **Juan in a Million:** 2300 Cesar Chavez St., Austin, TX
512-472-3872
www.juaninamillion.com
6. **Avalon Diner:** 2417 Westheimer Rd., Houston, TX
713-527-8900
www.avalondiner.com
7. **Rosie's Tamale House:** 13436 Highway 71 West, Bee Cave, TX
512-263-5245
Rosie's doesn't open on Tuesdays and generally stops serving by noon, sometimes as early as 11 a.m.

NACHOS JORGE
Houston, Texas

Pretty good nachos are everywhere; hugely bountiful ones aren't hard to find; Nachos Jorge at **Pico's Mex-Mex Restaurant** are in a class by themselves. *Cochinita pibil* puts them over the top. That's succulent,

Southwest

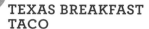

TEXAS BREAKFAST TACO

Nearly as popular as bacon-egg-cheese sandwiches elsewhere, the Tex-Mex breakfast taco is one of the Southwest's most portable and affordable meals. They're very good at Rosie's (page 349), and even better at Helen's Casa Alde in Buda, where Helen Alcala goes to the trouble of rolling out and cooking big golden flour tortillas every morning. Inside these tortillas you can get eggs, sausage, bacon, cheese, and potatoes (listed on the menu as the Fattie) or potatoes, beans, bacon, and cheese (known as the Same, for reasons no one seems to know). Bruce Bilmes and Sue Boyle, the friends who led us to Helen's, noted that "the combination of breakfast foods wrapped in these thick, warm tortillas is a positively terrific way to start the day, especially after they've been dabbed with a little of the fresh salsa served alongside." Buda (pronounced byouda) claims to be "The Outdoor Capital of Texas," and is known for its annual dachshund race in April.

Helen's Casa Alde Cafe: 108 Main St., Buda, TX 512-295-2053

pepper-marinated pork baked in banana leaves and is then shredded and placed on the top of the chips, along with marinated onions, black beans, guacamole, jalapeños, and plenty of creamy melted Chihuahua cheese. The pork is hot and sweet and savory all at once, juicy and chewy, impossible not to devour. Nachos Jorge is listed on Pico's huge and enticing menu as an appetizer, but it is a meal and then some for one person. Better to split it between two or four so you can enjoy sizzling fajitas or chicken mole as an entrée. Regarding a beverage to drink while eating nachos: Pico's margaritas are available in three sizes: 12-ounce, 27-ounce, and 48-ounce.

Pico's Mex-Mex Restaurant:
5941 Bellaire Blvd., Houston, TX
713-662-8383
www.picos.net

ONION-FRIED BURGER
El Reno, Oklahoma

An onion-fried burger fuses beef and onions into something far beyond a mere garnished hamburger. Known and admired throughout Oklahoma (which may be the most hamburger-conscious state in the nation), the onion-fried burger originated in the old frontier settlement of El Reno, just west of Oklahoma City. In this town, when you order a hamburger, you will get an onion-fried burger unless you specifically instruct the cook to leave out the onions. The best way to understand what makes it extraordinary, other than to taste one, is to see how it is made.

At **Johnnie's**, a 560-square-foot diner opened by W. J. "Johnnie" Siler in 1946, grill man Otis Bruce slaps a sphere of ground beef, one-quarter pound and 81 percent lean, onto a hot griddle. He grabs a fistful of very thinly sliced yellow onions — about the same cubage as the round of beef — and gingerly places them on top. Immediately he uses a spatula to flatten the onions and the meat together, creating a broad circular patty with an uneven edge. He presses this down three or four times, slightly changing the angle of attack with each press, and pressing only one half to two thirds of the patty each time. The ribbons of onion are mashed deep into the top of the soft raw meat, which assumes a craggy surface because the spatula hits it from multiple angles. Once the underside is cooked, the burger is flipped. The air around the grill clouds with the steam of sizzling onions. After another few minutes, the hamburger is scooped off the grill with all the darkened caramelized onions that have become part of it, and it is put it on a bun, onion side up.

Edward Graham, proprietor of **Robert's**, a counter-only cafe one block east of Johnnie's, says that his place has always been popular with children, who try to grab a few onion-fried hamburgers after school before they go home for supper. But the sneaked snack seldom goes undiscovered. "When they walk in the door at home, their mothers can smell exactly where they've been," Mr. Graham says. As we devoured a brace of Robert's hamburgers, made in an especially juicy configuration with glistening, limp squiggles of onion falling from inside the bun, we asked him who Robert was, figur-

In El Reno, OK, no one knows for sure who originated the incredible burger with caramelized onions.

ing that this restaurant must be the fountainhead of onion-fried burgers. It is a museum-piece town cafe, El Reno's oldest extant hamburger shop, going back to 1926. "Robert is gone," Mr. Graham told us. "But he was not the one who started this place. I believe it was built by two brothers who called it Bob's White Rock. They planned to open White Rocks all over the West." Graham was quite certain that the brothers were not the inventors of the onion-fried burger, just entrepreneurs who wanted to promulgate it.

Steve Gallaway, Johnnie's owner, told us that it was a pair of peripatetic railroad men who came up with the onion-fried burger concept sometime in the early 1900s, in an effort to settle down in one place. The genealogy of this regional delight is byzantine, and as we ate around town, we became more and more confused by the intricate relationships of the various hamburger chefs, all of whom

Southwest

THE WORLD'S LARGEST ONION-FRIED BURGER

To honor its heritage and pay tribute to decades of grill cooks who have created its reputation as America's foremost hamburger town, El Reno cooks a 400-pound onion-fried burger and serves it on a 350-pound bun on the first Saturday in May. Using specialized equipment designed by the local vo-tech school, the hamburger is cooked, flipped, and hoisted into its bun to resemble a normal-sized one but a thousand times bigger, and dressed with 10 gallons of pickles and plenty of mustard. After it is consumed (in portions cut out using the end of a tomato juice can), the town's restaurants serve more burgers inside the restaurants and on the street to some 20,000 celebrants who come from all over Oklahoma, a state that surely deserves to be known as America's Hamburger Heaven.

seem to like and admire each other (and many of whom have worked for each other), despite the fact that they are competitors. Finally we felt we had a good shot at determining onion-fried burger provenance when we walked into **Sid's**, another block east, where the proprietor, Marty Hall (who learned the business working at Johnnie's), has filled his place with archival photographs of El Reno. Mr. Hall makes a hamburger in which the onions are exquisitely caramelized by their term on the griddle, and yet despite his fondness for history, he couldn't tell us much about its origins. He did explain that the restaurant is named Sid's after his dad, whose dream was to open a hamburger place but who passed away before he and his son could do it together. As we left Sid's, still wondering when and where the unique burger began, Mr. Hall did provide us with a nice summary of how the onion-fried burger fits into the small town's allure. "A hamburger, good people, and Route 66: You won't get more American than El Reno."

The next morning, while at the Johnnie's counter eating Arkansas sandwiches (that's a pair of pancakes layered with a pair of eggs), we did at last find what seems like an authoritative description of the onion-fried burger's beginnings. Bob Johnson, who, as usual, came for breakfast, said with certainty that it was his father, along with a man named Ross Davis, who opened El Reno's first onion-fried burger restaurant, the Hamburger Inn, sometime in the 1920s. About ten years later, Mr. Johnson's uncle, Darrell Hurst, bought it; then in World War II it was taken over by a guy remembered only as Hindy. In the early 1950s, Ross Davis bought it back from Hindy. "That's when I lost track," Mr. Johnson confessed. "I moved to Alaska in 1957, and when I returned in 1975, Ross had opened Ross's Drive-In" (although the Hamburger Inn was still operating, under other management).

One piece of history we learned pretty much for certain over breakfast that day: Morgan Stafford, who owned a town burger shop about five decades ago, was the man who developed El Reno slaw. Yes, that is right: *El Reno slaw!* Amazingly, this Canadian River valley town of some 15,000 citizens has yet another food specialty all its own — the slaw that is used on local versions of the Coney Island frankfurter. A pickly-sweet, mustard-colored hash of finely minced cabbage, the slaw is vaguely like piccalilli or relish, but it has a taste and drippy texture like no other. Its usual place is atop the chili that adorns a weenie on a standard-issue El Reno Coney, transforming a tidy bunned hot dog into seriously messy fork-food. Nearly as popular as onion-fried burgers, slaw-and-chili-topped hot dogs are available at all the hamburger restaurants. Each has its own variation of the slaw recipe, the formulas for which have been passed down by generations of grill cooks. Several local eaters consider slaw El Reno's gastronomic pride every bit as much as the onion-fried burger. "We have some so crazy for it that they get it on their hamburgers!" Steve Galloway said, with sincere wonder at the aberration. (To our callow onion-fried burger palates, the combo is a great idea.) "And some come in and order nothing but a bowl of slaw and a spoon to eat it with!" *This* is a town of deep culinary passion.

THE BIG 3 OF EL RENO'S ONION-FRIED HAMBURGERS

1. **Johnnie's Grill:** 301 S. Rock Island Ave., El Reno, OK 405-262-4721
2. **Robert's Grill:** 300 S. Bickford Ave., El Reno, OK 405-262-1262

NATIONAL COWBOY & WESTERN HERITAGE MUSEUM

The Louvre of buckaroo life is a vast museum and interpretive center boasting an extensive collection of western art (classical and modern) and paeans to championship cowboys and the legendary bucking horses and rank bulls they rode. Permanent exhibits include the Fine Arms Gallery, the Rodeo Gallery, the Native American Gallery, and odes to pop culture icons of the West, from the 101 Ranch Wild West Show and John Wayne to Tom Selleck and TV's cowboy heroes. Each year in September the museum hosts the Traditional Cowboy Arts Association's Exhibition and Sale. If you are looking for the very best roping saddle or silver spurs with jingle-jangle jinglebobs, you will find them here to admire and, if you are a very high roller, to buy.

National Cowboy & Western Heritage Museum: 1700 N.E. 63rd St., Oklahoma City, OK 405-478-2250 www.nationalcowboymuseum.org

Southwest

3. Sid's Diner: 300 S. Choctaw Ave., El Reno, OK
405-262-7757

PECAN PIE
Texas

Please feel sorry for us. We keep eating pecan pies from the **Texas Pie Company** and **Royer's Round Top Café** and have had no success deciding which is best. We have little doubt that these are Texas's great ones — a determination of which we are pretty proud, given the fact that there's a passel of great pecan pies to eat in this state, which produces some 30 million pounds of pecans each year.

For the ultimate classic version, Bud Royer's takes the cake — a maximum dose of corn-syrup sweetness hand in hand with the huge toasty nut flavor of really fresh, crisp pecans. The nuts are jam-packed across the top of the pie, two or three deep in many places, so that no matter how syrupy the underside, it is still funda-

Ultra-rich chocolate pie studded with pecans, the pride of the Monument Cafe in Georgetown, TX

mentally a pie that honors pecans. It's hard to say whether the crust is crumbly or flaky, for it is both, and just savory enough to add minor harmony to the Karo-nut duet. Mention also must be made of Royer's chocolate Toll House pie. Although not a pecan pie by any stretch, it is studded with a copious number of pecans, which lend the ultra-chocolate flavor a luxury that is richer than cream. You've got to love the warning on the Round Top menu: "We reserve the right to charge you for pie and Häagen-Dazs even if you don't order it! It is a matter of principle . . . You don't drive all this way and not eat pie!!!!!"

Then there's the Texas Pie Company, the motto of which is "Life's Short — Eat More Pie." The pecans are crowded not just on top of the pie but seemingly all through the sweet-syrup part down below. One big plus for this place is that it makes tiny, whole single-serving pies. That means there is more excellent crust; and if any pie needs good crust to balance its hypersweet nature, it is pecan.

The Texas Pie Company makes its pies small, ensuring a greater ratio of crust to hypersweet filling.

We've cited our favorite traditional pecan pies, but we cannot abandon this exegesis without mention of the signature pie of the **Monument Cafe** in Georgetown. It is chocolate pie — a thick, fudgy cream topped with a ribbon of whipped cream and supported by a crust that is not a crust but rather a shelf of pecans stuck together in a sweet glaze. A sensational idea, rocketed into the stratosphere by the fact that these nuts are as crisp and buttery as if they just came out of the shell.

TOP 2 PECAN PIES (IN ALPHABETICAL ORDER, BECAUSE WE REFUSE TO CHOOSE)

Royer's Round Top Café: 105 Main St., Round Top, TX
979-249-3611
www.royersroundtopcafe.com
Royer's sells by mail-order and features a pie-of-the-month plan.

Texas Pie Co.: 202 W. Center St., Kyle, TX
512-268-5885
www.texaspiecompany.com

Also

Monument Cafe: 1953 S. Austin Ave., Georgetown, TX
512-930-9586
www.themonumentcafe.com

PICO DE GALLO
Tucson, Arizona

Pico de gallo, Spanish for "beak of the rooster," is a salsa traditionally made from chiles, tomatoes, and onions, but in south Tucson, pico de gallo is

Tucson's Taqueria Pico de Gallo replaces traditional salsa with a medley of chile-sprinkled fruit.

a gorgeous bouquet of giant chunks of watermelon, coconut, pineapple, mango, and even some jicama, just cut and glistening with moisture, that is spritzed with lime juice and liberally sprinkled with a red-hot chile-powder mix. The fruit is presented in a big red party cup, and it is stuck with four or five long wooden picks for fetching the pieces you want. The red-hot spice delivers a lip-tingling punch and elicits all the sweetness from the fruit it seasons. It's a heady culinary collusion that marshals taste buds at attention for the fine, low-cost Sonoran Mexican meal to come at **Taqueria Pico de Gallo,** the tiny restaurant that named itself for the refreshing fruit creation.

Southwest

Taqueria Pico de Gallo: 2618 S. Sixth Ave., Tucson, AZ 520-623-8775

SONORAN HOT DOG
Southern Arizona

We cannot say for sure whether this very local variant of the wiener actually came from Sonora or the Sonoran Desert or simply got its name because its flavor evokes Mexico. Found only in southern Arizona, particularly in Tucson, where it is sold by an estimated 250 taquerias, street carts, and eateries, it is perhaps the wildest and certainly the hottest of America's hot dogs, especially when served, as at **El Güero Canelo**, with a grilled yellow pepper. El Güero Canelo's chef, Arturo Contreras, begins with an all-beef frank wrapped completely in bacon. The swaddled dog is cooked in a pan until the bacon infuses it. Enough bacon grease remains in the pan from previous dogs that the process is close to deep-frying. The cooked dog, on which the bacon has become more a veil of flavor than a strip of meat, is nestled in an extra-large, extra-sturdy roll from a nearby Mexican bakery and topped with pinto beans, grilled onions, raw onions, and chopped tomatoes, then hot jalapeño sauce, mayonnaise, and mustard. How right it is with a bottle of made-in-Mexico Coca-Cola or Jarritos Mandarina soda pop!

Historians find evidence of the Sonoran dog as far back as the 1960s, but it was not until the mid-1980s that it became a popular street food in Tucson. El Güero Canelo opened in 1993 as a small hut and has since expanded to become two restaurants with full Mexican menus that range from *menudo* (tripe and hominy stew) for breakfast on the weekend to *carne asada caramelos* (mini quesadillas). For the full street-food experience, stroll along Fourth Avenue in south Tucson around midnight on a weekend. Sonoran hot dogs are dished out by dozens of street-corner carts, each with its own twist on the hot, hot hot dog.

TOP 2 SONORAN HOT DOGS (NOT COUNTING THOSE SOLD FROM STREET CARTS)

1. **El Güero Canelo:** 5201 S. Twelfth Ave., Tucson, AZ 520-295-9005
Second location: 2480 N. Oracle Rd., Tucson, AZ 520-882-8977
www.elguerocanelo.com

2. **BK Carne Asada & Hot Dogs:** 2680 N. First Ave., Tucson, AZ 520-207-2245
Second location: 5118 S. Twelfth Ave., Tucson, AZ 520-295-0105
www.bktacos.com

SOPAIPILLA
New Mexico

Every restaurant that serves true New Mex food has sopaipillas on the menu. If by some chance you have spent your life sopaipilla-deprived, know that these delightful breadstuffs are airy pillows of fried bread that generally come in the basket where dinner rolls might be at a mainstream restaurant meal. They are made from dough that is rolled out ultra-thin, then tossed into boiling lard so that they instantly puff up and become ever so slightly crisp but mostly very tender. It is essential that they be served hot and eaten warm. Nearly every place that serves them keeps a pitcher of honey on the table, as traditional a topping as butter is for bread.

Sopaipillas aren't just a bread substitute. Yes, they are wonderful for mopping chili off a plate, but they are also made for stuffing. Cut open hot from the fryer, they make a fantastic wrapper for carne seca, chili, or refried beans and rice. You'll get them on the side of every meal at **Rancho de Chimayó**, a romantic restaurant in the foothills of the Sangre de Cristo Mountains, where one of the essential dishes on the menu is *sopaipillas rellenas,* in which the triangular fried breads are stuffed with beef or chicken, beans, tomatoes, and Spanish rice and topped with your

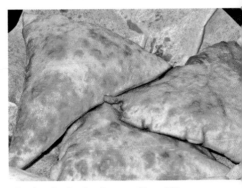

Cloud-soft, the fried sopaipillas of New Mexico tone down chili or sop up honey.

choice of red or green chiles. At **Las Trancas** down in Las Cruces, the stuffed sopaipillas, formally known as *sopaipillas compuesta,* are picture-perfect and, despite the town's proclivity for four-alarm food, stuffed with mild, sunshiny red chili. **Tortilla Flats** in Santa Fe offers a choice of tortillas or fine sopaipillas alongside every meal and also makes a specialty of a dessert called *sopaipilla helada,* sized for two or three: one big, hot sopaipilla loaded with vanilla ice cream, strawberries, chocolate chips, and whipped cream.

If you are looking for the best sopaipillas in the Southwest, go to the **Plaza Café** in Santa Fe just after 11 a.m. That's when baskets of them start to emerge from the kitchen, still glistening from their quick bath in the kettle and venting puffs of steam when opened up. Hot and cloud-soft, these golden pillows are simply wonderful to eat plain — no honey necessary — and as a dipping, mopping, and gathering tool when tackling the Plaza's green chili, a hearty stew loaded with big chunks of vegetables.

Southwest

Visit the Plaza in Santa Fe just after 11 a.m. for the best sopaipillas in the Southwest.

Whereas some sopaipillas tend to be small and chewy, those served at the very remote country eatery known as **El Farolito** ("little lantern") are large and tender. Tear off a broad piece and it makes one half of the simplest imaginable New Mex meal when dipped into a bowl of intense pureed red chili. If you are not going to use sopaipillas as a chili medium, the squeeze bottle of honey is handy for adding sweet avoirdupois to what surely must be the lightest breadstuff on earth.

Over 300,000 pilgrims a year visit the sanctuary in Chimayó, NM.

EL SANTUARIO DE NUESTRO SEÑOR DE ESQUIPULAS

The town of Chimayó is famous not only for Rancho de Chimayó's classic New Mex food and for the quality of cloth made by Chimayó weavers; it is also home to "the Lourdes of America," a tiny chapel erected in 1814 on land believed to have miraculous curative powers. The old stone *santuario* is adjoined by a small room filled with discarded crutches and touching letters of devotion left behind by true believers. Over 300,000 pilgrims visit each year to take some of the curative dirt available from the center of the floor of the small church.

Santuario: 1 mile south of the intersection of NM Route 76 and NM Route 520, Chimayó, NM
505-351-4889
www.archdiocesesantafe.org

NEW MEXICO'S BEST SOPAIPILLAS

1. **Plaza Café:** 54 Lincoln Ave., Santa Fe, NM
   505-982-1664
   www.thefamousplazacafe.com
2. **Rancho de Chimayó:** Santa Fe County Road 98 (State Route 520), Chimayó, NM
   505-351-4444 or 505-984-2100
   www.ranchodechimayo.com
3. **El Farolito:** 1212 Main St., El Rito, NM
   575-581-9509
4. **Las Trancas:** 1008 S. Solano Dr., Las Cruces, NM
   575-524-1430
5. **Tortilla Flats:** 3139 Cerrillos Rd., Santa Fe, NM
   505-471-8685
   www.tortillaflats.com

TAMALE PIE
Arizona and New Mexico

Few restaurants offer tamale pie, because its reputation is that of low-budget chow made at home for a hungry family. No dish could be further from that image than the tamale pie served at Tucson's **Cafe Poca Cosa**. Nothing in this superstylish culinary shrine is plebeian. In fact, most things written on the blackboard menu are not recognizable, even to Mexican-food lovers. When you order tamale pie, you will get a dish more like a soufflé — cream and cheese and corn masa whipped with a handful of kernels into an ethereal custard, sometimes around veins of green chile, sometimes not. There is a different variation every day. We've had it served in a tropical incarnation, smothered with leeks and a sweet mango sauce, as well as a version that our taste buds told us was Italian: *pastel de elote en berenjena,* the corn pie draped with a swarthy tomato-garlic mixture and big dark chunks of eggplant. With all the cream that is used, the pie is luxurious and yet maintains the honest virtues of the corn that is its essence. The menu lists tamale pie as a vegetarian entrée, and it is, but no carnivore should be dissuaded.

Cafe Poca Cosa in Tucson, where tamale pie meets haute cuisine

Green tamale pie at **Papa Felipe's Mexican Restaurant** in Albuquerque broadcasts the palmy essence of New Mexico chiles and is well apportioned with Papa's excellent carne adovada (page 302) as well as chopped vegetables larded into the corn masa medium. Up in Taos, you will find a cutting-edge variation at **Graham's Grille**, a high-consciousness cafe that is earnest in its cooking but fun in the serving (there aren't too many dishes more fun than the house Big Skillet: baked macaroni and cheddar with green chiles and bacon). At dinner, a big plate of Taos Tamale Pie is built around green chiles and jack cheese, includes black beans, and is decorated with roasted corn, tomatoes, and avocado.

GREAT TAMALE PIES

1. **Cafe Poca Cosa:** 110 E. Pennington St., Tucson, AZ 520-622-6400 www.cafepocacosatucson.com

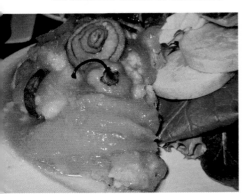

At its finest, tamale pie is a souffléed custard of corn, masa, cheese, and chile.

Southwest

OKLAHOMA STOCKYARDS

Many customers at the Cattlemen's Steak House work in and around the adjoining Oklahoma National Stockyards, which is the largest stocker-feeder cattle market in the world. The slaughterhouses and packing plants are gone, but the Monday-to-Wednesday auctions start at 8 a.m. and can run long into the night. A catwalk over the cow pens provides visitors a view of vast herds of cattle, and all around the yards is a district known as Stockyards City: a great place to buy boots, a Stetson, equestrian tack, and other necessary cowboy gear. The stockyards' website offers daily market reports as well as a link to live auctions around the nation.

Oklahoma National Stockyards: 107 Livestock Exchange Building, Oklahoma City, OK
405-235-8675
www.onsy.com

2. **Papa Felipe's Mexican Restaurant:** 9800 Menaul Blvd. NE, Albuquerque, NM
505-292-8877
www.papafelipes.com
3. **Graham's Grille:** 106 Paseo del Pueblo Norte, Taos, NM
575-751-1350
www.grahamsgrille.com

TESTICLES
Cattle Country

"Lamb fries are a lost art," declared Nancy Ann Clark, whose late husband, Warren, started the estimable **Clark's Outpost** up in Tioga, Texas, in 1974. Also known as prairie oysters, barnyard jewels, cowboy caviar, or, on jocular menus, tendergroin, these are the tenderest part of a young male animal. Mrs. Clark calls them lamb fries, but they are more common throughout the West in their bovine form. On frontier ranches, a young steer's balls were a special treat cowboys enjoyed for supper at the end of a hard day of branding and castrating. Mrs. Clark explained that you must be careful when you buy testicles, lest the butcher sell you big, tough ones from an old bull. "We use only the small ones," she says. "We skin them, we cut them, and we fry them to order. We go through so many that I have to tell our butcher to start accumulating fries as the spring approaches, because he doesn't slaughter in the summer and we can't go that long without them." Clark's cooks up over a ton of the delicate organ meat each year. Fried crisp but melting-soft inside, they do not taste like chicken. They remind us of sweetbreads: rich and smooth and, dare we say, nutty. Clark's serves the cattle-country treat with either rugged pan gravy or cocktail sauce for dipping.

At Denver's grand old **Buckhorn Exchange** (holder of Colorado liquor license #1), the Rocky

Whether you call them lamb fries, cowboy caviar, or prairie oysters, testicles taste good.

Mountain oysters are thickly sliced and fried long enough for the batter around them to get crisp and crumbly. The batter is full-flavored, so much so that the meat itself is elusive. For squeamish eaters, that is probably a good thing.

At the **Cattlemen's Steak House** in the Oklahoma City stockyards, lamb fries come as an hors d'oeuvre in a mound on a plate with a bowl of cocktail sauce for dipping and half a lemon to squeeze on top. Their flavor and texture are, to our taste, the cowboy cognate of New England fried clams but earthy rather than oceanic. Cattlemen's also uses gonads as a key ingredient in its superb steak soup, a lusty, eat-it-with-a-fork brew of thick-cut vegetables and chunks of tender steak.

We once filed a report that began "Greetings from the land of a thousand testicles." It was datelined Krebs, Oklahoma, which has been known for its Italian restaurants since 1925, when Pete Prichard, a local coal miner, opened **Pete's Place** to serve family-style meals and his home-brewed beer. For reasons still unclear, every one of those Italian restaurants serves lamb fries as the prelude to a big feed that includes spaghetti, meatballs, outsized ravioli, and garlic bread, plus steak, sausage, or chicken. While we weren't all that impressed by Pete's Italian fare, we did appreciate the way wickedly crisp cracker-crumb crust surrounds the painfully tender organ meat. In 1980, Pete's nephew Frank opened **Roseanna's** in McAlester (home of the annual Italian festival), where you can have the same big family-style dinners but no lamb-fry hors d'oeuvres. If you want to eat testicles here, you get them as an entrée. (The best Italian food in the area is not at a restaurant but at **Lovera's Family Grocery**, which is known for its hickory-smoked summer sausage and gourds of creamy caviocavallo cheese.)

NOTEWORTHY TESTICLES

1. **Clark's Outpost:** 101 Highway 377, Tioga, TX
940-437-2414
www.clarksoutpost.com
2. **Cattlemen's Steak House:** 1309 S. Agnew Ave., Oklahoma City, OK
405-236-0416
www.cattlemensrestaurant.com
3. **Buckhorn Exchange:** 1000 Osage St., Denver, CO
303-534-9505
www.buckhorn.com
4. **Pete's Place:** 120 S.W. 8th, Krebs, OK
918-423-2042
www.petes.org

Southwest

At the Cattlemen's Steak House in Oklahoma City, the testicle appetizer might be mistaken for fried clams.

5. Roseanna's Italian Food: 205 E. Washington, McAlester, OK 918-423-2055 www.roseannas.com

Also
Lovera's Family Grocery: 95 N.W. 6th, Krebs, OK 918-423-2842 www.iloveitalian.com

TOPOPO SALAD
Arizona

Monica Flin, founder of the **El Charro Café**, is said to have conceived topopo salad after seeing the volcano Popocatépeti outside Mexico City. *Topopo* means "volcano," and that is what this Mexican chef's salad looks like: a conical monument of lettuce and vegetables in a cilantro-lime dressing, with columns of cheese, carrots, and celery running up the outside, a wheel of tomato strewn with olive chunks on top, all resting on a foundation of a tostada. Chicken, shrimp, and carne seca can be included if you choose, and there is a vegan version as well. All around the monolith are tomato chunks, avocado slices, and chunks of red pepper. It is a dazzling sight and a bracing meal.

Most of the good restaurants in south Tucson serve topopo salad, and we've had it in Mexican restaurants as far away as Michigan and Washington State, but in our minds it is an Arizona dish. **Micha's** is a south Tucson Mexican food fiesta where its iterations are nearly endless: red or green chili, chicken, carne asada, carne seca, ground beef, or squash. In Scottsdale, **Los Olivos** adds cottage cheese on top. One of the biggest and best topopo salads is that served at **Maria Bonita Mexican Restaurant** on North Oracle Road in Tucson. What makes it a standout is the chicken, which in lesser versions is

A dazzling topopo salad rises from the plate like its volcanic namesake.

bland and boiled-tasting. Maria Bonita's white and dark meat shreds are moist and speckled with spice, excellently complemented by the black olives supplied in abundance.

TOP TOPOPO SALADS

1. **Maria Bonita Mexican Restaurant:** 5851 N. Oracle Rd., Tucson, AZ
520-293-6588
2. **El Charro Café:** 311 N. Court Ave., Tucson, AZ
520-622-1922
See www.elcharrocafe.com for additional locations.
3. **Micha's:** 2908 S. Fourth Ave., Tucson, AZ
520-623-5307
www.michascatering.com
4. **Los Olivos Mexican Patio:** 7328 2nd St., Scottsdale, AZ
480-946-2256

VALOMILK
Kansas City, Kansas

"Not to be personal, but are you going to eat this right away?" asks the lady behind the counter in a Kansas City souvenir store when we buy a couple of packs of Valomilks. When we tell her our intentions of immediate gratification, she reaches under the cash register and offers us each two squares of Bounty paper towels. "You'll need this," she advises, running her finger across the motto under the candy's name on its package: "The Original 'Flowing Center' Candy Cups."

No kidding! There is no way to eat one of these marshmallow-filled

Paper towels are recommended when you eat the "flowing center" candy called Valomilk.

chocolates gracefully without momentous spillage. The moment your teeth cut through the outside chocolate wall, the marshmallow inside cascades out. So, presuming you want to keep globs of it off your clothes and your chin, neck, and chest, the only possible strategy is to lean forward and eat it the way a dog eats, thus making certain that the filling falls on the plate, napkin, or table in front of you. If you like an old-fashioned creamy chocolate treat that is reminiscent of times long before chocolate became devilish and sinful, it is well worth the effort.

Valomilks are made in Merriam, a suburb of Kansas City, and are not directly available by mail-order. They can be found at Cracker Barrel, the Vermont Country Store, and a handful of groceries and drugstores in the K.C. area.
www.valomilk.com

Southwest

GREAT PLAINS AND WEST

NEBRASKA:
see below

Mountlake Terrace
Puyallup • Seattle
WASHINGTON
Sandpoint • Coram
Spokane • • Bigfork
• Coeur d'Alene

Cannon Beach • Seaside
Lincoln City • Tillamook
Oceanside • Vancouver
Newport • Portland
Waldport • South Beach
Florence • Yachats

Clinton •

MONTANA

Fairmont • Butte

Big Timber •

OREGON

IDAHO

West Yellowstone •

Boise •

Sheridan •

Shoshoni •

WYOMING

Marshall
San Francisco
Oakland
Berkeley
San Ramon • Reno
• Sacramento
Pleasanton
Redwood City
Pescadero
Palo Alto
San Jose
Gilroy
Castroville

Winnemucca •

Elko •

Brigham City •

Salt Lake City •
Sandy •

NEVADA

UTAH

CALIFORNIA

Nipomo
Guadalupe
Santa Maria
Casmalia

La Canada • Glendale
Hollywood • Los Angeles
Inglewood • Cabazon
Irvine • Palm Springs
Corona del Mar • Indio
Newport Coast
Solana Beach
Encinitas
Pacific Beach • Julian
La Jolla
Ocean Beach • Santa Ysabel
San Diego

Scottsbluff • South Sioux City
Gering • **NEBRASKA**
Omaha • Bellevue
Grand Island •

CALIFORNIA

Barbecued Oysters: Marshall, 367
Beef Jerky: Redwood City, 305
Beignets: Berkeley, 370
Chicken and Waffles: Los Angeles, 307
Chile Relleno: Glendale, 312
Chocolate Espresso Twinkie: Berkeley, 371
Cinnamon Raisin Toast: Berkeley, 419
Cream of Artichoke Soup: Castroville and Pescadero, 374
Cupcake: San Francisco, 376
Date Shake: Cabazon, Indio, Newport Coast, and Palm Springs, 378
Doughnut: Inglewood, Sacramento, San Francisco, and San Jose, 381
Fish Taco: Encinitas, La Jolla, Ocean Beach, San Diego, San Francisco, and Solana Beach, 384
French Dip: Corona del Mar, Irvine, La Canada, and Los Angeles, 386
French Fries: Corona del Mar and Ocean Beach, 247
Garlic Fries: Gilroy, Palo Alto, Pleasanton, and San Ramon, 387
Granola: La Jolla, 389
Hamburger: Ocean Beach and Sacramento, 328
Horchata: Los Angeles and San Francisco, 338
Hot Chocolate: Oakland and San Francisco, 390
Iced Coffee: San Francisco, 393
Ici Ice Cream: Berkeley, 393
Jersey Sauce: Oakland, 396
Key Lime Pie: Palo Alto, 173
Macaroon: Berkeley, 398
Morning Bun: Berkeley, Oakland, and San Francisco, 399
Pancakes: Hollywood and San Francisco, 402
Pie Crust Cookie: Julian and Santa Ysabel, 407
Pizza: Berkeley, 50
Pu-erh Tea: Oakland, 397
Rhubarb Tartlet: San Francisco, 412
Santa Maria Barbecue: Casmalia, Guadalupe, Nipomo, and Santa Maria, 413
Scrapple: Berkeley, 372
Sourdough Bread: Berkeley, Oakland, and San Francisco, 418
Stamina Noodles: Pacific Beach, 420
Taco Truck: Oakland and San Francisco, 420

IDAHO

Basque Dinner: Boise, 368
French Fries: Coeur d'Alene, 247
Hamburger: Coeur d'Alene, 328
Huckleberry Sweets: Sandpoint, 391
Idaho Spud Bar: Boise, 395

MONTANA

Huckleberry Sweets: Big Timber, Bigfork, Clinton, Coram, and West Yellowstone, 391
Pork Chop Sandwich: Butte and Fairmont, 412

NEBRASKA

Cabbage Burger (Runza): Gering, 411
Catfish: Omaha, 143
Coney Island: Grand Island, 233
Hamburger: Bellevue, 328
Plains Mexican: Scottsbluff, 408
Sour Cream Raisin Pie: South Sioux City, 287

NEVADA

Basque Dinner: Elko, Reno, and Winnemucca, 368

OREGON

Biscuits: Portland, 134
Crab Louis: Portland and Seaside, 371
Cup of Coffee: Portland, 374
Cupcake: Portland, 376
Doughnut: Portland, 381
Hazelnut Milk Shake: Portland, 389
Hot Chocolate: Portland, 390
Maple Bar: Portland, 382
Matcha Tea: Portland, 398
Oregon Clam Chowder: Cannon Beach, Florence, Newport, Oceanside, Portland, and Seaside, 400
Pancakes: Portland, 402
Triple-Berry Toast: Yachats, 375
Seafood Market/Cafes: Cannon Beach, Lincoln City, South Beach, Tillamook, and Waldport, 417

BARBECUED OYSTERS
North Coast California

Barbecued oysters are sold at seafood joints and stand-up oyster bars all along the northern stretch of California's Pacific Highway. At Tomales Bay, where the **Hog Island Oyster Company** has been harvesting Sweetwaters, Kumamotos, and Atlantics for years, they are sold by the dozen, ready to shuck and eat or take home and cook, but only a few years ago Hog Island installed a small restaurant in the **Marshall Store**, a few miles south of its wholesale/retail operation, and here you can enjoy cooked oysters on the spot, at their best.

Dining al fresco on wine barrels outside the Marshall Store in Marshall, CA

What makes these barbecued oysters especially good? Partly it is the al fresco tables made of boards set out on wine barrels by the side of the highway, where the Tomales Bay breeze wafts over your meal. Mostly it's just-opened Hog Island oysters that are big and sparkling with

Basted with butter and garlic and warmed on the grill, Hog Island oysters retain their plump sparkle.

briny flavor. "There is no secret," says the man at the grill. "Not as long as there is butter. Butter, lots of garlic, and parsley." This is the mixture he brushes over the oysters as they cook on the grate. He also advises that the fire cannot be too high or the oysters' moisture will boil and they will jump out of their shells. Once warmed in the shell with butter and garlic, they are dabbed with barbecue sauce and presented by the half-dozen with garlic toast. They aren't really cooked so much as warmed, thus retaining their plumpness and that detonation of juicy marine flavor that makes oyster-eating orgasmic. Oysters Rockefeller also are available, topped with a luxurious spinach and cheese mix as they cook.

Marshall Store: 19225 State Route 1, Marshall, CA
415-663-1339
www.themarshallstore.com

Hog Island Oyster Co.: 20215 State Route 1, Marshall, CA
415-663-9218
www.hogislandoysters.com

West

BASQUE DINNER
Idaho and Nevada

Three questions: (1) Are you extremely hungry? (2) Do you like garlic? (3) Do you really like garlic? If you answer yes to all of the above, you need to sit down for a traditional Basque dinner as served in Nevada, Idaho, and a few places in California. The legacy of shepherds who came to the American West in the late nineteenth century, they are big feeds designed to satisfy hungry men who have spent months living solitary lives and eating off the land. When these guys came to town, they brought formidable appetites.

At restaurants and hotel dining rooms that carry on the tradition, the way it works is this: You are seated at a table with strangers, once a custom suited to lonely shepherds, now ideal for travelers wanting to share and mingle. (Need we say that these places are not where you want to go for an intimate dinner or romantic assignation?) Hard-crusted bread, usually unsliced and ready to tear, is part of every meal; red wine is de rigueur. There may be a written menu or there may not. In either case, you have but one choice to make, and that is what entrée you want. Everything else, after the soup, is brought to the table family-style.

About the soup: It will be a hearty one, such as lentil, chowder, or chicken noodle; our favorite is known as drunkard's soup, occasionally available at **Louis' Basque Corner** in Reno. It is chicken stock loaded with garlic, croutons, and eggs cracked and dropped into the simmering broth. Another not-to-be-missed starter is the cabbage soup at the **Star Hotel**

COWBOY POETRY GATHERING

Of all the things we've written, the worst by far was a song. We didn't do it because the music muse beckoned, but because we were attending the National Cowboy Poetry Gathering and had signed up for a songwriting class taught by one of the legendary writer-performers of cowboy music, Ian Tyson. We thought we could sit in and observe, but Mr. Tyson insisted that everyone who attended had to write. The song is best forgotten, but we cherish memories of that week in Elko, when we had the opportunity to hear truly talented singers, poets, and storytellers; meet top practitioners of such frontier crafts as saddlemaking and horsehair braiding; view great western art; and hang out with thousands of people from around the country and the world who cherish the culture of the cowboy. The gathering is an annual event at the end of January, sponsored by the Western Folklife Center.

Western Folklife Center: 501 Railroad St., Elko, NV 775-738-7508 www.westernfolklife.org

in Elko. After the soup course, brace yourself for beans and salad and big dishes of what could be the entrée but is just its prelude: paella, tripe stew, pigs' feet, beef tongue, lamb stew, spaghetti, pickled tongue, and potatoes. The main course will be something significant, such as steak, lamb chops, or cod. Then comes dessert, which is

WOOLIES

If you are an equestrian planning to ride in severely cold weather, consider donning the buckaroo's warmest piece of apparel, wooly chaps. Traditionally made of white angora wool from sheep tended by Basque shepherds in Nevada and Idaho, "woolies" became an emblem of north-country cowboy life almost a century ago, then a symbol of dude-ranch style in the middle of the twentieth century. Whatever they represent, the fact is that there is no better protection against bitter cold. If the temperature is above freezing, you will swelter in them; but if it's 10 below, there's nothing cozier. Vintage leggings can sometimes be found in tack stores or online auctions. But if you want some made to order, expect to spend at least $1,000 (for all that good wool and expert leather tooling of the belt), and to wait several weeks.

Leather Legends: 121 W. River St., Fromberg, MT 406-668-7773 www.leatherlegends.com

generally the only course that isn't garlicked. Before and after this redoubtable meal, the beverage of choice is the bittersweet Basque *digestif* known as *picon* punch. Having shared one's feast with strangers, it is natural to linger and chat in the afterglow.

If you'd like to have a modest portion of Basque food, Winnemucca's **Martin Hotel**, a century-old gathering place that once was a shepherds' boardinghouse, serves single-dish lunches and chorizo sausage sandwiches Monday through Friday (as well as full-bore banquets each evening). Winnemucca is also the home of the **Ormacheas Dinner House**, a dinner-only place where all meals are served family-style, but at individual tables rather than the traditional eat-with-strangers setup.

Boise, Idaho, has a significant Basque presence, and **Leku Ona** is in the heart of it, on what is known as the Basque Block. While family-style banquets are available by request, the regular menu is organized in the more familiar course-by-course way, allowing you to order a single appetizer — perhaps a cod salad or red bean and chorizo soup — and an entrée as obscure as honeycomb tripe stewed in garlic-pepper sauce or whole squid tossed in its ink, or as familiar as T-bone steak. Leku Ona also has a tapas bar (tapas here are known as *pinxtos*), where you can feast on a big meal of little bites: leek pancakes, beef tongue, cod croquettes, and serrano ham with manchego cheese. We love the *madari egosiak*, a dessert of sweetened pears poached in red wine, which the menu advises "is also used as a palate cleanser."

Two perfect beignets blanketed in powdered sugar

BEIGNETS
Berkeley, California, and south Louisiana

Beignets are native to New Orleans, so why do we include them among the must-eats of the West? The answer is that the best beignets we've ever had are in Berkeley, California, at **Café Fanny**. Served two at a time accompanied by the house-made preserve du jour, they are barely dusted with powdered sugar; they are, in fact, just a little bit sweet. Their puffed-up, parchment-thin skin verges on crunch but is soft enough to chew and provides a toasty counterpoint to the fine sugar clinging to it. By volume, these flaky pillows are more air than pastry. By weight, air and pastry are so close to equal that it seems a good idea to lean a heavy butter knife against the beignet not being eaten, lest it float into the sky above the jolly outdoor tables.

The famous beignets at **Café du Monde** in the French Market of New Orleans are brought to the table still warm and accompanied by pale café au lait. We are not ones to complain about any freshly fried yeast dough covered with a blanket of powdered sugar, and there is nothing quite like sipping and noshing as the sun comes up over New Orleans. But if you are looking for a truly great beignet in Louisiana, head out to the bayous, where **Café des Amis** of Breaux Bridge dishes out crisp, savory beignets as free-form as a funnel cake and smothered with confectioner's sugar.

BEIGNETS AT THEIR BEST

Café des Amis: 140 E. Bridge St.,
   Breaux Bridge, LA
   337-507-3398
   www.cafedesamis.com
Café du Monde: 1039 Decatur St.,
   New Orleans, LA
   504-525-4544 and 800-772-2927

www.cafedumonde.com

Café Fanny: 1603 San Pablo Ave.,
Berkeley, CA
510-524-5447
www.cafefanny.com

Forget the other Twinkie: Bette's in Berkeley, CA, sets a new standard.

CHOCOLATE ESPRESSO TWINKIE
Berkeley, California

Other than its name and oblong shape, there is really nothing Twinkie-like about Bette's chocolate espresso twinkie. For one thing, the cake part of it is devil's food, moist and deeply chocolaty. The filling is not sugary "creme" but rather thick whipped cream flavored with a full measure of espresso and virtually no sweetener at all. And the exterior, encasing the cake on every surface but the bottom, is a sheath of deep, dark semisweet chocolate. The physical size of this pastry is that of a little Twinkie, but the size of its flavor is huge.

The magic twinkie is just one of the pastries at **Bette's To Go**, which adjoins the estimable Bette's Ocean-view Diner. Among the several other sweet essentials in the full cases are red velvet cake covered with pecans, twin-layer lemon bars (creamy on top, crunchy below), and macaroons in many flavors. Bette's To Go also has salads, sandwiches, and pizza, and the diner next door serves pancakes, thin waffles, and omelets in a setting that is retro-new but ingratiatingly unaffected.

Bette's To Go: 1807 4th St.,
Berkeley, CA
510-548-9494
www.bettesdiner.com

Bette's Oceanview Diner: retro-new but charmingly unpretentious

CRAB LOUIS
Northwest Coast

Crab Louis (or, if you wish, Louie, which is how it is pronounced) is defined by its dressing, which is mayonnaise, cream, lemon juice, red chili sauce, and usually green onions and spices. While similar to the Thousand Island dressing of the East, true Louis tends to be smoother and more sharply flavored and almost always

West

SCRAPPLE

San Francisco Bay scrapple? Scrapple of any kind, from anywhere? Does scrapple really belong in a book of must-eats? One of us Sterns answers with an emphatic "Perhaps." Equivocation is due to the fact that as a matter of principle, we believe in eating food in its natural habitat. For scrapple, that would be the mid-Atlantic states. The problem is that while there's some pretty good scrapple back east, the scrapple at Bette's Oceanview Diner in Berkeley, California, is better than pretty good. Smelling like the best possible sausage stuffing made from ground pork and cornmeal and flavored with sage, the loaf is cut so thick that when slices are pan-fried, the outside develops a golden crunch; the interior stays moist and perfumy. On the side of what the menu calls its Philadelphia Breakfast come poached eggs, toast, and fried green tomatoes.

Bette's Oceanview Diner: 1807 4th St., Berkeley, CA 510-644-3230 www.bettesdiner.com

the crowning touch for cool crab or shrimp. No one knows for sure where the Louis formula was created, or by whom, but food historians generally agree that the genesis of "the king of salads" was sometime early in the twentieth century, in either San Francisco or Seattle. And while it is available in restaurants all around the country, it is at its best in the Pacific

Perfect nuggets of Dungeness crab on "the king of salads" at Norma's in Seaside, OR

Northwest, home of what is arguably the king of crabs, the Dungeness.

Chandler's Crabhouse in Seattle serves an effulgent presentation: not only lump crabmeat and whole chunks of claw but also a school of salad shrimp, plus tomatoes, olives, and asparagus spears. If such a thing is possible, there is almost too much crab on the Louis served at the estimable **Dan & Louis Oyster Bar** in Portland. So as not to in any way veil the crustacean's flavor, the dressing comes on the side of the plate in a pair of silver ramekins. Also at the edges are a few halved hard-boiled eggs and hunks of cucumber and lemon wedges, but basically, it is a bowl full of crabmeat. No complaints here! Louis is not listed on the menu at Seattle's **Elliott's Oyster House**, but it is made at customers' request. Dressing is already mixed into the greens and the crab is surrounded by avocados, artichokes, and marinated asparagus.

The handsomest crab Louis we've come across is the one served at **Norma's Ocean Diner**, a happy-go-lucky joint in the Oregon resort town of Seaside. Norma's makes it with big, whole hunks of crab that are as fresh as the ocean itself. The size and integrity of each hunk make all the difference and set this version on a plane above lesser versions made with crab that is stringy and slack. Each piece

In Portland, Dan & Louis's salad comes with an extravagant load of fresh crabmeat.

ECOLA STATE PARK

Some of the most beautiful ocean views in the nation are from the lookout points around Cannon Beach, Oregon, where massive rock formations jut up from the water. The most majestic of these, especially at dusk, is the 235-foot-tall Haystack Rock. North along the shore is Ecola State Park, where a rainforest of lofty Sitka spruce trees backs to the Pacific. Year-round recreation in the park includes hiking in the footsteps of Captain Clark of the Lewis and Clark Expedition, surfing the waves at Indian Beach, and whale-watching in the winter and spring. One and a half miles in from the Indian Beach trailhead are the park's new primitive cabins for overnight stays. Picnic shelters can be reserved in advance.

Ecola State Park: Ecola Park Rd., 2 miles north of Cannon Beach, OR
800-541-6949 or
503-436-2844
www.oregonstateparks.org/park_188.php

is a silky, juice-laden nugget of marine opulence, a fully satisfying few mouthfuls even without Louis dressing. The splendid meat is accompanied by hard-boiled egg, lettuce, tomato, a few olives, and a warm, buttery tile of garlic toast. It arrives naked, the Louis dressing in a cup alongside the salad, allowing the customer to dollop or dip crab to taste.

CREAM OF THE CRAB LOUIS

1. **Dan & Louis Oyster Bar:** 208 S.W. Ankeny St., Portland, OR 503-227-5906 www.danandlouis.com
2. **Norma's Ocean Diner:** 20 N. Columbia St., Seaside, OR 503-738-4331
3. **Chandler's Crabhouse:** 901 Fairview Ave. North, Seattle, WA 206-223-2722 www.schwartzbros.com/chandlers.cfm
4. **Elliott's Oyster House:** 1201 Alaskan Way, Pier 56, Seattle, WA 206-623-4340 www.elliottsoysterhouse.com

West

CREAM OF ARTICHOKE SOUP
California

You can get artichoke anything at **Duarte's**, a 115-year-old tavern in Pescadero, the heart of artichoke country. Big, succulent-leaved globes are available simply steamed or stuffed with fennel sausage; there are artichoke omelets and chilled artichoke hearts with aïoli; best of all is cream of artichoke soup. Ron Duarte begins by cooking the hearts of the big local 'chokes in hot olive oil, a process that makes the flavor blossom. They are pureed and blended with chicken broth and plenty of garlic, and that potion is thickened with cream and enriched by butter. The result is a jade-green soup that is smooth and comforting but resolutely tonic. (Anyone who dines at Duarte's is required to finish the meal with a slice of olallieberry pie, made from the California fruit, which hums with fla-

vor buzz like a concentrated confluence of blackberry and raspberry.)

Because it is the Artichoke Capital of the World, Castroville hosts an annual festival devoted to the local crop in May, but all year long, you can visit the **Giant Artichoke**, a restaurant and produce stand heralded by a 20-foot-tall concrete sculpture of an artichoke. The kitschy place is most famous for its deep-fried artichokes, which are more about deep-fried than artichoke; nor are we enthusiastic about artichoke enchiladas or artichoke cake. But there is no faulting the handsome steamed artichokes and intriguing artichoke bread, and while the cream of artichoke soup is not up to the Duarte's standard, it is a true *goût de terroir*.

CREAM OF ARTICHOKE SOUP

Duarte's: 202 Stage Rd., Pescadero, CA
650-879-0464
www.duartestavern.com
Giant Artichoke: 11261 Merritt St., Castroville, CA
831-633-3501

Ron Duarte, of Duarte's in the heart of artichoke country, stirs his garlicky cream of artichoke soup.

CUP OF COFFEE
Portland and Seattle

Seattle gets the coffee glory, and there is no denying the deep, dark satisfaction of Italian espresso made at the beautiful **Caffè Umbria** and the urbane comfort of **Zeitgeist**, both in Pioneer Square, or the café con leche and Cubano (made with caramelized sugar) at **El Diablo**. But for us there is something even better about

TUMBLING TRIPLE-BERRY TOAST

At the Green Salmon of Yachats, Oregon, organic fair-trade coffee and espresso are only the beginnings of the story. How about a Cafe Oregonian, with hazelnut milk; a Cafe Mexico, with pepper, brown sugar, and cocoa; or a Kopi Jahe, which is a double-strength brew infused with the sparkle of ginger and the sweetness of cane sugar? Enticing as the coffees are, though, it's the eats that will keep us coming back. We visited in midsummer, the height of berry season, when the menu offered a stunningly beautiful breakfast called triple-berry toast: crunchy whole wheat spread with creamy Italian mascarpone and topped with freshly picked blueberries, strawberries, and raspberries, each at the peak of their natural, sunny fruitiness, the whole thing drizzled with honey and sprinkled with powdered sugar. Unbelievably delicious . . . although it became a tumbling tower of red and blue berries as soon as a slice was hefted off the plate.

Green Salmon: 220 Highway 101 North, Yachats, OR
541-547-3077
www.thegreensalmon.com

having coffee in Portland, Oregon. That something is the pastries. The variety at **Crema** is downright exasperating, right from this challenging decision: sweet or savory? Among the sweets that sing a siren song are Mexican chocolate cupcakes, still-

Midsummer day's dream: berries on mascarpone-slathered whole wheat bread at the Green Salmon coffeehouse in Yachats, OR

warm pear galettes, extra-goopy cinnamon rolls, and double chocolate earthquake cookies (including fault lines); savory essentials include manchego and mushroom biscuits and a cheddar corn biscuit that is rich and chewy and dotted with plump sweet kernels. Coffee choices include strong brewed Stumptown, French press, and espresso. Lattes come with artistic patterns in the foam on top.

Ristretto Roasters, a pint-sized coffee purveyor, roasts its own beans every day. Select the roast you want, and it will be ground and brewed to order. Ristretto notes that it does not make dark roasts because they overwhelm the flavor of the different beans. The small selection of pastries includes astounding "pound and a half cake" and chocolate espresso bread that is hugely chocolaty and just sweet enough to demand cup after cup of coffee as its companion.

West

Not that there is anything wrong with the coffee and espresso at **Random Order Coffeehouse**, but frankly, we find it hard to concentrate on the coffee when gazing upon a cornmeal-bacon-Tillamook-green-chile muffin or a tongue-enlightening chipotle brownie bar. The house specialty is pie, both savory and sweet. Brandied peach and organic banana cream ribboned with just-whipped cream earn top rank in the pie pantheon.

6 STELLAR CUPS OF COFFEE

1. **Ristretto Roasters:** 3520 N.E. 42nd St., Portland, OR 503-284-6767 Second location: 3808 N. Williams Ave., Portland, OR 503-288-8667 www.ristrettoroasters.com
2. **Zeitgeist Coffee:** 171 S. Jackson St., Seattle, WA 206-583-0497 www.zeitgeistcoffee.com
3. **Caffè Umbria:** 320 Occidental Ave. South, Seattle, WA

A temptation from the savory side of Crema: a cheddar biscuit nubbly with corn kernels and chewy cheese

206-624-5847 Second location: 303 N.W. Twelfth Ave., Portland, OR www.caffeumbria.com
4. **Crema:** 2728 S.E. Ankeny St., Portland, OR 503-234-0206 www.cremabakery.com
5. **El Diablo:** 1811 Queen Anne Ave. North, #101, Seattle, WA 206-285-0693 www.eldiablocoffee.com
6. **Random Order Coffeehouse & Bakery:** 1800 N.E. Alberta St., Portland, OR 503-331-1420 www.randomordercoffee.com

In the coffee-rich town of Portland, Crema serves some of the very best.

CUPCAKE
West Coast

We might have selected a single kind of cupcake from Portland's **Saint Cupcake** to list in this culinary aristocracy — maybe a turtle cupcake topped with molten caramel and hot fudge, or a banana–chocolate-chip pound-cake cupcake. But the truth is that each of the ones we have tasted has made us exclaim that it is the Platonic ideal of its flavor, and the frosting — vanilla cream cheese on red velvet, for instance — is nothing short of perfection. So we hereby recommend them all. One of us Sterns, the true cupcake connoisseur, declared the toasted coconut cream cupcake and the red velvet cupcake at Saint Cupcake the two best cupcakes she has ever eaten. The red velvet was especially appreciated for the buttermilk undertone of the bright red cocoa cake; the toasted coconut, she noted, came with toffee chips baked inside. The other Stern, who likes cupcakes as much as the next man, proclaimed his fudge-topped chocolate cupcake to be one of the three

Every choice at Portland's Saint Cupcake is the Platonic ideal of its particular flavor.

best chocolate things in Portland (the other two being Sahagún hot chocolate and Sahagún chocolate-covered glazed gingered Meyer lemon peels; page 390). A single at Saint Cupcake sells for $2.50; a two- to three-bite "dot" for $1.25.

Of special note at **Trophy Cupcakes** in Seattle are the chai tea cupcake; the hummingbird, which is pineapple, coconut, and banana in spicy cake topped with cream cheese frosting; and the chocolate cupcake topped with peanut butter frosting and crisp toasted nuts. A full-sized cupcake will set you back a full $2.99, or even $3.50 for a special flavor. High prices for a trivial pastry, but these are consequential, more like downsized adult cakes than children's snacks.

Candidate for sainthood: A toasted coconut cupcake secrets toffee chips within.

West

"A sophisticated twist on an old-fashioned favorite" is how San Francisco's **Kara's Cupcakes** bills its fare. Cases in point: the java, which is chocolate with espresso buttercream; a sweet vanilla cupcake topped with bourbon frosting; and a fleur de sel chocolate cupcake with caramel filling, powerful ganache frosting, and just enough salt to turbocharge the caramel-chocolate essence.

SUPERIOR CUPCAKES

1. **Trophy Cupcakes:** 1815 N. 45th St., Suite 209, Seattle, WA 206-632-7020 www.trophycupcakes.com
2. **Saint Cupcake:** 407 N.W. 17th Ave., Portland, OR 503-473-8760 Second location: 3300 S.E. Belmont, Portland, OR 503-235-0078 www.saintcupcake.com
3. **Kara's Cupcakes:** 3249 Scott St., San Francisco, CA 415-563-CAKE See www.karascupcakes.com for additional locations.

DATE SHAKE
Southern California

Long ago, when California was exotic and paradisiacal, dates were an emblem of its appeal. Grown in the stately palm groves of the Coachella Valley, the luxury fruit inspired a drink that has gone beyond the desert and has been embraced by all of Southern California: the date shake. As if an ordinary milk shake weren't sweet, creamy, and rich enough, chopped

At California's Shields Date Garden, you can slurp a date shake and watch a movie on the secretive fruit's sex life.

dates blended in with the ice cream make this beverage more sumptuous than manna itself. The classic place to slurp one up (straws are useless) is in Indio at **Shields Date Garden**, whose founder, Floyd Shields, actually invented the blonde and brunette varieties of date. Shields is a blast from a time when this part of California was proud of its resemblance to old Araby, and it still offers viewings of the ultra-kitsch movie *The Romance and Sex Life of the Date*, which explains the life cycle of what the narrator describes as "the least understood of all fruits." The date shake at **Palm Springs Fudge & Chocolates** is smoother than one you'll get at the desert's date orchards because it is made from puree rather than chopped-up dates. It is creamier more than it is date-intense, but thanks to high-quality ice cream, that is a good thing.

Opened in 1945 as the Crystal Cove Date Shack, the place now called **Ruby's Shake Shack** in Newport Coast has been scrubbed corporate-clean but remains a genuine shack with a million-dollar ocean view. Even if its new way of doing things feels disturbingly businesslike, the shakes and smoothies are delightful; the date shake, topped with whipped cream and a cherry, is pure SoCal.

In Cabazon, just off Interstate 10, **Hadley Fruit Orchard**, which claims to have invented trail mix, sells date shakes as well as banana date shakes. Made using date crystals rather than chopped-up dates, these prodigious drinks are as thick as a Midwest concrete (page 238) and available in regular, large, and giant sizes, the giant at least as satisfying as a pint of super-premium ice cream.

GREAT DATE SHAKES

Hadley Fruit Orchards: 48-980 Seminole Dr., Cabazon, CA 888-854-5655 www.hadleyfruitorchards.com

Palm Springs Fudge & Chocolates: 211 S. Palm Canyon Dr., Palm Springs, CA 760-416-0075

Ruby's Shake Shack: 7703 E. Coast Highway, Newport Coast, CA 949-464-0100

Shields Date Garden: 80-225 U.S. Highway 111, Indio, CA 800-414-2555 or 760-347-0996 www.shieldsdates.com

No better place to drink in all the West: The Mint Bar in Sheridan, WY, has been there for more than a hundred years.

DITCH
High Plains

In cowboy country, tipplers refer to whiskey and water as a ditch, and while the quality of the ditch itself depends on the taste of the booze and the water, the righteousness of the ditch-drinking experience is all about where you do it. There is no better drinking place in all the West than the **Mint Bar** of Sheridan, Wyoming. A Main Street fixture for over a hundred years, this ad hoc community center is where Sheridan's saddlemakers, gunsmiths, cowboy haberdashers, and wilderness guides gather to plan, palaver, and drink. It is a destination obligatory not only for its colorful clientele but for its sheer beauty, inside and out. Above the door, a multicolored neon sign shows a wrangler midair on a buck-

West

ing bronc with neon cattle brands like sparks around the hooves. The interior is lined entirely in cedar and gnarled pine burls, with rough-hewn log booths and shingle walls that gleam like slick leather and have hundreds of brands burned into them. The timber walls are hung with panoramic photographs of ranch life circa 1941, as well as portraits of rodeo stars, trick riders, and western celebrities of every stripe who consider this rugged woody grotto the ultimate cowboy bar.

Note: There is absolutely no food of interest. Nor do we recommend ordering a frozen froufrou margarita or a cosmo. At the Mint, you drink beer and whiskey.

Mint Bar: 151 N. Main St., Sheridan, WY
307-674-9696

KING'S SADDLERY

The equipment required for tending cows on horseback is a fast rope with a good lay and a sturdy saddle for anchoring both rope and cowboy to a pony. These tools of the trade, along with most other gear of cattle ranch and rodeo, are sold at King's Saddlery, across the street from the Mint Bar. To riders and ropers, as well as to city slickers who relish the accouterments of cowboy life, a visit to King's is a slice of High Plains heaven.

King's started making and selling ropes in 1963, but for many years before that, leatherwork was its fame. Built by Don King to withstand the tremendous stresses of roping but also famous for their beauty, King's saddles are among the most coveted of all modern brands, both by collectors and by serious horse people. In fact, in 1984, when Queen Elizabeth II came to Wyoming to visit Lady Jean Wallop Porchester, who grew up in Sheridan, she asked to see King's leather shop and was presented with a hand-tooled wastebasket. (Afterward, the Kings took the queen to the Maverick, a Sheridan steak house, where they explained to her how to order from a menu, and where Her Highness enjoyed hash-brown potatoes for the first time.)

One huge room at King's is an amazing family museum of western gear that includes woolies (angora chaps) and over five hundred saddles made over the past couple of centuries, ranging from a capacious pleasure seat built by the Visalia Stock Company of California for William Randolph Hearst to some swell-fork, high-cantle "beartraps" that put the squeeze on a rider's pelvis. "Saddles go in styles, just like ladies' clothes, but it takes twenty to thirty years for a certain style to take hold," saddle maestro Don King once explained to us. "But that doesn't have much effect on what we do. Here, cowboy gear is not a trend. It's our way of life."

King's Saddlery: 184 N. Main St., Sheridan, WY
800-443-8191 or 307-672-2702
www.kingssaddlery.com

DOUGHNUT
West Coast

We apologize to the West Coast. For years we have pontificated about doughnuts, claiming that all the great ones are in New England (page 19). We're not saying that the very best aren't in the Northeast, but it was wrong of us to dismiss Portland, Seattle, and California doughnut makers. Our West Coast fried-dough white-light experience happened in Mountlake Terrace, Washington, at **Countryside Donut House**, as we crunched

A double-circle shape gives Annie's doughnuts in Portland twice the crunch.

into the frail skin of a glazed doughnut whose weight we would estimate at negative 5 grams. Cake doughnuts, twists, and frosted doughnuts all are quite fine, but those glazed ones make us think of what Krispy Kreme wants to be when it grows up. Warning, though: Opening at 4:30 a.m., Countryside can run out of glazed doughnuts as early as 8 or 9 in the morning.

Praiseworthy **Top Pot** got its start in Seattle, and at its source, it is one of the best doughnuts in the land, with maximum crunchy surface and insides better than birthday cake. Alas, the Top Pots we've had in Starbucks around the country, served cold and heavy, are nightmarish. Seattle also is home of the socially conscious **Mighty-O**, where the cake doughnuts are vegan-friendly, made from all organic ingredients and containing no chemical preservatives, no artificial flavors, and no cholesterol. Nevertheless, they are delicious, especially the vanilla cake chocolate-frosted and the special French toast cake.

There's a whole case of vegan pastries at **Voodoo Doughnut** in

BIGHORN MOUNTAINS

Heading west out of Sheridan, the drive into the Bighorn Mountains is one of the most scenic routes anywhere. The huge wilderness that extends from central Wyoming north into Montana includes Crazy Woman Canyon, with spectacular rock formations; Outlaw Cave, where Butch Cassidy and the Sundance Kid hid out; Fort Phil Kearny, around which some of the fiercest fighting in the Indian wars took place; and the Pryor Mountain Wild Mustang Center, where wild horses still thrive. Whether your pleasure is to hunt, fish, climb, backpack, trail ride, bird-watch, or sightsee, you'll find unprecedented opportunity to do it here. For details, follow the links at www.bighornmountains.com.

West

Portland, which a tipster originally described to us as a Goth doughnut shop. It may or may not be that, but it sure gets the wacky award, and we are not referring to the fact that you can get married in the Voodoo Doughnut and Wedding Chapel for $175, which includes doughnuts and coffee for ten. We are talking about doughnuts with such names as Grape Ape (vanilla frosting and grape powder), Dirt (crumbled Oreos), and Tex-Ass (as big as a pizza). Kidding aside, the glazed old-fashioneds are elegant and as fresh-tasting as just-churned butter.

Voodoo's old-fashioned doughnuts, glazed and chocolate.

MAPLE BAR

Maple bars are the only good reason for not eating glazed doughnuts when you go to Countryside Donut House, just west of I-5 in Mountlake Terrace, Washington. (Well, maybe the apple fritters, too.) They are substantial without being the least bit heavy, and virtually slathered with maple flavor. Why the maple bar is such a favorite out west, we don't know. Virtually every shop mentioned above carries them. The best of the best, we believe, is Voodoo Doughnut's. It is a rectangular long john frosted with thick maple glaze and festooned with whole long strips of bacon that somehow, magically, retain a fresh-fried crunch. The harmony of maple and bacon is righteous, especially when it crowns a deep-fried pastry with buttermilk tang.

If Voodoo has all the attitude of an after-hours club, **Annie's Donuts** of Portland has the attitude of an open-all-night diner. Not that it is brusque. It's just that people come here solely to eat doughnuts and drink coffee, not to socialize, to see or be seen, or to connect via wi-fi. Humble though it may be, Annie's pastries are world-class. Cake doughnuts are made in the double-circle shape that yields nearly twice the exterior crunch, and while they are not hifalutin in any way, they are flawlessly cakey and infused with the savor of clean oil. A good part of Annie's appeal is that you can eat a half-dozen of these doughnuts and drink a couple of cups of coffee for what a single fancy latte would cost in a big-name coffeehouse.

We've never seen a butterfly doughnut anywhere other than **Marie's Do-Nut Shop**, a counter-only operation (no seating) in Sacramento. It is two pastry wings veined with cinnamon and blueberries. French crullers are also noteworthy, as are apple fritters and creme-filled glazed doughnuts and bars, and the hours of operation are a godsend if you are a person who gets struck by doughnut cravings in the middle of the night. Marie's opens at 1 a.m. and closes in midafternoon. Throughout most of the early morning, you will find varieties of doughnuts that are still hot. Down in San Jose, **Lou's** doughnuts are good-sized and weighty enough to be great dunkers. Have yours glazed with vanilla, chocolate, or maple, and depending on the whim of the bakers, there are chocolate ones with vanilla glaze, plain cake with maple glaze, blueberry, and honey wheat. If you have your heart set on a particular kind of doughnut, call first to make sure they've made it, then arrive early. Lou's opens at 6 a.m. and closes early in the afternoon; favorite flavors go quickly.

If you are in the Bay Area and it is glazed you like, to **Happy Donuts** you must go. Buttery and tender-crisp, the sugar veil encasing these tender hoops is exquisite, making them the sort of doughnut of which a dozen or so seems a reasonable portion. And if you are a doughnut fancier arriving at LAX, when you exit from the

Randy's iconic doughnut beacon in Inglewood, CA

parking lot, you may think you have been transported to the promised land. Atop the roof of **Randy's**, an otherwise ordinary drive-in, looms a 22-foot sculptured doughnut that looks as large as a Ferris wheel. Randy's doughnuts are classics — honey-glazed, chocolate-covered, jelly-filled, powdered, frosted, and filled with creme. Glazed twists are lighter than the standard sinkers, and the maple bars are superb.

9 SENSATIONAL WEST COAST DOUGHNUTS

1. **Countryside Donut House:** 21919 Sixty-sixth Ave. West, Mountlake Terrace, WA 425-672-7820 No website; additional locations can be found by calling.
2. **Voodoo Doughnut:** 22 S.W. Third Ave., Portland, OR 503-241-4704 Second location: 1501 N.E. Davis, Portland, OR 503-235-2666 www.voodoodoughnut.com

In the wedding chapel of Portland's Voodoo Doughnut, you can exchange wedding rings and doughnut rings.

3. **Annie's Donuts:** 3449 N.E. Seventy-second Ave., Portland, OR 503-284-2752

4. **Top Pot Hand-Forged Doughnuts:** 2124 Fifth Ave., Seattle, WA 206-728-1966 See www.toppotdoughnuts.com for additional locations.

5. **Marie's Do-Nut Shop:** 2950 Freeport Blvd., Sacramento, CA 916-444-5245

6. **Mighty-O Donuts:** 2110 N. 55th St., Seattle, WA 206-547-0335 www.mightyo.com

7. **Happy Donuts:** 100 Bush St., #101, San Francisco, CA 415-398-6769 No website; additional locations can be found by calling.

8. **Lou's Do-Nut Shop:** 387 Delmas Ave., San Jose, CA 408-295-5887

9. **Randy's Donuts:** 805 W. Manchester Ave., Inglewood, CA 310-645-4707 No website; additional locations can be found by calling.

FISH TACO
Southern California

For a while fish tacos were strictly a local thing in Baja, then in San Diego, to which restaurateur Ralph Rubio introduced them in the early 1980s. They became the city's signature dish and are now known to much of the country. The traditional and typical fish taco is a fast-food combo of deep-fried white fish in a spicy batter bedded on a yogurt-mayonnaise sauce in a soft tortilla, along with rough-cut shreds of cool white cabbage and a wedge of lime. You still can taste the original formulation (with chipotle sauce added, please) at the original **Rubio's Baja Grill**, which now has restaurants in five states.

There are magnificent upscale tacos in La Jolla, at **George's at the Cove**, where the corn tortilla is thin and crisp, the fish is marinated and grilled mahimahi, and instead of yogurt-mayo, the condiment is jalapeño-lime crème fraîche. Our favorite casual bungalow-eatery, the **Cottage**, also uses mahimahi, fire-searing it so the edges get crunchy and the inside stays clean and moist. Here it will be accompanied by a robust cilantro-avocado salsa, a ramekin of black beans, and a spill of chunky papaya relish. While these fish tacos can be picked up and eaten out of hand (with some risk of spillage), you'll never feel awkward about using knife and fork. After all, these tacos are served on a real china plate instead of disposable dishware!

The Cottage in La Jolla presents its fire-seared mahimahi tacos with avocado salsa and papaya relish on real china.

WINDANSEA SURF CLUB

Windansea, with its rickety beach hut and 12-foot waves, has been an icon of surfer life since the 1940s. It is a patch of sand and ocean that is home to the world-renowned Windansea Surf Club, which started as a group of devil-may-care watermen who went up to compete with the Malibu Surf Club in 1953 — an epic road trip that has become a celebrated tale of radical surfer mischief. They won, and subsequently dominated competition on the West Coast.

The Windansea Club remains surfing's elite. Anyone who wants to become a member must be "of outstanding character and advanced surfing ability" and be sponsored by three existing members in good standing. Those who can't make the cut — when they say "advanced surfing ability," they aren't kidding! — are invited to become Windansea Club Boosters. For a donation of $100 or more, you get a T-shirt and a window decal, plus an invitation to surf Windansea for one hour with only five other people in the water.

Windansea Beach: 6800 Neptune Place, La Jolla, CA 619-221-8874

In spirit the fish taco is beachside food, surfer fare offered with minimal amenities in shacks for maybe a couple of dollars each. At the end of Newport Street overlooking the pier in Ocean Beach, you will find a little bar with a little grill, known as **South Beach Bar & Grill**. Instead of corn tortillas, South Beach uses flour ones, and you get your choice of fried fish or grilled wahoo or shrimp. In Solana Beach, a neighborhood joint called **Fidel's Little Mexico** serves fried or grilled mahimahi tacos in a double layer of corn tortillas also piled with cabbage, peppery mayonnaise, and eye-opening salsa. And if you believe that when it comes to fish tacos, the more casual, the better, then the place to go is **Juanita's** in Encinitas. There are exactly two picnic tables to dine at once you get your tacos at the window, at which eaters from all walks of life crowd every day to get classic Baja tacos: battered fried fish with iceberg lettuce, salsa, thin white sauce, and a wedge of lime in a corn tortilla.

While the right and proper place to indulge in fish tacos is beachside in Southern California, San Francisco should not be neglected, a fact to which we were alerted when the *San Francisco Weekly* declared **El Metate**'s the best in the city. Its tacos are built around hunks of fried white fish encased in a highly seasoned, rugged-textured breadcrumb crust, and they come in a double corn tortilla with seasoned rice and cilantro salsa. It was a visit to El Metate that indirectly opened our eyes to the Bay Area's unbelievable wealth of inexpensive Mexican food, much of it served by street carts (page 420).

West

RANKING THE FISH TACOS
OF SO CAL

1. **Cottage:** 7702 Fay Ave.,
   La Jolla, CA
   858-454-8409
   www.cottagelajolla.com
2. **George's at the Cove:**
   1250 Prospect St., La Jolla, CA
   858-454-4244
   www.georgesatthecove.com
3. **Juanita's Taco Shop:** 290 N.
   Coast Highway, Encinitas, CA
   760-943-9612
4. **South Beach Bar & Grill:**
   5059 Newport Ave., #104, Ocean
   Beach, CA
   619-226-4577
5. **Fidel's Little Mexico:**
   607 Valley Ave., Solana Beach, CA
   858-755-5292
6. **Rubio's Baja Grill:** 4504 E.
   Mission Bay Dr., San Diego, CA
   858-272-2801
   See www.rubios.com for
   additional locations.

Also

El Metate Restaurant: 2406
   Bryant St., San Francisco, CA
   415-641-7209

FISHER SCONE
Puyallup, Washington

There is plenty to eat at the **Western Washington Fair** in Puyallup (say Pew-*al*-up), including crusty pups (a corn dog with an especially brittle skin) and half-pound Earthquake Burgers. The signature dish is a scone. Introduced by the Fisher bakery in 1915 at the Pan American Exposition in San Francisco as a way to promote its flour, the scones have been Fisher's presentation in Puyallup every year since, always from the same booth and in exponentially increasing numbers. At last count, approximately 75,000 are baked and sold every day for the two-week-plus duration of the fair. Visitors can watch the dough being kneaded and shaped, then baked in huge rotating ovens. Each scone is presented too hot to handle, and always the same way, with a filling of raspberry jam and honey butter. They have a scrumptious texture that is smooth and just a little bit flaky. The cost? One dollar each. (The ovens in Puyallup are permanent, but Fisher has mobile kitchens that take the celebrated scones to several other fairs in the Northwest.)

Western Washington Fair:
   770 Ninth Ave. SW, Puyallup, WA
   253-841-5045
   www.thefair.com
   Runs for two weeks in early
   September

FRENCH DIP
Los Angeles, California

One day in 1918 a counterman at Philippe's (now formally known as **Philippe the Original**) was preparing a sandwich when the roll fell into the gravy. Fetched out with tongs, the drippings-sopped bread looked so good that an impatient customer said, "I'll take it just like that." And so, according to Philippe's history of the world, the French dip was born: warm sliced roast beef on a gravy-soaked torpedo roll with ferociously hot mustard as a preferred condiment. The moistened bread melds with the mellow beef it wraps, and the result is a delicious mess. Los Angelenos considered this sandwich theirs for decades, and while no one knows how it got its Gallic name in L.A., similarly configured sandwiches throughout the Midwest and West are known as wet beef, beef Manhattan, hot beef, and dipped beef. Philippe's will also sell you French-dipped lamb, pork, turkey, and ham; options include hunks of cheese on top and having the sandwich double-dipped and thus dripping with gravy. The price of coffee is 10 cents per cup.

Most French dips are made from low-grade beef. At **Bandera** and **Houston's**, a couple of slick corporate restaurants, the meat is prime rib and almost too tender in comparison to the bread. We wonder, at what point does a French dip lose its blue-collar identity and become a blueblood steak sandwich? But as long as we are on the subject of deluxe French dips, we need to mention the one at **Taylor's Steakhouse**, a downtown dining establishment where marinated prime sirloin is carved into thick ribbons that throb with beef flavor. Good au jus soaking into the bread, creamy steak fries on the side: This is a single-sandwich orgy.

FINE FRENCH DIPS

1. **Taylor's Steakhouse:** 3361 W. 8th St., Los Angeles, CA
213-382-8449
Second location: 901 Foothill Rd., La Canada, CA
818-790-7668
www.taylorssteakhouse.com

2. **Philippe the Original:** 1001 N. Alameda St., Los Angeles, CA
203-628-3781
www.philippes.com
3. **Bandera:** 3201 E. Pacific Coast Highway, Corona del Mar, CA
949-673-3524

Also

Houston's: 2991 Michelson Dr., Irvine, CA
949-833-0977
National chain: See www .hillstone.com for additional locations.

GARLIC FRIES
California

Don't plan to work in a kissing booth if you eat even a half-order of garlic French fries at **Barney's** in the San Francisco Bay Area. They are festooned with spoonfuls of finely minced garlic and herbs, which are oily enough to cling to the rugged edges of the hot spuds, the heat of which transmits garlic essence all around the plate, even to lengths of potato that the garlic doesn't touch. Add a little salt and you have a taste you will be savoring as well as broadcasting for hours after you indulge. There are two ways to get garlic fries at Barney's: thick or thin. The former, known as "steak cut," provide lots of soft, starchy interior; the skinny ones are more about the crunch. Barney's burgers, the restaurant's main claim to fame, are quite all right, and they are available in dozens of configurations, including a California burger with grilled chiles, bacon, sour cream,

Hold the romance: The garlic-topped fries from Barney's are more important.

and cheese, as well as turkey burgers and garden burgers. But for us, Barney's (a ten-store chain) is a place where meat is a side dish for potatoes, which are primarily a garlic conveyance mechanism.

Coming up for air after garlic fries at Barney's, we came to realize that they are in fact a favorite item throughout the Bay Area. **Gordon Biersch**, which began as a single brewery restaurant in Palo Alto and has now grown to a multistate chain, packages regular garlic fries and red pepper garlic fries for supermarkets and started selling them at Candlestick Park (from which they have gained popularity at sports venues and concession stands in countless locations). Built on what used to be a hop field, the **Hop Yard**, a Pleasanton tavern with a branch in San Ramon, offers an inviting menu of some thirty beers on tap, nice burgers, and excellent garlic and Parmesan fries — not as knockout smelly as Barney's, but all the more luxurious for the generous application of cheese. We got our Hop Yard fries piping hot, and the potatoes' heat did wonders to release a fragrant garlic and cheese perfume into the air around our patio table.

If you want endless amounts of garlic fries and garlicked everything else, the place to go is the **Gilroy Garlic Festival** in late July. The self-proclaimed Garlic Capital of the World, Gilroy hosts a three-day blowout of eating, entertainment, and the crowning of Miss Gilroy Garlic. Of course you can try garlic bread, pastas of all kinds, scampi, sausage, and sandwiches. Samples of garlic ice cream and garlic shaved ice are given away for free. You can drink garlic beer and wine. The French fries are beer-battered, their crunchy coat spangled with flecks of garlic. But you know something funny? Of all the garlic fries we've eaten in California, these were the least garlicky.

EXTREME GARLIC FRIES

Barney's: Multiple Bay Area locations; see www .barneyshamburgers.com for specifics.

Gilroy Garlic Festival: Christmas Hill Park, 7050 Miller Ave., Gilroy, CA 408-842-1625 www.gilroygarlicfestival.com

Gordon Biersch: Multiple locations; see www.gordon biersch.com for specifics. 423-424-2000

Hop Yard: 3015-H Hopyard Rd., Pleasanton, CA 925-426-9600 Second location: 470 Market Place, San Ramon, CA 925-277-9600 www.hopyard.com

GRANOLA
La Jolla, California

We've eaten a lot of granolas over the years, but none is in the same league as that made by the **Cottage** of La Jolla, California. The cereal looks normal — dark brown rolled oats baked into chunky clusters — but close inspection and first bite reveal a sunburst of flavor that is much, much more than the usual musty mix with molasses saccharinity. This stuff has a vivid personality, each ingredient ringing a clarion call as bright as a fruit salad but with the added gravity of grain. While the exact formula remains a closely held Cottage secret, we can tell you that it contains dried cranberries, meaty chunks of toasted pecans, and just enough coconut to add a second note of sweetness.

Cottage: 7702 Fay Ave., La Jolla, CA
858-454-8409
www.cottagelajolla.com
Granola is available by mail-order.

Burgerville cures the winter blahs with hazelnut milk shakes.

HAZELNUT MILK SHAKE
Oregon

Every September, 99 percent of all the hazelnuts grown in the United States fall from trees in a patch of the Willamette Valley west of the Cascades and north of Eugene. Strangely enough, the best place to sample this luxury crop in all its glory is the Portland-area fast-food chain named **Burgerville**, dedicated to supporting locally grown ingredients. Burgerville offers a Pacific Northwest salad topped with salmon nuggets and a spill of crunchy roasted hazelnuts and is especially renowned for its hazelnut milk shakes. Executive chef George Brown explains that Burgerville offers hazelnut shakes in winter, although autumn is the harvesttime. "The chocolate hazelnut milk shake weans you out of the December choc-

At the Cottage in La Jolla, the vividly flavored granola isn't just for hippies.

West

oholic overload into the first of our spring fruits," he says. "By April we're getting strawberries, then raspberries, blackberries, and peaches, and huckleberries before our pumpkin shakes. Hazelnuts have a reassuring quality that gets you through the sad times when fresh fruits can't be had."

Burgerville: Multiple locations in Oregon and Washington; see www.burgerville.com for specifics.

HOT CHOCOLATE
West Coast

Our primary purpose here is to tell you that Elizabeth Montes's hot chocolate is as rapturous as love itself. But before we get there, please make note of a few other heartthrob specialties to be found in the earnest little Portland sweet shop called **Sahagún**: chocolate with raisins soaked in a distillation of cocoa bean pulp, lavender truffles, candied Meyer lemon peels, chile lemon soda, roasted cocoa beans, and hazelnut–sour cherry bark. As for the hot chocolate, it is made by melting the very best chocolate — "single-origin" chocolate, mind you (its country of origin listed on the board each time a new source is tapped) — and slowly mixing it with warm, hormone-free half-and-half and milk. To say that the resulting cup, sprinkled with cocoa around a bull's-eye of thick cream, is intensely chocolaty might give the impression that the flavor is overpowering and aggressive. No, it is deep, deep, deep more than it is strong, so entirely the spirit and essence of cocoa that it feels illicit, like a potable

drug too good to be true. While significantly thicker than commonplace hot chocolate, it is not too sweet, nor so insanely rich as to discourage a second cup, sipped even more slowly and lovingly than the first.

As its name suggests, the **Bittersweet Cafe** in San Francisco makes hot chocolate that is more about cocoa than sugar. Its sweetness is there only to remind you just how acutely chocolaty the brew is, so devoted to the dark cocoa bean that it contains no milk or cream whatsoever. If the drink is too, too much — and unless you are a professional chocoholic, it just might be — you also can get more normal hot milk chocolate, which is creamy to the nth degree.

Inspired by the chocolat chaud served at the Paris cafe Angelina's, the French hot chocolate at **Oh Chocolate!** in and around Seattle is also made from melted chunks of high-quality chocolate (rather than from cocoa powder). Oh Chocolate!, best known for its truffles, makes it so

A cup of bliss from Sahagún, a chocolate shop in Portland

thick that you might want to relax on the chocolatier's comfy couch and ingest it via spoon — an excellent idea, allowing you to accompany each spoonful with a dab of the freshly whipped cream that comes alongside.

SENSATIONAL HOT CHOCOLATE

1. **Sahagún:** 10 N.W. Sixteenth Ave., Portland, OR
503-274-7065
www.sahagunchocolates.com
2. **Oh Chocolate!:** 3131 E. Madison St., Suite 100, Seattle, WA
206-329-8777
See www.ohchocolate.com for additional locations.
3. **Bittersweet Cafe:** 5437 College Ave., Oakland, CA
510-654-7159
Second location: 2123 Fillmore St., San Francisco, CA
415-346-8715
www.bittersweetcafe.com

HUCKLEBERRY SWEETS
Idaho, Montana, and Wyoming

Wild huckleberries are the northern plains' treasured fruit, found only in the high mountains and only late in the summer, when they are a favorite snack of grizzly bears as well as of human beings. They are similar to blueberries but not quite as sweet, their wine-purple color hinting at a depth of flavor more satisfying than the richest chocolate. You'll find them in fruit salads and made into jam,

Singin' the blues: Deeper-flavored and not as sweet as blueberries, huckleberries are a happy match for ice cream.

and they are the basis of memorable huckleberry pie at the **Spruce Park Cafe**, an unlikely eatery attached to a gas station just south of Glacier National Park that inspires pie pilgrims to come from miles away.

Established in 1949, **Eva Gates** of Bigfork, Montana, sells a handful of products that reflect the fruity bounty of the Flathead Valley, including syrups made from rare blackcap berries and chokecherries, and her

West

progeny claim that Eva was the first to sell put-up huckleberry preserves to the public. The preserves are still made in five-pint batches, just as huckleberry syrup is produced using a hand-cranked press.

Because they are not aggressively sweet, huckleberries make particularly good companions for ice cream, and so milk shakes and sundaes made from them are a big deal in Idaho, Montana, and Wyoming. **Yellowstone Drug Store** in Shoshoni, Wyoming, boasts fifty-nine different flavors of milk shake; following close behind chocolate, vanilla, and strawberry in popularity is huckleberry. Shoshoni allows you to mix any two flavors, and although we are happy to drain huckleberry chocolate and huckleberry hazelnut from their icy silver beakers, huckleberry neat is the best way to go.

Dub's Drive-In in Sandpoint, Idaho, serves up pretty huckleberry sundaes starting in late summer. Inconspicuously wedged among shops in the Montana Outpost Mall in West Yellowstone, the **Outpost Restaurant** is known for its wild huckleberry sundaes, and the soda fountain of **Cole's Drug Store** in Big Timber, Montana, will allow you to include its devilishly dark huckleberry sauce on the mighty Big Timber sundae, which is nine scoops of ice cream, six sauces, whipped cream, and nuts. For a serious study of huckleberry cuisine, the place to go is **Ekstrom's Stage Station**, a short drive east of Missoula, Montana, where you can sample huckleberry pie, huckleberry and chocolate ice cream pie, huckleberry sundaes, and, at breakfast, huckleberry pancakes.

TOP SOURCES OF HUCKLEBERRY SWEETS

1. **Ekstrom's Stage Station:** 81 Rock Creek Rd., Clinton, MT

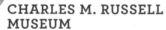

CHARLES M. RUSSELL MUSEUM

The paintings of Charles M. Russell were made from real life in Montana's Judith Basin — cowboys, Indians, horses, and fiery twilight skies with jaw-dropping natural beauty. But their intensity elevates them from documentary to mythology. Russell himself was one of the great characters of the Victorian-era West, and for those who prize his work, it is magical to visit the Charles M. Russell Museum in Great Falls, which was once his home. Here are his studio, his palates, his books, and, of course, some of his best paintings, which are now virtually priceless. Russell was a man who enjoyed drinking, and one of the crazy legends about him is that in the years after his death, in 1926, you could go into many local taverns and see his paintings or drawings on the wall. Supposedly, he used to trade his work for whiskey.

Charles M. Russell Museum:
400 13th Street North,
Great Falls, MT
406-727-8787
www.cmrussell.org

In late summer in Montana, huckleberries are the favorite treat of bears — and humans.

406-825-3183
www.ekstromstagestation.com

2. **Eva Gates Homemade Preserves:** 456 Electric Ave., Bigfork, MT
406-837-4356 and 800-682-4283
www.evagates.com
Huckleberry preserves and syrup are available by mail.

3. **Spruce Park Cafe & Bakery:** 10045 Highway 2 East, Coram, MT
406-387-5614

4. **Outpost Restaurant:** 115 Yellowstone Ave., West Yellowstone, MT
406-646-7303

5. **Cole's Drug Store:** 136 McLeod St., Big Timber, MT
406-932-5316

6. **Dub's Drive-In:** Highway 2 West, Sandpoint, ID
208-263-4300

7. **Yellowstone Drug Store:** 127 Main St., Shoshoni, WY
307-876-2539

ICED COFFEE
San Francisco

The coffee machine at **Blue Bottle Cafe**, made in Japan and known as a Siphon Bar, takes about 60 seconds to brew a cup using brass-trimmed halogen heating elements, glass globes, and bamboo paddles. It is the only coffeemaker of its kind in the United States, and it cost the cafe's owner, James Freeman, $20,000. This man is rather serious about making good coffee. He says that he practiced stirring plain water for months to develop proper muscle memory before attempting to make his first cup of siphon coffee, which requires that the coffee grounds be swirled with a bamboo paddle as vapor forces water through them. Using microroasted organic beans, the Siphon Bar produces coffee that is as smooth as velvet and sledgehammer strong, but what makes us weak-kneed is what it tastes like iced. Into a concentrate of his Bella Donna roast, Freeman stirs a full measure of Straus Creamery milk, yielding cold joe for God to drink on a hot day in heaven.
Blue Bottle Cafe: 66 Mint St., San Francisco, CA
415-495-3394

ICI ICE CREAM
Berkeley, California

Here is true love at first lick. Even before tasting the frozen rapture made at **Ici** in Berkeley, an impassioned ice cream lover is going to find himself in a state of extreme excitement,

KEANE EYES GALLERY

In the early 1960s, Walter and Margaret Keane were two of America's biggest artists — if not necessarily the best, certainly the best known. They were famous for "Big Eye" paintings: portraits mostly of children, but also of dogs, horses, and cats staring out from the canvas with huge, sorrowful eyes. Highbrow art critics despised their work as overly sentimental, and the Keane oeuvre has since become a paradigm of kitsch on canvas.

Walter and Margaret were divorced in 1965, and five years later, Margaret publicly proclaimed that she had painted all the Keane paintings, both hers and Walter's. Finally, in 1984, rights to the work went before a federal judge. Margaret set up an easel in the courtroom and created an unmistakable Keane original — a giant-eyed waif peeking over a fence. When the judge asked Walter to do the same, he said his shoulder was injured, preventing him from painting. Margaret won the case, and today her original work is on display and for sale at the Keane Eyes Gallery, across the street from Ghirardelli chocolate in San Francisco. Margaret claims that after the divorce she became a much happier woman, and the big eyes in her paintings are now filled with happiness and wonder instead of the dolor of her married days. Original Margaret Keane oil paintings sell for $15,000 to $30,000 and up. The gallery also carries canvas reproductions of many of them for around $1,000, and when we visited, we were able to buy T-shirts with her paintings on them for $25.

Keane Eyes Gallery: 3040 Larkin St., San Francisco, CA 415-922-9309 www.keane-eyes.com

---

because merely looking at the list of flavors posted along the walls of the small storefront parlor is devastating foreplay. What must it be like to feel mocha salted almond on the tongue? Sesame praline? Brandied cherry? To balance suave, fruity cool with smoky heat by swirling peach habanero sorbet around your mouth? Not everything here is sexy. The dowdiest flavor is one of the best: gingersnap cookie, a golden cream thickly veined with grainy streaks of peppery cookie. It is similar to the Indian pudding–flavored ice cream of New England (page 31), but bolder.

Unlike so many super-premium boutique ice creams, Ici's treasures depend neither on overloud flavorings nor on appetite-sating high butterfat content. The plain chocolate is actually quite plain and therefore perfect: big and dark and smooth, evocative of Mom's homemade pudding transmogrified by quality cream and rare chocolate. Likewise, coffee ice cream is not espresso nor bitter, not even dark roast. It is robust java, sweet and creamy. Flavors made with fruit — Santa Rosa plum, for instance — radiate a sunny ripeness into the cream.

For ice cream aficionados, Berkeley's Ici is mecca.

You can have your ice cream served in a cup for slow savoring, which is a good idea, considering that as it warms and softens, the flavor blooms. (If any flaw could be found at Ici, it is that the ice cream is sometimes too cold as presented, demanding that the eater wait patiently for a few minutes — no small task in the presence of such compelling goodness.) If you ask for a cone, you will get a modest-sized but hugely delicious one made here each day, and therefore occasionally in short supply. Crisp and elegant, the cones come with a surprise inside, in the form of a nugget of rich chocolate secreted in the point at the bottom.

While the inevitable wait in line and lack of seating might make Ici seem inconvenient, the staff is happy and helpful, offering little spoonfuls of anything you need to taste before committing to a flavor. And there are few food-service establishments of any kind more assertively earth-friendly. Among Ici's virtuous practices are the use of spoons made from potato starch and soy oil, biodegradable ice cream sandwich wrappers, and bowls made from material derived from sugarcane fibers recovered as crop residue.

Ici: 2948 College Ave., Berkeley, CA
510-665-6054
www.ici-icecream.com

IDAHO SPUD BAR
Boise, Idaho

Named for its potato shape and place of origin, the Idaho Spud Bar, made by the **Idaho Candy Company** in Boise, contains no potatoes. It is a clumsy-looking candy bar with a cocoa-flavored marshmallow center and a skin of dark chocolate sprinkled with shreds of coconut. First made in 1918, it was once billed as "the Healthful Candy Bar" (because of the coconut), and it enjoys a huge cult following throughout the Northwest. It is not gourmet candy, and if you are a chocolate connoisseur, you'll probably hate it — the chocolate is synthetic — but the ignominy of its elements gives it a wrong-side-of-the-tracks appeal that no high-class candy could match. We find the inelegant texture especially seductive. The center is firm and grainy rather than runny, reminiscent of a day-old Circus Peanut, and the chocolate tends to break away as you bite.

ICE CREAM TOPPING

The website of the Idaho Candy Company lists several ways to cook with the Spud Bar. Among them is this simple recipe for thick ice cream syrup. Mocha topping can be made by adding 1 tablespoon of instant coffee to the mix.

    4 Idaho Spud Bars
    1 cup milk

In a microwave oven, melt together the Spud Bars and milk in a bowl by cooking on high for about 30 seconds, stirring, cooking for 30 seconds more, and stirring again, until the ingredients are thoroughly softened.

MAKES ENOUGH FOR 4 SUNDAES

Idaho Candy Co.: 412 S. 8th St., Boise, ID
800-8-YUM-YUM or 208-342-5505
www.idahospud.com

IDLEBERRY PIE
Brigham City, Utah

Ahhh . . . idleberry pie! A sultry, dark extravaganza that resonates with blueberries, blackberries, and boysenberries, all packed into a crust that complements the berries with savory luxury. Idleberry pie is so complete that à la mode seems superfluous. It is especially welcome after a meal of pot roast with warm rolls and apricot marmalade at Utah's third oldest restaurant, the **Idle Isle Café**. Opened in 1921, Idle Isle is a nostalgic oasis of lunchroom charm, featuring its original handcrafted wooden booths, marble soda fountain, player piano, and grandfather clock. Across the street is Idle Isle's candy factory and store, home of Almond Crème Toffee, which Richard Nixon took as a hostess gift when he first visited China.
Idle Isle Café: 24 S. Main St., Brigham City, UT
435-734-2468
www.idleisle.com

JERSEY SAUCE
Oakland, California

You've got to think that Jersey sauce was named for the cow, not the state. It is a dairy creation of utmost richness: whipped cream infused with

A sundae at Fenton's Creamery overflows with Jersey sauce, a cocoa-malt whipped-cream glory.

PU-ERH TEA

If you want a hot caffeinated beverage to make your pulse pump and your brain snap to attention, have a cup of Pu-erh Tribute at L'Amyx Tea Bar in Oakland, California. The dark brown leaves, which begin as green tea, have been aged for what the tearista behind the counter assured us was "at least seven years, and all that time buried underground." L'Amyx literature boasts of some really rare Pu-erh teas that are aged for fifty years! However long it took to get the way it is, the tea in its loose form smells unbelievably earthy, something like tobacco leaves drying in a barn. When brewed, it turns as dark as coffee and rolls to the back of the tongue like a wave of warm mercury. We think it is delicious and, in its unique way, powerfully invigorating. It definitely is not for everyone, especially not for those people for whom sipping tea is an opportunity to find a place of delicate serenity. In addition to Pu-erh Tribute, L'Amyx offers Pu-erh Camel, which is a compressed version, somewhat less bold in flavor and named, according to the woman who gave us our strange lesson in the international trade of the Chinese exotic tea, "for the camels who carried the leaves all the way to England."

L'Amyx Tea Bar: 4179 Piedmont Ave., Oakland, CA
510-594-8322
www.lamyx.com

malt and just enough chocolate to give it a cocoa edge. It is one of ten toppings available for sundaes at **Fenton's Creamery**, which has been in the cow-milking business for well over a hundred years. Once the girl behind the counter explained what it was, we asked her which flavor ice cream we ought to put it on. Without hesitation, she pointed to Swiss milk chocolate, a tan concoction dotted with chocolate in the form of countless crunchy little shards. A small sundae, to go, is presented overflowing a pint container, the ice cream piled with clouds of Jersey sauce, chopped nuts, and a cherry. Big as it is, this is no death-by-chocolate dessert. Like the breed of cattle for which it is named — known for producing less milk than Holsteins, but the best — it is elegant rather than extreme. The ice cream is refined, and the Jersey sauce is beyond that. It is billowy stuff, as buoyant as well-whipped cream, its malt complementing chocolate with clarity of flavor but no added weight.

Note: Fenton's broad menu of ice cream treats includes a category titled "Sundaes for the Sophisticate," where you will find what many consider to be Fenton's signature sweet, a Black and Tan. It is layers of vanilla and toasted almond ice cream, caramel, and fudge, topped with toasted almonds, whipped cream, and a cherry.

Fenton's Creamery: 4226 Piedmont Ave., Oakland, CA
510-658-7000
www.fentonscreamery.com

West

MACAROON
Berkeley, California

The ice cream at **Sketch** is above reproach, slow-churned using organic milk and real fruit, without additives or stabilizers; the granitas are refreshment incarnate; and the house version of a Fudgsicle, a dairy-free frozen pudding that is as rich as fudge sauce, puts the brand-name treat to shame. But the main reason this place makes us blither with bliss is its macaroon. Not the usual sphere, it is nearly as flat as a cookie. That is a wonderful thing, because the broad, thin coconut cake is all toasty crunch and chew, nearly burned at its very edge. Here is a case where it is actually possible to improve upon perfection: Top one of these superb coconut disks with a scoop of Sketch's ice cream. We'll have burnt caramel or Venezuelan chocolate or Mariposa plum, please.

Sketch: 1809A Fourth St.,
   Berkeley, CA
   510-665-5650
   www.sketchicecream.com

MATCHA TEA
Portland, Oregon

If the color green has a taste, here it is, squared. Matcha tea, which is what's used in the Japanese tea ceremony, is the greenest thing you will ever eat or drink, outpowering even wheatgrass juice. Made into a powder from leaf tips of plants that are shade-grown to intensify the chlorophyll flavor, mat-

A taste of spring, chlorophyll-colored Japanese matcha tea contains antioxidants to the max.

cha tea is good for you, containing heaps of antioxidants.

We learned how to brew it at **Fox-fire Teas** in Portland, Oregon, by watching tea practitioner Quinn Losselyong. First he drops two small bamboo scoops (about half a teaspoon) of fine jade-green powder into the bottom of the bowl. Adding a bit of hot (not quite boiling) water from a kettle in one hand and stirring briskly with an elegant bamboo whisk in his other, he creates a dark green syrup topped with sparkling emerald foam. Then he stirs in more water, adjusting the tea's strength. To drink it is to know what it must be like for a horse to graze through dewy clover on a spring morning; there isn't a more salubrious-flavored beverage on earth.

Foxfire Teas: 2505 S.E. Eleventh
Ave., #105, Portland, OR
503-288-6869
www.foxfireteas.com
Matcha tea powder is available
retail and by mail-order; the cafe
is no longer open.

Top of the morning at La Farine
boulangerie

MORNING BUN
San Francisco Bay

Morning buns have become popular in coffee places almost everywhere, especially around San Francisco Bay. Most are pretty good. What could be wrong with an unsticky sticky bun veined with swirls of sugary butter (or maybe it's buttery sugar) and cinnamon, as tender and puffy as the best croissant, with enough crisp edge to make it a little bit noisy to chew? It is indeed made from croissant dough, which is rolled thin, cut into thick disks, then baked in muffin tins. The tins' hold on the dough concentrates flavor, making each bite an indulgence so delirious we want to describe it as ripe and quite nearly intoxicating.

Having never conducted a bun-to-bun taste-off, we cannot say with certainty where the best one is baked, but if you get yours at the **Bread Garden**, a vintage bakery just below the old Claremont Hotel in Berkeley, you will have no regrets. Its body is gossamer, but its top is a spiral of crisp caramel ridges that break when bitten and mix with the veils of buttery dough beneath. Nor is it ever wrong to get a morning bun at **La Farine** boulangerie, a neighborhood bakery that has become a bustling local legend (and sprouted branches on Fruitvale Avenue and Solano Avenue in Berkeley) since its inconspicuous opening on College Avenue in Oakland in 1974. La Farine's bun may be a bit heavier than the Bread Garden's, but only barely so; and we are especially fond of this place also for its sourdough bread (page 418) and for its chocoholic chocolatine, which

Ridges of cinnamon-sugar butter swirl
through croissant dough in a morning
bun at Berkeley's Bread Garden.

West

is the lovely croissant dough wrapped around thick sticks of cooked-tender chocolate.

The morning bun at **Hopkins Street Bakery** is yeastier than La Farine's and without such crisp edges, tilting more toward bread than croissant. A brilliant variation on the theme is Hopkins Street's cranberry morning bun, the berries' tartness a good balance for the cinnamon sugar on the surface. The charming little **Tartine** has morning buns with a subtle orange glaze that offers extra crunch, accentuating the tenderness at the pastry's heart.

EXTREMELY GOOD MORNING BUNS

1. **Bread Garden:** 2912 Domingo Ave., Berkeley, CA
   510-548-3122
   www.berkeleybreadgarden.com
2. **La Farine:** 6323 College Ave., Oakland, CA
   510-654-0338

See www.lafarine.com for additional locations.
3. **Tartine:** 600 Guerrero St., San Francisco, CA
   415-487-2600
   www.tartinebakery.com
4. **Hopkins Street Bakery:** 1584 Hopkins St., Berkeley, CA
   510-526-8188
   www.hopkinsbakery.com

OREGON CLAM CHOWDER
On the Coast

Let northeasterners argue about the merits of Manhattan chowder versus New England chowder versus Rhode Island chowder. Along the divinely scenic Pacific shoreline west of Portland, where icy gusts of wind skip in with the waves, thick and creamy is the only way to have it. **Norma's Ocean Diner**, in the semi-honky-tonk resort town of Seaside, displays a chalkboard list of what local seafood is fresh at every meal; you always can count on the kitchen's regal chowder. The menu boasts that it is pork-free, and yet it is saturated with luxury as plush as fatback, its extravagance augmented by a large pat of butter with every serving, which melts into a golden puddle on top. Seaside is also home to some of the most delicious chowder you can eat anywhere, but unfortunately, **Ambrosia** makes it only a few days a month (call ahead). This stuff is loaded with the tenderest full-flavored clams, corn, potato, and bacon and seasoned with dill and pepper. **Halibut's** in Portland is best known for fish and chips, made from Copper River salmon as

Halibut's in Portland serves a must-eat potato-clam chowder that supports a spoon.

SEA LION CAVES

Privately owned and operated for profit, Sea Lion Caves, just north of Florence, is an old-style tourist attraction well worth a visit by anyone traveling along the coast who has a fondness for sea lions. Discovered late in the nineteenth century, the immense grotto is a playpen for a herd of a couple hundred of the big mammals known as Steller sea lions. From road level, visitors take an elevator down 200 feet to an observation chamber at sea level, where you watch the finfoots play in the rough surf and battle each other for choice snoozing ground on the rocks. Spectators are kept at a respectful distance and separated from the cave by a wire fence. That's a good thing; cave literature advises, "The Steller sea lion would not deliberately attack a human; however, a descent by man into the midst of a harem during the mating season would be foolish."

Sea Lion Caves: 91560 Highway 101 North, Florence, OR 541-547-3111 www.sealioncaves.com

well as halibut. Before either of these, however, you must have chowder. It is stand-a-spoon-up thick, redolent of pork, loaded with nice-sized pieces of clam and potato chunks, and sprinkled with a green confetti of herbs.

Two places in Newport beckon to chowderheads: the longstanding favorite, **Mo's** (of which there are several branches along the coast), and the **Chowder Bowl**. Mo's bacony chowder is so thick that it actually rises higher than the edges of the bowl in which it's served, unless you get the Cannonball, which is a bread bowl filled with it. Clams far outnumber pieces of potato in Chowder Bowl chowder, making it sweeter and less dense-seeming, although it, too, is rich with cream and butter.

Chowder at **Roseanna's Oceanside Cafe** in Oceanside is as creamy as any and rich with bacon and potatoes (and plenty of clams), but its luxe is buoyed by the salubrious presence of fresh herbs. Nor is its enjoyment lessened by the divine view of the Pacific from the dining room. One of the most satisfying upscale chowders is the garlic- and spinach-enriched soup at Florence's charming **Sidestreet Bistro**, which serves it in a broad bowl sided by sourdough bread. There is no view from the plain dining room of **Ecola Seafoods Restaurant & Market**, although the Cannon Beach coastline is just about the most spectacular in the West. The view of Ecola's cases of fresh seafood is pretty impressive, too, as this place actually has two boats that fish Pacific waters. The chowder, sold by the cup, bowl, quart, and bread bowl, gets its texture from grated potatoes rather than heavy cream, so although it is hearty, it is not heavy. Vividly spiced with pepper and paprika, it is the most elegant of Oregon chowders, notwithstanding the fact that it comes in a Styrofoam bowl.

West

NATIONAL BESTS

PANCAKES

What's not to like about pancakes? With such playful nicknames as hotcake, griddle cake, flapjack, and flatcar, they are a food that defies seriousness (unless you start calling them crepes). Good ones are especially

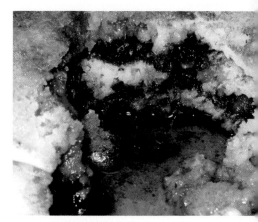

Batter is a side matter in the berry-berry pancakes from Dot's in Wilmington, VT.

appreciated by travelers in search of significant breakfast, and therefore we have long considered it our responsibility to seek out, sample, and praise extraordinary ones wherever they may be.

We are not the first culinary pilgrims to sing hoecake hosannas. In the 1940 edition of his pioneering guidebook *Adventures in Good Eating,* Duncan Hines rhapsodized about a new place he had discovered in Portland, Oregon, called simply the Pancake House: "No fancy menu, but the best homemade food. Pancakes, served two at a time, piping hot, for as long as you can sit and eat, for thirty cents." The price has risen in the past sixty-nine years, but the **Original Pancake House** is still a pancake lover's beacon for its unstinting use of fresh butter and heavy cream, and most of all for its top-of-the-line apple pancake. Oven-baked rather than fried, it occupies all of a large plate, a great puffed promontory of caramelized apples and sugar and butter and cinnamon and egg-rich pastry all intertwined, sizzling and gusting clouds of sweet steam into the air when it is set down on the table. It is a breakfast of the gods, a quorum of them.

The West Coast is particularly pancake-rich, ranging from the plate of eighteen elegant silver-dollar-sized "Swedish pancakes" that has made **Sears Fine Food** a San Francisco landmark nearly as well known as the cable car that trundles past its front door, to the most famous pancakes in Hollywood — **Musso & Frank**'s simple, satisfying, lunch-only special of Cinerama-wide pancakes that go by the name of flannel cakes because they are so thin and tender.

But if one region of the country can claim pancake hegemony, it is New England, with its prolific maple sugar bushes and a tradition of elemental grain cookery. **Polly's Pancake Parlor** is maple paradise in the White Mountains, where griddle cakes made of stone-ground buckwheat, corn, or whole wheat flour are available with nuts or blueberries and each table

Locals straddle the stools at Dot's.

is set with fancy-grade syrup, granulated maple sugar, and butter-thick maple spread, all made from local sap. Blanche Toth of **Blanche and Bill's Pancake House** in Bridgewater Corners, Vermont, makes pancakes from a recipe that is secret, but she did once reveal that part of the process is aging the batter three days. The result is a lacy cake with a faint bite reminiscent of sourdough but not as tangy. Local maple syrup is provided, or you can have Blanche's own wild blueberry sauce, which is warm and tart. At **Dot's** in Wilmington, Vermont, there are more berries per square inch than batter in the berry-berry pancakes, which contain blueberries, blackberries, raspberries, and strawberries. Yet for all their supreme fruitiness, they have real pancake integrity. In fact, before you ease into a stack with the edge of a fork, you might think you have been shortchanged, berrywise, for the surface of the cakes is mostly tan, with just hints of red, blue, and purple peeking up in little splotches. But once the fork descends into the griddle-cooked circle, behold! You hit the pay dirt of fruit, with just enough pancake around it to create a cobbler effect. Syrup isn't really necessary, but we love sopping berry-berries with a beaker of pure Vermont maple syrup (for 75 cents extra). The powerful sweetness of the maple and the varying sweetnesses of the four kinds of fruit are a rococo breakfast of dazzling intensity.

Santa Fe, New Mexico, is an oasis of griddled excellence. In particular we recommend the big whole wheat flatcars served with eggs and bacon in the lively corner eatery called **Cafe**

West

Blue Heaven's banana pancakes

The pancakes at Key West's Blue Heaven are made with fresh eggs from the chickens on the patio and one untraditional ingredient: Budweiser.

Pasqual's and the tawny buckwheat cakes studded with blueberries and accompanied by celestial apple-smoked bacon in the serene dining room of the **Inn of the Anasazi**. But the most interesting hotcakes in town are the ones that highlight the encyclopedic breakfast menu of the popular local gathering spot called **Tecolote Café**. They are pale blue because they are made from the region's beloved blue

cornmeal, and they are freckled with luxuriously smoky roasted piñon nuts.

Key West's **Blue Heaven** puts one in mind of eating eggs because its open-air dining patio is populated by crowing, cackling chickens, but it is also home to some of the most delicious pancakes anywhere. The menu notes they are made from scratch, which you will not doubt when you watch the edge of your fork press down against the slightly crisp surface, which yields, then snaps, as the fork falls into a thin ribbon of eggy cake. They're available plain or with a plentitude of pecans, pineapple bits, or sliced bananas mixed in, but there is something more to these pancakes than just good batter and fruit or nuts. They are sweet, but they also have an antisweet smack about them, and it is not the tang of sourdough. One time we asked our waitress what made them so special. She consulted with the cooks in the kitchen and returned with the secret ingredient that gives Blue Heaven pancakes that certain something extra: Budweiser.

Who says biscuits rule the South? You can't beat the buckwheat flapjacks at Nashville's Pancake Pantry.

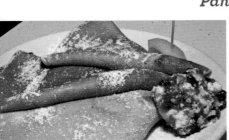

Swedish pancakes from the Pancake Pantry

Passionate as it is about biscuits, the South tends to give short shrift to pancakes, but not at Nashville's **Pancake Pantry**, a restaurant that is hugely popular (you will wait for a table). The repertoire goes from basic buttermilk and buckwheat to such astonishing creations as wild blueberry cakes, sugar-and-spice cakes, Swiss chocolate cakes, and Caribbean buttermilk cakes festooned with pecans, bananas, coconut, and powdered sugar. Our favorites are soft, fluffy

CHEDDAR CORN PANCAKES

It was sad when Gail's on the Common, in Ridgefield, Connecticut, closed last year; the friendly little cafe had been a pancake lover's breakfast destination for years, especially for its cheddar corn pancakes. Fortunately, we managed to secure the recipe. Lumpy with sweet corn kernels, the fluffy batter is webbed with enough sharp cheddar that each cake develops a mottled crust that is alternately cake-tender and cheese-chewy. Spread it with butter and pour on plenty of syrup. The result is unmitigated breakfast bliss.

1¼ cups all-purpose flour
1 tablespoon sugar
4 teaspoons baking powder
1 teaspoon salt
2 large eggs
1–1¼ cups milk
½ stick butter, melted and cooled
1 7-ounce can corn kernels, drained

Butter for frying
2 cups grated cheddar cheese
Softened butter and maple syrup

Mix the flour, sugar, baking powder, and salt in a large bowl. In another bowl, beat the eggs and stir in 1 cup of milk and the melted butter. Add the egg-milk mixture to the flour, then stir in the corn. Add the remaining ¼ cup milk if needed to make an easily pourable batter.

Melt a few tablespoons of butter on a griddle or in a heavy skillet over medium-high heat. Pour out pancakes 4 to 5 inches in diameter and sprinkle each with about 2 tablespoons of the cheddar cheese. When bubbles begin to pop on the surface of the pancakes, flip them and cook until the cheese on the underside is crusty gold.

Serve with softened butter and syrup.

SERVES 4

West

sweet potato pancakes accompanied by silky cinnamon cream — along with a serving of powerhouse country ham, of course.

The pancakes are swell at **Dwyer's**, in Lafayette, Louisiana, which has been the site of a kaffeeklatsch for Cajuns since the 1920s, but the real reason we recommend a visit is for the syrup. When you order a stack, the waitress will ask if you want maple or cane. Sugarcane is a major crop around here (you can't drive the back roads without getting stuck behind slow tractors hauling hoppers full of it), and the pancake syrup made from sugarcane is wild. It is resonantly sweet, but not white-sugar sweet. It is robust and thick, and it is a special treat to watch it swirl together with melting butter on a stack of sweet potato hotcakes.

Pancakes' warmth and substance are especially welcome when it's cold outside, and it is our belief that the very best ones are made in places where winters are severe. From October through April, the windows of **Al's**, a minuscule diner in the Dinkytown

Al's in Minneapolis may be tiny, but the griddle cakes pack a big taste.

district of Minneapolis, near the University of Minnesota, cloud with warm, breakfast-scented steam that makes it a most inviting breakfast destination. Onto Al's well-seasoned griddle is poured buttermilk batter that spreads into plate-sized circles, forming thin, fragile pancakes with a savory tang. The loquacious short-order chef will add berries to the batter or sprinkle corn kernels or walnuts into the uncooked cake; and as an alternative to syrup, sour cream is available to slather on top.

Thick, heavy pancakes are not what we seek; however, **Grove Cafe** of Ames, Iowa, is severe proof for that rule. When you order a pancake, you receive something that looks more like a layer for a layer cake, with a pleasant orange hue. Nearly an inch thick in its center and dinner-plate-sized, it comes with a couple of pats of butter and a pitcher of syrup (all of which this cake can absorb with ease). It is hugely, honestly satisfying, as only Iowa food can be.

In the opposite corner of the state, we discovered just how ethereal a pancake can be. In Stanton, known as "the Little White City" for all its pretty shipshape homes, the pancakes of **Susie's Kitchen** really are too thin to sever efficiently with the edge of a fork unless you fold one over on itself one or two times on the plate. They are eggy and cream-colored, with a muffled buttermilky tang, webbed with a fine gold lace pattern from their brief term on a hot grill, and they glisten with butter. You get two broad ones to an order, but these lovely slenderellas are so airy that we swear we easily could eat at least a dozen. They are served not with syrup but with the lingonberry jam Susie makes: just a little dab is all you want.

PREEMINENT PANCAKES

1. **Original Pancake House:** 8601 S.W. 24th St., Portland, OR 503-246-9007 Second location: 153 Greenbay Rd., Wilmette, IL 847-251-6000 Many locations around the country; see www.original pancakehouse.com for details. There are now many Original Pancake Houses around the country. We have never been to a bad one, but the original Original and Walker Brothers Original Pancake House in Wilmette, Illinois, are the standouts.

2. **Polly's Pancake Parlor:** 672 Route 117, Sugar Hill, NH 603-823-5575 www.pollyspancakeparlor.com Mail-order products are available at 800-432-8972.

3. **Cafe Pasqual's:** 121 Don Gaspar Ave., Santa Fe, NM 800-722-7672 or 505-983-9340 www.pasquals.com

4. **Dot's:** 3 W. Main St., Wilmington, VT 802-464-7284

5. **Pancake Pantry:** 1796 Twenty-first Ave. South, Nashville, TN 615-383-9333

6. **Inn of the Anasazi:** 113 Washington Ave., Santa Fe, NM 505-988-3030 www.innoftheanasazi.com

7. **Blue Heaven:** 729 Thomas St., Key West, FL 305-296-8666 www.blueheavenkw.com

8. **Al's Breakfast:** 413 14th Ave. SE, Minneapolis, MN 602-331-9991

9. **Susie's Kitchen:** 404 Broad Ave., Stanton, IA 712-829-2947

10. **Tecolote Café:** 1203 Cerrillos Rd., Santa Fe, NM 505-988-1362 www.tecolotecafe.com

11. **Sears Fine Food:** 439 Powell St., San Francisco, CA 405-986-0700 www.searsfinefood.com

12. **Blanche and Bill's Pancake House:** 586 U.S. Route 4, Bridgewater Corners, VT 802-422-3816

13. **Musso & Frank Grill:** 6667 Hollywood Boulevard, Hollywood, CA 213-467-7788

14. **Dwyer's Café:** 323 Jefferson St., Lafayette, LA 337-235-9364

15. **Grove Cafe:** 124 Main St., Ames, IA 515-232-9784

PIE CRUST COOKIE
Julian and Santa Ysabel, California

The **Julian Pie Company** is a California desert oasis at the base of Volcan Mountain, where the climate is perfect for growing apples. A sign on the door you push to enter advises, BEGIN SMELLING, and it is no joke. The moment you walk in, you are bowled over by the unbelievably appetizing aroma of cooking apples and spice and hot crust. There before you in the open kitchen, apples are loaded into crusts ready to be baked. Varieties include Dutch apple, with a crumb top; boysenberry apple crumb; natural strawberry apple; and apple rhubarb. You can eat here by the slice at a short counter or take whole pies home. However, even if you are passing through and in the mood for just a snack, you need to know that the Julian Pie Company makes one of the great snacks anywhere: bite-sized pieces of pie crust sheathed in cinnamon sugar and baked to become irresistibly delicious tan cookies that buzz savory-sweet and fall into flakes as you bite them.

Julian Pie Co.: 21976 Highway 79, Santa Ysabel, CA
760-765-2400
Second location: 2225 Main St., Julian, CA
760-765-2449
www.julianpie.com

An unnecessary cue: the sign at the entrance to the Julian Pie Company in Santa Ysabel, CA

The local drive-through in Scottsbluff, NE, where thousands of Latino residents work in nearby beet fields

PLAINS MEXICAN
Scottsbluff, Nebraska

Are you in need of a bracing bowl of garlicky menudo, thick with posole puffs and tripe, sparkling with fresh-squeezed lemon? Do you like your burrito festooned with bright pico de gallo that packs lip-searing jalapeño bite? How about a spill of smoky green chili to smother a pair of cheese-stuffed rolled corn enchiladas? To sate such cravings, we recommend a visit to Scottsbluff, Nebraska, a remote Great Plains town with 15,000 citizens and dozens of Mexican restaurants, markets, and bakeries.

In the panhandle at the northwestern corner of the state, Scottsbluff is anchored by the tall silos of the Great Western Sugar Company factory and surrounded by beet fields that have drawn Latino field workers from Texas and Mexico since the 1920s. The restaurants established by migrants who settled in the area as well as by their children and grandchildren make Scotts Bluff County a fabulous destination for travelers in

CARHENGE

If you drive to Alliance, an hour east of Scottsbluff, prepare to be amazed. In 1987, as a memorial to his dad, Jim Reinders built a replica of Stonehenge made out of cars instead of stones. Thirty-eight old vehicles, all painted gray, are arranged in a 96-foot-diameter circle along with three standing trilithons, a heel stone, a slaughter stone, and two station stones — just like the original, which Mr. Reinders had studied while in England. Admission to Carhenge is free; an adjoining shop sells souvenir T-shirts, coffee mugs, and shot glasses.

Carhenge: 2141 County Road 59, Alliance, NE www.carhenge.com

At Rosita's, a wait of an hour is common: Everything is made to order.

In Alliance, NE, cars form a replica of England's Stonehenge.

search of a noncorporate dining experience that sings of local character.

If you are just passing through (not likely, since Scottsbluff isn't on the way to anywhere), you needn't leave your car to taste what's good. **Taco Town**, the sign for which boasts, WE'RE THE TAC-O THE TOWN!, does have indoor seating and has been a favorite locals' gathering place for nearly forty years, but many customers simply drive through and pick up food at the window, just as one would do at any humdrum Taco Bell. Pork chili is sold by the pint and quart; there are plates of burritos, enchiladas, and flautas, and for $6.75 you can have a combo meal with all of the above plus rice and beans. The taco is a simple delight, its earthy corn shell audibly crisp but pliable enough not to shatter, loaded with a heap of ground beef filling that is creamy, rich, and peppery. Each taco comes wrapped in paper that is twisted tight at both ends to keep it secure until you've found a parking place and are ready to unwrap it and dine off the dashboard.

Rosita's has no drive-through service, and its menu warns, "Sometimes a wait of one hour or longer is common." In this homespun cafe with festive south-of-the-border decor, every dish is made to order, even the

West

Three of Rosita's specialties (*from top to bottom*): *panchos* (homemade chips with jalapeños, guacamole, refried beans, and cheese), tacos, and crisp-fried corn chips

corn chips — particularly the corn chips. Amazing chips they are, nearly as three-dimensional as a sopaipilla, fried so they puff up and become airy triangles with fragile skin. These are not munchies to be idly eaten while doing something else. Although they are not much larger than an ordinary flat chip, each one is a piece of food to ponder and extol. An order arrives almost too hot to handle; they come plain or as the foundation for the house specialty called *panchos*, a circle of chips topped with *frijoles*, melted cheese, guacamole, and jalapeños. *Panchos* are like nachos, but the chips' refined texture and their perfect poise between breakable and bendable make them far more satisfying than any bar grub.

The same quick-fry technique makes Rosita's taco shells an ideal crispy-chewy wrap for beef or chicken with piles of garnishes; flat tostadas are made the same way; and even taco salad includes the fine, fluffy chips. Rosemary Florez-Lerma, whose mother-in-law, Margarita Lerma, started the restaurant a half-century ago in the town of Lyman (25 miles away), told us that the extraordinary chips and shells are definitely Rosita's signature dish (so special that they have been trademarked), but they are also her Achilles' heel when it comes to catering. They cannot be made in advance or in bulk. Fresh out of the oil, they are fantastically hot and flaky, particularly wonderful when used to scoop up cool dabs of the kitchen's weighty guacamole. After ten minutes, the chips are still warm and beginning to develop a sturdier texture that is a pleasure. But as they cool, they lose their edge. That is one reason dining at Rosita's can take time, especially when the place is crowded and the kitchen gets backed up. You wouldn't want these beautiful crisp corn triangles going soft under a heat lamp.

Mrs. Florez-Lerma credits her mother-in-law with the recipes that make Rosita's food stand out in an area where so many places have similar menus. The cinnabar-red salsa that starts every meal and the stunning pico de gallo that adds eye-opening wallop to any dish are especially memorable. Mrs. Florez-Lerma's daughter, Selina, who is the family historian, told us that her grandmother invented the special way of cooking tortilla chips back at the restaurant in Lyman, where she was the only person working in the kitchen and there was just one server up front. Tortillas normally take time and attention to slow-cook on a griddle, so for efficiency's sake Mrs. Lerma took them straight from the press and tossed them into a kettle of hot oil. They cooked almost instantly and emerged unique. "It was a practi-cal thing to do," Selina reflects. "And it became the happy accident of our homemade history."

SCOTTSBLUFF MEXICAN RESTAURANTS

Rosita's: 1205 E. Overland, Scottsbluff, NE
308-632-2429
Second location: 710 W. 27th St., Scottsbluff, NE
308-632-5522
Taco Town: 1007 W. 27th St., Scottsbluff, NE
308-635-3776

The Gering Bakery's cabbage burger is a legacy from German immigrants who settled on the plains a century ago.

GERING BAKERY

As you leave Scottsbluff heading for Carhenge, drive through the town of Gering and stop at the Gering Bakery. Here you can get a cabbage burger, which is a delicious specialty found throughout the plains, where Volga Germans settled about a century ago. Known also as a *runza* or *bierok,* the cabbage burger is a soft-dough bread bun stuffed with ground beef and cabbage, peppered with spice. Locals get them to take home, but the Gering Bakery is happy to heat one up. (Its microwave works perfectly, softening the cabbage burger and retaining its savory moisture.)
Gering Bakery: 1446 10th St., Gering, NE
308-436-5500

West

PORK CHOP SANDWICH
Montana

On the roster of America's culinary shrines, 8 West Mercury Street is a windowless diner that is literally a hole in the wall adjoining Butte's old Chinatown. It was here, in 1932, when Butte was known as the Richest Hill on Earth for all its copper deposits, that "Pork Chop John" Burklund started serving pork chop sandwiches, both through a walk-up window and at his ten-stool counter. He had originally concocted the sandwich eight years earlier and had been selling them from a street cart at a time when Butte was a boomtown and its streets were bustling.

You can still get them at the window and counter of the original location, as well as at two other **Pork Chop John's** in Montana, on Harrison Avenue in Butte and in Bozeman, and they have become one of the Treasure State's defining culinary emblems. Vaguely similar to a Midwest tenderloin (page 288) but more uniform, the pork chop sandwich is a slab of boneless pork that is breaded, battered, and deep-fried, then placed in a bun and garnished with mustard, onion, and pickle chips. The deluxe version adds lettuce, tomato, and mayonnaise.

Pork chop sandwiches are common on menus throughout the region, but honestly, we never found an outstanding one until we came upon the **Springwater Cafe**, between Butte and Anaconda in a multiacre hot springs resort, where, on a menu among such finery as a mushroom merlot burger, a grilled salmon panini, and decadent chocolate cake, the pork chop sandwich is listed (along with the pasty, page 270) as a "Butte Tradition." This sandwich is bigger than most, the pork is juicier, and melted cheddar cheese is included.

PORK CHOP SANDWICHES

Springwater Cafe: at Fairmont Hot Springs Resort, 1500 Fairmont Rd., Fairmont, MT
406-797-3241
www.fairmontmontana.com

Pork Chop John's: 8 W. Mercury St., Butte, MT
406-782-0812
Second location: 2400 Harrison Ave., Butte, MT
406-782-1783
See www.porkchopjohns.com for additional locations.

RHUBARB TARTLET
San Francisco

Frog Hollow Farm is mainly in the business of selling fruit. Pears, peaches, apples, nectarines, plums, and grapes come from a 120-acre organic farm on the Sacramento River delta. You can buy the fruit at the **Frog Hollow Farm** in the Ferry Building Marketplace, and its freshness puts waxy supermarket fare to shame. The market also sells pastries made from the fruit: turnovers, galettes, tarts, and tartlets, and while we have never had one that didn't cause us to moan with ecstasy, the rhubarb tartlet is orgasmic. A delicate sheath of buttery pastry hugs fruit that is extremely sweet and extremely tart, the

GRAZING IN THE FERRY BUILDING MARKETPLACE

The Ferry Building, in which Frog Hollow sells its fruit and pastries, is a grazer's delight. There are nice sit-down restaurants and cafes, including a branch of Taylor's Refresher from up in St. Helena (get the tuna burger), as well as an Acme Bread Company (see sourdough bread, page 418) and countless opportunities to snack and sample. Herb-infused olive oils are offered with pieces of French bread to dip and taste. Recchiuti Confections sells its devastating burnt caramel chocolates piece by piece. Boccalone Salumeria makes little paper cones filled with slices of different, unusual salamis. And Cowgirl Creamery's Artisan Cheese Shop is practically guaranteed to make you faint with desire just from the way it smells.

Ferry Building Marketplace:
    1 Ferry Building, San Francisco, CA
    415-693-0996
    www.ferrybuildingmarketplace
    .com

antipodes generating unspeakable excitement among taste buds coaxed to do their damnedest. The coffee is swell (fair trade organic, natch), and if somehow you are not a rhubarb fan, how about the turnovers filled with gingered apples, the creamed scones (with Frog Hollow marmalade), or the fruit pockets, which are million-dollar Pop-Tarts? The highlight of summer, other than rhubarb, is Frog Hollow's fruity peach popsicle.

Frog Hollow Farm: Ferry Building Marketplace #46, San Francisco, CA
    415-445-0990
    www.froghollow.com

Frog Hollow Farm in San Francisco sells organic fruit and unspeakably good fruit pastries.

SANTA MARIA BARBECUE
California

Anchored by the heft of fire-charred red meat, Santa Maria barbecue is more than a distinct way of grilling or an especially tasty cut of beef. It is a whole precise feast, cooked and served in a ritual way, with a local history going back at least a hundred years and a harmony of flavors that evoke the bygone spirit of California cattle country as surely as the

West

sight of a cowboy in a silver saddle on a rearing golden palomino. The correct complement of side dishes is paramount. They must include pinquito beans, which are pink pillows half the size of red beans (also known as poquitos), cooked long and slow, seasoned with pork, pepper, garlic, and onion. After four or five hours in the bean pot, they develop a tongue-teasing snap, and the little pods are silk-soft, served in a soupy heap that mingles happily with juices from adjacent beef. Lengths of buttered and garlicked toasted French bread are important for mopping the plate. The other fundamental element is salsa, which can be used on everything: dolloped on the beans, spread on bread, and as relish for the meat. It is usually mild, mostly tomatoes, flavored with onion and perhaps a dash of horseradish, and laced with droopy bits of balmy canned green chiles, known to one and all hereabouts by their supermarket brand name, Ortegas.

Unlike exemplary barbecue in the South and Southwest, where meat

For Santa Maria barbecue, meat is cooked on an open grate over oak logs.

You can have your choice of meat at a Santa Maria barbecue, but the favorite is flavorful tri-tip.

is cooked for many hours by indirect heat in closed pits over smoldering wood, Santa Maria beef is always done in the open on a grate over a lively fire of oak logs. Almost any good cut of beef can be prepared this way. Eat your way through Guadalupe, Casmalia, Nipomo, and Los Alamos, and you will encounter oak-cooked prime rib, filet mignon, top sirloin, and rib eye. The most popular cut is tri-tip. Although it will never be as supple as filet mignon or as succulent as densely marbled prime rib, properly barbecued (and perhaps marinated) tri-tip is sheer pleasure to eat, packed with resounding flavor and a robust character that sings of

GOULDING'S LODGE

Goulding's is the only lodging around Monument Valley, and it has been an oasis for visitors since the 1920s, before John Ford used it as his headquarters while filming some of the greatest western movies, starting with *Stagecoach* in 1939. The building that appeared in *She Wore a Yellow Ribbon* as John Wayne's cabin is still standing, but the rest of Goulding's has been thoroughly modernized. There is a movie-themed museum on the premises, as well as plenty of Indian crafts to buy. Navajo guides are available for half-day or all-day tours of Anasazi ruins, movie locations, and the great monoliths that make Monument Valley such a dramatic site.

Goulding's Lodge: Monument Valley, UT
435-727-3231
www.gouldings.com

California's frontier days.

What's fun about Santa Maria barbecue for travelers is that the best of it is served al fresco and a capella, from stands and wagons in parking lots and on street corners throughout Santa Maria and surrounding towns. It's a weekend thing, so if you want it some other time, or prefer to sit at a table indoors, we recommend any of the following four restaurants.

4 RESTAURANTS SERVING SANTA MARIA BARBECUE

1. **Hitching Post:** 3325 Point Sal Rd., Casmalia, CA
866-879-4088 or 805-937-6151
www.hitchingpost1.com
2. **Far Western Tavern:** 899 Guadalupe St., Guadalupe, CA
805-343-2211
www.farwesterntavern.com
3. **Jocko's Steak House:** 125 N. Thompson Ave., Nipomo CA
805-929-3686
4. **Shaw's Steakhouse and Tavern:** 714 S. Broadway, Santa Maria, CA
805-925-5862

SCONE
Utah

A Utah scone is a puffy golden pastry about the size of a Barbie doll's pillow. At its best, it is so light and hollow that it threatens to rise up off the plate. It is served hot from the fry kettle so that when you pull it apart, the airy center sends forth puffs of steam that are on the verge of painful. But you want it good and hot, because you are about to add honey to it from the squeeze bottle on the table, and the heat of the pliable, crisp-edged pastry will make the honey less viscous. What a drippy delight!

No one knows why it is called a scone, when in fact it bears no resemblance to the dense biscuit that originally was English but has become a familiar morning pastry at Starbucks and its ilk. It is quite simply a small

West

piece of wheaty dough that gets quickly boiled in oil, emerging from the kettle all puffed up and ready to be squirted with honey or filled with jam. We're pretty sure a scone several hours old would be horrible, but hot and fresh, the puffy pastry has irresistible allure for anyone who enjoys a major carbo-splurge. Many regions have something like it: Portuguese malasadas in Hawaii, doughboys in New England (page 27), Amish funnel cakes in Pennsylvania, beignets in New Orleans (page 370), and zepoli in the Northeast's Italian neighborhoods. What the Utah scone most resembles is New Mexico's sopaipilla (page 356), with which, no doubt, it has common ancestry.

A thirteen-store state chain called **Sconecutter** offers white and wheat scones with honey butter or apple

BROWNING FIREARMS MUSEUM

What Picasso is to modern art, John Moses Browning is to gun design: the creative prodigy whose work eclipsed what went before him and overshadows all that has followed. Born in 1855 in Ogden, Utah Territory, where his Mormon father (himself a pioneer gunsmith) had settled after supplying Brigham Young's followers with weapons for their exodus to the Great Salt Lake, Browning took out 128 patents in his life for some of the most important rifles, machine guns, and handguns in history. His best-known invention is the .45-caliber semiautomatic pistol. It was patented in 1905, three years before Henry Ford introduced the Model T; and like Ford's assertively proletarian vehicle, the G.I. .45 became the kind of basic, rugged, but slightly quirky tool that its owner tends to develop an emotional bond with. Unlike the quaint Model T, however, Browning's .45 still dominates the market and is considered state-of-the-art by target shooters as well as many whose lifestyle or job description demands a surefire sidearm.

Browning's prodigious output is on display at the Browning Firearms Museum in Ogden's Union Station, a 1924 white sandstone Italian Renaissance–style edifice that has become a thriving multiuse community center as well as a railroad depot. Row upon row of glass-pylon cases display Browning-made prototypes at eye level and, just below that, the familiar production guns from Colt, Winchester, Remington, or Fabrique Nationale of Belgium. It is not unusual to hear visitors rhapsodize, whistle, gasp, even swoon from the intense pleasure of being in a room full of such inspired design. For those who like fine firearms, this cathedral of creativity north of Salt Lake City is the Louvre, Graceland, and Plymouth Rock all in one.

Browning Firearms Museum: Ogden Union Station, 2501 Wall Ave., Ogden, UT 801-393-9886 www.theunionstation.org

butter, as well as more than a dozen scone sandwiches with savory fillings that range from Hawaiian pork to hot pastrami. (Check out the website, where you are serenaded by "Everything Is Better on a Scone.") We are partial to the scones at **Johanna's Kitchen** in Sandy, where they are the standard companion to egg breakfasts and are beautifully crowned with Johanna's raspberry jam. They are also the basis for Johanna's Scone Alamode, made with vanilla ice cream, chocolate syrup, and whipped cream.

ESSENTIAL SCONES

Johanna's Kitchen: 9725 S. State St., Sandy, UT
801-566-1762

Also

Sconecutter: Multiple locations; see www.sconecutter.com for specifics.

SEAFOOD MARKET/ CAFES
Oregon Coast

If you like fish that is dramatically fresh and served at nautical food bars that offer do-it-yourself service and dispose-of-your-own cardboard plates, there is no road trip more rewarding than a drive along Oregon's Route 101. Dungeness crab, smoked salmon, and fresh tuna are the star attractions, although the **South Beach Fish Market** also offers fish and chips made with shrimp, scallops, oysters, calamari, or — best of all — creamy white halibut that is extremely swish in its golden crust. At the **Waldport Seafood Company** in Lincoln County, the fish to eat is tuna. It's cooked in the can, a process that supersaturates the meat with its own oils, exponentially increasing its creamy luxury, especially in the market's excellent tuna salad, served on homemade bread. About the best tuna we've eaten anywhere is at **Fresh Seafood NW**, across Route 101 from the huge Tillamook Cheese cooperative. It had come in only hours before we walked in the door. We watched proprietor Kari McGrath's father deftly use a knife to turn a whole fish into gorgeous dark pink tenderloins, which Kari then cut into thin little tiles and served us raw on a plate with wasabi and pickled ginger. Fresh-tasting? Stratospherically so!

For smoked fish, the place we like best is Lincoln City's **Crabpot**, a colorful roadside stand where the proprietor, Allen Black, loves to discuss the fine points of salmonology, from the vine maple he gathers to use in his smokehouse to his disdain for smoked salmon served cold. "Room temperature!" he insists. "Even if you have to put it in the microwave for a minute to sweat the fat, anything is better than smoked fish on ice." The place all salmon lovers need to know about is the **Ecola Seafoods Restaurant and Market**, named for Ecola State Park, just north of Cannon Beach. Ecola has its own boats bringing in wild salmon, and as casual and inexpensive as this cafeteria-style seafood market/cafe may be, there are few eats more regal than a juicy pink fillet grilled to a crusty edge, served with mango salsa on the side.

West

5 SUPERIOR OREGON COAST SEAFOOD MARKET/CAFES

1. **Ecola Seafoods Restaurant and Market:** 208 N. Spruce, Cannon Beach, OR
503-436-9130
2. **Fresh Seafood NW:** 3800 Highway 101 North, Tillamook, OR
503-815-3500
www.freshseafoodnw.com
3. **Crabpot:** 6019 S.W. Highway 101, Lincoln City, OR
541-996-2487
4. **Waldport Seafood Co.:** 310 Arrow St. (Pacific Highway 101), Waldport, OR
866-831-7494 or 541-563-4107
www.waldport-seafood-co.com
5. **South Beach Fish Market:** 3640 S. Coast Highway 101, South Beach, OR
541-867-6800
www.southbeachfishmarket.com

The packed house at Sam's, where the food is as good as the bread

Half-loaves of local sourdough start off every meal at Sam's Grill in San Francisco.

SOURDOUGH BREAD
San Francisco Bay Area

Lord knows the breadstuff selection around San Francisco Bay is cause to dance a jig of joy. Sourdough is the signature dish, and there is none better than the loaves baked at **Acme Bread Company**, opened in 1983 by Steve Sullivan, a former Chez Panisse busboy and leading light in defining America's artisan bread sensibility. Acme makes wonderful Italian bread, New York rye, cranberry walnut bread, elegant pain de mie, and authoritative pain au levain, its potent sourdough crumb encased in a dark and delicious crust. The sourdough at **La Farine** isn't as sour; it beams with the tang of a starter that has been nurtured long enough to develop a character that one wants to call dignified. If you like a lot of crisp crust, get a slim baguette. If you prefer a greater proportion of chewy center, with a crumb that is sturdy and cream-smooth, have a plump bâtard or circular muffaletta-shaped loaf. To gild this chewy lily,

Farine also offers sourdough loaves laced with salty Kalamata olives.

The minimum tab for dining at **Sam's Grill** is $5.75. We've never tested the policy, but it would make perfect sense to come to this brass-and-linen enclave and pay the tariff to eat only bread with water on the side. Not that Sam's meals aren't some of the best in San Francisco — from fresh abalone meunière to boned wild sand dabs à la Sam. Whether you come for the seafood, for liver and onions, or for epochal crab Louis, the meal will begin with half-loaves of habit-forming sourdough. Even before cocktails arrive, those white linen tablecloths will be strewn with shards of red-gold crust that break away as you grab slices from the bulbous hunk

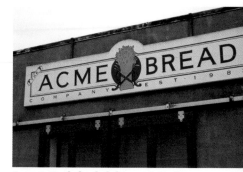

Acme in Berkeley led the way in artisan bread.

At Café Fanny in Berkeley, the cinnamon raisin toast is a breadstuff of your dreams.

of bread. Even butter is superfluous with this quintessential staff of life.

CINNAMON RAISIN TOAST

At Café Fanny in Berkeley, we fall to our knees and give praise to the cinnamon toast. Not that the sourdough toast isn't topnotch, and we have nothing against beignets, buckwheat crepes, and millet muffins, but this toast, rugged-crusted and dense, threaded with buttery veins of sweet cinnamon and dotted with raisins, maybe dabbed with some of the day's preserves, is a bread experience for the culinary memory book.

Café Fanny: 1603 San Pablo Ave., Berkeley, CA
510-524-5447
www.cafefanny.com

BEST SOURDOUGH BREAD

1. **Acme Bread Co.:** 1601 San Pablo Ave., Berkeley, CA
510-524-1327
Second location: Ferry Building Marketplace, 1 Ferry Building, San Francisco, CA
415-288-2978
2. **Sam's Grill:** 374 Bush St., San Francisco, CA
415-421-0594

West

3. La Farine: 6323 College Ave.,
Oakland, CA
510-654-0338
See www.lafarine.com for
additional locations.

STAMINA NOODLES
Pacific Beach, California

If you are in the market for a bowl of strength and succor, consider stamina noodles. A variation of the old-country cure-all *nabeyaki udon,* meaning a gallimaufry served in the iron caldron in which it has been cooked, this big bowl of food, which is a specialty of **Ichiban PB** (PB for Pacific Beach), is named because the buckwheat noodles on which it is based come in a package labeled *stamina.*

At the top of the heap of ingredients in the heavy metal serving vessel is a half a boiled egg surrounded by a glistening gyoza dumpling, a shrimp dumpling, two pink-rimmed slices of steamed fish cake, a tubular deep-fried scallop, a bundle of bright, limp greens, and a fistful of chopped scallions. Just below this first layer of food, submerged in the miso broth, you will find a shrimp (in its shell) and a thicket of buckwheat noodles. Then, among the noodles, surprise: big chunks of boneless chicken. Because of the immense variety of shapes, sizes, and textures of food in the bowl, plus the slipperiness of the big, thick noodles, this is a meal that demands full attention. There is no way to eat stamina noodles quickly. They are a dish to dawdle over, to explore, to contemplate as you inhale the scent and dip in to fetch

the contents with chopsticks and the shovel-like plastic soupspoon provided.

Ichiban PB: 1441 Garnet Ave.,
Pacific Beach, CA
858-270-5755

TACO TRUCK
San Francisco Bay Area

Taco trucks are huge in California, despite animosity from municipalities that don't like an enterprise that is so hard to regulate and control. Beyond tacos, most are great sources for burritos and tamales as well as *aqua fresca* (fruit drinks), *horchata* (rice milk; page 338), and smoothie-like concoctions called *liquados.* In our exploring around San Francisco Bay, we have been impressed with the following.

In our book, the best of all the taco trucks is a van called **El Paisa**, which you'll find parked in a lot off

The pork carnitas at El Paisa in Oakland are covered with a salsa so fine that it might almost be caviar.

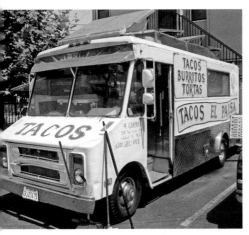

The El Paisa Taco Truck serves some of the best food ever to come out of a roving kitchen.

International Boulevard in Oakland. Here Abel Lopez offers unbelievably succulent pork carnitas — crusty-edged, big-spiced, and juicy — arrayed in double-layer corn tortillas along with parsley and pink salsa pulverized so fine it looks like caviar. Surrounded by crisp radishes, hot peppers, and slices of tomato, it is one of the most beautiful street foods anywhere.

It is said that the world's best burritos are made in Tonaya, in the Mexican province of Jalisco. Maybe so, but until we have the opportunity to taste them south of the border, we're perfectly content with a visit to San Francisco's Mission District and a meal of **El Tonayense** tacos filled with beef, chicken, pork, and even brains, tongue, and tripe. Even more wonderful are the burritos, giant street-food meals that are actually easy to eat straight off your lap with only minimal spillage.

Broad, full-flavored flour tortillas are tightly wrapped around loads of rice, beans, a good measure of salsa picante, and your choice of meats or vegetables. We really like the carnitas, *pollo asado,* and marinated pork, but it is the grilled veggies that win our loyalty. They are flame-flavored and cooked through but retain an ingratiating al dente snap, and they are complemented by slices of ripe red tomato.

If only for the salsa verde, we recommend a visit to **El Ojo de Agua** in Oakland. With the puckery tang of tomatillos and the smooth comfort of avocados, it doesn't quite upstage the crisp-edged, seasoned pork known as *al pastor,* or chicken, tongue, carne asada, or chorizo, but it is the taste of the salsa we remember long after our lunch. Alongside the tacos come sweet grilled green onions, known as *cebollitas,* jalapeño peppers, and wedges of lime.

There are indoor branches of **El Balazito**, known as El Balzano, in the Bay Area, but we much prefer to have our street food in the street or, in this case, at a counter seat behind the drive-in carwash underneath the freeway in San Francisco. The Burrito Vera Cruz is terrific, loaded with grilled-to-order seafood, and the fish tacos, made with red snapper in a double layer of warm corn tortillas, are not to be missed. There are vegetarian tacos and tongue tacos, but the must-eat taco at this beloved little taqueria is the *taco de nopales,* a soft corn tortilla containing an earthy, shockingly healthful-tasting medley of cactus braised with onions and tomatoes and topped with onion-sweet salsa fresca and fresh cilantro.

On the side, sip a refreshing *horchata*.

For a deep dive into the Los Angeles taco truck culture, we recommend a visit to the encyclopedic website tacohunt.blogspot.com.

FOUR FINE BAY AREA TACO TRUCKS

1. **El Paisa Taco Truck:** 2900 International Blvd., Oakland, CA 510-384-5465

2. **El Tonayense Taco Trucks:** Harrison at 19th and 22nd Streets, and Shotwell and 16th Sts., San Francisco, CA 415-550-9192

3. **El Ojo de Agua:** 3132 E. 12th St., Oakland, CA 510-535-9310

4. **El Balazito:** 2560 Marin St., San Francisco, CA 415-824-6684

MUDPUPPY'S TUB & SCRUB AND SIT & STAY CAFÉ

If you are eating your way around the East Bay in the company of your dog, here is a place you both want to know about: Mudpuppy's Tub & Scrub and Sit & Stay Café, located in Richmond at Point Isabel. It is a dog wash where you can get full service (leave your dog dirty, pick him up clean) or have access to wherewithal for a do-it-yourself dog bath, including rubber aprons to protect your clothes and deep raised tubs outfitted with short leashes to keep bath-averse dogs in place. It is also a pleasant outdoor cafe serving coffee and espresso drinks and pastries starting at 8 a.m. and such snacks and lunches as chili, nachos, hot dogs, and soup. It has a coin-operated dog-snack dispensing machine, and adjoining the cafe and washtubs is a large park where dogs are welcome to roam and play off the leash as well as go for a dunk in the bay. The water is not exactly sparkling clean, and the shoreline is a festival of mud, making the dog-wash aspect of this place all the more welcome.

Mudpuppy's Tub & Scrub and Sit & Stay Café: 1 Isabel St., Richmond, CA 510-559-8899 www.mudpuppys.com

A client awaits a bath at Mudpuppy's.

INDEX TO EATERIES

California (*cont.*)

CANDOR: Jim's BBQ Chicken, 80–81
ENDICOTT: Phil's Chicken House, 80, 81
FARMINGDALE: Hahn's Old Fashioned Cake Co., 85
HANCOCK: Delaware Delicacies Smoke House, 103–5
ITHACA: Hot Truck, 90–91; Shortstop Deli, 90, 91
LACKAWANNA: Steve's Pig & Ox Roast, 73
LIVERPOOL: Heid's of Liverpool, 113
MAMARONECK: Walter's Hot Dog Stand, 87–88
NEW YORK: Barney Greengrass, 97–98, 99, 105; Blue Smoke, 100–101; Café Edison, 93; Carnegie Deli, 93, 98, 99; Crif Dogs, 87–88; Grand Central Oyster Bar, 10, 11, 12; Barney Greengrass, 97–98, 99, 105; Gusto Ristorante e Bar Americano, 76; Katz's, 97, 99; Kossar's Bialys, 74; Margon, 96–97; Orwasher's, 100; Papaya King, 86, 87; Patsy's, 53, 57; Pearl Oyster Bar, 11; 2nd Avenue Deli, 90, 98, 99; Shake Shack, 334, 337; Wafels & Dinges, 98
ORCHARD PARK: Eckl's Beef & Weck Restaurant, 72–73
PLATTSBURGH: Clare & Carl's Hot Dog, 94, 95; Gus' Red Hots, 94, 95; McSweeney's Red Hots, 94–95
ROCHESTER: Nick Tahou Hots, 88–89
SEA BREEZE: Don's Original, 113
TONAWANDA: Ted's Jumbo Red Hots, 113
WEST SENECA: Schwabl's, 72, 73
WILLIAMSVILLE: Buffalo Brewpub, 73

NORTH CAROLINA

ASHEVILLE: Tomato Jam Cafe, 136
AYDEN: Skylight Inn, 210–11
CARY: Once in a Blue Moon Bakery & Café, 146
CHAPEL HILL: Crook's Corner, 171–72; Mount Carmel Baptist Church, 142; Sunrise Biscuit Kitchen, 135, 136
CHARLOTTE: Bill Spoon's Barbecue, 130–31, 132; Lupie's Café, 202, 203; Penguin Drive-In, 192, 330, 337
CLEVELAND: Keaton's, 171
GASTONIA: R. O.'s Barbecue, 131–32
GOLDSBORO: Wilber's Barbecue, 211
GREENSBORO: Stamey's, 131, 132, 172, 202, 203
HUNTERSVILLE: Lupie's Café, 202, 203

LEXINGTON: Bar-B-Q Center, 177, 178; Lexington Barbecue #1, 177–78
RALEIGH: Roast Grill, 157–58
SHELBY: Bridges Barbecue Lodge, 172
WILLIAMSTON: Sunny Side Oyster Bar, 200
WILSON: Parker's Barbecue, 131, 132
WINDSOR: Bunn's Barbecue, 131, 132

OHIO

AKRON: Or Derv Foods, 280; West Point Market, 263–64
BARBERTON: Belgrade Gardens, 254–55
BRIDGEPORT: Hocutt's Carolina Barbecue & Seafood Buffet, 172
CINCINNATI: Blue Ash Chili, 245, 247; Camp Washington Chili Parlor, 234, 235, 245–47; Chili Time, 245, 247; Empress Chili, 244–45, 247; Hathaway's Coffee Shop, 244
CLEVELAND: Freddie's Southern Style Rib House, 274; Hot Sauce Williams Barbecue, 274
DAYTON: Pine Club, 328–29, 337
LEBANON: Golden Lamb, 279, 288
WAYNESVILLE: Ohio Sauerkraut Festival, 279, 280
MULTIPLE LOCATIONS: Skyline Chili, 245, 247

OKLAHOMA

BARTLESVILLE: Murphy's Steak House, 248, 251
CLINTON: Jigg's Smoke House, 305
EL RENO: Johnnie's Grill, 350–51, 353; Robert's Grill, 351, 353; Sid's Diner, 352, 354
KREBS: Lovera's Family Grocery, 361, 362; Pete's Place, 361
MCALESTER: Roseanna's Italian Food, 361, 362
OKLAHOMA CITY: Cattlemen's Steak House, 361, 362; Classen Grill, 349
PONCA CITY: Enrique's, 301–2
SHAWNEE: Van's Pig Stand, 123, 124, 126, 129
TULSA: Cancun, 338–39; Coney I-Lander, 233, 235; White River Fish Market & Seafood Restaurant, 144, 145

OREGON

CANNON BEACH: Ecola Seafoods Restaurant & Market, 401, 402, 417, 418

GENERAL INDEX

Bourque's Supermarket, Port Barre, LA, 140, 141
Bowens Island Restaurant, Folly Island, SC, 172, 199–200
brats, Sheboygan, 280–82
Bread & Chocolate, St. Paul, MN, 231, 232
bread-baking school, 75
Bread Garden, Berkeley, CA, 399, 400
breads:
　bialys, 74
　biscuits, 134–37
　cinnamon raisin toast, 419
　Formica Bros. Bakery, 110
　hushpuppies, 171–72
　morning buns, 399–400
　pain de campagne, 47–49
　rye, 100
　scones, Fisher, 386
　sopaipillas, 356–58
　sourdough, 418–20
　Tomaro's, 189
breakfast. *See also* pancakes
　Café Pasqual's, 325
　cinnamon raisin toast, 419
　granola, 389
　hoppel poppel, 257–58
　horseshoes, 258–59
　huevos rancheros, 342–44
　kolaches, 345–47
　matzoh brei, 257
　migas, 347–49
　morning buns, 399–400
　oreille de cochon, 184
　streak o' lean, 201–2
　tacos, Tex-Mex, 350
　triple-berry toast, 375
Brenda's Dine In & Take Out, New Iberia, LA, 199
Brick Pit, Mobile, AL, 125, 129, 196
Bridges Barbecue Lodge, Shelby, NC, 172
brownies, killer, 263–64
Browning Firearms Museum, Ogden, UT, 416
Brunswick stew, 141–42
Sonny Bryan's Smokehouse, Dallas, TX, 298
Bryant House, Weston, VT, 13–15, 38
Arthur Bryant's BBQ, Kansas City, MO, 128, 129
Buckhorn Exchange, Denver, CO, 360–61
Buffalo Brewpub, Williamsville, NY, 73
Buffalo Grille, Houston, TX, 345
Bunn's Barbecue, Windsor, NC, 131, 132
buns, morning, 399–400
bureks, 239

burgers. *See also* cheeseburgers
　butter, 221–23
　cabbage, 411
　hamburgers, 328–38
　onion-fried, 350–54
Burgerville (multiple locations in Oregon and Washington), 337, 338, 389–90
burgoo, 142–43
burritos, beef, 301–2
Butler's Colonial Donut House, Somerset, MA, 19, 20–21, 22
butter:
　burgers, 221–23
　cake, gooey, 256–57
　-sculpture exhibit, 285
Buttonwood Farm, Griswold, CT, 31, 35
buzzards, 264
Byron's Hot Dog Haus, Chicago, IL, 276, 277

C

C&K Barbecue, St. Louis, MO, 278
C. W. Porubsky Grocery and Meats, Topeka, KS, 316, 317
La Cabañita, Glendale, CA, 313–14
cabbage:
　barbecue slaw, 130–32
　burgers, 411
　sauerkraut balls, 279–80
　smothered, 199
Café des Amis, Breaux Bridge, LA, 164, 165, 184, 370
Café du Monde, New Orleans, LA, 370
Café Edison, New York, NY, 93
Café Fanny, Berkeley, CA, 370, 371, 419
Cafe Pasqual's, Santa Fe, NM, 325, 403–4, 407
Cafe Poca Cosa, Tucson, AZ, 359
Caffè Umbria, Seattle, WA, 374, 376
Cahoots, Middlesex, NJ, 112
Cajun boudin sausage, 140–41
cakes:
　apple, Jewish, 91–92
　crumb, 84–85
　cupcakes, 376–78
　gateau sirop, 164–65
　gooey butter, 256–57
　red velvet, 196–98
　whoopie pie (recipe), 69
Calhoun's Country Hams, Culpeper, VA, 208
Camp Washington Chili Parlor, Cincinnati, OH, 234, 235, 245–47
Cancun, Tulsa, OK, 338–39

P

pain de campagne, 47–49
El Paisa Taco Truck, Oakland, CA, 420, 421, 422
Palm Springs Fudge & Chocolates, Palm Springs, CA, 378–79
Palo Duro Canyon State Park, Canyon, TX, 322
pan roast, 11
Pancake Pantry, Nashville, TN, 404, 405–6, 407
pancakes, 402–7
    Café Pasqual's, 325
    cheddar corn (recipe), 405
    gingerbread (recipe), 37
    jonnycakes, 36–38
Jack Pandl's Whitefish Bay Inn, Milwaukee, WI, 252, 253
Papa Felipe's Mexican Restaurant, Albuquerque, NM, 302, 303, 359, 360
Papaya King, New York, NY, 86, 87
Pappy's Orchard & Lisa's Kitchen, Coopersburg, PA, 91–92, 102
Parasol's Restaurant and Bar, New Orleans, LA, 194, 195
Park Avenue Coffee, St. Louis, MO, 256–57
Parker's Barbecue, Wilson, NC, 131, 132
Parkside Candy, Buffalo, NY, 74
Parkway Bakery & Tavern, New Orleans, LA, 194, 195
pasta:
    barbecue spaghetti, 132–34
    ravioli, toasted, 291
pasties, 270–71
pastrami sandwiches, 97–99
pastries (savory):
    bureks, 239
    Louisiana meat pies, 178–80
    oreille de cochon, 184
    pasties, 270–71
pastries (sweet). *See also* pies (sweet)
    beignets, 370–71
    cannoli, 75–76
    chocolate espresso twinkies, 371
    doughnuts, 381–84
    Dutch letters, 240
    kolaches, 345–47
    kringles, 264–65
    rhubarb tartlets, 412–13
    Utah scones, 415–17
Patrick Baker & Sons, Fairfield, CT, 17
Patsy's, New York, NY, 53, 57
Patty's Diner, Skokie, IL, 269
Paul Bond Boot Co., Nogales, AZ, 317

Payne's, Memphis, TN, 122, 123
peach:
    cobbler, 184–85
    ice cream, 185
Peachtree Café at the Lane Packing Company, Fort Valley, GA, 185
Peak Brothers Bar-B-Que Restaurant, Waverly, KY, 183
peanut(s):
    boiled, 138–39
    butter, 271–72
    pie, 185
    salt, 100–101
    soup, 185–87
Pearl Oyster Bar, New York, NY, 11
pecan pie, 354–55
Pella bologna, 240
Penguin Drive-In, Charlotte, NC, 192, 330, 337
Frank Pepes Pizzeria Napoletana, New Haven, CT, 50–51, 57
pepperoni rolls, 187–88
peppers:
    chiles rellenos, 312–14
    datil, 152–54
perch, boned and buttered, 218–20
perloo, 189–91
Ted Peters Famous Smoked Fish, South Pasadena, FL, 198–99
Pete's Place, Krebs, OK, 361
pharmacy, Champion's, 133
Philadelphia Soft Pretzels, Philadelphia, PA, 106–7
Philippe the Original, Los Angeles, CA, 386–87
Phillips Grocery, Holly Springs, MS, 334–35, 338
Phil's Chicken House, Endicott, NY, 80, 81
pico de gallo, 355–56
Pico's Mex-Mex Restaurant, Houston, TX, 349–50
pie crust cookies, 407–8
pie shakes, 272
pierogi, 49–50
pies (savory):
    chicken, 8–9
    Frito, 320–24
    meat, Louisiana, 178–80
    tamale, 358–60
pies (sweet):
    apple, baked in a bag, 215–16
    apple, crumb-top, 15
    apple, Dutch, 158–59
    cherry, 224–26

446 Index